A THING OF THIS WORLD

Topics in Historical Philosophy

# A THING OF THIS WORLD

## A History of Continental Anti-Realism

Lee Braver

Northwestern University Press
Evanston, Illinois

Northwestern University Press
www.nupress.northwestern.edu



Printed in the United States of America

10 9 8 7 6 5 4 3 2

**Library of Congress Cataloging-in-Publication Data**

Braver, Lee.
A thing of this world : a history of continental anti-realism / Lee Braver.
p. cm. — (Topics in historical philosophy)
Includes bibliographical references and index.
ISBN-13: 978-0-8101-2379-3 (cloth : alk. paper)
ISBN-10: 0-8101-2379-7 (cloth : alk. paper)
ISBN-13: 978-0-8101-2380-9 (pbk. : alk. paper)
ISBN-10: 0-8101-2380-0 (pbk. : alk. paper)
1. Knowledge, Theory of. 2. Realism. 3. Continental philosophy. I. Title.
II. Series: Northwestern University topics in historical philosophy.
BD161.B73 2007
149'.2—dc22

2007006120

∞The paper used in this publication meets the minimum requirements of the American National Standard for Information Sciences—Permanence of Paper for Printed Library Materials, ANSI Z39.48-1992.

For my mother, who taught me how to read

Truth is a thing of this world.
—Michel Foucault

The all-decisive question . . . [is] *What happens when the distinction between a true world and an apparent world falls away? What becomes of the metaphysical essence of truth?*
—Martin Heidegger

# Contents

# Acknowledgments

I must thank David Carr, who chaired the dissertation that was the seed of this work and who taught me so much about how to read, think, and write. John McCumber eased the process of publication greatly, and I have learned a lot about philosophy from him too. I want to thank John Koritansky and Rich Hall for reading and giving me helpful feedback on portions of this book. The two anonymous readers for Northwestern University Press combined to give me just the comments I needed. I owe a particularly high debt of gratitude to Colin Anderson for reading the entire manuscript and offering extensive and detailed comments which greatly improved its quality. Conversations with him have repeatedly refined my views and stimulated new thoughts. And I want to thank my wife, Yvonne, for her patience and support during the many hours I spent on this book.

# Abbreviations

## Donald Davidson

| | |
|---|---|
| *EAE* | *Essays on Actions and Events,* 2nd ed. |
| "Ext" | "Externalisms," in *Interpreting Davidson,* Kotatko et al. 2001 |
| *ITI* | *Inquiries into Truth and Interpretation,* 2nd ed. |
| "KVP" | "Comments on Karlovy Vary Papers," in *Interpreting Davidson,* Kotatko et al. 2001 |
| *PDD* | Replies to papers, in *The Philosophy of Donald Davidson,* Hahn 1999 |
| *Prob* | *Problems of Rationality* |
| *RD* | Replies to papers, in *Reflecting Davidson,* Stoecker 1993 |
| "SCT" | "The Structure and Content of Truth" |
| *SIO* | *Subjective, Intersubjective, Objective* |
| *TLH* | *Truth, Language, and History* |
| *TMK* | Replies to papers, in *Donald Davidson: Truth, Meaning and Knowledge,* Zeglen 1999 |

## Jacques Derrida

| | |
|---|---|
| *AF* | *The Archaeology of the Frivolous* |
| *Ap* | *Aporias* |
| *Dis* | *Dissemination* |
| *DN* | *Deconstruction in a Nutshell: A Conversation with Jacques Derrida* |
| *EO* | *The Ear of the Other: Otobiography, Transference, Translation* |
| *FWT* | *For What Tomorrow . . . A Dialogue* |
| *G* | *Of Grammatology* |
| *Gl* | *Glas* |
| *GT* | *Given Time: I. Counterfeit Money* |

*Ltd* *Limited Inc*
*MO* *Monolingualism of the Other; or, The Prosthesis of Origin*
*MP* *Margins of Philosophy*
*OS* *Of Spirit: Heidegger and the Question*
*PC* *The Post Card: From Socrates to Freud and Beyond*
*PoI* *Points . . . Interviews, 1974–1994*
*Pos* *Positions*
*SNS* *Spurs/Nietzsche's Styles*
"SOR" "Sending: On Representation," in Ormiston and Schrift 1990
*SP* *Speech and Phenomena and Other Essays on Husserl's Theory of Signs*
*TFS* *A Taste for the Secret*
*TP* *The Truth in Painting*
*WD* *Writing and Difference*

## René Descartes

*PWD* *The Philosophical Writings of Descartes,* 3 vols.

## Michel Foucault

*Ab* *Abnormal: Lectures at the Collège de France, 1974–1975*
*AK* *The Archaeology of Knowledge*
*BC* *The Birth of the Clinic*
*CS* *The History of Sexuality, Volume 3: The Care of the Self*
*DP* *Discipline and Punish*
*EW* *Essential Works of Foucault, 1954–1984,* 3 vols.
*FL* *Foucault Live*
*FR* *The Foucault Reader*
*FS* *Fearless Speech*
*HB* *Herculine Barbin*
*Herm* *The Hermeneutics of the Subject: Lectures at the Collège de France, 1981–1982*
*HS* *The History of Sexuality, Volume I: An Introduction*

*LCP* *Language, Counter-Memory, Practice*

*MC* *Madness and Civilization*

"MF" "Foucault, Michel, 1926–"; written under the pseudonym Maurice Florence; republished in Gutting 1994

*MIP* *Mental Illness and Psychology*

*OT* *The Order of Things*

*PK* *Power/Knowledge*

*PoT* *The Politics of Truth*

*PP* *Psychiatric Power: Lectures at the Collège de France, 1973–1974*

*PPC* *Politics, Philosophy, Culture*

*RC* *Religion and Culture*

*SMD* *"Society Must Be Defended": Lectures at the Collège de France, 1975–1976*

*TS* *Technologies of the Self*

*UP* *The History of Sexuality, Volume 2: The Use of Pleasure*

## G. W. F. Hegel

*DFS* *The Difference Between Fichte's and Schelling's System of Philosophy*

*HL* *Hegel's Logic,* trans. William Wallace (cited by page number and section number)

*PS* *Phenomenology of Spirit,* trans. A. V. Miller (cited by page number and section number)

*RH* *Reason in History*

## Martin Heidegger

*AM* *Aristotle's "Metaphysics" Θ 1–3*

*BCo* *Basic Concepts*

*BP* *The Basic Problems of Phenomenology*

*BQ* *Basic Questions of Philosophy: Selected "Problems" of "Logic"*

*BT* *Being and Time* (cited by page numbers of the English and German editions, respectively)

*BW* *Basic Writings,* rev. ed.

*CP* *Contributions to Philosophy* (cited by page number and section number)
*DT* *Discourse on Thinking*
*EF* *The Essence of Human Freedom: An Introduction to Philosophy*
*EGT* *Early Greek Thinking*
*EHP* *Elucidations of Hölderlin's Poetry*
*EP* *The End of Philosophy*
*ET* *The Essence of Truth*
*FCM* *The Fundamental Concepts of Metaphysics*
*FoS* *Four Seminars*
*H* *Heraclitus Seminar*
*HCT* *History of the Concept of Time*
*HH* *Hölderlin's Hymn "The Ister"*
*HPS* *Hegel's "Phenomenology of Spirit"*
*ID* *Identity and Difference*
*IM* *An Introduction to Metaphysics*
*IPR* *Introduction to Phenomenological Research*
*KPM* *Kant and the Problem of Metaphysics,* 5th enl. ed.
*MFL* *The Metaphysical Foundations of Logic*
*MHC* *Martin Heidegger in Conversation*
*Mi* *Mindfulness*
*N* *Nietzsche,* 4 vols.
*OBT* *Off the Beaten Track*
"OG" "'Only a God Can Save Us': The *Der Spiegel* Interview"
*OHF* *Ontology: The Hermeneutics of Facticity*
*OWL* *On the Way to Language*
*P* *Parmenides*
*PIK* *Phenomenological Interpretation of Kant's "Critique of Pure Reason"*
*PlS* *Plato's "Sophist"*
*PLT* *Poetry, Language, Thought*
*Pm* *Pathmarks*

*PR* *The Principle of Reason*

*PT* *The Piety of Thinking*

*QT* *The Question Concerning Technology and Other Essays*

*TB* *On Time and Being*

*TDP* *Towards the Definition of Philosophy*

*WCT* *What Is Called Thinking?*

*WIP* *What Is Philosophy?*

*WT* *What Is a Thing?*

*Zo* *Zollikon Seminars: Protocols—Conversations—Letters*

## Immanuel Kant

*C1* *Critique of Pure Reason* (cited by A and B, representing the original pagination of the 1st and 2nd editions, respectively)

*C2* *Critique of Practical Reason,* 3rd ed. (cited by page numbers of the English and German editions, respectively)

*FMM* *Foundations of the Metaphysics of Morals,* 2nd ed. (cited by page number of the English and German editions, respectively)

*PFM* *Prolegomena to Any Future Metaphysics* (cited by page number of the English and German editions, respectively)

## Friedrich Nietzsche (unless otherwise noted, all numbers refer to section number)

*A* *The Antichrist,* in *The Portable Nietzsche*

*BGE* *Beyond Good and Evil*

*D* *Daybreak: Thoughts on the Prejudices of Morality*

*EH* *Ecce Homo* (cited by chapter and section)

*GM* *On the Genealogy of Morals* (cited by essay and section)

*GS* *The Gay Science*

*HATH* *Human, All Too Human*

*TI* *Twilight of the Idols,* in *The Portable Nietzsche* (cited by chapter and section)

*WTP* *The Will to Power*

*Z* *Thus Spoke Zarathustra,* in *The Portable Nietzsche* (cited by part, chapter, and section, where applicable)

## Ludwig Wittgenstein

*LWP* *Last Writings on the Philosophy of Psychology,* 2 vols.

*OC* *On Certainty*

*PI* *Philosophical Investigations,* 3rd rev. ed. (part 1 cited by paragraph number; part 2 cited by section and page number)

*RFM* *Remarks on the Foundations of Mathematics,* rev. ed. (cited by page number and by section number)

*RPP* *Remarks on the Philosophy of Psychology,* 2 vols.

*Zet* *Zettel*

# Guide to Matrices

## Realism Matrix

R1 Independence: "The world consists of some fixed totality of mind-independent objects" (Putnam 1981, 49).

R2 Correspondence: "Truth involves some sort of correspondence relation between words or thought-signs and external things and sets of things" (Putnam 1981, 49).

R3 Uniqueness: "There is exactly one true and complete description of 'the way the world is'" (Putnam 1981, 49).

R4 Bivalence: "The primary tenet of realism, as applied to some given class of statements, is that each statement in the class is determined as true or not true, independently of our knowledge, by some objective reality whose existence and constitution is, again, independent of our knowledge" (Dummett 1981, 434).

R5 Passive Knower: "If, whenever I have to make a judgement, I restrain my will so that it extends to what the intellect clearly and distinctly reveals, and no further, then it is quite impossible for me to go wrong" (Descartes, *PWD* 2:43).

R6 Realism of the Subject: "In order that as a science metaphysics may be entitled to claim, not mere fallacious plausibility, but insight and conviction, a critique of reason must itself exhibit the whole stock of *a priori* concepts, their division according to their various sources (sensibility, understanding, and reason), together with a complete table of them. . . . Metaphysics alone can . . . be brought to such completion and fixity as to require no further change or be capable of any augmentation by new discoveries" (Kant, *PFM* 105/365, 106/366).

## Anti-Realism Matrix

A1 Mind-Dependence: "In pressing forward to its true existence, consciousness will arrive at a point at which it gets rid of its semblance of being burdened with something alien, with what is only for it, and with some sort of 'other,' at a point where appearance becomes identical with essence" (Hegel, *PS* 56–57, §89).

A2 Rejection of Correspondence Truth: "The criterion of truth resides in the enhancement of the feeling of power" (Nietzsche, *WTP* 534).

A3 Ontological Pluralism: "There are many kinds of eyes. . . . Consequently there are many kinds of 'truths,' and consequently there is no truth" (Nietzsche, *WTP* 540).

A4 Rejection of Bivalence: "If the Object, the product of this transition, be brought into relation with the notion, which, so far as its special form is concerned, has vanished in it, we may give a correct expression to the result, by saying that notion (or, if it be preferred, subjectivity) and object are *implicitly* the same. But it is equally correct to say that they are different. In short, the two modes of expression are equally correct and incorrect. *The true state of the case can be presented in no expressions of this kind*" (Hegel, *HL* 257–58, §193, final italics added).

A5 Active Knower: "The order and regularity in the appearances, which we entitle *nature,* we ourselves introduce. We could never find them in appearances, had we not ourselves, or the nature of our mind, originally set them there" (Kant, *C1* A125).

A6 Plural Subject: "The assumption of one single subject is perhaps unnecessary; perhaps it is just as permissible to assume a multiplicity of subjects, whose interaction and struggle is the basis of our thought and our consciousness in general? A kind of aristocracy of 'cells' in which dominion resides? . . . *My hypotheses:* The subject as multiplicity" (Nietzsche, *WTP* 490).

Empirical Directive (ED): "This I or he or it (the thing) which thinks . . . is known only through the thoughts which are its predicates, and of it, apart from them, we cannot have any concept whatsoever" (Kant, *C1* A346/B404).

### The Heideggerian Paradigm

Historical Phenomenological Ontology (HPO): "There is Being only in this or that particular historical character: *physis, logos, en, idea, energeia,* Substantiality, Objectivity, Subjectivity, the Will, the Will to Power, the Will to Will. . . . The manner in which it, Being, gives itself, is itself determined by the way in which it clears itself. This way, however, is a historic, always epochal character" (Heidegger, *ID* 66–67).

Mutual Interdependence (MI): "The fundamental idea of my thinking is exactly that Being, relative to the manifestation of Being, *needs* man and, conversely, man is only man in so far as he stands within the manifestation of Being. . . . One cannot pose a question about Being without posing a question about the essence of man" (Heidegger, *MHC* 40).

Impersonal Conceptual Scheme (ICS): "The thinking that proceeds from *Being and Time,* in that it gives up the word 'meaning of being' in favor of 'truth of being,' henceforth emphasizes the openness of being itself, rather than the openness of Dasein in regard to this openness of being. This signifies 'the turn,' in which thinking always more decisively turns to being as being" (Heidegger, *FoS* 47).

Unmooring: "For Hegel, there rules in history necessity. . . . For Heidegger, on the other hand, one cannot speak of a 'why.' Only the 'that'—that the history of Being is in such a way—can be said" (Heidegger, *TB* 52).

# A THING OF THIS WORLD

# Introduction: The Kantian Root

> If the established ground . . . has the character of a root, then it must be ground in such a way that it lets the stems grow out from itself, lending them support and stability. With that, however, we have already attained the direction we sought, by means of which the originality of the Kantian ground-laying can be discussed within its own particular problematic. This ground-laying becomes more original if it does not simply take the already-laid ground in stride, but if it unveils how this root is the root for both stems. (Heidegger, *KPM* 97)

Philosophy today faces a dilemma similar to the situation at the end of the eighteenth century. As we are now divided between analytic and continental branches, so philosophy was then split into rationalism and empiricism. Beginning from different assumptions and methods, the early modern schools grew farther apart as they developed. Starting from Descartes' commitment to a few absolutely certain innate ideas and reason's ability to determine some facts about reality a priori, Leibniz ended up making all ideas innate and deducing how God must have set up the universe. On the other side, Hume continued Locke's emptying out of the mind until there was no longer a there there, that is, not even a substantial mind to be emptied. Far from being rationally justifiable, Hume demonstrated that most of our beliefs are determined by an arational reflex, a process that has roughly the epistemological status of digestion.

Perhaps Kant's greatest accomplishment was reconciling these deeply heterogeneous schools, weaving a seamless system out of ideas taken from both sides. The linchpin of this synthesis was what he called his Copernican Revolution: the epoch-making claim that the mind actively processes or organizes experience in constructing knowledge, rather than passively reflecting an independent reality. To speak metaphorically, the mind is more like a factory than a mirror or soft wax. It is this idea that enabled Kant to incorporate the empiricist dependence on experience into the rationalist ideal of universal and necessary knowledge. At one stroke it both authenticated empirical science as genuine knowledge and placed traditional metaphysics beyond our ken, combining rationalism's ambition to attain genuine Truth with empiricism's insistence on humbly admitting our limitations into a single remarkable system which seems to flow naturally from this idea.

The contemporary situation of warring camps is considerably worse than the one that faced early modern philosophy. Although they were opposed in their starting points, methods, and overall Weltanschauungs, the empiricists and the rationalists at least talked to each other. They read each other's works and engaged in informed debate; to cite just one example, Leibniz chose the title *New Essays on the Understanding* as a direct response to Locke's *Essay Concerning Human Understanding*.[1] For much of the twentieth century, on the other hand, the level of engagement between analytic and continental thinkers has rarely risen above mutual disinterest, uninformed dismissal, or plain insult; it is hard to imagine a major figure from either side dedicating a work to the careful analysis of a text from the other tradition.[2] While the number of scholars who are doing work influenced by both or which defies easy categorization is growing, there is still a great deal of mutual misunderstanding, distrust, and even hostility.[3]

Having studied both traditions and found genuine wisdom in both, I consider this contemporary split detrimental to philosophy as a whole. We all specialize, but cutting oneself off a priori from an entire tradition is wasteful to the point of absurdity. Some believe that the other branch is "not really doing philosophy," thus presupposing that philosophy has an essence which is of course the sole possession of whichever tradition one happens to practice; while others justify mutual ignorance by claiming that the two branches are so divergent that they are no longer relevant to each other, if they ever were. Why put in the time and effort to understand the vocabulary and arguments of the other tradition if they have nothing to say about the issues one is interested in? Richard Rorty, perhaps the thinker best known for finding common ground between the traditions, has said that he expects philosophy to split into two distinct disciplines with their own names, departments, meetings, and so on, precisely because they lack sufficient common topics.[4]

I think that completing the split is the wrong way to end the dispute. The idea that one must choose between analytic and continental philosophy should and I think will become as obsolete as what were once regarded as the urgent and inescapable decisions between rationalism or empiricism, Augustine or Aquinas, Plato or Aristotle. The better resolution of the situation is not mutual ignoring and ignorance, but a dialogue between the two branches in which each sifts through the resources of the other to find elements that can address issues of interest as well as add new topics, and each deploys its own strengths to highlight and criticize the other's unnoticed presuppositions and biases. For this situation to come about, there would have to be common topics on which both branches have produced quality work. There would also have to be a way for those working in the different traditions to recognize and understand each other, since these discussions are embedded in vocabularies, extended conversations, and references to intellectual landmarks which require a considerable background. However, if there are such shared subjects and if a commensurable vocabulary could be constructed, the payoff could be enormous: thinkers could find new insights into topics they have long studied from fresh and unexpected approaches, and could confront unthought-of challenges to views and practices that have been taken for granted.

The project of this book is to demonstrate that there is at least one important topic shared by both analytic and continental philosophy, and to analyze it in a newly created vocabulary. Interestingly, the topic that I believe can best initiate this twenty-first-century rapprochement comes from the same figure who solved the parallel problem in the eighteenth century: Immanuel Kant. In fact, the seed for the reconciliation can be found in the very idea that forms the core of the *Critique of Pure Reason* and the linchpin of its rationalist-empiricist synthesis; namely, the idea that the mind actively organizes experience.

This idea, along with its various interpretations and ramifications, forms an important thread of what has become known as anti-realism in analytic philosophy. It represents one of that tradition's central topics and has been extensively discussed by such leading lights as Wittgenstein, Quine, Davidson, Putnam, Goodman, and Dummett.[5] Since Kant's work is the source of this idea and since he is certainly as influential on the continental tradition as on the analytic one, we should be able to find this core Kantian topic in the works of the great continental philosophers as well. If we can pierce the disparate vocabularies and styles to identify Kant's idea as seminal for both camps, we should be able to use it to bring about an informed dialogue and debate.[6] To initiate such a dialogue, this book traces the history of anti-realism in continental philosophy. I will show how the greatest continental philosophers of the last two centuries have been talking about the same subject as have many of the greatest analytic philosophers of the twentieth century, though generally unbeknown to both sides, since the two traditions have worked on it with such different vocabularies, interests, and approaches. This commonality should come as no surprise to anyone who believes that philosophy is deeply historical, since both traditions trace their lineage back to Kant,[7] for whose epistemology and metaphysics this anti-realist idea was the central innovation.[8]

In order to establish a commensurable vocabulary between the two camps as well as among the continental thinkers themselves (who tend to create their own terminology), I will use a set of theses derived from prominent analytic philosophers of anti-realism (particularly Putnam and Dummett) to define realism and, by negation, to supply an initial orientation on anti-realism. The set of theses defining anti-realism will then get refined and varied as we survey the continental philosophers and examine the various ways they reject realism and modify the positions of their predecessors. I will call these sets of theses the Realism and Anti-Realism Matrices,[9] and they will form a framework for a fine-grained analysis of the interrelations among these prominent continental thinkers as well as the foundation for a cross-divisional dialogue. The framework traces the specific ways in which Hegel, Nietzsche, and early Heidegger each modify the position and problems of their predecessors, thus highlighting the fact that, as heirs of Kant's revolution, the rejection of realism and the construction of a superior alternative is a central issue for their work. I will then modify the framework to analyze later Heidegger, Foucault, and Derrida, in order to show how they are still working in the wake of this issue.

Examining continental thought through the lens of an analytic issue (though one originating with Kant), as well as discussing these works in terms of theses, may concern some. The burden of proof, of course, rests with me to show that this topic can be found in the texts without procrustean readings and that my treatment of the texts is sensitive enough to avoid distortion. In order to establish this in detail as well as to introduce these figures to readers who might not be familiar with their work, I have quoted extensively, though I try to use the matrices to guide readers through these often difficult passages. I sprinkle many references to other works throughout the text in order to show that these themes appear throughout the thinkers' oeuvre, thereby demonstrating that these topics are present throughout the thinkers' works rather than cherry-picked from gerrymandered quotes. These copious references will also, I hope, make the book more useful for research. Throughout the book, I will mention supporting secondary literature where relevant and will direct interested readers to dissenting accounts, but extensive skirmishing is not my purpose here.

I hope to demonstrate to analytic philosophers that, once the context has been clarified and the vocabularies explained, continental philosophers have been working on topics that they can easily recognize as philosophical and of great concern to them, as well as that they have produced powerful insights on these issues. In order to do this, I have focused on the continental figures and texts that deal most directly with the topic of anti-realism, inevitably leaving out some quite important figures and movements (for example, Kierkegaard, Husserl, Deleuze, Merleau-Ponty, Gadamer, the Frankfurt school, and structuralism). However, the figures I have chosen—Kant, Hegel, Nietzsche, Heidegger, Foucault, and Derrida—are widely considered the greatest thinkers of the continental tradition (with some argument over an inclusion or exclusion here or there, of course). Because anti-realism is central to their thought, this study provides an illuminating overview of the history of continental philosophy that should prove useful to analytic philosophers and students approaching continental thought for the first time, as well as to specialists.

This tradition is still close to us, still alive, which makes its structure difficult to discern; anatomy is easier to make out during an autopsy than a surgery. Furthermore, many continental thinkers are difficult writers with a propensity to invent new vocabularies rather than using an agreed-upon set of terms. I believe that there are sound reasons for this—it is not just willful obscurantism for the sake of an appearance of profundity—but it certainly makes tracing interconnections and pinning down where and how they disagree with each other hard. I have found that arraying the major thinkers of the tradition along the trajectory of their positions on anti-realism imparts a surprisingly clear and intelligible structure to the last two centuries of philosophical thought. This book traces a fairly clean developmental arc from Kant to Derrida which strongly rejects the impression that their works come out of nowhere with no discernible relations to previous or later thinkers. On my reading, these thinkers have very powerful arguments when seen in their context, in relation to those who come before and after.

Although my goal here is to prepare the ground for and begin a dialogue between the traditions, I am not claiming that their divergence is illusory or due only to superficial misunderstandings which, once cleared up, will reveal that we're all really saying the same thing. Besides being untrue, this would not even be desirable. Philosophy thrives on disagreement; the problem today is not that we are arguing with each other, but that we aren't, that we have not yet risen to the point of disagreeing. Philosophical debate is productive, but it requires significant mutual understanding, as well as a basic recognition (in multiple senses of the word) of what the other is doing. Rather than trying to bring peace, this book attempts to instigate fruitful debate.

My narrative describes the history of continental philosophy in two phases: the Kantian Paradigm and the Heideggerian Paradigm. Loosely following Kuhn, I call them paradigms because each phase takes place within a broad framework of deep, organizing, orienting presuppositions that set the starting point, basic assumptions and outlook, and the issues of relevance for the thinkers working within it. Although each thinker modifies the framework significantly—indeed, it is this process of overlapping modification that forms the continuity of the tradition—they do so against the background of these structures.

After defining realism by deriving and discussing a set of theses from prominent analytic philosophers in chapter 1, I will examine Kant's partial rejection of realism through the lens of the Realism Matrix in chapter 2. Kant is of signal importance in the history of philosophy for his profound rejection of realism and his creation of a powerful alternative that establishes a fundamentally new conception of the self, metaphysics, and epistemology. Kant conceives of the mind as actively organizing experience, which entails a new aspect of reality—phenomena—and a new conception of truth—intersubjective "agreement," that is, what is necessary to experience for creatures like us. These pieces fit together to form the Kantian Paradigm, which rules over continental philosophy for the next century and a half. Although he initiates anti-realism, Kant retains two key elements of realism in his system. First, in order to secure the stability—that is, necessity and universality—of the knowledge organized by the subject, he has to make the experience-organizing faculties of the subject permanent and unchanging. Although it is no substantial object like Descartes' thinking thing, this view still amounts to a vestigial realism of the subject. Second, in order to escape what he considers to be the incoherence of complete idealism, he posits mind-independent reality in noumena.

In chapters 3 and 4, I show how both Hegel and Nietzsche work within the Kantian Paradigm by accepting the basic anti-realist picture of the subject actively organizing experience, but chafe against the remnants of realism in Kant's thought. Both reduce Kant's realism of the subject by introducing multiplicity into the subject's experience-organizing faculties—for Hegel this multiplicity is historical, while Nietzsche views it as a matter of corporeal drives—and they also seek an escape from positing noumenal reality. Although they make significant advances and verge on breaking with the Kantian Paradigm, I will argue that neither succeeds in getting free of it. Hegel's historical phases of consciousness end up getting gathered into a definitive totality at the end of history, while Nietzsche's drives are all incarnations of will to power, both ideas imposing limitations on what the subject can be. Furthermore, their conceptions of truth—the whole for Hegel and the pragmatic increase of power for Nietzsche—push them back to realist remnants, since Hegel's notion requires that there be a determinate whole, while Nietzsche needs at least a loose definition of power and what counts as increasing or decreasing it in order to evaluate various embodiments of will to power.

Heidegger's thought—particularly his *Kehre,* or the "turning" from his early to later periods—represents the turning point in my narrative of the history of continental philosophy. Chapter 5 shows how his early (roughly before 1930) work wrestles with the Kantian Paradigm as well as with Hegel and Nietzsche's attempts to break free of it. His background in phenomenology means that he begins unburdened by a noumenal realm, a notion that Nietzsche flirted with and that Hegel laboriously worked his way through. However, Heidegger's notion of authenticity commits him to a univocal realist conception of subjectivity that actually represents a step backwards from Nietzsche's multiple selves. In addition to phenomenological ontology which completely dispenses with the noumenal realm, Heidegger's other early breakthrough is his conception of truth as unconcealment. Unlike Hegel and Nietzsche, Heidegger has a conception of truth that works with his ontology to lay the groundwork for a decisive break with the Kantian Paradigm. If truth is unconcealment, then Heidegger is no longer sorting out false appearances from true reality; abandoning the reality-appearance distinction marks what he calls the end of metaphysics. Unfortunately, his fidelity to a deep, true structure of the self in authenticity compromises the potential of these discoveries in his early work.

Heidegger's later thought marks the next major phase in continental philosophy, the first genuinely non-Kantian rather than just post-Kantian philosophy, as described in chapter 6. Here he follows through on the promise of the ideas broached in the early work—primarily Phenomenological Ontology and Unconcealment Truth—with the important addition of history. Due to the new conceptions of reality and truth, history now permeates everything, and this removes any possibility of stable, unchanging reality, including a true self. Like everything else, the essence of human nature is fundamentally different in different epochs. Nothing can serve as an anchor or explanatory *arche*—not independent reality as in realism, not transcendental subjectivity as in Kantian anti-realism, and not Being. Later Heidegger maintains the anti-realist idea that beings and knowledge are organized around something like a conceptual scheme, but now he makes these schemes multiple "understandings of Being," removing them from the subject and claiming that they shift in history without reason or explanation.

With his later work, Heidegger breaks free of Kant's thought and takes his place as the unavoidable thinker for those who follow, as is shown in chapter 7 by demonstrating in detail how Foucault's thought works within the Heideggerian Paradigm. Foucault too immerses everything into history, especially the subject. He also believes that beings, knowledge, and subjectivity are organized differently at particular times by impersonal schemes which he variously calls *epistemes,* apparatuses, or games of truth. Foucault's more detailed examination of history and his focus on power and institutions in his genealogical phase make the epochal shifts more intelligible than Heidegger's profoundly mysterious "sendings of Being," but they too quickly reach a limit of explication. Heidegger's influence on Foucault, as well as Foucault's criticisms of Heidegger, are an extremely important topic which has received considerably less attention in the secondary literature than it deserves.

Finally I turn to Derrida, perhaps the most controversial and important continental philosopher after Heidegger. Derrida makes the dismantling of realism, what he calls the metaphysics of presence, a cornerstone of his thought, and he takes over many Heideggerian Paradigm tools to accomplish this. However, he is also extremely sensitive to just how difficult it is to escape metaphysics; Heidegger himself, in his estimation, is the greatest thinker of this escape, while still being mired in metaphysics. Ironically, it is Heidegger's very attempt to go outside of the history of metaphysics that locks him most firmly inside of it. In this way, Derrida's relationship to Heidegger resembles Heidegger's relationship to Kant: the earlier figure opened up essential new lines of thought, but remained fatally compromised by the very movement he sought to overcome. Derrida points the way to a new paradigm by recasting the idea of conceptual schemes as deeply unstable, and paradoxically succeeds in escaping metaphysics by problematizing the very idea of escape. These views effect profound changes across many issues, making Derrida's work disorienting and stunningly original, while at the same time fitting quite well into the two-hundred-year-long conversation I am sketching.

Arranging the philosophers in this organization with a commensurable vocabulary drawn from analytic philosophy shows a clear developmental trajectory in the history of continental philosophy. We can see how each thinker is responding to problems bequeathed him and is working on an inherited framework from within. In particular, we learn just how long Kant's shadow was. In fact, we can almost say of Kant what Nietzsche says of God, that he "is dead; but given the way of men, there may still be caves for thousands of years in which his shadow will be shown.—And we—we still have to vanquish his shadow" (Nietzsche, *GS* 108). In my reading, the century and a half following Kant was spent vanquishing his shadows. The major philosophers in his wake rejected his thought but still retained vestiges of it even in their attacks on it. I show how Hegel, Nietzsche, and early Heidegger all subscribe to important aspects of Kant's system while trying to surpass it.

The second lesson derived from this analysis is the significance and importance of Heidegger's later work. One of the most difficult and disorienting bodies of work in the canon, it has long served as a paradigm of unapproachable incomprehensibility to many. I will locate it in relation to the Kantian tradition, showing it to be the first work divested of the vestiges of Kant's thought. This shows its importance and makes its difficulty less suspect; if it is so groundbreaking—operating outside of assumptions that have guided thought for centuries—then it *should* appear strange to us. This history of continental anti-realism gives us a new way to understand the *Kehre* as the change from a thinker still fighting Kant's shadow to one who has broken free and taken his place, and makes Heidegger's enormous influence on continental thinkers understandable. It also makes him more important and, I hope, comprehensible to analytic philosophy. Although the early work of Hegel, Nietzsche, and Heidegger has been assimilated by analytic philosophers to varying degrees, Heidegger's later work remains terra incognita. If my narrative is correct, this body of work contains radically new insights into some of the basic problems of anti-realism and related issues. Whether they end up agreeing with this or not, analytic philosophers working on anti-realism could benefit enormously from his thought, and continental thinkers working on Heidegger should have the opportunity to hear their informed criticisms and suggestions.

1

# Defining Realism

> The world consists of some fixed totality of mind-independent objects. There is exactly one true and complete description of "the way the world is." Truth involves some sort of correspondence relation between words or thought-signs and external things and sets of things. I shall call this perspective the *externalist* perspective, because its favorite point of view is a God's Eye point of view. (Putnam 1981, 49)

Most writers on the topic agree that, as the name suggests, anti-realism is defined in contrast to realism: anti-realism is *not* whatever realism *is*. In J. L. Austin's phrase, realism wears the trousers in the pair,[1] so we must first understand it in order to grasp anti-realism. In this opening chapter I will draw on largely analytic sources to construct a definition of realism in the form of a set of theses (denoted R1–R6), or a Realism Matrix. During my examination of the continental philosophers, I will progressively construct a correlative Anti-Realism Matrix (A1–A6) by tracing these figures' various rejections and modifications of realism. These views arise from the historical conversation between the thinkers as they try to solve the problems and improve the positions left them by their predecessors. These matrices will then serve as the tool to analyze and organize much of the rest of the book. For the reader's convenience, I have listed these theses with representative quotes at the beginning of the book.

I have chosen this method for two reasons. First, although I dislike the clichéd division of virtues which awards clarity and rigor to analytic philosophers and relevance (whatever that means) to the continentals, in this case the conceptual tools offered by these analytic thinkers prove exceptionally useful in organizing and focusing the issue. Since I believe anti-realism is at the heart of continental thought as well, the resulting clarity greatly enhances comprehension of the central course of continental thought that I will be tracing. Second, deploying an analytic definition in the continental field will show that the two camps share this topic and thus supplies terms for a fruitful dialogue.

Of course, there are as many species of realism as there are kinds of objects, since realism can be type-specific or "local" rather than "global": one can be a realist about stars but not about the occurrence of the sequence "7777" in pi; a realist about the past, but not about the future; a realist about unobserveds, but not unobservables; or the reverse for each pair. For the most part, this study will abstract from such fine distinctions to examine the issue at a global level, that is, concerning all entities. Realism has also focused on different realms at various points in history, as documented by C. F. Delaney, who believes "not only that the *realism* dispute is an important issue in each philosophical age but in each it is viewed as *the* central issue" (Dahlstrom 1984, 2; see also 11).[2] According to Delaney, realism has serially taken on medieval nominalism, German idealism, and analytic semantic anti-realism as instantiated by Dummett. I will try to show that the latter two are not as far apart as they seem.

## Theses of Realism

Hilary Putnam's particularly clear and influential definition of what he calls "metaphysical (or external) realism" will supply several of my theses. This definition has become a touchstone in the literature, leading one of the few commentators who engages both the analytic and continental traditions to say of it: "This view obviously represents the dominant meaning of realism in Anglo-American philosophy (as well as the form of realism generally rejected by continental philosophy), so much so that it is generally the way in which 'realism' is defined" (Alcoff 1996, 166). Putnam certainly knows realism, being a prominent advocate of it before he converted to internal realism and became one of realism's principal critics in the late 1970s, only to move to some kind of Jamesian "natural" or "naive realism" in the mid-1990s (see Putnam 1994a, 487–89). In 1981, Putnam lists three components of metaphysical realism which together make up "a bundle of intimately associated philosophical ideas" (Putnam 1988, 107):

> [1] The world consists of some fixed totality of mind-independent objects. [3] There is exactly one true and complete description of "the way the world is." [2] Truth involves some sort of correspondence relation between words or thought-signs and external things and sets of things. I shall call this perspective the *externalist* perspective, because its favorite point of view is a God's Eye point of view.[3]

In a later book, Putnam repeats the definition (though now cast entirely in terms of truth) with names and one important addition: realism consists in "the ideas that truth is a matter of Correspondence [2] and that it exhibits Independence (of what humans do or could find out) [1], Bivalence [4], and Uniqueness (there cannot be more than one complete and true description of Reality) [3]" (Putnam 1988, 107, bracketed numbers added). I will name these defining theses of realism R1, R2, R3, and R4, and will discuss them individually.

### R1 Independence

The first component in the Realism Matrix is metaphysical: a set of objects or states of affairs, which does not rely upon us in any way, exists. The furniture of the universe does not rely upon us for existence or for essence, excluding trivial examples of things we have made or which depend upon us in relatively obvious and uninteresting ways, such as thoughts or beliefs. The fact that these entities are—and that they are what they are—is unaffected by the facts that and what we are, think, or say. Michael Devitt, one of the staunchest realists around, believes that this first component defines and, in fact, exhausts realism:

> An object has objective existence, in some sense, if it exists and has its nature whatever we believe, think, or can discover: it is independent of the cognitive activities of the mind. . . . It is not *constituted by* our knowledge, by our epistemic values, by our capacity to refer to it, by our imposition of concepts, theories, or languages. . . . For the realist, the world exists *independently of the mental.*[4]

In other words, objects are, in Nicholas Rescher's terms, "thought-invariant or thought indifferent" (Rescher 2000, 102).

### R2 Correspondence

The second component (in my ordering) is epistemological. It defines truth as the correspondence between (to cast my net widely—the differences don't concern me at this point) thoughts, ideas, beliefs, words, propositions, sentences, or languages on the one hand, and things, objects, states of affairs, configurations, reality, or experience on the other; that is, between something on the side of the mind or language and something on the side of the world. As Tarski points out,[5] this conception of correspondence truth goes back as far as Aristotle's definition of truth in the *Metaphysics* as "to say of what is that it is, and of what is not that it is not"

(1011b26–27; see also 1051b2–5). Some version of correspondence has been the most common view of truth throughout the history of philosophy, only receiving serious competition after Kant.[6]

Thinkers differ on how the metaphysical and epistemological components of Putnam's definition of realism relate to each other. Many philosophers run them together, as Putnam does in the quote above.[7] On the other hand, Devitt insists on defining realism solely in terms of metaphysical commitments. "Realism does not entail any doctrine of truth. . . . No doctrine of truth entails Realism. I conclude that no doctrine of truth is in any way constitutive of Realism. . . . Realism is about the nature of reality in general, about what there is, and what it is like" (Devitt 1997, 43). Michael Dummett, as I will discuss below, poses the question in semantic terms for greater clarity, since he finds the metaphysical version obscure and undecidable.[8] Crispin Wright favors epistemological factors for the defining feature of realism: "What seems essential [to realism] is the conception of truth as constituted by *fit* between our beliefs, or statements, and the features of an independent, determinate reality" (Wright 1993, 3; see also Walker 1995, 257; Zemach in Krausz 1989, 51).

I agree with Devitt that there is no relation of logical entailment between the metaphysical and epistemological components; reality can be mind-independent, while truth could be coherence or verification or *aletheia* or what have you. But even Devitt concedes that there is a natural fit between metaphysical realism and correspondence truth (see Devitt 1997, 49; see also 4; Kirkham 1995, 75). If the world is out there with a determinate, independent structure, then it would be odd not to define truth as capturing that structure even if this turned out to be unattainable. We may settle for something else, but then it would indeed be settling. Metaphysical realism does not force correspondence truth upon us, but one needs good reasons to match the former to a different partner. As Lynch puts it,

> Even if . . . the correspondence theory of truth does not entail metaphysical absolutism . . . some fairly simple considerations seem likely to lead a metaphysical absolutist to adopt the correspondence theory of truth. . . . It seems that the metaphysical absolutist, if she is to have any theory of truth at all, will be driven in the direction of the correspondence theory of truth. (Lynch 2001b, 124)

Vision makes the same point, calling the conjunction of correspondence truth with metaphysical anti-realism "highly unlikely" (Vision 1988, 18; see also 34). William P. Alston dissociates his "realism about truth from any commitment to such a metaphysical position, though the two positions do have an affinity for each other."[9]

Moving in the other direction—from correspondence truth to metaphysical realism—is highly plausible as well. If truth is correspondence, then there must be something to correspond to. Barry Allen writes of Aristotle's definition of truth that "one can say of *what is* that it is just in case there exists a *what* which is *there,* present with an identity, form, or nature of its own" (Allen 1993, 9). Wright puts the same point in Dummettian language: "There is an evident implication from objectivity of truth to objectivity of judgment: no one can coherently believe that the world is apt to confer potentially evidence-transcendent truth-values upon statements of a certain genre who does not believe that the world contains states of affairs of a kind appropriate to that genre" (Wright 1993, 7). It would be logically possible to define truth as correspondence, deny an independent reality, and simply claim that truth is unattainable, but it is hard to see what would lead one to such a position. If not mutually entailing, metaphysical realism and correspondence truth naturally go together, which explains why the pair has been so common for much of the history of philosophy.

### R3 Uniqueness

The third component in Putnam's definition follows from the first two.[10] If reality has a determinate structure independently of us (R1) and truth consists in capturing that structure (R2), then there will be one and only one way to do so accurately. Putnam spells out this connection with his usual lucidity:

> The metaphysics of realism traditionally included the idea that there is a definite totality of all objects . . . and a definite totality of all "properties.". . . It follows, on this picture, that there is a definite totality of all possible knowledge claims, likewise fixed once and for all independently of language users or thinkers. The nature of the language users or the thinkers can determine which of the possible knowledge claims they are able to think or verbalize, but not what the possible knowledge claims are. (Putnam 1994a, 466; see also Putnam 1992, 123; Putnam 1994b, 303)

There may be many partial truths, but there is only one Truth. There exists, at least in principle, a total, final account of the contents of the universe and their relations to each other. This Book of Truth can be scaled down to the point of single sentences, most philosophers having given up on words as not capturing facts.[11]

Plato was perhaps the first to explore the implications of a determinately structured, mind-independent reality to which true statements must correspond, a picture denied by both Parmenides (since articulated distinctions involve negation, which is incoherent) and Heraclitus (since no stable structure abides amidst the flux).[12] The articulation of a skeleton stands for the inherent structure of reality in the *Phaedrus;* the world divides at breaks that separate natural kinds in the way that joints separate bones. The proper way to gain knowledge through definitions or "dialectic" will then resemble a good butcher's technique: dialectic is the ability "to cut up each kind according to its species along its natural joints, and to try not to splinter any part, as a bad butcher might do" (Plato, *Phaedrus* 265e). When we set out to know the world, to give the kind of taxonomy so important to the later dialogues and Aristotle's thought, we must take care to analyze it into the correct categories, which means according to the classes that are really there, independent of us. Whatever we impose splinters recalcitrant bone rather than slicing through yielding joint. In the end, there are places which are bone and places which are joint, and our decisions about where to cut have no impact on where each lies.

Carving well requires knowledge of and obedience to the world's preexisting articulation. Socrates gives the art of dialectic his highest praise, calling himself "a lover of these divisions and collections, so that I may be able to think and to speak" (Plato, *Phaedrus* 266b). Thinking and speaking ("articulation" in its other meaning, a wordplay Heidegger sometimes employs) depend upon fidelity to reality; indeed, "the whole art of these definitions consists in finding these cleavages" (Plato, *Statesman* 262c). There exists, at least ideally, a full knowledge of all of the Forms which would constitute the complete knowledge of all natural kinds about which there could be no legitimate disagreement.[13] This view is also attributed to "Aristotelian realism, which posits that the species and genera into which the sciences divide reality are merely copies of the genera and species of this reality reflected more or less exactly, but ever more exactly, in the mirror of consciousness,"[14] that is, in my terms, R2 Correspondence Truth of R3 Unique Reality that is R1 Independent of us.

Putnam describes the interconnection between the three components well.

> What makes a metaphysical realist a *metaphysical* realist is his belief that there is somewhere "one true theory" [R3]. . . . In company with a correspondence theory of truth [R2], this belief in one true theory requires a *ready-made* world (an expression suggested in this connection by Nelson Goodman): the world itself has to have a "built-in" structure [R1], since otherwise theories with different structures might correctly "copy" the

> world (from different perspectives) and truth would lose its absolute (non-perspectival) character. (Putnam 1983, 211, bracketed comments added; see also Putnam 1988, 120)

Since the world is out there with a determinate structure, truth is the capturing of it, which can only happen in one way. Employing David Wiggins's phrase, Putnam says that "the world is, after all, being claimed to contain Self-Identifying Objects, for this is just what it means to say that the *world,* and not thinkers, sorts things into kinds" (Putnam 1981, 53).

Bernard Williams calls this third component "the absolute conception," that is, the conception of the world which does not depend upon any facts about our particular constitution, especially our perceptual or conceptual apparatus. It would describe "the world that is 'already there' . . . that is there *anyway,* independent of our experience" (Williams 1985, 138). Since it has filtered out all that is particular to us, "the absolute conception will, correspondingly, be a conception of the world that might be arrived at by any investigators, even if they were very different from us" (139). This will be "a conception consisting of nonperspectival materials available to any adequate investigator, of whatever constitution" (140). Since the materials are nonperspectival they are omniperspectival, that is, available in every perspective, and thus amount to "a systematized theoretical account of how the world really is" (135; see also Nagel 1986, 5, 90). For Williams, this sort of knowledge is Descartes' goal.

### R4 Bivalence

Michael Dummett—often credited with placing anti-realism in the foreground of analytic philosophy—organizes his discussion around bivalence. In framing the issue in semantic terms, he is following Frege and the early Wittgenstein—two of the greatest post-Kantian defenders of realism—who transpose realism into language, claiming that the very meaningfulness of a concept rests on its possession of an absolutely determinate range of application.[15] In order to be legitimate, a concept must divide in advance all objects into the set it applies to and the set it doesn't; for example, red is meaningful if and only if the universe can be exhaustively split into red and non-red objects. Frege calls this requirement "completeness" in "Principles of Definition" from his *Grundgesetze der Arithmetik* (*Basic Laws of Arithmetic*).

> A definition (of a possible predicate) must be complete; it must unambiguously determine, as regards any object, whether or not it falls under the concept. . . . Thus, there must not be any object as regards which the

> definition leaves us in doubt whether it falls under the concept; though for us men, with our defective knowledge, the question may not always be decidable. . . . A concept that is not sharply defined is wrongly termed a concept.[16]

This total subsumption of reality in advance of and even independent of our abilities to actually determine it is the modern heir to Plato's skeleton.

A great deal of Wittgenstein's later work amounts to a comprehensive assault on this realist intuition, which also informs his *Tractatus.* He shows bivalence at work in the realist conception of meaning in his famous discussion of rule- or order-following. The person who considers a rule or order such as "+2" has the intuition that it or, under its influence, the mind "contains" in advance a set of all the numbers that satisfy it: (2, 4, 6, 8, . . .).

> Your idea was that that act of meaning the order had in its own way already traversed all those steps: that when you meant it your mind as it were flew ahead and took all the steps before you physically arrived at this or that one. Thus you were inclined to use such expressions as: "The steps are *really* already taken, even before I take them in writing or orally or in thought." And it seemed as if they were in some *unique* way predetermined, anticipated—as only the act of meaning can anticipate reality. (Wittgenstein, *PI* §188; see also §352; Wittgenstein, *RFM* 84–85, §1.122)

All numbers are either within this set or not, with no third option; that is why Frege says that "the law of excluded middle is really just another form of the requirement that the concept should have a sharp boundary" (Geach and Black 1960, 159; see also Hacker 1996, 24, 104).

In an influential move, Dummett proposes to approach the metaphysical problem of realism via semantic issues. In a Wittgensteinian manner, he claims that the metaphysical debate about the mind-independence or -dependence of reality only presents us "with alternative *pictures.* The need to choose between these pictures seems very compelling; but the non-pictorial content of the pictures is unclear" (Dummett 1991, 10). In other words, posing the question in metaphysical terms just muddies the waters and gives us no way to come to a decision on the matter. Arguing back and forth on whether or not reality exists independently of us amounts to so much Johnsonian rock-kicking, so we should "[transpose] them from a metaphysical to a meaning-theoretical key."[17] Instead of the relatively meaningless and endless metaphysical discussion, we should examine the much more tangible implication of realism of bivalence: if reality is determinate independently of us, then propositions will have determinate truth values regardless of whether we can verify them or not.

Accordingly, this is how Dummett defines realism in order to escape the metaphysical metaphors of the realism debate.

> A common characteristic of realist doctrines is an insistence on the principle of bivalence—that every proposition . . . is determinately either true or false. Because, for the realist, statements about physical reality do not owe their truth-value to our observing that they hold . . . but . . . the statements' truth-value is owed to a reality that exists independently of our knowledge of it, these statements are true or false according as they agree or not with that reality.[18]

A realist who subscribes to all three of Putnam's factors must also accept bivalence; since the world is independently determinate and our sentences strive to correspond to it, their truth-values must be determinate. We saw Frege explicitly link conceptual completeness with the law of excluded middle, and, except for a few possible exceptions such as the debated category of "useful nonsense," the *Tractatus* also holds to the theory: "A proposition must restrict reality to two alternatives: yes or no."[19]

Dummett thus defines realism as the commitment to bivalence independent of our ability to verify or acquire sufficient evidence, and this doctrine connects to R3, that there is one true account of the world. The Book of All True Sentences has already been written and all possible sentences are either in it or not; the most we can hope for is to transcribe it. Our ability to determine the truth or falsity of sentences is wholly irrelevant here; truth is radically non-epistemic (Putnam 1978, 125; see also Moran 2000, 75) or verification-transcendent (Dummett 1978, 146). This means that human access to evidence is wholly irrelevant to what the truth is.[20]

### R5 Passive Knower

I want to add a fifth component to this definition of realism, one that is central to Kant's account and has remained important to continental thinkers, as well as playing at least a tacit role in analytic discussions. In order to be a realist who thinks there is any chance to attain correspondence truth about the world,[21] there must be a way for the mind to reach reality as it is. As we will see in the next chapter, Kant's anti-realism begins from his rejection of any such access, since all contact with the world bears the imprint of mental activity. As William James colorfully puts it, "The trail of the human serpent is thus over everything" (James 1963, 31). If our dealings with the world inevitably affect our experience of it, then the hope to achieve correspondence truth with the world as it is independently of us is futile. This is the meaning of Kant's transcendental idealism: we can never know noumena or things-in-themselves, but only phenomena or things-for-us as partially formed by us. Kenneth R. Westphal points out that

> the key underlying issue in this debate [between coherentism and foundationalism] is whether an activist epistemology is consistent with commonsense realism. Traditionally, both sides to this debate have assumed, even feared, that they are not; if the mind actively contributes to empirical knowledge, must it not inevitably obscure its intended objects. . . . The shared, underlying assumption is that realism requires some basic level of cognition that is purely passive, in which recognizing some purported individual state of affairs requires no interpretation of it. (K. R. Westphal 2003a, 72)

The view that correspondence knowledge of independent reality requires passive cognition has been around for a long time.

In *De anima,* Aristotle uses Plato's image of the mind as a wax tablet to describe the passivity of sense perception, the necessary origin of most knowledge (424a18–20). He then claims that the intellect which takes the forms from these impressions must itself be blank in order to avoid distorting the impression taken from reality. "The intellect is in a way potentially the objects of thought, although it is actually nothing before it thinks; potentially in the same way as there is writing on a tablet on which nothing actually written exists."[22] The mind must be passive and in some sense featureless so as not to distort what comes into it. If it interferes with its input, then, in a metaphor that permeates discussions of realism, the consequence is that (in Francis Bacon's words) "the human understanding is like a false mirror, which, receiving rays irregularly, distorts and discolors the nature of things by mingling its own nature with it" (Bacon 1960, 48, §1.41). Emmanuel Levinas, a thinker enjoying considerable attention in continental circles recently, describes the situation like this:

> The truth correlative to being—in which the subject, a pure welcome reserved for the nudity of disclosed being, effaces itself *before* that which manifests itself, and in which effort, inventiveness, and genius are all just the means, ways, and detours by which being is dis-covered, by which its phases come together and its structures are secured—remains, within the thought that issued from Greece, the foundation of every notion of truth. (Levinas 1996, 99)

Today the topic is sometimes discussed under the rubric of theory-free perception.

This fifth component captures realism's view of, for lack of a better term, humanity's place in the universe and a vague sense of its implicit philosophy of mind. And it is a peculiar view of humanity, as Crispin Wright points out, "a mixture of modesty and presumption" (Wright 1993, 1; see also French, Uehling, and Wettstein 1988, 25). On the one hand, we must humbly obey reality in order to know it; we have to find and follow the joints already there, since we're not strong enough just to cleave wherever we like. Giles Deleuze argues that the roles of sage and priest overlap in "the ancient conception of Wisdom: the sage was defined partly by his own submission, partly by his 'final' accord with Nature" (Deleuze 1984, 14). As pious knowers, we submit to reality, carrying the tablets down from the mountaintop without commenting in the margins. Indeed, when God is considered the direct author of the world, studying the world constitutes a form of worship, while altering the text becomes a kind of blasphemy.[23] As Rescher says of mind-independent reality, "In the main it has the whip hand and we merely respond to its causal dictates. And this is true in cognitive aspects as well" (Rescher 2000, 107).

On the other hand, if we do submit, our reward can be untold power. Patiently following after nature ultimately enables us, in Descartes' words, to "make ourselves, as it were, the lords and masters of nature" (*PWD* 1:142–43). Although there is doubt whether Bacon actually did speak of putting questions to nature stretched out on the rack, the image captures the relation perfectly. On the one hand, nature is bound and made to cough up her secrets; on the other hand, we're hanging on her every word, desperate for the information that only she can provide.

## Realist Foundations

It is no accident that analytic philosophy contains so many sophisticated analyses of realism; this topic has played a singularly important role in the movement's history from its beginning. By most accounts, analytic philosophy was born from Moore and Russell's revival of realism in rebellion against the British idealism that dominated their education. Russell recounts how

> at Cambridge I read Kant and Hegel, as well as Mr. Bradley's *Logic*, which influenced me profoundly. For some years I was a disciple of Mr. Bradley, but about 1898 I changed my views, largely as a result of arguments with

> G. E. Moore. I could no longer believe that knowing makes any difference to what is known. (Ayer 1959, 32)

Russell simply could not swallow the notion that the mind is not R5 Passive but affects what is known—the very centerpiece of Kant's Copernican Revolution, as we will see in the next chapter. Besides the doctrine of external relations (i.e., that many properties and relations possessed by an object are contingent and can be changed without fundamentally altering the underlying entity; see Russell 1959a, 54–55), he and Moore were primarily focused on "the rejection of the whole Kantian apparatus of *a priori* intuitions and categories, moulding experience" (Russell 1959b, 11–12; see also 38, 54, 172).

Russell especially emphasizes his disagreements in the realm of mathematics in his early work, insisting that "my views are, on almost every point of mathematical theory, diametrically opposed to those of Kant."[24] The overarching issue is the idea that "the mind is in some sense creative. . . . Some such theory is essential to every form of Kantianism." In his view, "all knowledge must be recognition, on pain of being mere delusion; Arithmetic must be discovered in just the same sense in which Columbus discovered the West Indies, and we no more create numbers than he created the Indians."[25] If mathematical knowledge is to have legitimacy, the mind must passively discover it (R5) without affecting it in any way; "mere delusion" results from any other view. Russell's thought thus links correspondence, bivalence, and independence: "It is always a fact, or many facts, that [R2] make the statement [R4] true or false as the case may be; and the fact or facts concerned, except in a linguistic statement, are [R1] independent of language and may be independent of all human experience" (Russell 1959a, 186, bracketed comments added; see also 132, 1959b 130). Extricating idealism from his own thought, as well as from the top ranks of the history of philosophy,[26] Russell finds models for proper philosophy in Kant's predecessors, the British empiricists. They had the right picture of the mind as a blank slate passively written upon by experience, as well as a healthy dose of good old British (broadly speaking) common sense; no subjectively constituted reality here!

Russell's great innovation (at least at one point in his career) was to combine an empiricist epistemology with his own extrapolations of Frege and Peano's logic to create "modern analytical empiricism . . . [which] differs from that of Locke, Berkeley, and Hume by its incorporation of mathematics and its development of a powerful logical technique. It is thus able, in regard to certain problems, to achieve definite answers, which have the quality of science rather than of philosophy" (Russell 1945, 834; see also Russell 1929, 62–63). Frege had already tried to stop "the devastation caused by the influx of psychology into logic . . . a widespread philosophical disease" (Frege 1972, 337). He rejected what he perceived as Husserl's view that knowledge changed the object known (a view enabled by confusing objects with their presentations), insisting instead that "in my opinion the bringing of an object under a concept is merely the recognition of a relation which previously already obtained" (324). Russell transferred the model of empiricist R5 Passive perception to logical relations in order to secure their R1 Independence and absolute validity: "It is plain that where we validly infer one proposition from another, we do so in virtue of a relation which holds between the two propositions [R1] whether we perceive it or not: the mind, in fact, is as [R5] purely receptive in inference as common sense supposes it to be in perception of sensible objects" (Russell 1996, 33, bracketed comments added; see also Russell 1959b, 98).

Knowledge by acquaintance, then, serves the same purpose for the link between mind and physical world by creating a connection in which "we are directly aware [of sense-data], without the intermediary of any process of inference or any knowledge of truths"; this is epistemologically foundational because it presents me with "things immediately known to me just as they are" (Russell 1959b, 46–47, bracketed comment added). In other words, the mind's passivity (R5) assures us of the accurate capturing (R2) of reality (R1). This is why Russell commits himself fully to R5: "I think we can, however imperfectly, mirror the world, like Leibniz's monads; and I think it is the duty of the philosopher to make himself as undistorting a mirror as he can. . . . To achieve such impartiality [as a God might have] is impossible for us, but we can travel a certain distance towards it. To show the road to this end is the supreme duty of the philosopher" (Russell 1959a, 213, bracketed comment added). Minimizing interference in one's apprehension of reality so as to render one's "observations and inferences as impersonal, and as much divested of local and temperamental bias, as is possible for human beings" represents "the chief merits of the philosophical school of which I am a member" (Russell 1945, 836).

G. E. Moore also attacks idealism, defining it (making no effort to distinguish British, Kantian, or German varieties or to show why they should be run together) as the identification of an entity with the experience of it (that is, *esse* with its *percipi*), whereas his entire "analysis of sensation has been designed to show . . . that whenever I have a mere sensation or idea, the fact is that I am then aware of something which is equally and in the same sense *not* an inseparable aspect of my awareness. . . . To have a sensation . . . is to know something which is . . . truly and really *not* a part of *my* experience" (G. E. Moore 1965, 27; see also 19). Here he seems to follow Aristotle, for whom "sensation is surely not the sensation of itself, but there is something beyond the sensation, which must be prior" (Aristotle, *Metaphysics* 1010b 35–38). The very nature of awareness seems to entail the R1 Mind-Independence of its object for Moore: "Awareness is and must be in all cases of such a nature that its object, when we are aware of it, is precisely what it would be, if we were not aware" (G. E. Moore 1965, 29). Awareness cannot affect the entity one is aware of in any way without compromising the truth of any beliefs based on this awareness, and it certainly cannot create or constitute the object of awareness. His non-negotiable starting point is, as the historian of analytic philosophy Peter Hylton puts it, "that there is an absolute independence of the objects of knowledge from the knowing mind" (Hylton 1990, 126; see also Hacker 1996, 7).

Russell defines knowledge by acquaintance in similar terms: "The faculty of being acquainted with things other than itself is the main characteristic of a mind."[27] Again this seems definitional, since (what he considers to be) the idealist view that "there can be nothing which is not experienced" would never have "flourished if people had taken the trouble to find out what the word 'experience' is capable of meaning" (Russell 1959a, 144). Frege similarly considers idealism defeated simply by "point[ing] out our intention in speaking or thinking" of a referent other than our own ideas (Geach and Black 1960, 61–62; Dummett 1981, 63–64), or by putting to Husserl the rhetorical question, "But might not the moon, for example, be somewhat hard to digest for a state of consciousness?" (Frege 1972, 324; see also 335). In other words, "the confusion of the subjective with the objective, the fact that no clear distinction is ever made between expressions like 'moon' and 'presentation of the Moon,' all this diffuses such an impenetrable fog that the attempt to achieve clarity becomes hopeless" (335). The problem, according to these fathers of analytic philosophy, arises from a simple confusion of two "expressions" easily cleared up with a little level-headed analysis.

Thus, Moore and Russell's revival of realism fit together with logic and empiricism to create analytic philosophy (see Soames 2003, 94–95). Robert Hanna claims that Russell and Moore's motivation for founding analytic philosophy was specifically to reestablish what I am calling R5 Passive Knower in the face of Kant's rejection: "Initially at least, Russell believed that [with the theory of descriptions] . . . he had finally realized Moore's original goal of a consistently anti-Kantian doctrine of judgement according to which no appeal whatsoever to consciousness, intentionality, or synthesizing subjectivity is required" (Hanna 2001, 58, bracketed comment added). Hylton states that for Moore and Russell,

> the object with which we are in contact [through mental acts] is, in all such cases, unaffected by the fact that we are in contact with it. If we can

> say that Idealism is a view according to which the mind (in some sense of "mind") is *active,* and plays a role in the constitution of reality, then we can equally say that Platonic Atomism is a view according to which the mind is completely passive, and in no way creative. (Hylton 1990, 110–11, bracketed comment added)

Analytic philosophy was at least partially founded on an insistence on what Hylton calls Russell's "extreme and naïve realism" (Hylton 1990, 371), a phrase echoed by Russell himself (see Russell 1959a, 61).

Russell considers his movement the beginning of a new epoch. Logic holds out the kind of philosophical promise to him that science did for Descartes; if used to its fullest potential, if lifted to its rightful place as First Philosophy, this tool can usher in a philosophical utopia.

> The study of logic becomes the central study in philosophy: it gives the method of research in philosophy, just as mathematics gives the method in physics. And as physics, which, from Plato to the Renaissance, was as unprogressive, dim, and superstitious as philosophy, became a science through Galileo's fresh observation of facts and subsequent mathematical manipulation, so philosophy, in our own day, is becoming scientific through the simultaneous acquisition of new facts and logical methods. . . . All this supposed knowledge in the traditional systems [of past philosophies] must be swept away, and a new beginning must be made.[28]

Compared with the rigor and exactness achieved with logic, previous philosophy can only appear as so much gassy superstition; logical analysis will now solve the problems that baffled generations. Just as Descartes touted his methods of analysis and clear and distinct ideas and used them to "reboot" philosophy, so Russell assures the reader that his own "methods . . . resemble those of science. I have no doubt that, in so far as philosophical knowledge is possible, it is by such methods that it must be sought; I have also no doubt that, by these methods, many ancient problems are completely soluble."[29]

The example of the method's power that Russell generally points to is his theory of descriptions, considered his "most important contribution to logic" (Russell 1959a, 83), which uncovers the logical or philosophical syntax hidden beneath ontologically misleading phrases such as "the golden mountain" or "the present king of France." His assessment of his own achievement is not exactly humble: "This clears up two millennia of muddle-headedness about 'existence,' beginning with Plato's *Theaetetus*" (Russell 1945, 831). The radical difference and astonishing success of this method, as well as the model of science, made studying the history of philosophy appear at best fruitless and quite possibly harmful. Physicians do not review the theory of the four humors, nor do chemists go through alchemical training, so why should philosophers be schooled in the history of mistakes? Although he ends one book by claiming, "Of the prospect of progress in philosophy, it would be rash to speak with confidence," in fact Russell consistently brims over with faith in its success as long as it meets "the one and only condition, I believe which is necessary in order to secure for philosophy in the near future an achievement surpassing all that has hitherto been accomplished by philosophers . . . the creation of a school of men with scientific training and philosophical interests, *unhampered by the traditions of the past*" (Russell 1929, 262–63, italics added). And his *History* closes with the promise of his own movement:

> Many questions, formerly obscured by the fog of metaphysics, can be answered with precision, and by objective methods. . . . Take such questions as: What is number? What are space and time? What is mind, and what is matter? I do not say that we can here and now give definitive answers to all these ancient questions, but I do say that a method has been discovered by which, as in science, we can make successive approximations to the truth, in which each new stage results from an improvement, not a rejection, of what has gone before. (Russell 1945, 835–36)

Of course, imploring his readers to be "unhampered by the traditions of the past" would make a rather awkward ending to an eight-hundred-page history of philosophy. But despite his rhetoric here, his faith in logic's vast superiority over and heterogeneity with all previous thought calls for more of a break with the past rather than a conversation with it.[30]

Science, often taken as a model for analytic philosophy, presents its history as one of progress which leaves mistakes behind, and it is the nature of both empiricism and logic, two movements at the heart of analytic philosophy's founding, to sift out the true from the historical. One of the reasons philosophers have perennially retreated to empiricist entitites like patches of color is that these seem to present a level of reality or experience untainted by chronological or cultural variation. No matter how differently we interpret what we see, surely we are all seeing the same thing at the most basic level. And logic has always served as the realm of the timeless; as Frege writes, "Analysis . . . has nothing to do with time; its applicability to occurrences in time is irrelevant" (Geach and Black 1960, 107; see also 134; Dummett 1994, 23). In combining these techniques into "modern analytic empiricism," Russell built a resistance to the incorporation of history into epistemology or metaphysics into the DNA of the movement. This feature has been noticed by commentators such as the historian of analytic philosophy Peter Hylton, who states that "analytic philosophy has largely rejected historical modes of understanding. . . . Analytic philosophy seems to think of itself as taking place within a single timeless moment" (Hylton 1990, vii; see also 16); or John McCumber, who claims that attitudes toward time form the central division between analytics and continentals (2003). Since (debatably) the first great continental philosopher after the split, Hegel, incorporates history into every aspect of his thought while the founders of analytic thought fully exclude it, we can see that this distinguishing characteristic was planted right at the birth of each.

Few other characteristics define the split as clearly as the differing attitude to history and the history of philosophy in particular. Talk of an analytic monopoly on such virtues as clarity or common sense is foolish; characteristics such as these are a matter of training and familiarity, not natural kinds. What one finds clear depends on one's education and background knowledge; Samuel C. Wheeler writes of his surprise when Derrida told him that he had trouble following Kripke's *Naming and Necessity* whereas he found Heidegger "very clear" (Wheeler 2000, 2). For a paragon of gnomic obscurity as well as a lack of argumentation, two criticisms often hurled at continental thinkers, one need look no farther than the greatest analytic philosopher, Wittgenstein, of whom Russell wrote (certainly with some personal animus): "He, himself, as usual, is oracular and emits his opinion as if it were a Czar's ukase, but humbler folk can hardly content themselves with this procedure" (Russell 1959a, 118).

Common sense is largely a matter of the ideas one is used to, as frequent handling rubs off the edges of strangeness. One of the figures responsible for giving analytic philosophy this value, Bertrand Russell (see, for example, 1959a 12), held at various points in his career that universals and numbers have real existence, that we only perceive color patches, that only indexicals like "this" are true names, and that solipsism is irrefutable, hardly beliefs we can expect the person in the street or on the Clapham Street omnibus to find natural. Other important analytic ideas have been Quine's indeterminacy of meaning, Kripke and his followers' serious analyses of multiple worlds, Putnam's Twin Earth investigations, and the logical positivists' relegation of vast amounts of mundane conversation to the dustbin of nonsense; I won't bother mentioning counterintuitive views from Wittgenstein's writings, since that's just shooting fish in a barrel. Continental thought has no monopoly on beliefs that look odd from the perspective of common sense, defined as what the non-philosopher unschooled in the issues would find plausible. This doesn't invalidate the views, of course, since we can understand how they were reached once we appreciate the problems they address and the alternatives they try to improve. The views can be seen to be at least reasonable options once we grasp the problems to which they are responses and the context in which they take place; the problem is that analytic philosophers lack this awareness for continental work, which makes it look willfully bizarre.

It is one of the fundamental aspects of Hegel's approach to philosophy which have become virtually ubiquitous in continental scholarship that, like other human endeavors, philosophy is a historical enterprise. This means that philosophical views and theories can only be fully understood and appreciated within the context of the concerns they are responding to and, at best, the criticisms and movements they influence. Whereas Russell's commitment to the doctrine of external relations and realist bivalence leads him to claim that "I still hold that an isolated truth may be quite true" (Russell 1959a, 63), continental philosophers prefer a kind of historical holism or context principle, analyzing philosophical ideas within a broader context. Since continental philosophers incorporate others' thought so deeply into their own, reading one without the background knowledge of the other figures he or she is responding to can be baffling, like eavesdropping on the middle of an extended conversation. This has been a significant obstacle to analytic philosophers who are interested in what continental thinkers are up to, but are unfamiliar with the intellectual landmarks that are so essential to this way of doing philosophy. This embeddedness contributes to the impression of continental obscurity and a lack of originality or inability to think for oneself, though I think this is a misunderstanding of philosophy and thought itself, as I will discuss in more detail in my book's conclusion.[31] One of the purposes of this book is to lay out one important thread of the continental conversation so that those who have not been listening can be brought up to speed and, hopefully, participate.

Part 1

# The Kantian Paradigm

# 2

# Kant's Revolution

> We suppose that our representation of things, as they are given to us, does not conform to these things as they are in themselves, but that these objects, as appearances, conform to our mode of representation. (Kant, *C1* Bxx)
>
> The order and regularity in the appearances, which we entitle *nature,* we ourselves introduce. We could never find them in appearances, had not we ourselves, or the nature of our mind, originally set them there. (Kant, *C1* A125)

When we examine the history of philosophy from the perspective of different issues, various philosophers take on greater or less weight depending on how directly, originally, and influentially they address the specific topic. For our topic of anti-realism, Descartes, for instance, recedes in importance. The basic structure of metaphysical realism prevalent throughout the history of philosophy continues in his thought, now just founded in the certainty of the subject. Subjectivity takes on new significance as the first bastion of knowledge, but it still functions as an inert stepping-stone; first in *ordine cognoscendi,* it can play no role in *ordine essendi.* Instead of the father of modern philosophy, it is Kant who forms the great fault line for realism. Although other philosophers had challenged individual tenets of realism, Kant was the first to undermine it radically and offer a coherent, powerful alternative account of reality, subjectivity, and knowledge. I will call this new conception the Kantian Paradigm and discuss it in this chapter. The next three chapters will then show how this framework dominates the continental tradition until Heidegger's definitive break with it in his later work.

Kant is keenly aware of how revolutionary his critical philosophy is. Although both Locke (Locke 1959, 1:9) and Hume both took their task to be the similar-sounding charting of a "mental geography, or delineation of the distinct parts and powers of the mind" (Hume 1975, 13) in order to determine its capabilities and limitations, Kant claims that his thought represents "a perfectly new science, of which no one has ever even thought, the very idea of which was unknown" (Kant, *PFM* 7/262). He believes that his transcendental or critical idealism is the first philosophy to challenge transcendental realism systematically, an assessment shared by many commentators. Hilary Putnam flatly claims that, "it is impossible to find a philosopher before Kant who was *not* a metaphysical realist" (Putnam 1981, 57; see also Putnam 1978, 1; Putnam 1990, xix). Robert B. Pippin dramatically states that "the implication of Kant's argument was a more comprehensive and wide-ranging revolution in conceiving mind-world and subject-subject relations than ever before effected within the Western tradition" (Pippin 1997, 9). Robert C. Solomon also stresses the contrast between Kant's transcendental idealism and the vast history of realism: "Kant denied . . . that the world was 'out there' and independent of our experience of it. The whole history of metaphysics depends upon the belief in the presence of a reality independent of us" (Solomon 1988, 28; see also H. Allison 1983, 16; Hyppolite 1974, 144).

Despite its virtually ubiquitous reign, Kant comes to the conclusion that realism is actually an obscure dogma.[1] Once we separate thought and being, there seems to be no rational way to demonstrate their unity (Kant, *C1* A369), so the connection simply gets assumed (see, for example, A197/B242). The unity of thought and being—that is, the claim that what we think correctly corresponds to what is—represents the essential condition for any further thought to have validity, yet rationally establishing it appears impossible, so philosophers just assert it dogmatically. Although there have been various attempts to underwrite it through biology (Aristotle) or a benevolent God (Augustine, Descartes), Kant considers these merely distractions from the emperor's nudity, since these proofs themselves require prior assurance of the reliability of our cognitive faculties.[2] The inevitable dilemma is either dogmatic realism or skepticism about external reality,[3] that great "scandal to philosophy and to human reason in general" (Bxl n.a). All realist philosophies require unjustified assumptions even to get started, a genuinely scandalous situation for the discipline that prides itself on rooting out all assumptions. Philosophy must start over with a new understanding of the relationship between subject and world or thought and being that actually establishes the connection rather than simply assuming it. A revolution is needed.

## The Copernican Revolution

Kant's solution to the problems of realism is his famous Copernican Revolution, the most profound change in the history of thought ever summed up in a single paragraph.

> Hitherto it has been assumed that all our knowledge must conform to objects. But all attempts to extend our knowledge of objects by establishing something in regard to them *a priori*, by means of concepts, have, on this assumption, ended in failure. We must therefore make trial whether we may not have more success in the tasks of metaphysics, if we suppose that objects must conform to our knowledge. (Kant, *C1* Bxvi)

This fundamentally alters the conception of knowledge and the role the subject plays in knowing, a change whose importance cannot be exaggerated. It marks the creation of a new paradigm, a new way of understanding subject-object relations. Gone is the inquiring subject (in both senses of the word) who must profess fealty to sovereign nature;[4] gone is the soft clay of the Platonic-Aristotelian soul or the blank paper of the Lockean mind passively taking on reality's imprint. In its place is the Baconian scientist who boldly questions, even tortures,[5] subservient nature (Kant, *C1* Bxiii) and the Cartesian ideal of humans as "the lords and masters of nature" (Descartes, *PWD* 1:142–43) made ontological. We do not find the order of (phenomenal) nature; we make it.

Whereas many early modern thinkers encouraged us voluntarily to take up an authoritative stance toward nature through experimental science, Kant claims that we are always already in this position (Kant, *C1* Bxiii). The ordering of experience is an autonomic process like regulating one's heart rate that constantly operates in the background rather than an attitude consciously taken on. In Pippin's words, Kant

> does not attempt, as in the popular essays, simply to encourage us to reject dependence and assert independence. Rather, Kant attempts to show that in all empirical experience . . . there simply are, necessarily, spontaneously self-legislated rules or conditions . . . whether recognized as such or not. (Pippin 1991, 50)

Any mastery of nature attained through scientific knowledge is secondary to and derivative of our prior, a priori constitutive role. This thought reverses realism's R5 Passive Knower which portrays the mind as a passive receptacle of information. The center of Kant's revolution is A5 Active

Knower—the thesis that the mind actively organizes and constitutes experience; it is more like a factory than wax or a mirror.

On this view the phenomenal world is partially due to features of the mind, specifically, the forms of intuition and the concepts of the understanding (themselves getting egged on and organized on a meta-level by the ideas of reason), imparting structure to the input of sensory data. Now, the idea that we affect experience is not exactly novel. It goes back at least as far as Democritus, for whom all that really exists are atoms and void, but the atoms' motion and inherent features interact with our body to produce other perceived characteristics which amount only to "what changes with the condition of our body" (Nahm 1964, 197, §9). Descartes and Locke both embrace this atomistic picture of secondary qualities arising from an interaction with us, while Hume attributes "perceived" features like causality to habit-induced subjective extrapolations from sense-data. The key point is that for all of these thinkers the subject's contributions amount to distortion, illusion, and generally untruth; they all take the faculties' meddling to be a damnable offense. This is the point of R5 as an epistemological method: the unquiet forces of the mind (senses, traditional belief, will, and so on) must be stilled to let the mirror, untroubled, reflect without distortion. Descartes and Locke seek true knowledge in mathematical or analytic relations which escape sensory influence; Hume takes the distortion to be inevitable, which functions as a *reductio* of the traditional conception of knowledge. As discussed in chapter 1, Russell revives this aspect of realism when he claims that "all knowledge must be recognition, on pain of being mere delusion" (Russell 1996, 451).

In the *Prolegomena,* Kant explicitly portrays his transcendental idealism as an extension of Locke's theory of secondary qualities (slightly qualified at Kant, *C1* A29/B45).

> Long before Locke's time, but assuredly since him, it has been generally assumed and granted without detriment to the actual existence of external things that many of their predicates may be said to belong, not to the things in themselves, but to their appearances, and to have no proper existence outside our representation. . . . I go further and, for weighty reasons, rank as mere appearances also the remaining qualities of bodies, which are called primary. (Kant, *PFM* 33/289)[6]

The astonishing thing about Kant's theory is not the fairly common view that our faculties contribute to experience, but the idea that this contribution does not compromise the knowledge claims based on experience so affected. Kant's revolution is to find this contribution not only acceptable but in fact *essential* for knowledge.

Kant's solution to the dilemma of either dogmatically assuming or skeptically denying the unity of thought and being in knowledge is to show that the unity can be wrought by thought's imposition of its forms on (phenomenal) being. It is this imposition of forms that makes reality accessible to us and thus knowable, and since Kant believes he can demonstrate this imposition, the ensuing unity is proven for the first time. Previous philosophers had merely assumed it, which is why Heidegger says that Kant "grounds [the 'correspondence' (*adaequatio*) of knowledge to the being] for the first time" (Heidegger, *KPM* 8, bracketed comment added; see also R. K. Hill 2003, 170; Deleuze 1984, 14). Whereas for earlier thinkers the fact that faculties contribute to experience was an objection to that experience serving as knowledge, Kant famously claims that "we can know *a priori* of things only what we ourselves put into them" (*C1* Bxviii).[7] Rather than being *ruled out* by subjective contributions, genuine knowledge actually *requires* the subject's imposition of form. Hume showed Kant that reliance on experience can only produce contingent information; as long as we depend just on what experience shows us, it can always surprise us. But a priori contributions which are necessary to the very act of thinking (proven in the "Deductions") must be present in all acts of thinking and thus in all that is thought. Therefore, we can never encounter an experience which violates or lacks those features which we always contribute, rendering these features necessary and universal to all experienced entities as experienced, that is, phenomena (see Bxxiii).

This reversal of attitude toward the subject's contribution to experience is stunning. Whereas Descartes cites sensory experience's "contamination" by the faculties as one of his main reasons for rejecting it as a source of knowledge, Kant cites this same interaction (broadened to include the understanding) as a reason that knowledge can *only* be of sensory experience. This epistemology fits Kant's central value of autonomy. While Descartes still subscribes to many aspects of an Augustinian kind of self-abnegation before reality, Kant insists on autonomy in all spheres. Rather than humbly following after God's creation or passively recording the intrinsic structure of the world, we boldly form phenomena. Deleuze describes this colorfully:

> The first thing that the Copernican Revolution teaches us is that it is we who are giving the orders. There is here an inversion of the ancient conception of Wisdom: the sage was defined partly by his own submission, partly by his "final" accord with Nature. Kant sets up the critical

> image in opposition to wisdom: we are the legislators of Nature. (Deleuze 1984, 14)

Reliance on anything external to the self, even God, (1) amounts to heteronomy and (2) can only be dogmatically asserted, not rationally proven. Both of these problems are fixed simultaneously by making the self first in the *ordine essendi* rather than just the *ordine cognoscendi,* as Descartes held. The subject is ontologically primary in that it constitutes the form of the phenomenal realm; Kant's adherence to what I am calling A5 Active Knower is the linchpin of his revolution. I will now turn to how this new position affects realism and then examine its ramifications for correspondence truth.

## (Anti-)Realism

Kant is often seen as the founder of anti-realism (see, for example, Plantinga 1982, 47; Putnam throughout); before him, realism was so common that it was more like the default obvious truth than a position actively held. Determining Kant's precise position on the issue, however, proves more difficult than might be expected. As we have already seen, the A5 Active Knower thesis forms the centerpiece of his thought, but rejecting R5 does not in and of itself entail the rejection of the rest of the theses of my Realism Matrix, like dominoes falling after the first is pushed. Indeed, one general lesson to be learned from examining the thinkers' positions in this book is how variously the realist and anti-realist ideas can be mixed and matched, as well as the way a view gets taken up and employed in a wholly unexpected way by a later figure. Kant ends up with a highly nuanced, though also rather problematic take on the other theses, which I will examine in turn.

### R1 Independence

Kant is famously split on the mind-independence of reality: noumena are, phenomena aren't. On the one hand, since phenomena are constituted by the mind, they require it to exist: "external objects (bodies), however, are mere appearances, and are therefore nothing but a species of my representations, the objects of which are something only through these representations. Apart from them they are nothing" (Kant, *C1* A370–71; see also A42/B59). Whether they are a separate group of entities (the "two-worlds" interpretation) or simply a different aspect or way of conceiving of the single world (the presently more popular "double-aspect" or "one-world" interpretation), phenomena depend upon the mind to exist. "If I remove the thinking subject the whole corporeal world must at once vanish: it is nothing save an appearance in the sensibility of our subject and a mode of its representations" (A383). This thesis is what led to the charges of idealism that infuriated him (see, for example, Kant, *PFM* 36–41/288–94).

It is important to note that the first *Critique* is not just about epistemology; this focus, common among neo-Kantians and analytic philosophers, forms one of Heidegger's main targets in his extensive interpretations of Kant (see, for example, Heidegger, *BP* 128). Once we understand that phenomenal reality is a genuine level of reality for Kant and appreciate what he calls the "highest principle of all synthetic judgments . . . that the conditions of the *possibility of experience* in general are likewise conditions of the *possibility of the objects of experience,*"[8] we can see that Heidegger is right to assert that the book is equally a book of ontology.[9] Since forms and concepts determine a great deal about the nature of phenomena, studying the mind's constitutive powers is just learning basic features of the phenomenal world. David Kolb writes that for Kant, metaphysics denotes "studies of the necessary structure of our knowing activity . . . and, therefore, the necessary structure of all rational actions or knowable objects in those areas."[10] This equation which follows from Kant's highest principle will be extremely important for the history of continental philosophy, as I will show. Kant's position is not, of course, full-blown idealism in which the world in toto is created by the subject; we merely supply the form for the given sensible manifold. However, this form's structuring is so profound that we cannot even speak of the phenomenal world as existing without it. We can only speak of the phenomenal world per se in relation to the subject, thus rendering it mind-dependent. "All appearances, are not in themselves *things;* they are nothing but representations, and cannot exist outside our mind" (Kant, *C1* A492/B520). Thus phenomena are not R1 Mind-Independent, but A1 Mind-Dependent.

On the other hand, it is undeniable that some entities or aspects of reality—noumena—do exist mind-independently for Kant.[11] One way to portray him as a realist is to stress this commitment to noumena, perhaps thinking of them as a set of existing, unknowable things. James Van Cleve claims that since "for Kant, things in themselves are things that exist independent of human cognition; they do not depend on human beings either for their existence or for their being the way they are"; that "on one important score, then, Kant is a metaphysical realist" (Van Cleve 1999, 134, 214).[12] According to the basic argument of the *Critique,* of course, we have no access to noumena, so we cannot directly establish their existence through experience; one indirect means of proving them is a Lockean-style argument that the very idea of appearance requires something behind it "causing" the appearance (Kant, *C1* Bxxvi). It simply makes no sense to talk about appearance without *something* appearing. This is problematic, however, because it takes the categories that are supposed to be limited to phenomena and stretches them to span the phenomenal and noumenal realms. This argument posits some kind of causal relation between the two (the famous affection problem) and applies at least the categories of causality and existence (and perhaps substance) to noumena, thus breaking the fundamental law of the first *Critique.*[13]

The second way of fleshing out the notion of noumena is by means of an appeal to God's intellectual intuition which can access the noumenal realm. According to this interpretation, noumena wear the pants in the noumena/phenomena contrast; they constitute true reality and knowledge of them would count as real knowledge but remains, alas, forever beyond our reach. Guyer depicts the position thus: "Kant's degradation of the very features of our cognition which he has discovered to be necessary for us is held to follow from his continuing attachment to the theological ideal of divine knowledge independent of all space and time" (Guyer 1987, 5; see also Findlay 1981, 19–20). This would place Kant in agreement with Berkeley's view that the only way to conceive of reality is by positing an observer, so we can only conceive of absolute reality as being perceived by an absolute subject. This is why Putnam famously calls this realist ideal the "God's Eye point of view" (Putnam 1981, 49). The problem with this option is Kant's reluctance to use God in any constitutive role in his work, a role many earlier philosophers assign Him without compunction. Kant sees philosophical reliance on God as a kind of deus ex machina; God provides miraculous solutions for many a thinker who has painted herself into a metaphysical corner.[14] Every idea supporting weight in his thought must pass the tribunal of reason which, of course, knowledge of God never can.[15] This position also implies that Kant saw the limits on our cognitive capacities as a defect, viewing our knowledge as a poor substitute for what we can never have, but the first *Critique* is just as much a vindication of empirical knowledge as it is an elimination of metaphysical knowledge.

The best alternative to these realist interpretations of noumena is Kant's own depiction of them as "limit-concepts."

> The concept of the noumenon is, therefore, not the concept of an object, but is a problem unavoidably bound up with the limitation of our sensibility—the problem, namely, as to whether there may not be objects entirely disengaged from any such kind of intuition. This is a question which can only be answered in an indeterminate manner, by saying that

> as sensible intuition does not extend to all things without distinction, a place remains open for other and different objects; and consequently that these latter must not be absolutely denied, though—since we are without a determinate concept of them (inasmuch as no category can serve that purpose)—neither can they be asserted as objects for our understanding. (Kant, *C1* A287–88/B344)

He says that noumena are "nothing to us" since we have no access to them (Kant, *C1* A105). However, once God has been removed from the picture as a constitutive entity (in theoretical thought), the difference between nothing to us and nothing at all becomes hard to pin down, a point that will be taken up by Hegel, Nietzsche, and the phenomenologists. The thing-in-itself, then, would not be an ontologically distinct entity but just the phenomenon considered as it is apart from the contributions of the subject. Henry E. Allison gives perhaps the best known version of this reading.

> To speak of appearances in the transcendental sense is simply to speak of spatiotemporal entities (phenomena), that is, of things insofar as they are viewed as subject to the conditions of human sensibility. Correlatively, to speak of things in themselves transcendentally is to speak of things insofar as they are independent of these conditions.[16]

Thus, rather than two metaphysically separate sets of entities, the distinction refers to different ways of conceiving of the same entities.

Kant's distinction between the positive and negative senses of noumenon corresponds roughly to this difference between the divine-perspective and limit-concept ways of conceiving of noumena.

> If by "noumenon" we mean a thing in so far as it is *not an object of our sensible intuition,* and so abstract from our mode of intuiting it, this is a noumenon in the *negative* sense of the term. But if we understand by it an *object* of a *non-sensible intuition* . . . this would be "noumenon" in the *positive* sense of the term. (Kant, *C1* B307)

Although Kant treats these as interchangeable sides of the same coin, they actually carry significantly different connotations. The positive sense gives noumena much more substance; they constitute a real, indeed *the* real realm of existence, while phenomena are merely these things squeezed into our forms of intuition and understanding. The negative sense, on the other hand, presents noumena as simply a conceptual counterpart or "intellectual shadow" cast by the notion of phenomena, if you will, without any further claims made about them. They are an empty thought, a mental placeholder. The former suggests a more realist perspective: things in themselves have identities which are by definition (at least human) mind-independent, thus downgrading our actively constituted knowledge to unavoidable distortions.[17] The latter interpretation is more compatible with the anti-realist line: noumena are nothing more than ideas we are forced to think because of the grammar (in Wittgenstein's sense) of the notions (see Putnam 1983, 226–27), but they are completely rather than just practically irrelevant to epistemological concerns (see Kant, *C1* A251–52).

Although Kant's inclusion of both the negative and positive senses of noumena prevents a decisive verdict on R1, he does severely qualify the thesis by profoundly separating noumena from our experience and rendering them unnecessary for our mundane and scientific endeavors. In the continental tradition R1 Independent reality never recovers from this blow.[18] No major continental thinker accepts the noumenal realm in the fashion that Kant understands it, the way he thought necessary to avoid absurdity, and one of the main arcs we will follow throughout the rest of part 1 of this book will be the attempts to hunt down and exterminate all vestiges of realism in Kant's basic framework. We will watch it erode over the next century and a half under continental philosophers' ever-increasing criticisms.

### R2 Correspondence

As discussed in chapter 1, the standard understanding of correspondence is that a statement/belief/judgment is true if and only if it corresponds to or correctly mirrors a fact in the world. The state of affairs is primary and the subject "pictures" it, in Wittgenstein's famous metaphor. This theory views the world as "prepackaged," so to speak: reality comes to us already organized into discrete facts or states of affairs which have R3 determinate states R1 Independently of us. We simply follow after nature, trying to reflect the facts adequately, cutting nature along its own joints. Kant undermines this conception; he "destroyed the basis of metaphysics and epistemology as they had been practiced for centuries" (Solomon 1988, 44; see also Prado 2003, 196). The world does not come prepackaged, allowing us only passive mimesis. Instead, the phenomenal realm is formed by the subject: "We give the orders." In the wake of this massive intellectual upheaval, it is difficult to know what truth means anymore. Although Kant still ostensibly subscribes to the traditional definition of correspondence truth which he calls "the nominal definition of truth,"[19] this can no longer mean what it did against the background of metaphysical realism, for what is being corresponded to?

On the one hand, our ideas obviously do not correspond to noumena; by definition these cannot be captured by human thought. Although we can think them with pure understanding, the notion of these thoughts "agreeing" with their objects in any significant way is unintelligible.[20] Kant explicitly rules out noumenal correspondence in the *Prolegomena* (77/336), and in the first *Critique* the limit-concept of noumena is so empty of content that there is virtually nothing in it to correspond to. He discusses the problem in his *Lectures on Logic.*

> *Truth,* it is said, consists in the agreement of cognition with its object. In consequence of this mere nominal explanation, my cognition, to count as true, is supposed to agree with its object. Now I can compare the object with my cognition, however, only by *cognizing* it. . . . Since the object is outside me, the cognition in me, all I can ever pass judgment on is whether my cognition of the object agrees with my cognition of the object. (Kant 1992, 557–58)[21]

Kant makes the same claim in an unpublished "Reflection" from the early 1780s:

> *If for truth* we require something more than the thoroughgoing harmony of intuitions according to the laws of the understanding, what would this be, if it were not at the same time the representation of a determinate object [?] Should it be in addition to this a further agreement with something else, which does not lie in our representations, how could we compare our representations with it [?] All objects (*crossed out:* are only determined by representations in me; what they may in addition be in themselves is unknown to me) are simultaneously in us; an object outside us is transcendent, i.e., entirely unknown to us and useless as a criterion of truth.[22]

Both of the above quotes claim that since noumena are inaccessible, correspondence with them is "useless as a criterion of truth," a common complaint against the correspondence theory of truth. As Donald Davidson writes, "The usual complaint about correspondence theories is that it makes no sense to suggest that it is somehow possible to compare one's words or beliefs with the world, since the attempt must always end up simply with the acquisition of more beliefs," citing Neurath, Hempel, Rorty, and himself as philosophers who have registered this complaint (Davidson, "SCT" 302).

The problem with this objection, as commentators such as Kirkham, Lynch, and Vision point out, is that the *criterion* of truth is distinct from the *definition or nature* of truth. The claim that correspondence offers no useful criterion or is completely inaccessible is irrelevant for the entirely different issue of whether correspondence is in fact the nature of truth. To believe otherwise—to use the usefulness or accessibility of the criterion as itself a criterion for a successful theory of the nature of truth—rests on the presupposition that truth is epistemic, that is, defined in terms of human beliefs and access. Davidson continues the quote given above with an exceptionally clear rebuttal:

> This complaint against correspondence theories is not sound. One reason it is not sound is that it depends on assuming that some form of epistemic theory is correct; therefore, it would be a legitimate complaint only if truth were an epistemic concept. If this were the only reason for rejecting correspondence theories, the realist could simply reply that his position is untouched; he always maintained that truth was independent of our beliefs or our ability to learn the truth. (Davidson, *SCT* 302–3; see also Davidson, *SIO* 183; McDermid 1998, 22–23)

In other words, the objection begs the question by assuming an epistemic conception of truth, that is, one where accessibility to humans is the relevant issue, which is one of the issues at stake.

Kant brings in this concern, but his situation is perhaps slightly stronger on this issue than most, since for him noumenal correspondence is not just uncertain but impossible in principle. As Guyer shows at length, Kant is "metaphysically immodest" in that he goes beyond the agnostic position that we cannot know whether temporality and spatiality apply to noumena to explicitly deny noumenal possession of these features (see Guyer 1987, 355; Schaper and Vossenkuhl 1989, 148; Houlgate 1991, 7). It isn't just that our beliefs *might not* accurately reflect reality; our experience is the end result of an inordinately complicated process of organization which injects features we know to be inapplicable to noumena and so *cannot* correspond to noumena. Thus Kant is forced to an epistemic truth—correspondence with phenomena—if he wants any kind of truth at all. Correspondence with noumena isn't merely unverifiable or useless, but wholly impossible. This is why he says that "if knowledge is to have objective reality, that is, to relate to an object, and is *to acquire meaning and significance* in relation to it, the object must be capable of being in some manner given" (Kant, *C1* A155/B194, italics added). For Kant it is not just the utility but rather the very existence of truth that is forfeit if truth resides entirely in the unknowable relation between a thought and a thing-in-itself.

This does not wholly escape the objection, of course. As we saw in chapter 1, Kant could simply opt for total skepticism, but avoiding this fate is one of the motivations behind his entire philosophy. This is what John

McCumber points to when he says that Kant's discussions "show that we need a *criterion* of truth because we can never have truth itself, in the traditional (dogmatic) sense of the [R2] agreement of our cognition with the world outside, or [R1] independent of, our minds" (McCumber 2003, 79n21, bracketed comments added; see also McCumber 2005, 25). Kant makes this transition to epistemic truth explicit when he says, "The question here is, namely, whether and to what extent there is a criterion of truth that is certain, universal, and useful in application. For this is what the question, *What is truth?* ought to mean" (Kant 1992, 558). In other words, he collapses the distinction between the nature and the criterion of truth, which is just what epistemic theories do.

When we turn from noumena to phenomena as the possible objects of correspondence, there are two candidates for the aspect of the object with which our beliefs correspond—the matter or the form (Kant explicitly makes this distinction at Kant 1992, 558–59). The matter would be the sensible manifold which comes to us from the outside and which forms our "contact" with things-in-themselves. However, this quickly becomes problematic, for how can a fully formed judgment of experience correspond to an unformed, nonunified sensible manifold? The comparison between a finished, processed item and its raw materials (the metaphor Kant employs at *C1* A1) is hard to cash out. In what sense does a window *correspond* to sand, heat, and bits of wood, or a Matisse painting to a piece of canvas and globs of colored paint?[23] Since perception is an active process, what comes out precisely does *not* correspond to what went in; that's the whole point. This is basically the same problem that confronts correspondence with noumena, which is unsurprising, since the sensible manifold is the closest we get to noumena (see, for example, Kant, *C1* A190/B235).

In fact, as that which precedes all of the shaping and molding necessary for experience, the sensible manifold is on a slippery slope towards noumena. We cannot talk intelligently about it until it is a phenomenon, that is, until it has been transformed into experience, but at that point it is precisely no longer the raw sensory data that were desired. Rorty describes the dilemma succinctly: "Insofar as a Kantian intuition is effable, it is just a perceptual judgment and thus not *merely* 'intuitive.' Insofar as it is ineffable, it is incapable of having an explanatory function" (Rorty 1982, 4).[24] Upon examination, the manifold too starts looking like a limit-concept, that is, something we must posit in order to avoid total idealism but about which we can have no real comprehension. Dermot Moran, following John McDowell, describes this well: "Kant's transcendental idealism . . . thinks of sensations only in so far as they can be *retrospectively* grasped as such, distilled out by thought experiment from the already spatially and temporally formed . . . whole. . . . Sensations as such don't exist as actual individual separable atoms of our experience."[25] This slide of sensory data coming into the mind *ab extra* into something at least quasi-noumenal is what leads to Hegel's idealism, as we will see in the next chapter.[26]

Now, there is a perfectly straightforward sense in which our judgments correspond with sensation: whatever we judge to be true of an object must be borne out by all further sensory data. If we determine that a car in the distance is blue and then see that it is red when it approaches, our judgment failed to correspond to the new sensory data; if the car is blue when it approaches, then the judgment's correspondence has been confirmed. This, however, is a matter of future observations—themselves full-fledged experience—not contradicting earlier judgments, a view closer to a coherence of experiences among themselves than a correspondence between experience and an external manifold. Kant sometimes even uses coherence-style language, as he does here when he describes a type of falsehood: "But even if our judgment contains no contradiction, it may connect concepts in a manner *not borne out* by the object."[27] Note that this language implies future disharmony, not present discord with reality. Some commentators have claimed that "Kant seems to dissolve this traditional notion of correspondence into something which sounds a good deal more like coherence."[28]

In fact, the only correspondence that really works in Kant's system is the conformity of objects to our forms of intuition and concepts of understanding, an unprecedented sense of the term since for the first time objects are required to correspond to human faculties rather than the other way around. Whereas some medieval philosophers believed that objects must conform to God's ideas in order to be true/real, now it is we who possess the "*a priori* concepts to which all objects of experience necessarily conform, and with which they must agree" (Kant, *C1* Bxvii–xviii; see also Heidegger, *PIK* 38). Kant makes this reversal of correspondence explicit in terms of the noumenon/phenomenon split: "We suppose that our representation of things, as they are given to us, does not conform to these things as they are in themselves, but that these objects, as appearances, conform to our mode of representation" (Kant, *C1* Bxx; see also A122, A177/B220). He is careful to limit the scope of the imposed conformity to only formal features in order to prevent dialectic, that is, Leibnizian or Hegelian-style aspirations to infer metaphysical facts about absolute reality from these formal conditions (A61/B85).

> The purely logical criterion of truth, namely the agreement of knowledge with the general and formal laws of the understanding and reason, is a *conditio sine qua non,* and is therefore the negative condition of all truth. But further than this logic cannot go. It has no touchstone for the

> discovery of such error as concerns not the form but the content. (Kant, *C1* A59–60/B84; see also Kant 1992, 559)

He downplays its importance here, but this negative condition is one of the fundamental achievements of the whole book. It is what allows him simultaneously to validate phenomenal knowledge and eliminate noumenal knowledge, since the former meets the condition and so counts as knowledge, while the latter does not.

Thus, although Kant claims to adhere to the nominal meaning of truth, correspondence in the traditional sense has no place in his thought: "There is no correspondence theory of truth in his philosophy" (Putnam 1981, 64; see also Putnam 1987, 43; Putnam 1991, 28; Apel 1999, 49). His system cannot accommodate the notion of experience corresponding to what is precisely non-experiential, whether it be noumena or pre-experiential sensible manifold. The kind of correspondence he does allow for is novel: phenomena must conform to our forms of experience. As W. B. Macomber says, "While empirical knowledge must correspond with its object, such knowledge is only possible because, in a deeper sense, things correspond with the structure of the human mind" (Macomber 1967, 14). Instead of following behind God, *nous,* or the cosmic logos to uncover the ground plan of the universe, inquiry actually amounts to retracing the steps that we ourselves have taken "autonomically," or "behind the back of consciousness," in Hegel's phrase. We try to comprehend consciously the way we have constituted the world unconsciously, thus relying on no one and nothing besides our own efforts. Autonomy is the central value in Kant's epistemology as well as his ethics.

### R3 Uniqueness

Kant insists that phenomena have stable, rule-governed identities that are not open to contingent fluctuation as Hume allowed. Without this stability, our experience would be a mere "rhapsody of perceptions" (Kant, *C1* A156/B195); not only would it not be amenable to scientific knowledge, it would not even count as genuine experience. Here Kant subscribes to the great tradition of epistemological realism that Plato expresses so well in his image of the divided line correlating self-identity and stability with knowability (see *Theaetetus* 183a; *Cratylus* 440a–b; *Republic* 509d–511e). The fundamental change the Copernican Revolution makes to this picture is that the entities do not possess this quality on their own, but rather have it imposed upon them by the knowing subject.

Kant makes the structure of phenomenal reality, which is all that is of concern for theoretical knowledge, A1 Mind-Dependent. The things of this world receive many of their essential features from us so if they enjoy stable, rule-governed, knowable natures it is only as our gift. Plato's ambition to divide up reality along the joints, to classify things according to their natural inherent "cleavages" (Plato, *Statesman* 262b–e), must be given up because these divisions are now introduced by us. Where God held reality in place for medieval philosophy and Berkeley, our faculties now reify the world into discrete, discernible piles. As one commentator puts it, "We still find in subjectivity the necessity, the intrinsic natures, the autonomy, the constructive power, the role as an always present conserver of determinacy, that earlier we had located in God" (Farrell 1994, 3).

This role makes the subject prior to reality in a profound sense since it is the subject that constitutes the phenomenal realm; nature follows us rather than the other way around. "The order and regularity in the appearances, which we entitle *nature,* we ourselves introduce" (Kant, *C1* A125). Although this is a radical innovation in the history of thought, Kant still wants to preserve the universality of knowledge so that all finite rational agents will find the same basic qualities in all places at all times.[29] As Barry Allen puts it, "Kant is no less certain than Heraclitus that this ordering of perceptions, this *kosmos,* is governed by a *logos* which transcends the merely local differences of history and power."[30] The problem with making reality mind-dependent (A1) is that it immediately seems to endanger uniqueness (R3), the idea that there is one true account of the world which we can all know. Although there are a few messy edges,[31] Kant is committed to R3. The three *Critiques* offer different accounts of the world, but Kant renders them compatible by assigning them different referents, so that for instance phenomena are deterministic while noumenal selves can be free. Within each realm, a unique account of all answerable questions is definitional of genuine knowledge.

The problem facing Kant is how to reject R5 Passive Knower and R1 Independence (for the knowable world) while securing R3 Uniqueness in the face of Hume's skeptical arguments. Up to this point, the generally accepted way to achieve R3, the One True Account of the World, had been to require the world to have an independent determinate structure, which the knower could acquire corresponding beliefs about (R5) without interference from their own beliefs or perceptual or conceptual structure. These theses fit together into a tightly interlocking, seemingly inevitable epistemo-metaphysical system. Kant's genius was to find a different solution.

## Realism of the Self

Here is Kant's key move in devising an alternative: if (A1) phenomenal reality does not possess an inherent order itself, but instead (A5) receives it from the subject's activity, then in order to preserve (R3) the universality, singularity, and determinacy of this order, that is, in order to make it permanent and intersubjectively reliable, Kant must require the organizing faculties of all subjects to remain the same at all times.[32] All finite rational agents must possess the same experience-organizing faculties so that they will constitute and thus know the same world: "If they serve for concepts, they are concepts of the necessary union of representations in [any] consciousness" (Kant, *PFM* 52/305). In order to keep relativism or the elimination of R3 from getting off the ground, which would amount to skepticism for Kant, he cannot allow the possibility of divergent conceptual schemes or organizing faculties. John Richardson puts it perfectly: Kantian idealism "denies the realist claim to be discovering entities as they intrinsically are—but it still permits the theoretical attitude to claim the next best thing to a perspectiveless sight: the one necessary perspective" (Richardson 1986, 164).

Thus, Kant, who is generally heroic in rooting out dogmatic assumptions, is forced to resort to what Solomon calls the "transcendental pretense," that is, "the unwarranted assumption that there is universality and necessity in the fundamental modes of human experience. . . . It is an aggressive and sometimes arrogant effort to prove that there are no . . . possible alternatives" (Solomon 1988, 7). It is essential to the securing of universal and necessary knowledge in the wake of the rejection of realism that, as Stephen Houlgate says, Kant's conceptual "framework is fixed and universal for all rational beings. It constitutes the unchanging, timeless grid which gives to human experience a uniform conceptual structure."[33] This claim of a fixed ahistorical human nature amounts to a realism in the one specific area of the subject, a topic so important that I will single it out as the final thesis of realism, R6 Realism of the Subject. This thesis allows Kant to claim that the ways that all A5 Active Knowers organize experience are identical and unchanging, thereby securing R3, unique and universal knowledge of the A1 phenomenal world. Since all subjects constitute in the same way, all constituted reality will be the same.

This claim sheds further light on Kant's epistemological innovations. He abandons objectivity in the sense of correspondence with independent reality since this is impossible, even senseless, in his system. Instead of objectivity, his epistemological goal is intersubjectivity, that is, what any similarly constituted finite rational being will put into—and so subsequently find—when combined with experience.

> Objective validity and necessary universality (for everybody) are equivalent terms, and though we do not know the object in itself, yet when we consider a judgment as universal, and hence necessary, we thereby understand it to have objective validity. . . . What experience teaches me under certain circumstances, it must always teach me and everybody. (Kant, *PFM* 46–47/298)

As Michael N. Forster notes, "Kant had argued that the concept of truth or objective validity was analyzable as necessary and universal intersubjective agreement, that 'true' or 'objectively valid' implicitly just meant 'necessarily and universally intersubjectively agreed on,' and that necessary and universal intersubjective agreement was hence a defining necessary and sufficient condition of truth or objective validity" (Forster 1998, 228). In Kant's system, truth could have no higher epistemological value.

An R6 Realist A5 Active Knower does the work that God performs in Leibniz's preestablished harmony and that R1 reality does for the realist: it makes sure that we all experience the same world, thus securing intersubjective knowledge and preventing relativism. Kant fervently insists that he has determined the structures of experience once and for all; after his critiques, there can be no more discussion of the subject (see Kant, *PFM* 106/366). After all, the *Prolegomena* are to *any* future metaphysics. He assures the reader over and over that there could not possibly be any other forms, categories, proofs, interests, and so on, besides the ones he outlines.[34] As Karl Ameriks writes, "In the general spirit of the sciences of his time, Kant was sure that, with this doctrine of forms of judgment and its related table of the categories, he had discovered substantive and irrevocable answers here" (Ameriks 2000a, 59). To some degree this thoroughness is just part of what he understands it to mean for thought to be systematic, but in securing a complete and unrevisable definition it amounts to a realism of the self.

Now, it is important to stress that this is no simple realism. The whole point of the "Paralogisms" is to keep us from transmuting necessary characteristics of experience into a metaphysical substantive notion of the noumenal self, like Descartes' thinking thing. Hegel praises the first *Critique* for this accomplishment: "Unquestionably one good result of the Kantian criticism was that it emancipated mental philosophy from the 'soul-thing'" (Hegel, *HL* 75, §47). Kant explicitly rules out knowledge of the noumenal self (except for problematic ethical awareness), but we do in fact learn a great deal about the *transcendental subject*—the thinker of our thoughts, the experience-organizing activity or faculty (Kant, *C1* A117n.a). This is the "I think" that must be able to accompany all of our thoughts, the transcendental unity of apperception that synthesizes them via the categories, and whose ontological status resembles an Aristotelian *energeia* or form. As long as we avoid identifying this aspect of ourselves with the noumenal self or defining it as a thing, Kant's system allows discussion of it; indeed, he must give an exhaustive account of the transcendental subject's processes in order to secure R3 as detailed above, and accordingly a great deal of the first *Critique* is taken up with providing just such a description.

Patricia Kitcher describes the situation well. In addition to the phenomenal and noumenal selves,

> many commentators have noted that the two official selves of the *Critique* are joined by a third self, who turns out to be its central character, the "I" of apperception, or the thinking self. Transcendental psychology is the psychology of the thinking, or better, knowing, self. . . . Although it provides only a highly abstract, functional description of a thinking self, the description is still positive. (Kitcher 1990, 21–22)

This transcendental subject is the book's "central character" because it is the active organizer of experience. It is the thinker or the "subject of the categories" as opposed to the empirical self which, being thought about, is the "object of the categories" (Kant, *C1* B422). Pippin also distinguishes the transcendental subject from the noumenal self. He believes that many of Kant's descriptions of the non-phenomenal self

> do offer a claim about necessary features of any "subject of experience," but that such a claim does not violate Kant's restriction that we do not know our substantial "selves," when "self" is considered apart from all relation to finite conditions of knowability. These arguments could be said to admit a non-noumenal relativization of the spontaneity claim to "subject qua possible knowing subject," and so can be said not to violate that restriction on knowledge of the subject simply as it is in itself. (Pippin 1997, 48–49)

Pippin's "subject qua possible knowing subject" is the transcendental subject.

Many commentators have noted just how much we learn about this transcendental subject. David Carr argues that Kant's repeated disavowals of any description of the "I" that accompanies all thinking

> are misleading in several respects. Kant is concerned to insist that no intuition is involved in transcendental apperception, and hence that none of the predicates that derive from intuition are available for charac-

> terizing the self. But it is not as if the self of transcendental apperception had no characteristics, no description at all. On the contrary, up to now we have been working out just what that description is, starting with the notion of *thinking*. Thinking has been further characterized in terms of acts of spontaneity through which combination occurs. And since Kant is dealing here with knowledge of the sensible world, that thinking has been further qualified: it is thought about objects in the world, thanks to the categories. . . . I construe myself strictly in terms of the activity of thinking—specifically, thinking about the sensible world.[35]

Carr goes on to distinguish the possibility of knowing things-in-themselves from the transcendental subject: "In the case of things-in-themselves we may know nothing but that they exist; but in the case of the transcendental subject, by contrast, we have the whole complex Kantian account of its functions as evidence that we are hardly in the dark about it" (Carr 1999, 117). In other words, if Kant really cannot talk about the transcendental subject, then the massive portions of the *Critique* dedicated to working out the inner processes of this subject's modes of experience-organization constitute a profound self-contradiction. Much of the book would consist in describing, in sometimes tedious detail, what should be just passed over in silence.

In fact, Kant believes that we can know a great deal about the transcendental subject as long as we place a few qualifications on this knowledge. First, as Hume showed (Selby-Bigge 1978, 252), we have no direct intuition of the transcendental subject.[36] We can only determine its features indirectly, via its effects on experience. Transcendental subjectivity is not a thing we can see but the activity of organizing experience through the concepts which, though they exist independently of experience, can only be known in application to experience: "The concept itself is always *a priori* in origin . . . but their employment and their relation to their professed objects can in the end be sought nowhere but in experience" (Kant, *C1* A240/B299; see also A737/B765). Transcendental subjectivity is prior in the *ordine essendi*, but experience is prior in the *ordine cognoscendi*. Kant thinks that because we cannot logically determine what our transcendental faculties must be, we depend on their empirical traces: "Human insight is at an end as soon as we arrive at fundamental powers or faculties, for their possibility can in no way be understood and yet should not be just arbitrarily imagined or assumed. Therefore in the theoretical use of reason only experience could justify their assumption" (Kant, *C2* 48/46–47). It is important to note that, although the traces of subjectivity are to be sought in experience, this subject itself is prior to and exempt from experience. It cannot be affected by empirical events without imperiling the R3 Uniqueness it is supposed to ensure.

Kant discusses this issue most explicitly in the first "Paralogism": "This I or he or it (the thing) which thinks . . . is known only through the thoughts which are its predicates, and of it, apart from them, we cannot have any concept whatsoever" (Kant, *C1* A346/B404). Wilfrid Sellars wrote a well-known paper on this quote in which he states that "if the relevant concepts are taken to include such concepts as that of a 'necessary condition of the possibility of experience,' not to go further afield, there is much that can be known *a priori* about an I. In this sense there is indeed, according to Kant, a body of knowledge which can be called 'transcendental psychology'" (Sellars 1974, 62–63). Kitcher follows Sellars in reviving a Kantian transcendental psychology, claiming that "even though we do not introspect a continuing subject of thoughts, we might infer the existence of a continuing thinker from the mental states with which we are presented" (Wood 1984, 124; see also Kitcher 1990, 13). Jean Hyppolite reverses the metaphor of the mind as mirror of the world: for Kant, "the world is 'the great mirror' in which consciousness discovers itself."[37]

I will call this strategy of seeking our modes of thinking in experience the Empirical Directive (ED). This approach differs markedly from many previous methods of investigating the self which primarily used a priori introspection to find facts about the mind directly. We will see that throughout the history of continental philosophy, the Empirical Directive gradually pulls subjectivity itself more and more into the field of experience—history, nature, causality, and community all come to claim constitutive power over the constituting subject. Although this immersion into this world would have horrified Kant, it is one of the unintended effects of the Empirical Directive that he initiated.

The second restriction laid on any knowledge of the transcendental subject follows directly from the first: we must not think that what we learn here tells us anything about the noumenal self, the central mistake criticized by the "Paralogisms." Since we can only know about the transcendental subject as it relates to experience, while the noumenal self is precisely the self considered separately from all experience, the two cannot be identified. It is tempting to infer noumenal facts, since the transcendental subject, being non-phenomenal, is a step closer to the noumenal self than the much more familiar empirical self. Although some commentators accuse Kant of making this mistake, most famously Strawson (1966, 173–74) and Ralph C. S. Walker (1978, 133–35), I think the distinction between the transcendental and noumenal subject clears him of this charge. Kant explicitly denounces this transference of properties as illegitimate, criticizing it as the mistake that the rational psychologists made (Kant, *C1* A350/B427, A356, B408–9, though see A492/B520). Ameriks directly rejects Walker's interpretation by appeal to "the basic point Kant was making in the Paralogisms . . . that we ought not to conflate the transcendental conditions of knowledge with properties of the self in itself" (Ameriks 2000b, 287; see also Kitcher 1990, 193, 201; Sellars 1974, 63). In other words, Kant himself originated the criticism now leveled at him. While it is certainly possible that he fell into the trap he was busy warning others of, the principle of charity requires a very high standard of proof in such a case, especially when a plausible distinction gets him off the hook.

The third qualification is not to think of the transcendental subject as a substance. It is easy to make this mistake, since the transcendental unity of apperception's basic function of unifying thoughts requires that it itself be deeply identical, an important feature of substantiality, and because Kant considers substance a pervasive category of all thought. However, the transcendental subject is an exception to the rule of universal category application; since the transcendental subject is in fact the *source* of the categories, they do not apply to it.

> Rational psychology owes its origin simply to misunderstanding. The unity of consciousness, which underlies the categories, is here mistaken for an intuition of the subject as object, and the category of substance is then applied to it. . . . The subject of the categories cannot by thinking the categories acquire a concept of itself as an object of the categories. For in order to think them, its pure self-consciousness, which is what was to be explained, must itself be presupposed. (Kant, *C1* B421–22)

Since the categories spring from the transcendental subject, capturing it by them is the primordial category mistake. Thus, the first "Paralogism" concludes, we may not conceive of the transcendental subject as a substance. Kant entertains various non-substantial possibilities for the noumenal basis of consciousness, such as thinking material things (contra Descartes) or a consciousness handed off among various objects as long as it itself stays unified, just to show that the necessary conditions of experience cannot indicate anything about the noumenal underpinnings of consciousness.[38]

Rather than a substance, Kant offers what some consider to be a protofunctionalist definition of the transcendental subject. For instance, Sellars says that

> the conceptual burden of the 'proposition "I think"' is carried by the verb "to think.". . . Kant's point, then, is that our concept of an I is the

> concept of *that which thinks,* in the various modes of thinking. . . . The idea that concepts pertaining to thinking are essentially *functional* in character raises the question: What non-functional characterization can be given of the processes which embody these functions. . . . Kant's answer is, essentially, that we are not able to give a non-functional characterization. We don't know these processes save as *processes which embody these functions.* (Sellars 1974, 66, 68)

All that we know about what the transcendental subject *is,* is what it *does.* This is fitting since it is defined by spontaneity which ED we only get to know through its organizing of experience. More recently, Terry Pinkard repeats the view that for Kant, "to have a mind is not to be made of any kind of particular 'stuff'; it is to be able to *perform* certain kinds of activities" (Pinkard 2002, 39). And R. Kevin Hill claims that "for Kant, the notion of a mind is a purely functionalist one. . . . The mind that happens is nothing above and beyond the fact that judgement happened" (R. K. Hill 2003, 159; see also Hanna 2001, 32; Kitcher 1990, 25).

Heidegger points out that the transcendental unity of apperception is an ability, "essentially an 'I am able'" (Heidegger, *KPM* 55), which is how he links the rational self of the first *Critique* with the practical self of the second. However, Heidegger's repeated verdict on Kantian subjectivity is that it remains trapped within the Cartesian substantial view of the subject: "Ontologically, Kant depends entirely on the traditional ontology of what is extant. . . . Kant retains the ontologically unclarified point of departure from the subject as inaugurated by Descartes."[39] Although I will qualify this below, this criticism seems somewhat unfair, as David Carr shows in detail: "The transcendental subject is the farthest thing from being a substance for Kant" (Carr 1999, 63). Kant thinks of the transcendental subject in functional rather than substantial terms—it is what it does—which actually forms an important step on the way from Descartes toward Heidegger's own Dasein in *Being and Time.* Charles M. Sherover, who tries to bring Kant and Heidegger together in his close reading of Heidegger's *Kant and the Problem of Metaphysics,* makes this point when he writes that "the self, *qua* knower, is not discovered as a 'thing' but as the dynamic demarcating and invoking of the cognitively possible. . . . The self then is not so much a subject as it is an act-ing" (Sherover 1971, 157; see also 209). Since Heidegger himself credits Kant with conceiving of the self as an ability, why does he accuse him of committing what has become in our time the common but unforgivable crime of maintaining a Cartesian subjectivity?

It is essential to Kant's preservation of R3 Uniqueness, the stability of the One True Account of the World, that the subject's contributions to experience never change; the "complete and necessary identity"[40] of the transcendental unity of apperception is one of the main points that comes out of the "Deductions." What is interesting about this transcendental subject is that, although it is responsible for undermining two or three of the theses of realism (depending on how one stands on R2 Correspondence Truth), it both ensures R3 Uniqueness and *fits the theses of metaphysical realism itself perfectly.* It founds anti-realism, but it is still conceived strictly along the lines of a realist metaphysics. In other words, R1–R3 are true of the transcendental subject, which is why Kant is committed to R6 Realism of the Subject.[41]

In a trivial sense, the transcendental subject is mind-dependent simply because it is a mind. But in a more significant sense, its R1 Mind-Independence is shown by Kant's argument discussed above that, as the source of the categories, these categories (such as causality) do not apply to it. It cannot be the effect of a previous cause, so obviously the mind cannot be A5 Active in relation to itself. Indeed, as the *transcendental* ego it could not be otherwise without giving birth to itself, sort of a reverse oroboro.[42] While the empirical ego is mind-dependent (Kant, *C1* B156), the transcendental unity of apperception is the fundamental condition for all experience, thus making it productive of and prior to all mind-dependent entities.[43] It is the unconstituted constitutor, the mind on which all mind-dependent things depend.

As I have tried to show at length above, it is essential to Kant's overall project that R3 Uniqueness hold of the transcendental subject. Although he boldly challenges the metaphysical underpinnings of the phenomenal world, he still wants to attribute a stable, rule-governed, and so knowable order to it. Since the world receives its order from the subject, the latter must now possess these realist qualities. The phenomenal world still enjoys R3, just not intrinsically but rather via the unchanging, universal experience-organizing features of the transcendental subject. Finally, there is no reason to doubt that Kant's account of the structure of the transcendental subject is true in the sense of corresponding to it (R2). And this, I think, is what Heidegger is getting at with his Cartesian criticism of Kant's subjectivity. Although we can easily absolve Kant of employing a substantial transcendental subject (Heidegger himself points out the different conception), he is still conceiving of it in realist terms; he has to for his revolution to work. As radical as his claims about external reality are, Kant's metaphysical system remains fairly conservative about the subject in order to preserve his traditional concerns about necessary and universal knowledge. As Heidegger says, "Even though in theory [Kant] has denied that the ontical foundations of the ontology of the substantial apply to the 'I,' he still slips back into *this same* inappropriate ontology" (Heidegger, *BT* 366/319; see also Heidegger, *PIK* 268).

The subject has ended up functioning as an epistemological foundation in Kant's system, albeit in a very different way than for Descartes. It is Descartes' foundation because it is the most knowable thing there is, accessible through the most immediate perception possible. Kant has eliminated this direct introspective access, considering the subject the unperceived perceiver. Instead, Kant's transcendental subject takes the place of Descartes' veracious God, guaranteeing that our true beliefs are actually about the world.

## Conclusion: The Kantian Paradigm

Kant is the first philosopher to pose an overarching challenge to the tenets of the metaphysical realism in which objects have stable identities (R3) independently (R1) of our experience, which are then reflected in our knowledge (R2). Sherover writes that "Kant's Revolution represents . . . the first serious attack on the traditional Plato-Aristotle approach to insight into the nature of things by focusing on that which is to be known."[44] Instead of abandoning realism altogether, however, he retains two important aspects of it: the mind-independent noumenal realm (R1) and the realist subject (R6). Although he makes the phenomenal world mind-dependent (A1) and changes the passive substantial knower to an active organizer of experience, he must keep the experience-organizing structures universal and unchanging (R6) in order to preserve the unique (R3) world. This requires a realist determination of the transcendental subject, even though neither as substance or noumena. As Kitcher says, it is the "central character" of the first *Critique,* the linchpin of Kant's system. And it does form a system: Kant's pieces—R1 noumena + A1 phenomena formed in one way only to establish R3 scientific knowledge of phenomena by the A5 transcendental and R6 (that is, R1–R3 about this entity) universal subject—combine to form a conceptual structure as coherent as the metaphysical realism it replaced. Kant's importance and greatness reside in the fact that he was the first to offer a systematic alternative to realism.

I will refer to this system as the Kantian Paradigm. It consists in a single type of transcendental subject forming components of reality which are then known in the same way by everyone. This paradigm reigned over the next century and a half of continental philosophy. Throughout the rest of part 1 I will show how Hegel, Nietzsche, and the early Heidegger all attacked, refined, and re-formed various parts of the Kantian Paradigm, but largely from within. This is why Heidegger says that "Kant towers so far above all who precede and follow that even those who reject him or go beyond him still remain entirely dependent upon him. . . . [The *Critique of Pure Reason* represents] a historical-intellectual basic position which carries and determines us today" (Heidegger, *WIT* 56, bracketed comment added). The story of the next 150 years that I will trace throughout part 1 describes the adaptation of various elements of the paradigm and the progressive erosion of the last vestiges of realism in Kant's system: R1 noumena and R6 Realist Subject.

# 3

# Hegel: The Truth of the Whole

> The divorce between thought and thing is mainly the work of the Critical Philosophy, and runs counter to the conviction of all previous ages, that their agreement was a matter of course. The antithesis between them is the hinge on which modern philosophy turns. (Hegel, *HL* 35, §22R)

> This absolute unrest of pure self-movement, in which whatever is determined in one way or another, e.g., as being, is rather the opposite of this determinateness, this no doubt has been from the start the soul of all that has gone before. (Hegel, *PS* 101, §163)

> What seems to happen outside of it, to be activity directed against it, is really its own doing, and Substance shows itself to be essentially Subject. When it has shown this completely, Spirit has made its existence identical with its essence; it has itself for its object just as it is. (Hegel, *PS* 21, §37)

The method of Hegel's *Phenomenology of Spirit*—his first masterpiece and the work of his I will be using more than any other—is to examine an idea on its own terms, letting that idea present its best arguments and develop itself until it unwittingly exposes its own limitations and self-contradictions, thus overcoming itself. Rather than refuting a theory from the outside, employing external criteria it never intended to meet and would not accept, Hegel's technique is to show how theories fail to meet their *own* standards, thus begging no questions. "If the refutation is thorough, it is derived and developed from the principle itself, not accomplished by counter-assertions and random thoughts from outside. The refutation would, therefore, properly consist in the further development of the principle, and in thus remedying the defectiveness" (Hegel, *PS* 13, §24; see also Gadamer 1976a, 5). As with the thought of many of the idealists, much of Hegel's thought can be viewed as just this kind of internal refutation through extension of Kant. As Tom Rockmore puts it, "Although he rejects the letter of Kant's critical philosophy, Hegel participates in the post-Kantian effort . . . to elaborate its spirit by thinking with Kant against Kant" (Denker and Vater 2003, 339). Hegel starts from Kant's position, but finds it internally inconsistent as well as unsatisfying for other reasons. He ends up extending it far beyond the limitations Kant imposed, but to where he thinks Kant *should* have gone had he consistently followed out his own best insights. Hegel's idealism is less a rejection of Kant's thought than its completion or fulfillment by working out flaws that even Kant should recognize; in other words, Hegel's thought is one enormous *Aufhebung*. According to Merold Westphal, "Hegel's philosophy [takes] the form of a continuous debate with the critical philosophy; and we should not be too surprised when he defines philosophy as the refutation of Kant."[1] Hegel's task is to be the Kant that Kant should have been were he sufficiently free of presuppositions to follow his own insights to their proper conclusions. Interestingly, Kant himself once described his own project as just this kind of overcoming-through-extension of his great predecessor, Hume: "If we start from a well-founded, but undeveloped, thought which another has bequeathed to us, we may well hope by continued reflection to advance farther than the acute man to whom we owe the first spark of light" (Kant, *PFM* 8/260).

As we will see, Hegel considers "the divorce between thought and thing" that Kant instigates by distinguishing between our phenomenal knowledge and noumenal reality to be "the hinge on which modern philosophy turns" (Hegel, *HL* 35, §22R). The gap between these two renders our knowledge false since it is not of true reality; it is only Kant's commitment to R1 noumena as reality existing independently from our thoughts about them that keeps the gap open. Thus, Hegel's philosophical mission is to overcome this chasm between thinking and being without resorting to the mere dogmatic assertion of unity that Kant sought to overcome in the first place. Another flaw in Kant's system is that even by his own lights Kant owes us an account of the specific table of categories he supplies. To say that our possession of precisely these categories instead of any others is a brute, inexplicable fact (see Kant, *C1* B145–46; Kant, *PFM* 65/318; Kant, *C2* 48/46–47) is dogmatic and compromises our autonomy.

This objection is crucial, since Hegel follows Kant in making autonomy the central value for both epistemology and morality; he also adopts the Empirical Directive (ED), that is, the strategy of studying transcendental subjectivity—the aspect of ourselves that is responsible for thinking and knowing—vicariously, through its activities in experience, instead of the rational psychologists' use of direct intuition. Kant studies transcendental subjectivity in its acting on experience, but this subject maintains a formal unity that can be considered separately from any content and bears a mysterious relationship to the noumenal self that never enters experience. Hegel ridicules the very idea of analyzing the knowing subject separately from experience—"To seek to know before we know is as absurd as the wise resolution of Scholasticus, not to venture into the water until he had learned to swim" (Hegel, *HL* 14, §10; see also 66, §41R1)—and dismisses any noumenal aspect of the self. All we are is what we do and have done: "Where Spirit is, or the concrete concept, manifestation itself is the essential. The criterion of Spirit is its action, its active essence. Man is his own action, the sequence of his actions, that into which he has been making himself."[2] This completes Kant's "functionalist" conception of transcendental subjectivity and represents one of Hegel's legacies to existentialism.

When we extend ED in this way and pay careful attention to what is manifest in experience, however, what we find according to Hegel is not the universal structures (R3) but vast diachronic heterogeneity, that is, enormous discrepancies in the ways that the world has been at different times. If our topic is transcendental subjectivity or the self as experience-organizer which we can only study via experience (ED), and it turns out that experience has been organized in fundamentally different ways throughout history, we must conclude that this self has fundamentally changed throughout history. Belief in an unchanging self in the face of such undeniable evidence can only be a dogmatic assumption; such was Kant's unfortunate commitment to R6 Realism of the Subject, which kept him from pressing his examination of experience to its logical conclusion. Since he is the one who insisted that we take our evidence for transcendental subjectivity from experience (ED), he fails by his own lights by ignoring the patent evidence of historical change in favor of the cherished prejudice for universal stability. Hegel's analysis of the "Paralogisms" concludes that the reason "that predicates like simplicity, permanence, etc., are inapplicable to the soul" is not because of Kant's explanation that "Reason, by applying them, would exceed its appointed bounds. The true ground is that this style of abstract terms is not good enough for the soul, which is very much more than a mere simple or unchangeable sort of thing" (Hegel, *HL* 76, §47R). Kant found antinomies because he clung to the assumption of a simple self; Hegel, on the other hand, sticks consistently to the Empirical Directive, so that when experience yields historical plurality, he accepts the implication of a multiple, changing self.

Hegel takes the next major step forward in the development of continental anti-realism by incorporating historical change and thus plurality into our conceptual schemes.[3] Kant maintains the unique determinacy of phenomena (R3) by means of a realist conception (R6) of an active transcendental subjectivity (A5). Together these theses entail the claim that there is only one conceptual scheme shared by all subjects across cultures and epochs which irrevocably freezes the structure of the phenomenal realm, thereby stabilizing intersubjective knowledge as the best alternative to objective knowledge. However, as Richard Rorty points out, "as soon as we have [the Kantian] picture of the mind in focus, it occurs to us, as it did to Hegel, that those all-important a priori concepts, those which determine what our experience or our morals will be, might have been different" (Rorty 1982, 3; Davidson makes the same point at *SIO* 40; see also Prado 2006, 11). In other words, the notion of *a* conceptual scheme shaping our experience naturally suggests the idea of *alternate* conceptual schemes forming vastly different phenomenal worlds. This suggestion becomes more pressing if we take history seriously, which Kant's strategy of investigating the traces of transcendental subjectivity within experience (ED) points us toward once history is taken seriously. Merold Westphal explicitly links this examination of history with Kant's transcendental ego: "The transcendental ego must be placed in the context of Spirit and its history. . . . Spirit is known through the interpretation of its words and deeds, i.e., through historical understanding."[4]

This historical proliferation of conceptual schemes seems to dissolve reality into the relativist, unknowable chaos that Kant tried to prevent by positing R6. After all, if reality is relative to multiple conceptual schemes, then there seems to be no adjudication between the differently formed worlds: your world corresponds to your concepts and so is "true," while mine corresponds to my concepts and so is also "true," even if the two contradict each other. Where Kant's challenge was to secure R3 Uniqueness without resorting to independent reality or God, Hegel's is to loosen this R3 restriction by allowing multiple schemes but without giving up knowledge altogether.

## Realism

The *Phenomenology of Spirit* is Hegel's Transcendental Deduction; it represents his attempt to uncover and justify the particular set of categories we have in a way that Kant should have but couldn't.[5] With a project of such enormous scope as the justification of all knowledge, it isn't surprising that getting starting requires considerable attention. Hegel rejects all types of foundationalism that lay claim to an indubitable starting point, since these have the unfortunate habit of getting doubted on a regular basis (see Hegel, *HL* 14, §10; 42, §24R3; 222, §159R). Rather than choosing a starting point that would inevitably appear arbitrary, Hegel does not start from his own view—what he calls the perspective of the phenomenological observer—at all, but rather with the beliefs held by natural consciousness. Nor does he start from *his* view of their views which they could easily reject as biased, but tries instead to present *their* views of their own views, giving them the best possible position, in order to show how even then these views turn out to be incoherent when fully examined. His job is

> to sink this freedom in the content, letting it move spontaneously of its own nature, by the self as its own self, and then to contemplate this movement. This refusal to intrude into the immanent rhythm of the Notion, either arbitrarily or with wisdom obtained from elsewhere, constitutes a restraint which is itself an essential moment of the notion. (Hegel, *PS* 36, §58; see also Hegel, *HL* 116, §81)

To the frustration of many of his readers, Hegel does not simply state the conclusions he has reached after thinking very hard about a set of issues, defend them with arguments, and counter possible objections. Instead, he wants us to think along with natural consciousness so that we may discover the contradictions and limitations within the positions that motivated philosophers to create successor systems of thought throughout history. If it works, the reader will come to what Hegel regards as the inevitable conclusion, but she will come to it as her own; she will, in contemporary pedagogical jargon, own it. One way to understand Hegel's method is to see it as a way of persuading the reader while still respecting—and even heightening—her autonomy, a methodological issue that plagues Kierkegaard and Nietzsche as well.

Hegel's understanding of successful refutation requires that he show a view to be incoherent by its own standards rather than by his, which are external to, and thus not recognized by, its holders. This can be done because each theory also contains a conception of what a satisfactory theory is by which the theory itself can be measured. In this way, "consciousness provides its own criterion from within itself, so that the investigation becomes a comparison of consciousness with itself. . . . Consequently, we do not need to import criteria, or to make use of our own bright ideas and thoughts during the course of the inquiry" (Hegel, *PS* 53–54, §84). The enormous advantage of such an internal refutation is that it does not beg any questions and so should be accepted by all proponents of non-Hegelian theories, until finally there are no more non-Hegelians left. "Hence they examine themselves: in their own action they must determine their limits, and point out their defects. . . . Instead of being brought to bear upon the categories from without, it is immanent in their own action."[6]

Hegel then adds a twist:

> But not only is a contribution by us superfluous, since . . . the criterion and what is to be tested, are present in consciousness itself, but we are also spared the trouble of comparing the two and really *testing* them, so that, since what consciousness examines is its own self, all that is left for us to do is simply look on. (Hegel, *PS* 54, §85; see also Hegel, *HL* 228, §163R2)

Not only *can* theories be tested by their own criteria, but history actually *consists* of this continual testing happening over and over again in a self-perpetuating series of "conjectures and refutations." Hegel sees the history of philosophy as an enormous Socratic dialogue, with views emerging and engaging in mutual elenchus, which exposes their weaknesses and contradictions and so invites new theories that solve the problems of the previous school but at the cost of engendering their own, thus perpetuating the process. Because ideas follow an internal logic, the way they have developed historically is neither random nor due to individual thinkers' idiosyncracies, but rather to intrinsic laws of thought itself (see Hegel, *HL* 228, §163R2). This is why the history of philosophy has the same content as logic, only cast in terms of temporal progression, the way, for instance, the category of causality is a hypothetical judgment put into time for Kant (see 19, §14; 125, §86R2). Science too follows this model that Hegel calls "determinate negation," where new theories arise in reaction to and out of conversation with those that came before as attempts to solve problems bequeathed to them. This view of philosophy as necessarily historical and engaged in conversation is largely taken for granted in continental philosophy (see McCumber 2003; also Beiser in Beiser 1993) and certainly informs this book.[7]

More debatable is Hegel's claim that events which have little obvious connection to intellectual movements are in some sense based on, emanations from, or even enactments of these self-developments and refutations of ideas. This is what Marx famously rejects, promising to put Hegel right side up so that the head (intellectual development) stands or depends upon the feet (labor). The degree to which this is a fair criticism is of course a matter of debate, but there is at least a kernel of truth in it.[8] As we will see in chapter 7, Foucault will reprise Marx's role to Heidegger's Hegel when they reenact a version of this debate a century later.

The upshot for our concerns is that discussing a particular view in the *Phenomenology of Spirit* presents it as a view held by a particular people at a particular time[9] which, through its self-development, comes to expose its own contradictions and gives way to a new theory that builds on its successes and improves on its failures. This is the famous *Aufhebung*—the new theory preserves features of the earlier one but in a new and better form (see Hegel, *HL* 126, §86R2). And the view examined throughout the first third of the book, "Consciousness,"[10] is realism, "the Metaphysic of the Past as it subsisted among us previous to the philosophy of Kant" (47, §26). The influential French Hegel interpreter Jean Hyppolite describes the *Phenomenology* as a "concrete history of consciousness [which] purifies itself of all prejudices—in particular, of the fundamental prejudice that things exist outside us, independent of knowledge" (Hyppolite 1974, 13), or my R1. In the words of another commentator, "The realist notion of objectivity [is] the fundamental assumption of 'consciousness'" (Pippin 1989, 146) and, since examination here amounts to refutation, the section "Consciousness" attempts "to undermine various realist alternatives in epistemology" (131; see also 134).[11] I will briefly demonstrate that "Consciousness" represents Hegel's account of realism by showing how it fits the theses of the Realism Matrix set out in chapter 1.

## R1 Independence

Hegel claims that Consciousness is[12] "a *knowing* which knows the object only because the *object* is, while the knowing may either be or not be. . . . [The object] is, regardless of whether it is known or not; and it remains, even if it is not known" (Hegel, *PS* 59, §93; see also 67, §111). In other words, for Consciousness the object's *percipi* has nothing to do with its *esse*, making reality mind-independent: "The Thing is what is true, i.e., it *possesses intrinsic being*" (73, §120; see also Hegel, *HL* 256, §193). As Jon Stewart writes,

> For Hegel, the most fundamental claim of common sense is that there are independent, external objects. . . . The task of the dialectic is to show common sense that this assertion of independent external objects is itself contradictory when one looks closely at the account that common sense gives of these objects. Hence, for Hegel, natural consciousness is simply a naïve realist. (Stewart 2000, 47; see also Flay 1984, 57)

As Moore and Russell will vehemently argue in their rejection of idealism, a realist considers it part of the very meaning of knowledge that it is of what is independent of the knower, whereas knowing what we non-trivially affect is not genuine knowledge. "Whatever is related to knowledge or knowing is also distinguished from it, and posited as existing outside of this relationship; this *being-in-itself* is called *truth*" (Hegel, *PS* 52–53, §82). Although the topics of pre-Kantian metaphysics "belong to reason that is, to the organized and systematically developed universe of thought [. . . they] were taken by the metaphysician as subjects made and ready" (Hegel, *HL* 51, §30).

### R2 Correspondence

In its self-examination, one of the central criteria that consciousness uses to evaluate its theories is whether or not they correspond to reality. "If we designate *knowledge* as the Notion, but the essence or the *True* as what exists, or the *object,* then the examination [by consciousness of itself] consists in seeing whether the Notion corresponds to the object" (Hegel, *PS* 53, §84, bracketed comment added). Among the failures that prod it to develop new theories, the most significant is when "consciousness thus finds that its knowledge does not correspond to its object" (54, §85). Consequently, Michael Forster comments, "natural consciousness conceives truth as consisting in the *correspondence* of 'knowledge' or representations to such facts" (Forster 1998, 234; see also Flay 1984, 57).

### R3 Uniqueness

This is Consciousness' Achilles' heel. It wants a single, final account of the Way the World Is and it conceives of reality in terms which would satisfy such a demand: "The object is the True and universal, the self-identical" (Hegel, *PS* 70, §116). Consciousness subscribes to Plato's doctrine of the divided line, i.e., that reality must be stable and self-identical or "ultimate and fixed" (Flay 1984, 57) in order to be known. The problem is that when Consciousness actually tries to fix the self-identical object of knowledge in a definite theory, the thing keeps changing, from sensory data to a collection of qualities to a nucleus to raw force to a law. Consciousness tries to achieve a simple immediate relation with determinate reality, but the harder it tries to make being stand still the more it changes. Like holding mercury, the tighter the grip, the more certain the escape, and Hegel narrates Consciousness' ever more desperate attempts to "preserve the self-identity and truth of the Thing, its being a One" (Hegel, *PS* 72, §119). The futility of these efforts is why consciousness' journey is a "way of despair":

> Natural consciousness will show itself to be only the Notion of knowledge, or in other words, not to be real knowledge. But since it directly takes itself to be real knowledge, this path has a negative significance for it, and what is in fact the realization of the Notion, counts for it rather as

> the loss of its own self; for it does lose its truth on this path. The road can therefore be regarded as the pathway of *doubt,* or more precisely as the way of despair. (Hegel, *PS* 49, §78)

This recurring disappointment continues as long as consciousness misunderstands itself and seeks the wrong kind of knowledge. "Observation which clings to passive, unbroken selfsameness of being, inevitably sees itself tormented just in its most general determinations . . . by instances which rob it of every determination."[13]

Although Consciousness' efforts to know the R3 Unique structure of reality are perpetually thwarted, it attributes these failures to its own mistakings of R1 Independent, determinate reality. The world is what it is and simply needs to be properly captured once and for all for final truth to be attained. Consciousness continually ignores earlier changes by treating them as mere mistakes which have now been corrected by dis-covering the real object that was there all along. "It usually seems to be the case . . . that our experience of the untruth of our first notion comes by way of a second object which we come upon by chance and externally, so that our part in all this is simply the pure *apprehension* of what is in and for itself" (Hegel, *PS* 55, §87). Previous scientists or philosophers distorted experience, but now we have finally eliminated these distorting influences to be able to gaze upon the true face of the universe; the fact that they believed the same thing is irrelevant because this time it's really true. "Natural consciousness, too, is always reaching this result, learning from experience what is true in it; but equally it is always forgetting it and starting the movement all over again" (64, §109). Discoveries simply uncover what was already present but masked by our predecessors' stubborn refusal just to look at reality, a refusal that is only visible retrospectively. The situation is rectified by getting rid of the presuppositions that interfered with the direct apprehension of reality, or by employing new technology which frees us from sensory distortions. In other words, full R5 Passivity of the Subject is the key to truth.

### R4 Bivalence

The way Consciousness treats previous phases of thought shows its subscription to bivalence. As opposed to Hegel's view that each period achieves partial insight on the way to total understanding, Consciousness simply rejects previous theories as false through and through, expressing impatience with the *Phenomenology*'s procedure of recounting refuted ideas: "Why bother with the false?" (Hegel, *PS* 22, §38). Hegel sums up the underlying view in this way: "'True' and 'false' belong among those determinate notions which are held to be inert and wholly separate essences, one here and one there, each standing fixed and isolated from the other, with which it has nothing in common" (22, §39). Commitment to bivalence is one of the central obstacles to progress in the *Phenomenology*, since it keeps consciousness from integrating all of the perspectives into the whole (see 78, §131).

> The more conventional opinion gets fixated on the antithesis of truth and falsity, the more it tends to expect a given philosophical system to be either accepted or contradicted; and hence it finds only acceptance or rejection. It does not comprehend the diversity of philosophical systems as the progressive unfolding of truth, but rather sees in it simple disagreements. (Hegel, *PS* 2, §2)

Pre-Kantian realism is "forced to assume that of two opposite assertions . . . the one must be true and the other false" (Hegel, *HL* 52, §32; see also 101, §65; 172, §119). This view then leads to understanding philosophical refutation "in a purely negative sense to mean that the system refuted has ceased to count for anything, has been set aside and done for," whereas the method of *aufheben* shows that "the earlier are preserved in the later; but subordinated and submerged" (126, §86R2; see also 132, §88R).

### R5 Passive Subject

This component explains Consciousness' continual failures to achieve the One True Account of the World. Consciousness is fully realist and pre-Kantian in its conception of the knowing subject. Any contribution the subject makes in grasping an object automatically amounts to error, Russell's "mere delusion": "It has only to *take* it, to confine itself to a pure apprehension of it, and what is thus yielded is the True. If consciousness itself did anything in taking what is given, it would by such adding or subtraction alter the truth" (Hegel, *PS* 70, §116). Consciousness has the epistemological duty of effacing itself: "Our approach to the object must also be *immediate* or *receptive;* we must alter nothing in the object as it presents itself" (58, §90; see also Hegel, *HL* 110, §76). In an earlier essay he ridicules the R5 realist epistemology which could only occur in

> a philosophical utopia in which the Absolute itself readies itself for being something true and known, and surrenders itself for total enjoyment to the passivity of a thinking which only needs a mouth agape. Strenuous creative construction, in assertoric and categorical statements, is banished from this utopia. A problematic and hypothetical shaking of the

> tree of knowledge, which grows in a sandy grounding, brings the fruit of knowledge down, already chewed and self-digested. (Hegel, *DFS* 185)

Consciousness must do nothing in coming to know objects since reality possesses its own organization, "already chewed and self-digested" independently of us.[14]

Thus, Consciousness posits a straightforward realism in which the pre-organized, independent world should be passively recorded by the mind. The knowing subject must root out the distorting influences that kept past thinkers from simply apprehending reality; the goal is to achieve passivity of the knower (R5) in order to get Correspondence True knowledge (R2) of (R1) Independent, (R3) Unique reality once and for all. This attempt, however, fails because the objects keep taking on new forms (A3). Hegel thinks that it is about time (literally—see Hegel, *PS* 44, §71; 486, §800) that we became self-aware and historically-minded enough to take a step back and understand this process as a whole. Instead of making the same mistake over and over again—thinking that somehow we will escape this ongoing process of self-correction if we could just . . . —we should instead reject the realist assumptions underlying this picture as a whole. Consciousness can escape this futile exercise only by "recollecting" or acknowledging the movements of experience as real and essential to itself and reality rather than "forgetting" them as mere accidental distortion. Consciousness must come to terms with its role in the formation of experience. In other words, philosophy must undergo a historically oriented Copernican Revolution to realize that, in Hegel's way of putting it, self-consciousness is the truth of Consciousness.

## Hegel's Kantian Copernican Revolution

The transition from Consciousness to Self-Consciousness, the second section of the *Phenomenology,* roughly recapitulates the transition from pre-Kantian philosophy to Kant's thought. In its first phase Consciousness tries to maintain realism. The different ways that people have understood reality in the past amount to so many mistakes or false representations which have finally been corrected, so that the final answer has been achieved, "or is at least in the works and will be finished by next Sunday, believe me" (Kierkegaard 1992, 106).[15] Consciousness is "fixated on the antithesis of truth and falsity," or (R4) Bivalence conceived of as (R2) Correspondence to (R1) Independent, (R3) Uniquely determinate reality; earlier systems of thought must be rejected as simply false because they do not correspond to independent objects. What Consciousness comes to realize, a realization that pushes it into Self-Consciousness, is that these changes in experience are not accidental distortions but are instead intrinsic to experience and necessary to knowledge. Self-Consciousness discovers Kant's great lesson: Consciousness actively contributes to experience. Merold Westphal delineates two steps in the "Consciousness" section: "(1) There is the presentation of the different ways in which the object is grasped. . . . (2) There is then the reflective discovery of the active role of consciousness in all that first order knowing." He understands this transition to be the "Copernican Revolution, the discovery of the transcendental role of the thinking subject" (M. Westphal 1998, 64, 65; see also Rockmore in Denker and Vater 2003, 338).

Natural Consciousness conceives of the historical changes of belief as thinkers alternately mis-taking and discovering independent reality. It remains unaware of its own role in the formation of experience, which goes on "behind the back of consciousness" (Hegel, *PS* 56, §87), as Kant would agree. "Such a style of Cognition does not recognize in itself the activity of the notion—an activity which it is implicitly, not consciously. In its own estimation its procedure is passive. Really that procedure is active" (Hegel, *HL* 284, §226R; see also 290, §232R; M. Westphal 1998, 110, 113). Only we, the phenomenological observers clued in by Hegel, are privy to the constituting activity of Consciousness. We understand that Consciousness is producing its own experience, that it is wearing pink sunglasses even though it believes the world to be pink: "*For us,* this object has developed through the movement of consciousness in such a way that consciousness is involved in that development" (Hegel, *PS* 79, §132; see also 55, §87). It is this discovery of A5 Active Knower that separates Kant from all previous thinkers.

Since reality is at least partially determined by Consciousness, and since Consciousness' goal is to understand reality, it can only fulfill its goal by studying itself. Instead of directly or immediately studying independent objects, we must study consciousness to see how it constitutes the objects; worldly inquiries actually turn out to be studying the mind's organization of the world. "The reason why 'explaining' affords so much self-satisfaction is just because in it consciousness is, so to speak, communing directly with itself, enjoying only itself; although it seems to busy with something else, it is in fact occupied only with itself" (Hegel, *PS* 101, §163; see also Pippin 1989, 138). Another way of putting this might be to say that "the order and regularity in the appearances, which we entitle *nature,* we ourselves introduce" (Kant, *C1* A125). The practice of science doesn't literally collapse into psychology, of course—if nothing else, ED prevents that—but *we* know that scientists are really studying the activity of their own minds. Although Consciousness would be scandalized at the idea that the mind unavoidably affects experience, considering such intermingling fatal for epistemological purposes, Kantian Self-Consciousness has shown how knowledge can reside peacefully with A5. In fact, Kant argues that the *only* way to defeat skepticism and secure knowledge is for Consciousness to find out that "what seems to happen outside of it, to be activity directed against it, is really its own doing" (Hegel, *PS* 21, §37). Consciousness' realism has not been rejected exactly, but *aufgehoben,* since Self-Consciousness is the only way to achieve its original goal of knowing reality: "Consciousness at once recognizes this aspect as its own and takes responsibility for it; by doing so it will obtain the true object in its purity" (72, §118). This is what Hegel means when he says that Self-Consciousness is the truth of Consciousness (see 102, §164), a phrase that summarizes Kantian idealism for Hyppolite (1974, 143).

Consciousness takes its first step toward its goal of Absolute Knowing by abandoning realism[16] in Self-Consciousness (see Hegel, *PS* 110, §177).

> Thus it becomes quite definite for consciousness how its perceiving is essentially constituted, viz. that it is not a simple pure apprehension, but *in its apprehension* is at the same time *reflected out of the True* [that is, independent object] *and into itself.* This return of consciousness into itself which is directly *mingled* with the pure apprehension [of the object]—for this return into itself has shown itself to be essential to perception—alters the truth. . . . Consciousness no longer merely perceives, but is also conscious of its reflection into itself, and separates this from simple apprehension. (Hegel, PS 71–72, §118, first bracketed comment added)

Instead of ignoring itself to focus exclusively on the object, Consciousness now understands that it "mingles" with being and contributes to it. In other words, the first step forward in the *Phenomenology* is the embracing of what I have called A5—the idea that the subject actively contributes to knowledge. In Hyppolite's words, "self-consciousness appears, in opposition to consciousness, as active consciousness" (1974, 146; see also Flay 1984, 61, 79). Consciousness now comes to realize that

> consciousness of an "other," of an object in general, is itself necessarily *self-consciousness,* a reflectedness-into-self, consciousness of itself in otherness. The *necessary advance* from the previous shapes of consciousness for which their truth was a Thing, an "other" than themselves, expresses just this, that . . . self-consciousness alone is the truth of those shapes. (Hegel, *PS* 102, §164)

All the advances in knowledge that realist Consciousness made were attributed to the discovery of "a Thing." It takes a leap forward when it realizes that the object is not simply "out there," independent of consciousness and waiting to be apprehended; rather, experience arises from "this *dialectical* movement which consciousness exercises on itself and which affects both its knowledge and its object" (Hegel, *PS* 55, §86).

This is Hegel's Copernican Revolution, his agreement with Kant that knowledge of the world must violate realism's sole focus on supposedly R1 Independent objects in order to take into account the A5 Activity of consciousness:

> What reflection elicits is a product of our thought. . . . To discover the truth in things, mere attention is not enough; we must call in the action of our own faculties to transform what is immediately before us. Now, at first sight, this seems an inversion of the natural order, calculated to thwart the very purpose on which knowledge is bent. But the method is not so irrational as it seems. . . . The real nature of the object is brought to light in reflection; but it is no less true that this exertion of thought is *my* act. If this be so, the real nature is a *product* of *my* mind, in its character of thinking subject. (Hegel, *HL* 34–35, §22R–23)

Many commentators have noted the Kantian legacy here. Stephen Houlgate, for instance, says that "Hegel is following in the footsteps of . . . Kant . . . [who] put forward the view that consciousness is not simply the passive recipient of the sensations which the things about us produce in our minds, but is also active in understanding those sensations in terms of certain categories."[17] In my terms, Hegel is following Kant in subscribing to A5, the view that the knowing subject actively contributes to experience.

### A6 Historicism

Self-Consciousness has turned out to be the truth of Consciousness; knowing the world means knowing my mind because the two intermingle. As discussed above, Kant and Hegel both subscribe to what I am calling the Empirical Directive, which means that transcendental subjectivity is understood from its effects within experience rather than apart from experience, as with rationalists Descartes or Leibniz. Hegel introduces an important difference in the application of this strategy, however. Kant sifts through historical changes in knowledge for permanent structures (R3) in the disciplines of mathematics, science, and ethics in order to maintain a single set of constituting faculties in the knower (R6). Hegel follows ED more consistently and broadly to emphasize the study of history among the disciplines and the way theories have changed across time as indications of the nature of subjectivity: "History itself must be taken as it is; we have to proceed historically, empirically" (Hegel, *RH* 12; see also Gadamer 1976a, 104–5). Once he has rejected the noumenal self (which I will discuss in a moment), only the empirical and transcendental selves are left, and the profound changes in experience indicate that both are historical. "It is wrong therefore to take the mind for a processless *ens,* as did the old metaphysic which divided the processless inward life of the mind from its outward life. The mind, of all things, must be looked at in its concrete actuality, in its energy; and in such a way that its manifestations are seen to be determined by its inward force" (Hegel, *HL* 54, §34R).

Although often caricatured as an otherworldly metaphysician, Hegel steadfastly insists on discussing only what appears within experience, even concerning what seems the most ghostly element of his thought: *Geist,* translated as either "spirit" or "mind." Although it might sound a bit noumenal, in fact "Spirit is only that into which it makes itself" (Hegel, *RH* 69). Whereas the noumenal self is what is separate from the phenomenal realm, "in regard to Spirit one cannot set aside its manifestation. . . . It is this manifestation that we have to investigate in the form of states and individuals" (51). Without a noumenal realm in which permanently unactualized possibilities can be stored as in Kant's ethics, "a man is what he does" (Hegel, *HL* 199, §140R). Spirit cannot be distinguished from its manifestation, anticipating Heidegger's description of ec-static Dasein as always already "outside itself" or in-the-world, as well as Sartre's denunciation of the perpetual dreamer who defines himself in terms of what he would have done. Rejecting just the kind of abstract metaphysics he is often accused of, Hegel insists that "with such empty and other-world stuff philosophy has nothing to do. What philosophy has to do with is always something concrete and in the highest sense present" (138, §94R). Empiricism's great benefit was to tell philosophers to "'stop roaming in empty abstractions, keep your eyes open, lay hold on man and nature as they are here before you.'. . . The everyday world, what is here and now, was a good exchange for the futile other-world—for the mirages and the chimeras of the abstract understanding" (62, §38R).

Thus, following ED more rigorously than Kant did leads Hegel to accept the historical diversity of experience (A3) rather than cling to its uniqueness (R3). This in turn undermines Kant's R6 Realism of the Subject; we are only considering consciousness as organizer of experience,[18] like Kant's transcendental subjectivity, so if the organizations of experience altered, then the organizer changed. As one commentator puts it, Hegel "argues on broadly empirical grounds for the fundamental diversity of human cognitive nature and against the Kantian view . . . that in respect of cognitive nature all men share a large amount in common."[19] Hegel adds a major innovation to continental anti-realism in inaugurating a new thesis which I will call A6 Plural Subject, meaning minimally that there is more than one type of subjectivity or set of experience-organizing faculties, which Hegel ties to specific historical periods.

Many commentators have noticed that this amounts to a "general 'historicization' of Kant's transcendental enterprise."[20] Forster writes that

> Hegel had discovered a serious problem with Kant's analysis and criterion of truth, as they stood—namely, that they rested on [R6] an assumption that human nature, and in particular human *cognitive* nature, was basically the same in everybody. Hegel now realized, in light of [ED] a much greater interest in, and knowledge of, the actual history of human thought than Kant ever had, that this assumption was a mistake. . . . Hegel then goes on to criticize this Kantian position on the grounds that [A6] human nature is in fact much more diverse, much less shared in common, than it assumes. (Forster 1998, 229, bracketed comments added; see also 244)

When ED is followed to its logical conclusion it undermines R6, thus legitimating Hegel's claim that a consistent Kantian turns out to be a Hegelian, since Hegel's work is really an internal-overcoming-through-extension (*Aufhebung*) of Kant.

At this stage, both agree that consciousness contributes to experience (A5) but, fascinatingly, they are diametrically opposed on just what gets contributed. Whereas Kant sees the forms of intuition and understanding conferring necessary, universal laws and thus *stability* to experience (R3), Hegelian consciousness introduces *movement* or historical change to experience.[21] Here is how A5 and A6 come together: A5 Active Knower states that consciousness contributes features of the mind to experience and A6 Plural Subject specifies that since it changes, the way it organizes experience must do so as well. In an idea that Nietzsche will incorporate into the self-overcoming *Übermensch* and Heidegger into ecstatic Dasein, Hegel paradoxically makes this constant flux part of the very definition of consciousness: "Consciousness . . . is something that goes beyond limits, and since these limits are its own, it is something that goes beyond itself" (Hegel, *PS* 51, §80; see also Hegel, *HL* 292, §237; Hyppolite 1974, 16). Since the knower is constantly changing (A6) and she organizes experience (A5), experience is constantly changing too. This then leads to another thesis: A3 Ontological Pluralism, the idea that experience and/or reality (I will address this below) take on fundamentally different forms, thus spoiling R3 Uniqueness. Natural Consciousness desires stable identity in reality (R3) and is constantly frustrated by its mercurial transformations (A3), making the search for knowledge into a highway of despair. The idea that dawns on it in Self-Consciousness is that it itself is responsible for these changes in experience (A5 + A6): the subject "constitutes the determinateness, i.e., the differentiated content and its movement" (Hegel, *PS* 37, §60). Hegel says that the movement "and unfolded becoming" of experience "is just this unrest that is the self" (12, §22). He sums up the central realization of Self-Consciousness here: "This absolute [A3] unrest of pure self-movement, in which whatever is determined in one way or another, e.g., as being, is rather the opposite of this determinateness, this no doubt has been from the start [A5] the soul of all that has gone before" (101, §163, bracketed comments added).

For Kant, self-identical transcendental consciousness maintains a constant conceptual scheme (R6) which allows it to contribute (A5) stable forms to phenomena, thus securing their rule-governed essence and knowability over time (R3). For Hegel, on the other hand, Spirit sheds patterns of consciousness like a snake shedding its skin, which are then transferred to experience. This continual movement or self-transcendence is precisely what *prevents* the simple self-identity of reality, although, as we shall see, it is ultimately the key to knowledge for Hegel. Using parallel argument structures but with reversed valences, Kant states that unchanging consciousness constitutes phenomena the same way universally, while Hegel claims that constantly changing consciousness shapes experience in fundamentally different ways. To translate Kant's phrase into Hegel's idiom, this *dis*order and *ir*regularity in the appearances, which we entitle *history*, we ourselves introduce (note: this is only true at this stage of the *Phenomenology*).

Thus what the combination of ED and A5 yield for Hegel is A6 Plural Subject and, when added to his system, A3 Ontological Pluralism results. He describes the various phases of consciousness' development as "the formative stages of universal Spirit" (Hegel, *PS* 16, §28) or, variously, moments, shapes, or "*patterns of consciousness*" (56, §89) which are roughly multiple instances of Kant's single conceptual scheme.[22] Each phase is a historical instantiation of a different conceptual scheme which constitutes experience in a wholly new way: "As the knowledge changes, so too does the object" (54, §85). This accounts for the radical revolutions science has undergone without having to consider our predecessors idiots who couldn't see what was right in front of their noses. Like Kuhn's scientists, "the proponents of competing paradigms [read 'shapes of consciousness'] practice their trades in different worlds" (Kuhn 1970, 150, bracketed comment added). Hegel analyzes transcendental subjectivity in the *Phenomenology* by reconstructing each epoch's shape of consciousness from its understanding of reality, self, and truth (see Forster 1998, 120), in order ultimately to piece together "the system of structured shapes assumed by consciousness as self-systematizing whole of the life of Spirit—the system that we are considering here, and which has its objective existence as world-history" (Hegel, *PS* 178, §295; see also 413, §679; 487, §801).[23] Before we examine this conception of the self in greater depth, we must look at two specific criticisms of Kant.

### A2 Rejection of Correspondence Truth

We saw in chapter 2 that Kant still holds onto some version of R2 Correspondence Truth, even though just what is being corresponded to is problematic. It must be something phenomenal since noumena are off-limits, but precisely what proved difficult to pin down. Hegel makes precisely this criticism; as many have pointed out, he anticipates many twentieth-century philosophers by attacking Sellars's " myth of the given" in his *Meditations Hegeliènnes*.[24] One of the conclusions to come out of the refutation of realism in "Consciousness" is that the idea of starting immediately with immediately given sensory data immediately collapses into incoherence.[25]

As usual, Hegel views his argument as extending ideas already present in Kant. One of the ways that Kant insists that he has avoided full-blown idealism is by anchoring sensory data—the raw material input of our representations—onto external reality as its source.[26] But he also claims that nothing from the "outside" can play an epistemological role until it has been unified by the mind, a process which eliminates its status as raw sense data (Kant, *C1* B160n.a; see also McDowell 1996, 9, 41; Beiser 1993, 453–54). Paradoxically, sensory data cannot even determine how we synthesize it until after it has been synthesized. Kant insists that a sensory packet cannot simply be given to consciousness or impressed upon the mind so that it could just copy its inherent qualities; that was the empiricists' mistake. A sensible manifold must be synthesized or combined; "Combination does not, however, lie in the objects, and cannot be borrowed from them, and so, through perception, first taken up into the understanding. On the contrary, it is an affair of the understanding alone, which itself is an affair of the combining *a priori*, and of bringing the manifold of given representations under the unity of apperception" (Kant, *C1* B134–35). But if this is true, then the raw data cannot determine what we make of them, in which case they simply fall out of the equation as having no role to play. As Heidegger puts it, "they are data only in so far as we are *conscious* of them. What kind of function do they have in knowing beings? Just that the data get eliminated. They are the X of the knowledge equation that is to be solved" (Heidegger, *TDP* 69). Ralph Walker interprets Kant as holding to a coherence theory of truth for these reasons.

> There is no consciousness of the raw data of intuition prior to synthesis; to be conscious of what is empirically given we must synthesise it first,

> and if to synthesise is not to make a judgement about it (and thus to hold a perceptual belief) it is essentially very similar. . . . There is no part left for the data to play: if they lack any character of their own prior to synthesis, there is no way in which they can determine the course of our experience. . . . Indeed, it no longer makes sense to talk of them in their unsynthesised state at all. (Stevenson and Walker 1983, 164, 166)

Kant criticizes Leibniz for reducing sensation to a confused form of thought (Kant, *C1* A271/B327), but he cannot stop his own position from sliding into something similar, which then forms Hegel's beginning point. Although Kant "starts originally from the distinction of elements presented in the analysis of experience, viz. the matter of sense, and its universal relations," Hegel argues that "the Critical Philosophy however widened the contrast in such a way, that the subjectivity comes to embrace the *ensemble* of experience, including both of the aforesaid elements; and nothing remains on the other side but the 'thing-in-itself'" (Hegel, *HL* 65, §40; 66, §41). Kant could not sustain the distinction, since subjective concepts and synthesis swallow up anything from "outside" which is supposed to have an epistemic impact on our thoughts. "In pressing forward to its true existence, consciousness will arrive at a point at which it gets rid of its semblance of being burdened with something alien, with what is only for it, and with some sort of 'other'" (Hegel, *PS* 56–57, §89). Davidson makes the same Sellarsian criticism of Kant:

> I had been persuaded by Wilfrid Sellars of the absurdity of an unconceptualized "given.". . . If one agreed with Kant that "Thoughts without content are empty, intuitions without concepts are blind," one could not conceive of intuitions as occurring separately and so serving as a basis for empirical knowledge. But in saying this, one would still be assuming that it is possible to distinguish between the conceptual element and the experiential element in thought, and it is the distinction itself I questioned. (Davidson, *PDD* 51)

Davidson also turns to a coherence theory of knowledge where "nothing can count as a reason for holding a belief except another belief," since "a confrontation between what we believe and reality . . . is absurd" (Davidson, *SIO* 141, 137; see also 164).

Hegel argues that Kant "fails equally with Scepticism to bring together its contradictory thoughts of pure consciousness being all reality, while the extraneous impulse or sensations and ideas are equally reality. Instead of bringing them together, it shifts from one to the other" (Hegel, *PS* 144, §238; see also Hegel, *DFS* 115). Kant wants to posit a reality that is wholly external to thought, but Hegel claims that he cannot achieve such a thing. Raw data can't affect us epistemologically; cooked data does not stave off idealism. Thus in Kant "thought (and the universal) is not a mere opposite of sense: it lets nothing escape it, but, outflanking its other, is at once that other and itself" (Hegel, *HL* 31, §20; note that this is stated in a different but related context). As we will see below, this is one of the internal tensions in Kant's work that Hegel develops into full-blown idealism.

Another problem with Kant's correspondence truth arises when we consider one of the vestiges of his realism, the noumenal realm. Whatever aspect of phenomena our beliefs correspond to, it is certain that they do not correspond to things-in-themselves; they cannot in principle.[27] This means that our beliefs can never correspond to reality in itself, which makes it farcical to call these intersubjectively shared beliefs true. I think Hegel would have liked the way Heidegger describes Kant's ersatz substitution of intersubjectivity for objectivity: "Critical concern, it is true, intends to arrive at something absolute, but it would like to manage it without the absolute" (Heidegger, *OBT* 101).

If our beliefs do not correspond to reality as it is in itself, then Hegel thinks that they simply cannot be considered true, and Kant's abandonment of this goal for a truth redefined as mere intersubjective agreement constitutes a betrayal of philosophy's fundamental quest.

> This inner world is determined as the *beyond* of consciousness. . . . If no further significance attached to the inner world and to our close link with it through the world of appearance, then nothing would be left to us but to stop at the world of appearance, i.e., to perceive something as true which we know is not true. Or, in order that there may yet be something in the void . . . which is even called the *holy of holies* . . . we must fill it up with reveries, *appearances*, produced by consciousness itself. It would have to be content with being treated so badly for it would not deserve anything better, since even reveries are better than its own emptiness. (Hegel, *PS* 88–89, §146)

As we will see below, Hegel holds the idea of a thing-in-itself with no relation to us whatsoever to be perfectly empty, meaningless, a void. If skepticism is the idea that our beliefs may not match up with what reality is actually like, then one can see how Kant's "solution" that of course they don't match up might appear somewhat unsatisfactory. To prevent the obvious travesty of a void, Kant resorts to the disguised travesty of "reveries," that is, phenomena made up by us and so intersubjectively shared, even if not true. But a mass hallucination is still a hallucination, rendering Kant's "subjective idealism" incapable of yielding genuine truth. "Objectivity of thought, in Kant's sense, is again to a certain extent subjective. Thoughts, according to Kant, although universal and necessary categories, are *only our* thoughts—separated by an impassable gulf from the thing, as it exists apart from our knowledge" (Hegel, *HL* 67, §41R2; see also 93–94, §60R1; Hegel, *DFS* 97).

Kant botched the job, in Hegel's view, because of the way that he set up the issue:

> The pure Reason of this idealism, in order to reach this "other" which is *essential* to it, and thus is the *in-itself,* but which it does not have within it, is therefore thrown back by its own self on to that knowing which is *not* as knowing of what is true; in this way, it condemns itself of its own knowledge and volition to being an untrue kind of knowing, and cannot get away from "meaning" and "perceiving," which for it have no truth. It is involved in a direct contradiction; it asserts essence to be a duality of opposed factors, the *unity of apperception* and equally a *Thing;* whether the Thing is called an extraneous impulse, or an empirical or sensuous entity, or the Thing-in-itself, it still remains in principle the same, i.e., extraneous to that unity. (Hegel, *PS* 145, §238)

Hegel cannot accept Kant's transcendental idealism because it presupposes a transcendent *realism:* the commitment to a realm that in principle can never be experienced by humans. The first problem with this setup is that it has the unfortunate consequence of invalidating all knowledge: "In common with Empiricism the Critical Philosophy assumes that experience affords the sole foundation for cognitions; which however it does not allow to rank as truths, but only as knowledge of phenomena" (Hegel, *HL* 65, §40). Here Hegel reinstates precisely the distinction between intersubjectively universal knowledge of phenomena and genuine truth that Kant wants to collapse. If this is Kant's position, then he should be honest and call it skepticism and make way for someone who can actually give us true knowledge. Once again, in order to get what he wants Kant must become a Hegelian.

## A1 Mind-Dependence

Hegel's second major revision of Kant's framework is to reject the coherence of the very idea of noumena. This is the beginning[28] of one of the central threads in the history of continental philosophy that I will be following out: the erosion of noumena.[29] Hegel rejects both Consciousness' realist claim that true ideas correspond to a wholly external, independent reality and Self-Consciousness' Kantian view that the mind creates mere "reveries" that cannot match up with reality-in-itself. While these two might seem to exhaust the possible positions, like many great philosophers Hegel seeks hidden assumptions shared by both parties to a disagreement which, when discarded, allow new alternatives to emerge. Here both views share the assumption of R1 Independent reality, merely differing on whether we can know it or not. Hegel's strategy will be to show that this idea is historically generated and unsustainable.

Despite his reputation as an otherworldly metaphysician, as shown above Hegel is an "immanentist" of the first order (see Beiser 1993, 289; Houlgate 1986, 125–26, 173). Although the definition of "noumena" is something with no relation to us whatsoever, Hegel wants to see this precisely as an idea that humans came up with which needs to be examined in that context. The thing-in-itself is a category that arose within the human quest to know reality, and it can only have meaning within this context.

> The Logic of Understanding . . . believes thought to be a mere subjective and formal activity, and the objective fact, which confronts thought, to have a separate and permanent being. But this dualism is a half-truth: and there is a want of intelligence in the procedure which at once accepts, without inquiring into their origin, the categories of subjectivity and objectivity. Both of them, subjectivity as well as objectivity, are certainly thoughts. (Hegel, *HL* 255, §192R)

As long as knowledge is imperfect there will be a disparity between it and reality (see Hegel, *PS* 491, §805). The notion of independent reality arises out of and functions within this perfectly intelligible gap between belief and reality as a kind of placeholder in our inquiries: that-which-is-not-yet-known. The problem comes when this goal of inquiry which *is not* known gets hypostatized into a separately existing thing which *cannot* be known. At that point, a mundanely meaningful concept has been taken out of the context that gives it sense and is stretched beyond intelligibility. John McCumber expresses this reading of Hegel's views on the thing-in-itself better than anyone else.

> Both things for us and things in themselves are ingredients in the empirical realm. . . . Hegel does not deny the notion of the "in-itself,". . . rather, he rejects what might be called the Kantian *chōrismos:* the separation of the in-itself from experience. . . . The Hegelian in-itself is not an indeterminable something beyond experience, but an indeterminacy—a potentiality—which is found as such within experience and which we

> call such because it goes on to determine, or actualize, itself within experience. (McCumber 2002, 47; see also Hegel, *HL* 181, §124R)

Hegel reforms Kant's notion of the in-itself by returning it to the context of our normal usage, thus fulfilling what Beiser calls "the aim of the *Phenomenology* . . . to show the possibility, indeed the necessity of a strictly immanent metaphysics based upon experience alone" (Beiser 1993, 20).

Since our concepts determine all the meaning that ideas like "existence" or "thing" can have, the idea of a thing wholly independent of a conceptual scheme is at best meaningless, at worst an outright contradiction. Hegel considers the Kantian noumenon, the object beyond all access to experience, not ultimate reality but rather a confusion. Since things are constituted by us (the truth that Kant hit upon), removing this contribution does not yield true reality but just "a pure direction or a blank space" (Hegel, *PS* 47, §73; see also Forster 1998, 156n72).

> The Thing-in-itself . . . expresses the object when we leave out of sight all that consciousness makes of it. . . . It is easy to see what is left—utter abstraction, total emptiness, only described still as an "other-world.". . . Nor does it require much penetration to see that this *caput mortuum* is still only a product of thought, such as accrues when thought is carried on to abstraction unalloyed. (Hegel, *HL* 72, §44; see also 162, §112)

This is just what Nelson Goodman has said of the noumenal realm, using the term "version" for "world considered under a particular conceptual scheme": "Nor can we factor out the contributions of the several systems and discover the common features that underlie them. For to factor out everything version-dependent is to factor out everything" (Goodman and Elgin 1988, 51). To quote Wittgenstein, "in order to find the real artichoke, we divested it of its leaves" (*PI* §164). Any world beneath the versions would be Rorty's famous "world well lost," that is, "a world without kinds or order or motion or rest or pattern—a world not worth fighting for or against" (Goodman 1978, 20; see also 4).[30] Of course, for Hegel, immediately following Kant, it was very much worth fighting against.

The thing-in-itself would be an object stripped of all the features that make objects objects, leaving nothing; Kant's Being (thing-in-itself) turns out to be nothing (wholly indeterminate and meaningless; see Hegel, *HL* 127, §87). Kant says that things that are in principle outside of our experience are "nothing to us" (*C1* A105; see also A370–71, A383), but he leaves a noumenal remainder which simply exists. Hegel downgrades this "nothing to us" to "nothing at all": "What is not present for consciousness as something existing in its own right, i.e., what does not appear, is for consciousness nothing at all" (Hegel, *PS* 151, §249).[31] Hegel's strategy here is quite reminiscent of the later Wittgenstein's dissolution of problems by showing that our terms only make sense in mundane contexts, whereas philosophy confuses itself by taking them out of the language-games where they do work. It is then that we tend to misconstrue notions in bizarre, that is, philosophical ways: "When we do philosophy we are like savages, primitive people, who hear the expressions of civilized men, put a false interpretation on them, and then draw the queerest conclusions from it."[32] Within normal conversation or during standard inquiry, we can make perfect sense of an idea corresponding to reality as it really is or the world apart from our conceptions, but once we stop these mundane endeavors and become bewitched by the sublime vision of an unknowable world existing in absolute isolation from all human contact, it has gotten away from us.

In his final work, Wittgenstein demonstrates such metaphysical confusion with the slightly different example of the knowledge claim, "I know that I am now sitting in a chair."

> In its language-game it is not presumptuous. There, it has no higher position than, simply, the human language-game. For there it has its restricted application. But as soon as I say this sentence outside its context, it appears in a false light. For then it is as if I wanted to insist that there are things that I *know.* God himself can't say anything to me about them. (Wittgenstein, *OC* §554; see also §347, §482)

It is the "false light" in which Kant makes noumena appear that Hegel is trying to correct, so that we can rehabilitate this concept in an intelligible way. Wittgenstein cures philosophical maladies by bringing "words back from their metaphysical to their everyday use" (Wittgenstein, *PI* §116; see also §108). The essential therapeutic question is, "But how is this sentence applied—that is, in our everyday language? For I got it from there and nowhere else" (§134; see also §235), firmly rejecting the philosophical "tendency to sublime the logic of our language" (§38).[33, 34]

If "reality" can only be intelligibly discussed in terms of the role it plays in our attempts to know the world, this leaves no room for even the ideal notion of comparing our ideas with a wholly extra-experiential reality, that is, R1 and R2. Jonathan Lear notes that "thought, for both Hegel and the later Wittgenstein, should be seen as embedded in activities, projects, customs and institutions" (Lear 1984, 239; see also Stewart 2000, 48–49; Lamb 1980, 88). Somewhat like Peirce, Hegel holds that the notion of a disparity between our best understanding of reality at present and reality in itself can only be cashed out in terms of future beliefs correcting our present understanding: "The noumenal is the futural" (McCumber 2002, 47).

When we return the notions of reality and correspondence back to our epistemological practices, we find that the comparison of our ideas or beliefs with the world happens all the time, which means that whatever we are comparing our beliefs to is something that we have access to. "The distinction made above [between knowledge for us and reality in itself] falls within [consciousness]. . . . These two moments, 'Notion' and 'object,' 'being-for-another' and 'being-in-itself,' both fall *within* that knowledge which we are investigating" (Hegel, *PS* 53, §84, bracketed comments added).[35] We are the ones who make the distinction between the in-itself and the for-us; both are "certainly thoughts" that we employ in our epistemological endeavors. We're constantly encountering disparities between reality and our beliefs, finding that what we had believed did not match up with reality, precisely because we *do* experience reality and compare it with our thoughts. Hegel is hardly cavalier about this process—the entire *Phenomenology* is a complex analysis of how this happens—but *that* it happens is simply undeniable for him (see Kolb 1986, 93). These notions of reality or thing-in-itself have meaning because they play a role in our experience, just not the role that Kant gives them; that role is both unintelligible in itself and doesn't match our actual employment of the concept of reality in our continuous quest to know it. "Hegel shows that what must be presupposed is not a distinction between the 'in-itself' and the 'for-us' as two worlds, or even as two ontologically or epistemologically separable worlds. Rather, the in-itselfness of the world is an aspect of experience which belongs to appearance itself" (Flay 1984, 77).

Although Consciousness was wrong to believe that it had contact with unmediated reality, Self-Consciousness conceived as Kantian transcendental idealism, or what Hegel calls subjective idealism, is also wrong to think that it only has contact with phenomena, mere "reveries" as opposed to true reality.

> Objectivity of thought, in Kant's sense, is again to a certain extent subjective. Thoughts, according to Kant, although universal and necessary categories, are *only our* thoughts—separated by an impassable gulf from the thing, as it exists apart from our knowledge. But the true objectivity of thinking means that the thoughts, far from being merely ours, must at the same time be the real essence of the things, and of whatever is an object to us.[36]

Unfortunately, Kant's commitment to the noumenal realm structures his system in terms of the subject-object opposition, which prevents the possibility of genuine knowledge from the beginning: "Nonidentity is raised to an absolute principle. Nothing else was to be expected, once . . . the Idea had been posited in absolute opposition to being" (Hegel, *DFS* 81).

As Wittgenstein says (about a different topic): "(The decisive movement in the conjuring trick has been made, and it was the very one that we thought quite innocent)—And now the analogy which was to make us understand our thoughts falls to pieces" (Wittgenstein, *PI* §308).

Hegel singles out Reinhold, a contemporary popularizer of Kant's ideas who takes a step toward idealism, for believing that "thinking has its antithesis (a) in an application of thinking and (b) in absolute materiality" (Hegel, *DFS* 97). Beginning from the notion that "the formal and the material are absolutely opposed," the application of thought to the entirely alien raw material coming in *ab extra* can never "arrive at an absolute synthesis—which must be more than a mere fitting together" (181). Kant's R1 realism thus left an insoluble problem to modern philosophy: "The divorce between thought and thing is mainly the work of the Critical Philosophy. . . . The antithesis between them is the hinge on which modern philosophy turns" (Hegel, *HL* 35, §22R). Hegel takes as his central task to overcome this deep schism and to create a new conception that allows for knowledge. Of course, the only way to solve an insoluble problem is to change the terms; in his architectonic, this means moving from the Understanding, which is hung up on polar opposition to Reason, the faculty of *Aufhebung.*

> The sole interest of Reason is to suspend such rigid antitheses. . . . With respect to the given dichotomy the need is the necessary attempt to suspend the rigidified opposition between subjectivity and objectivity; to comprehend the achieved existence of the intellectual and real world as a becoming. . . . In the infinite activity of becoming and producing, Reason has united what was sundered and it has reduced the absolute dichotomy to a relative one, one that is conditioned by the original identity. (Hegel, *DFS* 90–91)

Identity is achieved in what Hegel famously calls "Absolute Knowing," but we have to be careful with this term. Many have taken him to be undoing Kant's revolution by proposing a pre-Kantian metaphysics, whereas he is actually absorbing Kant's lesson and going beyond him. "People in the present day have got over Kant and his philosophy: everybody wants to get further. But there are two ways of going further—a backward and a forward. The light of criticism soon shows that many of our modern essays in philosophy are mere repetitions of the old metaphysical method" (Hegel, *HL* 67, §41R1).

Absolute Knowing takes its start from Kant's "highest principle of all synthetic judgments . . . that the conditions of the *possibility of experience* in general are likewise conditions of the *possibility of the objects of experience*"

(Kant, *C1* A158/B197). What Hegel then does (and all of the thinkers we will examine follow him in this in various ways) is to remove the final qualifying phrase "of experience," so that the conditions of the possibility of experience are the conditions of objects. Or better, he leaves the phrase in place but eliminates the contrast that gave it its previous meaning, since the only reality we can speak intelligibly of is the one accessible to us. After all,

> it argues an utter want of consistency to say, on the one hand, that the understanding only knows phenomena, and, on the other, assert the absolute character of this knowledge, by such statements as "Cognition can go not further"; "Here is the *natural* and absolute limit of human knowledge.". . . No one knows, or even feels, that anything is a limit or defect, until he is at the same time above and beyond it. (Hegel, *HL* 91–92, §60)[37]

Hegel argues that if we cannot know noumena, then there is no reason to call them real, and the world we experience simply becomes the world. What appears to us is not *mere* appearance but reality full stop, since we cannot talk about another realm which would supply the invidious contrast. Without a contrasting term, there should be no hesitation in calling the world we experience the real world, or even the really real (*ontos on*) world.

This *Aufhebung* of subjectivity and objectivity isn't a "mere fitting together" (Hegel, *DFS* 181) which would retain the object in its unknown otherness. Instead, Hegel shows that there is an *internal* connection between the two which fundamentally changes the meaning of both and allows him to unite them from the inside: "the absolute identity" is "the identity of subject and object which suspends both in their opposition and grasps them within itself" (97; see also 101, 112). This move eliminates (while in some sense preserving) the subject-object opposition: "Laying aside therefore as unimportant this distinction between subjective and objective, we are chiefly interested in knowing what a thing is: i.e., its content, which is no more objective than it is subjective" (Hegel, *HL* 71, §42R3). I think Hegel should have said that the distinction is meaningless rather than unimportant, but the point is that he goes on to talk about knowing what things are full stop, which, without the phenomenon-noumenon distinction, is beyond subjectivity and objectivity alike. Without the conception of objective raw matter being supplied to us from the outside and getting organized on the inside by subjective processes—a conception we saw above that Kant could not maintain—the whole distinction of subjective and objective falls away. In a way, he is agreeing with Davidson's conclusion that "in giving up the dualism of scheme and world, we do not give up the world, but re-establish unmediated touch with the familiar objects whose antics make our sentences and opinions true or false."[38] Hegel even says that "philosophy [has] no other task than to overcome this antithesis" (Hegel, *HL* 261, §194R2) which is accomplished in the Idea, the culmination of his system, where "the implicit unity of subjective and objective is now realized" (274, §212).

The best way to understand Absolute Knowledge is the realization that there is no higher court of appeal for our beliefs than our community, that there is no other meaningful reality than the one reached by making our understanding of it as consistent and intelligible as possible to as many people as possible. Appeals to wholly independent, external reality are still *our* appeals; they are "certainly thoughts." As Goodman says,

> We cannot test a version by comparing it with a world undescribed, undepicted, unperceived. . . . While we may speak of determining what versions are right as "learning about the world," "the world" supposedly being that which all right versions describe, all we learn about the world is contained in right versions of it; and while the underlying world, bereft of these, need not be denied to those who love it, it is perhaps on the whole a world well lost. (Goodman 1978, 4)

Over a hundred years before Goodman's work, Hegel completed the A1 Dependence that Kant only began. Kant retained an R1 Independent level or aspect of reality, which depicts experience as the projecting of a form over a given and alien content which thus prevents genuine knowledge. The fact that there is a reality out there which we project features onto or organize holds open a logical space between the world as we encounter it and the world as it really is. The elimination of noumena closes this space, or, in Hegel's thought, stretches it out temporally.

Kant's A5 Activity is indicated by the difference between the world as it is in itself and the experience we make of it, but Hegel cannot employ this distinction, since he has gotten rid of independent noumena. Instead, he spreads his "levels" of reality across history (see Hegel, *HL* 181, §124R); we can see Spirit's Activity in the different ways it has A5 organized experience at different periods, with the difference that now it isn't just subjective experience that is being organized but reality full stop: "As the knowledge changes, so too does the object" (Hegel, *PS* 54, §85). This is not pre-Kantian realism, but a post-Kantian *Aufhebung* of subjectivity and objectivity.

The eradication of independently existing noumena supplying raw material to our minds to organize marks an important change in the Kantian Paradigm, one that Hegel criticizes Reinhold for not making:

> If Reinhold were truly serious about the identity and non-subjectivity of this thinking, he could not make any distinction between thinking and its application. If thinking is true identity, and not something subjective, where could this application that is so distinct from it come from, let alone the stuff that is postulated for the sake of the application? (Hegel, *DFS* 97; see also 181; Findlay 1958, 22)

Hegel anticipates here one aspect of Davidson's well-known criticism of conceptual schemes (I will take up the other main one in chapter 5). Davidson views conceptual schemes in a Kantian way as necessarily involving a scheme and content that are independent of each other, as he acknowledges in his "Intellectual Autobiography." Here he talks about ruminating on Quine, Carnap, and C. I. Lewis in 1971 as "example[s] of the dualism of scheme and content," commenting that "these variously described dualisms had a common origin in Kant, who clearly had the distinction though he thought there could be only one conceptual scheme" (Davidson, *PDD* 51). Kant's version of conceptual schemes posits separate sensory data as raw material, so Davidson holds that "it is essential to this idea that there be something neutral and common that lies outside all schemes" (Davidson, *ITI* 190; see also Davidson, *SIO* 41; Davidson, *TLH* 48). Nicholas Rescher shows the problem with this analysis when he writes,

> The animus of various recent writers against the idea of conceptual schemes is largely due to their construing the notion as committed to the Myth of a Ubiquitous Scheme-Neutral Input (as per the deliverances of Kant's *sensibility*) and the Myth of Form-Content Separability (as per the schematizing labor of Kant's *understanding*). But this perspective unjustly visits upon conceptual schemes a construction geared too closely to the Kantian processing-faculty model, a construction from which this resource can certainly be extricated and from which it is in fact free throughout most of its recent invocations. (French, Uehling, and Wettstein 1980, 340)

Davidson's criticism is that we cannot reach such a raw given except through or as linguistically formed beliefs (see Davidson, *SIO* 164–65), thus cooking the desired rawness, and that perceptual data can only play a causal role in our beliefs, not an evidential one (see Davidson, *PDD* 105–6; Davidson, *TLH* 321). He concludes that "if we reject the idea of an uninterpreted source of evidence no room is left for a dualism of scheme and content" (Davidson, *ITI* xx), leaving us in "unmediated touch with the familiar objects whose antics make our sentences and opinions true or false" (198). This is remarkably similar to Hegel's (more opaque) criticisms of

Kant's scheme-content distinction as preserving an independent content (R1) where "the assimilation of the matter, therefore, as a datum, presents itself in the light of a reception of it into categories which at the same time remain external to it" (Hegel, *HL* 284, §226; see also 256, §192R). Hegel solves the problem by eliminating content that is separate from the scheme: "Form does not supervene upon matter from without, but as a totality involves the principle of matter in itself. . . . Both are at bottom the same" (185, §128R–29; see also 223, §160; 226, §162). Like Davidson, Hegel concludes that in light of this *Aufhebung* of subjective form imposed on external matter, the world as we encounter it is simply the world: "In the transcendental intuition all opposition is suspended, all distinction between the universe as constructed by and for the intelligence, and the universe as an organization intuited as objective and appearing independent, is nullified" (Hegel, *DFS* 111). This is why he claims that at the final stage of consciousness' development, "the antithesis between form and content has also vanished" (Hegel, *HL* 274, §212). Just as Davidson examines and undermines the metaphors of conceptual schemes organizing or fitting content which "conceive language as an inert (though necessarily distorting) medium independent of the human agencies that employ it; a view that surely cannot be maintained" (Davidson, *ITI* 185), so Hegel shows the incoherence of subjective idealism's metaphor of knowledge as an instrument or refracting ray which distorts its content (Hegel, *PS* 46–47, §73–74).[39]

As discussed above, Kant resists assimilation into complete idealism with the notion of sensory data coming in from the outside, which Hegel shows to be untenable. Hegel's idealism is not the metaphysical, Berkeleyan claim that only minds and ideas exist,[40] but rather the negative, antirealist claim that we have no way of talking about input *ab extra*. When noumena go, discussion of genuinely external sensory data must follow. As Hegel puts it: "Now, because, in this way, the pure essentiality of things, like their difference, belongs to Reason, we can, strictly speaking, no longer talk of *things* at all, i.e., of something which would be for consciousness merely the negative of itself" (Hegel, *PS* 143, §236). Although Hegelian idealism has been frequently depicted as a ridiculously overblown metaphysical scheme, it has its roots in the same epistemological criticism of Kant's system that has been made by philosophers like Sellars and Davidson:

> Emphasis on sensation or perception in matters epistemological springs from the obvious thought: sensation are what connect the world and our beliefs, and they are candidates for justifiers because we often are aware of them. The trouble we have been running into is that the justification seems to depend on the awareness, which is just another belief. (Davidson, *SIO* 142)

Although experience comes in from the outside in *some* sense, when we try to pin down what this means, it ends up becoming "an otherness which is superseded in the act of grasping it" (Hegel, *PS* 143, §237). The sensible manifold loses its "outsideness" or "otherness" as it gets synthesized, which is necessary to "the act of grasping it." "The Thing is superseded; in itself it is nothing; it has meaning only in the relation, only *through the 'I'* and its *connection* with it" (481, §791). In other words, "otherness as an *intrinsic being* vanishes" (140, §233; see also 22, §37; 491, §805); thus A1 Mind-Dependence is completed. Hegel criticizes Kant for not taking his subjective idealism to its logical conclusion in what Hegel calls Objective or Absolute Idealism:

> Self-consciousness and being are the same essence. . . . It is only the one-sided, spurious idealism that lets this unity again come on the scene as consciousness, on one side, confronted by an *in-itself,* on the other. But . . . its essence is just this, to be immediately one and selfsame in *otherness,* or in absolute difference. The difference therefore *is,* but is perfectly transparent, and *a difference that is at the same time none.* (Hegel, *PS* 142, §235, last italics added)

Reason posits the difference but also realizes that it isn't one. This isn't idealism in the sense that all of reality becomes subjective since, without a contrast, subjectivity loses its traditional meaning. If everything is subjective, then nothing is.

We can no longer contrast our subjective contributions with reality's objective contributions even theoretically, as Kant does. The categories are in some sense our contributions, but Kant's notion of raw matter coming in from the outside has collapsed, and with it the entire projectionist or scheme-content conception as well. "The one-sided subjectivity and the show of objective independence confronting it are both cancelled" (Hegel, *HL* 273, §212). Subjectivity and objectivity have been *aufgehoben:* "The principles of logic are to be sought in a system of thought-types or fundamental categories, in which the opposition between subjective and objective, in its usual sense, vanishes."[41] The reality which we contribute to is reality itself, and the features we give it are its actual features, not mere subjective projections onto phenomena (see Margolis 2003, 49–50, 54–55). Hegel's version of Kant's highest principle is: "*Logic therefore coincides with Metaphysics*" (Hegel, *HL* 36, §24).[42]

Hegel's phrase "Absolute Knowing" has misled many into thinking of it as some kind of omniscience; Russell gets it about as wrong as one can: "If we saw the universe whole, as we may suppose God sees it, space and time and matter and evil and all striving and struggling would disappear, and we should see instead an eternal perfect unchanging spiritual unity" (Russell 1959b, 143). Hegel means the term "absolute" more literally, in the sense of that which is free of relations to anything external to it (*ab solus*): "Thought is always in its own sphere: its relations are with itself, and it is its own object" (Hegel, *HL* 49, §28R; see also Hegel, *DFS* 96; Rockmore in Denker and Vater 2003, 341). Once we have freed ourselves of the illusion that we can check our theories against external reality or that the world determines how we think of it, the highest authority possible can only be the latest outcome of the history-long internal debate. Once again, Hegel and Davidson are surprisingly close (though I don't want to claim that they're saying exactly the same thing here): "A community of minds is the basis of knowledge; it provides the measure of all things. It makes no sense to question the adequacy of this measure, or to seek a more ultimate standard" (Davidson, *SIO* 218; see also 83).

Here is how I read the *Phenomenology*. The entire history of consciousness leading to Absolute Knowing has been (1) Consciousness constituting reality but unknowingly and so believing in realism, then (2) converting to Kantian subjective idealism in Self-Consciousness with a scheme-content duality which prevents genuine knowledge, until finally (3) Reason achieves Objective or Absolute Idealism where there is no difference between the world we constitute in experience and reality full stop. "Consciousness, however, as essence is this whole process itself, of [1] passing out of itself as simply category . . . into the object [A5], and of [2] contemplating this process in the object, nullifying the object as distinct [from it], *appropriating* it as its own [A1], and [3] proclaiming itself as this certainty of being all reality, of being both itself and its object" (Hegel, *PS* 144, §237, bracketed comments added). Realism's problems lead to subjective idealism which then morphs into Objective Idealism which, strangely enough, ends up being a very sophisticated form of realism. As Hegel says at the end of the book, "The movement is the circle that returns into itself, the circle that presupposes its beginning and reaches it only at the end" (Hegel, *PS* 488, §802); and, at the beginning, "It is the process of its own becoming, the circle that presupposes its end as its goal, having its end also as its beginning, and only by being worked out to its end, is it actual" (10, §18; see also Hegel, *HL* 23, §17).

An important point about this derivation of Kant from realism and then of Objective Idealism from Kant is that it occurs as the development of views within the history of philosophy. Bare experience can never teach us idealism; it insists on commonsense realism, which is why Hegel begins there. But the failed attempts to spell out a coherent theory of realism are what lead to Kantian subjective idealism, at which point the attempts to understand correspondence truth and the anchoring of experience on noumena via the sensible manifold end up in antinomies. Thus, Kant's thought has been *aufgehoben* or cultivated to grow almost on its own into Objective Idealism, which drops all discussion of reality in itself as completely outside human experience. Consistent with Hegel's understanding of how philosophy works, we have reached this position through an internal thinking through of our predecessors.

> Self-consciousness is all reality, not merely *for itself* [that is, it understands itself to be all reality] but also *in itself,* only through *becoming* this reality, or rather through *demonstrating* itself to be such. It demonstrates itself to be this *along the path* in which . . . otherness as an *intrinsic being* vanishes. . . . Anyone who has not trodden this path finds this assertion incomprehensible when he hears it in this pure form. (Hegel, *PS* 140–41, §233, bracketed comment added)

Idealism outrages common sense and seems bizarre when baldly stated. It only makes sense when seen as the logical culmination of a long process of philosophical thought and dialogue which has explored and exhausted (a more contentious claim) all other options. This is one reason Hegel insists in his preface that "the real issue is not exhausted by stating it as an aim, but by carrying it out, nor is the result the actual whole, but rather the result together with the process through which it came about. . . . The bare result is the corpse which has left the guiding tendency behind" (Hegel, *PS* 2–3, §3; see also Hegel, *HL* 14, §10; 222, §159R). The point is never just the conclusion, but must include how it was reached: "Error or other-being, when superseded, is still a necessary dynamic element of truth: for truth can only be where it makes itself its own result" (Hegel, *HL* 274, §212R).[43] It is only the difficulties of making sense of the sensible manifold and noumena that convinces people to stop talking about such things (see Lamb 1980, 91–97).

Once we understand Hegel, claims like "self-consciousness . . . is all reality" (Hegel, *PS* 236, §394) really mean roughly the same as Putnam's denial of the coherence of a God's-eye view. Without an external view of our contributions and that to which we contribute, what John McDowell calls the "sideways on" view of our relations to the world (McDowell 1996, 34), "our language cannot be divided up into two parts, a part that describes the world 'as it is anyway' and a part that describes our conceptual contribution" (Putnam 1992, 123), so all we can say is that "the mind and the world jointly make up the mind and the world" (Putnam 1983, xi).[44] Putnam is in agreement with Hegel's dismissal of appeal to the *ab extra* when he says that his own position "does not deny that there are experiential *inputs* to knowledge; . . . but it does deny that there are any inputs *which are not themselves to some extent shaped by our concepts*" (Putnam 1981, 54).

Given these views, Putnam proclaims that "the time has come for a moratorium on the kind of ontological speculation that seeks to describe the Furniture of the Universe and to tell us what is Really There and what is Only a Human Projection" (Putnam 1990, 118). The essential insight of Objective Idealism is that rejecting the latter distinction between the in-itself and the merely projected is precisely what allows us to talk about the Furniture of the Universe. It was only that distinction that maintained a set of objects which counted as True Reality but couldn't be encountered. As Putnam writes, "The sharp distinction between what really is the case and what one judges to be the case is precisely what constitutes metaphysical realism" (Putnam 1981, 71). On my reading, Hegel agrees with this sentiment and therefore has no hesitation in talking about "what really is the case" after metaphysical realism has been abandoned. In other words, as he says in the last paragraph of the introduction, once consciousness "gets rid of its semblance of being burdened with something alien . . . appearance becomes identical with essence" (Hegel, *PS* 56–57, §89; see also Hegel, *HL* 186, §131). Now the things of this world can enjoy what Putnam calls "a kind of objectivity, *objectivity for us,* even if it is not the metaphysical objectivity of the God's Eye view" (Putnam 1981, 55). I think that this phrase "objectivity for us," which is not the same as subjectivity, is just what Hegel is after. Of course, we need to be careful, for the phrase "for us" seems to reintroduce the distinction we are trying to undermine, since only one option is a genuine, coherent option (see Wittgenstein, *PI* §140). What the phrase means, however, is that this is an objectivity, just not a pre-Kantian metaphysical kind of objectivity.

On this reading, Objective Idealism resembles Wittgenstein's argument in the *Tractatus* that "solipsism, when its implications are followed out strictly, coincides with pure realism" (Wittgenstein 2001, 5.64). Absolute Knowing amounts to a kind of solipsism en masse or solipsism of Spirit, that is, the human community. There is nothing to contrast our experience of the world with, certainly not the world in-itself; hence what Spirit experiences at the end of history simply is what is. In his reading of Wittgenstein as an idealist, Jonathan Lear calls this phenomenon "the strange case of the disappearing 'we'" (Lear 1984, 238; see also 242; Williams in Vesey 1974). Objective Idealism, when followed out strictly, coincides with a pure but sophisticated realism which shows that Hegel's Absolute Knowing is not transcendent at all (contrary to Walker 1989, 134). "The Absolute," according to Daniel J. Cook, "is nothing but the experience and expression of consciousness—individual and collective—and has no existence or meaning beyond them" (Cook 1973, 180; see also Lamb 1980, 92, 175). Heidegger writes of Hegel that "catching sight of the interior of the thing in itself does not mean going directly behind appearance, as it were, through a back door, leading straight to the interior of the thing in itself. Rather, it always means going solely and precisely *though appearance*" (Heidegger, *HPS* 109).

Hegel holds to a radically epistemic view of truth in that it has a necessary relation to humans, and therefore so does reality, since reality is whatever true statements claim exists.[45] When Hegel says that we know reality absolutely, he is not saying with the realists that he knows that our ideas reach out to an independent reality and capture it accurately, but rather that whatever it is that we know is the only thing that can sensibly be considered real. Rather than existing in splendid isolation of each other and hoping to make contact, thinking and being are inextricably linked. As Hans-Georg Gadamer says of Hegel's dialectic, "The object known can never be separated in any way from the knowing subject" (Gadamer 1976a, 11). Since the only reality there is is what we are in contact with, and since this contact molds reality into its own shape (as shown by the diversity of periods), every paradigm or epoch has a kind of truth or reality to it; in Kuhn and Goodman's phrase, it is its own world. Without noumena existing independently of thought, there is no persistent remainder which could even in theory validate one shape over the others. This is how Hegel can lay claim to divergent realities without Davidson's scheme-content division; there is no content or scheme independent of each other, just various realities at different points in history, with the self and the cross-epochal internal logic of the moments allowing sufficient continuity for cross-epochal reference. This is the radical fallout of Hegel's completion of A1 which Kant only began (see McCumber 2002, 44).

## Autonomous Thinking

Hegel's final criticism of Kant that leads to his development of his own position focuses on Kant's analysis of the table of categories. As we saw in chapter 2, it is essential to Kant's project to determine a complete list of the categories that transcendental subjectivity uses to organize experience once and for all. Since knowledge of the world consists in tracing the effects of our organizing faculties, he can only secure necessity and universality for knowledge by attributing these qualities to the transcendental subjectivity: he must give a definitive account of our categories. But, Hegel dryly notes, "Kant, it is well known, did not put himself to much trouble in discovering the categories. . . . Fortunately, the common logic offers to our hand an empirical classification of the kinds of *judgement*" (Hegel, *HL* 68, §42).

Hegel lays out his criticism at the beginning of "Reason," the third section of the *Phenomenology,* when he turns to Kant's mere assertion of the set of categories.

> The assertion as such, as also the assertion as to any *specific number* of species of categories, is a new assertion which, however, itself implies that we no longer have to accept it as an assertion. For since the difference [among the categories themselves as well as between them and the transcendental unity of apperception] originates in the pure "I," in the pure Understanding itself, it is thereby made explicit that the *immediacy,* the making of assertions and [mere] finding of differences, is here given. . . . But to pick up the plurality of categories again in some way or other as a welcome find, taking them, e.g., from the various judgements, and complacently accepting them so, is in fact to be regarded as an outrage on Science. (Hegel, *PS* 142–43, §235, bracketed comment added)

Hegel is not complaining, as many have, that it is illicit for Kant to take the categories from the table of logical judgments that just happened to be standard in his day; he is making the more general criticism that Kant took the categories from *anywhere.* It is "the assertion as such," the fact that they are merely being asserted rather than "demonstrated as a necessity," i.e., that the categories are "given," "picked up," "found," "complacently accepted" rather than derived or demonstrated that violates autonomy. What is worse, Kant violates it at the very heart of the self; the above quote continues: "Where else should the Understanding be able to demonstrate a necessity, if it is unable to do so in its own self, which is pure necessity?" To solve the great "scandal to philosophy and to human reason in general" (Kant, *C1*Bxl n.a), Kant resorts to "an outrage on Science."

This has been a sore spot for idealists almost from the publication of the first *Critique,* when Fichte objected to the moral law that we simply find that we must obey. Although Kant claims that it is our true self issuing moral commands, so that obeying it does not compromise our autonomy, the idealists consider themselves more faithful to Kant's spirit in rejecting his letter; autonomy demands that we not accept anything as issuing from our true self if we haven't created and given it to ourselves. "Fichte's philosophy, and most of the whole era of German idealism, can be seen as a massive attempt . . . to argue that whatever seems to be a given of nature is in some hidden sense the product of an autonomous mind" (Ameriks 2000a, 227). This is certainly Hegel's view: "To the philosophy of Fichte belongs the great merit of having called attention to the need of exhibiting the *necessity* of these categories and giving a genuine *deduction* of them" (Hegel, *HL* 69, §42). Ameriks makes it a central thesis of his book that

> it is obviously from Reinhold that Fichte got the main idea here, namely that Kant's transcendental deduction, with its mysterious dependence on the metaphysical deduction and its "given" list of categories, should be replaced by a "fundamental thesis" from which all further basic concepts would be derived in order and in such a way that the possibility of such a deduction would itself be reflexively explained. (Ameriks 2000a, 176)

While I certainly yield to Ameriks's greater knowledge of Reinhold, I question the need for a historical explanation of the idealists' demand for a derivation of the categories. Once one realizes that "whatever transcendental idealism exactly means, Kant stresses that it is not an account that even purports to give any positive 'explanation' of how we come to have the basic powers of mind that we exhibit" (Ameriks 2000a, 63), the heteronomous air of just accepting them seems obvious.[46]

Kant frees us from heteronomous dependence on external objects for our knowledge,[47] since they must be synthesized by us in order to be known, but he enslaves us to these specific ways of synthesizing sensory data, that is, these particular forms of intuition and concepts of understanding. The mere fact that they are internal to us does not by itself make them *ours* in the strong sense needed for autonomy; witness the inclinations which are in some sense internal. Ironically, it was Kant himself who imparted this strong sense of autonomy to philosophy. "Kant was instrumental in rejecting the empiricist notion of the *given* in experience. But he replaced it, according to Hegel, by introducing a *given* in the Understanding" (Solomon in Inwood 1985, 43). Once again Hegel is completing Kant, performing an *Aufhebung* or internal overcoming rather than an external refutation. By Kant's own (occasional) admission (*C1* B145–46; Kant, *PFM* 65/318; Kant, *C2* 48/46–47), he fails to prove the necessity of this specific set of categories, one of his own criteria for satisfactory knowledge.[48] As Pippin puts it, at this point "the 'critical spirit' had begun to devour itself" (in Magnus and Higgins 1996, 253).

Kant believes that there can be no explanation of why we have this particular set of categories and forms of intuition since they are the very source of all explanation, making them appear an arbitrary, heteronomous imposition that the idealists must overcome in order to secure full epistemological autonomy. Heidegger expresses the difference colorfully: "We can say that Fichte and Hegel are looking for a ground where for Kant there could only be an abyss. . . . Speculation becomes autonomous. This unveils a power of speculation that was impossible for Kant."[49] The best commentator on this issue is Robert B. Pippin, who places autonomy at the center of his reading of post-Kantian philosophy in general.

> Roughly, for his immediate successors in the Idealist tradition, Kant was perceived to have succeeded decisively in his negative task, in undermining "dogmatism" in prior philosophy, . . . (that is, he succeeded in elevating freedom or self-determination to the supreme philosophic principle of modernity). But he was thought to have failed to account for any truly self-legislated constraints on experience or action. Instead, it was alleged, he reverted to some form of dogmatism himself, appealing to "characteristics" of the human species, the nature of our pure forms of intuition, a non-derived, supposedly complete "table of concepts.". . . Kant's powerful critical spirit was invoked against the Master himself. Fichte was the first to suggest that even the Kantian appeal to reason or to philosophy might be viewed as dogmatic or ungrounded unless we could show how such a commitment could be viewed as the "product" of a subject's purely self-determining, or absolutely free activity. (Pippin 1999, 57; see also 161)

The *Phenomenology* is an attempt to use history as a superior Transcendental Deduction, one that would show how we had to come to have these and only these categories, and to show how nothing external to us (not even our own given nature) gave them to us, rendering our knowledge *ab solus* and our selves absolutely autonomous. "This is the true business of logic: to show that those thoughts, which as usually employed merely float before consciousness neither understood nor demonstrated, are really grades in the self-determination of thought. It is by this means that they are understood and demonstrated" (Hegel, *HL* 176, §121R). Just as the moral law "is valid for us as men, inasmuch as it has arisen from our proper self" (Kant, *FMM* 79/461; see also 48/431, 75/457), so the laws of logic should claim the same justification. For Kant the proper self means the noumenal self; for Hegel, as I will discuss below, it is the historical process of *Geist.*

The *Phenomenology* demonstrates how humanity did and had to come to this way of thinking, since every other form leads here. By the end of the book we can see that we (considered collectively) developed them ourselves: the Idea is both "the free notion giving character to itself, and that character, reality" (Hegel, *HL* 275, §213). This is why Spirit is, in my image, a reverse oroboro, that is, a snake giving birth to itself, or a "hyper-original" self, to use Pippin's term (1999, 58).

> In Kant's actual theory, . . . the understanding's spontaneity is constrained by the forms of human intuition, reason's spontaneity by a preexisting, internal architectonic, and so on. Hegel's project, by contrast, or his experiment, insists on a rejection of all such qualifications; and the attempt at a complete avoidance of any reliance on the "positive." It radicalizes, that is, critical philosophy's attempt at reason's reliance on itself alone in accounting for experience or evaluating action, but it attempts to do so without any certifying appeal to intuitions, facts of reason, or logical forms, and by avoiding or denying any assumption that such self-determination should be understood as "imposing" itself on a foreign manifold or object.[50]

Thus Hegel wants to complete Kant's autonomy to a degree that Kant, and indeed most philosophers, would find impossible, even absurd (see *C1* B422 and Kant, *FMM* 68–69/451, where Kant rules out the possibility). He wants to show how we must have "chosen" and "given" to ourselves just these ways of thinking. The self must arise from a purely internal process which is somehow of its own making, instead of preceding experience as already made. In this way, Hegel saves autonomy by stretching it across all of history and at the same time demonstrates the necessity and, to his mind, the validity of our conceptual scheme. Although he introduced plurality into the schemes, he ultimately saves them from the relativism which Kant only dogmatically denies.

## A6 Anti-Realism of the Self

Kant maintains a kind of R6 Realism of the Subject by conceiving of the concepts of the understanding as identical for all rational entities at all times: we are all outfitted a priori with the same ways of organizing reality which do not change across cultures or times. However, the idealists thought that this "issuance" of a certain set of mental tools compromised autonomy. "Theoretically, the question was: how has it come to be that we require experience to be categorized in various, ineliminable ways, in just *these* ways? No one in this tradition was content with Kant's reliance on some innate 'logical form' in human judgment as an answer" (Pippin 1991, 64; see also 58). Kant limits the autonomy that consciousness can achieve in principle by assigning certain forms to it a priori. He links the transcendental subject to experience (ED), bracketing the noumenal self for purposes of knowledge, but the transcendental subject is still pure, a priori, untouched by the causal fluctuating chain of experience (R6).

Hegel, on the other hand, plunges the self into history. "Thoughts become fluid when pure thinking, this inner *immediacy*, recognizes itself as a moment, or when the pure certainty of self abstracts from itself—not by leaving itself out, or setting itself aside, but by giving up the *fixity* of its self-positing" (Hegel, *PS* 20, §33). "Leaving itself out" would mean ignoring A5 Active Knower to return to a realist exclusive focus on things themselves, while the "fixity" of the self is R6 Realism of the Subject, even when conceived as an experience-forming activity rather than a thing. Kant's commitment to R6 "made the categories into static, dead pigeonholes of the intellect" (Hegel, *DFS* 80). Hegel, on the other hand, dissolves this static self into the "fluid" flux of history.

In a wonderfully self-aware passage, he writes of history that

> in this movement the [R5] passive Subject itself perishes; it [A6] enters into the differences and the content, and constitutes the determinateness, i.e. [A3] the differentiated content and its movement, instead of [R6] remaining inertly over against it. The solid ground which argumentation has in the passive Subject is therefore shaken.[51]

There is no self-identical subject outside time and change which forms reality the same way at all times from the outside. Rather, consciousness "enters into the differences and the content" of experience, "mingling" with the various periods. Instead of an a priori self separate from experience, Hegel posits "the immanent self of the content. . . . [It] is an activity that results in its own dissolution, and makes itself a moment of the whole" (Hegel, *PS* 33, §54; see also Hegel, *DFS* 120–21). This is a much stronger version of ED, which in Kant only connects an a priori subject to experience. It is in this historical process, the millennia-long *elenchus* described above, that we ourselves forge our own categories, thus achieving a much greater sense of autonomy.

If the categories that we have are the inevitable result of the use of any categories, then they are thoroughly "deduced" or justified. If we constitute the categories ourselves through the collective conversation of humanity's quest for knowledge, then our employment of them cannot compromise autonomy; we are *genuinely* giving them to ourselves rather than just finding them inside of us. "Hegel thus agrees with Kant that thought constitutes its own objects, but takes a step beyond him in arguing that it also constitutes the very means by which it constitutes those objects, its own categories (which for Kant remain a fixed given, not produced by thought itself)" (Dudley 2002, 313–14n5; see also Stewart 2000, 466). Although the shapes or "past existence . . . appears externally to [natural consciousness] as his inorganic nature," the way Kant's objects appear wholly independent of us, the phenomenological narrator shows natural consciousness (and the reader) that what we have been doing throughout our reading of the *Phenomenology* has been *Bildung*, that is, "taking possession of it for himself" (Hegel, *PS* 16, §28). Spirit is the truth of Self-Consciousness. Hegel's thought enables us to identify ourselves with "Spirit," that is, the entirety of human intelligence which has been brought to bear on the problem of knowing reality throughout history, so that its products become our own.

Spirit isn't a giant super-being or anything like traditional notions of God, contra some readings that take Hegel's metaphors and desires to unify all of philosophy and religion within his system too literally. Once again, Russell presents the authoritative misreading: "A person is a complex whole, having a single life; can there be a super-person, composed of persons as the body is composed of organs, and having a single life which is not the sum of the lives of the component persons? If there can be such a super-person, as Hegel thinks, then the state may be such a being" (Russell 1945, 744; see also Taylor 1975, 97). Rather, Spirit is the communal intelligence that comes about when linguistic communication (see Hegel, *RH* 78) allows for group analysis and mutual self-correction across generations, which renders human intelligence exponentially greater than any individual could ever be. Because I can publish my findings, the smartest people in the world can criticize them, enabling me to improve my views in ways I never could working by myself. Something I discover can touch off a line of research somewhere else or in the next generation that I could never have pursued, and which could not have occurred without the catalyst of my discovery. Thus human intelligence takes a quantum leap forward when it goes communal and historical by becoming linguistic. Sellars recognizes Hegel, "that great foe of 'immediacy,'" as the pioneer in rejecting

> the Robinson Crusoe conception of the world as generating conceptual thinking. . . . It was not until the time of Hegel that the essential role of the group as a mediating factor in this causation was recognized, and while it is easy for us to see that the immanence and transcendence of conceptual frameworks with respect to the individual thinker is a social phenomenon, and to find a recognition of this fact implicit in the very form of our image of man in the world, it was not until the nineteenth century that this feature of the manifest image was, however inadequately, taken into account.[52]

The accumulation of written records gives the "conversation" of humanity a continuity and longevity that generates astonishing epistemological power, as Popper discusses (see Hacking 1975, 184–86, for a discussion of this comparison). Later periods possess a tendency to be more advanced than earlier ones because, for one thing, they have access to more stores of written dialogue—"spirit preserves," if you will—and so can improve their positions by accommodating more beliefs and answering more objections. We can see how later eras have greater truth without resorting to realist claims to have gotten the external world right.

Autonomy comes about through our identification with the progression of Spirit, the simultaneously historical and logical development of just these particular categories (Hegel, *HL* 19, §14). "Such a 'collective historical subject' is viewed as completely self-forming in time, and so is supposed to do justice to, at some trans-individual level, the critical demand for spontaneous self-determination . . . [which] can clearly be said to be extensions of Kant's critical project" (Pippin 1999, 66). Hegel tries to show in great detail that any other theory leads to his particular configuration, so the end result is as necessary and inevitable as Kant's single conceptual scheme. This is how Hegel escapes the common criticism of the coherence theory of truth that many alternate coherent sets of belief can be generated which, since they are all coherent, would all be equally true. Hegel limits candidates to those which actually occur historically (see Hegel, *HL* 155, §104R3) and then shows that only one is fully consistent; all other candidates fall away or, rather, transform into that ultimate one under examination. So we are autonomous because we as Spirit have given ourselves as individuals these concepts, this government, and so on: "Thought must not be taken in the sense of a method or form, but in the sense of the self-developing totality of its laws and peculiar terms. These laws are the work of thought itself, and not a fact which it finds and must submit to."[53] In obeying it, I am obeying myself; consistent disobedience is futile anyway, since any alternative I try to set up will, when followed out far enough, lead back to this way.

In different eras consciousness takes on various shapes which constitute reality in alternate ways. Consciousness does not regally precede experience as the unformed former, but A6 changes along with it. However, since R6 was Kant's way of securing knowledge, the question is how Hegel can lay claim to absolute knowledge without this stability.

## R6 Realism of the Self

Although Hegel posits a plurality of conceptual schemes (A6) which in turn introduce multiple forms of reality (A3), he still wants a definitive, final account of the self (R6) and the world (R3). Absolute Knowledge is metaphysically modest in the sense of giving up pre-Kantian claims of corresponding with reality as it is wholly independent of us, but it is epistemologically ambitious in that knowledge should be incorrigible. As I will discuss below, Hegel's famous claim that the true is the whole assumes a closure to the object of true descriptions. By definition a whole must be complete, which pushes Hegel back to more traditional, realist ideas concerning the transcendental subject; despite the variety he introduces into the subject, he wants to end up with a list of the subject's "categories" that is as complete and final as Kant's. Hegel achieves this closure by placing firm limits on the changes the subject can undergo. Thus, although he greatly expands the possibilities of what both self and reality can be, he ends up merely loosening R6 Realism of the Subject and R3 Unique knowledge rather than dissolving them. In this way, he is still operating within the Kantian Paradigm. The tension in his thought results from the fact that his conception of truth as the whole keeps him within the Kantian Paradigm, while his Objective Idealism pushes him to surpass it. This return to R6 occurs in two ways which I will examine in turn: Hegel (a) limits the transformations of the subject and (b) gives a definition of the self.

### Totality: The True Is the Whole of the Subject

Although the self continually changes, there is a set number of shapes that it can take on, namely the ones depicted in the *Phenomenology*. Hegel disapproves of the idea he calls "bad infinity," which portrays infinity as an unending, ever-receding line of changes. Instead of this indeterminate trailing off, the progress of Spirit as depicted in the *Phenomenology* achieves the infinity of "the circle that presupposes its end as its goal, having its end also as its beginning" (Hegel, *PS* 10, §18). This is infinity but with completeness and order since, although it can continue forever, its course is laid out and limited in advance. This closure is the key to Hegel's alternate solution to Kant's problem. Kant wanted to secure unique knowledge of reality (R3), which he thought could only be secured by a universal and static self (R6): there must be one and only one set of categories which cannot vary across time or culture. This conflicts with the historical evidence of dramatic epochal differences that we should take seriously if we follow the Empirical Directive; the heterogeneous data of history indicates a plurality of experience-organizing conceptual schemes (A6) for Hegel. The problem now is that consciousness and reality seem hopelessly dispersed among the various shapes, becoming "as many-coloured and diverse a self as I have representations" (Kant, *C1* B134), just as Kant warned.

But that would only be the case for a bad infinity where the self keeps altering in unpredictable ways and so constituting reality in arbitrary configurations forever. Although the self has dissolved into the various historical periods (ED + A6), these epochs are connected by an internal logic which links them into a necessary order which brings them to a close at the end of history, after which no new ones can emerge. The shapes of consciousness described in the *Phenomenology* exhaust all of the conceptual schemes that consciousness is capable of taking on. Hegel believes he has proven this by showing how all others naturally transform into just these, which then naturally develop into Absolute Knowing the way acorns grow into oak trees (Hegel, *HL* 224, §161R). Since there is a limit to the number of schemes, we can collect them all and piece them together into an interlocking system (that is, the *Logic*); this system then will be a complete account of consciousness' workings. Kant makes the faculties of the mind timelessly contemporaneous while Hegel spreads them across history, but both thinkers posit a limited totality that can be described once and for all. This description is the purpose of both the *Critique of Pure Reason* and the *Phenomenology of Mind.*

The *Phenomenology* sifts through history to gather together all of the faculties that consciousness has ever had.

> Immersed in the material, and advancing with its movement, scientific cognition does come back to itself, but not before its filling or content is taken back into itself. . . . Through this process the simple, self-surveying whole itself emerges from the wealth in which its reflection seemed to be lost. (Hegel, *PS* 32–33, §53)

Although it seemed lost or wholly dissolved into the historical richness, compiling them and comprehending their inner logic achieves a knowledge of the totality of the conceptual schemes—"the simple, self-surveying whole itself emerges from the wealth in which its reflection seemed to be lost." Time spreads them out but thought re-collects them. The important point is that this compilation of consciousness' concepts is *just as complete and final* as Kant's analysis of the single scheme. This parallel is strengthened by the fact that Hegel is as insistent that he has captured the totality and necessary order of the schemes as Kant is about having listed all possible forms and concepts in his one scheme. "This pathway, through the movement of the Notion, will encompass the *entire* sphere of secular consciousness in its *necessary* development."[54] As discussed above, Hegel claims a key superiority over Kant in that his developmental account shows the necessary logic and autonomous self-derivation of the schemes, whereas Kant presents his set as brute facts to be accepted: "All the forms of finite thought will make their appearance in the course of logical development, the order in which they present themselves being determined by necessary laws" (Hegel, *HL* 42, §24R3).

Since consciousness has been dissolved into its various moments, the re-collection of the totality of these moments constitutes the self in its completeness; there is nothing else to it. And as Hegel reveals at the end of the book, assembling these pieces into a systematic totality by showing how each shape must lead to the next, which demonstrates the necessity of each phase as well as the completeness of the set, is exactly what the entire *Phenomenology* has been:

> For this Notion is, as we see, the knowledge of the Self's act within itself as all essentiality and all existence, the knowledge of this subject as substance and of the substance as this knowledge of its act. Our *own* act here has been simply to *gather together* the separate moments, each of which in principle exhibits the life of Spirit in its entirety. (Hegel, *PS* 485, §797)

The purpose of the book is in fact to achieve R6, a full, determinate (R3) knowledge of subjectivity, conceived with Kant as constituting activity (A5) but contra Kant as inseparable from reality (ED) and as encompassing a diachronic multiplicity (A6). The only way to reach this understanding is by going through all of the phases which inevitably lead to the final realization—one that retroactively shows all of the previous phases precisely *as* leading to this conclusion and as fitting into the system of *Geist,* Hegel's version of transcendental subjectivity. This is why Hegel says that what we learn at the end of the long journey is just the content of the journey itself, but with the new perspective that the journey is all there is:

> To speak of the absolute idea may suggest the conception that we are at length reaching the right thing and the sum of the whole matter. . . . Its true content is only the whole system of which we have been hitherto studying the development. . . . The content of the absolute idea is the whole breadth of ground which has passed under our view up to this point. Last of all comes the discovery that the whole evolution is what constitutes the content. . . . We have had the content already, and what we have now is the knowledge that the content is the living development of the idea. (Hegel, *HL* 292–93, §237R)

Indeed, the end result of philosophy as a whole is that "the mind . . . comes to itself; for thought is its principle, and its very unadulterated self" (Hegel, *HL* 15, §11). The fact that Hegel has "the aim of repatriating and reappropriating oneself, of returning close to oneself in the infinite richness of one's determination," is Derrida's main objection to him precisely because it retains too much realism of the subject (Derrida, *Pos* 96; see also Derrida, *Gl* 108).

The task of phenomenology or Science is to collect and internalize (to achieve *Er-innerung* of) all of the shapes of consciousness, so that the book could only have been written after they have all been run through implicitly or in-themselves. This is what Hegel means when he says that history has ended.

> This past existence is the already acquired property of universal Spirit which constitutes the Substance of the individual, and hence appears externally to him as his inorganic nature. In this respect formative education, regarded from the side of the individual, consists in his acquiring what thus lies at hand, devouring his inorganic nature, and taking possession of it for himself. (Hegel, *PS* 16, §28)

Education consists in explicitly appropriating the moments of consciousness which Spirit has already been through without self-awareness, making what we are "in-itself" become "for us." In a phrase that Nietzsche will pick up and adapt, Hegel says that "this Substance which is Spirit is the process in which Spirit *becomes* what it is *in itself*" (Hegel, *PS* 487, §802; see also 14, §25). In order for this to be possible, however, the circle must be closed; the number of shapes must be finished and therefore finite, otherwise there will continue to be new undigested shapes which compromise the claim of absolute knowledge.[55]

If the path of Science is circular, closed, and complete, then we can achieve Absolute Knowledge by listing the totality of all possible conceptual schemes. Since reality is wholly determined by these without noumenal remainder (A1), this list also captures the entirety of reality the way Euclidean geometry and Newtonian physics set the unalterable parameters of phenomenal reality for Kant.

> This is the movement of *consciousness,* and in that movement consciousness is the totality of its moments. Equally, consciousness must have related itself to the object in accordance with the totality of the latter's determinations and have thus grasped it from the standpoint of each of them. This totality of its determinations establishes the object as an *implicitly* spiritual being, and it does truly become a spiritual being for consciousness when each of its individual determinations is grasped as a determination of the Self, or through the spiritual relationship to them that was just mentioned. (Hegel, *PS* 479–80, §798)

This is how I understand Hegel's famous statement that "the True is the whole. But the whole is nothing other than the essence consummating itself through its development" (Hegel, *PS* 11, §20). The whole is the entirety of the shapes of consciousness and so too all of the correlative constitutions of reality, outside of which there can be nothing, not even nothing (see Heidegger, *N* 1:68; Heidegger, *Mi* 46, 107). Although Absolute Knowing is not divine omniscience in the sense that one will know specific events that will happen, readers who have mastered the system are familiar with all possible conceptual schemes and their internal logic, and so understand the basic outlines of all possible entities and events as well as the overall direction that history takes.

In the end, Hegel recaptures a realism of the subject by imposing closure on its possible changes. Like Heraclitus's logos, Hegel draws stability out of controlled, lawful movement. Consciousness constantly changes and introduces differences, but these differences are ultimately recaptured into a unity more profound than realism's simplistic self-identity, the earlier idealists' "night in which . . . all cows are black" (Hegel, *PS* 9, §16). Hegel's mediated unity,

> the absolute Notion . . . is neither disturbed nor interrupted by any difference, but rather is itself every difference, as also their supersession; it pulsates within itself but does not move, inwardly vibrates, yet is at rest. It is self-*identical,* for the differences are tautological; they are differences that are none. (Hegel, *PS* 100, §162)

Here we have an updated version of Heraclitus's logos of flux ("by changing it rests") and Plato's "moving image of eternity."

If we focus narrowly on a particular shape, it will always be in the process of transforming into another, thus lacking self-identity or determinateness; it will be "false." When we achieve absolute knowledge, though, we see that history as a whole, Spirit, the totality of shapes of consciousness, possesses those qualities we have been searching for since the beginning of our quest in Consciousness' naive realism: stability and self-identity. "The self-knowing Spirit, just because it grasps its Notion, is the immediate identity with itself which, in its difference, is the *certainty of immediacy,* or *sense-consciousness*—the beginning from which we started."[56] At the end of this long journey, we have achieved a mediated and successful form of the self-identity we sought at the start in simple realism; the beginning is in the end. As Kojève says, "In spite of the *Negativity* which it encloses and presupposes, the final *Totality* is just as much one and unique, homogeneous and autonomous, as the first and primordial *Identity*" (Kojève 1969, 202–3). By compiling the systematic totality of limited becoming, we achieve Being: "Through this movement the path by which the Notion of knowledge is reached becomes likewise a *necessary and complete process of becoming*" (Hegel, *PS* 20, §34, italics added).[57]

### Definition of the Subject

Although at first Hegel seems to dissolve consciousness completely into history, defining humanity solely in terms of what it is within a particular shape without any transcendental ego remaining the same outside of time, he does end up sifting through these patterns of consciousness for an essence of the self, a defining feature of consciousness which maintains self-identity throughout historical change. He explicitly states on occasion that: "Once it has liberated its own view from contingencies and limitations, Reason necessarily finds itself throughout all the particular forms" (Hegel, *DFS* 88; see also 114), or "seeing that there is in it no transition, or presupposition, and in general no specific character other than what is fluid and transparent, the Absolute Idea is for itself the pure form of the notion, which contemplates its contents as its own self" (Hegel, *HL* 292, §237). Being a good student of Kant, of course, Hegel does not conceive of the self as a Cartesian thinking thing or static substance but rather as a kind of process or activity, a way of organizing experience. Hegel defines subjectivity as being "*self-moving*" or "pure negativity," a transformative power of mediation: "The realized purpose, or the existent actuality, is movement and unfolded becoming; but it is just this unrest that is the self."[58]

After the "Paralogisms," philosophers rarely think of the self as some*thing*. Both Kant and Hegel are able to claim knowledge of the self by conceiving of it as a determinate process, however, a definable activity. Hegel views the self as "an absolute unrest of pure self-movement" (Hegel, *PS* 101, §163). Although this movement is a constant self-surpassing in the sense of always entering into new shapes, the formal structure of this movement as *Aufhebung* remains the same throughout all of these changes. This is what allows Hegel to make his claims about the necessity of the order of the patterns in the *Phenomenology:* once we grasp how consciousness works, we can know with certainty what course it will take in any situation. Just as Kant's phenomenal realm derives its determinateness (R3) from the determinate structure of transcendental subjectivity (R6), so Hegelian history as a whole gets its necessity, closure, and order (R3) from the inner process of consciousness (R6). Although more fully dissolved into history and time than most earlier conceptions of the self, Hegelian consciousness ends up with an essential definition to which whatever particular shape it happens to reside in at any point in time is in some sense accidental. Houlgate states that "for Hegel, there is no given, immutable human self, no 'entity' called the self which would be available for scientific scrutiny. There is only the human *activity* of producing our world. . . . For Hegel, that activity of historical self-production, self-construction and self-determination *is* thus what we are. It is the universal form of all human activity" (Houlgate 1991, 20–21; see also 35).

Absolute Knowledge consists in the complete comprehension of the self. Natural consciousness puts the emphasis on individual shapes; even when it perceives the role of consciousness in experience (A5) in Self-Consciousness, it still tries to stop at a single pattern and declare it the whole of the self, as Kant did. This inevitably leads to antinomies which should not, in Hegel's opinion, be simply shrugged off. Absolute Knowledge is the realization that this perpetual movement, this constant transition of shapes is what reality and the self are and that any particular slice is necessarily limited or "false." At this point, consciousness understands itself completely and knows itself for what it is. "Substance shows itself to be essentially Subject. When it has shown this completely, Spirit has made its existence identical with its essence; *it has itself for its object just as it is*" (Hegel, *PS* 21, §37, italics added). Spirit understands itself completely and this knowledge corresponds to the "essence" or nature of Spirit. In "true knowledge," Spirit appropriates the shapes of history "so that it may purify itself for the life of the Spirit, and achieve finally, through a completed experience of itself, *the awareness of what it really is in itself*" (49, §77, italics added).

Here we have a traditional correspondence conception of truth (R2) of what the (R6) subject really is, albeit achieved through history (ED) rather than direct intuition. Absolute Knowledge means that our conception of the self corresponds to its true essence.

> This last shape of Spirit—the Spirit which at the same time gives its complete and true content the form of the Self and thereby realizes its Notion as remaining in its Notion in this realization—this is absolute knowing; it is Spirit that knows itself in the shape of Spirit. (Hegel, *PS* 485, §798)

All along the self-movement of Spirit has animated experience, making it shift and twist into new shapes and patterns. Absolute Knowledge consists in fully understanding this history of movement by grasping the movement of history, that is, the self that has been driving it. As Hegel says in the final paragraph of the book, "Its fulfillment consists in perfectly *knowing* what *it is*" (Hegel, *PS* 492, §808, italics in original). Consciousness achieves satisfaction by understanding and accepting the structure of its own continuous movement; it achieves identity in fully understanding its self-transcendence.

## A4 Non-Bivalent Truth of the Whole

Truth and knowledge are central topics for Hegel; he even says that the *Phenomenology*'s "goal is Spirit's insight into what knowing is" (Hegel, *PS* 17, §29). However, as mentioned previously, natural Consciousness objects to the lengthy procedure of examining earlier, "false" moments of consciousness—"Why bother with the false?" (22, §38)—perhaps preferring "the rapturous enthusiasm which, like a shot from a pistol, begins straight away with absolute knowledge, and makes short work of other standpoints by declaring that it takes no notice of them" (16, §27). Given the isomorphism between logic and history, though, Hegel insists that "since the Substance of the individual, the World-Spirit itself, has had the patience to pass through these shapes over the long passage of time . . . and since it could not have attained consciousness of itself by any lesser effort, the individual certainly cannot by the nature of the case comprehend his own substance more easily" (17, §29). The process that was necessary for Spirit to achieve its great insights throughout history is equally necessary for us to go through in order to grasp these insights properly, though happily we can go through it intellectually rather than via wars and revolutions. His general epistemological position is that "the view already discussed, namely that we should begin with Science [that is, the true results] straight away, is to be answered at this point by examining the nature of the negative in general regarded as what is *false*. This is a topic regarding which established ideas notably obstruct the approach to truth" (22, §38, bracketed comment added). In other words, focusing exclusively on truth and truths actually keeps us from both.

Resistance to Hegel's method can be viewed in light of bivalence—something is either true or it is not, such truth being a matter of yes or no without degrees. If this is the case, then beliefs which have been refuted can only be false and there is little reason to spend time on them. Instead of Hegel's elaborate examination of other views from the inside, what is needed is to refute these outdated views, shelve them, and get on to the truth. "The more conventional opinion gets fixated on the antithesis of truth and falsity, the more it tends to expect a given philosophical system to be either accepted or contradicted; and hence it finds only acceptance or rejection" (Hegel, *PS* 2, §2). In this way, "'true' and 'false' belong among those determinate notions which are held to be inert and wholly separate essences, one here and one there, each standing fixed and isolated from the other, with which it has nothing in common." Hegel believes, however, that "against this view it must be maintained that truth is not a minted coin that can be given and pocketed ready-made" (22, §39). Truth isn't merely a matter of conclusions for Hegel; a true result separated from how it was determined is what he sometimes calls merely correct (Hegel, *HL* 237, §172 R). It's not that it has no epistemological merit whatsoever, but it is only a shadow of the genuine truth that philosophy should strive for.

> *Dogmatism* as a way of thinking, whether in ordinary knowing or in the study of philosophy, is nothing else but the opinion that the True consists in a proposition which is a fixed result, or which is immediately known. To such questions as, When was Caesar born? or How many feet were there in a stadium? etc. a clear-cut answer ought to be given. . . . But the nature of a so-called truth of that kind is different from the nature of philosophical truths. (Hegel, *PS* 23, §40)

Answers to some factual questions can be separated from their method of determination and perhaps are bivalent, but philosophy does not consist in such matters.

What Hegel is doing here is incorporating knowledge's requirement of justification into truth. As Socrates suggests in the *Theaetetus,* knowledge must be a justified true belief; without an account of why one believes what one believes, it's just a lucky guess. Since truth is radically epistemic for Hegel, not just knowledge but *truth* too requires an account. "Only out of this error does the truth arise. In this fact lies the reconciliation with error and with finitude. Error or other-being, when superseded, is still a necessary dynamic element of truth: for truth can only be where it makes itself its own result" (Hegel, *HL* 274, §212R). A conclusion without an account does not count as a full truth; rather, "it is only when it is taken as the result of that from which it emerges, that it is, in fact, the true result" (Hegel, *PS* 51, §79; see also Hegel, *DFS* 99). This is why the beginning point is so difficult: "Where knowledge by thought is our aim, we cannot begin with the truth, because the truth, when it forms the beginning, must rest on mere assertion. The truth when it is thought must as such verify itself to thought" (Hegel, *HL* 222, §159R). Being able to give an account, to justify one's beliefs, is a necessary component in a full understanding of the idea in question, changing it from in-itself to for-itself in Hegel's terms (see Hegel, *PS* 12, §21). Although a schoolchild who has memorized the Pythagorean theorem can in some sense be said to know it, this comprehension pales in comparison to the grasp of the geometrician who can prove it: "We should be even less inclined to regard anyone as a geometer who knew Euclid's theorems *outwardly* by rote, without knowing their proofs" (24, §42).[59]

As discussed above, the accounts of philosophical views come about in history by people holding and examining particular views in conversations across generations and educating themselves by coming up to speed on how the conversation has led up to the present. Since ideas have an intrinsic logic, the historical development of philosophy is also the logical analysis, refutation, and improvement of views which leads to Absolute Knowledge. The proof of Absolute Knowledge, and Hegel's thought as a whole, can only be the entire history of thought which has led to it. This is why "the True is the whole. But the whole is nothing other than the essence consummating itself through its development" (Hegel, *PS* 11, §20). He also describes this whole as the system: "Truth, then, is only possible as a universe or totality of thought. . . . Unless it is a system, a philosophy is not a scientific production. . . . Apart from their interdependence and organic union, the truths of philosophy are valueless" (Hegel, *HL* 20, §14; see also 3, §5). We can only genuinely know a philosophical view if we can justify it, and we can only justify it by giving an account of it which rebuts objections and shows its superiority to alternatives, both of which must be done historically for Hegel. This treatment of knowledge is similar to Sellars's explicitly social epistemology where "the essential point is that in characterizing an episode or a state as that of *knowing,* we are not giving an empirical description of that episode or state; we are placing it in the logical space of reasons, of justifying and being able to justify what one says" (Sellars 1963, 169; see also 6, 16–17). Hegel, I think, would call it "the logical *time* of reasons" and put a great deal of emphasis on the way this dialogue has actually happened in addition to how it might still unfold, but basically agree.

The "motor" of Hegelian dialectic—how we get from Consciousness to Absolute Knowing—is determinate negation. This means that a particular thing—a theory, a plant, a government—reacts to some internal shortcoming by rejecting it while also preserving elements of it: the *Aufhebung.* The *Phenomenology* as a whole shows how the history of philosophy has been one long process of this activity, leading eventually to its own self-understanding in Hegel. He compares "the diversity of philosophical systems as the progressive unfolding of truth" to the growth of a plant: "The bud disappears in the bursting-forth of the blossom, and one might say that the former is refuted by the latter; similarly, when the fruit appears, the blossom is shown up in its turn as a false manifestation of the plant" (Hegel, *PS* 2, §2; see also 43, §70). But of course, this kind of simplistic refutation as mutual exclusion isn't at all how we understand the development of a living thing. Stages don't "refute" or "reject" each other but build upon and elevate the previous ones, so that "the child is the father to the man." "Their fluid nature makes them moments of an organic unity in which they not only do not conflict, but in which each is as necessary as the other; and this mutual necessity alone constitutes the life of the whole" (2, §2). Hegel finds this a much more accurate depiction of how individuals think, how schools of thought and societies develop, and how organic entities grow than the one forced on us by simple bivalence.

Bivalent propositions can never capture this kind of movement.

> If the Object, the product of this transition, be brought into relation with the notion, which, so far as its special form is concerned, has vanished in it, we may give a correct expression to the result, by saying that notion (or, if it be preferred, subjectivity) and object are *implicitly* the same. But it is equally correct to say that they are different. In short, the two modes of expression are equally correct and incorrect. *The true state of the case can be presented in no expressions of this kind.* (Hegel, *HL* 257–58, §193, final italics added)

Hegel gives us an account of a linguistic form that is proper to the expression of philosophical truths in his notion of the speculative proposition (see Hegel, *PS* 38–41, §61–66). Discussing it here would take us too far afield, but suffice it to say that it provides a linguistic model that incorporates the dynamism Hegel sees in the world. Clearly, it will not be bivalent ("the two modes of expression are equally correct and incorrect").

Furthermore, since Hegel accepts a conception of developmental truth where each stage incorporates and elevates what came before, he apportions truth to previous phases in degrees. Spirit "embodied in each shape as much of its entire content as that shape was capable of holding" (Hegel, *PS* 17, §29; see also Hegel, *HL* 41, §24R2). Since the ultimate truth of the *Phenomenology of Spirit* is the accurate portrayal of Spirit, each shape has truth to the degree that it contains Spirit, which can only be partial until the end (Hegel, *PS* 491, §805). This is why we must study each of these shapes rather than rejecting them as simply false. Nothing is simply anything for Hegel, but certainly no belief that has been held in history is simply false. He takes great care in explaining just what he means by these partial truths.

> To know something falsely means that there is a disparity between knowledge and its Substance. But this very disparity is the process of distinguishing in general, which is an essential moment [in knowing]. Out of this distinguishing, of course, comes their identity, and this resultant identity is the truth. But it is not truth as if the disparity had been thrown

> away, like dross from pure metal, not even like the tool which remains separate from the finished vessel; disparity, rather, as the negative, the self, is itself still directly present in the True as such. Yet we cannot therefore say that the false is a moment of the True, let alone a component part of it. To say that in every falsehood there is a grain of truth is to treat the two like oil and water, which cannot be mixed and are only externally combined.[60]

To treat theories as if they were made up of groups of theses from which later thinkers accept some and reject others falsifies the way earlier philosophers exert influence and later ones adapt earlier ideas, as well as presenting truth and falsity as distinct, even if interwoven threads.[61] It's much more fluid and complex than that. We cannot simply reduce the transitions between thinkers to selective acceptance and rejection; we have to be sensitive to the holistic ways that these changes alter the entire character or flavor of a system of thought. Obviously I have tried very hard to maintain this standard in this book.

> Dogmatism consists in the tenacity which draws a hard and fast line between certain terms and others opposite to them. We may see this clearly in the strict "either—or": for instance, The world is either finite or infinite; but one of these two it must be. The contrary of this rigidity is the characteristic of all Speculative truth. . . . The half-truth, instead of being a fixed or self-subsistent principle, is a mere element absolved and included in the whole. The metaphysic of understanding is dogmatic, because it maintains half-truths in their isolation. . . . Idealism would say: The soul is neither finite only, nor infinite only; it is really the one just as much as the other. (Hegel, *HL* 52, §32R; see also 101, §65; 172, §119)[62]

Once we understand all of this, Hegel thinks we will lose our fixation on R4 Bivalence and study "the process which begets and traverses its own moments, and this whole movement constitutes what is positive [in it] and its truth. This truth therefore includes the negative also, what would be called the false" (Hegel, *PS* 27, §47). This is what he presents in his books.

## Conclusion

Hegel's greatest contributions to continental anti-realism are the introduction of historical change (A6) into the self with the concomitant plurality into conceptual schemes and reality (A3), and the complete dismissal of noumena (A1). He rigorously follows out the implications of A1 to reach Objective Idealism, which eliminates the distinction between an objective given and our subjective projection. This is a profound breakthrough which will be highly influential and could have led to a much larger break with the Kantian Paradigm. However, although he disperses the subject across history (ED) and makes subjectivity social, he ends up with a complex but ultimately realist notion of the self (R6), since the subject's ways of forming experience are limited and the various shapes can be compared by how well they correspond to the true reality of the self as a specific logical function. In this way, Hegel preserves a realism of the subject (R6) in order to determine a unique knowledge (R3) that shows his continued allegiance to the Kantian Paradigm, despite his substantial innovations. His account of truth as the whole and his demand for a definite Absolute Knowing require a closed totality of forms of subjectivity, thus reinstating R6.

Another lasting contribution Hegel makes to continental philosophy in general, as well as to its forms of anti-realism, is his treatment of history. Without a noumenal realm, phenomena exhaust reality and phenomena are deeply historical. The changes the world undergoes cannot be merely apparent or subjective, since the very distinction between subjective and objective has been undermined. Given the importance of justifying ideas against genuine alternatives, the evaluation of a position requires understanding these alternatives which are found in the history of philosophy. Positions arise and can only be fully understood within their intellectual context, even if this does not entirely determine their truth. This is implied by his idea of determinate negation: thinkers do not come out of nowhere or create ideas out of a direct confrontation with bare reality, but react to the positions and problems left them by their predecessors. Doing philosophy necessarily takes place in a historical manner. Even Moore and Russell's anti-historical founding of analytic philosophy is usually and is best explained as a reaction to their education in British idealism. Some version of this view is virtually ubiquitous in continental thought and it certainly guides this book, in that I am showing how each thinker develops his own position out of various adaptations to the framework that was bequeathed to him.

# 4

# Nietzsche's Will to Truth

> It is *we* alone who have devised cause, sequence, for-each-other, relativity, constraint, number, law, freedom, motive, and purpose: and when we project and mix this symbol world into things as if it existed "in itself," we act once more as we have always acted—*mythologically*. (Nietzsche, *BGE* 21)

> The criterion of truth resides in the enhancement of the feeling of power. (Nietzsche, *WTP* 534)

Nietzsche is perhaps the most enigmatic thinker I will be discussing. Although he discusses realism and anti-realism and their consequences for truth and reality extensively, he is notoriously difficult to pin down. Karl Jaspers got it right when he said that "one had not thoroughly read Nietzsche until, for every claim, he or she had also found the contradiction" (paraphrased in Solomon and Higgins 1988, viii). Derrida makes the similar comment that "he said the most mutually incompatible things, and he said that he said them" (Derrida, *EO* 15); and Lacoue-Labarthe as well: "Nietzsche, of all the 'philosophers' (Kierkegaard included), was the one who distinguished himself the most systematically . . . by his contradictory and multifarious, enigmatic and, let us say, disruptive practice of writing" (Lacoue-Labarthe 1993, 39). However, Nietzsche advances the history of continental anti-realism in important ways. His major innovations are to place the concepts that organize experience (A5) under the voluntary control of a few strong individuals, to greatly reduce R6 Realism of the Subject, and to explore the full consequences of anti-realism on R2 Correspondence Truth.

Nietzsche spent a great deal of his professional life railing against various "types": the ascetic, the Christian, the reactive, weak, herd, slave, and so on. These types, whom I will group under the umbrella title "the weak," were dangerous because they were plunging headlong into nihilism themselves and taking the rest of Europe with them. Nietzsche's philosophical mission is to diagnose this psychological and philosophical malady and to find a way to stave off the nihilism that is its inevitable end. And the underlying theoretical assumption shared by all of these types, the view that is dooming all of Western civilization, turns out to be realism.

## Realism

Since realism is what leads to the kind of nihilism he wants to overcome, Nietzsche studies it thoroughly, dissecting its contradictions and incoherencies at great length. But Nietzsche considers philosophy as much a matter of psychology as of logical analysis of arguments; understanding a belief does not just mean grasping its truth conditions but appreciating why it is believed, which means studying those who believe it. Thus he is very interested in the psychological and even physiological motivations that cause people to find certain views persuasive, diagnosing the popularity of ideas somewhat like a disease. "It is my purpose here to bring to light, not what this [ascetic] ideal has *done,* but simply what it *means;* what it indicates; what lies hidden behind it, beneath it, in it" (Nietzsche, *GM* 3.23, bracketed comment added). Arguments haven't driven people to accept realism; instead "a certain *impoverishment of life* is a presupposition" (3.25; see also Nietzsche, *GS* 370). This is why I have grouped realism's adherents under the heading of the weak: they resort to it because they are incapable of dealing with certain features of reality—its flux in particular—and certain features of themselves—especially their bodily drives. Nietzsche views realism as a symptom, as a massive metaphysical and ethical system that certain types have developed in order to posit and justify the kind of world in which they can thrive, or at least survive: "*The ascetic ideal springs from the protective instincts of a degenerating life* which tries by all means to sustain itself and to fight for its existence" (Nietzsche, *GM* 3.13; see also Nietzsche, *A* 15). The relationship between asceticism and realism is not one of logical entailment but rather a natural affinity or even Freudian wish-fulfillment, since this philosophical position legitimates the way of life most conducive to their state.

> The consensus of the sages—I comprehended this ever more clearly—proves least of all that they were right in what they agreed on: it shows rather that they themselves, these wisest men, agreed in some *physiological*

> respect, and hence adopted the same negative attitude to life—*had to* adopt it. Judgments, judgments of value, concerning life, for it or against it, can, in the end, never be true: they have value only as symptoms. (Nietzsche, *TI* 2.2; see also Nietzsche, *GS* 34–35)

The best entrance into Nietzsche's account of realism will therefore be his account of realists.

## R5 Passive Knower and R1 Independence

In order to understand realism and dissuade people from it, we need to understand why so many find it attractive. Nietzsche thinks that philosophical views are often more psychologically than logically motivated: "Gradually it has become clear to me what every great philosophy so far has been: namely, the personal confession of its author and a kind of involuntary and unconscious memoir."[1] To give a brief sketch of his account which I will fill out below, Nietzsche believes that reality is actually in continuous flux, but most people are incapable of dealing with this; through concepts, language, and the crudeness of the senses, people simplify and stabilize this roiling chaos. However, this A5 organization destroys R2 Correspondence Truth, so awareness of it is suppressed. People want a stable world of self-identical objects, but they don't want to be responsible for it; they simply want the world to be that way.

In addition to external chaos, the weak person is also overwhelmed by the cacophony of competing drives within himself or herself, each fighting for its own perspective and thus its own version of reality: "Before knowledge is possible, each of these instincts must first have presented its onesided view of the thing or event; after this comes the fight of these one-sided views" (Nietzsche, *GS* 333). This plurality of perspectives requires us to choose among them, which the weak do not want to do, so they are drawn to whatever will reduce the competing drives and render the decision unnecessary. Since the weak lack the strength simply to eliminate the drives themselves, they "turn *reason* into a tyrant" (Nietzsche, *TI* 2.10) and yoke their drives to its simplifying "will to truth."

> The belief that the world as it ought to be *is*, really exists, is a belief of the unproductive who [R5] do *not desire to create a world* as it ought to be. They posit it as [R1] already available, they seek ways and means of reaching it. . . . Whoever is incapable of [R5] laying his will into things, lacking will and strength, at least lays some *meaning* into them, i.e., the faith that [R1] there is a will in them already. . . . The philosophical objective outlook can therefore be a sign that will and strength are small.

> For strength [A5] organizes what is close and closest; "men of knowledge," who desire only to [R5] ascertain [R1] what is, are those who cannot *fix* anything *as it ought to be.* (Nietzsche, *WTP* 585A, bracketed comments added)

The weak believe in "the apparent *objective* character of things," i.e., "that things possess a constitution in themselves quite apart from interpretation and subjectivity,"[2] in order to avoid the effort and responsibility of actively constructing and choosing. John Richardson describes this well:

> Why does the theorist (typically) pursue truth? He needs that detachment or objectivity, that stilling or forgetting of his drives; he needs it because he can't (successfully) enact these drives themselves, directly. . . . The effort to conform one's beliefs to an external reality is a way of evading the responsibility for choosing and creating one's beliefs oneself. So *WP*585 [1887] asks "what kind of human being" mistrusts and disvalues becoming and seeks an unchanging, uncontradictory "true world," and answers, "An unproductive, *suffering kind,* a kind weary of life. . . . 'Will to *truth'—as the impotence of the will to create.*" (Richardson 1996, 233)

The realist believes that attaining correspondence to independent reality requires maximal passivity, so that nothing will interfere with the awareness of reality as it really is. In Nietzsche's interpretation of realism, the causal order is reversed: it is *because* the weak knower is insufficiently active that they create the idea of an independent world that they can just mirror. This self-conception is attractive because it relieves them of the internal chaos of the drives (A6) and the responsibility to choose and create (A5). "The objective person" can simply "become a passageway" (Nietzsche, *BGE* 207).

An independent reality also gives authority to dictates of knowledge and morality, leading to the ultimate authority of God who, not coincidentally, is the being that necessarily exists independently of everything else.

> We see: an authority speaks—who speaks?—One may forgive human pride if it sought to make this authority as high as possible in order to feel as little humiliated as possible under it. Therefore—God speaks! One needed God as an unconditioned sanction, with no court of appeal, as a "categorical imperator." (Nietzsche, *WTP* 275; see also Nietzsche, *GS* 143; Nietzsche, *A* 9)

Although God is the oldest and most obvious example of an independent reality issuing commands, it is by no means the only one. Nietzsche holds that science "is not the opposite of the ascetic ideal but rather *the latest and noblest form of it*" (Nietzsche, *GM* 3.23). It succeeded Christianity because the religion undermined itself when its demand for honesty revealed its own reliance on lies. Science, on the other hand, maintains the essential structure of submission to external, independent reality—"science and the ascetic ideal both rest on the same foundation" (3.25)—without the same vulnerability. Although the atheistic scientists of his day considered themselves daring and free—one thinks of the nihilist scientist in Turgenev's *Fathers and Sons*—Nietzsche considers them "far from being *free* spirits: *for they still have faith in truth*" (3.24). The legitimation and passivity of reflecting an independent world are irresistible to the weak, whether the commands come from God or reality. Let's now turn to this truth.

## R2 Correspondence

The easiest form of knowledge would simply be mirroring what is there. This is comforting, since it consists in an epistemological submission to something external. As Rorty puts it, "The notion of reality as having a 'nature' to which it is our duty to correspond is simply one more variant of the notion that the gods can be placated by chanting the right words" (Rorty 1991a, 80). Putnam, too, compares "the world (THE WORLD) which dictates a unique description to us" to "the Fundamentalist's God" who "dictated the bible to Moses" (Clark and Hale 1994, 265). A century earlier Nietzsche had seen how science was really a zealous faith in truth and reality.

> The nihilistic question "for what?" is rooted in the old habit of supposing that the goal must be put up, given, demanded *from outside*—by some *superhuman authority*. Having unlearned faith in that, one still follows the old habit and seeks *another* authority that can *speak unconditionally* and *command* goals and tasks. The authority of *conscience* now steps up front. . . . Or the authority of *reason*. Or the *social instinct* (the herd). Or *history* with an immanent spirit and a goal within, so one can entrust oneself to it. One wants to get around the will, the willing of a goal, the risk of positing a goal *for oneself;* one wants to rid oneself of the responsibility. (Nietzsche, *WTP* 20)

As we saw above, independent, external reality is another superhuman authority we seek to submit ourselves to epistemologically. Nietzsche agrees with Kant that realism compromises autonomy, but thinks that people actually seek heteronomy out of laziness rather than wickedness (if only!);

holding up a mirror is infinitely easier than shaping the inchoate forces of chaos. Once again, Richardson has it right.

> It's not just that what happens to be true is harmful, but it's harmful *as* the truth. That is, even the bare logical structure of truth imparts a reactive and damaging aspect to the project and possession of it. The goal of truth is a certain passive state: to "mirror," or correspond to, how things already are, and not to make them a particular way. Instead of creating one's own viewpoint, one has it prescribed from outside. (Richardson 1996, 235)

Specific Christian doctrines are harmful, but it is also the very structure of correspondence to independent reality as such that is bad for us. Using the standard image for realist correspondence truth, Nietzsche writes: "The objective man is indeed a mirror: he is accustomed to submit before whatever wants to be known, without any other pleasure than that found in knowing and 'mirroring'" (Nietzsche, *BGE* 207).

### R3 Uniqueness

If the weak embrace realism in an attempt to escape responsibility for the creation of reality, in order to be as passive and submissive as possible, then they will certainly want reality to issue an unambiguous set of instructions. After all, an independent reality that offers options among which they must choose would require their active participation once again, now at the level of decision among presented options rather than constitution. For us to be passive recipients—the pure white paper on which the world writes—reality must write clearly, allowing only one correct reading. Therefore realists will "prefer a handful of 'certainty' to a whole carload of beautiful possibilities."[3] After all, "the doctrine of being, of things, of all sorts of fixed unities is a hundred times easier than the doctrine of becoming, of development" (Nietzsche, *WTP* 538).

This insistence that its own view is the only truth is one of the most pernicious features of Christianity, in some ways more dangerous than any of its specific doctrines.[4]

> Extreme positions are not succeeded by moderate ones but by extreme positions of the opposite kind. Thus the belief in the absolute immorality of nature, in aim- and meaninglessness, is the psychologically necessary affect once the belief in God and an essentially moral order becomes untenable. . . . One interpretation has collapsed; but because it was con-

> sidered *the* interpretation it now seems as if there were no meaning at all in existence. (Nietzsche, *WTP* 55)

This is the great irony of the history of values: the realist account of values as coming from an ultimate authority provided the highest possible guarantee of those values, thus making them as safe as possible. But due to the rise of science, among other factors, belief in these super-values eroded and now, addicted to super-values, we find human-sized values weak substitutes. Nihilism consists in the withdrawal symptoms of our millennia-long addiction to divinely sanctioned realism. By insisting on R3, we deprived ourselves of auxiliary value systems which might have proven useful now that the dominant one is failing, and by insisting on R1 we cursed our own ability to create new values as sacrilegious. Thus, realism is the root of nihilism.

### R4 Bivalence

One of Nietzsche's most frequent complaints against philosophers is their tendency to black-or-white thinking. As he states at the beginning of a chapter titled, "On the Prejudices of Philosophers," "The fundamental faith of the metaphysicians is *the faith in opposite values*" (Nietzsche, *BGE* 2). He describes this faith this way:

> "How *could* anything originate out of its opposite? for example, truth out of error? or the will to truth out of the will to deception? . . . Such origins are impossible; whoever dreams of them is a fool, indeed worse; the things of the highest value must have another, *peculiar* origin—they cannot be derived from this transitory, seductive, deceptive, paltry world, from this turmoil of delusion and lust. Rather from the lap of Being, the intransitory, the hidden god, the 'thing-in-itself'.". . . This way of judging constitutes the typical prejudgment and prejudice which give away the metaphysicians of all ages. (Nietzsche, *BGE* 2; see also Nietzsche, *HATH* 1.1)

This conception of truth helps eliminate the need for interpretation or decision on the part of the knower: claims are either true or not, so we need only passively reflect the right ones.

### R6 Realism of the Subject

Nietzsche is fascinated with the way a core, atomistic self behind or beneath all actions and thoughts, that is, a subjective *hypokeimenon,* was invented. This entity is originally suggested by the structure of our language, which separates nouns from verbs, thus assuming a doer for every deed: "If I say 'lightning flashes,' I have posited the flash once as an activity and a second time as a subject, and thus added to the event a being that is not one with the event but is rather fixed, *is,* and does not 'become'" (Nietzsche, *WTP* 531).[5] Christianity, latching onto this "*soul-atomism*" (Nietzsche, *BGE* 12), attributed free will and thus responsibility to it as ways of taming the strong.

> Just as the popular mind separates the lightning from its flash and takes the latter for an *action,* for the operation of a subject called lightning, so popular morality also separates strength from expressions of strength, as if there were a neutral substratum behind the strong man, which was *free* to express strength or not to do so. . . . Thus they gain the right to make the bird of prey *accountable* for being a bird of prey. (Nietzsche, *GM* 1.13; see also 2.4)

A self which is separate from its actions can control them, and so is responsible for them. Hence it deserves rewards and punishments for what it chooses to do, hence it will receive them, hence people must obey the priests who know the rules of the game and are rumored to have influence with the referee.

Of course, when we look around we see that the good suffer and the wicked prosper. Aristotle's substance metaphysics, however, supplies a way to think of the unchanging self as that which underlies change; one merely has to apply this template to death as the relevant alteration in order to get an eternal soul which can enjoy rewards or suffer punishment in the next life. Since the body obviously decays, Christianity needed an aspect of the self that could survive death and enjoy the rewards promised those submissive to the priests; the atomistic, self-identical soul-thing which is both the transcendental origin of all actions and thus responsible for them, and impervious to change and so immortal, fitted this function perfectly (Nietzsche, *BGE* 12; Nietzsche, *HATH* 1.2).

## Anti-Realism

Realism is the belief system the weak resort to in order to escape the stress of internal and external conflict and flux, as well as the responsibility of choice and creation forced on them by these conditions. The strong, however, embrace and even celebrate these conditions; they accept that the world is of their own making, and, at the highest, take control of this process. In other words, they are anti-realists. Once again, the entry point of our examination of Nietzsche's views will be the role of the knower.

### A5 Active Knower

One of Nietzsche's most frequently repeated assertions is that we are at least partially responsible for the organization of the world, a view he explicitly attributes to Kant: "When Kant says: 'the understanding does not draw its laws from nature, it prescribes them to nature,' this is wholly true with regard to the *concept of nature*" (Nietzsche, *HATH* 1.19).[6] Following the basic point of Kant's anti-realism, Nietzsche claims again and again that we contribute various forms to reality.

> Our subjective compulsion to believe in logic only reveals that, long before logic itself entered our consciousness, we did nothing but introduce its postulates into events: now we discover them in events—we can no longer do otherwise—and imagine that this compulsion guarantees something connected with "truth." It is we who created the "thing," the "identical thing," subject, attribute, activity, object, substance, form. . . . The world seems logical to us because we have made it logical. (Nietzsche, *WTP* 521; see also Nietzsche, *HATH* 1.11, 1.18)

In addition to reason (*TI* 3.2), Nietzsche attributes this categorical formation of experience to various processes that do their work before conscious thought comes on the scene, such as language,[7] the senses,[8] and instinctive drives (Nietzsche, *WTP* 544; see also Blondel in Ormiston and Schrift 1990, 82–84). Since this organization takes place at the preconscious level, our conscious experience shows us stable, apparently independent objects, which accounts for the plausibility of realism; it certainly seems as if all we do is open our eyes and encounter a premade world. The similar "optical illusion" of the sun appearing to rise is one of the reasons Kant chose the title "Copernican Revolution" (see Nietzsche, *TI* 3.5, for a reference to this phenomenon). But this illusion of passivity should not fool us; Nietzsche even appropriates some of Kant's specific terms in describing the doctrine of A5 Active Knower.

> It is *we* alone who have devised cause, sequence, for-each-other, relativity, constraint, number, law, freedom, motive, and purpose: and when we project and mix this symbol into things as if it existed "in itself," we act once more as we have always acted—*mythologically*. (Nietzsche, *BGE* 21)

Directly echoing Kant (*C1* Bxviii), Nietzsche claims that humanity "always found in things only that *which he had put into them*."[9]

Fundamentally rejecting the idea of a direct confrontation with the bare world—"Facts is precisely what there is not, only interpretations. We cannot establish any fact 'in itself'" (Nietzsche, *WTP* 481; see also 555, 556)—Nietzsche agrees with Kant and Hegel that all knowledge is mediated: "*Rational thought is interpretation according to a scheme that we cannot throw off*" (522). Michel Haar puts this idea well:

> Nietzsche attacks the myth of a "pure" objective knowledge that could hover over reality without being implicated in it, that could, without prejudice or point of view, be the faithful mirror of reality. The illusion peculiar to knowledge, i.e., the illusion of objectivity, consists in imagining that it is possible to penetrate the essence of things, right down to its innermost recesses, while merely reflecting it. However, knowledge is essentially active even when it takes itself to be passive. (Haar 1996, 14–15)

Many critics have noted this connection with Kantian anti-realism, in particular with the idea I am calling A5.[10] Recently attention has been paid to the connection between Kant and Nietzsche via various neo-Kantians. In *Nietzsche's Critiques: The Kantian Foundations of His Thought,* R. Kevin Hill writes that "Nietzsche's relationship to Kant should be modelled on Hegel's. For Nietzsche, as for Hegel, Kant is *the* philosopher with whom one must come to terms" (R. K. Hill 2003, 6). Hill points out that Schopenhauer and the neo-Kantian philosopher Lange[11] were two of Nietzsche's most important influences. My way of putting this is that both Hegel and Nietzsche work within the Kantian Paradigm. Hill specifically focuses on my A5: "For Nietzsche, as for Kant, our minds are independent sources of activity, striving to subjugate and reduce to order the sensory states that arise in us" (194). In *Nietzsche and the Transcendental Tradition,* Michael Steven Green (along with Robin Small in *Nietzsche in Context*) makes the connection with Kant through the nineteenth-century neo-Kantian Afrikan Spir. Green argues that Nietzsche is "firmly grounded in the Neo-Kantian tradition," so "it is to these writers that we should primarily look to understand what Nietzsche was talking about, not Derrida or Foucault and not Tarski or Quine" (Green 2002, 3). My strategy is to show how Nietzsche can be more fruitfully related to people like Foucault and Quine precisely by exploring his relation to Kant.

### A1 Mind-Dependence

Nietzsche repeatedly states that the apparently stable world is actually chaos or will to power that consists only in extreme flux or continual becoming: "The total character of the world, however, is in all eternity chaos" (Nietzsche, *GS* 109; see also Nietzsche, *WTP* 569, 604). "And do you know what 'the world' is to me? Shall I show it to you in my mirror? . . . a sea of forces flowing and rushing together, eternally changing, eternally flooding back, with an ebb and flood of its forms. . . . *This world is the will to power—and nothing besides!*" (Nietzsche, *WTP* 1067). We generally recoil from this incomprehensible and uncontrollable roiling chaos, unconsciously stabilizing it through the various means mentioned above. In this way the world we experience—this realm of stable, relatively unchanging objects with knowable identities—is our creation and hence mind-dependent. "We need 'unities' in order to be able to reckon: that does not mean we must suppose that such unities exist" (635).

Nietzsche's early work comes quite close to the Kantian view, considering the idea of noumena fully coherent but inaccessible: "*Metaphysical world.*—It is true, there could be a metaphysical world; the absolute possibility of it is hardly to be disputed. We behold all things through the human head and cannot cut off this head; while the question nonetheless remains what of the world would still be there if one had cut it off" (Nietzsche, *HATH* 1.9). Speculation about what the world would be like without our contributions, implying that the world itself makes a separate contribution, is inevitable but, equally, unanswerable. Of course, any information about such entities would be of no help to people living in the phenomenal realm: "Even if the existence of such a world were ever so well demonstrated, it is certain that knowledge of it would be the most useless of all knowledge: more useless even than knowledge of the chemical composition of water must be to the sailor in danger of shipwreck" (1.9, translation modified). This pragmatic objection to noumena—that it is of no concern, since it could not be of any use to us—is repeated in Step Five of his famous attack on noumena, "How the 'True World' Finally Became a Fable": "The 'true' world—an idea which is no longer good for anything, not even obligating—an idea which has become useless and superfluous—*consequently*, a refuted idea: let us abolish it!" (Nietzsche, *TI* 4.5, italics in original).

Later, however, he goes beyond merely objecting that noumena would be useless to rejecting the coherence of the very idea. In 1887 he writes: "Questions, what things 'in-themselves' may be like, apart from our sense receptivity and the activity of our understanding, must be rebutted with the question: how could we know that things exist? 'Thingness' was first created by us" (Nietzsche, *WTP* 569). Just talking about an uncategorized reality is already applying categories like "thingness" to it, and hence is precisely *not* talking about something uncategorized (see Wilcox 1974, 73; Priest 2002, 81–82). If we were to remove *all* categories, then existence, substance, and causality would have to go, and they are the materials from which Kant built his concept of noumena as the source of our sensory data. Indeed, they are the conceptual resources that any discussion must draw upon; withdraw them all and we are left with, as Hegel said, just "a pure direction or a blank space" (Hegel, *PS* 47, §73). Goodman puts it succinctly: "We are confined to ways of describing whatever is described" (Goodman 1978, 3), or "talk of unstructured content or an unconceptualized given or a substratum without properties is self-defeating; for the talk imposes structure, ascribes properties" (6).

### A6 Multiple Selves

This is Nietzsche's greatest advance in my narrative of continental antirealism. Kant links transcendental subjectivity to experience (ED) but maintains its transcendental status and unique definition (R6); Hegel makes the self historical and multiple (A6) but still obedient to necessary logical laws, and ultimately collected into a closed circle of possibilities (R6). Nietzsche plunges the self completely into the physical, empirical world (ED) without closure or identity, law or reason (A6). Whereas Hegel gathers up the temporally spread but logically linked phases of the subject and reality into a limited, rationally structured totality, Nietzsche scatters an irreconcilable multiplicity of power-hungry drives (A6). Nietzsche puts his disagreement with Hegel (not explicitly named) this way: "The sole fundamental fact, however, is that [the world] does not aim at a final state. . . . Becoming does not aim at a *final state,* does not flow into 'being'" (Nietzsche, *WTP* 708). As Deleuze contrasts the two thinkers, "There is no possible compromise between Hegel and Nietzsche. Nietzsche's philosophy . . . forms an absolute anti-dialectics and sets out to expose all the mystifications that find a final refuge in the dialectic" (Deleuze 1983, 195).

The first significant innovation in Nietzsche's conception of the self is the way he extends the Empirical Directive; he inserts the self fully into the empirical, physical world by identifying the self with the body, allowing nothing like a soul, noumenal or transcendental subject, Spirit, and so on, to supply any further identity to the self. He considers such extra dimensions to be Kant and Hegel's vestiges of superstition and Christianity; Nietzsche goes all the way into naturalism: "We no longer derive man from 'the spirit' or 'the deity'; we have placed him back among the animals" (Nietzsche, *A* 14; see also Nietzsche, *WTP* 487). Everything about us must be explained empirically, in terms of our animal nature interacting with the environment, with some accommodation of a historical dimension.

> There exists neither "spirit," nor reason, nor thinking, nor consciousness, nor soul, nor will, nor truth: all are fictions that are of no use. There is no question of "subject and object," but of a particular species

> of animal that can prosper only through a certain relative rightness; above all, regularity of its perceptions. (Nietzsche, *WTP* 480; see also Nietzsche, *Z* 1.4)

Instead of transcendent or transcendental explanations, Nietzsche wants to make "the body and physiology the starting point" (Nietzsche, *WTP* 492).

Nietzsche agrees with Kant that we project categories (A5), but, extending ED even farther than Hegel, he rejects all transcendent and transcendental origins of these categories; only natural, evolutionary, or genealogical explanations are allowed. Knowledge "is to be regarded in a strict and narrow anthropocentric and biological sense" (Nietzsche, *WTP* 480). As Maudemarie Clark writes,

> In [*GS* and *BGE*], Nietzsche seems to accept a naturalized version of Kant's theory of knowledge. He agrees with Kant's denial that the form or structural features of our representations derive from experience, but explains these features naturalistically, in terms of their contribution to the survival of the species. (M. Clark 1990, 121)

Like Hegel, Nietzsche is dissatisfied with Kant's simple assertion of the categories instead of justifying them (see R. K. Hill 2003, 180). But where Hegel shows Spirit developing itself within a rational, lawful history in order to generate the strong or "hyper" autonomy that is lacking in Kant, Nietzsche sees only the evolution of an animal out of the blind play of chance forces locked in a violent struggle. As Hill puts it, Nietzsche wants to "'Darwinize' Kant's transcendental Aesthetic."[12] Our particular categories evolved not because they are logically entailed by the unification processes of the transcendental unity of apperception or because they are the inevitable culmination that any sentient being must reach if they think through their ideas consistently; they just helped primitive humans have sex and not get eaten. "The utility of preservation—not some abstract-theoretical need not to be deceived—stands as the motive behind the development of the organs of knowledge—they develop in such a way that their observations suffice for our preservation."[13]

The general effect of our concepts is reification and simplification; they form stable, manageable beings out of chaotic becoming: "To impose upon becoming the character of being—that is the supreme will to power" (Nietzsche, *WTP* 617). Nietzsche subscribes to the ancient incompatibility of becoming and knowledge stated clearly by the follower of Heraclitus, Cratylus, when he said that "about that which changes no true statement can be made" (Aristotle, *Metaphysics* 1010a 6–9). Nietzsche inverts this statement: "In order to think and infer it is necessary to assume beings: logic handles only formulas for what remains the same. . . . Knowledge and becoming exclude one another. . . . Supposing everything is becoming, then knowledge is possible only on the basis of belief in being."[14] We need to understand and predict nature in order to survive, but only stable, self-identical objects yield to such treatment; hence this is the shape into which we fit reality. Where Kant's categories unify for the purpose of knowledge and Hegel's volatize for progress, Nietzsche's simplify and stabilize beings in order to master them. "The entire apparatus of knowledge is an apparatus for abstraction and simplification—directed not at knowledge but at taking possession of things" (Nietzsche, *WTP* 503).

Nietzsche's second innovation is that when the self is wholly corporeal, it loses the unity that is central to the "soul-superstition." While a transcendent entity may be simple, the things of this world are complex and changing. This internal multiplicity creates the "happiness of the historian . . . who, in contrast to the metaphysicians, is happy to harbour in himself, not 'an immortal soul,' but *many mortal souls*" (Nietzsche, *HATH* 2.17). Nietzsche sometimes follows Plato in using governmental metaphors to describe the self, though as multiple drives and selves that do not reduce to a unified one.

> The assumption of one single subject is perhaps unnecessary; perhaps it is just as permissible to assume a multiplicity of subjects, whose interaction and struggle is the basis of our thought and our consciousness in general? A kind of aristocracy of "cells" in which dominion resides? . . . *My hypotheses:* The subject as multiplicity. (Nietzsche, *WTP* 490)

Once the "soul-superstition" is defeated, "the way is open for new versions and refinements of the soul-hypothesis; and such conceptions as 'mortal soul,' and 'soul as subjective multiplicity,' and 'soul as social structure'" (Nietzsche, *BGE* 12; see also 19), views he clearly favors. Our internal plurality is regulated by the external pressure of other wills exerting force on it and by the internal pressure of individual aspects trying to increase their power. These are not rational processes—the wills and drives are not debating each other in a mock United Nations; indeed, rationality itself arises from this interplay of forces as a tool for the satisfaction of the drives, like everything else about us (Nietzsche, *WTP* 515–16; Nietzsche, *GS* 333). This development certainly cannot be described as an intelligible, necessary process like that in Hegel's *Phenomenology*. No, we are the result of "those iron hands of necessity which shake the dice-box of chance" (Nietzsche, *D* 130; see also Nietzsche, *TI* 1.26).

Stephen Houlgate contrasts Hegel's conception of the self with Nietzsche's in his book-length study of the two:

> Authentic subjectivity is understood by [Nietzsche] as the antithesis of what he sees as the traditional conception of the soul. The authentic subject for Nietzsche is natural and instinctual, rather than spiritual; it is multiple and ever-changing, rather than unified and continuous. . . . Like that of Hegel, Nietzsche's "subject" is dynamic; but, unlike that of Hegel, its dynamism is rooted in its instinctual "life," rather than in its social and historical character. Such a subject is the embodiment of chaotic, pulsating reality. (Houlgate 1986, 183; see also Schürmann 1979, 165)

The apparent stable self that we experience and identify with is in fact a mask hiding the true self—will to power. Nietzsche completes the passage in *Will to Power* quoted earlier by adding: "*This world is the will to power—and nothing besides!* And you yourselves are also this will to power—and nothing besides!" (Nietzsche, *WTP* 1067).

### A2 Non-Correspondence Truth: Pragmatic versus Correspondence

Since correspondence truth is an important factor in realism-induced nihilism, changing this traditional understanding of truth is one of the central components in Nietzsche's proposed cure: "Let us not underestimate this: *we ourselves,* we free spirits, are nothing less than a 'revaluation of all values,' an *incarnate* declaration of war and triumph over all the ancient conceptions of 'true' and 'untrue'" (Nietzsche, *A* 13; see also Danto 1965, 72–73). No conception is more ancient or venerable than correspondence, which he takes as his principal target in a rather complex attack.

As Kant himself acknowledged, the idea that the mind organizes experience (A5) renders (transcendent) correspondence truth (R2) impossible. The fact that space, time, and the categories are transcendentally ideal means that they do not correspond to noumena and thus, according to a strict understanding of correspondence truth, should be considered transcendentally false, though Kant does not follow it out to this conclusion (Kant, *C1* A369). This was Hegel's assessment when he ridiculed Kant's epistemological substitute—intersubjectively shared knowledge organized the same way (A5) by all people (R6)—as "an untrue kind of knowing" (Hegel, *PS* 145, §238). Hegel's solution is Objective Idealism, which overcomes the entire structure of a subject actively organizing an independent content by rejecting the notion of an independent source of content; after all, it was this way of framing the problem that created the problem in the first place. Absorbing and surpassing Kant's subject-object opposition keeps skepticism from getting off the ground not by finding a secure way to make contact with R1 Independent reality, but by showing that very idea to be incoherent.

Nietzsche's puzzling position is to keep Kant's scheme-content structure while agreeing with Hegel's verdict that it condemns us to permanent falsification: the one truth that humanity may know for sure is "the truth that he is eternally condemned to untruth."[15] The reason Nietzsche does not feel the need to overcome a structure that condemns us to ubiquitous falsehoods the way Hegel does is that Nietzsche redefines the value of the true-false dichotomy: "The falseness of a judgment is for us not necessarily an objection to a judgment; in this respect our new language may sound strangest."[16] Indeed. Nietzsche sums up these "strange" views on truth in his aphorism, "Truth is the kind of error without which a certain species of life could not live" (Nietzsche, *WTP* 493). Now, to call truth itself an error is obviously a contradiction committed right at the beginning of his account. As commentator Wilcox says, Nietzsche's views on truth aren't even internally consistent "unless some rather careful distinctions are made."[17] It is precisely such careful distinctions I now want to introduce into Nietzsche's discussions.

Nietzsche switches between different senses of "true" and "false," sometimes within a single discussion, often without drawing attention to this fact. Sometimes "true" picks out claims that must be accepted by certain people under certain circumstances for practical reasons; let us call this sense "truth$_P$" since these are determined pragmatically, that is, by the criterion of the survival and, at best, the increase of power of individuals or species (see Nietzsche, *WTP* 534; Nietzsche, *BGE* 13). When Nietzsche uses "truth" in this sense, he seems to endorse a pragmatic theory of truth: "The categories are 'truths' only in the sense that they are conditions of life for us" (Nietzsche, *WTP* 515; see also 532). Or, appearance "is perfectly true for *us;* that is to say, we live, we are able to live in it: proof of its truth for us" (568). His general view of truths$_P$ is that they are A5 forged by the processes mentioned above, with the purpose of stabilizing and making the disorienting chaos around us more regular and easier to deal with.

At other times, however, Nietzsche uses "truth" in its traditional sense of corresponding with mind-independent reality; let us call this "truth$_C$." The truest$_C$ account of the world would be the description he occasionally gives of the formless, seething chaos of will to power; of course, due to its uncontrollability, this account is false$_P$ in that it is impossible for most people to live with. Thus Nietzsche's point, once we disentangle his various meanings, is that truths$_P$ are not necessarily and, given his commitment to A5 Active Knower, in fact cannot be true$_C$. In a relatively clear statement of this idea, he writes that synthetic a priori judgments "must be *believed* to be true, for the sake of the preservation of creatures like ourselves [that is, they are true$_P$]; though they might, of course, be *false* judgments for all that [false$_C$]" (Nietzsche, *BGE* 11, bracketed comments added). This is similar to the Kantian empirically valid but transcendentally inapplicable distinction, that is, they are true of phenomena but do not apply to noumena, but Nietzsche prefers to push Kant's system to what he sees as its logical conclusion: the A5 projection of categories amounts to a falsification$_C$ (see R. K. Hill 2003, 183–84).

Nietzsche clearly employs correspondence truth rather than pragmatic truth at times, since he occasionally says that the utility of a belief is *not* equivalent to its truth: "Something might be true while being harmful and dangerous in the highest degree" (Nietzsche, *BGE* 39); or "We have arranged for ourselves a world in which we can live . . . without these articles of faith nobody could now endure life. But that does not prove them. Life is no argument. The conditions of life might include error."[18] He achieves the rhetorical effect he desires by bringing these two conceptions of truth together and letting them interfere with each other. As discussed above, one concept he considers necessary for controlling our environment, for example, is that of stable self-identical objects. "There would be nothing that could be called knowledge [truth$_P$] if thought did not first [A5] re-form the world in this way into 'things,' into what is self-identical. Only because there is thought is there untruth$_{[C]}$" (Nietzsche, *WTP* 574, bracketed comments added). Although the concept of "things" is necessary for us and thus constitutes pragmatically true "knowledge," it is still "untruth" in that such things do not actually exist in the sea of chaos.

Nietzsche muddies the waters, intentionally I think, by using words like "truth," "falsehood," "knowledge," or "lies" without indicating which sense he is employing. His paradoxical claims are designed to point to the divergence between the pragmatic conception of truth built into the naturalized version of Kant he is advocating and the traditional correspondence truth that philosophers still hang onto. He is playing these two conceptions of truth against each other in order to persuade us to drop correspondence altogether in favor of pragmatic truth because (1) correspondence is impossible for us to attain, given our (A5) interpretive projections and the irreconcilable differences between chaos and language or thought; and (2) it would be much better for us simply to hold beliefs that enhance our lives. It's better to be wrong$_C$ than dead: throughout the history of evolution, "innumerable beings who made inferences in a way different from ours perished; for all that, their ways might have been truer$_{[C]}$" (Nietzsche, *GS* 111, bracketed comment added). The impossibility of correspondence frees us from attempted allegiance to reality, liberating us to create new views for the purpose of making a better life.

## A3 Ontological Pluralism

If reality is actually fluctuating chaos which cannot be known, captured, or immediately experienced, then correspondence truth is impossible; we should reject this goal and instead try to acquire what will benefit us (A2). If correspondence is impossible we should turn to pragmatic truth, albeit for pragmatic reasons, since the uselessness of the criterion doesn't in and of itself disprove the nature of truth as correspondence, as we saw in chapter 1. Once we accept pragmatic truth, we realize that since both reality and our drives are constantly changing, our beliefs and conceptual schemes need to be in flux as well in order to keep our health or power on the rise. Ironically, this move is based on a correspondence claim about the true nature of reality. The move from correspondence to pragmatic truth is made on pragmatic grounds—correspondence truth is rejected because it's useless—and then the pragmatic move to A3 Pluralism is made on correspondence grounds—the fact is that the world out there is actually chaos which therefore is constantly throwing new challenges at us, requiring an epistemological flexibility in order to prosper. These kinds of twists are typical of Nietzsche's thought.

Nietzsche wants us to become aware of the fact that we are A5 Active Knowers, that we are always already organizing experience, so that we can take control of that ability. Rather than meekly trying to copy the world which we have in fact created, we ought to take the reins of this power in our hands to use it for our benefit. "No longer joy in certainty but in uncertainty; no longer 'cause and effect' but the continually creative; no longer will to preservation but to power; no longer the humble expression, 'everything is *merely* subjective,' but 'it is also *our* work!—Let us be proud of it!'" (Nietzsche, *WTP* 1059; see also 495; Nietzsche, *Z* 1.3). Hegel criticized Kant's subjective idealism for compromising our autonomy and substituting intersubjective falsification for genuine knowledge. Nietzsche, on the other hand, criticizes Kant's subjective idealism because Kant (1) fails ED by resorting to a ghostly transcendental subjectivity, (2) places the constitution of experience outside of our control, and (3) still holds to a form of R2 Correspondence Truth, leaving him, like Hegel, ashamed that we are not in contact with the "really real" world.

Nietzsche follows the thread of Kant's thought which says that knowing phenomena is better than knowing noumena could ever be, since the former are our creation. Kant links this to autonomy, while Nietzsche connects it to empowerment.

> The aberration of philosophy is that, instead of [seeing] in logic and the categories of reason means toward the adjustment of the world for utili-

> tarian ends (basically, toward an expedient *falsification* [false$_C$, truth$_P$]), one believed one possessed in them the criterion of truth and *reality* [truth$_C$]. The "criterion of truth" was in fact merely the biological utility [truth$_P$] of such a system of systematic falsification [false$_C$]. . . . Instead of employing the forms as a tool for making the world manageable and calculable [truth$_P$], the madness of philosophers divined that in these categories is presented the concept of that world to which the one in which man lives does not correspond. . . . This is the greatest error that has ever been committed, the essential fatality of error on earth: one believed one possessed a criterion of reality in the forms of reason [truth$_C$]—while in fact one possessed them in order to become master of reality [truth$_P$], in order to misunderstand reality [false$_C$] in a shrewd manner [truth$_P$]. (Nietzsche, *WTP* 584, bracketed comments added; see also 495)

Correspondence truth is the "aberration of philosophy" that blocks the way to greater life because it keeps people from wielding categories for their own benefit. Nietzsche sees the combination of Kantian anti-realism with naturalism and purposeful control over the categories as the key to untold greatness (see Conway 1998, 404).

Realism, and in particular R3 Uniqueness, have been zealously protected by the weak ("The good *must* crucify him who invents his own virtue" [Nietzsche, *Z* 3.12.26]), which forms one of Nietzsche's central criticisms of views like Christianity or science. Although *On the Genealogy of Morals* actually praises the ascetic spirit in a number of ways, its unforgivable sin is that "it permits no other interpretation, no other goal; it rejects, denies, affirms, and sanctions solely from the point of view of *its* interpretation" (Nietzsche, *GM* 3.23). Religions, especially monotheistic ones, are guilty of R3: "Monotheism . . . this rigid consequence of the doctrine of one normal human type . . . was perhaps the greatest danger that has yet confronted humanity. It threatened us with the premature stagnation" (Nietzsche, *GS* 143). It is the "greatest danger" precisely because "no *other* perspective is conceded any further value once one's own has been made sacrosanct with the names of 'God,' 'redemption,' and 'eternity'" (Nietzsche, *A* 9; see also 32; Nietzsche, *GS* 143).

Since Nietzsche views all of reality, including people, as roiling multiplicities, no single scheme or set of values can benefit any individual, much less an entire society or all of humanity (see Nietzsche, *Z* 1.15; Nietzsche, *BGE* 221, 228). But in order to secure their power over others and reassure their own insecurities, ascetics insist on their views as the sole truth.

> *Morality in Europe today is herd animal morality*—in other words, as we understand it, merely *one* type of human morality beside which, before

> which, and after which many other types, above all *higher* moralities, are, or ought to be, possible. But this morality resists such a "possibility," such an "ought" with all its power: it says stubbornly and inexorably, "I am morality itself, and nothing besides is morality." (Nietzsche, *BGE* 202)

This insistence on univocal truth closes off all alternatives, thus enforcing "premature stagnation." A6 Multiple Selves plus A2 Pragmatic Truth leads to A3 Ontological Pluralism and its epistemological counterpart, Multiple Truths: A2 states that truth is what benefits us and A6 claims that we are made up of a variety of aspects, hence we can be benefited in many different ways (see Schacht 1983, 75).[19]

Nietzsche's preferred position is "perspectivalism," the view that there are indefinitely many interpretations of phenomena, none of which can be legitimated as the *one* that gets things right: "There are many kinds of eyes. . . . Consequently there are many kinds of 'truths,' and consequently there is no truth" (Nietzsche, *WTP* 540). Once again, he is using "truth" in different senses, the latter meaning the R3 Unique interpretation; thus the statement claims that A3 perspectivalism eliminates R3, commonly assumed to be a necessary characteristic of truth. Nietzsche sees the embracing of perspectivalism as both a sign of strength and a key to increasing strength. It is a sign of strength because it shows the ability to tolerate tension and ambiguity: "Inertia needs unity (monism); plurality of interpretations a sign of strength. Not to desire to deprive the world of its disturbing and enigmatic character!"[20] It allows increases of strength by enhancing our adaptability to the changes that inevitably occur within ourselves and our environment. The effect of Christianity's intolerance of innovation was devastating—it started out helpful, but once the conditions prevalent at its birth changed, it became harmful to many. Unfortunately, by linking its claims to an eternal, omniscient, jealous, and vengeful God, it effectively prevented us from changing it to adapt to new circumstances. Our values, which are really our creation, have become alienated from us in Marx's sense of the word. The change in our sociological environment that Nietzsche calls the death of God has undermined those values, but Christianity's initial legitimation strategy prevents us from forging a new set. This results in nihilism, "the ultimate logical conclusion of our great values and ideals" (Nietzsche, *WTP* preface).

Nihilism is a two-step process, the first of which is weak or passive nihilism, that is, a dependence on the highest values of truth, being, or God for meaning and legitimation, combined with their erosion. Nietzsche describes the development of Western thought as a kind of Hegelian *Aufhebung* in which the Platonic-Christian exhortation to truth turns on itself, unraveling the very support it stands upon. "Atheism . . . is the awe-inspiring *catastrophe* of two thousand years of training in truthfulness that finally forbids itself the *lie involved in belief in God*" (Nietzsche, *GM* 3.27). Atheism, the complete disintegration of the credibility of these ideals, represents

> a triumph achieved finally and with great difficulty by the European conscience, being the most fateful act of two thousand years of discipline for truth that in the end forbids itself the *lie* in faith in God. You see what it was that really triumphed over the Christian god: Christian morality itself, the concept of truthfulness that was understood ever more rigorously. (Nietzsche, *GS* 357; see also Nietzsche, *WTP* 1)

Christianity's practice of confession requires penitents to be honest regardless of personal consequences; Christ's incarnation makes history essential rather than just an accidental appendage to eternity. Applying merciless honesty to history then forces us to recognize the genealogical origin of Plato-Christianity in our weakness, vengefulness, and insecurity, which breaks its hold on us. "The insight into some *pudenda origo* certainly brings with it a *feeling* of a diminution in value of the thing that originated thus and prepares the way to a critical mood and attitude toward it" (Nietzsche, *WTP* 254). Once genealogy reveals the all-too-human origin of these supposedly transcendent ideals, they can no longer support the values that give our lives meaning.

Genealogy uncovers a normative anti-realism, that is, the idea that values are our creation, which is intricately related to ontological/epistemological anti-realism.[21] "Verily, men gave themselves all their good and evil. Verily, they did not take it, did not find it, nor did it come to them as a voice from heaven. Only man placed values in things to preserve himself—he alone created a meaning for things" (Nietzsche, *Z* 1.15). Just as nature lacks form and order until we impose them on it, so too it lacks values.

> Whatever has *value* in our world now does not have value in itself, according to its nature—nature is always value-less, but has been *given* value at some time, as a present—and it was *we* who gave and bestowed it. Only we have created the world *that concerns man!*—But precisely this knowledge we lack. . . . We are *neither as proud nor as happy* as we might be. (Nietzsche, *GS* 301; see also Heidegger, *N* 4:80)

Western civilization was raised on normative realism, so the anti-realism that accompanies the death of God shakes us to the core. "The categories 'aim,' 'unity,' 'being' which we used to project some value into the world—we *pull out* again; so the world looks *valueless*" (Nietzsche, *WTP* 12). Since these ultimate, transcendent, independent values are what had been giving our actions cosmic significance, their withdrawal is existentially deflating.

Nietzsche's proposed solution to this crisis of despair is to let passive nihilism run its course as a necessary step toward its fulfillment in the second phase of active nihilism. This phase, liberated from the obligation to submit to supernatural authority of either internal (transcendental subjectivity, Spirit) or external (God) origin, welcomes the death of God as an opportunity to create new and better values. Whereas realism had enforced adherence to a rigorous set of often stifling universal guidelines "as if there were but a single path to the future" (Nietzsche, *Z* 2.4), now we can see that "there are a thousand paths that have never yet been trodden—a thousand healths and hidden isles of life. Even now, man and man's earth are unexhausted and undiscovered" (1.22.2). Once we understand that we were creating these ideals all along, we realize that we are not bound to the ascetic, anti-life values inherited from tradition; we can discard those to make more life-affirming ones. This is the celebration of A3 Ontological Pluralism: the path is now open to create as many interpretations of the world as we find beneficial. We can see how far Nietzsche's evaluation of this situation is from Sartre's, who "finds it extremely embarrassing that God does not exist, for there disappears with Him all possibility of finding values in an intelligible heaven. . . . It is nowhere written that 'the good' exists, that one must be honest or must not lie, since we are now upon the plane where there are only men" (Solomon 2005, 211).

First passive nihilism clears away forced conformity to a narrow set of divinely commanded values (R1–R3), then active nihilism encourages experimentation to create new values (A2, A3, A5). In a metaphor of land and sea that plays throughout *The Gay Science*, Nietzsche says that once we have left firm ground, that is, a realist justification of a single set of values, "the secret for harvesting from existence the greatest fruitfulness and the greatest enjoyment is—to *live dangerously!* . . . Send your ships into uncharted seas" (Nietzsche, *GS* 283). Without God handing down a list of rules on a mountaintop, we must discover what works for us through trial and error.

> We philosophers and "free spirits" feel, when we hear the news that "the old god is dead," as if a new dawn shone on us. . . . At long last the horizon appears free to us again . . . at long last our ships may venture out again . . . the sea, *our* sea, lies open again; perhaps there has never yet been such an "open sea." (Nietzsche, *GS* 343)

The death of God completes the lion's "no" of passive nihilism and, for those who are strong enough to take up the child's active nihilist task of creation (see Nietzsche, *Z* 1.1), it presents an unprecedented opportunity to create new values for ourselves. The attitude Nietzsche finds appropriate to post-atheistic active nihilism is experimentation, the constant taking up of new perspectives, values, or concepts to find what works for each of us at various times. Using the language of health, he claims that, "'*your* virtue is the health of *your* soul.' For there is no health as such." Thus there can be no civilization- or species-wide morality, no universal $truth_P$. Given the plurality of selves within each individual, he goes farther:

> Even the determination of what is healthy for your *body* depends on your goal, your horizon, your energies, your impulses, your errors, and above all on the ideals and phantasms of your soul. Thus there are innumerable healths of the body; and the more we allow the unique and incomparable to raise its head again, and the more we abjure the dogma of the "equality of men," the more must the concept of a *normal* health . . . be abandoned. (Nietzsche, *GS* 120)

An individual needs a variety of perspectives just to keep up with his own internal multiplicity and the ever-changing world, which is why Nietzsche praises those nimble enough to look at the world from multiple perspectives: "Opinions grow out of *passions; inertia of the spirit* lets them stiffen into *convictions.*—He, however, whose spirit is *free* and restlessly alive can prevent this stiffening through continual change" (Nietzsche, *HATH* 1.637; see also Nietzsche, *GS* 301). This is one way to read his famous pronouncement: "There is *only* a perspective seeing, *only* a perspective 'knowing'; and the *more* affects we allow to speak about one thing, the more complete will our 'concept' of this thing, our 'objectivity,' be" (Nietzsche, *GM* 3.12). This idea will be one of his strongest influences on Foucault, as we will see in chapter 7.

Let me summarize my reading of Nietzsche so far. He agrees with Kant that we organize the chaos around us into stable forms (A5, A1), but for naturalistic purposes (ED)—primarily for control in order to help our survival and the increase of power. Once we understand that R2 Correspondence Truth is impossible, we can take control of these experience-forming abilities (A5) to create a better world and values for ourselves (A2). However, since our nature consists of multiple fluctuating wills to power and a collection of battling drives with varying needs (A6), we must employ multiple conceptual schemes (A3), each of which possesses the degree of $truth_P$ correlative to its benefit (A4). This kind of experimental flexibility is what distinguishes his ideal type, the *Übermensch.*

> We premature births of an as yet unproven future need for a new goal also a new means—namely, a new health. . . . Whoever has a soul that

> craves to have experienced the whole range of values and desiderata to date . . . whoever wants to know from the adventures of his own most authentic experience how a discoverer and conqueror of the ideal feels, and also an artist, a saint, a legislator, a sage . . . needs one thing above everything else: the *great health*. . . . Another ideal runs ahead of us, a strange, tempting, dangerous ideal . . . the ideal of a spirit who plays naively—that is, not deliberately but from overflowing power and abundance—with all that we hitherto called holy, good, untouchable, divine . . . it is perhaps only with him that *great seriousness* really begins, that the real question mark is posed for the first time, that the destiny of the soul changes, the hand moves forward. (Nietzsche, *GS* 382; see also Nietzsche, *BGE* 205)

The *Übermensch* possesses such internal richness and multiplicity of roles/perspectives/values that he can adapt fruitfully to whatever conditions the world and his internal battles create (see Schacht 1983, 102).

### A4 Rejection of Bivalence

Nietzsche embraces perspectivalism; he believes that there can be many true views of the world (A3), and he encourages taking a wide variety of perspectives. Since none of them can be true$_C$, we should evaluate them by how they benefit us, that is, by their truth$_P$: "The criterion of truth resides in the enhancement of the feeling of power" (Nietzsche, *WTP* 534). The "us" that gets benefited is in constant flux without identity (A6), so there is no reason to believe that any particular perspective or proposition will benefit or harm us as a totality, and thus be true or false in a simple way. Hence, R4 Bivalence is untenable.

Nietzsche makes bivalence, along with traditional logic as a whole, relative to a particular perspective:

> Not "to know" but to schematize—to impose upon chaos as much regularity and form as our practical needs require. In the formation of reason, logic, the categories, it was *need* that was authoritative. . . . No pre-existing "idea" was here at work, but the utilitarian fact that only when we see things coarsely and made equal do they become calculable and usable to us. . . . The subjective compulsion not to contradict here is a biological compulsion: the instinct for the utility of inferring as we do infer is part of us, we almost *are* this instinct—But what naïveté to extract from this a proof that we are therewith in possession of a "truth in itself"!—Not being able to contradict is proof of an incapacity, not of "truth."
>
> We are unable to affirm and to deny one and the same thing: this is a

> subjective empirical law, not the expression of any "necessity" but only of an inability.[22]

This is Nietzsche's naturalized Kant: logic, reason, and the categories are simply ways that our species has evolved to deal with the world. R4 Bivalence is an occasionally helpful organizing principle, but that in no way establishes its application to the world as it really is, nor its necessity if enough changes were to occur.[23] Furthermore, Nietzsche holds that bivalence often hinders us by leading us to reject wholesale views or perspectives which don't work at one time but which might work perfectly well at another time, or by leading us to cling to views or perspectives as absolutely true because they helped at one time, even though they have long since become harmful; for example, religion. Since the benefit yielded comes in degrees, so does truth: "What forces us at all to suppose that there is an essential opposition of 'true' and 'false'? Is it not sufficient to assume degrees of apparentness?"[24]

## Error

According to my interpretation, Nietzsche frequently claims that our categories are generally pragmatically true in that they evolved for our survival but are correspondently false.

> *Life no argument.*—We have arranged for ourselves a world in which we can live—by [A5] positing bodies, lines, planes, causes and effects, motion and rest, form and content; without these articles of faith nobody now could endure life [$\text{truth}_P$]. But that does not prove them. Life is no argument. The conditions of life might include error [$\text{false}_C$]. (Nietzsche, *GS* 121, bracketed comments added)

The question I now want to ask is, if he denies noumenal reality—the world as it is apart from how we experience it—how can he employ the concept of falsification? What exactly is being falsified? And if there is something being falsified, how could we find out that we are not capturing it accurately? To put it in contemporary anti-realist terminology, if truth is epistemic, that is, if by definition truth does not transcend evidence, experience, verification, or justification that is in principle available, then what sense can we give to the claim that all of our beliefs are false, precisely the kind of claim that epistemic truth tries to rule out? Many commentators have pointed out that Nietzsche does not seem to be entitled to his claim that all views of the world are false—what Clark calls Nietzsche's falsification thesis. Heidegger, perhaps the earliest and still one of the best critics on this point, asks, "If there is no longer a [R2] measuring and estimating with regard to [R1] something true, how is the [A1] world that arises from the [A5] 'action' of life still supposed to be branded and comprehended as 'semblance' [$false_C$] at all?" (Heidegger, *N* 3:129, bracketed comments added). I find Nietzsche using two separate strategies to establish this falsity: (a) letting reason undermine itself through an antinomy with the senses, and (b) illicitly making "$true_C$" claims about universal chaos, that is, committing metaphysics.

### Rational Self-Undermining

One way that Nietzsche tries to show that our conceptual schemes do not correspond to reality is by tracing out a quasi-Hegelian process by which reason, specifically science, undermines itself in its attempts to know the Real World. Honest inquiry leads to "the realization of general untruth and mendaciousness that now comes to us *through science*—the realization that delusion and error are conditions of human knowledge" (Nietzsche, *GS* 107, italics added). The goal of the scientific attitude is to R2 capture R1 reality as it is in itself without interference (R5) from the observer (see, for example, Williams 1978, 65–66). In pursuing this goal, science makes the surprising discovery that the subject's perspective, particularly our sensory apparatus, plays an ineliminable role in observation.[25] Thus, it is the "non-perspectival" scientific analysis of our perceptual faculties which reveals the *impossibility* of "non-perspectival" science.

The knowledge made possible by science on the basis of our conceptual scheme leads to considerable advances in tools of observation, such as microscopes, telescopes, and so on. The resulting observations, though, undermine the very categories which made their construction possible. For instance, two logical categories built into science are equality and substance; scientific laws are universal in that they apply equally to all things of a certain sort, and these things must constitute stable objects in order to be knowable. This scheme enables tremendous improvement in our perceptual tools, but what we find when we use the resulting microscopes and telescopes is that nothing is quite like anything else and that reality is in constant flux.

> The dominant tendency, however, to treat as equal what is merely similar—an illogical tendency, for nothing is really equal—is what first created any basis for logic. In order that the concept of substance could originate—which is indispensable for logic [$truth_P$] although nothing

> real corresponds to it [$truth_C$]—it was likewise necessary that for a long time one did not see nor perceive the changes in things. The beings that did not see so precisely [$truth_C$] had an advantage [$truth_P$] over those that saw everything "in flux." (Nietzsche, *GS* 111, bracketed comments added; see also Nietzsche, *TI* 3.2)

The irony is that science relies on this falsifying logic precisely to discover the "truth" that it has in fact been falsifying all along. The scheme vastly improves our ability to perceive features of reality, which then shows us empirically that reality does not fit the very categories that enabled us to make the discovery. Science's attempt at correspondence truth implodes when it discovers that reality is "a deception through the coarseness of organs" (Nietzsche, *WTP* 580). This sets up an antinomy between the two equally important sources of knowledge of macroscopic experience and scientific results (see R. K. Hill 2003, 127). Since it is not an option just to accept one and dismiss the other, the conflict between the two leads us to distrust the whole idea of getting things right (R3).

On this reading, the charge of falsification is not legitimated by metaphysical claims about reality in-itself outside of experience, but by just the kind of careful empirical evidence that science values.

> For there to be communication something has to be firm, simplified, capable of precision (above all in the [so-called] *identical* case). . . . The material of the senses adapted by the understanding, reduced to rough outlines, made similar, subsumed under related matters. Thus the fuzziness and chaos of sense impressions are, as it were, logicized. . . . The antithesis of this phenomenal world is not "the true world," but the formless unformulable world of the chaos of sensations—*another kind* of phenomenal world. (Nietzsche, *WTP* 569)

Here Nietzsche justifies the claim of falsification from within experience, from sharper empirical perception. As the last sentence makes clear, he is careful not to invoke extra-experiential reality as a contrast with experience, but only the evidence you get when you "think through your own senses to their consequences" (Nietzsche, *Z* 2.2).

Jorge Luis Borges's wonderful short story "Funes the Memorious" illustrates Nietzsche's point nicely. Funes suffered a childhood accident which paralyzed him while vastly enhancing his perceptual and mnemonic capabilities. These changes have a profound effect on him.

> Locke, in the seventeenth century, postulated (and rejected) an impossible language in which each individual thing, each stone, each bird and

> each branch, would have its own name; Funes once projected an analogous language, but discarded it because it seemed too general to him, too ambiguous. In fact, Funes remembered not only every leaf of every tree of every wood, but also every one of the times he had perceived or imagined it. . . . Not only was it difficult for him to comprehend that the symbol *dog* embraces so many unlike individuals of diverse size and form; it bothered him that the dog at three fourteen (seen from the side) should have the same name as the dog at three fifteen (seen from the front). (Borges 1962, 65)

Funes would be one of the "innumerable beings who made inferences in a way different from ours [and] perished [making the inferences false$_P$]; for all that, their ways might have been truer$_{[c]}$" (Nietzsche, *GS* 111, bracketed comments added). Funes sees and indelibly remembers the vast detail and flux we usually pass over but can occasionally make out with enough effort and equipment. The fact that this perspective is accessible to us, even prioritized by science, allows Nietzsche to show how our normal thoughts and perceptions can be considered false$_C$ without relying on the kind of separate "true" reality (R1) he wants to eradicate. Our conceptualized experience is false because more careful and exact observations do not bear it out; even without the epistemological priority that science awards them, the fact that we can't decide between the two accounts leaves us in an antinomy. Borges also agrees with Nietzsche on the enormous impracticality of such "truer$_C$" abilities, that is, their pragmatic falsity: "I suspect, however, that [Funes] was not very capable of thought. To think is to forget differences, generalize, make abstractions. In the teeming world of Funes, there were only details" (Borges 1962, 66).

### Metaphysical Chaos

At other times, however, the structure of the Kantian Paradigm in which concepts are projected (A5) onto a reality (R1) draws Nietzsche into discussing the world as it is apart from human interpretations, describing it as either chaos or will to power. He says that "the total character of the world, however, is in all eternity chaos" (Nietzsche, *GS* 109). The ability to see chaotic reality for what it is without masking it even serves as a measure of strength: "Indeed, it might be a basic characterization of existence that those who would know it completely would perish [false$_P$], in which case the strength of a spirit should be measured according to how much of the 'truth[$_C$]' one could still barely endure" (Nietzsche, *BGE* 39; see also Nietzsche, *WTP* 1041). The *Übermensch* would have the greatest strength, since he "conceives reality *as it is,* being strong enough to do so; this type is not estranged or removed from reality but is reality itself" (Nietzsche, *EH* 4.5). He can know reality as it really is because he embodies it most fully, thus combining commitments to both R1 and R6.[26] The famous final aphorism of *The Will to Power* also describes the world as "a sea of forces flowing and rushing together, eternally changing . . . a becoming that knows no satiety, no disgust, no weariness. . . . *This world is the will to power—and nothing besides!* And you yourselves are also this will to power—and nothing besides!" (Nietzsche, *WTP* 1067; see also Nietzsche, *GM* 2.11).

Passages like these form the basis of Heidegger's famous reading of Nietzsche as the last metaphysician who overturns Plato's divided line without abandoning it. Nietzsche privileges becoming over being (see Nietzsche, *EH* 3.1.3; Nietzsche, *WTP* 584; Nietzsche, *TI* 3.6), but such an inversion still counts as metaphysics, since it describes the flux as true reality—what actually exists—in opposition to the "false" phenomenal world of self-identical beings we constitute or the Gods and Forms we make up. For Heidegger it is the appearance/reality distinction itself that defines metaphysics, rather than any particular assignment of these values; since Nietzsche's inversion of Plato's hierarchy is still in the business of sifting out reality from appearance, he is a metaphysician. "Metaphysical thinking rests on the distinction between what truly is and what, measured against this, constitutes all that is not truly in being. . . . The distinction persists even when the Platonic hierarchy of suprasensuous and sensuous is inverted."[27] It is this contrast with the chaotic and violent will to power as the really real that creates the logical space for Nietzsche to accuse our normal perceptions and conceptions of falsehood or deception. "The condition of the existence of the good is the *lie:* put differently, not *wanting* to see at any price how reality is constituted fundamentally" (Nietzsche, *EH* 4.4; see also Nietzsche, *Z* 3.12.7). This setup also allows him to praise his own honesty: Zarathustra's "doctrine, and his alone, posits truthfulness as the highest virtue; this means the opposite of the cowardice of the 'idealist' who flees from reality" (Nietzsche, *EH* 4.3, see also Nietzsche, *Z* 1.3). Chaotic becoming is real and asserting it is truth$_C$, whereas stable being is projected and false$_C$; although a reversal, this conception retains R2 Correspondence Truth to R1 Independent reality and its presuppositions.

Heidegger observes that Nietzsche's use of the concept of error only works given the presuppositions of R2 Correspondence with R1 true reality.

> If for Nietzsche truth is a kind of error, then its essence consists in a way of thinking that always, indeed necessarily, falsifies the real, specifically insofar as every act of representing halts the continual "becoming" and,

> in erecting its established facts against the flow of "becoming," sets up the supposedly real something that does not correspond—i.e., something incorrect and thus erroneous. Nietzsche's determination of truth as the incorrectness of thinking is in agreement with the traditional essence of truth as the correctness of assertion.[28]

Nietzsche can accuse certain views of falsity only by claiming genuine insight into true reality for himself. As Clark says, "The falsification thesis commits him to a 'true' world, which makes sense only on the assumption that reality is something in itself" (M. Clark 1990, 117).[29]

In addition to the Kantian picture of the self as organizing experience (A5) made naturalistic (ED), Nietzsche also takes up Kant's transcendental realism. However, whereas Kant only says about noumena that they exist and are *not* spatial, temporal, and so on, Nietzsche goes so far as to give a positive characterization of the world in itself, that is, will to power or chaos: it is in continual flux, interacts causally, is indefinitely interpretable, lacks a final cause, and so on. This chaos is what the world is like once our contributions have been subtracted; in other words, this is the R1 Independent world.

> For Nietzsche, as for Kant, imagination (or what Nietzsche calls "interpretation") is essential to the constitution of experience. However, given that we are partly passive in relation to experience, both Kant and Nietzsche write of a prime matter of sensation that the mind works up into experience. . . . Nietzsche identifies both the source of the chaos and the organizing system we are with the will to power.[30]

This "prime matter of sensation" is precisely what Hegel rejects as virtually noumenal and thus unintelligible: "Whether the Thing is called an extraneous impulse, or an empirical or sensuous entity, or the Thing-in-itself, it still remains in principle the same, i.e., extraneous to that unity" (Hegel, *PS* 145, §238).

In a note from 1888, Nietzsche audaciously totals up our contributions to experience, as well as what remains when these are removed.

> We need "unities" in order to be able to reckon: that does not mean we must suppose that such unities exist. . . . The following are therefore phenomenal: the injection of the concept of number, the concept of the thing. . . . If we eliminate these additions, no things remain but only dynamic quanta, in a relation of tension to all other dynamic quanta: their essence lies in their relation to all other quanta. (Nietzsche, *WTP* 635; compare with Quine 1960, 5)

This represents subjective idealism at its worst (although the note was unpublished, it is surprisingly late). After attacking Kant's "right to his distinction 'appearance' and 'thing-in-itself'" (Nietzsche, *WTP* 553) and claiming in 1887 that the view "that things possess a constitution in themselves quite apart from interpretation and subjectivity, is a quite idle hypothesis" (560), Nietzsche goes on to discuss precisely this independent constitution. Note too that the late dates of these writings throw doubt on Clark's developmental theory, i.e., that Nietzsche came to reject this Kantian subjective idealism, what she calls the falsification thesis, in his last years. One of the ways she maintains her interpretation is by ruling out the *Nachlass* (M. Clark 1990, 25), which contains many conflicting passages post-dating Nietzsche's supposed conversion. Although the *Nachlass* certainly deserves a lower status than the published work,[31] it seems implausible that Nietzsche would continue writing extensively about ideas that he had come to realize were incoherent (see R. K. Hill 2003, 137n14).

Nietzsche wants his claims to correspond (R2) to the world:

> Nietzsche acknowledges his philosophical "truths" to be simplified, perspectival, interpretive, and therefore unjust. But these "truths" are also more appropriate to his sense of what life is, more *realistic* than metaphysical concepts. They describe chaos, becoming, will, rather than substance, being and identity. Nietzsche thus relies on an albeit attenuated concept of correspondence between his own "truth" and human life. (Houlgate 1986, 54; see also 239n90; Richardson 1996, 280)

He *has* to claim to have gotten it right about chaos in order to accuse metaphysics, Christianity, and so on of getting it wrong in positing stable things, heaven, and so on. Nor does he brook any disagreement about the true nature of this chaos, coming up with elaborate explanations of ulterior motives for those who disagree. In these ways, Nietzsche lapses back into elements of Kant's subjective idealism with its concomitant realism, even after Hegel's important criticisms of it.

## A Healthy Realism of the Self

In Kant's system, a moderately realist conception of the self (R6) as a determinate activity existing apart from changing reality, but constituting it (A5), is what ensures the knowability and stability of the phenomenal realm (R3). Nietzsche is committed to a strong version of A6 Plural Subject, allowing the forms of the self to multiply indefinitely, which entails a wide-open A3 Ontological Pluralism; he rules out Hegel's use of the end of history to bring closure to the possible types of subjectivity and conceptual schemes, a closure that reinstates a loosened form of R3 and R6. This move allows Hegel to evaluate the various moments of consciousness by how close they are to the end and, what is basically the same, how closely they resemble genuine subjectivity. Once Nietzsche has eliminated correspondence truth (R2) as the guide to inquiry and liberated those strong enough to constitute reality as they wish, he faces the problem of the criterion: how are they to decide? Even if one is strong enough to accept the responsibility and scorn the passive quest of merely capturing an independent reality, one still needs some way to determine which concepts to adopt.

We saw above that many claims generally accepted as true are validated pragmatically: they are true$_{P}$ because they enhance our survival and power, or at least contributed to our species' survival at one point in its evolution (see, for example, Nietzsche, *HATH* 1.2). Passive nihilism brings us to the realization that these concepts and beliefs are not true$_{C}$, i.e., that our language, survival conditions, and logic do not correspond to the chaos of reality itself, which drives the weak who cling to correspondence truth to despair that nothing has value or truth anymore, since this kind of Truth is unattainable. Those strong enough to withstand the honest gaze into the abyss, however, are liberated from fidelity to a prescribed, ascetic way of life and are freed to create new values in active nihilism. The defining value of active nihilism would then be a power-based pragmatism.

> If the morality of "thou shalt not lie" [truth$_{C}$]is rejected, the "sense for truth" will have to legitimize itself before another tribunal:—as a means of the preservation of man, as *will to power* [truth$_{P}$]. . . . The sense for the real is the means of acquiring the power to [A5] shape things according to our wish. The joy in shaping and reshaping—a primeval joy! (Nietzsche, *WTP* 495, bracketed comments added)

In this self-consciously pragmatic and creative will to truth, "the criterion of truth resides in the enhancement of the feeling of power" (Nietzsche, *WTP* 534; see also Houlgate 1986, 58). The increase of power takes the place of corresponding to independent reality as the fundamental criterion of truth$_{P}$ (see Schrift 1990, 180).

In order for this litmus test to work, though, there must be some definition to this life or power which certain beliefs enhance and others harm, a definition Nietzsche does not hesitate to name as "will to power."

The *Übermensch* assesses beliefs in terms of "the really fundamental instinct of life which aims at *the expansion of power*" (Nietzsche, *GS* 349; see also Nietzsche, *A* 2) because life actually is power.

> Life operates *essentially,* that is in its basic functions, through injury, assault, exploitation, destruction and simply cannot be thought of at all without this character. . . . A legal order thought of as sovereign and universal, not as a means in the struggle between power-complexes but as a means of *preventing* all struggle in general . . . would be a principle *hostile to life,* an agent of the dissolution and destruction of man. (Nietzsche, *GM* 2.11)

Universal pacifism must be rejected because it violates the essence of life as exploitation and expanding its own influence. In *Beyond Good and Evil* §259, Nietzsche reiterates the point that a society organized around preventing injury would be a denial of life, and again justifies this evaluation by a description of the true nature of life: "Life itself is *essentially* appropriation, injury . . . imposition of one's own forms. . . . Life simply *is* will to power."

Although Nietzsche takes the step from correspondence to pragmatic truth, his pragmatic truth itself rests upon one particular correspondence truth (R2) about our essence (R6) in order to determine what will benefit us. He spells out the links quite clearly here: "There is nothing to life that has value, except the degree of power—*assuming that life itself is the will to power.* Morality guarded the underprivileged against nihilism . . . by placing each in an order that *did not agree with the world order of rank and power*" (Nietzsche, *WTP* 55, italics added). The evaluation of beliefs is based on their compatibility with life as will to power, a definition which generates a "world order of rank and power" according to an "essential priority of the spontaneous, aggressive, expansive, form-giving forces that give new interpretations and directions" (Nietzsche, *GM* 2.12; see also Nietzsche, *A* 6). Deleuze's influential interpretation of Nietzsche starts from the idea that his genealogy is organized around and presupposes an active-reactive polarity which is simply embedded in the nature of the will to power (see Deleuze 1983, 40, 60).

Although Nietzsche makes the self multiple, corporeal, and natural, the definition of the self as will to power seems to be a fundamental assumption of his thought, rather like a wilder version of Kant's transcendental faculties. He himself believes that thinkers' systems are informed by deep assumptions, *arches* where, in Wittgenstein's phrase, their spade is turned.

> At the bottom of us, really "deep down," there is, of course, something unteachable, some granite of spiritual *fatum*, of predetermined decision and answer to predetermined selected questions. Whenever a cardinal problem is at stake, there speaks an unchangeable "this is I." (Nietzsche, *BGE* 231)

This is why "most of the conscious thinking of a philosopher is secretly guided and forced into certain channels by his instincts," exposing "every great philosophy so far" as actually "the personal confession of its author and a kind of involuntary and unconscious memoir" (Nietzsche, *BGE* 3, 6; see also Nietzsche, *EH* 1.2). In his own case, at least one aspect of this fundamental layer is the view of the self as will to power (see Heidegger, *N* 4:73, 4:134).

Heidegger views Nietzsche's critique of traditional values and endorsement of new ones as parasitic on a metaphysical definition of the self and its health.

> Man hitherto is called this, according to Nietzsche's metaphysics, because, although his essence is indeed determined by the will to power as the fundamental characteristic of all that is, he still has not experienced and accepted the will to power as that principal characteristic. Man who surpasses man up to now takes the will to power, as the principal characteristic of all that is, up into his own willing and in that way wills himself in the manner of will to power. (Heidegger, *QT* 98; see also 95)

Humanity has always been will to power, but only the *Übermensch* realizes and accepts this. Thus, his superiority is determined by his life matching the R6 Realist definition of the Subject.

> Will to power is a name for the basic character of all beings. . . . Nietzsche's decisive consideration runs as follows: if we are to establish what properly should be, and what must come to be in consequence of that, it can be determined only if truth and clarity already surround whatever *is* and whatever constitutes *Being*. How else could we determine what is to be? (Heidegger, *N* 1:31; see also 1:32, 3:202)

In other words, Nietzsche's ethics is grounded in a realist ontology; it is only because we *are* will to power that we *ought* to increase our power.[32] Nietzsche's command to become who you are presupposes that there is something that you are which can then be appropriated and consciously willed. The *Übermensch* is the one who, like Hegel's Spirit at the end of history, has become who he is by accepting his essence, here defined as will to power, and living in conformity with this nature, rather than mendaciously denying it (while secretly satisfying it) through Christian love. "With the name *Übermensch* Nietzsche designates those who recognize themselves as will to power *qua* play of forces" (Schrift 1990, 69; see also D. B. Allison 1977, 26).

Genealogy also presupposes a specific ideal justified by the conception of health, namely, the state in which a person explicitly lives their will to power rather than denying or disguising it. *On the Genealogy of Morals* bases its evaluations of master and slave moralities on the former's activity and the latter's reactivity (Nietzsche, *WTP* 1009), as Deleuze believes, but why prefer one to the other? What justifies "the essential priority of the spontaneous, aggressive, expansive, form-giving forces" is that these constitute "the essence of life, its *will to power*" (Nietzsche, *GM* 2.13). Maudemarie Clark sums up this problem nicely:

> Some radical interpreters insist that the reason to accept Nietzsche's perspective is not cognitive superiority—its greater truth [$_C$]—but its superiority in serving a noncognitive end, for example, that it is more life-affirming [$_P$] (Kofman) or that it reflects the active rather than the reactive position (Deleuze). But this only pushes the self-reference problem back one step. The question naturally arises as to whether it is only a perspectival truth that Nietzsche's position is more life-affirming than the Christian position. (M. Clark 1990, 151, bracketed comments added; see also Houlgate 1986, 72)

In order to justify his pragmatic evaluations, Nietzsche must have recourse to correspondence truth claims; he must ground his judgments that a certain belief is better for us in a definite description of what the self is in order to determine what increases and what decreases that self's health. "The judgment that one interpretation is more life-affirming than another seems to require for its justification claims presented not simply as life-affirming, but also as true" (M. Clark 1990, 16–17). The pragmatic criterion of life-affirmation rests on correspondence truth claims about the essence of the subject (R6).

Artists serve as Nietzsche's model for the person who is comfortable creatively shaping reality. In an aphorism titled "Our ultimate gratitude to art," Nietzsche writes that art can prepare us for active nihilism's conscious forming of reality.

> If we had not welcomed the arts and invented this kind of cult of the untrue, then the realization of general untruth and mendaciousness that

> now comes to us through science—the realization that delusion and error[$_C$] are conditions of human knowledge[$_P$] and sensation—would be utterly unbearable. *Honesty* would lead us to nausea and suicide. But now there is a counterforce against our honesty that helps to avoid such consequences: art as the *good* will to appearance. (Nietzsche, *GS* 107, bracketed comments added)

Followed to its end, honesty concludes that truth$_C$ is impossible, thus allowing us to discard honesty and fidelity together. In active nihilism, we eschew this ascetic and subservient will to truth and embrace appearance, masks, illusion. "This faith in truth attains its ultimate conclusion in us—you know what it is: that if there is anything that is to be worshipped it is *appearance* that must be worshipped, that the lie—and *not* the truth—is divine!" (Nietzsche, *WTP* 1011).

Strongly disagreeing with the traditional interpretation of art as mimesis or imitation, Nietzsche sees art as one of the only human pursuits that rejoices in the creative shaping of reality. Although we are the source of many features of reality, we generally deny it, attributing them to reality in-itself or God the way that Hegel's Consciousness "forgets" its contributions to experience that go on "behind its back." Art offers a model of accepting our own creativity as something positive. "Man must be a liar by nature, he must be above all an *artist.* And he *is* one: metaphysics, religion, morality, science—all of them only products of his will to art, to lie [false$_C$]" (Nietzsche, *WTP* 853, bracketed comment added). In other words, we are continuously shaping reality (A5) without realizing it. "Basically and from time immemorial we are—*accustomed to lying.* . . . One is much more of an artist than one knows" (Nietzsche, *BGE* 192; see also Haar in D. B. Allison 1977, 27). The problem isn't that we are artists; it's that we are but don't know it which condemns us to remain bad artists.

Active nihilism makes us aware of this fact without forcing us to give up the necessary organizing process: "I suddenly woke up in the midst of this dream, but only to the consciousness that I am dreaming and that I must go on dreaming lest I perish" (Nietzsche, *GS* 54). Realism and passive nihilism recommend that we renounce our (A5) creative interpretations, since they necessarily falsify$_C$. Active nihilism, on the other hand, tells us to take control of them and bend them to our will, making them true$_P$. We should not try to become R5 Passive Knowers but "become who we are," that is, artistic interpreters. As Heidegger puts it, for Nietzsche "the fault in naïveté is not the humanization of things, but the fact that the humanization is not *consciously* carried out" (Heidegger, *N* 4:80; see also 81, 83). Nietzsche encourages us to embrace this ability joyously.

> How much artists triumph in the feeling of power!—Man has once again become master of "*material*"—master of truth!—And whenever man rejoices, he is always the same in his rejoicing: he rejoices as an artist, he enjoys himself as power, he enjoys the lie[$_C$] as his form of power. . . . But truth[$_C$] does not count as the supreme value. . . . The will to appearance, to deception, to becoming and change (to objectified deception) here counts as more profound, primeval, "metaphysical" than the will to truth[$_C$], to [R1] reality. (Nietzsche, *WTP* 853, bracketed comments added)

The irony is that art's freedom from correspondence to reality is valued so highly precisely because it corresponds to our essence as A5 Active Knowers! In Haar's words, "If art has to become the highest value, it is because art corresponds best to, is most adequate to, the essence of the Will to Power as permanent growth of the self."[33]

Although Nietzsche protests that he is not a systematic thinker (see Nietzsche, *TI* 1.26), in fact A1–A6 combine in his thought to form a powerful, coherent view. We are A5 Active Knowers, which renders R2 Correspondence Truth impossible; that goal should be given up for truth$_p$, that is, for beliefs that benefit us (A2): "*Genuine philosophers, however, are commanders and legislators:* they say, '*thus* it *shall* be!' They first determine the Whither and For What of man. . . . Their 'knowing' is *creating*, their creating is a legislation" (Nietzsche, *BGE* 211). However, since the subject to be benefited is actually a plurality of drives (A6), each with its own interests which are benefited differently, and each with its own perspectives determining different truths, we must amass a plurality of perspectives (A3) to adapt to this internal variety[34] and external change. "The fundamental laws of self-preservation and growth demand the opposite [of the universal requirements of traditional and Kantian moralities]—that everyone invent *his own* virtue, *his own* categorical imperative" (Nietzsche, *A* 11, bracketed comment added; see also Nietzsche, *BGE* 228). This gives us degrees of truth indexed to the benefit that a perspective yields to our present state (A4). What I have just been arguing is that this system also rests on a certain realism.

Nietzsche qualifies or rejects the notion of a core, atomistic self behind or beneath all actions and thoughts, a *hypokeimenon*. He variously sees this idea as the source of our category of causation (Nietzsche, *WTP* 488), the result of the structure of our language (Nietzsche, *BGE* 17), or a tool of Christianity to tame the master type (Nietzsche, *GM* 1.13). He multiplies the self (A6) and immerses it into time, nature, causality, corporeality, instincts, and power struggles (ED). These moves indefinitely extend the multiplicity that Hegel introduces into the self, thus preparing the way for the later Heidegger and Foucault's profound innovations. Nietzsche, however, is only attacking one particular conception of the self, namely the atomistic, self-identical, immortal, and free soul-thing as the transcendental origin of our actions. His criticism is that this conception does not accurately capture the self's true nature, thus retaining the traditional notion of correspondence truth.

Rather than dismissing the very idea of "getting it right," Nietzsche posits his conception of the self as a multiplicity of drives fighting for mastery as a more accurate depiction. He still claims truth for "*my hypothesis:* The subject as multiplicity" (Nietzsche, *WTP* 490) or "a social structure composed of many souls" (Nietzsche, *BGE* 19), thus, by his own lights, remaining one of those who "are far from being *free* spirits: *for they still have faith in truth*" (Nietzsche, *GM* 3.24). Nietzsche extends the multiplicity and change that Hegel introduced into the self, positing a similar idea of a continuously self-overcoming movement of unrest: "We ourselves keep growing, keep changing, we shed our old bark, we shed our skins every spring" (Nietzsche, *GS* 371). Although it never reposes in a single essence like Kant's transcendental subjectivity, nor can it be collected into any kind of totality like Hegel's Spirit, the struggle for control between the various drives does operate via the specific set of active-reactive values which determine some beliefs and actions as appropriate to its nature and others as violations. This is the essence of will to power (R6) on which Nietzsche bases his values.

## Step Six Physics

Many commentators, especially French scholars (for example, Granier, Kofman, De Man), believe that Nietzsche avoids the vestiges of realism I have saddled him with. These interpreters, often reacting against Heidegger's reading of Nietzsche as a metaphysician, argue that Nietzsche escapes the conceptual trap of Kantian subjective idealism, whose very notion of projection (A5) brings the concept of an unformed raw matter to be organized in its wake. As Rorty puts it in talking about another philosopher,

> The picture called up by Williams's terminology is of some mighty immaterial force called "mind" or "language" or "social practice"—a force which shapes facts out of indeterminate goo, constructs reality out of something not yet determinate enough to count as real. The problem for

> antirepresentationalists is to find a way of putting their point which carries no such suggestion. (Rorty 1991a, 5)

The "goo" turns out to be a very sticky problem indeed.

These "postmodernist" commentators emphasize Nietzsche's criticisms of the intelligibility of the notion of a world in itself. On this reading, Nietzsche is much closer to Hegel's Objective Idealism, which dismisses this idea as incoherent. Just as Hegel said that subtracting knowledge leaves only "a pure direction or a blank space" (Hegel, *PS* 47, §73), so Nietzsche sometimes writes that "the 'thing-in-itself' is nonsensical. If I remove all the relationships, all the 'properties,' all the 'activities' of a thing, the thing does not remain over."[35] There are certainly passages that support such a reading.

> *To the realists.*—You sober people who feel well armed against passion and fantasies and would like to turn your [R5] emptiness into a matter of pride and an ornament: you call yourselves realists and hint that the [R1] world [R2] really is the way it appears to you. . . . You are still burdened with those [A5] estimates of things that have their origin in the passions and loves of former centuries. . . . That mountain there! That cloud there! What is "real" in that? Subtract the phantasm and [A5] every human *contribution* from it, my sober friends! If you *can!* If you can forget your descent, your past, your training—all of your humanity and [ED] animality. There is no [A1] "reality" for us—not for you either. (Nietzsche, *GS* 57, bracketed comments added)

Here Nietzsche follows a strategy similar to Hegel's in tracing the origin of the category of the in-itself back to our usage: "We have no categories at all that permit us to distinguish a 'world in itself' from a 'world of appearance.' All our categories of reason are of sensual origin: derived from the empirical world" (Nietzsche, *WTP* 488, from 1887). And just as Hegel insists that "both of them, subjectivity as well as objectivity, are certainly thoughts" (Hegel, *HL* 255, §192R), so Nietzsche claims that "the psychological derivation of the belief in things forbids us to speak of 'things-in-themselves.'"[36]

If we do not overemphasize the empiricist tone of *Will to Power* 488 quoted above, we can see Nietzsche making the same point here that I attributed to Hegel (and Wittgenstein) in chapter 3, namely that all of our ways of thinking and talking emerge from dealing with experience and can only make sense within that context. They cannot intelligibly be used to handle or refer to a world wholly independent of experience. Similarly, a claim like "in so far as the word 'knowledge' has any meaning, the world is knowable" (Nietzsche, *WTP* 481) fits in perfectly with Objective Idealist epistemology. It isn't so much a denial of noumenal reality, which would require superhuman access to a meta-physical realm in order to ascertain its emptiness, but rather a delimitation of the very sense of the concept of knowing similar to Wittgenstein's strategy in *On Certainty*.

Although he uses misleading terminology, Nietzsche comes close to Objective Idealism in another note from 1887: "The apparent *objective* character of things: could it not be merely a difference of degree within the subjective?—that perhaps that which changes slowly presents itself to us as 'objectively' enduring, being, 'in-itself'—that the objective is only a false concept of a genus and an antithesis *within* the subjective?" (Nietzsche, *WTP* 560; see also 567; Nietzsche, *TI* 3.2). The notion of R1 Mind-Independence emerges from our encounters with the experiential world—where else could it come from? Due to certain features (here slowness of change), we introduce distinctions which rigidify into the metaphysical dichotomy of subjective and objective, even though both have meaning only within experience. But in that case the qualification "subjective" falls away, at least in its absolute metaphysical sense. This would be Nietzsche's way of putting Hegel's point: "These two moments, 'Notion' and 'object,' 'being-for-another' and 'being-in-itself,' both fall *within* that knowledge which we are investigating" (Hegel, *PS* 53, §84). I think Nietzsche's use of the terms "objective" and "subjective" here is a mistake since they tend to pull the discussion back into the orbit of subjective idealism, but he seems to be making the same point. We would then see the terms as the ladder to be kicked away once his point is grasped.

A note from 1888 states:

> The "in-itself" is even an absurd conception; a "constitution-in-itself" is nonsense; we possess the concept "being," "thing," only as a relational concept. . . . We possess no categories by which we can distinguish a true from an apparent world. (There might only be an apparent world, but not *our* apparent world). (Nietzsche, *WTP* 583A)

This is a very interesting quote. The first part dismisses the in-itself as absurd and non-sense rather than as inaccessible and useless. These are importantly different arguments, as I will discuss in a moment. The second part treats the idea that our categories evolved to help us deal with the world we experience and so are simply not designed for a realm wholly cut off from us. But the most interesting part of this quote is the parenthetical aside. He is using potentially misleading terms again, but to make a powerful point. Just thinking subjective idealism assumes the third-person omniscient view, what John McDowell calls the "sideways on" view of our concepts interacting with the world (McDowell 1996, 34). God could see the noumena on one side and us locked into our phenomenal interpretations on the other, forever barred from the truth, but *we* cannot see this or even understand it any further than just as a picture.

This argument resembles Putnam's refutation of the Brain in a Vat hypothesis, that is, the skeptical idea that we might be experiencing a completely false world. Even entertaining this hypothesis requires us to take up the alien scientists' point of view who can see our brains floating in the vats and compare the real world outside the vats with the illusory program feeding impulses into the brains' synapses. But *ex hypothesi* the brains are cut off from just this point of view and thus unable to think such a thought: "The supposition that such a possibility makes sense arises from a combination of two errors: (1) taking *physical possibility* too seriously; and (2) unconsciously operating with a magical theory of reference, a theory on which certain mental representations necessarily refer to certain external things" (Putnam 1981, 15). In other words, just because the scientists can establish the physical state of the brains as artificially stimulated doesn't mean that the brains can think or state such an idea. As Peter van Inwagen puts it, "*Someone* may be a brain in a vat. . . . But no one can coherently say that *he* is in [this situation]" (French, Uehling, and Wettstein 1988, 101). According to Putnam's externalism, reference and sense are achieved through interactions with society and referents, not through a magical link that simply exists between words and things. As Wittgenstein argues over and over again, just having an image in one's head isn't enough to secure reference; a "total way of being situated in the world and in his linguistic community" is needed (Putnam 1975, 247). Nietzsche makes the similar claim here that even if we have an image that "there might only be an apparent world," it could never be "*our* apparent world"; we cannot think of it as merely apparent to us, since we have nothing more real with which to compare it.

The touchstone for this non- or post-metaphysical rather than anti-metaphysical reading of Nietzsche is the final transition from Step Five to Step Six in his famous "How the 'True World' Finally Became a Fable." Step Five marks the pragmatic refutation of noumena as inaccessible and useless that, as I showed above, he accepted in his early work: "The 'true' world—an idea which is no longer good for anything, not even obligating—an idea which has become useless and superfluous—*consequently,* a refuted idea: let us abolish it!" (Nietzsche, *TI* 4, italics in original). The important word here is the italicized "*consequently,*" which shows the argument to be purely pragmatic: since we can never get noumenal knowledge, it makes no difference, so why bother about it? Importantly, this objection says nothing about the conceptual coherence of the idea, but only its utility and historical or sociological status.

Step Six, on the other hand, is the climax of the entire history of philosophy, the epoch-making breakthrough that brings the "end of the longest error; high point of humanity": "the true world—we have abolished. What world has remained? The apparent one perhaps? But no! *With the true world we have also abolished the apparent one*" (Nietzsche, *TI* 4, italics in original). This moves from the pragmatic rejection of a metaphysical world as useless to conceptually overcoming the very distinction between real and apparent. Once we get rid of the idea of a true world beyond this one (*meta-physis*), this world does not then become the true one. The meaning of a true or real world depends on a contrast, as J. L. Austin points out: "A definite sense attaches to the assertion that something is real, a real such-and-such, only in the light of a specific way in which it might be, or might have been, *not* real" (Austin 1962, 70). Without the contrast, this world is neither false nor true, neither apparent nor real; it's just the world. I will call this position Step Six Physics (physics not as the scientific discipline but as opposed to *meta-physis*); it is Nietzsche's counterpart to Hegel's Objective Idealism, that is, his point of a potential break with the Kantian Paradigm.[37] Nietzsche's own estimation of the importance of this breakthrough is indicated by the fact that it occupies an entire step in his history, the equivalent of the change from Plato to Christianity, or Christianity to Kant, and that it represents the final, culminating climax.[38]

Another clear presentation of Step Six Physics comes in an unpublished note titled "Against the word '*appearances.*'"

> N.B. *Semblance* as I understand it, is the actual and sole reality of things—that to which all present predicates belong and which can best be characterized by all predicates, even the opposite ones. With the word, however, nothing more is expressed than its inaccessibility to logical procedure and distinctions: thus "semblance," "illusion" in relation to "logical truth"—which however, itself is only possible in an imaginary world. I thus place "*Schein*" not in opposition to "reality" but rather on the contrary accept semblance as the reality which resists transformation into an imaginative "truth world." A more determinate name for this reality would be "the will to power," that is, characterized from the inside and not from its incomprehensible, fluid Protean nature.[39]

This is one of his better expressions of an idea that is very hard to express (see D. B. Allison 1977, 136). Since "all present predicates belong" to it, "even the opposite ones," A3 Ontological Pluralism and A4 Rejection of Bivalence both hold of it. Nietzsche does not contrast this world of semblance with the real world but, in a proto-phenomenological move, claims that appearance is reality (see Hegel, *HL* 186, §131). Furthermore, he explicitly states that he is characterizing it from the inside, whereas many of his descriptions of reality as chaos or will to power seem to illicitly take an external perspective.

So what should we make of all the claims about chaos and will to power? Some, like Michel Haar, see Nietzsche as a proto-Derridean who uses will to power or chaos not as metaphysical descriptions but as self-deconstructing concepts which intentionally disrupt attempts to read them as depictions of reality (R2). He claims that it "deliberately shatters the logic of identity. . . . Appearance . . . never comes to the point of referring to an ultimate foundation . . . nor to anything 'in itself.'"[40] Simply stating that there are no noumena ties one up in metaphysics, since this amounts to "the attempt to say that *from a God's-Eye View there is no God's-Eye View*" (Putnam 1990, 25; see also Putnam 1995, 39). So perhaps Nietzsche is trying to *show* the incoherence of noumena rather than *saying* it. Whereas Hegel uses the speculative proposition whose subject and predicate interfere with each other to introduce fluidity into static assertions, Nietzsche would be deliberately provoking antinomies to disrupt the metaphysics inherent in our language. Saying that Being is becoming isn't metaphysics on this reading, but a reason-frustrating koan meant to break down our expectations of realist truth; Nietzsche's strategy of using two different senses of "truth" that I outlined above certainly fits this pattern. This would give further prominence to his doctrine of the eternal return. Besides its usefulness as a litmus test of one's strength, it shatters identities and generates paradoxes by the dozen: the past is the future,[41] free choice is fate, I am just me but also all the other selves throughout time, each cycle is the same but different, and so on. Rather than saying that metaphysical entities don't exist, Nietzsche replaces them with concepts that "crumble before their own meanings" (Conway 1998, 367; see also D. B. Allison 1977, 33, 34).

Others, such as Barry Allen, point to "the ironic, performative quality of affirmation in Nietzsche." Rather than making assertions in the traditional sense of putting forth a claim as true, he uses sentences playfully, "*indifferent* to the difference between truth and error" (Allen 1993, 49). *Beyond Good and Evil* §22, where Nietzsche describes the hypothesis that the world is will to power and then happily accepts the criticism that his hypothesis is itself "only an interpretation," is the best example of this distancing from the commitments of his own claims (see also Nietzsche, *BGE* 43, 230). It is in criticizing Heidegger's dismissal of any ironic reading of Nietzsche (see Heidegger, *N* 2:148) that Derrida repeatedly points out the effects of his writing rather than just its content: "The virulence of Nietzschean thought could not be more completely misunderstood."[42]

No doubt, these ingenious readings tell us something of Nietzsche's rhetorical strategies in the surprisingly difficult quest to shed metaphysics.

At times he does seem to be playing a new, different game, one close to Hegel's Objective Idealism. However, his many apparently straightforward metaphysical descriptions of what reality is really like are integral to his accusations of the falsehood of Platonism, Christianity, scientific categories, and so on. Besides their frequency, these claims play too important a role in his overall thought to be dismissed. Without his R6 conception of the self as will to power, Nietzsche loses the criteria to generate values or evaluate perspectives; without his R2 correct depiction of reality as will to power, he cannot accuse Christianity of deception or praise the strong for their honesty.

Ultimately, I do not think either interpretation, subjective or objective idealism, Step Five or Step Six, holds for all of Nietzsche's oeuvre; he seems to alternate between the two strategies, and I have tried to show the presence of both views in his work. Some commentators have noted this ambiguity.

> Sometimes he seems to be a "demystifying" interpreter, one whose aim is to clear away symbols and masks and illusions in an attempt to get down to the true and solid reality of "things" [R1–R3]. At other times, he appears as a *re*-mystifier, as one who wants to say that there is no such thing as a thing—that every "thing" is only a mask for some other "thing," which in its turn will be seen to be only a mask as well [A1–A3]. (Megill 1985, 85, bracketed comments added; see also Rorty 1989, 105)

When Nietzsche claims an honest glimpse of the chaos that really exists which others falsify, he is employing the realist logic of true and false descriptions of reality. When he dispenses with the reality/appearance distinction on the other hand, then he is right to claim that he has "found the exit out of the labyrinth of thousands of years" (Nietzsche, *A* 1).

Contrary to the common impressions of Heidegger's reading of Nietzsche as simplistic, Heidegger sees these contradictory impulses in Nietzsche; that is, the impulse to make claims about reality in itself as chaos, as well as the denial of any kind of "non-subjective" metaphysics.[43] On the one hand, he approvingly quotes *The Gay Science* 374: "We cannot see around our own corner," jokingly calling it "mankind's Little-Jack-Horner essence." Here is Nietzsche's full original:

> *Our new "infinite."*—How far the perspective character of existence extends or indeed whether existence has any other character than this; whether [R1] existence without interpretation, without "sense," does not become "nonsense"; whether, on the other hand, all existence is not essentially actively engaged in *interpretation*—that cannot be decided

> even by the most industrious and most scrupulously conscientious analysis and self-examination of the intellect; for in the course of this analysis the human intellect cannot avoid seeing itself in its own perspectives, and *only* in these. We cannot look around our own corner. . . . We are at least far from the ridiculous immodesty that would be involved in decreeing from our corner that [R6] perspectives are permitted only from this corner. Rather has the world become "infinite" for us all over again, inasmuch as we cannot reject the possibility that *it may include infinite interpretations.* (Nietzsche, *GS* 374, bracketed comments added)

From my perspective, this is one of Nietzsche's best criticisms of Kant and an excellent statement of Step Six Physics. We cannot make a distinction between our contributions and the world's since we only ever experience an amalgamation, even in positing two separate sources. Nor can we rule out other perspectives, as Kant's R6 does. This passage even supplies a non-metaphysical way to read chaos as the idea that the world is indefinitely pliable to various interpretations, rather than possessing the specific characteristics of flux, violence, and so on.

Heidegger praises this strain in Nietzsche: "Nietzsche achieves waxing clarity concerning the fact that human beings always think within the confinements of their little 'corner' of the world, their tiny angle of space-time" (Heidegger, *N* 2:117). But he sees this strain as incompatible with the metaphysical thread in Nietzsche's work which imagines chaos as the remainder left over once our humanizing contributions have been removed.

> Hence the interpretation of the world's nature as a necessitous chaos is also impossible in the intended sense—namely in the sense that it would strip away all humanization. . . . The intention to put out of action all humanizing tendencies in our thoughts on the world's essence cannot endure side by side with acknowledgement of mankind's Little-Jack-Horner essence. If this particular intention is held to be practicable, then man would have to get a grip on the world's essence from a location outside of every corner; he would have to occupy something like a standpoint of standpointlessness[44]. . . . How does Nietzsche decide in this either/or? . . . Nietzsche decides for both—for the will to dehumanize being as a whole and also for the will to take seriously the human being as a creature of corners. (Heidegger, *N* 2:117–18)

Although Heidegger is often seen as offering a one-sided reading of Nietzsche, I find this interpretation quite nuanced and correct. Both strains can be found in Nietzsche, as I have tried to show. They don't seem to me to fall neatly into developmental stages, as Clark claims, though I grant that Step Six Physics doesn't appear until late.

Heidegger also ties these two views to Steps Five and Six of "How the 'True World' Finally Became a Fable." Step Five is still metaphysical since

> the vacant niche of the higher world remains, and so does the blueprint of an "above and below," which is to say, so does Platonism. The inquiry must go one step farther. . . . That Nietzsche appends a sixth division here shows that, and how, he must advance beyond himself and beyond sheer abolition of the supersensuous. (Heidegger, *N* 1:207–8)

Since Heidegger believes that "metaphysical thinking rests on the distinction between what truly is and what, measured against this, constitutes all that is not truly in being" (Heidegger, *N* 2:230; see also Heidegger, *Mi* 339), the only way to get beyond metaphysics is to dispense entirely with this distinction rather than merely overturn it. This is what Hegel's Objective Idealism accomplishes as well as Nietzsche's Step Six Physics, but unfortunately it is not consistently maintained. Despite his own sensitivity to the power of metaphors and the traps and confusions built into our language, it seems that Nietzsche is often seduced by his own metaphors. As Putnam says, "Referring to alternative conceptual schemes as 'perspectives,' of course, makes it sound as if there must be ways of describing the world as it is apart from the descriptions. This is just the disastrous Kantian error that we need to avoid" (Clark and Hale 1994, 291n25). Similarly, the metaphor of interpretations brings in the idea of the text that gets interpreted, masks imply an original face, and so on. We will see Derrida take on this issue directly in chapter 8. Regardless of Nietzsche's awareness of the problem and intentions to avoid it, I do not find his solution satisfactory. The Kantian way of framing the issues is strewn with conceptual traps; getting out from his shadow and escaping the problems of his position requires a profoundly different approach to these issues. Another revolution is needed.

## Conclusion

Like Hegel, Nietzsche develops a genuine alternative to the Kantian Paradigm, which I am calling Step Six Physics to emphasize its focus on the changing empirical world of experience (*physis*) rather than any kind of *meta-physis* realm. Unfortunately, this alternative exists in tension with the rest of his system, which is composed of active knowers (A5) who should consciously structure their experience in ontologically plural (A3) ways according to the criterion of pragmatic truth (A2), which itself rests on a slight realism of the subject as will to power (R6). Although he weakens R6 by making the self indeterminately multiple (unlike Hegel's collectable totality), this multiplicity emanates from a basic will to power, and the various instantiations are evaluated by how well they accord with this essence. This definition of the self plays a central role in his work in that it allows Nietzsche to make the judgments that pervade his work. Due to this and what certainly look like discussions of reality as will to power (R1), Nietzsche is not free of the Kantian Paradigm.

# Transition

# 5

# Early Heidegger: Fundamental Ontology

> This characteristic is not to be understood as merely a way of taking them, as if we were talking such "aspects" into the "entities" which we proximally encounter, or as if some world-stuff which is proximally present-at-hand in itself were "given subjective colouring" in this way. . . . *Readiness-to-hand is the way in which entities as they are "in-themselves" are defined ontologicol-categorially.* (Heidegger, *BT* 101/71)

> The most primordial and basic existential truth, for which the problematic of fundamental ontology strives in preparing the question of Being in general, is the *disclosedness of the meaning of the Being of care.* (Heidegger, *BT* 364/316)

As anyone who has fallen under its spell can attest, *Being and Time* is an astonishing work.[1] The first impression it makes is one of stunning originality; on further readings one sees that the book is equally a synthesis of ideas taken from a wide range of previous philosophers, primarily Husserl, Kierkegaard, Kant, Hegel, and Nietzsche. This realization increases the impression the book makes, since its synthesis of these disparate figures is so natural that the seams can only be detected on close inspection. The last three influences listed are the representatives of what I am calling the Kantian Paradigm, so it should come as no surprise that I read *Being and Time* as the culmination of this movement. Or rather, simultaneously the paradigm's highest point and its undermining; for although Heidegger's early work is still working within this system, it also lays the ground for its overcoming in his later work. Heidegger's *Kehre* or "turning" from his early to his later phase, which I will discuss in chapter 6, inaugurates a turn away from the Kantian Paradigm in the history of continental philosophy, which is why I describe Heidegger's early thought as the Transition point in my narrative.

The sense that something has been lost permeates *Being and Time.* Heidegger claims that Dasein, roughly his term for the structured awareness which he considers our defining feature, has become "alienated" so that it "*has lost itself,* and, in falling, 'lives' *away from itself*" (Heidegger, *BT* 223/179). We have become disconnected from the deep structure that defines us—"this alienation *closes off* from Dasein its authenticity" (222/178), or proper way of living—and the point of the book is to put us back in touch with the meaning of *our* Being in addition to the meaning of Being per se in order to recover a whole, "true" way of life.

The method employed is hermeneutic phenomenology, which depicts human inquiry as locked into "the hermeneutic circle" (Heidegger, *BT* 27/7). Heidegger responds to Meno's paradox—that is, the dilemma that inquiry is impossible since a completely ignorant inquirer would not recognize the answer if she came across it, while a knowledgeable inquirer would not need to inquire in the first place—by adapting Plato's solution of recollection: we have a "pre-ontological" understanding of Being, including our own way of Being, which orients all of our actions and thoughts at all times (32/12). This is a pre-theoretical, unthematic understanding that guides and gets expressed in our behavior, something like Ryle's concept of intelligence as knowing-how.[2] Like Plato's method of maieutics, though stripped of its metaphysical-mythical trappings, hermeneutic phenomenology works by reminding us of the experience we live in all the time and the wisdom contained therein. Although we are so to speak "primordially" familiar with these phenomena, conscious reflection tends to misconstrue, cover up, or disguise them. "*The entity which in every case we ourselves are, is ontologically that which is farthest.* . . . The ontology which is directed towards this entity is denied an appropriate basis. . . . The laying-bare of Dasein's primordial Being must rather be *wrested* from Dasein" (359/311; see also 61/36). And what is it that has covered over and disguised the primal phenomena of our daily life, consigning us to inauthenticity? In a word, realism.

## Realism

*Being and Time* as we have it (only one-third of what Heidegger originally planned to write was published) is largely an analysis of realism—its origins, limitations, dangers, and cure. Realism has inflicted philosophical trauma upon humanity for millennia, and it must be dismantled before we can reconnect with our selves to achieve authenticity. Since the book concerns Being, Heidegger gets at the issue by asking the question of the meaning of Being in a wholly new way. He admits that he has no idea how to ask such a bizarre question, much less how to answer it, so he first undertakes "the ontological task of a genealogy of the different possible ways of Being" (Heidegger, *BT* 31/11). In other words, he will approach what it means to be by examining the various ways there are to be. Of course, this approach already involves us in the hermeneutic circle, since we have to know what Being is even to identify the various ways of Being, but Heidegger views this circularity as enabling rather than disabling our investigations (see 27/7, 195/153, 362/314).

The first (and last and constant) thing to understand about Being is Heidegger's continual insistence on the ontological difference, i.e., that Being is not a being. A common and highly misleading interpretation of his thought is that Being is the great being in the sky, God, or the subject, or something like that, but it is the very key to his work that Heidegger is not thinking of Being as a thing at all. *Sein* is sometimes translated as "Be-ing" to stress the dynamic, temporal quality Heidegger emphasizes, meaning that ways of Be-ing are closer to ways that entities be-have than to properties they have. *Being and Time* outlines three modes of Being which are ways that individual entities can be: readiness-to-hand (sometimes translated as "availableness" or "handiness"), presence-at-hand (variously rendered as "occurrentness," "on-handness," or "extantness"), and existence.[3] Equipment, objects or things, and Dasein are then, respectively, the entities that *are* (read actively) in these different ways.

Realism is singled out by its exclusive focus on presence-at-hand as the sole mode of Being. It interprets all experience in terms of this one mode, which profoundly distorts our daily lives.

> The Being of what is proximally ready-to-hand gets passed over, and entities are first conceived as a context of Things (*res*) which are present-at-hand. "*Being*" acquires the meaning of "*Reality*." Substantiality becomes the basic characteristic of Being. . . . In this way "*Being in general*" acquires the meaning of "*Reality*.". . . The other modes of Being become defined negatively and privatively with regard to Reality. (Heidegger, *BT* 245/201)

Realism insists that only one kind of Being is real, while everything else gets relegated to bastard status (see Caputo 1983, 668; Frede in Donagan, Perovich, and Wedin 1986, 136).

### R3 Uniqueness

In his early work, Heidegger claims that realism arises for two very different kinds of reasons: it is endemic to Dasein's structure, and the history of philosophy gave rise to it. These two explanations are interrelated, of course: the reason that realism emerged in and persisted through history is because of our natural affinity for it. However, they are still heterogeneous kinds of explanations; in particular, the former essential argument makes realism seem inevitable, whereas the historical account renders it more contingent. According to the historical account, realism originates with the ancient Greeks and receives a boost from Descartes, who both gave it a powerful philosophical theory and integrated it into science. Scientific knowledge's need to be universal, certain, and unchanging made mathematics attractive; although this combination started as an epistemological criterion, it soon took on ontological significance (see Mensch 1996, 16, 29).

> Mathematical knowledge is regarded by Descartes as the one manner of apprehending entities which can always give assurance that their Being has been securely grasped. If anything measures up in its own kind of Being to the Being that is accessible in mathematical knowledge, then it *is* in the authentic sense. Such entities are those *which always are what they are.* Accordingly, that which can be shown to have the character of something that *constantly remains* . . . makes up the real Being of those entities of the world which get experienced. That which enduringly remains, really *is*. . . . His ontological orientation in principle [is] towards Being as constant presence-at-hand, which mathematical knowledge is exceptionally well suited to grasp. (Heidegger, *BT* 128–29/95–96; see also Heidegger, *IPR* 168, 230)

Descartes' conception of scientific knowledge requires aspects of reality which are constant across time, space, and observers so that results can be multiply verified.

> "Validity" means . . . the validity of the meaning of the judgment, which is valid of the "Object" it has in view; and thus it attains the signification of an "*Objectively valid character*" and of Objectivity in general. . . . The meaning which is thus "valid" *of* an entity, and which is valid "timelessly" in itself, is said to be "valid" also in the sense of being valid for *everyone who judges rationally.* "Validity" now means a *bindingness,* or "universally valid" character. (Heidegger, *BT* 198/156; see also Heidegger, *IPR* 188)

Universally discoverable features become the sole true facts, and only mathematical characteristics of present-at-hand objects meet this criterion, so science and scientific philosophy recognize nothing else as real. In science an "entity is admitted only insofar as it is determined by laws of motion which remain invariant, unaltered, always the same for every possible approach and regard" (Heidegger, *HCT* 218).

Descartes is so impressed by the security and power of this approach that he takes these features to define reality exhaustively.

> The idea of Being as permanent presence-at-hand not only gives Descartes a motive for identifying entities within-the-world with the world in general, and for providing so extreme a definition of their Being; it also keeps him from bringing Dasein's ways of behaving into view in a manner which is ontologically appropriate. . . . He takes the Being of "Dasein" (to whose basic constitution Being-in-the-world belongs) in the very same way as he takes the Being of the *res extensa*—namely as substance. (Heidegger, *BT* 130–31/98; see also 150/114–15; Heidegger, *IPR* 170)

The problem isn't the scientific description or analysis of presence-at-hand per se; Heidegger is not anti-science. The problem is scientism, the view that science gives us the whole and sole truth so that anything that cannot be captured in its terms gets discounted. There can only be one type of Being which will be the same for everyone, which means that variations such as the wax's changing empirical qualities or differing aesthetic qualities cannot be fully real or actually in the object. As John Richardson puts it, "Heidegger has no quarrel with the theoretical attitude in itself. But he thinks that it naturally tends to generalize itself in a certain way, and to take all Being as presence-at-hand, or to claim that this is the fundamental way in which entities 'really' are" (Richardson 1986, 51; see also 76). In Heidegger's terms, Descartes takes one mode of Being—presence-at-hand—to be the only one and so understands beings with different modes such as Dasein, equipment, and the world as present-at-hand objects (see Heidegger, *IPR* 217–19). These other entities get distorted when defined by this procrustean bed and, since Dasein is one of these misunderstood entities, we become alienated from ourselves.

### R1 Independence

One of the primary features of present-at-hand objects is that they are independent of us; they do not depend on the encounter with humans in order to be. Heidegger often discusses this in terms of the traditional definition of substance: "The Being of a 'substance' is characterized by not needing anything" (Heidegger, *BT* 125/92; see also Heidegger, *HCT* 172; Heidegger, *MFL* 32). He acknowledges how traditional this idea is: "It is customary to point out that the world is first there not on account of a subject, the world is rather '*in itself*'" (Heidegger, *HCT* 197; see also Heidegger, *MFL* 128–29). I will return to this below.

### R2 Correspondence

Once beings are viewed as present-at-hand objects, truth naturally becomes a matter of correctly corresponding to them. This conception of truth seems inevitable because

> the *logos* has been Interpreted in a way which is ontologically inadequate. . . . The *logos* gets experienced as something present-at-hand and Interpreted as such, while at the same time the entities which it points out have the meaning of presence-at-hand. This meaning of Being is left undifferentiated and uncontrasted with other possibilities of Being. (Heidegger, *BT* 203/160; see also 85–86/59; Heidegger, *MFL* 124)

Once again, the culprit is the interpretation of everything in terms of presence-at-hand. Once entities are seen as bare, inert objects, the only kind of relationship that language or thought can have with them is also an inert one of corresponding to them. "*The uncoveredness (truth) becomes, for its part, a relationship between things which are present-at-hand (intellectus and res)—a relationship that is present-at-hand itself*" (Heidegger, *BT* 267/225; see also Heidegger, *BP* 206–7; Heidegger, *TDP* 155).

### R4 Bivalence

And this static relationship can only be either correct or incorrect, true or false. Once again, the problem lies in the fact that "the traditional logic . . . has its foundation in an ontology of the present-at-hand. . . . So no matter in how many ways this logic may be improved and expanded, it cannot in principle be made any more flexible" (Heidegger, *BT* 166–67/129). This conception of the entitites involved predetermines the relations they can sensibly enter into. In the transitional essay (1930) "On the Essence of Truth," Heidegger defines the traditional conception of truth in terms of correspondence and bivalence.

> The formula for the essence of truth (*veritas est adaequatio intellectus et rei*) comes to have its general validity as something immediately evident to everyone. Under the domination of the obviousness that this concept of truth seems to have but that is hardly attended to as regards its essential grounds, it is considered equally obvious that truth has an opposite, and that there is untruth. The untruth of the proposition (incorrectness) is

> the nonaccordance of the statement with the matter. (Heidegger, *BW* 119; see also Heidegger, *FCM* 337–38)

### R5 Passive Knower

Interestingly, Heidegger agrees with traditional realism that our best mode of access to present-at-hand objects is as a disengaged observer: "When something present-at-hand has been uncovered, it is encountered most purely if we just look at the entity and let it be encountered in itself" (Heidegger, *BT* 309/264; see also Heidegger, *BP* 118). This is how the knowing relation has been understood since Parmenides: "Being is that which shows itself in the pure perception which belongs to beholding, and only by such seeing does Being get discovered. Primordial and genuine truth lies in pure beholding. This thesis has remained the foundation of western philosophy ever since" (Heidegger, *BT* 215/171).

Passive observation has long been considered the zenith of intellectual apprehension, as evinced, for instance, by Descartes' preparations for his *Meditations:* he reassures the reader that he has "expressly rid my mind of all worries and arranged for myself a clear stretch of free time" (Descartes, *PWD* 2:12), "fortunately having no cares or passions to trouble me" (1:116). Or we can look further back to the *Phaedo,* where Socrates decides that "surely the soul can best reflect when it is free of all distractions such as hearing or sight or pain or pleasure of any kind—that is, when it ignores the body and becomes as far as possible independent" (Plato, *Phaedo* 65c). This is particularly true because "the body provides us with innumerable distractions . . . loves and desires and fears and all sorts of fancies and a great deal of nonsense, with the result that we literally never get an opportunity to think at all about anything" (66b–c). In other words, any kind of practical engagement, emotional stirrings, or interests cloud the mirror of the mind. One can only conclude that "*scientific* knowing is characterized by the fact that the existing Dasein sets before itself, as a freely chosen task, the uncovering of the beings which are already somehow accessible, *for the sake of their being uncovered*. . . . Thus all those purposes of comportment are omitted which aim at employment of what is uncovered and known" (Heidegger, *PIK* 18–19). Heidegger initially follows the traditional contrast between practical dealing with and theoretical knowing of beings. Like Descartes' retiring to the leisure of his warm room,

> if knowing is to be possible as a way of determining the nature of the present-at-hand by observing it, then there must first be a *deficiency* in our having-to-do with the world concernfully. When concern holds back from any kind of producing, manipulating, and the like, it puts itself

> into what is now the sole remaining mode of Being-in, the mode of just tarrying alongside. . . . This kind of Being towards the world is one which lets us encounter entities within-the-world purely in the *way they look*. (Heidegger, *BT* 88/61; see also 200–201/158)

The restriction of practical engagement for the sake of mere looking reveals present-at-hand objects. Of course, for Heidegger, as we will see, these objects represent only one aspect of reality (A3), rather than all of or even the most important part of reality.

### R6 Realism of the Subject

This is Heidegger's primary criticism of realism in what we have of *Being and Time*. Traditional philosophy wrongly takes all beings to be present-at-hand objects, but defining Dasein this way is particularly alarming.

> Even if one rejects the "soul substance"[4] and the Thinghood of consciousness, or denies that a person is an object, ontologically one is still positing something whose Being retains the meaning of present-at-hand, whether it does so explicitly or not. Substantiality is the ontological clue for determining which entity is to provide the answer to the question of the "who." Dasein is tacitly conceived in advance as something present-at-hand. . . . Yet presence-at-hand is the kind of Being which belongs to entities whose character is not that of Dasein. (Heidegger, *BT* 150/114–15)

This category mistake is Heidegger's frequent charge against previous thinkers, including Kant, as we have seen. "If we posit an 'I' or subject as that which is proximally given, we shall completely miss the phenomenal content of Dasein. *Ontologically*, every idea of a 'subject'—unless refined by a previous ontological determination of its basic character—still posits the *subjectum*" (Heidegger, *BT* 72/46). Although it has historical roots (41/20), the tendency toward this misunderstanding is embedded in our nature: "In understanding its own Being, it has a tendency to do so in terms of that entity towards which it comports itself proximally and in a way which is essentially constant—in terms of the 'world' " (36/15; see also 42/21, 245/201).

The picture of a substantial subject separate from the world is what gives rise to traditional epistemology, especially the question of how to get outside of our heads to establish contact with the external world. The central goal of *Being and Time* as we have it is to offer a new understanding of our nature, one which is more accurate and which will undermine or dissolve all of the insoluble pseudo-problems thrown up by the misunderstandings of the history of philosophy, and that will thus allow us to become who we are.

## Anti-Realism

### A3 Ontological Pluralism

Realism forces all beings into a single way of Being (R3) which creates an inappropriate and alienating conception of ourselves. Hence, the "ontological task of a genealogy of the *different possible ways* of Being" (Heidegger, *BT* 31/11, italics added) will open up new understandings of Being that will allow us to construct a superior conception of our Being.

> The concept of Reality [that is, presence-at-hand] has a peculiar priority in the ontological problematic. By this priority the route to a genuine existential analytic of Dasein gets diverted, and so too does our very view of the Being of what is proximally ready-to-hand within-the-world. It finally forces the general problematic of Being into a direction that lies off the course. The other modes of Being become defined negatively and privatively with regard to Reality. Thus not only the analytic of Dasein but the working-out of the question of the meaning of Being in general must be turned away from a [R3] one-sided orientation with regard to Being in the sense of Reality. We must demonstrate that [A3] Reality is . . . only *one* kind of Being *among* others. (Heidegger, *BT* 245/201, bracketed comments added)

Heidegger wants to show, against realism's exclusive focus on the present-at-hand, that "among the modes of Being of entities within-the-world, Reality has no priority, and that Reality is a kind of Being which cannot even characterize anything like the world or Dasein in a way which is ontologically appropriate" (Heidegger, *BT* 254–55/211). We must come to understand that Dasein's way of Being is fundamentally distinct from presence-at-hand ("extantness"), which thus disrupts its claim to ubiquity: "If the being of the subject should reveal itself as other than extantness, then a fundamental limit would be set to the hitherto prevailing [R3] equation of being with actuality, or extantness, and thus to ancient ontology" (Heidegger, *BP* 125, bracketed comment added). Grasping our own mode of Be-ing can then enable us to be it or to become authentic.

*Being and Time* describes the three fundamentally different modes of Being as "equi-primordial," which means that they cannot be derived from or reduced to one another. Presence-at-hand characterizes the bare, inert objects that philosophical and scientific theory study; they are the substances that underlie change and possess constant, objective qualities. Readiness-to-hand or equipmentality, on the other hand, is the most common mode we encounter in our daily lives. It denotes the way the entities we use for various purposes all the time fit into chains of means and ends and tend to dissolve inconspicuously into these chains during use. Their significance is holistically determined by their position in their overall network of references so that, for example, a pen's significance lies in its relationships to paper, desks, and jobs that require writing. Heidegger calls the coherent totality of all of these chains anchored on and organized by the jobs and roles we take on "world" or "worldhood." Dasein lives "in" this world the way that one is "in" love or "in" a family; rather than spatial containment, this is a relationship of involvement and constitution. Dasein exists by taking herself to be a certain sort of person, for example, a professor. In order to fulfill this role, she must use certain tools (computers, offices, chalk, books) in certain ways and interact with others (students, administrators, colleagues) in certain ways. Most roles require both the Dasein to take herself to be that role and others to take her to be it, or at least participate somehow; one cannot be a professor unconsciously or without the proper institutions, nor without students taking one to be a professor or in a society without an educational system. All of these factors and many more collectively make up one's world and are needed if one is to be that kind of person. In all of these ways, Heidegger is an "externalist" about subjectivity and meaning.

Heidegger's strategy is to show that the other two modes of Being cannot be derived from or explained by present-at-hand objects. "The sense of worldhood can *not* be read off from mere nature. The environmental references, in which nature is present primarily in a worldly way, tell us rather the reverse: *nature as reality can only be understood on the basis of worldhood*" (Heidegger, *HCT* 199). Realism's insistence on the dominance of presence-at-hand downgrades or dismisses all other features as mere subjective projections: "If one is oriented primarily by Thinghood, these latter qualities [like beautiful or useful] must be taken as non-quantifiable value-predicates by which what is in the first instance just a material Thing, gets stamped" (Heidegger, *BT* 132/99, bracketed comment added; see also 141/106). This theoretical perspective acts as a blinder, sheering off the richness of our normal experience and relegating these features to the dustbin of subjectivity. According to realism, what is variable is subjective, what is subjective is not fully real or true, and therefore should be ignored by serious endeavors to know the world. Reality must be built entirely out of universally valid, self-identical blocks; whatever doesn't fit this model must be downgraded to a lesser form of reality and should not form the basis of knowledge.

The problem is that by this criterion, the vast majority of what makes up our daily experience and self-understanding gets screened out so that our theoretical reconstructions of ourselves and our world become profoundly divorced from our mundane experience.

> One tries to conceive the relationship between world and soul as grounded in these two entities themselves and in the meaning of their Being—namely, to conceive it as Being-present-at-hand. And even though Being-in-the world is something of which one has pre-phenomenological experience and acquaintance, it becomes *invisible* if one interprets it in a way which is ontologically inappropriate. (Heidegger, *BT* 86/59)

Heidegger's solution, similar to later Wittgenstein's (see *PI* §66, §112, §340), is to remind us of what we already know by giving a detailed phenomenological description of those features of our daily experience that get covered up or ignored by theoretical explanations.

> That wherein Dasein already understands itself in this way is always something with which it is primordially familiar. This familiarity with the world does not necessarily require that the relations which are constitutive for the world as world should be theoretically transparent. However, the possibility of giving these relations an explicit ontologico-existential Interpretation, is grounded in this familiarity with the world. . . . This possibility is one which can be seized upon explicitly in so far as Dasein has set itself the task of giving a primordial Interpretation for its own Being and for the possibilities of that Being, or indeed for the meaning of Being in general. (Heidegger, *BT* 119/86)

We live these relations knowingly, and phenomenology dredges up this pre-theoretical grasp of the world in order to undo or "destroy" the traditional realist interpretations that have covered it over.

One of the things we discover in this pre-theoretical experience is that beings have many ways to be (A3). In particular, we ourselves exist in a fundamentally different way than substances: we are temporally stretched out, free (in some sense), self-interpreting, purposive, and so on, none of which can be accounted for in terms of substances. "It has to be shown that the mode of being of human Dasein is totally different from that of all other entities" (in Husserl 1997, 138). This ontological pluralism could be explained as a simple dichotomy, however—those entities which are Dasein have one mode of Being, non-Dasein another. Heidegger goes farther, however, to state that one and the same entity can be in different ways. When a pen is being used to write, inconspicuously withdrawing from attention, it is in the mode of ready-to-hand. On the other hand, if it runs out of ink and draws attention to itself as a useless thing to be stared at, it changes over to present-at-hand.[5] Which is the real pen? Heidegger's position is that this is a bad question; entities simply can be in more than one way. "Beings have stages of discoverability, diverse possibilities in which they manifest themselves in themselves. There are diverse stages—and one cannot say that, for example, physics has the genuine knowledge of the solar sphere, in contrast to our natural grasp of the sun" (Heidegger, *MFL* 167; see also Heidegger, *HCT* 38; Heidegger, *BP* 68). The demand that things must *really* be only one way (R3) is a realist prejudice, an assumption that becomes self-confirming by filtering out all disconfirming experience. Actual attention to our experience suggests openness to widely disparate ways of Being: "Even in a rough analysis a multiplicity of intrinsically founded levels of being are manifested within the being of things and of equipment alone" (Heidegger, *BP* 305).

Present-at-hand objects are real—he's not overcompensating by denying them—but they only represent one type of Being; science is true, but only one kind of truth. Heidegger inherits from Husserl the project of regional ontology, that is, the description of the various kinds or "regions" of beings that respects their differences without reducing them to a single kind. Although presence-at-hand is a distortive category when applied to other types of beings (or beings in certain situations), it is perfectly appropriate within its own region (see an interesting discussion at Heidegger, *OHF* 70). The problem isn't that presence-at-hand is false or inapplicable full stop, but that it is limited, while philosophers apply it to everything that is. "Descartes' discussion of possible kinds of *access* to entities within-the-world is dominated by an idea of Being which has been gathered from a definite realm of these entities themselves" (Heidegger, *BT* 130/97; see also Heidegger, *HCT* 219). Just as Nietzsche acknowledges asceticism's benefits, objecting primarily to its presumption to be the only way, so Heidegger criticizes metaphysics' exclusive employment of one mode of Being, which perpetuates itself by blinding us to other modes.

Since, as we will see, an entity's mode of Being depends on our attitude toward it, entities can possess different qualities for different observers, violating R3 Uniqueness even for an individual entity, as well as science's ambition for universal validity. For Heidegger, though, this demand for uniqueness is a contingent historical occurrence which we do not have to agree to.

> The original sense of this concept of truth does not yet include objectivity as universal validity, universal binding force. That has nothing to do

> with truth. . . . Something can indeed be true which is not binding for everyone but only for a single individual. At the same time, in this concept of truth, truth as uncovering, it is not yet prejudged that genuine uncovering has to be by necessity theoretical knowledge or a determinate possibility of theoretical knowledge. (Heidegger, *PlS* 17)

Even within a single mode of Being, ready-to-hand tools offer multiple perspectives. Since they are defined by their context of referential significance, that is, their position in the network of instrumental relations which ultimately depends on our roles, a tool can change character as our roles change. A flat tire will be very different to a professor trying to get to work than to a mechanic, being an obstacle to work for one but work itself to the other. Rather than rejecting this instability as evidence of subjectivity and unreality, Heidegger wants us to accept it as the fully legitimate nature of this mode of Being.

> It is precisely when we see the "world" unsteadily and fitfully in accordance with our moods, that the ready-to-hand shows itself in its specific worldhood, which is never the same from day to day. By looking at the world theoretically, we have already dimmed it down to the uniformity of what is purely present-at-hand, though admittedly this uniformity comprises a new abundance of things which can be discovered by simply characterizing them. (Heidegger, *BT* 177/138; see also 141/106)

Presence-at-hand is itself a legitimate perspective which reveals real beings, but it denies the reality of the ready-to-hand tools that it covers over in its ontological Gestalt switch.[6]

## A5 Active Knower

*Being and Time* pursues the inquiry into the meaning of Being by means of "fundamental ontology," so called because it will provide the foundation for ontology as a whole. Our appropriate interactions with different kinds of beings (that is, the fact that we deal with tools differently from people and generally don't confuse the two) show that we possess a pre-ontological (or tacit) understanding of Being. Hence, Heidegger takes his orientation from the analysis of one specific kind of being—ourselves or Dasein—because it has and continually expresses a grasp of the meaning of the modes of Being: "*Fundamental ontology,* from which alone all other ontologies can take their rise, must be sought in the *existential analytic of Dasein.*"[7] If we are looking for this strange thing that we don't even know how to look for—an understanding of Being—and we know that it occurs in Dasein's behavior, then that is what we should study.

As I will discuss in some detail further below (in the section "A1 Dependence"), Heidegger makes his commitment to epistemic truth fairly clear: "If we are inquiring about the meaning of Being, our investigation does not then become a 'deep' one, nor does it puzzle out what stands behind Being. It asks about Being itself in so far as Being enters into the intelligibility of Dasein" (Heidegger, *BT* 193/152). Being can only be meaningful to an understanding entity, so, in true anti-realist fashion, the question of the meaning of Being asks about Being insofar as it is in principle accessible to human awareness. Whatever conditions Dasein's understanding of Being conditions Being and all beings insofar as they are experienced by Dasein, and thus insofar as they can be objects of study, knowledge, discussion, and so on. To briefly anticipate the argument, without noumena, the experienced realm that is affected by Dasein is reality itself; hence our effects on it are not distortive but constitutive, and must be studied in order to understand the world. This is another reason why the analysis of Dasein must form the foundation of all ontology—because beings get their characteristics from Dasein's organizing features (A5). "Since the being of the world becomes comprehensible in the encounter, the understanding of the entity in itself is as such revealed *only in a radical interpretation of Dasein*" (Heidegger, *HCT* 218). Heidegger ultimately concludes that since Dasein's essence is temporality, our understanding of Being and therefore all beings' ways of Being must be temporal as well. He states the argument succinctly in a lecture course from 1927: "If Dasein harbors the understanding of being within itself, and if temporality makes possible the Dasein in its ontological constitution, then *temporality* must also be the *condition of the possibility* of the *understanding of being*."[8]

What is striking about this argument which forms the organizing core of *Being and Time* as we have it (though the unwritten third division of the book would have "reversed" it somehow) is just how Kantian it is, even down to the phrase "condition of the possibility." Like Kant, Heidegger approaches ontology via the way the subject actively organizes phenomena. Although Heidegger radically redefines both subject and phenomena, there is a strong continuity with Kant's thought, as he himself recognizes:

> The direction of the path [Kant] follows, by returning to the subject in its broadest sense, is the only one that is possible and correct. It is the direction of the interpretation of being, actuality, existence that was followed not just by modern philosophy since Descartes, by expressly orienting its philosophical problems to the subject . . . or toward what is basically meant by it, namely, our Dasein. (Heidegger, *BP* 73; see also 155)

The strategy is right, he thinks, just carried out poorly by previous philosophers. Phenomenology allows Heidegger to examine Being through the prism of Dasein's understanding in a full, unprejudiced way (to put it simplistically). Somewhat like Hegel, Heidegger considers his early work to be a "radicalization" of Kant's project.

> If we radicalize the Kantian problem of ontological knowledge in the sense that we do not limit this problem to the ontological foundation of the positive sciences and if we do not take this problem as a problem of judgment but as the radical and fundamental question concerning the possibility of understanding being in general, then we shall arrive at the philosophically fundamental problematic of *Being and Time*.[9]

Despite the differences, credit is given to Kant who, "for the first time, came upon this primordial productivity of the 'subject'" (Heidegger, *MFL* 210); in other words, Kant discovered A5 Active Knower. In a 1927 letter to Husserl, Heidegger is quite explicit about how important this issue is to his book: "What is the mode of being of the entity in which 'world' [in Husserl's sense] is constituted? That is *Being and Time*'s central problem—namely, a fundamental ontology of Dasein. . . . As the mode of being that it is, it harbors right within itself the possibility of transcendental constitution" (Husserl 1997, 138, bracketed comment added). Obviously, Heidegger is making some concessions to Husserl's terminology here, but the connection to Kant is consistent with his other works.

One of the ways that Heidegger radicalizes Kant is by showing the "subject" to be active in multiple ways rather than limiting it to theoretical knowing (see Heidegger, *PIK* 136). We are doers before we are knowers, and our theoretical activity is parasitic upon our practical activity. Initially and for the most part, Dasein exists in the mode of concerned interaction.

> In thus being preoccupied with the world, Dasein always already finds its world, and this finding is not theoretical apprehension. *The "already-being-involved-with" is care in being concerned.* As concerned preoccupation with the world Dasein lets itself *encounter* its world. Concern as the basic mode of Dasein permits encounter. . . . All knowing, which as a mode of being of concern is built upon concern, merely *lays out, interprets* the disclosed world and happens on the basis of concern. (Heidegger, *HCT* 168; see also 185)

It is our care about who we are that motivates us to choose a role (professor, father, friend) to attempt to settle the issue of our Being, which in turn, like a magnet dropped onto a plate of iron filings, organizes the world into interrelated groups of tools and people that have determinate functions within our projects. Care is what reveals a meaningful world to us in the first place, and everything we experience must find its place within this practically structured world, including purportedly autonomous theory. "Knowing is a mode of Dasein founded upon Being-in-the-world" (Heidegger, *BT* 90/62; see also 409/358).

In order to minimize presuppositions, Heidegger starts by examining Dasein in its "average everydayness," that is, what we are like most of the time. Picking an exceptional state such as theoretical knowing as our topic of study requires a justification of that choice, which then pushes the inquiry back to the examination of those supporting arguments, and so on. In order to avoid as much of that as possible (similar to the way Hegel begins), Heidegger just looks at our normal mundane living, where he finds that

> the kind of dealing which is closest to us is as we have shown, not a bare perceptual cognition, but rather that kind of concern which manipulates things and puts them to use. . . . Such entities are not thereby objects for knowing the "world" theoretically; they are simply what gets used, what gets produced, and so forth. (Heidegger, *BT* 95/67; see also Heidegger, *HCT* 30)

These entities are the ready-to-hand tools we are constantly using without paying explicit attention to. It is essential to Heidegger's project to take them as they present themselves and not interpret them in present-at-hand terms, as we are wont to do when we think about them.

> This is the way in which everyday Dasein always *is:* when I open the door, for instance, I use the latch. The achieving of phenomenological access to the entities which we encounter, consists rather in thrusting aside our interpretive tendencies, which keep thrusting themselves upon us and running along with us, and which conceal not only the phenomenon of such "concern," but even more those entities themselves *as* encountered of their own accord *in* our concern with them. . . . In addressing these entities as "Things" (*res*), we have tacitly anticipated their ontological character. When analysis starts with such entities and goes on to inquire about Being, what it meets is Thinghood and Reality. (Heidegger, *BT* 96/67–68)

It is when we have assumed this theoretical state (similar to Dewey's spectator theory of knowledge) that we find the highly distortive picture of ourselves as primarily knowers facing bare substances plausible, and then are baffled by the epistemological problems that arise from this picture. Heidegger wants to short-circuit these problems by putting us back in touch with a more accurate picture of our Being-in-the-world as practical dealing or concern.

If it is so unlike our actual experience, then where does this present-at-hand ontology come from and why does it press upon us so insistently? "Why does natural Dasein, in the elucidation of the world in which it is, simply *pass over* the environing world? Why, in the categorical characterization of the being of the world, does it always already apply developed categories like thingness as *the* basic determinations?" (Heidegger, *HCT* 219). Heidegger has two answers to this question. One is a narrative of the history of philosophy which was to be the second part of *Being and Time* and of which we have chunks in his contemporary lecture series. This kind of history takes center stage in his later work for important reasons, however, and I will discuss it at length in the next chapter.

Another reason we fall into present-at-hand ontology has to do with the ready-to-hand's inconspicuousness.[10] "The ready-to-hand is not grasped theoretically at all. . . . The peculiarity of what is proximally ready-to-hand is that, in its readiness-to-hand, it must, as it were, withdraw in order to be ready-to-hand quite authentically" (Heidegger, *BT* 99/69). When we are working on a task, we rarely pay conscious attention to the tool we use. We think about the goal, or the next step, or something altogether unrelated: "The tool thus becomes absorbed in the reference" (Heidegger, *HCT* 191). We only pay attention to the tool when it breaks down, malfunctions, or is missing, thus becoming conspicuous. At this point we see it thematically, but as a present-at-hand object; the fluid network of instrumental assignments (that is, the worldhood of the world) has hardened, cracked, and dried up, leaving just bare things. In an early lecture, Heidegger says that when this happens, "the 'it worlds' has already been extinguished. The thing is merely there as such, i.e., it is real, it exists. . . . It is a specifically theoretical characteristic. The meaningful is de-interpreted into this residue of being real. Experience of the environment is de-vivified into the residue of recognizing something as real" (Heidegger, *TDP* 75).

Our experience of ready-to-hand equipment is primary and most common. "To lay bare what is just present-at-hand and no more, cognition must first penetrate *beyond* what is ready-to-hand in our concern" (Heidegger, *BT* 101/71), a process he sometimes calls "unworlding" (Heidegger, *HCT* 219; see also Heidegger, *BT* 147/112). Although the world is our natural and virtually constant environment, unworlding comes easily because it has its roots in our attempts to pay attention to inconspicuous equipment; for instance, when tools break and so show up as present-at-hand things. Constructing hypotheses in philosophy or science, as conscious thinking, takes place completely within this horizon of presence-at-hand, so that recapturing the experience of readiness-to-hand becomes very difficult. Theorizing about the ready-to-hand is a self-defeating enterprise, like trying to see the inside of a refrigerator with the light off: the very attempt to accomplish it prevents it. "Thematical perception of Things is precisely not the way equipment ready-to-hand is encountered in its 'true "in-itself"'; it is encountered rather in the inconspicuousness of what we can come across 'obviously' and 'Objectively'" (Heidegger, *BT* 405/354). Equipment is really inconspicuous readiness-to-hand, but it is hard to see and talk about while in this mode; conspicuous present-at-hand objects, on the other hand (excuse the pun), are easy to see and talk about, but that is not how equipment really is.

> Why is it that what we are talking about—the heavy hammer—shows itself differently when our way of talking is thus modified? . . . Because we are looking *at* the ready-to-hand thing which we encounter, and looking at it "in a new way" as something present-at-hand. *The understanding of Being* by which our concernful dealings with entities within-the-world have been guided *has changed over.* (Heidegger, *BT* 412/361)

This explains why the vast majority of metaphysical systems have been realist: theoretical looking naturally finds present-at-hand objects which give rise to a realist philosophy.

But the point is that theory *finds* present-at-hand objects because it *forms* them. In his early phase, Heidegger is committed to a Kantian-style A5 Active Knower: Dasein, specifically Dasein's temporality, is responsible for specific features of Being and thus of beings. Heidegger himself compares the modes of Being or "the *Being* of entities" (Heidegger, *BT* 59/35) that phenomenology seeks to Kant's forms of intuition (54–55/31). He has taken from Hegel and Nietzsche's criticisms of Kant the lesson that there is a plurality of conceptual schemes (A3) and thus of ways for beings to be; non-Dasein entities can be either present-at-hand or ready-to-hand. But what determines which mode they are in is how Dasein approaches them, or what Heidegger sometimes calls Dasein's "projecting" or "projecting a being on its Being."

Heidegger explicitly ties Dasein's different ways of projecting to the two modes of non-Dasein Being. One way to project is scientific "thematizing" where the "aim is to free the entities we encounter within-the-world, and to free them in such a way that they can 'throw themselves against' a pure discovering—that is, that they can become 'Objects.' Thematizing Objectifies" (Heidegger, *BT* 414/363). On the other hand, if I become preoccupied with something else while using a pen and let it fade from conscious awareness, then I make it ready-to-hand. Of course, the pen has to cooperate, writing roles must be available within my society, and so on, but it is still my action that gives it its ontological character. "What determines an entity as such ready-to-hand equipment, then, is that we have adopted a certain attitude or relationship to it" (Richardson 1986, 17; see also 19). If I then stop writing and stare at the pen, letting its usefulness and emotional resonances fade out, I have rendered it present-at-hand. As Guignon says, "Our projections determine the Being of entities" (Guignon 1983, 201; see also Versényi 1965, 27; Pöggeler 1970, 293). Placing at least some control over conceptual assignment, as well as focusing on the basic dichotomy between temporal and non-temporal categories, are two distinctly Nietzschean elements in Heidegger's early thought.

From Hegel, Heidegger learns to incorporate a degree of historical flux into our nature (see Gadamer 1976b, 48–49). Although the three fundamental modes of Being outlined in *Being and Time* appear to be the permanent modes of Being, the more specific features of equipment vary from society to society and period to period as the roles and projects change. To cite an example from the secondary literature, although a sword might remain the same physical entity, it simply cannot enjoy the same place within a network of self-defining equipment and roles when placed in a museum case for me as it did in the hands of a twelfth-century samurai. Also with Hegel and against Nietzsche, Heidegger sees these categories as permeating an entire society. There is little rhetoric of the strong mastering their concepts and breaking through ascetic stability to face raw chaos in early Heidegger; everyone lives in the same temporal, dynamic modes of Dasein and ready-to-hand while frequently thinking in the mode of present-at-hand. A touch of Nietzschean elitism does remain in Heidegger's praise of phenomenology's perceptive powers and the occasional hint that authenticity itself rests on an accurate understanding of Dasein's mode of Being.

## A1 Phenomenological Ontology

Heidegger follows Hegel and Nietzsche in rejecting noumena. Like them, he condemns most of traditional metaphysics and Kant for employing the notion of reality in itself (R1) which automatically relegates experience to a lesser degree of reality. "We must adhere to this genuine sense of *phainomenon* employed by the Greeks. But we must also see that at first it has absolutely nothing to do with our term '*appearance*' or still less '*mere appear-*

*ance*.' Probably no word has caused as much havoc and confusion in philosophy as this one" (Heidegger, *HCT* 81). In a discussion which amounts to a summary of the first half of Nietzsche's "How the 'True World' Finally Became a Fable," Heidegger recounts how appearance turns into *mere* appearance, culminating in the complete separation of appearance and reality, or what I quoted McCumber refering to as "the Kantian *chōrismos*": "If we now take this degraded entity, the appearance versus the essence in this sense of mere appearance, then this mere appearance is called semblance. Confusion is then carried to extremes. But traditional epistemology and metaphysics live off this confusion" (Heidegger, *HCT* 83; see also Heidegger, *IPR* 33). Once again philosophy's problems originate from a set of presuppositions whose removal would keep these *aporiai* from arising, and thus dissolve rather than solve the problems. "The concept of 'thing in itself' and all the absurd problems related to it die away in the thoroughgoing critique and restriction of the realm of validity of the ancient concept of being and of the metaphysics which is determined by this concept, from the ancients up to and beyond Kant" (Heidegger, *PIK* 69). Heidegger's "destruction of the tradition" is meant to dismantle these presuppositions in order to clear the ground for an entirely new epistemology and metaphysics, which would be simultaneously the oldest and the most familiar.

Hegel's profoundly new Objective Idealism resulted from showing that all metaphysical systems committed to anything like noumena fall apart due to their internal incoherence, while Nietzsche justified Step Six Physics by uncovering the unhealthy psychological/physiological motivations of belief in noumena, as well as the harm it does. Having been trained in phenomenology, Heidegger enjoys the distinct advantage of beginning his career virtually free of noumenal baggage. Husserl describes his school of thought in terms rather similar to Objective Idealism in the article he "coauthored" with Heidegger for the 1927 edition of *Encyclopaedia Britannica:*

> In the systematic work of phenomenology . . . the old traditional ambiguous antitheses of the philosophical standpoint are resolved—by themselves. . . . *Subjectivism* can only be overcome by the most all-embracing and consistent subjectivism (the transcendental). In this [latter] form it is at the same time objecticism [of a deeper sort], in that it represents the claims of whatever objectivity is to be demonstrated through concordant experience, but admittedly [this is an objectivism which] also brings out its full and genuine sense, against which [sense] the supposedly realistic objectivism sins by its failure to understand transcendental constitution. (Welton 1999, 334, all bracketed comments in original)

As in Objective Idealism, we reach a new realism by working all the way through subjectivism to grasp the "counter-sense" of the idea of an object that is in principle cut off from experience (see Welton 1999, 328; Husserl 1982, §47).

The starting point of phenomenology, as shown by its name, is to suspend or "bracket" speculation about what the world might be like independently of us and just study the world as it appears to us, that is, phenomena; hence Heidegger decrees that "philosophical research . . . deals with phenomena and only with phenomena" (Heidegger, *HCT* 85). Like Putnam's internal realism, phenomenology gives up the age-old quest for a God's-eye view of reality; Kant's positive sense of noumena depends on this concept of intellectual or absolute intuition being coherent even if inaccessible to us, but phenomenology dismisses it out of hand, thus allowing no conceptual space for any other realm. And, as we have seen in our discussions of Hegel and Nietzsche, removing one partner of such a dyad fundamentally changes the other's meaning.

> Along with the assumption of an absolute intuition . . . the concept of a thing in itself also dies away. But things do not thereby vanish into phantoms and images—phantoms and images which we produce for ourselves. For *appearances are the things themselves,* and they are the things that they are without these things having to be thought as things in themselves on the basis of an untenable concept of being and on the basis of the assumption of a representing God. (Heidegger, *PIK* 68–69, italics added; see also Heidegger, *MFL* 164, 198)

Heidegger is not just removing noumena while leaving Kantian phenomena in place or performing some kind of simple reversal, as he accuses Nietzsche of doing; the elimination of noumena fundamentally redefines Being. Much of his work is an exploration of the ramifications of this profound change.

Discussion of entities that are separated from contact with us in principle is not just unproductive (Nietzsche's Step Five), but incoherent (Step Six).

> It is phenomenologically absurd to speak of the phenomenon as if it were something behind which there would be something else of which it would be a phenomenon. . . . One cannot ask for something behind the phenomenon at all, since what the phenomenon gives is precisely that something in itself. (Heidegger, *HCT* 86; see also 81; Heidegger, *BT* 51–55/28–31)

Here Heidegger is using Kant's terminology against itself. Whereas Kant defines phenomena precisely in contrast to things-in-themselves, Heidegger rejects this dichotomy, so that what appears should be called reality without qualification.

> We are not simply taking over unaltered the concept of the transcendental in Kant, although we are indeed adopting its original sense and its true tendency, perhaps still concealed from Kant. We are surmounting beings in order to reach being. Once having made the ascent we shall not again descend to a being, which, say, might lie like another world behind the familiar beings. The transcendental science of being has nothing to do with popular metaphysics, which deals with some being behind the known beings. (Heidegger, *BP* 17; see also Heidegger, *BT* 60/36)

Heidegger's most basic tenets entail this rejection of noumena. His definition of Being as the presencing[11] of that which is present (which represents his "granite of spiritual *fatum*," in Nietzsche's term)[12] on the one hand, and the identification of beings with the totality of that which presents itself on the other, are flip sides of the same coin. Starting from this definition of Being, it is virtually tautological that anything that in principle cannot present itself to us cannot be considered real, while whatever is present to us has real Being without needing an absent Idea, God, or noumenon for support. Going in the other direction, once we reject noumena, the realm of beings left is coextensive with the realm of phenomena or what shows itself to us. "*The question of being is thus raised, it is even answered.* We have to do solely with the genuinely *scientific way of answering it,* which attempts to define the sense of the reality of something real insofar as it manifests itself in consciousness."[13] The raising of the question of Being guides its own answer, since the only way we can possibly investigate it is by appealing to evidence that is in principle available to the inquirer. The only Being we can talk and think about is not evidence- or experience-transcendent. Thus, the meaning of the Being of beings is ultimately whatever is involved in becoming present to Dasein, or what he calls "presence within the clearing."

This view represents Heidegger's early theory of Being, which I will call Phenomenological Ontology (PO). It represents his counterpart to Hegel's Objective Idealism and Nietzsche's Step Six Physics; that is, the strain of his thought that has surpassed the Kantian Paradigm and twisted free of meta-physics by rejecting even the coherence of a realm inaccessible to human experience. What we experience is what is real, with no need or possibility to posit something behind or beyond, below or above it. "Appearance as appearance or object does not need at all still to *correspond* to something actual, because appearance itself *is* the actual" (Heidegger, *PIK* 69). Like Hegel, Heidegger does not hesitate to call what Dasein experiences objective, real, or even the in-itself since, with nothing further to reality, the for-us *is* the in-itself. "The phenomenological research which breaks through to objectivity arrives at the form of research sought by ancient ontology. There is no ontology *alongside* a phenomenology. Rather, *scientific ontology is nothing but phenomenology*" (Heidegger, *HCT* 72, italics in original; see also Heidegger, *IPR* 200–202). Merleau-Ponty makes the same point nicely when he says, "We must not, therefore, wonder whether we really perceive a world, we must instead say: the world is what we perceive" (Merleau-Ponty 1962, xvi). By saying that "philosophy is universal phenomenological ontology" (*BT* 62/38; see also 60/35), Heidegger means two things. First, philosophy is the study of "the Being of entities, its meaning, its modifications and derivatives" (60/35). He calls these the categories and existentialia, that is, the modes in which entities are, all ultimately rooted in temporality and which Heidegger compares to Kant's forms of intuition (55/31).

Second, he means that, like all disciplines, philosophy studies that which is, and it can only do this by studying what presents itself to us, that is, what we can become aware of.[14] These are the phenomena which Heidegger equates with beings as a whole. Heidegger vastly expands the ways phenomena can be present to us, but ultimately they must enter the "clearing" of our awareness in order for us to be able to say that and what they are, not for the trivial reason that otherwise we wouldn't be able to *say* it, but because otherwise it would not be *intelligible* to say. As Theodore R. Schatzki puts it, Heidegger "would side with Hegel against Kant and claim that, since Kant attributes existence to the thing in itself, the Kantian conception of the thing in itself is a conception of a way things are for us and not a conception of how things are independently of any way they are for us" (Dreyfus and Hall 1992, 96). In other words, "both of them, subjectivity as well as objectivity, are certainly thoughts" (Hegel, *HL* 255, §192R). Phenomenological Ontology explains why Heidegger repeatedly rejects the subject-object and realism-idealism distinctions as traditionally conceived: "Only with the aid of a radical interpretation of the subject can an ungenuine subjectivism be avoided and equally a blind realism."[15] There is no independent reality to get formed by us upon contact, as in the scheme-content division Davidson criticizes; Heidegger rejects the idea of unformed matter "as if some world-stuff which is proximally present-at-hand in itself were 'given subjective colouring'" (Heidegger, *BT* 101/71). Instead, the world is Dasein-dependent all the way down, removing the problems of the content-scheme structure. I will now show in turn how Heidegger considers Being, ready-to-hand tools, and present-at-hand objects to be each A1 Dasein-Dependent.

### Being

In Heidegger's sense, the idea that Being needs Dasein is uncontroversial, even obvious: presencing requires someone to whom or a site in which to be present; meaning needs an understanding to be meaningful to. "Of course only as long as Dasein *is* (that is, only as long as an understanding of Being is ontically possible), 'is there' Being" (Heidegger, *BT* 255/212; see also Heidegger, *BP* 19). Thus we arrive at Dasein-dependent Being, the rejection of R1 Mind-Independence at this level: "Being 'is' only in the understanding of those entities to whose Being something like an understanding of Being belongs" (Heidegger, *BT* 228/183). A transcendent Being would be of no relevance (not just of no use) to human thought, since it could not sustain intelligible discussion. Heidegger puts this most directly when he says that "our investigation . . . asks about Being itself in so far as Being enters into the intelligibility of Dasein" (193/152). For the realist, Being itself and Being insofar as it enters into the understanding of Dasein are importantly distinct, and identifying the two fatally compromises inquiry as the search for true reality or "what is there anyway." For the Phenomenological Ontologist who has completed the mounting break with the noumenal realm (A1), however, the claim amounts to little more than a truism: we can only think, talk about, and attribute Being to what is in principle encounterable. Being just is Being as it shows itself to Dasein (see Versényi 1965, 46).

### Equipment

Ready-to-hand equipment is obviously Dasein-dependent as well. Equipment, also called "the in-order-to," hangs from the goal or "towards-which" of the task at hand; a hammer is only a hammer insofar as it is related to hammering. The towards-which, however, only functions within the context of a "for-the-sake-of-which," that is, a broader, self-defining role or project we take up as a (futile) attempt to settle the issue of our Being (see Heidegger, *BP* 301). Without Dasein's care for its own Being driving her to pursue projects via tools (again, widely construed), there simply would be no such thing as equipment, since what it means to be a tool is to occupy a place within or be "involved in" the network of instrumental chains anchored on our roles. "The fact that it has such an involvement is *ontologically* definitive for the Being of such an entity, and is not an ontical assertion about it."[16] Heidegger leaves no doubt that the tool's mode of Being is due to our activities: "Ontically, 'letting something be involved' signifies that within our factical concern we let something ready-to-hand *be* so-and-so *as* it is already and *in order that* it be such" (Heidegger, *BT* 117/84). As Richardson puts it, "What determines an entity as such ready-to-hand equipment, then, is that we have adopted a certain attitude or relationship to it" (Richardson 1986, 17; see also 19; Prauss 1999, 36; Okrent 1988, 80).

What is particularly important for our discussion is the way Phenomenological Ontology gets evinced in Heidegger's treatment of equipment. Although he admits that readiness-to-hand is due to our projection and that a tool can also be a present-at-hand object if we change our attitude, these facts do not render readiness-to-hand a merely subjective or secondary quality. Instead, Heidegger makes the ontologically shocking claim that

> this characteristic is not to be understood as merely a way of taking them, as if we were talking such "aspects" into the "entities" which we proximally encounter, or as if some world-stuff which is proximally present-at-hand in itself were "given subjective colouring" in this way. . . . *Readiness-to-hand is the way in which entities as they are "in-themselves" are defined ontological-categorially.*[17]

This quote represents a clear expression of Heidegger's Phenomenological Ontology. Although the ready-to-hand is fully Dasein-dependent (A1) and variable (A3), it is fully real, the tool in-itself even. How we experience it is how it is, even if we can trace its constitution to our projection (A5) and determine that these features can change (A3), offenses that would have eliminated these features from the entity's essence for traditional metaphysics. This is how Heidegger radicalizes Kant's "highest principle of all synthetic judgments . . . that the conditions of the *possibility of experience* in general are likewise conditions of the *possibility of the objects of experience*" (Kant, *C1* A158/B197) sans noumena, similar to Hegel's version that "*logic therefore coincides with Metaphysics*" (Hegel, *HL* 36, §24) or "appearance becomes identical with essence."[18]

Gerold Prauss, in his generally insightful study of practice and theory in *Being and Time,* criticizes Heidegger for anthropomorphizing instruments, that is, for confusing our subjective impressions of them with their objective characteristics (Prauss 1999, 37). This objection misses the point of PO, which refuses precisely this distinction. As Richardson puts it,

> Heidegger disputes a conception that is natural to us: that the hammer "really is" as the theoretical attitude discovers it, while its use and the

> other involvements encountered in it from a position of everyday concern are external relationships added secondarily, "subjectively," to that bare, present-at-hand subsistence. Both modes of Being possible for the hammer originate in our own understanding. (Richardson 1986, 50)

The charge of anthropomorphism arises from taking the bare, inert present-at-hand object as the thing's true nature and thus relegating all other qualities to a lower ontological status as subjective. But Heidegger insists that "among the modes of Being of entities within-the-world, Reality has no priority" (Heidegger, *BT* 254–55/211). When we use the hammer, it presents itself as a tool with all of the qualities we normally and without hesitation use to describe it—too heavy, ugly, fits nicely into my palm; it is only metaphysical presuppositions that make us look beyond these features for a different type of characteristic that remains the same across observers, is mathematically measurable, and so on. The demand that reality show one face only—that it respect R3 by remaining consistent across all observers—might be a good criterion for scientifically useful information, but that is no reason to take it as a criterion for reality full stop. If, in different contexts, the hammer presents itself in different modes, then it really is different kinds of beings (notice the way one must fight grammar here). The fact that it shows itself differently in various circumstances does not force us to proclaim one real at the expense of all others. Depending on the attitude we take up, entities show themselves as and thus truly are ready-to-hand tools or present-at-hand objects; the need to reduce this diversity in order to proclaim one the real one is simply a metaphysical bias.

Furthermore, things really possess the qualities we relegate to subjective projection when under the spell of traditional metaphysics:

> Concerned being-in-the-world can be addressed originally by the *threatening* and the *non-threatening*, in short, by the world as meaningfulness. It is only because Dasein itself is in itself care that the world is experienced in its threatening character, in its meaningfulness. This does not mean that the caring Dasein thus construes the world "subjectively." That would be a complete inversion of the elements invoked. Rather, the caring in-being discovers the world in its meaningfulness.[19]

Heidegger is clear that these emotional features of the world are due to Dasein ("it is only because Dasein itself is in itself care that the world is experienced in its threatening character"), but he refuses to call them merely subjective or less real on those grounds. As he says in an early lecture series, "Care is nothing subjective and does not feign what it takes care of; care allows it rather to come to its genuine being" (Heidegger, *IPR*

43). Calling such features subjective presupposes a more fundamental objective level of present-at-hand objects that those features are accidentally attached to or projected over: "If one is oriented primarily by Thinghood, these latter qualities must be taken as non-quantifiable value-predicates by which what is in the first instance just a material Thing, gets stamped" (Heidegger, *BT* 132/99).

This view seems plausible when confronted with present-at-hand objects within the theoretical attitude. But

> such an Interpretation would overlook the fact that in this case these entities would have to be understood and discovered beforehand as something purely present-at-hand, and must have priority and take the lead in the sequence of those dealing with the "world" in which something is discovered and made one's own. But this already runs counter to the ontological meaning of cognition, which we have exhibited as a *founded* mode of Being-in-the-world. To lay bare what is just present-at-hand and no more, cognition must first penetrate *beyond* what is ready-to-hand in our concern. (Heidegger, *BT* 101/71)

It is the phenomenologically unjustified assumption of a substance "standing under" these various ways of presenting themselves which underwrites the desire to determine a single "true reality" of the entity; without this picture, a being goes back to being what it presents itself as. Initially and for the most part, beings present themselves as ready-to-hand tools. "What is ready-to-hand in the environment is certainly not present-at-hand for an eternal observer exempt from Dasein: but it is encountered in Dasein's circumspectively concernful everydayness" (Heidegger, *BT* 140/106). Having rejected the God's-eye view, phenomenology tries to capture the human-level perspective.

Once we describe how we actually experience the world without the presupposition of present-at-hand ontology, once we accept appearance as real in Phenomenological Ontology, the distinction between "really there" and "mere subjective projection" vanishes, as shown in Heidegger's treatment of moods. For instance, "boredom is not simply an inner spiritual experience, rather something about it, namely *that which bores* and which lets being bored arise, comes toward us precisely *from out of things themselves*. It is much rather the case that boredom is outside, seated in what is boring, and creeps into us from the outside" (Heidegger, *FCM* 83). If we describe how we experience it, we should say that *things* are boring, not that we have within our private sphere of emotions a subjective feeling. So what if someone else finds the same thing interesting? Why does reality have to be the same for everyone? The entire history of realist metaphysicians demands this, but our daily experience shows the opposite.

## Objects

Recently a considerable body of literature concerning Heidegger's position on realism has sprung up, with many commentators taking the position that, although Heidegger is an anti-realist about Being and equipment—that is, considering them to be Dasein-dependent—he is a realist about present-at-hand objects.[20] According to these commentators, Heidegger holds that present-at-hand objects are independent of Dasein and Dasein's awareness. That and how they are does not depend upon us; our encounters with them discover them (R5) as they already are (R1). There are certainly passages which can be read as supporting such a position, the locus classicus being his claim that "Being (not entities) is dependent upon the understanding of Being; that is to say, Reality (not the Real) is dependent upon care" (Heidegger, *BT* 255/212; see also 272/230). The parenthetical qualifications appear to use the ontological difference between Being and beings to combine an ontological idealism with an ontic realism. According to this interpretation, Heidegger would be maintaining the position discussed earlier, that Being is Dasein-dependent, but also claiming that some entities are independent; reality or presence-at-hand is a way of Being and so Dasein-dependent, but the entities that are real aren't. There are other similar passages which speak of the entrance into the clearing—that is, Dasein's becoming aware of an entity—as unnecessary to an entity's reality. Dasein uncovers them just as they already were, implying that they preexisted Dasein's awareness with a determinate essence.[21]

These passages present a problem for my interpretation, since they seem to consider at least one class of entities R1 Independent, whereas I am arguing that Heidegger is fully committed to A1 Dependence. Because of their frequency and apparent realism, one option I could take is simply to admit that Heidegger's position is not consistent; he had some realist tendencies about the present-at-hand that he shouldn't have had, since these views do not fit into his overall view.[22] If the point of phenomenology is to study phenomena exclusively as they appear, then why theorize about what pre-apparent or non-apparent reality might be like? This seems like just the kind of speculation phenomenology is supposed to end. Furthermore, it is admitted on all sides that Being is Dasein-dependent, and of course presence-at-hand is a mode of Being, so these non-apparent entities cannot be present-at-hand, their purported mode according to this interpretation. In fact, they can't be anything; being something means having a mode of Being, which reverts them back to Dasein-dependence again. I don't see how to make such an interpretation fully consistent.

Fortunately, there is an alternate way of reading these passages that does not saddle Heidegger with noumena, one that I think makes more sense of the texts.[23] What should have tipped off the ontic realist commentators is that Heidegger occasionally describes even equipment as preceding encounters with Dasein:

> Ontically, "letting something be involved" signifies that within our factical concern we let something ready-to-hand *be* so-and-so *as* it is already and *in order that* it be such. The way we take this ontical sense of "letting be" is, in principle, ontological. And therewith we Interpret the meaning of previously freeing what is proximally ready-to-hand within-the-world. Previously letting something "be" does not mean that we must first bring it into its Being and produce it; it means rather that something which is already an "entity" must be discovered in its readiness-to-hand, and that we must thus let the entity which has this Being be encountered. (Heidegger, *BT* 117/84–85)

Now, equipment is unequivocally constituted by Dasein's behavior. Without Dasein equipment cannot be ready-to-hand, and without individual Dasein pursuing specific roles, specific tools cannot be.[24] A similarly realist-sounding remark about equipment occurs in the sentence immediately following what I quoted above as one of the most important and direct statements of Phenomenological Ontology, that "*readiness-to-hand is the way in which entities as they are 'in-themselves' are defined ontologico-categorially.* Yet only by reason of something present-at-hand, 'is there' anything ready-to-hand" (Heidegger, *BT* 101/71). This second sentence seems to completely contradict the entire paragraph it ends, as well as Heidegger's overall view that "we do not, so to speak, throw a 'signification' over some naked thing which is present-at-hand, we do not stick a value on it" (190/150; see also Heidegger, *HCT* 207). That sentence appears to revert to the traditional metaphysical view that presence-at-hand substances ground all of reality and that tools really are present-at-hand things with subjective features stuck into them.

What's going on here and in the realist-sounding passages in general, I believe, is that Heidegger is doing phenomenology, that is, he is describing how the world presents itself to Dasein in pre-theoretical average everydayness. Karin de Boer makes the illuminating comparison between *Being and Time* and Hegel's *Phenomenology of Spirit* that each allows its version of common sense to have its say, so that it will discover the limitations of its own views itself and rise to a higher understanding of authenticity and Absolute Knowing, respectively (De Boer 2000, 44–45). For instance, Heidegger states that

> like any ontological Interpretation whatsoever, this analytic [that is, the existential analytic of Dasein] can only, so to speak, "listen in" to some previously disclosed entity as regards its Being. . . . Phenomenological

> Interpretation must make it possible for Dasein itself to disclose things primordially; it must, as it were, let Dasein interpret itself. Such Interpretation takes part in this disclosure only in order to raise to a conceptual level the phenomenal content of what has been disclosed, and to do so existentially. (Heidegger, *BT* 179/139–40, bracketed comment added)

Hegel's version of this claim runs: "But not only is a contribution by us superfluous, since . . . the criterion and what is to be tested, are present in consciousness itself, but we are also spared the trouble of comparing the two and really *testing* them, so that, since what consciousness examines is its own self, all that is left for us to do is simply look on" (Hegel, *PS* 54, §85). Throughout his career Heidegger employs the rhetorical device of presenting views he disagrees with initially in his own voice before going on to refute them (see Löwith 1994, 45, for a description of how this worked in the classroom). For phenomenology, this strategy has the additional virtue of fully unpacking the way phenomena present themselves before analyzing their conditions and limitations. Heidegger always accepted Husserl's notion of categorial intuition—the anti-reductionist idea that we directly perceive meanings and categories rather than just patches of color—which means that phenomenological descriptions of our experience can include theoretical or propositional ideas. The aspect of our experience he is capturing in these passages is the impression that they preexist our experience of them.

I propose that Heidegger's supposed ontic realism is best understood as a description of how present-at-hand objects present themselves to average everyday Dasein. These objects appear as permanent, unchanging, independent objects, so that is how he describes them when reporting their manifest character. Although he often does not explicitly explain that this is what he is doing, there are passages where it is relatively clear when read closely. For instance: "To say that before Newton his laws were neither true nor false, cannot signify that before him there were no such entities as have been uncovered and pointed out by those laws" (Heidegger, *BT* 269/227). This initially sounds like a straightforward denial of ontic idealism: *of course* the things Newton's laws talk about preexisted the *Principia;* we just didn't understand them properly. The passage continues: "Through Newton the laws became true and with them, entities became accessible in themselves to Dasein" (269/227). This is a step closer to ontic idealism or anti-realism because the laws only became true with Newton, but that can still be explained by an unusual sense of truth. The entities still are independent, and it is only our access to them that is newly created, not the entities themselves.

The next sentence is the kicker: "Once entities have been uncovered, they show themselves precisely as entities which beforehand already were" (Heidegger, *BT* 269/227). This is now Heidegger the philosopher talking about average everyday Dasein's ontically realist experience of the world. In other words, part of the way objects appear to us is as not dependent on appearing to us. That does not mean that they really *are* independent of their manifestation, just that they manifest themselves that way; paradoxically, they depend on Dasein to manifest themselves as *in*dependent of all manifestation (this line of thought is intimated in the *Encyclopaedia Britannica* article at Welton 1999, 335). As Joseph P. Fell states, "When Heidegger asserts that nature has its own being, this in effect says that it must be *meant as* existing *apart from* all meaning and all human design" (Dreyfus and Hall 1992, 75). Of course, this is still a meaning. Heidegger makes the contrast explicit here: "Every realism is right to the extent that it attempts to retain Dasein's natural consciousness of the extantness of the world. But it immediately falls short in attempting to explain this reality by means of the real itself" (Heidegger, *HCT* 223). In other words, realism correctly depicts Dasein's "natural consciousness" and its commitment to extantness or presence-at-hand, but it mistakenly takes this to be the final word and "explanation" of the matter. Reading another of his supposedly realist passages carefully, we see that he actually claims that "*it must be stated that* the entity as an entity is 'in itself' and independent of any apprehension of it" (Heidegger, *HCT* 217, italics added). The realism of the entity here is simply what characterizes the manifest character of entities. Heidegger would be agreeing with Nietzsche that "'it is considered' is the real 'it is,' the sole 'this is'" (Nietzsche, *WTP* 556). The rest of the *HCT* sentence makes the anti-realist case more explicit: "Accordingly, the being of the entity is found only in encounter and can be explained, made understandable, only from the phenomenal exhibition and interpretation of the structure of encounter."

Heidegger's considered opinion is that as a mode of Being, presence-at-hand is as dependent on Dasein as any mode. The problem is that discussion of this mode immediately runs into paradoxes, since one of its apparent features is independence of Dasein. Ultimately, Heidegger wants to acknowledge phenomenologically that we do find this feature, but still claim that it is founded in Dasein, "that to which all understanding of being-at-hand, actuality, must be traced back" (Heidegger, *BP* 119).

> Of course only as long as Dasein *is* (that is, only as long as an understanding of Being is ontically possible), "is there" Being. When Dasein does not exist, "independence" "is" not either, nor "is" the "in-itself.". . . *In such a case* it cannot be said that entities are, nor can it be said that they are not. But *now,* as long as there is an understanding of Being and

> therefore an understanding of presence-at-hand, it can indeed be said that *in this case* entities will still continue to be. (Heidegger, *BT* 255/212)

This passage solves the puzzle. As long as Dasein is around and has an understanding of Being—including an understanding of presence-at-hand which claims Dasein-independence—we can intelligibly say that present-at-hand objects do not need Dasein, that is, they can exist before or after Dasein as a whole arose or will pass away. However, this Dasein-independence itself is dependent on Dasein, since it is a meaning which can only manifest itself within a clearing. Paradoxically, Dasein-independence is itself Dasein-dependent (see Heidegger, *BT* 412/361). Piotr Hoffman puts this well:

> Heidegger takes away with one hand what he gives with the other. Even in the same key passage of *Being and Time* the "unworldly" and "unmeaning" status of nature is itself identified as nature's "ontological characteristic." But Dasein, and Dasein alone, posits ontological characteristics of entities, all the way down to entities' very existence. The present-at-hand as such and, we now see, the peculiar meaning of the present-at-hand as "unworldly" and "unmeaning," is dependent upon Dasein's understanding of being. . . . We *conceive* entities as independent of us. (Hoffman 2000, 405; see also Blattner 1994, 186)

This solution is the same position that Nelson Goodman adopts decades later. In arguing for a strong anti-realism, Goodman claims that the world is made by our "versions," roughly equal to conceptual schemes, and that we can make no sense of reality outside all versions:

> Once we recognize that some supposed features of the world derive from—are made and imposed by—versions, "the world" rapidly evaporates. For there is no version-independent feature. . . . The objects themselves and the time and space they occupy are version-dependent. No organization into units is unique or mandatory, nor is there any featureless raw material underlying different organizations. Any raw stuff is as much the creature of a version as is what is made out of that stuff. (McCormick 1996, 154)

As discussed above, this resembles Hegel's attack on Kant's use of the sensible manifold to anchor experience to external, independent reality; appeals to raw material outside of thought quickly get brought within its boundaries.

Goodman's colleague Israel Scheffler challenges him on the counterintuitive implication of his theory that gives the collection of essays *Star-*

*making* its title: how could we puny and recently arisen humans have made the ancient, massive stars? Andrew Cortens considers Goodman's view, as well as what he understands to be Derrida's "linguistic idealism," "to be simply crazy, not serious options at all, in light of certain obvious empirical facts" (Alston 2002, 54; see also 45). The facts that Derrida and Goodman are presumably unacquainted with are that stars are actually rather old and have been around much longer than people; since they were here when we were not, they cannot depend upon us. If only Derrida had picked up an astronomy book or two instead of so much literature! In analytic philosophy, this line of criticism goes back to Russell's claim to have refuted Kant and Hegel by marshaling certain "results from astronomy and geology" which show on the one hand that the mind is of recent date and on the other that "the great processes of nebular and stellar evolution proceed according to laws in which mind plays no part" (Russell 1959a, 16). Q.E.D.

For Heidegger, this objection confuses the ontic with the ontological, as well as commonsense prejudices with philosophy.

> It is customary to point out that the world is first there not on account of a subject, the world is rather "*in-itself.*" The frequent use of this expressions "*in-itself*" of course never tells us anything about its sense. The opinion seems to be that the self-evidence in which this character of the environing world is experienced is tantamount to a categorial self-evidence. But what is clearly experienced as *ontically* self-evident need not be *ontologically* clear at all. The opposite holds true here and in all similar cases. Nothing at all has been said ontologically when the expression "in-itself" is used without further clarification. (Heidegger, *HCT* 197; see also 202)

Obviously we didn't ontically make the stars in the sense of physically constructing those bright, faraway things. But ontologically we are responsible for their having the mode of Being that they do as things that we experience which, for Phenomenological Ontology, is what they are. "The independence of things at hand from humans is not altered through the fact that this very independence as such is possible only if humans exist. The being in themselves of things not only becomes unexplainable without the existence of humans, it becomes utterly meaningless; but this does not mean that the things themselves are dependent upon humans" (Heidegger, *AM* 173–74). There is no ontic dependence since we do not make the vast majority of entities, but their mode of Being, even presence-at-hand's independence, would be "utterly meaningless" and hence impossible without us.

Goodman makes a parallel distinction between making stars and making versions: "If stars like constellations are made by versions, how can the stars have been there eons before all versions? Plainly, through being made by a version that puts the stars much earlier than itself in its own space-time" (McCormick 1996, 156; see also 145, 167). Time and time-ordering are version-dependent and hence version-relative. Different versions determine different orderings, and it isn't a problem that a version could project the existence of something "inside" it before itself, as long as we recognize that this ordering is precisely the projection of a version. (Ernest Sosa makes the same argument in terms of possible worlds in Van Inwagen and Zimmerman 1998, 406.) Goodman does not shy away from the paradoxes his view generates, for example: "One might say that there is only one world but this holds for each of the many worlds" (McCormick 1996, 153). Catherine Z. Elgin makes the similar temporal paradox: "Once the criteria are fixed, they apply timelessly" (Elgin 1997, 169).

My reading of Heidegger is further confirmed by the many points at which he explicitly states that presence-at-hand is Dasein-dependent, a claim he should not make on the realist reading. Although he rejects both realism and idealism, in his early work he has specific criticisms of Kantian subjective idealism that can be corrected, namely that it employs the scheme-content conception and that it has never worked out a proper conception of the "subject." However,

> as compared with realism, *idealism,* no matter how contrary and untenable it may be in its results, has an advantage in principle. . . . If idealism emphasizes that Being and Reality are only "in the consciousness," this expresses an understanding of the fact that Being cannot be explained through entities. . . . Reality is possible only in the understanding of Being. . . . Only because Being is "in the consciousness"—that is to say, only because it is understandable in Dasein—can Dasein also understand and conceptualize such characteristics of Being as independence, the "in-itself," and Reality in general. Only because of this are "independent" entities, as encountered within-the-world, accessible to circumspection. (Heidegger, *BT* 251/207)

Independence is understandable and can only *be* for Dasein.

In *The Metaphysical Foundations of Logic,* called by one commentator on this issue the "high-water mark for [Heidegger's] realism" (Blattner 1994, 194), he makes three consecutive claims:

> 1) Beings are in themselves the kinds of beings they are, and in the way they are, even if, for example, Dasein does not exist. 2) Being "is" not, but being is there, insofar as Dasein exists. . . . 3) Only insofar as existing

> Dasein gives itself anything like being can beings emerge in their in-themselves, i.e., *can the first claim likewise be understood at all* and be taken into account. (Heidegger, *MFL* 153, italics added)

No. 1 initially looks like straightforward ontic realism: the existence and essence of beings are wholly independent of Dasein. No. 2 is then ontological idealism—Being is Dasein-dependent. But no. 3 once again is the kicker: because of the ontological idealism of no. 2, no. 1 has to be reconceived so that even beings "in their in-themselves" can only "emerge," an idea tantamount to "be" for Heidegger, insofar as Dasein is there. As Goodman says, "'Being already there' needs further examination, and finding what is already there may turn out to be very much a matter of making" (McCormick 1996, 155). In fact, we cannot say what seems undeniably obvious, that beings are wholly independent of us, without considerable qualification, since this independence is itself a meaning assigned by us. "If Dasein does not exist, there is no truth, and then there is nothing at all" (Heidegger, *KPM* 198), though even this is saying too much.

Presence-at-hand is constituted by the attitude in which we refrain from practical interaction and merely stare. Although there is a resemblance to it, Heidegger rejects the traditional idea that this "merely tarrying and staring" means achieving R5 Passive Knower, which allows us to see reality as it really is.

> When we have to do with anything, the mere seeing of the Things which are closest to us bears in itself the structure of interpretation, and in so primordial a manner that just to grasp something *free,* as it were, *of the "as,"* requires a certain readjustment. When we merely stare at something, our just-having-it-before-us lies before us *as a failure to understand it any more.* This grasping which is free of the "as," is a privation of the kind of seeing in which one *merely* understands. It is not more primordial than that kind of seeing, but is derived from it. (Heidegger, *BT* 190/149)

Theoretical seeing is still practical and as full of presuppositions as any other mode of access. It is not genuinely passivity but a different type of activity that generates a specific mode of Being.

> Care, as a primordial structural totality, lies "before" every factical "attitude" and "situation" of Dasein, and it does so existentially *a priori;* this means that it always lies *in* them. . . . When we ascertain something present-at-hand by merely beholding it, this activity has the character of care just as much as does a "political action" or taking a rest and enjoying oneself. (Heidegger, *BT* 238/193; see also 99/69, 409/358)

One of the reasons Heidegger calls his method *hermeneutic* phenomenology is that he considers interpretation inescapable: "An interpretation is never a presuppositionless apprehending of something presented to us" (Heidegger, *BT* 191–92/150; see also 213/169), hence true R5 Passive Knower is impossible. This leads Heidegger to echo Nietzsche's claim that "in principle there are no 'bare facts'" (414/362).

If practice and interpretation are ubiquitous, then all modes of Being are dependent on Dasein and the notion of Dasein-independence becomes incoherent. What we have is "Dasein-independent" present-at-hand objects where the scare quotes indicate that the objects present themselves as independent, but this character actually arises from specific practices and attitudes of Dasein. "The 'in-itself' is not an original character; it still has a phenomenal genesis."[25] As Heidegger tells Husserl in a 1927 letter, "We are in agreement on the fact that entities in the sense of what you call 'world' cannot be explained in their transcendental constitution by returning to an entity of the same mode of being. . . . The eksistence-structure of Dasein makes possible the transcendental constitution of everything positive" (Husserl 1997, 138).

## A2 and A4: Rejection of Correspondence Truth and Bivalence

Heidegger adopts the "metaphysics" of Phenomenological Ontology, where beings are and are only what they present themselves to us as. This frees us from presence-at-hand realism, which he considers the foundation of traditional metaphysics and epistemology. We no longer have to look underneath the fluctuating appearance of equipment or of boring or beautiful things for a steady, faceless substance; we can accept these qualities as fully real. Now I will turn to "epistemology" which undergoes a radical transformation in Heidegger's thought along with metaphysics: "Just as truth must undergo a 'widening,' so too must 'being'" (Heidegger, *HCT* 55). Hegel and Nietzsche took philosophy to the edge of the Kantian Paradigm but retreated from making a full break with it. One of the main factors keeping them from doing so was their conceptions of truth. It is Kant's demand for necessary, universal knowledge (R3) that sets up the paradigm's requirement of R6 Realism of the A5 Active Knower. Hegel's understanding of truth as the whole gave closure to truth and preserved an overall realism of the subject as the totality of the shapes of consciousness that fit into a logical system. Nietzsche introduced a chaotic multiplicity but he, too, ended up with a form of R6 by embracing a power-based pragmatic truth which needs the criterion of active will to power to make judgments. Their conceptions of truth worked at cross-purposes with their metaphysics to close down the elements in their thought that could have led to a more thorough breach of the Kantian Paradigm.

Heidegger's conception of truth, on the other hand, is profoundly original, and it works *with* his Phenomenological Ontology to lay the foundation for a complete break with the Kantian Paradigm, though this does not fully emerge until his later work. As John Sallis puts it,

> The phenomenological analyses of *Being and Time* issue in a redetermination of truth, one which does not metaphysically oppose truth to appearances, true world to apparent world, but rather displaces the opposition: truth as the opening/openness of the very site of self-showing. It is precisely for the sake of enforcing this displacement that Heidegger insists on distinguishing between truth as [*aletheia*] and truth as correctness. (Sallis 1995, 165)

Heidegger derides traditional epistemology for sticking with correspondence truth for so long, for having made "no headway . . . in over two thousand years" (Heidegger, *BT* 259/216). This theory is only self-evident in the context of a particular set of metaphysical assumptions; its ubiquity is due to this picture's long hegemony, not its accuracy or quality. "The definition of truth as *adaequatio* is the starting point, not yet the answer; it is the point of departure for posing the problem, but is not yet the solution!" (Heidegger, *MFL* 125).

Heidegger criticizes "the *traditional conception of truth*" for claiming "(1) that the 'locus' of truth is assertion (judgment); (2) that the essence of truth lies in the 'agreement' of the judgment with its object" (Heidegger, *BT* 257/214). As throughout, the culprit is presence-at-hand: "Even the traditional logic . . . has its foundation in an ontology of the present-at-hand" (166–67/129). This took root right at the beginning of philosophy.

> The Greeks . . . took the primary phenomenon of *Logos* to be the proposition, the *theoretical* assertion of something about something. Insofar as *Logos* was primarily determined on this basis, the entire subsequent logic, as it developed in the philosophy of the Occident, became propositional logic. . . . What we commonly know as logic is merely one particular, determinately worked out, logic, given direction by the research impetus within Greek philosophy, but by no means is it *the* logic.[26]

Propositional logic, which has dominated Western thought for two millennia, is based on the metaphysics of presence-at-hand; since there are other modes of Being, there should be other logics, too. A3 Ontological Pluralism's claim that there are multiple modes of Being has very far-reaching implications if Heidegger is right that the ways we think should be tailored to individual ways of Being. Just as traditional philosophy has insisted on only one way of Being (R3), so it has also insisted on only one way of thinking, when in fact this way might be inappropriate for many subjects.

It is when we stop wending our way knowingly through the meaningful world to just stop and stare that bare present-at-hand objects confront us. At that point the dynamically interwoven processes of language, thought, and reality all congeal into inert objects which are only capable of supporting correspondence.

> The relation itself now acquires the character of presence-at-hand by getting switched over to a relationship between things which are present-at-hand. The uncoveredness of something becomes the present-at-hand conformity of one thing which is present-at-hand—the assertion expressed—*to* something else which is present-at-hand—the entity under discussion. . . . *The uncoveredness (truth) becomes, for its part, a relationship between things which are present-at-hand (intellectus and res)—a relationship that is present-at-hand itself.* (Heidegger, *BT* 267/224–25; see also 203/160; Heidegger, *TDP* 155)

However, just as the present-at-hand is grounded in the ready-to-hand, so its correlate assertional or propositional truth is also parasitic on a more fundamental form of truth. "Assertion is grounded in Dasein's uncovering, or rather in its *disclosedness.* The most primordial 'truth' is the 'locus' of assertion; it is the ontological condition for the possibility that assertions can be either true or false—that they may uncover or cover things up" (Heidegger, *BT* 269/226). The original locus of truth is Dasein's uncovering or clearing, that is, her experience of beings which enables them to be corresponded to in the first place. Assertions are only derivative truth-relations that occur after Dasein's switch-over to the non-engaged attitude (see 57/33; Heidegger, *BW* 122).

Although propositional truth possesses R4 Bivalence, this is because of Dasein's attitude, not the inherently determinate constitution of the world. This means that Heidegger accepts A4, qualifying him as a Dummettian anti-realist.

> As assertion, the *Logos apophantikos* certainly has the possibility of being true or being false, but this manner of being true, of becoming manifest,

> is grounded in a manifestness which, because it lies *prior* to *predication* and the assertion, we designate as *pre-predicative manifestness,* or better, as *pre-logical truth*. . . . This original manifestness grounds the possibility of the *Logos* being true and being false. (Heidegger, *FCM* 340–41; see also 314–15)

Further down the page, he clarifies the source of this condition for bivalence: "Where then is this originary manifestness? It is surely not outside man, but must be man himself in a deeper sense, man himself in his essence" (Heidegger, *FCM* 341). In other words, in direct contradiction of realist R4, the condition for assertional bivalence is not reality but humanity. Take away Dasein and neither truth nor falsity remains. "There is truth—unveiling and unveiledness—only when and as long as Dasein exists. If and when there are no 'subjects,' taken in fact in the well-understood sense of the existent Dasein, then there is neither truth nor falsehood" (Heidegger, *BP* 219; see also 220; Heidegger, *KPM* 198; Heidegger, *BT* 269/226). Since "the principle of contradiction, any truth whatever" (Heidegger, *BT* 269/226) depends on Dasein, the truth of the law of the excluded middle or bivalence must as well. Heidegger specifically states that without Dasein, Newton's laws are neither true nor false, a clear violation of bivalence.

Just as present-at-hand objects emerge out of and are dependent upon ready-to-hand tools, so propositional correspondence is derivative of and founded on our more common practical engagement with the world.

> The truth of statements is founded primarily on comportments which do not have the character of statements, such as intuiting and the like. The latter have the character of disclosing and, as ontic truth about beings, they are grounded in the understanding-of-being, i.e., in what makes the disclosability of beings possible. That is, however, world-entry.[27]

As we have seen, it is our use of tools in pursuit of projects and self-defining roles that makes world-entry possible. Heidegger's project is a Kantian transcendental inquiry into the "conditions for the possibility" of correspondence truth as a whole (rather than just of R3 universal scientific knowledge, as in the first *Critique*). He clearly states that "our analysis takes its departure from the *traditional conception of truth,* and attempts to lay bare the ontological foundations of that conception. . . . In terms of these foundations the *primordial* phenomenon of truth becomes visible. We can then exhibit the way in which the traditional conception of truth has been *derived* from this *phenomenon*" (Heidegger, *BT* 257/214; see also 258/215).

Heidegger looks for the presuppositions of correspondence truth in phenomenological descriptions of our experience with truth, in particular of the paradigmatic experience of confirmation or demonstration.

> We must . . . try to bring into view a phenomenon which is characteristic of knowledge—the phenomenon of truth. When does truth become phenomenally explicit in knowledge itself? It does so when such knowing demonstrates itself *as true*. By demonstrating itself it is assured of its truth. Thus in the phenomenal context of demonstration, the relationship of agreement must become visible. (Heidegger, *BT* 260/217)

Since "asserting is a way of Being towards the Thing" (Heidegger, *BT* 260/218), Heidegger wants to examine how this comportment actually occurs and what comes to light in it. He examines propositions in their actual use or real-life context, instead of a detached contemplation of "The cat is on the mat."[28] In this way Heidegger is in sympathy with recent analytic philosophers of language like Dummett for whom "the meaning of a statement . . . is determined by what has to be done by a speaker to vindicate the claim that he makes by means of that statement" (Dummett 1993, 475). As Mark Okrent points out (Okrent 1988, 101–2), Heidegger's strategy here also fits with Quine's somewhat verificationist idea that "the meaning of a sentence turns purely on what would count as evidence for its truth" (Quine 1969, 80). Heidegger does not go so far as to identify the meaning of the statement with its truth conditions or its means of verification, but based on his phenomenological method, he is counting these as important in determining its meaning as well as the meaning of truth.

We encounter truth when we find an assertion to be true, that is, "demonstrate" it. Heidegger's example is demonstrating the truth of the assertion that a painting is hanging askew on the wall. I make this assertion with my back to the wall and then turn around to see that it is indeed askew, thus proving and experiencing the assertion's truth. If we closely examine how this confirmation actually takes place, at no point do we find a representation or proposition interposing itself between the painting and myself.

> In the simple apprehension of an object, nothing like a consciousness of a picture[29] [that is, mental image] can be found. It goes against all the plain and simple findings about the simple apprehension of an object to interpret them as if I first perceive a picture in my consciousness when I see that house there, as if a picture-thing were first given and thereupon apprehended as picturing that house out there. There would thus be a subjective picture within and that which is pictured outside, transcen-

> dent. Nothing of the sort is to be found. Rather, in the simple sense of perception I see the house itself. (Heidegger, *HCT* 42, bracketed comment added)

Although he raises some conceptual problems for this view, "the real reason for rejecting this transposition [is that] it does not correspond to the simple phenomenological findings" (Heidegger, *HCT* 42). Rather than logically refuting it, Heidegger shows that this view does not accurately capture the way we actually experience demonstration. Employing Husserl's analysis of intentionality, Heidegger claims that "what one has in mind is the Real picture, and nothing else. Any Interpretation in which something else is here slipped in as what one supposedly has in mind in an assertion that merely represents, belies the phenomenal facts of the case" (Heidegger, *BT* 260/217).[30]

Phenomenology shows that we do not relate to representations or assertions; these are philosophical reconstructions after the fact that distort the actual experience. At all times, even through the assertion, one relates to the entity. When language is used (successfully) in real-life situations, the sounds and letters generally fade away inconspicuously and we simply grasp the meanings or entities referred to.

> Suppose someone here in the classroom states the proposition "the board is black" and does so in an immediately given context of question and answer. To what do we then attend in understanding the statement? To the phonetic articulation? Or to the representation that performs the making of the statement and for which then the sounds uttered are "signs"? No, rather we direct ourselves to the blackboard itself, here on the wall! . . . What the statement immediately presents is that *about which* it states something.[31]

Retrospective theoretical reconstructions freeze this fluid process, making proposition and object static and divorced present-at-hand objects, which then require a relation of comparison (Heidegger, *BT* 267/225). The problem again is the inappropriate ontology: "When considered philosophically, the *Logos* itself is an entity, and, according to the orientation of ancient ontology, it is something present-at-hand" (201/159). As with many traditional separations (for example, man and world, subject and object), Heidegger wants to preserve the primordial unity preceding and underlying the split (see 170/132). He wants to show assertion and demonstration as moments in a single, fluid process of unconcealing rather than as separate static items that need to be stitched together. Assertion is already *apophansis*—an uncovering/pointing out which reveals the entity to an interlocutor (196–97/154–55); turning around to look at the entity to confirm the statement is just an extension or modulation of this process.

On the one hand, the picture of holding up a mental representation to the object is phenomenologically refuted since we have no experience of it; on the other hand, any such comparison would still presuppose the entity's manifestation. "The confirmation is accomplished on the basis of the entity's showing itself" (Heidegger, *BT* 261/218; see also Heidegger, *BP* 210). I can only form and confirm propositions about entities if they are revealed to me, that is, if I am aware of them. "An assertion can finally be true, be adequate in propositional content to that about which the statement is made, only because the being it speaks of is already in some way disclosed" (Heidegger, *MFL* 127). Since an entity's manifestation is the necessary condition of the traditional agreement of a true assertion with its object, Heidegger redefines truth as this condition. He makes this argument clearly in "On the Essence of Truth," a transitional essay written three years after the publication of *Being and Time*.

> But if the correctness (truth) of statements becomes possible only through this openness of comportment, then what first makes correctness possible must with more original right be taken as the essence of truth. Thus the traditional assignment of truth exclusively to statements as the sole essential locus of truth falls away.[32]

This argument is a bit odd, as he realizes late in his career (see Heidegger, *BW* 446–47); the necessary condition for X seems to be a very different thing than its essence. The most charitable reading is simply to grant Heidegger a technical use of the word "essence" here as the necessary condition or what makes something possible, as he states on the next page: "In this connection 'essence' is understood as the ground of the inner possibility of what is initially and generally admitted as known" (123). While often quite legitimate, Heidegger's propensity for using standard terms in unusual ways is another reason for his obscurity.

We can see that Heidegger does accept R2 Correspondence Truth, but redefines (see Heidegger, *HCT* 51) and limits it. It is only true of present-at-hand objects, and it necessarily presupposes the more primordial truth of uncovering or disclosure (A2), which he calls *aletheia.* As Wrathall says, "Heidegger takes the traditional understanding of truth seriously and attempts to clarify its foundations rather than abandon it altogether. . . . The inquiry into unconcealment, far from being intended as a replacement for the correspondence view of truth, in fact seeks to elucidate the way in which propositional truth is founded" (Wrathall 1999, 70; see also Carman 2003, 259). This is the deeper meaning of truth which is presupposed in any experience Dasein can have. "The Being of truth is connected primordially with Dasein. And only because Dasein i s [*sic*] as constituted by disclosedness (that is, by understanding), can anything like Being be understood. . . . Being and truth 'are' equiprimordially" (Heidegger, *BT* 272/230).

Hegel's and Nietzsche's conceptions of truth held them back from fully developing the implications of their more progressive Objective Idealism and Step Six Physics, drawing them back at least to aspects of a relatively conservative metaphysics. Heidegger's conception of truth as unconcealment, on the other hand, is the key to his advance beyond the Kantian Paradigm in that it dispenses with the reality-appearance distinction, the defining feature of metaphysics for him. Ernst Tugendhat famously notes a progressive change in the definitions of truth in §44 of *Being and Time* from uncovering the entity "just as it is in itself" to simply uncovering the entity. Dispensing with the "as it is in itself" clause prevents us from comparing the appearance with the real entity, thus closing down the traditional logical space of correspondence truth and falsity. Heidegger identifies truth with uncovering in general rather than with *accurate* uncovering, prompting Tugendhat to object that "this theory leaves out of account precisely the phenomenon of truth in its specificity" (Wolin 1993, 251–52, 257).

Tugendhat is right to see radical implications in Heidegger's thought. "A true assertion is not directed at the entity as it shows itself immediately, but instead at the entity as it is in itself. This difference intrinsic to self-manifestation between an immediately apparent givenness and the thing itself is not taken into consideration by Heidegger" (Wolin 1993, 255). However, the radicality of this new conception of truth actually fits Heidegger's dismissal of the in-itself, for what is the appearance to be compared with in order to generate falsity?[33] Given Heidegger's Phenomenological Ontology, the thing-in-itself cannot even serve as the "regulative idea of critical questioning" that Tugendhat suggests (260). "Appearance as appearance or object does not need at all still to *correspond* to something actual, because appearance itself *is* the actual" (Heidegger, *PIK* 69). There simply is nothing else to correspond to for PO.

The problems that Kant's Copernican Revolution raised for correspondence with the thing-in-itself get exacerbated in Heidegger's thought. Whereas Kant has R3, "the next best thing to a perspectiveless sight: the one necessary perspective" (Richardson 1986, 164), Heidegger has given that up. Kant's categories form the world into the sole scientific form in order to protect Newtonian physics from Hume's doubts. These fundamental laws of phenomenal reality—that is, that objects must be substantial, causally related, and so on—must be preserved in all objects if they are to be "true" objects. But Heidegger considers this supposedly ultimate level to be one region among many.

> The Kantian ontology does not prove to be the ontology which ought to be equated with *metaphysica generalis*. This equation is legitimate only insofar as and as long as "being" is equated with "being extant" and its concomitant determinations—an equation which has remained self-evident for the whole philosophical tradition up to now, but fundamentally without justification. (Heidegger, *PIK* 136)

Presence-at-hand or "being extant" is only one of at least three modes of Being that entities can have (A3), and "among the modes of Being of entities within-the-world, Reality has no priority" (Heidegger, *BT* 254–55/211). Even readiness-to-hand has only the relative primacy of being how things are "proximally and for the most part," a mode which has been neglected, but it has no absolute priority in the sense of being more real or true. "Circumspective concern, or even that concern in which we tarry and look at something, uncovers entities" (263/220; see also Heidegger, *OHF* 70). In other words, both of these attitudes uncover genuine Being, even though of quite heterogeneous types. According to PO, if they are uncovered, they are real. Although Heidegger only discusses three modes of being in *Being and Time,* there is nothing in his early thought to limit them to just these; in theory there could be as many modes as there are attitudes Dasein can take toward beings.[34] Where Hegel's "truth is the whole" imposes closure on history, Heidegger's "truth is unconcealment" opens us indefinitely to whatever appears. This way of thinking cannot place a priori restrictions on experience, since whatever is unconcealed is what is real and true; experience teaches us what is necessary and possible.[35]

Since Heidegger has jettisoned any kind of stable sub-stance behind or beneath these various appearances (R1), all unconcealment is true. Without something beyond the appearances to serve as a standard of truth, we have no object for comparison and thus no criterion of the correctness or accuracy of revelations; all revelations have truth and truth just is this uncovering. What Tugendhat sees as a fundamental flaw in Heidegger's notion of truth is the logical—albeit radical—implication of his Phenomenological Ontology. Joseph Fell puts it like this: "Unless one insists *a priori* and arbitrarily that there is one and only one method of disclosing, and one and only one true aspect of beings, one can be open to the possibility of different *but complementary*[36] disclosures of one and the same being" (Dreyfus and Hall 1992, 73). We cannot talk about correspondence or lack thereof between the appearance and something else, since we must have some contact with this object of comparison in order to use it in a constitutive role, and, of course, this contact brings it into appearance broadly construed. As Nietzsche says, "Even supposing there were an in-itself, an unconditioned thing, it would for that very reason be unknowable! Something unconditioned cannot be known; otherwise it would not be unconditioned!" (Nietzsche, *WTP* 555).

A further rejection of R4 Bivalence follows from defining truth as unconcealment. Heidegger expands and applies Husserl's notion of "adumbrations"—the idea that we only see objects from one side at at time—to the multiple modes of Being. The switch-over from ready-to-hand to present-at-hand is a Gestalt switch, so that revealing an entity as an object hides it as a tool and vice versa. This means that *every* unconcealment by its very nature conceals or covers up alternate ways of revealing the entity (see, for example, Heidegger, *BW* 134). Thus, whereas before we saw that without Dasein there would be neither truth nor falsity, we can now see that with Dasein there are always both. Since truth is unconcealment and untruth is concealment, and since every unconcealment also conceals, truth and untruth are inextricably intertwined for Heidegger. As Hegel thought (until the end of history, at least), there can be no simple truth or falsity; they are always mixed. Although Heidegger sometimes interprets this untruth in terms of inauthentic or idle grasping of thoughts which could be overcome through effort (see Heidegger, *BT* 264/222), he also recognizes a structural, necessary intermingling: "Dasein is equiprimordially both in the truth and in untruth,"[37] thus eliminating bivalence.

## A6 and ED: Dasein Is Its World

The defining feature of modern philosophy for Heidegger is that it places the subject at the center of all thought but, to his dismay, no one seems to undertake a genuine examination of the subject's mode of Being.

> Modern philosophy made a total turnabout of philosophical inquiry and started out from the subject, the ego. It will be surmised and expected that, in conformity with this fundamental diversion of inquiry to the ego, the being now standing at the center would become decisive in its specific mode of being. It will be expected that ontology now takes the subject as exemplary entity and interprets the concept of being by looking to the mode of being of the subject—that henceforth the subject's *way of being* becomes an ontological problem. But that is precisely what

> does not happen. (Heidegger, *BP* 123; see also Heidegger, *HCT* 156; Heidegger, *IPR* 195)

As we have seen, Heidegger criticizes Kant, Hegel, and Nietzsche—the thinkers of the Kantian Paradigm—for adopting traditional conceptions of the subject; even phenomenology betrays itself by falling back on an understanding of the self which is actually "alien to consciousness" (Heidegger, *HCT* 106), one that is derived from the tradition rather than from careful descriptions of experience (107; Heidegger, *IPR* 42, 208).

The method of investigation Heidegger employs in his early work represents a further development of the Empirical Directive. Although Kant posited the existence of a noumenal self, he ruled out speculation about it in theoretical philosophy and science. Only discussion of the transcendental and empirical subjects was allowed in these areas, and they are both studied in relation to experience, the latter being studied *in* experience, the former *from* experience. What began as an epistemological strategy then led over the course of the nineteenth century to the ontological doctrine of A6, that is, the various denials of our possession of an identity beyond this empirical, physical world of history and change. Hegel plunges the transcendental subject into history, allowing change in its conceptual schemes, but only according to logical laws which necessarily culminate in a final totality. Nietzsche seems to open up the experience-organizing subject into multiple animal drives, but he ultimately defines and evaluates them according to a spectrum of the underlying core active/reactive will to power.

For Heidegger, the strategy of ED is implicit in phenomenology itself, a fact he credits to Husserl in a footnote: "Edmund Husserl has not only enabled us to understand once more the meaning of any genuine philosophical empiricism; he has also given us the necessary tools" (Heidegger, *BT* 490n10/50). Phenomenology insists that *everything* must be studied within experience, though Dasein still retains the experience-organizing features (A5) of transcendental subjectivity, as shown in the switch-over of equipment to object when Dasein changes attitudes from use to mere staring or theorizing.[38] "If the intentional [that is, the quality that distinguishes subjectivity] is to be interrogated regarding its manner of being, then the entity which is intentional must be originally given, that is, it must be originally experienced in its manner of being" (Heidegger, *HCT* 110, bracketed comment added; see also Heidegger, *MFL* 126). Just as Kant ruled out the rationalists' direct a priori intuition of the self so that we must examine the ways that the forms of intuition and concepts organize phenomena, Heidegger insists that we analyze Dasein via the world. "It is not a matter of perceptually tracking down and inspecting a point called the 'Self,' but rather one of seizing upon the full disclosedness of Being-in-the-world *throughout all* the constitutive items which are essential to it . . . their Being-alongside the world and their Being-with Others" (Heidegger, *BT* 187/146; see also 184/144).

The traditional conception of subjectivity is false in Heidegger's sense because it is not true to our experience.

> Even the positive Interpretation of Dasein which we have so far given, already forbids us to start with the formal givenness of the "I," if our purpose is to answer the question of the "who" in a way which is phenomenally adequate. In clarifying Being-in-the-world we have shown that a bare subject without a world never "is" proximally, nor is it ever given. And so in the end an isolated "I" without Others is just as far from being proximally given. (Heidegger, *BT* 152/116)

If we carefully describe our normal experience of engaged daily dealings, we find no ego there; it is only theoretical speculation on what we assume must have been the case that retrospectively injects a doer back into the deed. Heidegger is supplying a phenomenological explanation for Nietzsche's "conspiracy theory" of the creation of a subject for every action. "Simple inspection does not discover anything like an 'I.' What I see is just that 'it lives,' moreover that it lives towards something."[39] Against Husserl's Cartesian leanings, Heidegger believes that the "I" is not a primary phenomenon, but only arises from specific situations and assumptions. Just as careful description unveiled the ready-to-hand rather than the present-at-hand as the most common type of being we encounter on a daily basis, so we must find a more accurate mode of Being for the self. This is the further unraveling of R3 Uniqueness by showing that like readiness-to-hand, Dasein's mode of Being cannot be captured in present-at-hand terms either.

Heidegger calls Dasein's mode of Being "existence," which etymologically means being outside of oneself, the phenomenon Heidegger defines as "Being-in-the-world." We are never locked up in the closet of our mind (see Locke 1959, 148–49) but rather, to the degree the metaphor makes sense, always already outside of ourselves in the world among things and people. "Dasein finds 'itself' proximally in *what* it does, uses, expects, avoids—in those things environmentally ready-to-hand with which it is proximally *concerned*" (Heidegger, *BT* 155/119; see also 368/321; van Buren 2002, 164–65).

This is Heidegger's rejection of a realist self that is even conceptually separable from the empirical world. He takes this idea farther than any of the thinkers in the Kantian Paradigm by virtually dissolving Dasein into the world: "What one pursues, that wherein one tarries for a while—

one-self 'is' this world. Whatever one-self is, one is it in the world with the others" (Heidegger, *OHF* 72). This intertwining of ED and A6 is one of the most insistent refrains in Heidegger's early work:

> Dasein does not first need to turn backward to itself as though, keeping itself behind its own back, it were at first standing in front of things and staring rigidly at them. Instead, it never finds itself otherwise than in the things themselves and in fact in those things that daily surround it. It *finds itself* primarily and constantly *in things* because, tending them, distressed by them, it always in some way or other rests in things. Each of us is what he pursues and cares for. In everyday terms, we understand ourselves and our existence by way of the activities we pursue and the things we take care of. We understand ourselves by starting from them because the Dasein finds itself primarily in things. (Heidegger, *BP* 159; see also Heidegger, *MFL* 127; Heidegger, *HCT* 244)

His conclusion is that "in so far as Dasein exists factically, it understands itself in the way its 'for-the-sake-of-itself' is thus connected with some current 'in-order-to'. . . . Dasein *is* its world existingly" (Heidegger, *BT* 416/364; see also Heidegger, *BP* 171; Heidegger, *HCT* 202). Translated, this says that Dasein always understands herself in terms of a specific role ("its 'for-the-sake-of-itself'") which unfurls networks of connected places and equipment ("some current 'in-order-to'") in and by which she can *be* that kind of person. I am a professor in a college and by means of classrooms, books, students, and so on. In some sense, the college enables me to be what I am and, reciprocally, a college is partially made up of its faculty, so the clear distinction between it and me only rests upon the presupposition of a present-at-hand ontology. This is how Heidegger can retain a form of constitution without transcendental subjectivity: "Transcendental constitution is a central possibility of the eksistence of the factical self . . . the concrete human being" (in Husserl 1997, 138).

One idea that frequently appears in these discussions is Dasein's necessary relations with both entities and other Dasein: "Just as the Dasein is originally being with others, so it is originally being with the handy and the extant."[40] Heidegger takes Aristotle and Hegel's views that humanity is inherently social a step farther by arguing that intersubjectivity is primary. Our membership in society isn't an accidental, contingent feature added to our Being (Heidegger, *HCT* 239); rather, there cannot be a full Dasein who is not a member of society, since our ability to disclose Being—the defining feature of being a Dasein—is tied to our socialization. Here is how it works: through our upbringing, we internalize the goals and roles that allow us to become someone. Heidegger claims, in a view that Sartre exaggerates, that Dasein has less determinate essential content than other beings; it is up to us to fill out our selves, and we can only get the material for this content from society and tradition. Heidegger rules out the idea of roles supplied or even assigned to us by God, Reason, the universe, our own Nature, and so on; in addition to mortality, existential angst arises from our realization of "the impossibility of projecting oneself upon a potentiality-for-Being which belongs to existence" (Heidegger, *BT* 393/343).[41] We absorb these roles through socialization, and then articulate the various instrumental chains we use to pursue them: being a parent highlights babysitters, the toy section of Wal-Mart, and so on. I could have grasped the significance of these before having kids, of course, but only by imaginatively projecting myself into this role. Thus it is the role that anchors the entities that form the nodes along its network[42] which combine to form the world I only perceive or live in by taking over these roles from society. This is one reason Heidegger does not take seriously skeptical problems like other minds or the external world (two problems which, we can now see, are deeply interrelated rather than just parallel). Simply raising the skeptical question requires the kind of intelligence and skill that could only be obtained from socialization (see 246–47/202–3, 279/205).

If we refrain from automatically applying present-at-hand ontology in order to analyze how the subject actually exists, we find that for the most part, in fact, there is no subject. As Sartre puts it, I generally exist in "a pure mode of losing myself in the world, of causing myself to be drunk in by things as ink is by a blotter" (Sartre 1992, 348). In a state of "flow," the self is as inconspicuous as tools; it is actually quite rare that I explicitly think about myself as I go about my daily business. "The Self must forget itself if, lost in the world of equipment, it is to be able 'actually' to go to work and manipulate something" (Heidegger, *BT* 405/354). In what will become an important theme for Foucault, Heidegger interprets self-consciousness in terms of conformity. He thinks that our anxiety about lacking a defining content drives us to identify ourselves completely with our roles. For the most part, we neither distinguish ourselves from what we do (see 163/126, 283/239) nor from others: "This Being-with-one-another dissolves one's own Dasein completely into the kind of Being of 'the Others'. . . . We take pleasure and enjoy ourselves as *they* take pleasure" (164/126; see also 154/118, 163/126). Thus, in a strong version of ED, the self is rarely differentiated from others or its world.

## R6 Authenticity

Ironically, the roles we take up in order to be someone are actually impersonal and can be filled by just about anyone (see Heidegger, *BT* 283/239).

To live authentically would only consist in an explicit and willed choosing of these roles, since there is nothing else to the self but interactions with people, tools, and things in the pursuit of self-defining roles (ED). We have no noumenal repository of imperatives that can issue extra-mundane instructions; we can only modify the everyday ways we live in this world.

> Resoluteness, as *authentic Being-one's-Self,* does not detach Dasein from its world, nor does it isolate it so that it becomes a free-floating "I." And how should it, when resoluteness as authentic disclosedness, is *authentically* nothing else than *Being-in-the-world?* Resoluteness brings the Self right into its current concernful Being-alongside what is ready-to-hand, and pushes it into solicitous Being with Others. (Heidegger, *BT* 344/298; see also 168/130, 346/299)

Guignon gives this interpretation: "Far from being an autonomous and isolated subject, the self is pictured as the 'Anyone' (*das Man*), a 'crossing point' of cultural systems unfolding through history. To be human, in Heidegger's view, is to be a place-holder in a network of internal relations, constituted by a public language, of the communal world into which Dasein is thrown" (Guignon 1983, 86; see also 19, 108, 127).

This interpretation of the self as completely defined by societal structures would be the fulfillment of ED and A6, the complete immersion of the self into the world without remainder. This would complete the progressive erosion of R6 Realism of the Subject, one of the processes we have been watching since Kant inaugurated it by distinguishing the noumenal self from transcendental subjectivity and focusing the attention of theoretical knowledge on the latter. However, Heidegger does not maintain this position in his early work. Like Hegel and Nietzsche, he falls back into an attenuated R6 Realism of the Subject in two different ways which I will discuss in turn. This backsliding constitutes the major compromise of his early work and is why it has not fully broken free of the Kantian Paradigm.

### Formal Structure

The true revelation of Dasein is the exception to Heidegger's general A2 Rejection of Correspondence Truth; that is, his re-formation of truth into unconcealment per se without allowing for incorrect or false unconcealment. And it is an exception of great importance, seeing how the distinction between true and false conceptions of Dasein is the central, guiding thread of what we have of *Being and Time.* Derrida is the main critic of this realist strain in Heidegger (though he does not use this term), arguing that the idea of a true or authentic (*eigentlich*) idea of Dasein compromises the book's overall innovations and tendencies. Although it offers significant challenges to traditional metaphysics, the idea of a correct, realist self in fact structures the entire work.

> The extraordinary trembling to which classical ontology is subjected in *Sein und Zeit* still remains within the grammar and lexicon of metaphysics. And all the conceptual pairs of opposites which serve the destruction of ontology are ordered around one fundamental axis: that which separates the authentic from the inauthentic. (Derrida, *MP* 63)

This is no small misstep, but one that informs the entire nature of the system: "In *Sein und Zeit* the opposition of *Eigentlichkeit and Uneigentlichkeit* was organizing the existential analytic. Once there has been a certain valuation of the proper-ty (*propre*) and *Eigentlichkeit,* it can never be interrupted."[43] The overall project of *Being and Time* as it stands can be described as the attempt to correct traditional theories of man, soul, ego, or mind as a present-at-hand object (see, for example, Heidegger, *BT* 255/212). I have shown that this revision demonstrates A3 Ontological Pluralism, that beings have more than this one way to be, and thus undermines realism, which insists that all reality has the features of presence-at-hand (R3). However, unlike non-Dasein entities which can be either as objects or tools (and possibly other ways), depending on the circumstances, Heidegger creates a single defining set of terms called "existentialia" for Dasein, firmly walling them off from "categories" which are only appropriate for non-Dasein entities (71/44, 81/54). As we saw with Heidegger's own criticism of Nietzsche, correction presupposes correctness, thus resurrecting the supposedly dead epistemology and metaphysics, since it must be talking correctly about something.

Heidegger's definition of Dasein's distinct mode of Being as existence has occasionally been misconstrued, as Sartre does. Sartre understands the statement that "*the 'essence' of Dasein lies in its existence*" (Heidegger, *BT* 67/42; see also 255/212) to mean that consciousness'[44] bare fact of existing or being there precedes its having any essence whatsoever, since there is no creator God to give us one; we are deeply blank slates who create our own essence through the choices we make. On this view, there could be nothing like a definition of the "for-itself" (Sartre's name for human awareness), though, of course, *Being and Nothingness* seems to be just this kind of an extended analysis of the necessary essence of the inauthentic for-itself. This Sartrean line has been attributed to Heidegger, for instance by Barry Allen: "No God or Nature or Human Nature predetermines our essential possibilities once and for all. . . . Heidegger claims that human beings lack essence in this sense. There is no *what* which is what a human being essentially is" (Allen 1993, 79).

I don't think Heidegger should be read like this (although there are passages which seem to support it such as Heidegger, *BT* 303–4/259). When Heidegger defines Dasein's way of Being as "existence," he means the term as a specific, precisely articulated structure, not just what happens to occur in a person's life. It is true that the content that makes up a particular Dasein's role is contingent and historically variable, and these roles do partially define each Dasein. But it remains the case that the formal structure, that is, the set of existentialia, is neither contingent nor historically variable, but permanent and essential. Most of *Being and Time* as we have it consists of a detailed analysis of these formal aspects of existence, which he repeatedly calls essential and necessary. "There are certain structures which we shall exhibit—*not just any accidental structures, but essential ones* which, *in every kind* of Being that factical Dasein may possess, persist as *determinative* for the character of its Being" (38/17, all italics added). These qualities are formal and need to be filled in by content from one's particular society, but they are the definite ways that any and every Dasein incorporates it. In Caputo's words, "The goal of *Being and Time*—a very Husserlian and neo-Kantian goal indeed—was to 'formalize' these factical structures, to give them a formal-ontological conceptualization that would be ontologically neutral as to their concrete instantiation" (Caputo 1993, 172).

Like Kant and Hegel, Heidegger repeatedly insists that his existential analysis exhaustively captures all of Dasein's basic features: "With this analysis, the whole existential constitution of Dasein has been laid bare in its principle features" (Heidegger, *BT* 224/180; see also Heidegger, *HCT* 152; Heidegger, *BP* 59). On this point, Heidegger takes a step backward from Nietzsche's A6 open proliferation of selves. While Nietzsche posited an R6 essence to will to power which allows the evaluation of particular instantiations, it could be fulfilled in indefinitely many ways, whereas Heidegger demands that in order for his project to succeed, "the formally existential totality of Dasein's ontological structural whole must therefore be grasped" (Heidegger, *BT* 237/192). This formal totality of Dasein's structural whole is Dasein's essence in the traditional sense. In accordance with Kant's "Paralogism" which guides all of the thinkers of the Kantian Paradigm, these features are comportments or active ways of Be-ing rather than properties of an object, but they are the determinate set of ways of Be-ing that every Dasein must have in order to be Dasein, and there can be no others. "The existential analytic of the Dasein . . . must aim at bringing to light the ground of the basic structures of the Dasein in their unity and wholeness."[45] In fact, it is the lack of this wholeness in *Being and Time*'s first division's account of Dasein that requires the second division.

The early Heidegger is still playing the game of providing a more accurate definition of the self. Foucault's criticism of Sartre equally applies to early Heidegger: "From the theoretical point of view, Sartre avoids the idea of the self as something which is given to us, but through the moral notion of authenticity, he turns back to the idea that we have to be ourselves—to be truly our true self" (Foucault, *FR* 351). Heidegger expresses concern about this possibility: "It must still have seemed that Being-in-the-world has the function of a rigid framework, within which Dasein's possible ways of comporting itself towards its world run their course without touching the 'framework' itself as regards its Being" (Heidegger, *BT* 221/176). As we will see in chapter 6, he comes to conclude that his early work did in fact end up committed to this position, and he explicitly states that this element kept him in metaphysics and Kantian transcendental philosophy. In my architectonic, it kept him at least partially within the Kantian Paradigm.

Although Heidegger does not explicitly limit the number of true forms that non-Dasein beings can have, there is a correct understanding of Dasein and a false one. The correct understanding, "the laying-bare of Dasein's primordial Being" (Heidegger, *BT* 359/311), pierces the false view of the self common to both philosophy and everydayness as a present-at-hand object or solely in terms of worldly things (168/130) in order to get to its true nature as temporal mortal care. There is a true self behind the traditional and everyday understandings which allows the distinction between a true unconcealment of Dasein and false ones, a distinction that violates Heidegger's conception of truth. In one early work he even calls the fallen view a "mask" that Dasein "holds up before itself," a metaphor that implies a true face lying beneath (Heidegger, *OHF* 26). Charles Taylor writes that this kind of argument "purports to show us more of what we really are like—to show us, as it were, something of our deep or authentic nature as selves" (Baynes 1987, 482–83; see also Rorty 1989, 110; Haar 1993, 184).

Heidegger even endows this true self with the traditional qualities of Being that he refuses other entities. One of the main targets of *Being and Time* is the view that "that which can be shown to have the character of something that *constantly endures* . . . makes up the real Being of those entities of the world which get experienced" (Heidegger, *BT* 128/96; see also 125/92). This age-old prioritization of constant endurance or presence is based on present-at-hand ontology and its concomitant temporality. However, Dasein's existential structures are awarded the status of being the real ones precisely because "in every kind of Being that factical Dasein may possess, [they] *persist* as determinative for the character of its Being" (38/17, italics added). In other words, the formal existentialia are constantly present throughout ontic fluctuations in content, so they must constitute the true nature of the self. Correlatively, one of the flaws of the average everyday self is that it "has been *dispersed* into the 'they,' and must first find itself" (167/129). The they-self has been dispersed into projects which come and go like ephemeral fads, "driven about by its 'affairs.' So if it wants to come to itself, it must first *pull itself together* from the *dispersion* and *disconnectedness* of the very things that have 'come to pass'" (441/390). If this happens, a new possibility that was prevented by the hustle and bustle of fallen everydayness emerges.

> The phenomenon of this authentic potentiality-for-Being also opens our eyes for the *constancy of the Self. . . . The constancy of the Self,* in the double sense of steadiness and steadfastness, is the *authentic* counter-possibility to the non-Self-constancy which is characteristic of irresolute falling. Existentially, "*Self-constancy*" signifies nothing more than anticipatory resoluteness. (Heidegger, *BT* 369/322)

The obvious question here is, if we have rid ourselves of the traditional bias that favors constant presence, why should we value self-constancy? What makes this better than the mercurial change and multiplicity endorsed by Nietzsche and some postmodernists? Besides the kind of cultural commentary he always denies indulging in, it seems that the only argument for self-constancy rests on just the kind of traditional ontology Heidegger is trying to overcome. Charles Guignon describes this problem well.

> [Heidegger's] criticism of the Cartesian tradition is concerned with undermining the assumptions that underlie all of philosophy when this is understood as the quest for timeless, immutable truths. But if this is the case, then the question arises: Why is it that the quest for eternal truths of traditional philosophy is "nonsense" while fundamental ontology is in order and perfectly meaningful? (Guignon 1983, 197)

Although Heidegger denies that his analysis of Dasein contains any ethical prescriptions, it is obvious that authenticity is some kind of ideal. The basis for this evaluation seems to be the very old argument, summed up nicely in Aristotle's "function" argument, that once we have determined our essence—whether it be contemplation (Plato), moderate rational citizenship (Aristotle), worship (Augustine), obeying reason's universal laws (Kant), motivating historical change (Hegel), or joyous creation

(Nietzsche)—the ethical goal is to live in accordance with this essence, that is, to do it with excellence. The specific motivations differ considerably, from biological nature to grateful duty to desire for autonomy, but the fundamental idea is always the same: we should act in a certain way because it coheres with our nature. Heidegger neatly sums up this idea with the connotations of the German word *eigentlich,* which means "authentic" but also what is one's own, or what is "proper" to one. Authentic existence means living in a way that is "appropriate" to the kind of creatures that we are. We are not present-at-hand objects, so we must reconcile ourselves to the fact that we determine much of our content without foundation, and we are not worldly ready-to-hand entities, so we cannot identify ourselves *completely* with our for-the-sake-of-which's. We must carefully examine our Be-ing so that we can know how to be—ethics through phenomenology.

Joseph Fell correctly points out that this ideal of authenticity ties into Nietzsche's (and Hegel's) exhortation to "become who you are," an idea Heidegger refers to approvingly (see *BT* 186/145, 188/148). "This means recognition of Dasein as Dasein, of one's real ontological situation. . . . It can only be a matter of being what one already is with explicit awareness" (Fell 1979, 39; see also 50–51). We always are Dasein, but we normally live in a way that is unaware of and inappropriate to this mode of Being. Although Heidegger's definition of Dasein's essence as temporal care is quite innovative, and his insistence on the importance of the roles taken from society represents an important step toward A6, his ideal of authenticity as willed self-coincidence is perhaps the most conventional aspect of *Being and Time* and constitutes a regression to R6 Realism of the Subject in that it presupposes a self to appropriate and live in conformity with. "Dasein becomes 'essentially' Dasein in that authentic existence which constitutes itself as anticipatory resoluteness. Such resoluteness, as a mode of the authenticity of care, contains Dasein's primordial Self-constancy and totality" (Heidegger, *BT* 370/323). When Dasein coincides with itself to achieve authenticity, it captures itself in its constancy and totality, traditional metaphysical qualities that Kant and Hegel award their realist conceptions of the self as well.

The obvious presupposition of Heidegger's argument is that there is a way that we really are, a way that gets covered up and disguised by our fallen average everyday understanding. Phenomenology or, in its less thematic form, conscience, dredges up and clarifies our pre-ontological understanding of existence, "summoning" (Heidegger, *BT* 314/269) us to our necessary structure of selfhood so that we can explicitly live in "the *loyalty* of existence to its own Self" (443/391). If falling into everydayness is the covering up, disguising of, or fleeing from our authentic self (see Heidegger, *OHF* 26), that is, the false disclosure of the self, then conscience provides the true or correct revelation; it "gives us 'something' to understand; it *discloses*" (Heidegger, *BT* 314/269). "And to what is one called when one is thus appealed to? To one's *own Self*" (317/272; see also 333/287).

As we saw above, one of the claims that makes Heidegger a leading proponent of A6 and ED is that Dasein is always in-a-world: there is nothing like a noumenal self, since one is defined by what one does. Because one is what one does and what one does is wholly derived from historically changing societies, the door is open for a complete A6 in which people from different communities or different periods are deeply different types of subjects, the view he takes up in his later work. However, *Being and Time* does not follow through on this line of thought. The experience of anxiety and the anticipation of death teach Dasein a necessary lesson for authenticity. In anxiety, my usual pressing forward into roles and goals loses its momentum; instrumental chains in turn fall slack, since the roles they depend on now lack meaning. Anticipating death can also rob my projects of meaning; why should I show up for work if I and all of my students will be dead and forgotten one day and no one will ever care if I showed up or not? Why should I do anything in the shadow of this thought? As in anxiety, I disengage from the world that partially defines me. And this is exactly what I learn: that the world only *partially* defines me; that a thin but decisive layer of "nothingness" seeps in between the world and myself, whereas before there had been only seamless unity. Although my roles could be performed by others, the fact that there is a mineness to my life that can't be taken over by anyone else comes out vividly when we consider that which can never be taken over by anyone else—my death.[46]

These phenomena prepare the ground for authenticity as Dasein's "ownmost possibility." I want to quote this passage at length because it contains a lot of important material for this point.

> The ownmost possibility is *non-relational.* Anticipation allows Dasein to understand that that potentiality-for-being in which its ownmost Being is an issue, must be taken over by Dasein alone. . . . Death *lays claim* to it as an *individual* Dasein. The non-relational character of death, as understood in anticipation, individualizes Dasein down to itself. . . . It makes manifest that all Being-alongside the things with which we concern ourselves, and all Being-with Others, will fail us when our ownmost potentiality-for-Being is the issue. Dasein can be *authentically itself* only if it makes this possible for itself of its own accord. . . . As structures essential to Dasein's constitution, these have a share in conditioning the possibility of any existence whatsoever. Dasein is authentically itself only to the extent that, *as* concernful Being-alongside and solicitous Being-with,

> it projects itself upon its ownmost potentiality-for-Being rather than upon the possibility of the they-self. (Heidegger, *BT* 308/263)

Dasein's "ownmost possibility," what allows it to be itself, is non-relational, which means that each of us faces his own death by himself. Other people and things are of no relevance to this possibility, so death inserts a wedge between ourselves and everything else, even though up to now involvements with things and others have been presented as pervasive, defining features of Being-in-the-world. Heidegger confirms even here that these two relations are essential features of Dasein in the traditional sense of always being part of all Dasein ("as structures essential to Dasein's constitution, these have a share in conditioning the possibility of any existence whatsoever"), but the fact that they "will fail us when our ownmost potentiality-for-Being is the issue" fundamentally changes our "appropriate" relationship to them. Anxiety and death "bracket" or suspend the roles that I usually take for granted and that unthinkingly link me to things and others. This suspension allows me to distinguish between their contingency and, in some sense, externality to me, on the one hand, and the absolute necessity and mineness of my death, on the other. Roles come and go with different societies, but death is part of what it means to be Dasein, so it can reveal "not just any accidental structures, but essential ones which, in every kind of Being that factical Dasein may possess, persist as determinative for the character of its Being" (Heidegger, *BT* 38/17).

Now it is very important that, in line with Heidegger's partial commitment to A6, even when it has achieved authenticity Dasein has nowhere else to go but back to society, the world, and *das Man* (roughly the average inherited background intelligibility of society) for the content to live a life and be a self (see Heidegger, *BT* 168/130, 434/383). There is no possibility of transcending the world for a Form- or God-given nature or role. However, it is equally important to his partial commitment to R6 that we only learn the truth about the world and *das Man* by disengaging with the world to discover our true, mortal structure.

> In the anticipatory revealing of this potentiality-for-Being, Dasein discloses itself in the Being of the entity so revealed—namely, to exist. Anticipation turns out to be the possibility of understanding one's *ownmost* and uttermost potentiality-for-Being—that is to say, the possibility of *authentic existence.* The ontological constitution of such existence must be made visible by setting forth the concrete structure of anticipation of death. . . . Here it can become manifest to Dasein that in this distinctive possibility of its own self, it has been wrenched away from the "they." (Heidegger, *BT* 307/262–63)

Death is the ultimate breakdown of all of my projects which renders the formal structure of existence conspicuous, that I may authentically live in accord with it.

It is precisely when the content of Dasein's particular or "existentiell" self-definitions has been bracketed that she can grasp her formal or "existential" structure for the first time. The possibilities we press ourselves into and occupy ourselves with suddenly "*abandon us to ourselves.*"[47] Using boredom instead of anxiety as another fundamental mood in which all of my possibilities go slack (see Heidegger, *BW* 99), Heidegger sums up the view nicely: "This peculiar impoverishment which sets in with respect to ourselves in this 'it is boring for one' first *brings* the *self* in all its nakedness *to itself* as the self that *is there* and has taken over the being-there of its Da-sein. For what purpose? *To be that Da-sein*" (Heidegger, *FCM* 143). Usually I lose myself in the "one-self" of daily occupations and preoccupations where I simply am my roles of professor, father, friend, and so on. But fundamental moods like anxiety or boredom represent the equipmental breakdown writ large; then the entire world is suspended, distanced, no longer involving me and absorbing my self inconspicuously. Authenticity which follows the call of conscience, that is, which grasps the structure of the self in order to take it up, gives death the power of "dispersing all fugitive Self-concealments" (Heidegger, *BT* 357/310). Drained of content, since during these times our roles have no meaning and do not involve us, we have nothing but the formal structure of our existence or pure Dasein to cling to: "Anxiety leaves us hanging because it induces the slipping away of beings as a whole. . . . Where there is nothing to hold onto, pure Da-sein is all that is still there" (Heidegger, *BW* 101). Our "duty" at that point is to "actively complete the transformation of man into his Da-sein that every instance of anxiety occasions in us" (102). Once the covering content has drained away, we can grasp what we are and become it resolutely, that is, with excellence.

This argument follows Kant's positing of autonomy as the central value in his analysis of the moral law. Kant insists that we must turn away from the material content of inclinations that come from our empirical self as illegitimate sources of morality, leaving nothing else to guide our actions but the formal structure of the rational self which prescribes the universal form of lawfulness. For Heidegger, once anxiety brackets the roles given and enforced by "the real dictatorship of the 'they'" (Heidegger, *BT* 164/126), we have nothing but the structural features of pure Dasein to give us guidance. Just like for Kant, this guidance is formal and needs to be applied to the specifics which can only be derived from concrete life, but the purified structure of the self gives us direction: specifically, roles need to be taken up in full acknowledgment of their contingency, our mortality, and so on.

Since Kant's moral law generally ignores the agent's happiness, his justification for why we ought to be good is that obeying this law constitutes autonomy, in that the law is issued by our true self. This law legitimately "interests us because it is valid for us as men, inasmuch as it has arisen from our will as intelligence and hence our *proper self*" (Kant, *FMM* 79/461, italics added; see also 48/431, 75/457). Although Heidegger's notion of thrownness severely compromises autonomy, he still claims that "resoluteness constitutes the *loyalty* of existence to its own Self. As resoluteness which is ready for *anxiety*, this loyalty is at the same time a possible way of revering the sole authority which a free existing can have" (Heidegger, *BT* 443/391). Authenticity is announced to us in the call of conscience which, like Kant's moral law, "calls, against our expectations and even against our will. On the other hand, the call undoubtedly does not come from someone else who is with me in the world. The call comes *from* me and yet *from beyond me and over me*" (320/275). The call of conscience comes from me but not from me, mapping the true Dasein/superficial one-self distinction neatly onto Kant's ethical noumenal/phenomenal selves distinction. For both philosophers, the self is "the sole authority which a free existing can have."

## Transcendental Temporal Ground

Heidegger often describes his fundamental ontology as an extension of Kant's transcendental inquiry. Kant sought to found a stable, self-identical phenomenal realm (R3) in the subject's unchanging form-giving faculties (A5, R6): phenomena have a unique, unchanging character which is susceptible to scientific analysis because that is how we organize them (Kant, *C1* A111). As discussed above, Heidegger does not make presence-at-hand and scientific knowledge the sole or even fundamental mode of Being and knowledge like this (see, for example, Heidegger, *WT* 128), exploring other modes instead (A3).

Despite this difference, there is a deep accord between the two projects. Just as Kant interprets the categories as forms of unification and traces them all back to the primitive unity of the transcendental unity of apperception, so Heidegger founds the three modes of Being on Dasein's innermost core of primordial temporality. To support this claim, he will show in the second division of *Being and Time* how all the existentialia discovered in the first division (that is, the concepts describing Dasein's way of Being) can be redescribed in temporal terms.

> The primordial phenomenon of temporality will be held secure by demonstrating that if we have regard for the possible totality, unity, and development of those fundamental structures of Dasein which we have

> hitherto exhibited, these structures are all to be conceived as at bottom "temporal" and as modes of the temporalizing of temporality. Thus, when temporality has been laid bare, there arises for the existential analytic the task of *repeating* our analysis of Dasein in the sense of Interpreting its essential structures with regard to their temporality. (Heidegger, *BT* 352/304; see also 384/335)

As an added bonus for R6 Realism of the Subject, if we can give an account of time and the existentialia in terms of each other, the completeness of both accounts will be further confirmed. The second division of *Being and Time* is largely taken up with this redescription.

Heidegger's argument takes the form of a Kantian-style idealism transcribed into a temporal key. Dasein is the source of the categories that shape Being, and time is the deepest level of Dasein's Being; Heidegger even says at times that "*Dasein itself* . . . is *time*."[48] Therefore the various ways that entities are, that is, the ways that Dasein organizes them, are actually the different forms that time can take, just as Kant's categories are the various ways consciousness brings experience into a unity. Since Being is as it presents itself to Dasein and Dasein is deeply temporal, it is obvious why the theme of *Being and Time* is "the Interpretation of *time* as the possible horizon for any understanding whatsoever of Being" (Heidegger, *BT* 19/1; see also 40/19). As temporal beings, we cannot but experience everything temporally; then, according to Phenomenological Ontology, everything actually is temporal, so time is the only way that things can be, that is, time is the meaning of Being. William Blattner explores the parallel with Kant's temporal idealism in some detail: "We discover—as in Kant—that being is always understood in terms of time, and that time depends on us" (Blattner 1994, 196; see also 191; Blattner 1999, 245–47).

Being must be temporal since Dasein's clearing, the only site where Being can be, temporalizes whatever appears within it. Heidegger explicitly connects this idea to Kant's.

> Temporality is the basic constitution of human Dasein. On the basis of Dasein's original constitution it is possible for Dasein to have pure understanding of being and of determinations of being. Understanding of being in general is constituted on the basis of the temporality of Dasein. And only because something like this is possible can Dasein as an existing being comport itself toward beings that are not Dasein and simultaneously toward a being that Dasein itself is. Although Kant did not unfold the problem of ontological knowledge in such a fundamental way and did not push the possibility of a radical resolution this far, nevertheless he offers a hint at the problem. (Heidegger, *PIK* 288–89)

One of the ways in which Heidegger's work is more radical than Kant's is that Heidegger does away with the objective deduction. Briefly, the subjective deduction says that we must use the categories since they are the only way we can have experience, while the objective deduction demonstrates that we are justified in using them since they really form characteristics of the phenomena. Heidegger's rejection of the phenomenon-noumenon distinction (A1) undermines this distinction: "From this we infer that a juridical inquiry makes no sense and that one can no longer ask how a pure concept of understanding is to have ob-jective validity, once it belongs to informed subjectivity. *For belonging to subjectivity sufficiently disclosed is just the elucidation of the manner and possibility of the ob-jective reality of categories*" (Heidegger, *PIK* 260). This is exactly the conclusion that accepting A5 Active Knower while rejecting R1 Independent noumenal reality should lead to. Since reality simply is what we experience, it is the way we form it; there is no motivation for a concern about whether we are justified in our organizing when there isn't a separate thing having a scheme imposed upon it. The noumenal realm and its correlate scheme-content distinction are what make something above and beyond the subjective deduction necessary. Without them, the transcendental deduction "is identical with the disclosure of the dimension of origin, that is, with the ontological explication of the subjectivity of the subject" (261).

Repeating Hegel's objection, Heidegger complains that Kant's categories aren't unified or well grounded, but his solution is to trace them back to time.

> More than Kant, we attempted to render visible the unitary character of the original dimension, in order to let the essence of the categories spring from it. Now, even if Kant not infrequently strives toward this original dimension, i.e., toward the boundaries of subjectivity as the unity of time and the I-think, of receptivity and spontaneity, nevertheless Kant does not proceed from this dimension of the origin disclosed in advance in its unity. (Heidegger, *PIK* 273–74; see also 291)

Although Kant was on the right track with the "Schematism," he did not emphasize time enough, nor did he unify the categories and faculties. Fortunately, both problems can be remedied with the same solution, since the categories and faculties are unified in time as the fundamental essence of Dasein (see Heidegger, *PIK* 268).

What is relevant for my discussion is that, just as Heidegger insists that he has gathered up all of Dasein's existentialia, he also claims to have dug down to the deepest level in his analysis of the layers of Dasein's self. First there is the surface level of Dasein's average everydayness; this is made possible by Being-in-the-world, whose unifying condition is care, which in turn rests on time. Like Kant, this analysis explains our organizing structures: "The eksistence-structure of Dasein makes possible the transcendental constitution of everything positive" (in Husserl 1997, 138; see also Heidegger, *KPM* 199). Importantly, Heidegger does not say that this is how Dasein appears at this point in history, nor that these are just various aspects of Dasein, as presence-at-hand and readiness-to-hand are just possible alternate modes of non-Dasein beings. Instead, he arranges the levels in a definite order of nesting, founding layers that, importantly, comes to a specific end:

> The series . . . of projections as it were inserted one before the other—understanding of beings, projection upon being, understanding of being, projection upon time—has its end at the horizon of the ecstatic unity of temporality. We cannot establish this here in a more primordial way. . . . At this horizon each ecstasis of time, hence temporality itself, has its end. . . . If anyone wished to protest that the description of that to which the ecstasis as such is carried away, the description of this as horizon, is after all only an interpretation once more of the whither in general to which an ecstasis points, then the answer would be as follows. The concept "Horizon" in the common sense presupposes exactly what we are calling the ecstatic horizon. There would be nothing like a horizon for us if there were not ecstatic openness for . . . and a schematic determination of that openness, say, in the sense of praesens [the conception of temporality employed in this work]. (Heidegger, *BP* 308, bracketed comment added)

Heidegger knows this to be the ultimate level, he reassures us. If someone suggests that there might be other layers or arrangements of the layers he does not retort, as Nietzsche does, "Supposing that this also is only interpretation—and you will be eager enough to make this objection?—well, so much the better" (Nietzsche, *BGE* 22). Instead, he trots out a transcendental argument proving that his thesis *can't* be just another interpretation, that it *must* be the final level, making his version the ultimate truth. Heidegger insists that his thought has encompassed the horizontal (existentialia) and vertical (levels of transcendental conditions) boundaries of Dasein in their totality and, right or wrong, he can only entertain this as a goal if he believes that there is a single way that Dasein really is. In "On the Essence of Ground," he changes the final level from time to transcendence but still claims ultimacy for his account: "Transcendence designates the essence of the subject. . . . It is the fundamental structure of subjectivity. . . . To *be* a subject means to be a being in and as transcendence" (Heidegger, *Pm* 108; see also Haar 1993, 56). Derrida gets it right when he makes a point parallel to Heidegger's criticism of Kant against Heidegger: "*Dasein* cannot be reduced to a subjectivity, certainly, but the existential analytic still retains the formal traits of every transcendental analytic," which leads to the fact that "in spite of everything it opens up and encourages us to think, to question, and to redistribute, *Dasein* still occupies a place analogous to that of the transcendental subject" (Derrida, *PoI* 258, 273; see also 267; Derrida, *PC* 363). As we will see in chapter 8, Derrida is deeply committed to protesting that any description "is after all only an interpretation," to put it a bit crudely.

## Historicism

So far we have seen Heidegger allow for the (possibly) indefinite proliferation of the modes of Being of non-Dasein beings (A3) without trying to determine an ultimate form which could differentiate between their true and false unconcealments (A2). Just appearing is their truth, however they appear. On the other hand, he does make this distinction in the uncovering of Dasein, even building his entire project around it:

> Dasein *can* understand *itself* in terms of the "world" and Others or in terms of its ownmost potentiality-for-Being. The possibility just mentioned means that Dasein discloses itself to itself in and as its ownmost potentiality-for-Being. This *authentic* disclosedness shows the phenomenon of the most primordial truth in the mode of authenticity. The most primordial, and indeed the most authentic, disclosedness in which Dasein, as a potentiality-for-Being, can be, is the *truth of existence.* (Heidegger, *BT* 264/221)

And, even more directly: "The most primordial and basic existential truth, for which the problematic of fundamental ontology strives in preparing the question of Being in general, is the *disclosedness of the meaning of the Being of care*" (Heidegger, *BT* 364/316; see also Heidegger, *KPM* 163). This disclosedness of our true self as temporal care sets the ethical goal of accepting this mode of existence rather than trying to live an inappropriate mode of Being, and, via temporal idealism, it determines the basic ontological meaning of Being as temporality. To follow out the connotations of the German word for "authenticity," we need to own the kind of life that is our own but which we usually don't own up to. Or we need to appropriate what is appropriate or proper for beings like us. This essential, authentic self constitutes "the sole authority which a free existing can have" (Heidegger, *BT* 443/391), following Kant and the idealists in prioritizing autonomy.

Not only does Heidegger's formal R6 Realism of the Subject represent a step backward from Nietzsche in the progression we have been tracing, and not only does the idea of a true revelation of the self as opposed to false revealings violate his new A2 conception of Unconcealment Truth, but this analysis of Dasein's structure also presents an internal inconsistency in his treatment of historicity. In one of the last sections of the book, Heidegger claims that Dasein's temporality finds its concrete manifestation in history (Heidegger, *BT* 434/382). Dasein's temporality is not the empty, formal fact that moments pass, but rather the concrete inheritance of understandings of Being and roles and projects from tradition and society. Since PO Being is what Being presents itself as and since we always experience the world within a historical context, Being is historical.

> The consideration of being takes its start from beings. This commencement is obviously always determined by the factual experience of beings and the range of possibilities of experience that at any time are peculiar to a factical Dasein, and hence to the historical situation of a philosophical investigation. It is not the case that at all times and for everyone all beings and all specific domains of beings are accessible in the same way. . . . Because the Dasein is historical in its own existence, possibilities of access and modes of interpretation are themselves diverse, varying in different historical circumstances. (Heidegger, *BP* 22)

As with Dasein's transcendental temporality "making" Being temporal, so Dasein's historicality should make beings vary from era to era, including Dasein itself.

The roles we get from society change historically, and since these make up a significant aspect of ourselves, so too should we. However, although historicity is part of the essential nature of Dasein, this nature itself is ahistorical. The existentialia are themselves constant and unchanging throughout history and end up functioning, despite his own warning, as "a rigid framework, within which Dasein's possible ways of comporting itself towards its world run their course without touching the 'framework' itself as regards its Being" (Heidegger, *BT* 221/176). Paradoxically, since historicity is one of these existentialia, historicity is ahistorical. Guignon poses this dilemma concisely: "Is historicity itself to be conceived of as absolute, or is it also historical?" (Guignon 1983, 82; see also 63, 208). The former leads to an obvious contradiction, while the latter restricts this ostensibly universal existential to a particular period of time. As we will discuss in the next chapter, this tension might have been a factor in Heidegger's later abandonment of fundamental ontology.[49] Guignon goes on to say that

> if the goal of *Being and Time* is limited to unfolding the meaning of Being "insofar as Being enters into the understandability [*Verständlichkeit*] of Dasein" (152), then it seems that the account should be subject to the same cultural and historical limitations that are found to shape Dasein's understanding in general. (Guignon 1983, 67)

Since understandings of Being are necessarily historical and since Being only is what it is within the context of these understandings, Being and Dasein are necessarily historical. They change as the various interpretations of them do. Only the illicit notion of a quasi-transcendental authentic self (illicit because it violates ED and A6) gives content to the distinction between the false everyday they-self and the true resolute self, allowing Heidegger the logical space to state that *Being and Time*'s first division's description of the average everyday self "*cannot lay claim to primordiality*" (Heidegger, *BT* 276/233), whereas in the second division "we have now arrived at that truth which is most primordial because it is *authentic*" (343/297). As Derrida asks,

> Is not the opposition of the *primordial* to the *derivative* still metaphysical? Is not the quest for an *archia* in general, no matter with what precautions one surrounds the concept, still the "essential" operation of metaphysics? . . . Is there not at least some Platonism in the *Verfallen?* Why determine as *fall* the passage from one temporality to another? (Derrida, *MP* 63; see also Derrida, *Ap* 14)

Here Derrida poses the same question about Heidegger's temporality that I asked about Nietzsche's dualism of activity and reactivity in the previous chapter: on what grounds other than a metaphysical definition does one get prioritized over the other?

To be consistent with his Phenomenological Ontology and Unconcealment Truth, as well as with his recognition of the historicality of Dasein, Heidegger should not seek the single, true essential structure of Dasein. The average everyday self described in the first division of *Being and Time* is not a false self in comparison with the true self of the second division; they are merely different selves, both of which show themselves, and should therefore be considered real and true by his lights. Both are persuasively unconcealed by Heidegger's descriptions and so meet his criterion of truth. The desire to make one *eigentlich,* real, or true and the other false is a holdover from the metaphysics he attacks so well when it comes to non-Dasein beings. Here, though, he is still under the influence of the Kantian Paradigm's R6 Realism of the Self.

What would an inquiry that was free of these concerns look like? It would apply A3 across the board, to the "Subject" as well as to the rest of the world, thus fully embracing A6 to take every manifestation of Dasein as a true unconcealment. It would admit the open-endedness of Dasein-analysis rather than founding everything in the *arche* of primordial temporality, or for that matter any *arche*. It would recognize its own historical situatedness and therefore acknowledge the inherent lack of closure to its inquiry.[50] Unlike the passage where Heidegger posits an end to the series of layers, determining an ultimate level to Dasein's Being and scoffing at the suggestion that his view too could be simply another interpretation, he should begin from the fact that his own account is historically bound.

Heidegger ought to recognize each historical manifestation of Dasein as true without a final closure into one truth. He should employ what Derrida calls a general economy, as opposed to restricted economies which settle all diversity and play into a set, closed system (Hegel is the poster child here). Heidegger should accept the field of historical fluctuation as lacking the self-identical, stable structure of Dasein to support it, leaving "a play of forms without a determined and invariable substance" (Derrida, *MP* 15). We must see this field as one which "excludes totalization. This field is in effect that of *play*, that is to say, a field of infinite substitutions only because it is finite . . . there is something missing from it: a center which arrests and grounds the play of substitutions" (Derrida, *WD* 289). Rather than anxiously fleeing *to* an authentic self, philosophy should be "the joyous affirmation of the play of the world and of the innocence of becoming, the affirmation of a world of signs without fault, without truth, and without origin" (292). Without fault means no accusations of fallenness or inauthenticity; without truth means no holding up of authentic existence as the true ideal we really are and should try to be; without origin means (for the early Heidegger) eliminating all traces of the transcendental subject founding and forming experience. This is the landscape in which Heidegger's later work moves; this is the Heideggerian Paradigm which marks the next great phase of continental philosophy.

## Donald Davidson's Understanding of Understanding

At the risk of interrupting the flow of my narrative, I will now turn to Donald Davidson's well-known argument against the coherence of the very idea of conceptual schemes. It is important for me to discuss this argument because my reading commits all of the continental philosophers treated in this book to some form of multiple conceptual schemes (A3). If my interpretation is correct, then Davidson's attack on this idea poses a serious threat to this central lineage of continental philosophers. However, I will show that his argument is based on a very questionable (and often questioned) conception of interpretation and communication. Continental philosophers generally, and early Heidegger in particular, have a very different understanding of interpretation which, while being superior on its own merits, has the additional advantage of not allowing Davidson's objection to arise. What is particularly interesting is that Heidegger's early attack on traditional conceptions of knowledge and interpretation not only anticipates three criticisms of Davidson's theory of interpretation made by several prominent analytic figures, but gives a detailed alternative account of interpretation, though I can only give a sketch of the potential response to Davidson here.[51]

I briefly talked about one of Davidson's criticisms of the idea of conceptual schemes, namely that it presupposes the incoherent notion of unformed matter, in my chapter on Hegel. I discussed that objection there because Hegel anticipated it in his attacks on Kant's conception of conceptual schemes, and offered an alternative version of schemes without this problematic element. This shows that Davidson's argument does not refute the *very idea* of conceptual schemes, but rather one particular formulation of them; continental philosophers after Hegel are generally committed to the A1 Mind-Dependence of Phenomenological Ontology (or Step Six Physics), which avoids this problem. Davidson's other main objection is based on the role that the principle of charity plays in interpreting others. Since language and understanding are central to Heidegger's early work, this seems like the best place to respond to this topic. Also, Davidson's work has been repeatedly linked to Heidegger,[52] and since the topic of this book is bridging the analytic-continental divide, the heavy traffic here makes this a felicitous place to engage with Davidson.

The traditional conception of meaning that Davidson is rejecting is the view that transparent meanings get attached to conventional sounds and marks within the epistemologically sterile and secure environment of the mind. The individual consciousness wholly determines meaning, rendering the relationship to words and others accidental. Davidson credits Quine with leading the revolt against this view: "Quine's way of approaching language by way of the radical translator . . . made the public aspect of language do the fundamental work it should and in the process permanently altered the way we think of meaning."[53] This approach reverses the traditional conception by viewing meaning as primarily communicative and public, which means that all accounts of it must use only publicly available phenomena. I will call this view the "public theory of meaning": if we want to explain how people understand each other (the locus of meaning), we cannot appeal to something inaccessible to the hearer such as the speaker's inner thoughts, so these factors, like Wittgenstein's beetles, fall out as irrelevant to the establishment of linguistic meaning.

Davidson is fully committed to this thesis: "The ultimate evidence, as opposed to a criterion, for the correctness of a theory of truth[54] must lie in available facts about how speakers use the language. When I say available, I mean publicly available."[55] No one has independent access to what is inside another's head, so communication takes place entirely on the basis of "external" factors; whatever meaning is, it can only be found here. Quine's thought experiment of the radical translator helps us resist assumptions about the role played by inner mental meaning that seem so plausible for conversations in known languages with fluent speakers: "Perhaps the most important thing he taught me was that there can be no more to the communicative content of words than is conveyed by verbal behavior. . . . This helps explain Quine's (and my) concentration on the tableau containing two people (teacher and pupil, jungle linguist and informant, speaker and hearer) in a shared environment" (Davidson, *PDD* 80; see also 192; Grandy 1973, 439–40). Assuming the position of someone trying to understand another's utterances with no previous knowledge of their language makes explicit what public resources are available to us. Thus, the perspective of radical translation (or interpretation, in Davidson's formulation) is the appropriate framework for this public conception of meaning because it shears off the features that tempt us into misleading pictures.

Without telepathic access or magical meanings, we have only publicly accessible sounds and behavior to go on in understanding another; this fact is dramatically demonstrated by radical translation, which is why, as Quine writes, "it is only radical translation that exposes the poverty of ultimate data for the identification of meanings" (Quine 1987, 7; see also Quine 1960, 28; Quine 1992 46). When we "bracket" our knowledge of a language in radical ignorance, only meaningless noises and movements remain for us to go on, a terribly meager source of information. I will call this idea the "paucity of evidence claim," which Davidson expresses by repeatedly stating that the only information available to radical interpretation is "thin" (Davidson, *ITI* 74) or "anaemic bits of evidence" (Davidson, "SCT" 314), namely the "noises" (Davidson, *ITI* 144) or "sound patterns" (277; Davidson, *SIO* 13–14; Davidson, "SCT" 309) emitted by the speaker. It is the combination of these claims—that we only have publicly available clues to go on and that these are meager—that makes interpretation such a puzzle.

> An interpreter cannot directly observe another person's propositional attitudes; beliefs, desires, and intentions, including the intentions which partly determine the meanings of utterances, are invisible to the naked eye. The interpreter can, however, attend to the outward manifestations of these attitudes, including utterances. Since we are able to discover from such manifestations what an agent thinks and means, there must be some intelligible relation between evidence and attitude. How do we bridge this gap? (Davidson, *SIO* 210)

This is the question to which radical interpretation is the answer.

Moreover, it is an urgently needed answer, since radical interpretation is not limited to jungle encounters. Since the gap between observable manifestations and unobservable intentions is ubiquitous, radical interpretation is as well. This is the final piece of the problem, which I will call the "ubiquity of radical interpretation thesis." The idea is that the thought experiment of the jungle translator is privileged only in being particularly illuminating; what it illuminates is actually the inescapable condition of all speech (see Quine 1969, 46; Quine 1992, 48). We never have more than public, impoverished data to go on, forcing us to interpret radically whenever we understand another. "As a matter of principle, then, meaning, and by its connection with meaning, belief also, are open to public determination [public meaning]. I shall take advantage of this fact . . . and adopt the stance of a radical interpreter when asking about the nature of belief. What a fully informed interpreter could learn about what a speaker means is all there is to learn [ubiquity]."[56] All there is to meaning is what occurs in social exchanges, which is in principle observable by a radical interpreter wholly ignorant of the language. Paraphrasing Quine, Davidson writes that "the problem of interpretation is domestic as well as foreign: it surfaces for speakers of the same language in the form of the question, how can it be determined that the language is the same? . . . All understanding of the speech of another involves radical interpretation" (Davidson, *ITI* 125).

The principle of charity enters to help with this seemingly impossible task of constructing meaning from meaningless sounds and movements. It states that an interpreter who is truly radical, meaning that they are not relying on any familiarity with the previous meanings of the speaker's words, intentions, actions, or beliefs, must start by assuming that the speaker's most basic assertions are true and her beliefs, desires, and actions largely consistent, else interpretation could find no purchase. Without a lot of auxiliary understanding, we would not be able to recognize a profoundly alien way of thinking, desiring, valuing, and so on, *as* a way of thinking, desiring, valuing, and so on, and without these initial identifications we could never reach the critical mass of auxiliary understanding required even to find that the interlocutor thinks or values differently. Thus we must a priori find any interlocutor carrying on in recognizable and recognizably rational ways. Since it is not the mind that is the source of meaning but interpersonal communication, successful interpretations determine what the speaker is actually saying; there is no further fact of the matter about what the speaker means beyond what successful interpretations make her out to mean.[57] So, putting the pieces together, the process of interpretation requires us to find others rational, what we find really is there, so others do think basically the way we do, that is, they must be by and large right and rational. "We must find others largely consistent and right in what they believe as a condition of making them intelligible, that is, as having thoughts at all. But since what we find is what is really there, it follows that rational creatures, creatures with thoughts, must be largely consistent and correct in their beliefs" (Davidson, *TLH* 245).

Davidson considers the principle of charity necessary to all understanding, calling this claim "the precept of unavoidable charity in interpretation."[58] Davidson's most persuasive argument for this point is the appeal to what would happen if a speaker were to stop making sense. If the speaker violates fundamental laws of logic or denies easily observed features of reality, the interpreter is faced with a choice: she can decide that her understanding is faulty (that is, some kind of miscommunication is going on), or that the interlocutor is not a rational being and thus not capable of carrying on a dialogue.[59] The principle of charity instructs us always to prefer the first choice, abandoning it only when overwhelmingly difficult to maintain, since, as Quine puts it, "the common sense behind the maxim is that one's interlocutor's silliness, beyond a certain point, is less likely than bad translation" (Quine 1960, 59; see also Davidson, *ITI* 101; Davidson, *Prob* 68–69).

Quine allows a third option here, namely ontological relativity. This is the possibility that the speaker is operating with a fundamentally different conceptual scheme (A3) which generates beliefs that are false by our lights, but which make sense within the boundaries of his way of organizing reality (A5). Davidson, however, extends Quine's principle of charity to rule out ontological relativity as an option open to a radical interpreter.[60] For Davidson, once the number of the interlocutor's beliefs that are false and/or incoherent by our lights reaches a critical mass (which, of course, has no set amount), the ability to interpret such a speaker becomes vanishingly small; we could never get a foothold in order to bootstrap ourselves up to the level of sophistication which could then allow us to construct an alternative conceptual scheme that would enable us to identify such a dissenting belief. Since such a speaker cannot be interpreted as speaking intelligibly, thoughts cannot be attributed to him and he is not a rational being. "If we cannot find a way to interpret the utterances and other behaviour of a creature as revealing a set of beliefs largely consistent and true by our own standards, we have no reason to count that creature as rational, as having beliefs, or as saying anything."[61] Simply to function as an interlocutor, one must have a sufficiently large body of correct beliefs and, since we can only evaluate correctness as we judge it, interlocutors must largely agree with us. Thus, it is the difficulties involved in radical interpretation and its situation of paucity of evidence that require such a strong principle of charity which in turn rules out alternative conceptual schemes: "*Given the underlying methodology of interpretation,* we could not be in a position to judge that others had concepts or beliefs radically different from our own" (Davidson, *ITI* 197, italics added; see also xx). This dependence is key because it implies that a different conception of interpretation might allow us to reach this judgment.

Davidson's view of interpretation has given rise to many criticisms, including one particularly well-known objection common to Ian Hacking and Michael Dummett's comments on Davidson's "A Nice Derangement of Epitaphs," as well as a paper by Tyler Burge. They all object to what I am calling Davidson's ubiquity of radical interpretation thesis. While conceding that it is perfectly plausible to speak of interpretation in circumstances such as learning unknown languages, figuring out nautical misdescriptions, malapropisms, and so on, they complain that Davidson has extrapolated features from these atypical situations to all linguistic encounters. According to Hacking, Davidson

> holds that radical interpretation is needed for domestic commerce as well as foreign. Davidson says that this surfaces in the question of how we know that we are speaking the same language. It is as if every time that I enter into conversation with another, I have to hold before me the possibility that he is an alien. . . . Something more plausibly called interpreting comes into play when we turn to malaprops and other mistakes or tropes. A philosophy of language couched in terms of domestic interpretation needs and feeds on things like malaprops. (Lepore 1986, 451)

Calling mundane instances of communication "interpretation" misuses the term, since "the vast majority of things we say to our peers in ordinary conversation are not interpreted at all" (Lepore 1986, 451). Explaining normal communication by means of a model derived from the abnormal situation of interpretation can only lead to a highly distorted picture of language.

Dummett agrees that interpretation occurs when comprehension is hindered by particular obstacles, and that here Davidson's work is applicable and illuminating. "They are, however, in the nature of things, atypical cases: if taken as prototypes for linguistic communication, they prompt the formulation of an incoherent theory" (Lepore 1986, 472; see also 463; Gorman in Dasenbrock 1993, 214). What usually occurs in communication is better captured by a more ordinary description: "In the normal case, the speaker simply says what he means. . . . In the normal case, likewise, the hearer simply understands. . . . There is nothing that his understanding the words consists in save his hearing them" (Lepore 1986, 471). Tyler Burge makes the same point (Hahn 1999, 235), differentiating the activity of interpretation that operates in the kinds of examples Davidson focuses on from an "understanding that is epistemically immediate, unreasoned, and non-inferential" (236), which he calls "comprehension," which is what usually happens in understanding utterances. Denying the first-person asymmetry of understanding that Davidson subscribes to, Burge claims that "barring anomaly, understanding an interlocutor's speech, on ordinary topics, seems no less immediate than understanding one's own speech in thinking out loud."[62]

Let me summarize these criticisms of Davidson's theory of radical interpretation in three objections:

1. Most communication takes place unproblematically and immediately without involving anything that we would normally call interpretation, that is, an evidence-based process of making inferences about meaning.
2. Cases of interpretation do occasionally occur, usually when some difficulty in comprehension arises, but these are by their very nature atypical and should not form the basis for a theory of communication.
3. Theoretical knowledge is in general a bad model for linguistic competence.[63]

Once the explicit references to Davidson are removed from these objections, the combined analysis bears a startling resemblance to Heidegger's analysis of Being-in-the-world. Heidegger's criticisms of traditional and in particular Cartesian conceptions of the mind and understanding anticipate to a large degree the objections these three prominent analytic philosophers pose to Davidson. Furthermore, Heidegger also offers a rich, fully worked out analysis of (to speak loosely) human nature, thought, knowledge, and language comprehension that connects these three objections into an organic whole, just the kind of analysis Dummett calls for at the end of his piece (see Lepore 1986, 475–76). Heidegger's early work not only criticizes the model of understanding Davidson adopts, but also explains why philosophers are continuously tempted to depict linguistic mastery as theoretical knowledge based on atypical instances of comprehension breakdown. Since it is this theoretical model that leads to Davidson's rejection of conceptual schemes, Heidegger's alternative view of communication offers a coherent way of thinking about them. Let us now turn to the individual objections.

1. Average everyday Dasein is characterized as Being-in-the-world, which is defined as "a non-thematic circumspective absorption in references or assignments constitutive for the readiness-to-hand of a totality of equipment" (Heidegger, *BT* 107/76). First and foremost Dasein is an active participant using ready-to-hand tools, rather than a disengaged observer or theoretical knower (Heidegger, *PIK* 15; Heidegger, *HCT* 30). This means that while she uses tools intelligently and so demonstrates her understanding of them, this understanding takes the form of a non-thematic and non-theoretical "circumspection" (see Heidegger, *BT* 98–99/69), an idea similar to Ryle's know-how.[64] Rather than focusing on theoretical knowledge as most epistemologists do, Heidegger is interested in the kind of understanding that "is not made thematic, remains unobjectified, and is preconceptual."[65]

The early Heidegger applies this non-thematic circumspective comprehension to our normal use of language as well as tools, both of which occur primarily within the meaning-generating context of ongoing projects. Heidegger views understanding as immediate rather than as a two-part process of meaningless raw data followed by its interpretation. A hammer presents itself as to-drive-in-nails-with rather than as a group of color patches that have to be fitted together and given a purpose before we understand what it is; similarly, grasping language does not generally occur in two distinct steps—first bare sounds and then the act of interpretation, which yields meaning—but encounters significance right from the start.

> What we "first" hear is never noises or complexes of sounds, but the creaking wagon, the motor-cycle. We hear the column on the march, the north wind, the woodpecker tapping, the fire crackling. It requires a very artificial and complicated frame of mind to "hear" a "pure noise.". . . Likewise, when we are explicitly hearing the discourse of another, we proximally understand what is said. . . . Even in cases where the speech is indistinct or in a foreign language, what we proximally hear is *unintelligible* words, and not a multiplicity of tone-data.[66]

Thus Heidegger anticipates Hacking, Dummett, and Burge in rejecting the paucity of evidence claim. A good phenomenological description would never allow such a finding: "It is not as if there were first verbal sounds which in time were furnished with meanings. On the contrary, what is primary is being in the world, that is, concerned understanding and being in the context of meanings" (Heidegger, *HCT* 210).

The objection to Davidson here isn't that he is doing bad phenomenology, of course, since that is not his intention (though, as Heidegger points out, one needs an accurate description of a phenomenon just to ensure that one's explanation accounts for it). Rather, the paucity of evidence claim poses an internal problem for Davidson because, by separating interpretation into the two steps of mere noise and meaningful language, it resurrects the third dogma of empiricism, that is, the insistence on "an uninterpreted source of evidence" (Davidson, *ITI* xx) independent of the significance we place on it. Since he makes the rejection of this dogma an important part of his objection to conceptual schemes, its resurfacing in the theory of radical interpretation that is supposed to supplant conceptual schemes is highly problematic. It is this view of words as mere noise that justifies the ubiquity of radical interpretation: since all we ever have to go on are patterns of sound with no intrinsic significance, a second step of interpretation is required to infuse them with meaning, and the difficulty of doing so much with so little is what demands the principle of charity's homogenization. This view is the target of the first criticism by Dummett and others, and it seems to presuppose the dogma that Davidson rejects.[67]

Davidson often claims a more commonsense epistemology that takes the macroscopic mundane entities we normally think we are talking about to be the genuine referents of sentences in an "unmediated touch with the familiar objects" (Davidson, *ITI* 198, see also Davidson, *TLH* 53) of our world, rejecting any kind of intermediaries like color patches or ideas. Perhaps Davidson's main objection to the third dogma of empiricism is its vulnerability to skepticism.

> What matters is that there should be an ultimate source of evidence the character of which can be wholly specified without reference to what it is evidence for. Thus patterns of stimulation, like sense data, can be identified and described without reference to "what goes on around us." If our knowledge of the world derives entirely from evidence of this kind, then not only may our senses sometimes deceive us; it is possible that we are systematically and generally deceived.[68]

His solution? "The moral is obvious. Since we can't swear intermediaries to truthfulness, we should allow no intermediaries between our beliefs and their objects in the world" (Davidson, *SIO* 144; see also Davidson, *TLH* 135; Davidson, *PDD* 106). We must abolish these intermediaries in order to reestablish unmediated contact with the world, a contact that involves nothing like an act of interpretation of meaningless color patches.

The problem is that Davidson only goes halfway; he abolishes intermediaries between ourselves and things while keeping them between us and other people. In fact, the theory of radical interpretation is *based on* the empiricist-style picture of bare noise forming an uninterpreted intermediary between ourselves and our interlocutors, which is the "ultimate evidence" (Davidson, *TLH* 49) for theories of meaning. The only legitimate data for all instances of linguistic interpretation is "evidence we can imagine the virgin investigator having without his already being in possession of the theory it is supposed to be evidence for" (Davidson, *ITI* 143; see also 128). Any utterance must be described "without reference to what it is evidence for" in order to keep the radical interpreter's virginal ignorance pristine, yet this places it back into the framework of the uninterpreted given of the third dogma that Davidson works hard to reject.

Heidegger, on the other hand, rejects intermediaries across the board, in speech as well as perception. Words immediately strike us as meaningful communication from others.

> We do not first need to process and shape a tumult and medley of feelings; we are right from the start involved with what is understood itself. . . . Even in hearing discourse we first in fact hear what is said. Even when we do not understand the discourse, when it is unclear or perhaps the language is foreign, even then we first hear *incomprehensible* words and not mere phonetic data. We first hear what is said and not its being said, not the process of discourse as such but the about-which of the discourse. (Heidegger, *HCT* 266–67)

Rather than requiring a special act to infuse faceless bits of sonic material with significance, we constantly live in an atmosphere of meaning. The worldhood of Dasein is made up of the teleological chains of tools that structure our projects, which significantly refer to their utility: I grab my keys in order to drive my car to my office, where I start up the computer in order to check my e-mail. . . . (see Heidegger, *HCT* 203, 213; Heidegger, *TDP* 61). This is the world I live in and am and it is made of significance. Thus Heidegger's extensive analysis of worldhood shores up objection no. 1, supplying a comprehensive conception of unproblematic, non-interpretive, immediate understanding.

2. Heidegger also gives an extensive explanation of objection no. 2, those atypical cases in which fluid comprehension turns into active, conscious interpretation when confronted with a problem. In light of Dasein's primary mode of active engagement, he accounts for these cases of ex-

plicit interpretation in terms of equipment breakdowns. Although inconspicuous while functioning properly, when it malfunctions a tool shatters our absorbed flow, forcing us to switch to some degree of thematic awareness. This alteration in attitude induces a correlative "changeover" in the tool's mode of Being from ready-to-hand to, at its most extreme, mere present-at-hand object just sitting there, its referential meaning-giving connections cut. This attitude of theoretical observation constitutes "*a new stance of the being of Dasein* toward that which is known" (Heidegger, *HCT* 163; see also Heidegger, *BT* 412–14/361–63); instead of engaged absorbed use, one is now merely observing or "thematizing."

When this stance is assumed, "being-in-the-world is now modified to a state of solely *looking*, a mere looking which *interprets*" (Heidegger, *HCT* 195). An act of interpretation is now required because we are confronted with faceless entities, mere things lacking significance: "In the pure perception of a thing, the world shows itself instead in a *deficient meaningfulness*. . . . The traditional categories of thingness, which for definite reasons are also identified as *the* categories of being—thingness, substance, accident, property, causality—have their phenomenal genesis in this deficient meaningfulness" (219; see also Heidegger, *BT* 200–201/158, 412/361). Present-at-hand things have no intrinsic meaning, since they lack referential relations with other entities. Although presence-at-hand is only one possible mode of Being, due to the fact that it is what is apparent to thematic attention, it is what philosophers and scientists have always latched on to as genuine reality. Presence-at-hand has an intrinsic propensity to present itself as the sole mode of reality (R3), and so tends to form the basis for theories.

When language is studied and thereby thematized, "the *Logos* itself is an entity, and, according to the orientation of ancient ontology, it is something present-at-hand. Words are proximally present-at-hand; that is to say, we come across them just as we come across Things" (Heidegger, *BT* 201/159; see also Heidegger, *BP* 205). Put out of play, words become inert sounds that need to be figured out; in other words, the position of the radical interpreter corresponds to the theoretical attitude. Although situations of active interpretation are rare exceptions which behave very differently from normal linguistic experience, Heidegger shows why it is almost inevitable that thinkers base their theories of communication on just such instances. Fluid, successful speech is inconspicuous and difficult to study; it is only when easy comprehension breaks down in mistakes, metaphors, or malaprops that language calls attention to itself and invites study. Philosophers prioritize the phenomena most apparent to thematic analysis (presence-at-hand) while ignoring what is much more common but inconspicuous (ready-to-hand).[69] Davidson explicitly states that the most important linguistic phenomena for his work are the cases of difficult but successful communication,[70] just the cases of partial linguistic breakdown that criticism no. 2 accuses Davidson of taking as the norm. Heidegger's analysis explains why philosophers are attracted to this mode as well as why it is inadequate.

3. The inappropriateness of the model of theoretical knowledge for all sorts of phenomena concerning Dasein, including linguistic competence, is one of Heidegger's main topics. A disengaged thinker presses all entities into the only ontological mold available in this stance: present-at-hand objects. Likewise, the only epistemological relation apparent in that mode is the thematic hypothetico-explanatory inquiry he is presently engaged in. Now Heidegger is not antagonistic to theory per se; he merely wants to unseat its presumed hegemony and return it to one mode of knowing among others. Theory has its place, and Heidegger is trying to put it in its place. One of his main criticisms of Husserl's form of phenomenology, sometimes under the guise of Descartes (see Heidegger, *HCT* 172; Heidegger, *BT* 122/89; Heidegger, *IPR* 160), is that it focuses exclusively on this mode of knowledge and views all experience in terms of it.

> This primary kind of experience, which provides the basis for every further characterization of consciousness, turns out to be a theoretical kind of experience and not a genuinely natural one. . . . The manner in which what is experienced gives itself here is defined by the feature of an objectivity for a theoretical consideration of nature, and nothing else. It thus follows that the starting point for the elaboration of pure consciousness is a *theoretical* one. (Heidegger, *HCT* 117; see also 91, 111)

Engaged in theoretical analysis, the Husserlian phenomenologist projects this attitude and its ramifications on to the object of his study. Although phenomenology's basic ambition is to capture life as it is actually lived, Husserl views phenomena through the atypical and distorting brackets of the theoretical phenomenological attitude.

> Inasmuch as [Husserlian] phenomenological investigation is itself theoretical, the investigator is easily motivated to make a specifically theoretical comportment to the world his theme. Thus a specifically theoretical apprehension of the thing is put forward as an exemplary mode of being-in-the-world, instead of phenomenologically placing oneself directly in the current and the continuity of access of the everyday preoccupation with things.[71]

In a theoretical attitude, all experience looks like theory and everyone a theoretician, but this is hardly our "everyday" state.

Davidson is sensitive to the other functions that language has, but in principle language always comes down to truth conditions and literal (what he calls "first") meaning (see Davidson, *SCT* 312, 312–13n56). Any other functions necessarily depend on language's truth conditions, which are understood by the construction of truth theories. Propositional knowledge which gets expressed in assertions is for him an ineliminable component of linguistic competence. When Richard Rorty puts objection no. 3 to him by suggesting that the non-theoretical knowing how to ride a bicycle is a better model for language comprehension, Davidson responds this way:

> Knowing a language is, in some respects, like knowing how to ride a bicycle. In both cases, as Rorty points out, we talk of knowing how, and in neither case is it necessary or common to know a theory that explains what we do. But there are also striking differences. There are endless things a speaker or interpreter must know: the truth conditions a hearer will probably take her utterances to have, the truth conditions that most of the sentences she hears will have, relations of entailment, contradiction, and evidential support among sentences. And this is just a start. . . . Bicycle riding requires no propositional knowledge at all. (Davidson, *TLH* 325)

Although admitting that such knowledge is rarely consciously entertained (see Davidson, *TLH* 112; see also Davidson, *SIO* 90), Davidson holds that unlike know-how, language comprehension requires some form of propositional knowledge.

And Davidson conceives of the meaning of these sentences in terms of theories of truth. Calling them "theories" is not a chance word choice, but indicates the tenor of his entire analysis. Since we cannot rely on linguistic conventions (Davidson, *TLH* 107; Davidson, *PDD* 80), Davidson must construct a complex machinery of theory to account for how we succeed in understanding each other on the basis of so little data. In this context, comprehension occurs by means of making hypotheses about the meaning of utterances, hypotheses that get tested and, in light of evidence, either stand, get refuted, or retooled: "Your knowledge of what my words mean has to be based on evidence and inference: you probably assume you have it right, and you probably do. Nevertheless, it is a hypothesis" (Davidson, *SIO* 66). Davidson explicitly compares having a mundane conversation to engaging in a scientific investigation: "Finding out what others think is in the same general line of business with finding out how hydrogen and oxygen combine to make water. . . . We learn how to talk about other people's states of belief, desire, intention, hope, and doubt using the normal sort of observable evidence."[72] Pascal Engel is right when he says that although continental hermeneuticists and Davidson all focus on what they call "interpretation," they conceive it very differently: "On Davidson's view, the interpretation of action is not a scientific explanation but, like it, consists in testing hypotheses against data. The data and the hypotheses differ . . . but it is a form of hypothetico-deductive explanation nevertheless" (Engel 1991, 143).

Davidson depicts mundane conversations as Hempel-style scientific investigations involving the generation and modification of hypotheses on the basis of evidence. Along with the paucity of evidence claim, Davidson often justifies this analysis by what I will call Davidson's uncertainty principle. This principle claims that no matter how familiar the circumstances and the interlocutor, one can never be sure of the meaning of her words or language, or even that she is speaking a language and so is rational at all. This uncertainty is a necessary part of all communication, and it shows why we should explain language comprehension in terms of scientific-style evidence, inference, hypothesis, and so on. Davidson responds to Burge's criticism by saying that he "was not supposing one had to go through the absurdly artificial maneuvers of radical interpretation, or that one had to search for evidence, consult a theory, or in general do any complicated thinking. My point was simply that it is always an empirical question, though one we normally do not raise, whether what we take for granted others mean is what they do in fact mean" (Davidson, *PDD* 252). We do not *actually* go through the procedure of radical interpretation, he says here (a point he is inconsistent on), but it is important to show that it is always *possible,* since it is a real issue whether the meanings that we take for granted are correct (see Davidson, *RD* 81; though see also Davidson, *PDD* 330). Although not normally raised, it is a genuine question whether my wife's utterance, "The cat is on the mat," in response to my query as to the location of the cat really means that the cat is on the mat, or whether she has suddenly started speaking another language which happens to contain an expression that sounds exactly like the English sentence, or if her vocal mechanisms have undergone a random spasm that by chance produced a sound that perfectly resembles an appropriate answer. Since a sufficient number of errors amounts to her irrationality, it is by implication also a real question whether she is or will continue to be rational.

Davidson's view is that although we did not consciously think out hypotheses while listening, the fact of perpetual uncertainty retrospectively exposes our communication as resting on presuppositions. Communication turns out to be a theoretical activity. Since it is merely an assumption that the speaker's utterance means what I think it does, my quick and dirty interpretation has written a check that only radical interpretation can cash. Since the uncertainty is ubiquitous, so are assumptions about what language the speaker is using and thus what her words mean.

> The problem of interpretation . . . surfaces for speakers of the same language in the form of the question, how can it be determined that the language is the same?[73] Speakers of the same language can go on the assumption that for them the same expressions are to be interpreted in the same way, but this does not indicate what justifies the assumption. (Davidson, *ITI* 125)

Even when we have no reason whatsoever to doubt our comprehension of our interlocutor's utterances or her rationality, the threat of communication breakdown is always present, and it is what justifies the theoretical model which portrays our conversations as a set of inferences resting on assumptions. Given only meaningless noise (paucity of evidence) and an unjustified assumption that the emitter of the noise is a rational, competent language-user using the sounds as words the way I do (uncertainty principle), and given that all of these interactions take place by means of theoretical knowledge which must be assessed by a logical rigor appropriate to the making of hypotheses, the conclusion that "in any normal utterance there is a presumption that the speaker knows what he means, while there is no such presumption in our understanding of others" (Davidson, *RD* 211–12; see also 248; Davidson, *SIO* 66) is inevitable. Davidson's proof that radical interpretation is possible is then what justifies these assumptions (see Davidson, *RD* 264; Davidson, *EAE* 257).

Heidegger's diagnosis would be that Davidson has fallen victim to the problem that bedevils philosophy in general. Davidson focuses on moments of communicative breakdown which present words as meaningless present-at-hand sound and understanding as theoretical knowledge. These two ideas combine to form his central notion of radical interpretation. Heidegger sees all three of the objections raised by Hacking, Dummett, and Burge arising together as an organic whole from this single starting point: "Starting with the logos as a verbal sequence leads directly to misinterpretation of the remaining constituents of the logos" (Heidegger, *BP* 206; see also Heidegger, *BT* 267/224). The only way to construct a better account of interpretation is to begin from a better description of communication.

The teleological chains that make up Heidegger's conception of worldhood "resist any sort of mathematical functionalization; nor are they merely something thought, first posited in an 'act of thinking.' They are rather relationships in which concernful circumspection as such already dwells" (Heidegger, *BT* 122/88). Traditional philosophy assumes that actions must be founded on something like truth-functional propositional beliefs; my standing up presupposes a belief that the ground is solid, for example. Heidegger reverses this relation, concluding that although "it has long been held that the way to grasp the Real is by that kind of knowing which is characterized by beholding . . . knowing is a *founded* mode of access to the Real" (246/202). Our primary and much more common way of relating to things is through active engagement, which is why Dreyfus calls Heidegger's hermeneutics practical holism, as opposed to Davidson's theoretical holism (see Dreyfus 1980). Although we do engage in conceptual thought and evidence-based inference, the vast majority of the time we react unthinkingly, albeit intelligently, to the world and others: "Interpretation is carried out primordially not in a theoretical statement but in an action of circumspective concern—laying aside the unsuitable tool" (Heidegger, *BT* 200/157). The stance of disengaged observer retroactively inserts the belief "this tool is unsuitable" into the behavior, but this is an artifact of the theoretical attitude. Heidegger insists that "I cannot adequately define the concept of understanding if, in trying to make the definition, I look solely to specific types of cognitive comportment" (Heidegger, *BP* 275; see also Heidegger, *BT* 185/145). Instead, he conceives the term "understands in the sense of being skilled or expert at it, has the know-how of it" (Heidegger, *BP* 276). This know-how cannot be spelled out in terms of thematic beliefs, but must be accepted as its own primitive mode of understanding, what he calls circumspection. In fact, Heidegger considers theoretical knowledge to be based on practical engagement, not the other way around: Dasein "is in a particular but primarily non-cognitive and not merely cognitive mode of being. . . . Knowing understood as apprehending has sense only on the basis of an *already-being-involved-with.* This already-being-involved-with, in which knowing as such can first 'live,' is not first 'produced' directly by a cognitive performance" (Heidegger, *HCT* 162; see also 299).

This means that the theoretical model cannot capture our fundamental relationship to the world and other people; attempts to do so always end up distorting the situation. Speaking in 1925 of the "problem" of skepticism toward the external world, Heidegger says,

> Nothing exists in our relationship to the world which provides a basis for the phenomenon of belief in the world. I have not yet been able to find this phenomenon of belief. Rather, the peculiar thing is just that the world is "there" *before* all belief. The world is never experienced as something which is believed any more than it is guaranteed by knowledge.

> Inherent in the being of the world is that its existence *needs no guarantee in regard to a subject*. . . . Any purported belief in it is a theoretically motivated misunderstanding. This is not a convenient evasion of a problem. The question rather is whether this so-called problem which is ostensibly being evaded is really a problem at all. (Heidegger, *HCT* 215–16)

The whole model of theoretical, cognitive beliefs is a fundamentally inappropriate way to characterize our most common and most basic interactions with the world and others, and it is the source of pseudo-problems when we find that these "beliefs" cannot be justified. Heidegger speaks of the uncertainty of the external world here, but it is equally applicable to the uncertainty of the meaning of words and the rationality of interlocutors, that is, external-world skepticism and solipsism. When plugged into the theoretical model and viewed as beliefs in need of justification, assumptions seem to pop up everywhere one looks and we scramble to find reasons for them. This is the purpose of radical interpretation. Heidegger's alternative is to reject the theoretical model that creates the pseudo-problem in the first place.

This approach is strikingly similar to Wittgenstein's later work. I will briefly examine this work both in order to illuminate Heidegger's position and to break down the view of analytic and continental philosophy as monolithic movements that are internally unified and mutually opposed. Heidegger and Wittgenstein are in fact much closer to each other on this important issue than Wittgenstein is to Davidson, even though Davidson often invokes Wittgenstein (or Kripkenstein) as an inspiration. Whereas Davidson argues that communication is based on an assumption that the interlocutor is a rational being which then requires radical interpretation to secure, Wittgenstein believes that justifications come to an end at assertions that cannot and need not be justified, such as that other people have minds or that there is an external world. The entire theoretical model of justification and inference loses application at this point. Although it is true that we do not doubt such basic ideas, it is a deep mistake to consider them assumptions. "I would like to regard this certainty, not as something akin to hastiness or superficiality, but as a form of life. . . . But that means I want to conceive it as something that lies beyond being justified or unjustified; as it were, as something animal" (Wittgenstein, *OC* §358–59; see also §538). Like Heidegger, Wittgenstein grounds our fundamental outlook on practical engagement rather than on theoretical thought. "As if giving grounds did not come to an end sometime. But the end is not an ungrounded presupposition: it is an ungrounded way of acting."[74] Davidson sees unjustified assumptions in communication because of the constant uncertainty, leading to the need for radical interpretation. Wittgenstein agrees that there is no ultimate justification here, but also thinks that none is needed, since these are not the kinds of practices for which justification is relevant.

Skepticism-induced vertigo results when we judge our most basic beliefs or believing tout court by the standards used to evaluate individual beliefs and inevitably find them wanting. This kind of evaluation, though, is based on a category mistake: it applies a technique that is perfectly reasonable and practical within its context to exceptional assertions or to the language-game as a whole. The theoretical view considers our language-game as a whole in need of justification by establishing a set of facts, but "why should the language-game rest on some kind of knowledge?" (Wittgenstein, *OC* §477). Instead, in words that almost directly echo Heidegger's, "the language-game . . . is not based on grounds. It is not reasonable (or unreasonable). It is there—like our life" (Wittgenstein, *OC* §559; see also Wittgenstein, *PI* II.xi, p. 171; II.xi, p. 192). The parenthetical addition here is crucial; the lack of grounds does not render the language-game irrational, but rather arational, since this practice lies outside the bounds of justification. Accepting what Heidegger would call an "abyssal ground" is hard, though. "The difficult thing here is not, to dig down to the ground; no, it is to recognize the ground that lies before us as the ground. . . . Our disease is one of wanting to explain."[75] One reason for this drive to explain is the paucity of evidence that is induced by exiting from our normal flowing interactions, what Heidegger sometimes calls "unworlding" and which Wittgenstein identifies with philosophy's language going "on holiday." Staring at a phenomenon stopped in its tracks, no longer functioning in its normal context, renders its usual effectiveness in practice deeply mysterious. Interpreting an arrow from the perspective of one radically ignorant of "sign language" instead of just following it automatically (something like the radical interpreter) makes me realize how arbitrary its conventional direction is; in that frame of mind, a rule does not seem capable of directing me, since "any interpretation still hangs in the air along with what it interprets, and cannot give it any support" (Wittgenstein, *PI* §198). To help the stupefied theoretical observer, Wittgenstein does not construct a conceptual machinery for determining the meaning of the rule, since that is impossible, but rather assembles reminders of the immediate meaningfulness of our usual flowing interactions, showing us that deliberative interpretation is not necessary in these situations: "'How can one follow a rule?' That is what I should like to ask. But how does it come about that I want to ask that, when after all I find no kind of difficulty in following a rule? Here we obviously misunderstand the facts that lie before our eyes."[76] Like Heidegger, Wittgenstein is fighting the bewitchment of philosophy by returning us to our average everyday circumstances.

The theoretical model presents relations to others as based on assumptions, plugging mundane interactions into the language-game of theory within which they are notoriously difficult to justify. This is Davidson's position, where an interlocutor's rationality is an uncertain assumption that must be justified by the possibility of radical interpretation. For Wittgenstein, viewing others as having minds is one of these unjustified and unjustifiable "beliefs" that needs no justification. He agrees with Heidegger's diagnosis:

> How does the philosophical problem about mental processes and states and about behaviourism arise?—The first step is the one that altogether escapes notice. We talk of processes and states and leave their nature undecided. . . . But that is just what commits us to a particular way of looking at the matter. . . . (The decisive movement in the conjuring trick has been made, and it was the very one that we thought quite innocent.)—And now the analogy which was to make us understand our thoughts falls to pieces. (Wittgenstein, *PI* §308; see also §152, §154)

The starting point (a picture for Wittgenstein, an ontological definition for Heidegger) sets the parameters for all that follows and if they are set badly, unanswerable problems ensue.

In this case, defining relations to others as based on beliefs activates an inappropriate conceptual machinery:

> "I believe that he is suffering."—Do I also *believe* that he isn't an automaton? It would go against the grain to use the word in both connexions. (Or is it like this: I believe that he is suffering, but am certain that he is not an automaton? Nonsense!) . . . . My attitude towards him is an attitude towards a soul. I am not of the *opinion* that he has a soul. (Wittgenstein, *PI* II.iv, p. 152; see also *RPP* §268)

Wittgenstein draws a distinction here between opinion or belief and attitude, where the former fits into the epistemic structure of reasons and justification, while the latter is connected to practical engagement. The mistake made by both the skeptic and the one who responds to the skeptic's challenge is to treat the attitude as if it were a matter of knowledge. Under this picture, one is forced to conclude that "'then they make a tacit presupposition.' Then what we do in our language-game always rests on a tacit presupposition" (Wittgenstein, *PI* II.v, p. 153). This is precisely how

Davidson talks about our relations to others, but Wittgenstein regards it as a reductio ad absurdum (see Wittgenstein, *LWP* 2:87; Wittgenstein, *OC* §627, for the absurdities of ubiquitous qualifications). As Wittgenstein says dismissively about the uncertainty of others' mental states, "'But, if you are *certain,* isn't it that you are shutting your eyes in face of doubt?'—They are shut" (Wittgenstein, *PI* II.xi, p.191). Wittgenstein rejects Davidson's Uncertainty Principle, responding to the skeptic that "a doubt is not necessary even when it is possible" (Wittgenstein, *OC* §392; see also Wittgenstein, *RPP* §342; Wittgenstein, *Zet* §235).

Early Heidegger, like later Wittgenstein, treats our relations to others as primarily practical rather than cognitive and as immediate rather than mediated through evidence and inference: another's "being-there-with in the environing world is wholly immediate, inconspicuous, obvious, similar to the character of the presence of world-things" (Heidegger, *HCT* 239), that is, tools. The inferential conception of our relations to others is based on viewing them as present-at-hand objects to which sole relation is explicit theoretical beliefs. This view falsifies our pre-philosophical experience as recovered by careful phenomenological description: "When we interpret Dasein without any theoretical distortions we can see it immediately as 'Being-alongside' the world with which it concerns itself. . . . They are not encountered as person-Things present-at-hand: we meet them 'at work,' that is, primarily in their Being-in-the-world" (Heidegger, *BT* 156/120). However, just as equipment switches over under the theoretical gaze, so others are misunderstood as person-Things, and "the problem of other minds," that is, how we could possibly communicate with or know the inner workings of such opaque creatures, arises and appears primary.

> The theoretical problematic of understanding the "psychical life of Others" . . . gets taken as that which, primordially and "in the beginning," constitutes Being towards Others and makes it possible at all. This phenomenon, which is none too happily designated as "*empathy,*" is then supposed, as it were, to provide the first ontological bridge from one's own subject, which is given proximally as alone, to the other subject, which is proximally quite closed off. (Heidegger, *BT* 161–62/124)

This bridge is exceedingly difficult to build, but luckily, it is gratuitous; it is an impossible bridge being built over solid land.

However, it is just this gap that Davidson's radical interpretation intends to span. The uncertainty principle that I have been attributing to him, that is, the claim that we must take it as an open question whether or not my interlocutor is speaking my language or is even a rational agent, entertains skepticism toward other minds as a serious possibility. This skepticism inevitably follows from treating utterances as mere sounds and the sole evidence we have for inferring others' mental states;[77] it is the problem to which radical interpretation is the solution. The irony, as mentioned above, is that Davidson repeatedly criticizes Quine's proximal stimulus of nerve irritations for leading to skepticism toward the external world.

> If we are not to be skeptics about the possibility of knowledge of the external world or other minds we must reject the view that all knowledge of the world depends on objects . . . taken as epistemically basic, and therefore as epistemic intermediaries between our minds and the rest of the world. . . . Empiricism . . . claims that the ultimate evidence for beliefs about the external world is something nonconceptual that is directly given in experience.[78]

Utterances as mere sounds (paucity) represent the ultimate evidence for a speaker's rationality that is nonconceptual in the sense that their meaning and even their meaningfulness are bracketed. And the result is exactly what Davidson warns us of: the possibility of skepticism (uncertainty) is built into his theory of radical interpretation; staving off this possibility is what motivates the principle of charity. The constant possibility of skepticism toward any *individual* mind (he effectively rules out wholesale solipsism) is integral to his approach, inasmuch as we are forced to adjust our interpretations in order to prevent the conclusion that the other is not rational.

Since skepticism "about the possibility of the external world or other minds" is based on empiricism's reliance on epistemic intermediaries, Davidson claims in his later work that "the only alternative to subjectivism is externalism, a view that makes the connection between thought and the world intrinsic rather than extrinsic—a connection not inferred, constructed, or discovered, but there from the start" (Davidson, "Ext" 1–2; see also Davidson, *PDD* 732). He tries to build relations to others and world directly into the holistic triangle that is necessary for thought and language so that skepticism "cannot get started" (Davidson, *TMK* 155; see also Davidson, "KVP" 287). However, this project is hobbled from the beginning because radical interpretation is still retained in triangulation, and it rests upon the idea that knowledge of others *is* "inferred, constructed, or discovered." The two legs of the triangle are on fundamentally different footings, since perception of things is unmediated, while perception of others must be inferred from meaningless sounds. Davidson's triangulation tries to make the connection between thought and others intrinsic or there from the start, but its retention of radical interpretation prevents it. Heidegger's early work, however, does give such an analysis. He frequently claims that "*as being-in-the-world, Dasein is at the same time being with one another*—more rigorously, '*being-with*'. . . . Being-with signifies a character of being of Dasein as such which is *co-original* with being-in-the-world" (Heidegger, *HCT* 238; see also Heidegger, *BT* 156/120, 162/125). "Co-original" or "equi-primordial" means that it is as integral to Dasein's makeup as the other basic constituents; it could not simply be added on to a fully composed Dasein.

Both early Heidegger and Davidson insist on quite similar tripartite holisms of self, world, and others, though of course Davidson casts the parts in terms of knowledge.[79] Look at Davidson's discussion:

> The conceptual connections between our knowledge of our own minds and our knowledge of the world of nature are not definitional but holistic. The same is true of the conceptual connections between our knowledge of behavior and our knowledge of other minds. There are, then, no "barriers," logical or epistemic, between the three varieties of knowledge. On the other hand, the very way in which each depends on the others shows why none can be eliminated, or reduced to the others. (Davidson, *SIO* 214; see also 121, 220)

Now Heidegger:

> Because being-in-the-world belongs to the basic constitution of the Dasein, the existent Dasein is essentially *being-with* others *as being-among* intraworldy beings. . . . Being-in-the-world is with equal originality both being-with and being-among. (Heidegger, *BP* 278; see also 297; Heidegger, *HCT* 296–97)

Here is Davidson:

> Knowledge of other minds and knowledge of the world are mutually dependent; neither is possible without the other. . . . Knowledge of our own minds and knowledge of the minds of others are thus mutually dependent. (Davidson, *SIO* 213; see also Davidson, *Prob* 18)

And here Heidegger:

> Because Dasein's Being is Being-with, its understanding of Being already implies the understanding of Others. . . . Knowing oneself is grounded in Being-with. (Heidegger, *BT* 161/123–24)

Besides rejecting the model of theoretical knowledge, the main difference between the two is that Heidegger's holism is stronger and constitutes an absolute starting place. Davidson tries to explain how the triangle comes about to enable us to construct our knowledge of the other, which means that this awareness is *not* "there from the start." Heidegger, on the other hand, does make Dasein's connection to both the world and to others primordial: "Dasein is determined from the very outset by being-with others" (Heidegger, *BP* 296; see also Heidegger, *BT* 152/116). Heidegger argues that any attempt to establish intersubjectivity by starting from separate subjects will prove futile.

> It is wrong to oppose to objects an isolated ego-subject, without seeing in the Dasein the basic constitution of being-in-the-world; but it is equally wrong to suppose that the problem is seen in principle and progress made toward answering it if the solipsism of the isolated ego is replaced by a solipsism en deux in the I-thou relationship. . . . Being-in-the-world is with equal originality both being-with and being-among. (Heidegger, *BP* 278; see also Heidegger, *HCT* 246)

Bringing together a group of traditionally conceived subjects does not surmount the fundamental problem; it amounts to merely a group solipsism.

Davidson maintains that the farther our interpretations depart from our own beliefs, the more probable it becomes that we are misinterpreting the speaker, until we must conclude that either we do not understand the language or the speaker is not a rational agent. Although the theory of triangulation prevents wholesale solipsism, since other minds in general have to exist in order for me to have thought,[80] the threat is there in every particular encounter, no matter what other reasons there are for believing in the other's rationality. This uncertainty principle is essential to his entire system, since it is this possibility that shows that all of our relations with others are based on assumptions in need of justification. It also enforces the principle of charity by constantly holding the ultimate threat over the interpreter's head: any interpretation that yields largely false propositions ends up absolving the speaker of rationality and hence language. The act of finding others to be deeply heterogeneous believers becomes a performative contradiction in that it undermines the very act of interpretation. On pain of failure, interpretations must produce generally homogeneous translations, rendering the very idea of alternate, and thus any, conceptual schemes incoherent.

The important point to notice here is that the threat that I might find a speaker irrational or her words meaningless regardless of other indications of her rationality is based on the claims that I only have noise and behavior available, and that these operate as evidence on which I construct disprovable hypotheses. In my terms, Davidson bases his uncertainty principle on the paucity of evidence and ubiquity of radical interpretation claims, all structured by the model of theoretical knowledge. It is only if we accept this model and the view of words as an unconceptualized evidential intermediary that we are led to find uncertainty a genuine problem, and so feel the need to enforce the principle of charity so strictly that alternate conceptual schemes are unacceptable.

Early Heidegger and later Wittgenstein offer an alternative view which rejects the paucity of evidence claim as well as the model of theoretical knowledge. They posit an engaged, non-epistemic relation that immediately grasps the other as a rational agent without a process of cognitive interpretation or evidence-based inference. My friend could always stop making sense, but that doesn't mean that this possibility does or should play a role in my smoothly running daily interactions, nor does it inform our understanding of them in any significant way. "Here one must realize that complete absence of doubt at some point, even where we would say that 'legitimate' doubt can exist, need not falsify a language-game" (Wittgenstein, *OC* §375; see also §392), nor need it teach us anything about the language-game. Since our being-in-the-world or form of life is not epistemic or knowledge-based, Davidson's view that it rests on unjustified assumptions and his consequent attempts to justify them distort the matter. It isn't that, even unconsciously, we hold the proposition, "This speaker is a rational agent, hence I can trust that the noises coming from her mouth are meaningful and therefore should continue the process of interpretation," a proposition located within the space of reasons and justification. Rather, we are talking with our friend, a being-with that should be taken as primitive.[81]

The early Heidegger and later Wittgenstein's views of human nature and interaction lead to a very different conception of interpretation than Davidson's, which in turn alters the prospects for alternative conceptual schemes. First, the option of eliminating speakers' rationality is vastly reduced. Davidson's radical interpretation holds truth stable, while solving for meaning and keeping the threat of the verdict of irrationality in the wings at all times. Heidegger's picture, on the other hand, holds the speaker's rationality stable; there is a much stronger presumption that the other is a competent speaker engaged in the world with me: "The strangest man whom we encounter is with me in my world and is experienced as such in avoiding and passing each other by" (Heidegger, *HCT* 240). Bizarre things can always happen which would cause me to radically revise my view of my interlocutor, but then my mode of dealing with the situation will change into an entirely different one. By definition, these unusual events do not arise under normal circumstances, and they should not be used to define the norm. It is also the case that continental philosophers generally find their examples of alternate conceptual schemes in the texts of tradition; it is harder to condemn Plato for a wholesale lack of rationality than thought experiments like Martians or made-up jungle-dwellers. Rather than a bridge we construct to reach a presupposed other, language is an original connection we have to others: "Listening to . . . is Dasein's existential way of Being-open as Being-with for Others. . . . Being-with develops in listening to one another" (Heidegger, *BT* 206/163).

Second, the paucity of evidence claim is firmly rejected; we do not confront noise but hear meaning. Third, the model of theoretical knowledge is an atypical way of relating to others; our usual mode of interacting does not rest on assumptions, but is a practical being-with that behaves very differently. Fourth, relations with others are as basic as relations with the world, so that, in Davidson's terms, social externalism is on all fours with perceptual externalism. Heidegger's view of the holism between the three kinds of understanding or relations is that their unity must be preserved from the beginning; it cannot be built up out of separate pieces as in Davidson's triangulation.

> The essential thing is the portrayal of the specific *contextural interconnection* of these phenomena which belong essentially to the whole of the logos. This contexture must not merely come about after the fact by a process of composition under the constraint of things. Instead, this relational whole of word, signification, thinking, what is thought, what *is* must be determined in a primary way beforehand. . . . We free ourselves from the start from the isolated and isolating orientation toward the complex of spoken words of the problem of assertion. (Heidegger, *BP* 207)

Finally, the radical ignorance restriction on background knowledge is relaxed. Since this is not our true condition, it does not characterize communication in general, but only those instances in which we actually confront an unknown language. In other cases, we do and can legitimately rely on our familiarity with the language being spoken until there is a reason not to.

If the possibility that the speaker is not making meaningful statements is greatly reduced, and if background knowledge gives us a more generous entering wedge for comprehension, then the threat of finding the speaker irrational is greatly reduced. This gives us much greater latitude in the meanings the interpreter can attribute to the speaker. Under this system, interpreters have a much higher tolerance for speakers holding beliefs that do not make sense to them, which, along with Hegel's matterless schemes, removes Davidson's other major objection—the principle of charity—to the coherence of multiple conceptual schemes.[82]

## Conclusion

Heidegger's early work marks a transitional phase from the Kantian Paradigm to its successor in the Heideggerian Paradigm. On the one hand, the early work still operates within the Kantian Paradigm in important ways, most particularly in that *Being and Time* is organized around a realist conception of the subject (R6). Though it is inseparable from the world (ED), fundamental moods and the anticipation of death reveal a formal structure of Dasein that is permanent and universal (R6), allowing us to appropriate it in order to live appropriately. Heidegger also employs a Kantian temporal idealism which posits an ultimate definition of Dasein as temporality. On the other hand, Phenomenological Ontology leaves his thought more fully divested of noumenal reality (R1) for non-Dasein reality than any system we have examined. Furthermore, his conception of Unconcealment Truth (A2) works with his metaphysics rather than against it—unlike Hegel and Nietzsche, whose conceptions of truth interfered with their metaphysics—to create an exit from the Kantian Paradigm and, indeed, from traditional metaphysics tout court. The main concept holding Heidegger back is his commitment to an ahistorical, permanent structure of the self, and this is the piece that he will get rid of in his later work, allowing him, after Kant, to create the first genuinely non-Kantian position in the continental tradition.

Part 2

# The Heideggerian Paradigm

# 6

# Later Heidegger: "The Great Turning Around"

> *Any kind* of metaphysics has and must come to an end, if philosophy is to attain its other beginning. (Heidegger, *CP* 121, §85)
>
> Truth is defined as this very unconcealment in its essence, in disclosure, in terms of the beings it sanctions; it shapes each configuration of its own essence on the basis of Being thus defined. In its own Being, therefore, truth is historical. (Heidegger, *N* 3:187)

Hegel, Nietzsche, and the early Heidegger were all engaged in the project of working out the implications of Kant's anti-realism while simultaneously trying to break free of certain of his ways of framing the issue. I have argued that they only succeeded in liberating themselves from parts of it, while retaining much of its basic structure. For the thinkers of the Kantian Paradigm, the A5 Active Knower's faculties partially constitute A1 Dependent reality by either organizing it with space, time, and the categories (Kant), volatilizing historical movement (Hegel), congealing chaotic flux (Nietzsche), or temporalizing into the forms of engaged instrumentality or disengaged inertness (early Heidegger). The latter three figures developed "metaphysical" systems (Objective Idealism, Step Six Physics, and Phenomenological Ontology, respectively) that dispensed with noumena, Kant's remnant of realism's R1 Mind-Independence. Without independent reality, the distinction between our subjective contribution and the world's objective raw matter—ultimately, the distinction between appearance and reality that defines metaphysics for Heidegger—cannot be maintained. These thinkers establish the presence of human activity (A5) in experience in other ways than Kant's strategy of positing a difference between the way the world appears to us and the way it really is (R1); namely, by noting (A3 Ontological Pluralist) differences among historical periods (Hegel), among the experiences of various kinds of people (Nietzsche), or between tools and objects depending on whether we use or stare at them (early Heidegger). These differences are linked to some form of human agency in order to show A5. At their most progressive, these thinkers complete A1 by considering the variously constituted phenomena to be reality itself, since there are no noumena beyond them.

The Kantian Paradigm embraces what I am calling the Empirical Directive by changing the conception of the self from a substance like Descartes' thinking thing to a functional experience-organizing *energeia* which can only be studied by the way it organizes experience. Kant retained R6 Realism of the Subject by insisting on a unique definition of the self as one specific set of forms of intuition and concepts, but as ED took hold and evidence of historical and cultural diversity became increasingly persuasive over the nineteenth century, the paradigm's single definition of the subject loosened (A6). Seeking evidence of a transcendental subject within experience brought the subject into the gravitational pull of the empirical world, so to speak, which drew it in more and more completely over the next 150 years (see Schürmann 1987, 46). Whereas Kant maintains a single, static set of experience-organizing processes necessarily linked to experience and so not transcendent but transcendental, Hegel posits an evolving chain of conceptual schemes within history that transform according to an internal logic. Nietzsche liberates this multiplicity from the organizing rule of reason that limits its possible forms, allowing the schemes to proliferate according to needs, albeit needs founded on a somewhat determinate will to power. The unchanging content of the self for Nietzsche is slight—just a loose group of drives seeking increased power in indefinitely many ways—but it must engage in active appropriation in order to be healthy, that is, to be in accordance with its true nature. Although the trajectory of these thinkers is one of decreasing content to the self, each of them ends up giving the subject some kind of R6 functional identity which remains constant throughout external historical change (see Rorty 1989, 4). While the Kantian Paradigm thinkers were fairly successful in undermining R1 or realism for external reality (Nietzsche's stand on this is ambiguous, as I showed), they only weakened R6.

*Being and Time* represents a step backward in this progressive erosion of R6 Realism of the Subject. On the one hand, it gives ED a strong ontological grounding by defining Dasein as Being-in-the-world, but on the other hand it regresses to Kant's single definition of the faculties of the subject, that is, the existentialia. The existential analysis or examination of Dasein's structure is the organizing and motivating focus of the book as we have it, as well as the key to authenticity, since we must know our essence in order to take it up and live in accord with it. Although Heidegger incorporates history into the structure of Dasein, this permanent, formal structure itself does not change across history. However, the discussion of truth in *Being and Time*—the section which least fits the book's architectonic—contains the seeds of a radical breakthrough to a new form of thought, the first philosophy in a century and a half with a structure different from the Kantian Paradigm's, as Heidegger himself realizes. "Transcendental philosophy too must fall. What, then, is to take the place of ontology? . . . In the end, through our unfolding of the problem, we altogether lose the *place* in which we could replace ontology by something else. It is only thus that we shall ultimately come completely into the open" (Heidegger, *FCM* 359). When his later work follows his new conceptions of truth and Being to their logical conclusions, it breaks out of the very framework of the Kantian Paradigm, thus inaugurating the next major phase in continental philosophy.

Freeing himself completely from R2 Correspondence Truth which was rendered problematic but still retained in the Kantian Paradigm, Heidegger defines truth as unconcealment (A2), revelation, appearance. As discussed in the previous chapter, this conception eliminates the distinction between correct and incorrect unconcealment. I see this radically new conception of truth as the culmination of a long development of thought—the final nail in the metaphysical coffin and a new beginning in the history of Western thought, albeit one that is unwelcome to many. Whereas Hegel's and Nietzsche's conceptions of truth worked *against* their metaphysical systems to reincorporate vestiges of realism into their thought, Heidegger's Unconcealment Truth *reinforces* his Phenomenological Ontology, enabling him to break fully with the Kantian Paradigm. Heidegger compromised the potential of *Being and Time* by trying to discover the one deep, true structure of the self, even making this "the most primordial and basic existential truth" (Heidegger, *BT* 364/316). Perhaps the third division of the book would have reversed this, but, as we shall see, Heidegger himself came to consider *Being and Time*'s starting point in fundamental ontology too entrenched in Kantian thought to allow him a decisive departure from the tradition.

Abandoning his earlier quest for the self's true essence (R6)—which should have been ruled out by his commitment to Unconcealment Truth and Phenomenological Ontology, had they been applied consistently—frees him from the Kantian Paradigm. Heidegger recognizes the long dominance of this paradigm, claiming that "the era in which European thinking came to this opinion [roughly my A5] continues to cast its last shadow over us" (Heidegger, *Pm* 303, bracketed comment added). However, in a seminar given late in his career, he is quoted as saying that "with the relation of letting-presence to *aletheia,* the whole question about the Being of beings is removed from the Kantian framework of the constitution of objects" (Heidegger, *TB* 46; see also Gadamer 1981, 42; Apel 1998, 104). It is his definition of truth as *aletheia,* or unconcealment, working in tandem with his PO conception of Being that allows him to escape *both* realism and Kant's form of anti-realism to create a fundamentally new position. It is no accident that the discussion of truth dominates his writings of the 1930s, the period of his turning.

In his later work, Heidegger places everything within history; there is nothing essential and self-same that transcends historical change. The main idea that held his early work back was R6 Realism of the Subject; following out the joint implications of Phenomenological Ontology (PO) and Unconcealment Truth (UT) more consistently, he now rejects this idea. Although he talks about the "essence of man" a great deal in the later work, he has in effect eliminated the traditional notion of essence as a definite, permanent set of characteristics or functions inherent in all humans (R6),[1] an idea that in some form or other has been central to philosophy virtually since its inception. Removing the realist conception of the self then allows him to rethink Being and truth in a new way. This breakthrough to the first truly non-Kantian rather than just post-Kantian philosophy is the reason Heidegger's later work is so important in the history of philosophy: for anyone who wishes to escape the subject-centered philosophy of the Kantian Paradigm, later Heidegger is the unavoidable thinker.

This rejection of R2 Correctness is one reason why recent continental philosophy can appear so strange: it operates outside of assumptions that have widely been considered necessary for all discourse almost since the beginning of philosophy (see, for example, Searle 1993). As we saw with Hegel's account of idealism, though, these initially bizarre ideas become much more intelligible when seen as solutions to problems that have been inherited, rather than as ideas coming out of the blue. I have tried to show that the problems facing these thinkers—the difficulties inherent to correspondence, determining truth without realism, and so on—are shared by analytic philosophers as well, and that some well-respected analytic figures have even staked out positions that are not that far from the continental ones. If this is the case, then Heidegger's later work should be of great interest to analytic philosophers, since it offers a highly innovative and powerful alternative conception that either solves or dissolves many of these problems. Whereas much early analytic thought followed Moore and Russell's combination of empiricist realist epistemology and logical analysis, a significant amount of later analytic philosophy (though of course far from all) takes up some version of Kant's Paradigm, often substituting language for transcendental psychology. Rorty, for instance, is well known for portraying analytic philosophy's "linguistic turn" as a

Kantian move (see Rorty 1979, 257; Rorty 1992, 17). The later Heidegger offers a profoundly different approach that conceives of the most basic issues in radically new ways; this is one of the reasons for its difficulty but also its promise. My exegetical strategy will be to render Heidegger's later position more intelligible by indicating the specific features of the Kantian Paradigm it rejects and what it puts in their place, thus showing it to be a new take on ancient topics, a new solution to some very old problems that tries to improve on the solutions of its predecessor, the Kantian Paradigm.

## A3 Epochs of Being: Historical Phenomenological Ontology

Perhaps the single most important difference between Heidegger's two phases is the way history permeates everything in the later work. In *Being and Time,* the changeover in the mode of Being of tools to objects occurred because Dasein altered her attitude toward them. This was evidence that she "constituted" their mode of Being (A5), but there wasn't a whiff of historical variability in these modes; although never explicitly stated, everything in the book suggested the permanence of these categories. The book's second part was to trace the history of philosophy, but the sketch of it in the introduction promised a narrative of continuity: "Kant took over Descartes' position quite dogmatically" (Heidegger, *BT* 45/24), while "what presents itself in Descartes' case is . . . no break, but instead a process of seizing upon a prefigured possibility . . . that *Greek philosophy* specified" (Heidegger, *IPR* 83; see also 233), with the result that "Kant's basic ontological orientation remains that of the Greeks" (Heidegger, *BT* 49/26). Presumably Aristotle's hammer was ready-to-hand while he used it and present-at-hand when he stared at in virtually the same way as my hammer, even if he incorporated hammering into different roles.

While his early work emphasized the variety of modes of Being at a particular time (A3), Heidegger's later work posits a general uniformity of Being within a historical period, that is, synchronic homogeneity. Now what he calls a period's truth or understanding of Being sets the parameters for *all* the beings that can appear and actions that can be taken for that time. "The fundamental characteristic of all beings . . . must, so to speak, be 'encountered' by the thinking of this thought in every region of beings: in nature, art, history, politics, in science and in knowledge in general" (Heidegger, *N* 3:19). He calls an age's clearing its understanding of Being, its truth, or its "sending of Being," all names for the period's conception of what is real that founds and shapes all human practices and discourse at that time. "Every sort of thought, however, is always only the execution and consequence of a mode of historical Dasein, of the fundamental position taken towards Being and toward the way in which beings are manifest as such, i.e., toward truth."[2] As I will discuss in greater detail below, the fact that these understandings influence everything we can think or do greatly accentuates Dasein's thrownness, that is, the fact that we find ourselves in (among other factors) a period and society that is not of our choosing but which affects a great deal about us. Whereas this was just one element in the early work, even a subordinate one, now we are completely beholden to our epoch's truth or unconcealment for everything we are, can be, and can think and experience. "Always the destining of revealing holds complete sway over men" (Heidegger, *BW* 330; see also Heidegger, *CP* 169, §122).

Heidegger still recognizes the diversity of types of beings and occasionally discusses this fact, such as in the first section of "The Origin of the Work of Art," where he shows how artworks cannot be described in categories taken from equipment or things, the two types of non-Dasein beings from *Being and Time.* However, the emphasis is now on the single conception of Being that rules each period but, importantly, *varies across epochs.* A clearing, that is, the horizon within which all beings appear, is now historical and only admits or "constitutes" certain kinds of beings in each era, thus establishing diachronic diversity (A3). Each period has its own understanding of what it means to be: the Greeks understood beings as nature emerging on its own (*physis*), the medievals saw beings as divine creations, and the moderns think of them as objects or resources to be technologically manipulated to satisfy our needs and desires. Heidegger no longer believes that there is just one set of modes of Being for all times, but variously "[a being] in its *emergence* unto itself (Classical Greece); *caused* by a supreme [being] of the same essence (Middle Ages); [a being as] the extant as *object* (modernity)" (Heidegger, *CP* 120, §84, bracketed comments in original; see also Heidegger, *Zo* 99; Heidegger, *PR* 91). Each time a new epoch dawns, the understanding of Being or the way beings present themselves to us completely alters, which means that each clearing is like a different version of Kant's single set of forms of intuition and concepts of understanding or Hegel's shapes of spirit (see Kolb 1986, 202, 254; Apel 1998, 112; Thomson 2005, 54). As Heidegger claims, "The 'new life' meant here is a new way of standing in the midst of beings as a whole; it is a new kind of truth and thereby a metamorphosis of beings."[3]

Heidegger's later work takes Dasein's multiple (A3) constitutive (A5) attitudes that are her permanent structures (R6) in *Being and Time* and spreads them across history (as well as detaching them from Dasein, as we will discuss below). In the early work, a being undergoes a changeover in its mode of Being from readiness-to-hand to presence-at-hand when Dasein stops using it and just stares at it (or vice versa); now modes of Being change over for an entire society at these epochal shifts: "At the inception of the modern age the beingness of beings changed" (Heidegger, *N* 3:220; see also 3:215; Heidegger, *P* 42). Whereas the early work took up "the ontological task of a genealogy of the different possible ways of Being" (Heidegger, *BT* 31/11) which, despite the name, were founded on Dasein's permanent structure (R6) since it determined (A5) these modes of Being, the later inquiry into Being examines "the changing forms in which Being shows itself epochally and historically" (Heidegger, *TB* 52). Questions about Being are now indexed to a historical period rather than to Dasein's comportments or ways of interacting with beings (see Heidegger, *WCT* 90, 136; Heidegger, *PR* 23). Instead of engaging in fundamental ontology which bases the examination of Being on existential analysis, that is, the analysis of Dasein's ahistorical existence, we need to study "the history of Being, which Being itself 'is' as Being" (Heidegger, *N* 4:221; see also Heidegger, *WCT* 121; Heidegger, *CP* 348, §273).

This view represents a logical step from the early work because it preserves the anti-realist notion that the character of beings—their "beingness"—is determined by something "outside" of them. "The decisive insight is this: in its truth being can never be obtained from *beings*" (Heidegger, *Mi* 125). He fundamentally rejects realism, here understood as the attempt to understand beings solely in terms of themselves, where "it appears as though that which presences . . . were self-sufficient" (Heidegger, *Pm* 313; see also Heidegger, *CP* 80–81, §55; Heidegger, *IM* 138; Heidegger, *Mi* 75). This would amount to my R1 Independence where "the existing being is thereby taken as a thing-in-itself, i.e., without attending to the conditions of its possible givenness" (Heidegger, *EF* 159; see also Heidegger, *BW* 132; Heidegger, *BQ* 170). Realism is a form of Heidegger's great nemesis—the forgetfulness of Being, which "keeps to beings and even considers beings to be being" (Heidegger, *Pm* 231). Like Kant, Heidegger wants to show us how much goes into the apparently simple event of encountering beings: people "already stand, without *their* knowing it, in a relation to being. Only from the truth of being that prevails on each occasion do they receive a light that first enables them to see and observe *as such* the beings represented by them" (Heidegger, *Pm* 318; see also 277, 315). Although he had already claimed that every relation to beings presupposed the clearing, now he adds the key phrase, "the truth of being that prevails *on each occasion*," to indicate that unconcealment is always historically specific.

This new conception of the clearing as imparting a particular character to all beings of an epoch is the later Heidegger's version of the anti-realist conceptual scheme (A5) whose history we have been tracing; it is his rejection of the realist claim that beings simply come with their characters stamped onto their nature so that all we have to do is open our eyes to receive them. He describes the epochal clearing in standard anti-realist language as "the application of a determination of the thing, which is not experientially derived from the thing and yet lies at the base of every determination of the things, making them possible" (Heidegger, *BW* 289; see also Heidegger, *P* 150; Heidegger, *ET* 45). It is the condition for their possibility which cannot be derived from them alone. Beings do not sort themselves into neat piles with determinate natures on their own; the world does not have inherent joints but receives its organization. Against realism's R1 Independence of beings, he argues that "truth is never gathered from things at hand" (Heidegger, *BW* 196; Heidegger, *WCT* 66). Heidegger wants to retain the part of Kant's model that claims that beings get organized according to a kind of conceptual scheme, which is why he is an heir to continental anti-realism despite his significant adaptations of it. Linking different languages to the periods when their thinkers dominated world philosophy, he states that "what in Greek is called *ta onta,* in Latin *ens,* in French *l'être,* in German *das Seiende* [beings] has in every case already been decided by the epochal clearing and lighting of being" (Heidegger, *PR* 84). In other words, the beings of each era receive their character or beingness from their "epochal clearing."

Like the wearer of Kant's pink sunglasses who assumes that things are independently pink, we usually don't suspect that anything goes into the "presencing" of something, that is, our becoming aware of it; it's the simplest thing in the world to just open your eyes and have an object present itself (Heidegger, *AM* 8, 102). And of course, the thing's properties naturally reside within it; it is what it is (R3). But Heidegger thinks this view is naively absorbed into the immediate context.

> We call "natural" (*natürlich*) what is understood without further ado and is "self-evident" in the realm of everyday understanding. . . . In the Middle Ages everything was "natural" which obtained its essence, its *natura,* from God. . . . Therefore, it follows: what is "natural" is *not* "natural" at all, here meaning self-evident for any given ever-existing man. The "natural" is always historical. A suspicion creeps up from behind us. What if this so "natural" appearing essential definition of the thing were by no means self-evident, were not "natural"? Then there must have been a time when the essence of the thing was not defined in this way. Consequently, there also must have been a time when the essential definition of the thing was first worked out. The formation of this essential definition of the thing did not, then, at some time just fall absolute from

> heaven, but would have itself been based upon very definite presuppositions. (Heidegger, *WT* 39–40; see also Heidegger, *IM* 56)

Although we tend to take our own understanding of Being for granted as obvious and inevitable, seeing the deeply different ways that other epochs understand Being gives us a critical distance from our own understanding: "What did we seek from this 'historical reflection'? To obtain a *distance* from what we take as self-evident, from what lies all too close to us" (Heidegger, *ET* 6).

Studying other epochs performs a kind of bracketing on our present understanding of Being, suspending our naïveté; in what might be called Heideggerian genealogy, we come to realize that our way of perceiving is (in one sense of the word) an interpretation rather than a direct, unmediated taking up of what is simply there, and that it is only one among indefinitely numerous ways of Being (A3).[4] Nothing lasts, not even the present mode of Being that seems inevitable and blindingly obvious to us.[5] In perhaps a reference to Kant's (R3) assumption that Newtonian physics is the only way humans will ever organize experience (Heidegger was a close personal friend of Werner Heisenberg), Heidegger says that "everything which we are inclined to regard as a 'necessary element of the culture' can one day pass away. So, for example, the 'objectifying' knowledge of physics rests upon the historical destining disclosure of Being" (Heidegger, *PT* 69). Studying Being in the way it naturally reveals itself to us tends to lead to the realist assumption that this is the necessary way things are in themselves (R1, R3), just as Hegel's Consciousness keeps forgetting its previous self-corrections or Kant's sunglasses-wearer thinks the world is pink. This is why "discourse about Being and beings can never be pinned down to *one* epoch in the history of the clearing of 'Being'" (Heidegger, *ID* 51). One reason the history of metaphysics is so important is that it calls our attention to the *multiplicity* of clearings, which in turn reveals the contingency of any particular way of understanding Being. Ironically, for Kant the transcendental clue to anti-realism, that is, the thesis that we impose an organization on experience, is suggested by the necessity and universality of math and science; for the later Heidegger as for Hegel, the idea that beings do not possess their features intrinsically comes from their historical fluctuations. Against Kant and his own early work which insisted on the necessity and universality of its understanding (R3), Heidegger states that "no one kind of thinking has a hegemony. Thought becomes a product of sheer fantasy when we represent it as a universally human faculty" (Heidegger, *PT* 57).

As Foucault will also argue, we can only understand something within the context of its period's understanding of Being. Just as Putnam's internal realism claims that "*what objects does the world consist of?* is a question that it only makes sense to ask *within* a theory or description" (Putnam 1981, 49), so for what we might call Heidegger's "epochal realism," "the question 'What is a thing?' is a historical question" (Heidegger, *WT* 52; see also Heidegger, *WIP* 37). Reality must always be indexed to an epoch because each epoch's understanding of Being determines the way issues are settled; for instance: "We shall now name the kind of presence *belonging* to that which presences that appears in the modern age as object: *objectness*" (Heidegger, *QT* 163). Importantly, this modern character, though limited to one specific period, nevertheless *is the entity's real character:* "This is first of all a character belonging to that which presences itself" (163; see also Heidegger, *ID* 51; Heidegger, *AM* 64; Heidegger, *Mi* 13). This is the logical consequence of his Phenomenological Ontology: how things present themselves is how they are; if they present themselves differently at different points in history, then they *are* in different ways.

An ontology based on presence-at-hand would reject this view: as transient, these epochal modes of Being lack stability and permanence; entities could possess profoundly different modes of Being at different points in history, leaving it indeterminate which one would be the real one. Heidegger questions this ontology's assumptions: "But why should what comes into existence and passes away count as non-being? Only when beingness is already established as constancy and presence" (Heidegger, *CP* 137, §100). Dismissing qualities or entities because they change and refusing to allow beings to have deeply different ways of Being is based on a metaphysical presupposition (albeit one of the oldest; see Heidegger, *Mi* 249), not argumentation or evidence. If looked at without prejudice, all the evidence argues against this view. Since Heidegger wants to base his ontology on the world as we experience it rather than filtered through a presupposed ontology, pluralism simply does not present a problem for him. Just as he did not hesitate to call readiness-to-hand the tool's in-itself in *Being and Time* even though it involved Dasein's projection (A5) and change (A3), so he now calls each epoch's version of reality fully real even though these are transient. This represents a refinement and extension of his earlier metaphysics which I will call Historical Phenomenological Ontology (HPO). He is still practicing PO by taking Being as it appears—for example, "What matters is to see appearance as the reality of presence" (Heidegger, *OWL* 40)—but he is now committed to the claim that Being appears differently at different points in history.

Heidegger believes that the understanding of Being which rules a period, determining how individual beings are then, is best captured in that age's metaphysical writings. "Metaphysics grounds an age, in that through a specific interpretation of what is and through a specific comprehension of truth it gives to that age the basis upon which it is essentially formed. This basis holds complete dominion over all the phenomena that distinguish the age" (Heidegger, *QT* 115; see also Heidegger, *Pm* 232). Metaphysicians capture their epoch's understanding of Being in their analyses of "the totality of beings as such with an eye to their most universal traits" (Heidegger, *Pm* 287); they attempt "to find words for what a being *is* in the history of its Being" (Heidegger, *N* 4:7). These thinkers look beyond the proliferation of various individual beings to their horizon, the mode of Being or beingness upon which they are projected. Uncovering the understandings of Being underneath the different epochs constitutes "the most covert history of the West. This history is the poet's and thinker's struggle for a word for beings as a whole."[6] Much of Heidegger's later thought (though not all, as I will discuss below) is taken up with this project: "My whole work in lectures and exercises in the past 30 years has been in the main only an interpretation of Western philosophy" (Heidegger, "OG" 109). This history, rather than historiography which only records surface events, is what is essential, since an age's understanding of Being is what determines what beings can be encountered and what actions will make sense. "Actual historical situations and conditions are seen as merely the *consequences* of this hidden history; as *consequences,* they have no control over their ground."[7]

Since HPO considers whatever appears to be the real, Heidegger neither needs nor wants to place limitations on what can count as reality. Whereas Hegel demanded that the shapes of consciousness and their correlative phases of reality snap together into a coherent whole, and Nietzsche only endorsed embodiments of will to power that actively increase health, moves which allowed these thinkers to evaluate either individual shapes of consciousness by how well they approximated completed Spirit or specific incarnations of will to power by how honestly and flexibly they let their inner power flow and increase, Heidegger's thought precludes these kinds of requirements or expectations from the ground up. That which shows up simply is true reality, and he considers it very important to release all pretensions to control or comprehend this process. After listing his standard three epochal revealings of ancient, medieval, and modern, he claims that "at each time there happened unconcealment of beings" (Heidegger, *BW* 201), which, given his understanding of truth as unconcealment, means that each is true. This is how his conception of truth (UT) works in tandem with his ontology (HPO) to form the Heideggerian Paradigm. A parallel cooperation between similar elements once operated in Greek thought: "The Greek essence of truth is possible only together with the Greek essence of Being as *phusis.* On the grounds of the unique essential relation between *phusis* and *alētheia,* the Greeks could say: beings as beings are true" (Heidegger, *IM* 107; see also Heidegger, *Mi* 280–81). Together, these elements eliminate unfortunate metaphysical distinctions such as those between reality and appearance, history's long preparation and its climactic conclusion, active health and reactive weakness, or authentic and inauthentic Dasein.

Accepting all historical appearings as real or true leads to some form of historical relativism, though a significantly qualified form, as I will discuss below. Since reality is and is only what appears within a particular epoch's understanding of Being, that is, roughly as constituted by its conceptual scheme without remainder, then what occurs within each era is fully real without reservation. This means that multiple periods' philosophical and scientific views can be true even if they contradict each other, as modern and Aristotelian physics do. In Heidegger's terms,

> neither can we say that the Galilean doctrine of freely falling bodies is true and that Aristotle's teaching, that light bodies strive upward, is false; for the Greek understanding of the essence of body and place and of the relation between the two rests upon a different interpretation of beings and hence conditions a correspondingly different kind of seeing and questioning of natural events. No one would presume to maintain that Shakespeare's poetry is more advanced than that of Aeschylus. It is still more impossible to say that the modern understanding of whatever is, is more correct than that of the Greeks.[8]

Given HPO, this A3 Ontological Pluralism is not just about different interpretations of entities that have an essential nature independently of these interpretations, something standing under the interpretations we throw over them; these are wholly different kinds of beings. Reality is what appears within particular epochal clearings without remainder, so there is nothing even in principle that could serve as a basis for comparing the correctness of different epochal understandings.

Discussing Galileo's experiment at the tower of Pisa—often cited as a paradigm of modern science's commitment to empirical results instead of faith or ad hoc rationalizations—Heidegger describes how

> both Galileo and his opponents saw the same "fact." But they interpreted the same fact differently and made the same happening visible to themselves in different ways. Indeed, what appeared for them as the essential fact and truth was something different. Both thought something along with the same appearance but they thought something different, not only about the single case, but fundamentally, regarding the essence of a body and the nature of its motion. (Heidegger, *WT* 90; see also Heidegger, *PIK* 22)

This is Heidegger's 1935–36 anticipation of the famous Duhem-Quine thesis that, due to the fact that observation is laden with holistic theories, there is no such thing as a truly crucial experiment that forces us to abandon a theory; we can always revise assumptions or interpret observations differently instead. Kuhn similarly comments that "all these natural phenomena [Galileo] saw differently from the way they had been seen before" (Kuhn 1970, 119), and Norwood Hanson gives a negative answer to the question, "*Do Kepler and Tycho see the same thing in the east at dawn?*" since "theories and interpretations are 'there' in the seeing from the outset" (Hanson 1958, 5, 10). Just as Hanson believes that "seeing is a 'theory-laden' undertaking. Observation of *x* is shaped by prior knowledge of *x*" (19; see also 54, 157), so for Heidegger, we are always "thinking something along with the appearance." Heidegger insists on the radical differences of the historical theories that inform our observations, leading him to reject R2 Correspondence Truth with an R3 Unique reality and to agree with Kuhn: "That claims . . . [that science is zeroing in on, getting closer and closer to, the truth] are meaningless is a consequence of incommensurability."[9]

Heidegger concludes that "in principle the objectness in which at any given time nature, man, history, language, exhibit themselves always itself remains only *one* kind of presencing, in which indeed that which presences can appear, but never absolutely must appear" (Heidegger, *QT* 176). The Empirical Directive's emphasis on paying attention to experience and, by Hegel's extension, to historical diversity, combined with Phenomenological Ontology's commitment to take what appears as real, culminates in a strong A3 Ontological Pluralism. Beings have existed in radically different ways at different points in time, and instead of sorting through these for the right one or fitting them together to form a coherent totality, we should accept this heterogeneous multiplicity as true reality. Unlike Lockean accidents or Kantian phenomena, the various manifestations "are not signposts for something else. They are the manifold shining of presencing itself" (Heidegger, *EGT* 98). Leo Strauss gets it right when he says that "the relation of Heidegger to his own existentialism is the same as that of Hegel to Kant. . . . Existence cannot be the clue, the clue to the understanding of that by virtue of which all beings are."[10] Just as Hegel included history in the experience Kant studied as evidence for transcendental subjectivity, so Heidegger's later work vastly expands and deepens the role of history in his own early work.

Occasionally, Heidegger comes close to admitting that he had not appreciated the full significance of history in his earlier work. After running through his three epochal modes of Being, he claims that in modern times

> the fundamental position of Being as reality attains an assumed self-evidence which has remained decisive ever since for all subsequent

> understanding of the beingness of beings. . . . Herein lies the reason for the necessity of the "destruction" of this distortion, when a thinking of the truth of being has become necessary (see *Being and Time*). But this destruction, like "phenomenology" and all hermeneutical-transcendental questions, has not yet been thought in terms of the history of Being. (Heidegger, *EP* 14–15; see also Heidegger, *Mi* 91)

The modern period's understanding of Being—here called "reality"—lays claim to R3 Uniqueness, that it is the only way that beings can be. This is why the "destruction" of tradition by surveying other periods is required to undermine its self-evidence. However, the destruction projected for the second part of *Being and Time* did not fully recognize the profound heterogeneity of the various philosophers' positions, since it hadn't been thought "in terms of the history of Being," nor had phenomenology or "all hermeneutical-transcendental questions," which is how he described his own method in the first part of *Being and Time.* At the end of his long career, he admits that "there was not yet in *Being and Time* a genuine knowledge of the history of being, hence the awkwardness and, strictly speaking, the naïveté of the 'ontological destruction'" (Heidegger, *FoS* 78).

In the later work, studying man and reality within experience (ED) inescapably points to the fact that they change historically: "Be-ing itself announced its historical essential sway" (Heidegger, *CP* 318, §262). In his early work, Heidegger repeatedly emphasized that Being is always the Being of a being. In the later work this becomes the claim that Being is always the *epochal* Being of a being, so that we can only examine Being in the various historical ways it has revealed itself. "There is Being only in this or that particular historical character: *physis, logos, en, idea, energeia,* Substantiality, Objectivity, Subjectivity, the Will, the Will to Power, the Will to Will."[11] We must study the way Being manifests itself; this, after all, is what phenomenology means for Heidegger: to Being itself! It turns out, however, that Being has revealed itself in fundamentally different ways throughout history. As Heidegger told David Farrell Krell, "Being takes on varied significance in the different epochs of the history or sending of Being" (Krell 1986, 103). If we are not to begin with presuppositions that tell us what reality must be like—especially unchanging, univocal, and so on—then we must take Being as it occurs in these various forms without dismissing them as merely transitory and thus unreal. "The thinking that thinks into the truth of Being is, as thinking, historical."[12]

*Being and Time* was organized around an ahistorical subject, the accurate depiction of which functioned as an ahistorical foundation for all individual truths, since R6 Dasein was the A5 experience-organizing clearing (Heidegger, *BT* 171/133). Dasein's temporality "shaped" the clearing and thus rendered all beings appearing therein temporal, but neither time nor history affected its own permanent structure. The breakthrough to the Heideggerian Paradigm comes when Heidegger follows through on the implications of Unconcealment Truth, the most radical element of his early thought (the key point of PO having been anticipated by Hegel's Objective Idealism and Nietzsche's Step Six Physics). This conception of truth removes all vestiges of correspondence (R2) with a unique (R3) and independent (R1) reality which sorts out correct and false, and instead encourages us to take Being as we find it. This allows us to openly and honestly confront the flux we experience without trying to explain it away in favor of Forms or substances or to capture it in any kind of conceptual closure.

This conception of truth takes the momentous step of making truth itself historical: "Truth is defined as this very unconcealment in its essence, in disclosure, in terms of the beings it sanctions; it shapes each configuration of its own essence on the basis of Being thus defined. *In its own Being, therefore, truth is historical*" (Heidegger, *N* 3:187, italics added; see also Heidegger, *BW* 238). This move follows from the other elements of the Heideggerian Paradigm, though it is difficult to overestimate its importance (see Haar 1993, 181). Being simply (HPO) is what it appears to us as—there is nothing else to it (A1)—and it appears differently at different periods (A3). Since truth is the unconcealment of these changing beings, truth is historical. This is the application of ED to truth: "But perhaps we have learnt to understand that it is precisely *here,* and *only* here, in such *history,* that we experience the *presencing* of truth. . . . We can reach what truth is, and how it presences, only by *interrogating* it in respect of its own *occurrence*" (Heidegger, *ET* 228). All of these points form a tightly interwoven system in Heidegger's thought.

He occasionally puts these pieces (A1-HPO-UT) together fairly explicitly: "Unhiddenness [UT] does not [R1] persist somewhere by and in itself, or as a property of things. Being [ED, A1] occurs as the history of man, as the history of a people" (Heidegger, *ET* 104, bracketed comments added; see also Heidegger, *BW* 186). Being, which isn't a being, simply isn't the kind of thing that could exist apart from its appearing to people throughout history; it is its appearings, which occur historically. The fact that it cannot be independently of us is why we cannot distinguish between "its own" properties and what we project onto it; if we experience it historically, then it is historical.[13] This is his new reading of Kant's highest principle that the conditions of knowing are also conditions of the objects of experience whose evolution we have been tracing. Heidegger is fully aware of the importance of this idea and his relationship to it, calling it "a fundamental posture of the history of man, which we can neither avoid, leap over, nor deny in any way. But we have to bring this by an appropriate transformation to fulfillment in the future" (Heidegger, *WT* 183). Bringing Kant's highest principle to fulfillment is a good way to describe what all of the thinkers we have looked at have been trying to do in their various ways.

Embracing HPO-UT-A3 leads to a position similar in some ways to Nietzsche's perspectivism, where no particular unconcealment can be ruled out as false unless it commits the one unforgivable sin of insisting that it is the only true one.

> The [Greek] *on* is not [medieval] *ens* in the sense of the *ens creatum* of the medieval scholastics, beings created by God. Nor is [Greek] *on* the [modern] object with respect to its objectness. What determines beings with respect to their being in Aristotle's sense, and how this happens, is experienced differently than in the medieval doctrine of *ens qua ens*. Yet it would be silly to say the medieval theologians misunderstood Aristotle; rather, they understood him differently, responding to the different manner in which being proffered itself to them. Then again, the *Geschick* [sending] of being is different for Kant. *A different understanding becomes a misunderstanding only where it comes to a peak in a uniquely possible truth and is subsumed under the order of what is to be understood.* (Heidegger, *PR* 79, bracketed comments added, italics added; see also Heidegger, *EGT* 43)

Different, even incompatible understandings can all be true insofar as they appear at various times. They only become misunderstandings when they insist on being recognized as the "uniquely possible truth" or simply "what is to be understood" rather than one among many truths. In other words, when they claim R3 Uniqueness.

Any particular epoch's understanding of Being that insists on permanence and exclusive truth is the new version of presence-at-hand's claim to be the only true aspect of the world which was always already there (R3), independently of us (R1). Now it is a matter of beings rejecting the fact that they depend for their character on a historical and transient sending of Being, so that it looks like their character is just their inherent, permanent nature.

> The "is" which *so to speak* is innate to beings [R1], indicates being in the sense of constant presencing. Remaining unquestioned . . . this "is" seizes up the determination of being and steers *all modes of being* [R3]. . . . The projecting-opening of be-ing as constant presencing takes beings themselves as the pre-given support and site of be-ing [R1]. . . . All the while a being is itself a being to the extent that it towers already within the unexperienced clearing of projecting-open [A1]. (Heidegger, *Mi* 75, all italics added)

Although this can happen to any period, the modern mode of revealing called "enframing" is especially prone to R3 Uniqueness: "It drives out every other possibility of revealing."[14] Heidegger frequently criticizes this understanding of Being, which is tied to modern science, for refusing to acknowledge any other kind of Being. Enframing only admits as real what is "countable" (Heidegger, *Pm* 235) or causally related: "What effects and is effected . . . is, in our eyes, the whole of what is real" (Heidegger, *PR* 59), so that in general "only that which becomes object in this way *is*—is considered to be in being."[15] In these ways, "the domain of producedness that is projectable within the horizon of *techne* . . . becomes normative for the later interpretation of all beingness of beings" (Heidegger, *Mi* 155). It is scientism that is Heidegger's enemy, not science: "In no way is science as such rejected. Merely its claim to absoluteness—that is, as the standard measure for all true propositions—is warded off as an arrogant presumption."[16]

## R5 and A1: Mutual Interdependence

Working in a modified Kantian manner, Heidegger's early work portrayed the analysis of Dasein as *fundamental* ontology, that is, the foundation of all ontology, since Dasein played a constitutive role in experience.

> Being and its distinction from beings can be fixed only if we get a proper hold on the understanding of being as such. But to comprehend the understanding of being means first and foremost to understand *that* being to whose ontological constitution the understanding of being belongs, the Dasein. Exposition of the basic constitution of the Dasein, its existential constitution, is the task of the preparatory ontological analytic. (Heidegger, *BP* 227)

Philosophy had to begin with Dasein because it determines (A5) the features of Being via temporality (with the constant reservation that we do not know what would have taken place in the third part of *Being and Time*'s "reversal"). Organizing one's system around the A5 Active Knower is an essential feature of the Kantian Paradigm: the examination of anything else, including history, must start from the analysis of the structures of the self because it is these structures that constitute the rest. The subject is the prism whose configuration accounts for the rainbow. Heidegger was explicit in comparing his early project to Kant's: "If we radicalize the Kantian problem of ontological knowledge" by broadening the understanding of Being to all encounters rather than just scientific theorizing, "then we shall arrive at the philosophically fundamental problematic of *Being and Time*" (Heidegger, *PIK* 289; see also Heidegger, *BP* 73).

In addition to its superficial treatment of history, the other main criticism that Heidegger levels against his earlier thought is that it was too subjectivistic. He comes to think that *Being and Time* was infected by the thought which preceded it, what he often calls transcendental philosophy and which I am calling the Kantian Paradigm, so that although the work tries to challenge traditional conceptions of the subject, "the attempt and the path it chose confront the danger of unwillingly becoming merely another entrenchment of subjectivity" (Heidegger, *N* 4:141). In discussing *Being and Time*'s view that the meaning of Being is a projection based in Dasein's understanding, he says that

> what is inappropriate in this formulation of the question is that it makes it all too possible to understand the "project" as a human performance. Accordingly, project is then only taken to be a structure of subjectivity—which is how Sartre takes it, by basing himself upon Descartes (for whom *aletheia* as *aletheia* does not arise). In order to counter this mistaken conception and to retain the meaning of "project" as it is to be taken (that of the opening disclosure), the thinking after *Being and Time* replaced the expression "meaning of being" with "truth of being." (Heidegger, *FoS* 40–41; see also Heidegger, *TB* 28; Heidegger, *Mi* 125, 187)

The meaning of Being, the goal of the entire book, was the temporality that human Dasein projects which makes Being possible, similar to the way Kant's transcendental subject projects time and space (Heidegger, *BT* 54–55/31). Although Dasein is thrown into this structure and opens Being autonomically rather than through a willed choice, it is still Dasein that makes the clearing (Heidegger, *Mi* 284). His student Gadamer repeatedly describes Heidegger's turn as a break with these elements of the Kantian Paradigm: "Heidegger himself, after the 'turning,' abandoned his transcendental conception of self, on the one hand, and *Dasein's* understanding of being as the point of departure for posing the question about being, on the other."[17]

Heidegger's later work attempts to fulfill the stated intention of the third division of *Being and Time* by analyzing Being without going through the lens of Dasein. In direct opposition to the A5 element of the Kantian Paradigm, the subject—usually called "man" now[18]—is not responsible for Being or the clearing. This denial of the linchpin of Kant's system is one of the most common refrains throughout the later texts. For instance: "Man only *inhabits* the keeping of what gives him food for thought—he does not create the keeping" (Heidegger, *WCT* 151). "Truth, as we translate this word, is of the origin, i.e., it is essentially not a characteristic of human knowing and asserting. . . . Rather, truth as self-revealing belongs to being itself" (Heidegger, *Pm* 230). And, tying his later work to the section on truth in *Being and Time*—the part of the book which I consider most continuous with the later work—"if the essence of the unconcealment of beings belongs in any way to Being itself (see *Being and Time,* section 44), then Being, by way of its own essence, lets the free space of openness (the clearing of the There) happen."[19] Over and over again, Heidegger claims that it is not man who establishes or forms our relation to beings, but Being. Michel Haar summarizes this point nicely: "The formulation *it is not we* who (it is not we who give ourselves freedom, language, thought . . .) is the fundamental formulation of the poverty of man" (Haar 1993, 60).

This is a new, revised form of R5 Passive Knower. The clearing or relation to beings is not created or instituted by us, as in the Kantian Paradigm; rather, it is "granted" or "sent" to us and we receive it. Later Heideggerian man is an exceedingly passive being. This is not the passivity of the empiricist soft-wax or blank-slate mind, since interpretation is always at work, but the controlling and inaugurating activity of the Kantian active knower is now rejected. Man could not have created the clearing, since any activity on our part presupposes awareness of some kind. Awareness is the ultimate "always already," the transcendental condition for the possibility of everything.[20] Starting with Descartes, modern philosophy has given credit for the clearing to the subject: "Apprehending has become a setting-forth-before-itself in the *perceptio* of the *res cogitans* taken as the *subiectum* of *certitudo*" (Heidegger, *BW* 235; see also Heidegger, *Mi* 257–58). As I will discuss below, Heidegger believes that "we moderns, or, to speak more broadly, all post-Greek humanity, have for a long time been so deflected that we understand looking exclusively as man's representational self-direction toward beings. . . . It is understood only as a self-accomplished 'activity,' i.e., an act of re-presenting. To re-present means here to present before oneself, to bring before oneself and to master, to attack things" (Heidegger, *P* 103). This rise in the A5 Active Subject is one of the defining trends of modernity, but Heidegger is trying to bring it to a close.

Of course, man hardly drops out of the picture. We still occupy an essential place as the necessary partner in the clearing of Being. Although man does not create Being or the clearing, they cannot be without him; this is the new version of A1 Dependence. "Man should be understood, within the question of being, as *the* site which being requires in order to disclose itself. Man is the site of openness, the there" (Heidegger, *IM* 205). "The world cannot be what it is or the way that it is through man, but neither can it be without man. . . . Being . . . needs man for its revelation, preservation, and formation" (Heidegger, "OG" 107). This follows from Phenomenological Ontology's definition of Being as appearing: given this sense, it cannot appear without someone to appear to (see Heidegger, *ET* 52, 75; Heidegger, *Mi* 119). He puts this new relationship, which goes beyond both realism's R1 Independence and Kantian anti-realism's A1 Dependence, fairly explicitly here: "Does such revealing happen somewhere beyond all human doing? No. But neither does it happen exclusively *in* man, or definitively *through* man."[21]

This is not so much a new claim added on as it is an organic development of his understanding of Being. One of the implications of the ontological difference—that Being is not a being—is that Being should be conceived as the appearing itself rather than as a thing which either could appear or not. As presencing, Be-ing can only *be* in the act of appearing to the perceiver. Hence "both have to belong mutually and fundamentally to each other" (Heidegger, *Mi* 133; see also 367; Heidegger, *ID* 33). Unfortunately, language constantly hypostasizes Being into a being for which appearance and the relation to humans seem optional.

> Presencing ("being") is, as presencing, on each and every occasion a presencing directed toward the human essence. . . . The human essence as such is a hearing. . . . That which is the Same each time, the belonging together of call and hearing, would then be "being"? What am I saying? It is no longer "being" at all—if we attempt fully to think through "being" . . . as presencing. . . . We would then have to relinquish the isolating and separating word "being" just as decisively as the name "human being." The question concerning the relation between the two revealed itself to be inadequate, because it never attains to the realm of what it seeks to ask after. In truth we cannot then even continue to say that "being" and "the human being" "are" the Same in the sense that *they* belong together; for when we say it in *this* way, we continue to let both subsist independently. (Heidegger, *Pm* 308–9; see also Heidegger, *BW* 235; Heidegger, *ID* 31; Heidegger, *Mi* 281)

Grammar fights us here. Even saying that Being and man belong together implies that they are two independent things which are "constantly conjoined," which is not what Heidegger wants to say. The point is that they are conceptually inseparable, but to make the point we have to name them separately in order then to state that they are one.

One reason for Heidegger's often bizarre writing style is that he resorts to rhetorical tricks such as tautologous phrases, neologisms, or crossing out the word "being" in order to highlight and resist language's ontic tendencies, that is, its propensity to treat all phenomena as entities: "Language in principle has an ontic character, so that thinking finds itself in the situation of having to use ontic models for what it wishes to say ontologically" (Heidegger, *TB* 51; see also Heidegger, *BT* 63/39). Since his primary goal is to discuss Being, this is a serious problem.

> The crossing out of this word initially has only a preventive role, namely, that of preventing the almost ineradicable habit of representing "being" as something standing somewhere on its own that then on occasion first comes face-to-face with human beings. In accordance with this way of representing matters, it appears as though the human being is excepted from "being." However, he is not only not excepted, i.e., not only included in "being," but "being," in needing the human being, is obliged to relinquish this appearance of independence. (Heidegger, *Pm* 310)

The ontic representation of Being as a being makes us think of it with realist R1 Independence, but its ontological nature means that it can only be in the presence of man. This is one reason why Heidegger stresses the ontological difference so much. Equally, man can only be when Being presences to him. In a late interview, Heidegger goes so far as to say that

> the fundamental idea of my thinking is exactly that Being, relative to the manifestation of Being, *needs* man and, conversely, man is only man in so far as he stands within the manifestation of Being. Thus, the question as to what extent I am concerned only with Being and have forgotten man, ought to be settled. One cannot pose a question about Being without posing a question about the essence of man. (Heidegger, *MHC* 40)

Neither can be understood by itself, since neither can be by itself; the very meaning of each is to be related to the other, though again language frustrates the expression of this fact.

> Every philosophical—that is, thoughtful—doctrine of man's essential nature is *in itself alone* a doctrine of the Being of beings. Every doctrine of Being is *in itself alone* a doctrine of man's essential nature. . . . Generally the question of this relation existing between man's nature and the Being of beings—this is in fact the one single question which all traditional thinking must first be brought to face. . . . But it is a question of abysmal difficulty, simply because our seemingly correct posing of the question in fact muddles the question fundamentally. We ask what the relation is between man's nature and the Being of beings. But—as soon as I thoughtfully say "man's nature," I have already said relatedness to Being. Likewise, as soon as I say thoughtfully: Being of beings, the relat-

> edness to man's nature has been named. Each of the two members of the relation between man's nature and Being already implies the relation itself. To speak to the heart of the matter: there is no such thing here as members of the relation, nor the relation as such.[22]

This idea that neither properly exists except in relation with the other is the fulfillment of *Being and Time*'s Being-in-the-world. Although Heidegger claimed there that ED Dasein could only be understood in the world and in terms of worldly projects, anxiety and anticipation of death revealed structural aspects of Dasein that couldn't be defined wholly in terms of the world. Now, however, "man" virtually means relatedness to beings and Being.

Rather than either realism's R1 Independence or Kantian anti-realism's A1 Dependence of beings and/or Being on the subject, the Heideggerian Paradigm proposes the new doctrine that I will call "mutual interdependence." Being and man need each other and can only be and be thought of in relation to each other. This is his version of Parmenidean unity: "Beings are only where perceiving is, and perceiving is only where beings are" (Heidegger, *N* 3:49; see also Heidegger, *TB* 38; Heidegger, *QT* 130–31; Heidegger, *Mi* 178).

> Man *is* essentially this relationship of responding to Being, and he is only this. . . . And Being? Let us think of Being according to its original meaning, as presence. Being is present to man neither incidentally nor only on rare occasions. Being is present and abides only as it concerns man through the claim it makes on him. For it is man, open toward Being, who alone lets Being arrive as presence. Such becoming present needs the openness of a clearing, and by this need remains appropriated to human being. This does not at all mean that Being is posited first and only by man. . . . Man and Being are appropriated to each other. They belong to each other.[23]

This unites A6 Non-Realism of the Subject and A1 Dependence. Man is only what he is in relation to Being and beings (A6), and Being and beings are what they are only in relation to man (A1). This is one of the ways in which Heidegger is still heir to anti-realism: Being only is in relation to human awareness, so there can be no experience-transcendent Being in principle. "By no means is there somewhere and somehow something present outside the duality. . . . Anything outside of presencing . . . is impossible" (Heidegger, *EGT* 96; see also Heidegger, *Zo* 180).

Despite this mutuality, though, it is hard to deny Being's place as first among equals: "The point is that in the determination of the humanity of man as ek-sistence what is essential is not man but Being" (Heidegger, *BW* 237). Being approaches us first (logically; temporal order makes no sense here) to enable us to think at all. We are the necessary site, but we do not control, constitute, or create this site; we depend entirely on the fact and character of Being's approach. "The field of vision is something open, but its openness is not due to our looking" (Heidegger, *DT* 64). Thinking does not found or create itself, but responds to Being's call. "Thinking accomplishes the relation of Being to the essence of man. It does not make or cause the relation. Thinking brings the relation to Being solely as something handed over to it from Being."[24] This receptivity is one of the constant themes in Heidegger's later work and constitutes an important part of his rejection of the Kantian Paradigm. I discuss this more below.

## A6 and Impersonal Conceptual Scheme: The Unmooring

The most important vestige of realism in Heidegger's early work was his commitment to R6 Realism of the Subject in Dasein's permanent, ahistorical structure. This idea retained significant elements of the Kantian Paradigm, even while his PO ontology and UT epistemology were undermining it. This produced deep tensions in the early work, as he occasionally admits:

> The adequate execution and completion of this other thinking that abandons subjectivity is surely made more difficult by the fact that in the publication of *Being and Time* the third division of the first part, "Time and Being," was held back. . . . Here everything is reversed. The division in question was held back because *thinking failed in the adequate saying of this turning [Kehre] and did not succeed with the help of the language of metaphysics.* (Heidegger, *BW* 231, italics added)

Although Heidegger intended to throw off the subjectivism of the first two divisions in the third, he found that he could not do so because the work as a whole was too deeply structured around the Kantian subject. In order to escape this framework, he had to start from scratch with a new approach. So far we have discussed his deeper integration of history into, and his removal of the status of A5 constituting origin from, the subject. Now we can examine the consequences of these changes.

The later Heidegger is still an anti-realist in that we can only talk about Being in relation to man (mutual interdependence), but he rejects the Kantian Paradigm's attempt to ground Being in man. His new thinking analyzes man in a different way:

> As mindfulness of be-ing, philosophy is necessarily self-mindfulness. The foregoing claim regarding this interconnection is essentially different from any way of securing the "self"-certainty of the "I" for the sake of "certainty" and not for the sake of the truth *of be-ing*. But this claim reaches deeper still, into a domain that is more originary than the one which the "fundamental ontological" approach to Da-sein in *Being and Time* had to set forth in *crossing*. (Heidegger, *CP* 34, §19; see also 53, §34)

He now realizes that "in *Being and Time* Da-sein still stood in the shadow of the 'anthropological,' the 'subjectivistic,' and the 'individualistic,' and so on—and yet the opposite of all of this is what we have in view" (Heidegger, *CP* 208, §172; see also 212, §176). He characterizes his early work as a "transcendental manner of questioning" which "must still in a way speak the language of metaphysics" so that "the fundamental experience of *Being and Time* is thus that of the oblivion of Being" (Heidegger, *TB* 29, qualified slightly in the next sentence). His verdict is that "the fundamental flaw of the book *Being and Time* is perhaps that I ventured forth too far too early" (Heidegger, *OWL* 7; see also 12). Not the humblest admission of error, but an admission nonetheless.[25]

The later work throws off the vestiges of subjectivist realism by eradicating all traces of an R6 ahistorical self. Following HPO and UT all the way, man is whatever he appears as, which means that he changes throughout history like everything else. "Overall [it is a question of] rethinking being-historically (but not 'ontologically') the whole of human being, as soon as it is grounded in Da-sein" (Heidegger, *CP* 71, §49, bracketed comment in original). Heidegger now believes, contra Kant and his own earlier work's single set of existentialia, that "grounding time-space does not design an empty table of categories. Rather . . . thinking is historical in its very core."[26] Just as Being varies radically in different epochs, so do man and thought; Heidegger is reported to have said that "the becoming of being (*Seins-Geschick*) is meant always for the historical human being . . . that is, for the Hellenic, the Christian, and so on" (Sallis 1970, 26; see also Heidegger, *HH* 124). Completing ED as well, man has fully entered into history and alters along with everything else at the epochal shifts. In a direct reference to Dasein's ahistorical structure in his early work, Heidegger now says that "the ek-sistence of man is historical as such" (Heidegger, *BW* 239; see also Heidegger, *EHP* 57).

Heidegger is particularly interested in the modern epochal changeover of man into subject, which is as important an event as there has ever been, in his view:

> Being as a whole has already experienced a different interpretation through that in which subjectivity finds its origin; that is, through the *truth* of beings. By virtue of the transformation of the human being into the subject, the history of modern mankind does not merely receive new "contents" and areas of activity; rather the course of history itself takes a different direction.[27]

He explicitly denies that it is only our content that alters with time, the more superficial historical change that took place in the early work, and drops *Being and Time*'s facade of neutrality by blatantly attacking the subjective turn history has taken. Importantly, however, modern man *really has become* a subject; in keeping with HPO, Heidegger cannot say that this is an illusory appearance behind which the real, permanent self awaits liberation. "What is decisive is . . . that the very essence of man itself changes, in that man becomes subject" (Heidegger, *QT* 128; see also 151; Heidegger, *N* 3:221). If this is how man appears now, then this is how he actually is.

Since our essence is historical, however, it is neither permanent nor universal, and we must take care not to read our present form back into earlier periods. "Not every way of being a self is necessarily subjectivity. As long as we fail to see this, then every time a priority is accorded to the self we will run the risk of misinterpreting it as 'subjectivity' or even 'subjectivism'" (Heidegger, *P* 138; see also Heidegger, *Pm* 285; Heidegger, *Mi* 98). Man has existed in very different forms, each of which is fully real, even if they are incompatible with each other, and in all likelihood he will change again. In a passage that strikingly presages Foucault's famous conclusion to *The Order of Things,* Heidegger writes that

> being subject as humanity has not always been the sole possibility belonging to the essence of historical man, which is always beginning in a primal way, nor will it always be. A fleeting cloud shadow over a concealed land, such is the darkening which that truth as the certainty of subjectivity—once prepared by Christendom's certainty of salvation—lays over a disclosing event that it remains denied to subjectivity itself to experience. (Heidegger, *QT* 153; see also Heidegger, *DT* 77–78; Heidegger, *Pm* 334)

One of the goals of the later work is to delimit the self-evidence of subjectivity in order to allow for alternate and future conceptions of the self, which would be one aspect of what he sometimes calls "the other beginning." In contrast to the Kantian Paradigm's ethical goal, the Heideggerian Paradigm's emphasis on historical flux invites us to become what we are *not.* "If our thinking should succeed in its efforts to go back into the ground of metaphysics, it might well help to bring about a change in the human essence" (Heidegger, *Pm* 279; see also Heidegger, *Mi* 37). Historicality brings contingency and openness to various ways of Being (A3), for nonhuman beings as well as ourselves.

Later Heideggerian man is deeply historical. Where *Being and Time* insisted that it had determined the totality of Dasein's structure once and for all (R6), Heidegger now allows that "when understood historically, the relationship between ontic interpretation and ontology is always a correlative relationship insofar as new *existentialia* are discovered from ontic experience" (Heidegger, *Zo* 207). New existentialia can be discovered from ontic findings (ED), since historical openness prevents any closure or a priori limits to what we may find or be. In contrast to Hegel's "truth is the whole" in which the subject succeeds when it completes itself, when "Spirit has made its existence identical with its essence; it has itself for its object just as it is" (Hegel, *PS* 21, §37), UT presumes no a priori whole but remains open to whatever appears. This is an important way in which Heidegger's conception of truth cooperates with his ontology, whereas Hegel's conception closed down the opportunity for his Objective Idealism to surpass the Kantian Paradigm.

In his early temporal idealism, Dasein's temporality was primitive and Being derived its temporality from Dasein (A5). Heidegger explicitly rejects this approach in his later work: "One tries in vain to interpret this occurrence [of the destiny of Being only as history] in terms of what was said in *Being and Time* about the historicity of man (*Dasein*) (not of Being)" (Heidegger, *TB* 9, bracketed comment added; see also 28–29). The earlier argument amounted to a kind of foundationalism: Being is grounded in Dasein, which was unpacked as a series of nesting layers which (R6) come to an end in temporality (or transcendence), which thus constitutes the meaning of Dasein and, via Dasein (A5), Being. Heidegger sided with Kant against the idealists in believing that the reason for these particular faculties must remain mysterious and ungrounded,[28] but he still posited a single set of existentialia.

Now Heidegger says that each new epoch will "bestow on [man] the foundation of a new essence. This need displaces man into the beginning of a foundation of his essence. I say advisedly *a* foundation for we can never say that it is the absolute one" (Heidegger, *BQ* 139; see also Heidegger, *TB* 35, 45). Man has foundations, but now they're multiple, transient, and can yield no ultimate or final *arche*. Each era gives us new ones which do not come together into a logical progression toward a totality. Whereas the analysis of existence reached at least a provisional answer to the meaning of Being in *Being and Time*, now "1. The determination of the essence of the human being is *never* an answer, but is essentially a question. 2. The asking of this question and its decision are historical" (Heidegger, *IM* 149). Heidegger even gives a quasi-Socratic interpretation of questioning and ignorance as the sole proper conclusion: "Here questioning already counts as knowing, because no matter how essential and decisive an answer might be, the answer cannot be other than the penultimate step in the long series of steps of a questioning founded in itself" (Heidegger, *BQ* 7; see also Heidegger, *OWL* 12).

In one of his more disingenuous rereadings of his early work, he claims that "time, which is addressed as the meaning of Being in *Being and Time,* is itself not an answer, not a last prop for questioning, but rather itself the naming of a question" (Heidegger, *TB* 28). This description fits the various "answers" he comes up with every decade or so in his later work, but I don't think this is how he thought of time in his early work. He's a better reader of his early writings at times like this: "But *Being and Time* after all aims at demonstrating 'time' as the domain for projecting-opening be-ing. Certainly, but if things had remained that way, then the question of being would never have unfolded as *question* and thus as en-thinking of what is most question-worthy" (Heidegger, *CP* 317, §262). *Being and Time* did in fact seek a final answer which would have imposed closure on questioning, and he denied alternative interpretations.

In perhaps his best discussion of his "*Kehre*" or turning, Heidegger states that

> meaning in *Being and Time* is defined in terms of a project region, and [A5] projection is the accomplishment of Dasein, which means the ek-static instancy in the openness of being. By ek-sisting, Dasein includes *meaning.* The thinking that proceeds from *Being and Time,* in that it gives up the word "meaning of being" in favor of "truth of being," henceforth emphasizes the openness of being itself, rather than the openness of Dasein in regard to this openness of being. This signifies "the turn," in which thinking always more decisively turns to being as being. (Heidegger, *FoS* 47, bracketed comment added; see also Heidegger, *Pm* 361)

The opening of the clearing was the result of Forms or God in pre-Kantian realism (onto-theology) and it was the "accomplishment of Dasein" (A5) in the Kantian Paradigm and Heidegger's own early work: "Metaphysics recognizes the clearing of Being either solely as the [R1] view of what is present in 'outward appearance' (*idea*) or critically as what is seen as a result of [A5] categorial representation on the part of subjectivity. This means that the truth of Being as the clearing itself remains concealed for metaphysics" (Heidegger, *BW* 235, bracketed comments added; see also Heidegger, *Mi* 347). Heidegger rejects both of these options and turns to Being's opening of itself instead.

Now Being's historicality is primitive, and humans derive their features from it rather than the other way around (see Marrati 2005, 106). Heidegger's rejection of the A5 Kantian subject founding aspects of reality is one of the primary sources of the backlash against "humanism" that has reigned over continental thought ever since. This anti-humanism is the culmination of ED and A6 in a fully empirical, historical subject completely determined by the various historical determinations or "sendings" of Being rather than their origin. The transcendental project of fundamental ontology—the grounding of all projections of Being (A5) in the unchanging focal point of the subject (R6)—has virtually been inverted. But neither does he retreat to a pre-Kantian realism of looking to individual beings (R1) by themselves; they cannot explain our access to them or their propensity to undergo fundamental, essential shifts. The Heideggerian Paradigm turns to the historical truths or understandings of Being, which informs postmodernism and post-structuralism's move away from the subject to focus on the impersonal structures that organize and enable the subject's actions and thoughts.

Heidegger's epochal clearings, also called the truths or understandings of Being, *Geschicken,* destinings/sendings, or the mathematical, are similar to the Kantian Paradigm's conceptual schemes in that they determine (A5) the general character of beings of their period. However, Heidegger introduces a major change here by not basing the schemes in the subject. In this way he wants his later work, as he puts it, "to re-enact *Kant's* main steps but to overcome the 'transcendental' point of departure through Da-sein" (Heidegger, *CP* 123, §88; see also 169, §122; 315, §262). Thus the Heideggerian Paradigm is simultaneously close to and far from Kant, as appropriating his thought but also profoundly modifying it: "[What is needed is a] transcendental and ontological inquiry, that is, a fundamental ontological inquiry which is reminiscent of Kant, and yet radically different at the same time" (Heidegger, *Zo* 194). This characterization might sound rather empty, yet it actually describes his later project quite well. Haar shows both its connection to and distinction from Kant by calling the clearing a "quasi-transcendental":[29] it is "a radical making-possible," but "its illumination does not come from the subject or from its transcendence" (Haar 1993, 99). In the next chapters we will see both Foucault and Derrida make the same move, which is common to many continental thinkers after Heidegger.

Heidegger maintains the Kantian Paradigm's idea of conceptual schemes or ways of organizing beings, but detaches them from the subject; indeed, they have become Unmoored from any *arche,* principle, or ground whatsoever. Both traditional ways of accounting for the way things are have been rejected: beings are not the basis for their own nature as in realism, and Dasein or man is no longer the organizing source of concepts, as in the Kantian Paradigm. In a late seminar, Heidegger dismisses the metaphor of a foundation as simply inappropriate for a subject with variability (A6), since nothing stable could be built on such a "foundation":

> What is fundamental in fundamental ontology is incompatible with any building on it. Instead, after the meaning of Being had been clarified, the whole analytic of Dasein was to be more originally repeated in a completely different way. Thus, since the foundation of fundamental ontology is no foundation upon which something could be built, no *fundamentum inconcussum*, but rather a *fundamentum concussum* . . . whereas the word "foundation" contradicts the preliminary character of the analytic, the term "fundamental ontology" was dropped. (Heidegger, *TB* 32)

Without a realist subject as source or foundation, we must look to the epochal clearings as what shape the beings of their eras. I will call this thesis of the Heideggerian Paradigm—its non-subjectivistic version of A5—Impersonal Conceptual Scheme (ICS). The idea is that beings are organized at a particular time into a general way of Being, but the subject is now organized along with everything else rather than being the source of the scheme. This is what Ricoeur once called, in discussing structuralism which adheres to basically the same thesis, "a transcendentalism without a subject" (Ricoeur 1974, 53).

Heidegger distinguishes two levels of history: the covert history of the epochs of Being, and the surface sequence of events made possible by the former (Heidegger, *Mi* 199). The former is the history of metaphysics, which describes an epoch's mode of Being that forms the basis for everything that happens within that period (Heidegger, *P* 64; Heidegger, *N* 3:8). This is what takes the place of A5 Active Knower, now rendered anonymous rather than being located in the subject. Being reveals itself in these sendings, which we study through contemporary metaphysicians' attempts to express their epoch's understanding of Being. "Metaphysics alone is able to ground an epoch insofar as it establishes and *maintains* humankind in a truth concerning beings as such and as a whole" (Heidegger, *N* 3:188; Heidegger, *DT* 82). Rather than the subject opening and structuring a field of experience, Being maintains us in unconcealment, so we must examine this structure in order to study Being and man, a new form of fundamental ontology (see Marx 1971, 244).

One point that Heidegger never tires of making in his later work is the utter mystery of Being's revealings. Although Dasein's features are grounded in what Being "sends" at a particular time, it is essential that

> if we ever wanted to ground our plans and recourses among beings—our using and shaping of things—immediately upon being, if we wanted to

> assess the reliability of the everyday according to how being is grounded in its essence there, and how this essence is familiar to us, then we must just as soon experience that none of our intentions and attitudes can be built directly upon being. Being, otherwise constantly used and called upon, offers us no foundation and no ground upon which we can immediately place whatever we erect, undertake, and bring about every day. Being thus appears as the groundless, as something that continually gives way, offers no support, and denies every ground and basis. . . . *Being is the most reliable and at the same time the non-ground.* (Heidegger, *BCo* 53; see also Heidegger, *Mi* 283)

Being is, on the one hand, the most reliable since it is the most basic, necessary, and ubiquitous feature of experience—that there are beings and that we can experience them. But this fact gives us nothing specific to do, no directives to fulfill. This is Heidegger's new version of *Being and Time*'s "impossibility of projecting oneself upon a potentiality-for-Being which belongs to existence" (Heidegger, *BT* 393/343) and his view that "death, as possibility, gives Dasein nothing to be 'actualized'" (307/262; see also 434/383). Although Being is the only foundation we have, it cannot fulfill the function traditionally served by rational foundations (Forms, God, nature) of explaining all of the whys and wherefores of life and giving us the right way to live. This is why he calls it an "abyssal" or "groundless ground":

> Being . . . offers us a reliance whose reliability cannot be surpassed anywhere. And yet Being offers us no ground and no basis—as beings do—to which we can turn, on which we can build, and to which we can cling. Being is the rejection of the role of such grounding: it renounces all grounding, is abyssal [*ab-gründig*]. (Heidegger, *N* 4:193; see also 3:90)

Although it is all the ground we have, it is a groundless or ungrounded ground.

As we have seen, grounding the structures of thinking was a central concern for the Kantian Paradigm. Kant did not succeed in making them fully intelligible or necessary, by his own admission. Hegel tries to overcome the raw contingency of simply being "thrown" into this fact of reason by depicting all of history as the process of Spirit coming to choose our present form of the self, thus creating total autonomy and self-choice. He imputes an intrinsic and necessary logic to the movement of ideas, such that no rational being could have ended up anywhere else but at Hegel's own Absolute Knowing.

Heidegger has reversed the A5 grounding relation—Being isn't grounded on temporal Dasein, man is grounded on historical Being—

and he has made Being a groundless ground. In this way it resembles Derrida's "*différance*" which "governs nothing, reigns over nothing, and nowhere exercises any authority. . . . *Différance* instigates the subversion of every kingdom" (Derrida, *MP* 22). As Gadamer often points out, what I am calling Heidegger's notion of Impersonal Conceptual Schemes indexed to historical epochs is his inheritance from Hegel (Gadamer 1976a, 104, 1981 41). For instance: "It is not *we* who frame the notions. . . . The notion is the genuine first; and things are what they are through the action of the notion, immanent in them, and revealing itself in them" (Hegel, *HL* 228, §163R2). However, Heidegger rejects Hegel's attempts to organize the epochs along a logical self-development: "Thinking no longer enjoys the favor of the 'system'; it is historical in the singular sense that being itself as en-owning above all sustains all history and thus can never be calculated. Historical preparedness for the truth of be-ing replaces the systematization and deduction" (Heidegger, *CP* 171, §125; see also Heidegger, *Mi* 39, 206, 313). The epochs are groundless in that they can neither be traced to an R6 ahistorical subject nor arranged along an internal developmental logic: "In no way can it be seen that individual philosophies and epochs of philosophy have emerged from one another in the sense of the necessity of a dialectic process" (Heidegger, *WIP* 63; see also Heidegger, *QT* 39). Heidegger's conclusion is that finitude entails, among other things, that

> the origin of the principles of thinking, the place of the thinking that posits them, the essence, i.e., essential presencing of this place and its locality—all that remains in the dark for us. This darkness is perhaps always in play, in all thinking. Human beings cannot avoid it. Rather, they must learn to recognize the dark as the ineluctable and to keep at a distance those prejudices which destroy the lofty sway of the dark. . . . The dark is rather the secret mystery of what is light. . . . It is hard to keep the dark pure and clear, to preserve it from admixture with a brightness that does not belong to it. (Heidegger, *PT* 55–56; see also Heidegger, *BW* 204)

Although Heidegger applauds Hegel's incorporation of history, Kant had a better appreciation of finitude, in that he accepted the basic givenness of our ways of thinking (see the brief comparison at Heidegger, *KPM* 166, and Heidegger, *AM* 27). I will return to this issue in my conclusion.

Heidegger's argument for the necessary groundlessness of Being as a ground is that since it itself is the source of our way of reasoning—the way that we ask for and accept reasons and grounds—it cannot in turn be justified. To legitimate it would require a further, more encompassing set of criteria and way of reasoning which would then stand in need of similar grounding. However much we try to ground or found our lives on principles, we can always ask for the justification of these principles. Indeed, this very demand for grounds—the principle of reason itself—must remain ungrounded for this reason: "The principle of reason is, as the supreme fundamental principle, something underivable, the sort of thing which puts a check on thinking" (Heidegger, *PR* 45). Thus "insofar as being essentially comes to be as ground/reason, it has no ground/reason. However, this is not because it founds itself, but because every foundation—even and especially self-founded ones—remain[s] inappropriate to being as ground/reason. . . . Being *qua* being remains ground-less" (111). As the source of rationality, it can neither be rational nor irrational; to evaluate it by these standards would be a category mistake.

> Wonder displaces man into and before beings as such. . . . It displaces him into that on which and in which word, work, and deed, as historical, can be *based* and history can begin. The basic disposition, however, can neither be simply brought about by man's will [the Kantian Paradigm] nor is it the effect of a cause issuing from beings and operating on man [realism]. This displacement is beyond explanation, for all explanation here necessarily falls short and comes too late, since it could only move within, and would have to appeal to, something that was first encountered as unconcealed in the displacement. (Heidegger, *BQ* 147, bracketed comments added)

Explanations are shaped by the particular way of thinking that we have, by the way thoughts occur to us, by what reasons strike us as plausible, and by what answers appear acceptable. None of this is under our control, but conforms to the way of thinking we are thrown into, which has changed significantly throughout history (see Heidegger, *Pm* 293). We cannot use any of these particular epochal ways of reasoning to judge reason itself, nor the sequence of epochs. As a student in a late seminar transcribes, "For Hegel, there rules in history necessity. . . . For Heidegger, on the other hand, one cannot speak of a 'why.' Only the 'that'—that the history of Being is in such a way—can be said."[30] The key point for our discussion is that once Heidegger has Unmoored the epochs from the founding self, he does not turn to an internal or objective logic of the epochs themselves for closure or necessary order, but simply accepts raw, ultimate contingency. This "Unmooring thesis" is the culmination of UT, HPO, and ICS—reality is whatever appears in whatever manner it appears and so cannot be based on a principle that will place limits on what it can be the way that realism and the Kantian Paradigm do in their respective ways.

Heidegger often calls these epochal understandings of Being "destinings" or "fate." These seem like exactly the wrong words to use, given their connotations of necessity and planning by an intelligent agent. Of course, these understandings cannot be planned by a supernatural agent because God is just another being; invoking him just begs the question of how God came about with the nature that he has, how he decided to create the world in this way, and so on—what Heidegger calls onto-theology. This explanation presupposes and is only acceptable within a particular understanding, and so cannot account for the fact of understandings as a whole. Indeed, any explanation takes place within a particular way of reasoning, rendering it incapable of explaining the fact of reasoning or the multiplicity of ways of reasoning. This rules out questions about the rationality or irrationality, the necessity or randomness of the sequence of epochs. As what enables us to think at all, they are not subject to these kinds of determinations. "One cannot inquire into the 'correctness' of a projecting-open at all—and certainly not into the correctness of *that* projecting-open through which on the whole the clearing as such is grounded. . . . Is then the projecting-open pure caprice? No, it is the utmost necessity, but of course not a necessity in the sense of a logical conclusion" (Heidegger, *CP* 229–30, §204). Since the traditional trappings of these words are inapplicable in this case, Heidegger applies "destinings" (he also likes the word's etymological connections) or "utmost necessity," just as he applied "in-itself" in *Being and Time,* even though he knows it could be misleading. "Why it gave itself in this way and not another, of this we admittedly know nothing, at least in the sense where knowledge is the definition of a scientific law. Concerning this, I have risked speaking of the 'destiny of being'" (Heidegger, *FoS* 9; see also Gadamer 1976a, 109).

Heidegger repeatedly denies any necessary order or logic to the series of epochs, but he does occasionally impute some intelligible relationship among them. "The sequence of epochs in the destiny of Being is not accidental, nor can it be calculated as necessary. Still, what is appropriate shows itself in the destiny, what is appropriate shows itself in the belonging together of the epochs" (Heidegger, *TB* 9). He often justifies calling Nietzsche the last metaphysician, for instance, because Nietzsche's metaphysics hits upon the final permutation of the being-becoming dyad set up by Plato, which presupposes that there is a set number of variations (Heidegger, *HH* 24). He also frequently traces a pattern of decline in the history of metaphysics as an increasing concealment or forgetfulness of Being, though with qualifications. The discussion quoted above which says that we cannot say why but only that the history of Being has occurred as a certain way continues: "Within the 'that' and in the sense of the 'that,' thinking can also ascertain *something like* necessity in the sequence, *some-*

*thing like* an order and a consistency. Thus *one can say* that the history of Being is the history of the oblivion of Being escalating itself" (Heidegger, *TB* 52, italics added; see also 9; Heidegger, *PR* 108). He uses the term "legacy" at one point to name this inter-epochal connection: "The epochs can never be derived from one another, much less be placed on the track of an ongoing process. Nevertheless, there is a legacy from epoch to epoch" (Heidegger, *PR* 91; see also Sallis 1978, 4). I will show in the next section of this chapter how this legacy shapes Heidegger's thoughts on truth.

Although it is more difficult to relate the Heideggerian Paradigm to analytic philosophy than it was for the Kantian Paradigm—indeed, this heterogeneity is part of the promise Heidegger holds for analytic philosophers—there is a clear resemblance here with Wittgenstein's later work, especially post-*Philosophical Investigations.* Just as Heidegger calls Being both a ground and groundless, neither necessary nor contingent, so Wittgenstein too calls our form of life or language "akin both to what is arbitrary and to what is non-arbitrary."[31] Wittgenstein agrees with Heidegger's anti-realist interpretation of the understanding of Being, i.e., that it cannot be empirically derived. As the Gestalt psychologists would say, observation is a top-down process, so that once an understanding is in place, experience confirms it; but without the understanding in place, indefinitely many others could have arisen.

> But isn't it experience that teaches us to judge like *this,* that is to say, that it is correct to judge like this? But how does experience *teach* us, then? *We* may derive it from experience, but experience does not direct us to derive anything from experience. If it is the *ground* of our judging like this, and not just the cause, still we do not have a ground for seeing this in turn as a ground. (Wittgenstein, *OC* §130; see also Wittgenstein, *Zet* §331, §357)

Experience underdetermines interpretations; interpretations organize what we make of experience in the first place (see Heidegger, *BW* 168; see also 354).

Wittgenstein also points to the infinite regress (Wittgenstein, *RFM* 79, §1.112) involved in the rational justification of forms of life, using the very same term as Heidegger: "The difficulty is to realize the groundlessness of our believing" (Wittgenstein, *OC* §166; see also §253; Wittgenstein, *RFM* 61, §1.63). Like Heidegger's truth of Being which opens and guides all further truths, Wittgenstein discusses "the inherited background against which I distinguish between true and false" (OC §94), which "is not based on grounds" (Wittgenstein, *OC* §559; see also Wittgenstein, *PI* 2.II.192). Given its overwhelming importance, we desperately try to find a ground for our ground, to give it a deep justification. We want to, so to speak, sublime our epistemology, "as if I wanted to insist that there are things that I *know.* God himself can't say anything to me about them" (Wittgenstein, *OC* §554). This is both futile and potentially harmful, so Wittgenstein wants to cure us of it. His solution, like Heidegger's, is to acknowledge the ultimate contingency of our form of life while still living it, not demeaning it due to this fact: "It is true that we can compare a picture that is firmly rooted in us to a superstition; but it is equally true that we *always* eventually have to reach some firm ground, either a picture or something else, so that a picture which is at the root of all our thinking is to be respected and not treated as a superstition" (Wittgenstein 1980a, 83). Heidegger, of course, goes further than "respect" to recommend treating the sendings as well as our general ability to receive any sendings at all with awe and gratitude, but the point is roughly the same. The groundlessness of the ground actually does not diminish its ability to ground, as long as we break our metaphysical addiction to "super-justifications." After repeating his famous demonstration that we cannot show all necessary conditions for someone's following a rule or the rule for following rules, Wittgenstein concludes, "but the most important thing is: The rule is not needed. Nothing is lacking. We do calculate according to a rule, and that is enough" (Wittgenstein, *OC* §46). The fact that we don't doubt all of the propositions that skepticism shows that we could and perhaps should rationally is wholly unimportant: "Why do I not satisfy myself that I have two feet when I want to get up from a chair? There is no why. I simply don't. This is how I act."[32, 33]

## A2 and A4 Rejections of Correspondence Truth and Bivalence: The Ancient History of Truth

In his later work, Heidegger preserves the distinction he had earlier laid out between truth as correspondence or propositional correctness (R2) on the one hand, and truth as unconcealment (UT) on the other. He also still maintains that the former presupposes the latter.

> Yet why should we not be satisfied with the essence of truth that has by now been familiar to us for centuries? Truth means today and has long meant the conformity of knowledge with the matter. However, the matter must show itself to be such if knowledge and the proposition that forms and expresses knowledge are to be able to conform to it. . . . How

> can the matter show itself if it cannot itself stand forth out of concealment, if it does not itself stand in the unconcealed? A proposition is true by conforming to the unconcealed, to what is true. Propositional truth is always, and always exclusively, this correctness. . . . The essence of truth which is familiar to us—correctness in representation—stands and falls with truth as unconcealment of beings.[34]

In the earlier work, the fact that there were two conceptions of truth, as well as the fact that correspondence obscured unconcealment, received two different kinds of explanations: brief allusions to a historical narrative of correspondence coming to dominate unconcealment; and a detailed structural account of Dasein, which showed how once the present-at-hand lay inert before the theoretical gaze, only a relationship of correspondence could bridge the gap between proposition and thing.

The later work gives up the structural account entirely for the historical narrative.[35] This is because the later work's pervasive historicality sweeps away any ahistorical structure of man that could explain the cross-epochal suppression of unconcealment for correspondence. Since man and Being (HPO) are only how they appear at particular times determined by the epochal unconcealment of Being (ICS), we cannot appeal to permanent facts about either to explain long-term processes such as the fate of truth. Thus, when Heidegger discusses the dominance of correspondence or correctness now, it has to be in terms of the course of its history rather than our innate tendency to fall into it, since nothing about us is natural or inevitable.[36] He makes his preference for the historical account explicit in a lecture series from 1935:

> "Being" has the meaning we have indicated, which recalls the Greek conception of the essence of Being—a definiteness, then, which has not come to us from just anywhere, but which has long ruled our historical Dasein. At one blow, our search for the definiteness of the meaning of the word "Being" thus becomes explicitly what it is: a meditation on the provenance of our *concealed history.* The question, "How does it stand with Being?" must maintain itself within the history of Being if it is, in turn, to unfold and preserve its own historical import. (Heidegger, *IM* 96–7)

The destruction of tradition could only have played a secondary role to the existential analysis's structural account in *Being and Time;* now Heidegger believes that the study of Being as well as truth (see, for example, Heidegger, *P* 50) cannot be separated from a discussion of how they have been historically. Hegel too claimed that "the same evolution of thought which is exhibited in the history of philosophy is presented in the System of Philosophy itself" (Hegel, *HL* 19, §14; see also 18, §13; 125, §86R2), but that was because the system "possesses an internal source of development" (20, §14) which necessarily guides consciousness both in its concrete progress and its logical analysis. Heidegger, on the other hand, subscribes to HPO and the completed ED, so there can be nothing more to Being and truth than their historical instantiations.

The historical victory of correspondence over unconcealment is a profoundly fateful event; it is one of the central aspects of this Greek "legacy" that determines all ensuing epochs which I will trace in this section.

> "History," conceived essentially, that is, thought in terms of the ground of the essence of Being itself, is the transformation of the essence of truth. It is "only" this . . . from which as ground the other essential features of history spring forth as essential consequences. History "is" the transformation of the essence of truth. Historical beings receive their Being from such transformation. . . . If unveiling is the essence of truth, and if in accordance with the transformation of this essence of truth the assignment of Being is also transformed, then the essence of "history" is the transformation of the essence of truth.[37]

Heidegger believes that the character of our present epoch, which he wants to help bring to a close, is deeply bound up with R2 Correspondence Truth, so his goal is "to revise, no matter the cost, what has come down to us, i.e., to take the traditional theory of truth as correctness ultimately for granted no longer, but to experience it instead as a source of uneasiness" (Heidegger, *BQ* 20). His early work linked correspondence to Dasein's comportment of disengaged staring, so the way to delimit it and open a space for other conceptions of truth at that point was to show the existence of a different comportment, namely, engaged activity. He had to dis-cover the covered-over existentialia of Dasein's structure (implying R6 Realism of the Subject) that did not support R2 Correspondence Truth in order to break that theory's hegemony (A2).

This cannot be Heidegger's strategy in the later work. Changes in man cannot explain the changes in truth, since it is precisely the epochal changes in truth that form man; the order of determination has been reversed. "Whatever happens with historical human beings always derives from a decision about the essence of truth that was taken long ago and is never up to humans alone" (Heidegger, *Pm* 182). He still aims to break the monopoly of correspondence truth, to show (A2) that "the positing of the essence of truth as the correctness of an assertion is obviously only *one* essential determination among others" (Heidegger, *BQ* 65). But now his strategy is to show us how a series of historical events—especially in ancient Greek and Roman times—closed off alternative conceptions, making the definition of truth as correspondence seem self-evident and necessary: "Because the Greek *homoiosis* [likeness] turned into *rectitudo* [correctness], the realm of *aletheia,* disclosure, still present for Plato and Aristotle in *homoiosis,* disappeared" (Heidegger, *P* 50, bracketed comments added). This is one reason why Heidegger keeps returning to the ancients throughout his career. He explicitly rejects "mere restoration and uncreative imitation" (Heidegger, *IM* 133; see also Heidegger, *Pm* 280) as motives; he considers it neither desirable nor possible to go back.[38] The importance of this period is that it was here that the fateful switch in the conception of truth happened: "This transition itself, of *aletheia qua* unhiddenness to truth *qua* correctness, is an *occurrence,* indeed nothing less than *the* occurrence wherein, already at the beginning of its history, Western philosophy takes off on an erroneous and fateful course" (Heidegger, *ET* 12). Plato and Aristotle's discussions of truth represent "the beginning of that history through which Western man lost his ground as an existing being, in order to end up in contemporary groundlessness" (87; see also 105; Heidegger, *Mi* 337). If we are to correct this catastrophe and recover the lost possibilities, we must understand the point at which we went off track. As in Foucault's genealogy, even being able to see correspondence as a conception rather than what truth simply must be is aided by seeing how it came to be through a series of historical events. Heidegger pinpoints the central event variously in Plato, Aristotle, and the medievals; I will examine his depiction of Plato as the transitional figure of unconcealment to correspondence, since this is the most frequent and detailed account he offers.

According to Heidegger, the pre-Platonic Greeks understood truth as unconcealment pertaining primarily to beings rather than propositions; beings were unconcealed or taken out of hiddenness and then could be captured in assertions if desired. This contrasts with truth as correctness or correspondence: "Unconcealedness (truth as understood by the Greeks) is a determination of beings themselves and not—as is correctness—a character of assertions *about* beings."[39] The Greek understanding of Being was *physis,* meaning nature as self-emerging into unhiddenness (see Heidegger, *Pm* 230; Heidegger, *EGT* 15; Heidegger, *IM* 107). This process highlights the dynamic quality of coming from not-Being into Being, much like the alpha-privative in *a-letheia* emphasizes the transition from concealedness into the open (see Heidegger, *Pm* 171, 206). The dynamism and reference to potential non-Being or concealment implicit in this original meaning of "truth" remind us that the being in question could have remained hidden. This awareness of contingency instills wonder at beings' Being or unconcealment, preventing us from taking it for granted or "forgetting" Being.

Plato's focus on the *idea* or "look" of beings rather than on the being's occurrence as the locus of truth and knowledge begins the fundamental transformation in the history of truth. He does not behold and wonder at the entity's presence—its "that-it-is"—but rather wants to understand its essence, that is, how it is or its whatness.

> When *phusis* changes into *idea,* the *to estin* (what-Being) comes forth and the *hoti estin* (that-Being) distinguishes itself in contrast to it. . . . As soon as the essence of Being comes to consist in whatness (idea), then whatness, as *the* Being of beings, is also what is most in being about beings. . . . Whatness is now what *really* is, *ontōs on.* Being as *idea* is now promoted to the status of what really is, and beings themselves, which previously held sway, sink to the level of what Plato calls *mē on*—that which really should not be and really *is* not either. (Heidegger, *IM* 196; see also Heidegger, *Pm* 170, 172; Heidegger, *Mi* 337–39)

Although the *idea* or look is initially intertwined with beings, as soon as it becomes the focus it starts undergoing a *chorismos* or separation such that it can be contemplated and be on its own. Ultimately, the separation becomes metaphysical and the *ideas* can only be fully captured when abstracted from the distracting particulars.

Once this separation has occurred, truth becomes a matter of *orthotes,* or correctly capturing the *idea,* which has little to do with the being and its emergence from concealment. Indeed, the *idea* is easier to capture the more stable it is, thus turning against the emergence of *physis* itself. The emergent being is relegated to the status of an impure approximation of or a confusing distraction from the unchanging Forms. The allegory of the cave

> contains Plato's "doctrine" of truth, for the "allegory" is grounded in the unspoken event whereby *idea* gains dominance over *aletheia.* . . . *Aletheia* comes under the yoke of the *idea.* When Plato says of the *idea* that she is the mistress that allows unhiddenness, he points to something unsaid, namely, that henceforth the essence of truth does not, as the essence of unhiddenness, unfold from its proper and essential fullness but rather shifts to the essence of the *idea.* The essence of truth gives up its fundamental trait of unhiddenness. (Heidegger, *Pm* 176)

The *idea* is now separate from beings which come and go, emerging into unhiddenness from time to time, so that the *idea* can instantiate the new sense of Being—constant presence—to the fullest extent. *Ideas* are permanent and unchanging, having nothing to do with concealment or emergence; indeed, their status as the true beings is due to their having nothing to do with change. This then relegates the empirical realm to a lesser truth and appearance becomes mere seeming, a new concept (see Heidegger, *IM* 111, 197) which will wreak havoc for some twenty-five centuries until Heidegger's UT can overcome it.

*Ideas* do not emerge or submerge the way *physis* does; they are always there. As Heidegger reads Plato's allegory of the cave, the purpose of education is to redirect our gaze away from mere seeming to true being in order to achieve correct knowledge of the constantly present *ideas*, which itself transforms the understanding of truth from unconcealment to correspondence.

> The movement of passage from one place to the other consists in the process whereby the gaze becomes more correct. Everything depends on the *orthotes*, the correctness of the gaze. Through this correctness, seeing or knowing becomes something correct. . . . What results from this conforming of apprehension, as an *idein*, to the *idea* is a *homoiosis*, an agreement of the act of knowing with the thing itself. Thus the priority of *idea* and *idein* over *aletheia* results in a transformation in the essence of truth. Truth becomes *orthotes*, the correctness of apprehending and asserting. (Heidegger, *Pm* 177)

Changing the object of truth from emerging beings to unchanging Forms leads to a transformation of truth from dynamic un-concealment to static correspondence. Accompanying this transformation is a change in the primary locus of truth from beings to assertions. This is particularly important, since assertions are the mind or soul's attempts to capture a state of affairs. Not only does this reinforce the static nature of correspondence, but it marks the beginning of the long development of the subject's activity in knowing (A5). "In Plato's simile of the cave there is already a falling away from the beginning. . . . *Aletheia* is nevertheless carried over into a 'representation' of the soul" (Heidegger, *Mi* 91). This representation then gets ossified into an assertion.

> The assertion of a judgment made by the intellect is the place of truth and falsehood and of the difference between them. The assertion is called true insofar as it conforms to the state of affairs and thus is a *homoiosis*. The determination of the essence of truth no longer contains an appeal to *aletheia* in the sense of unhiddenness; on the contrary *aletheia* . . . is thought of as correctness. From now on this characterization of the essence of truth as the correctness of both representation and assertion becomes normative for the whole of Western thinking. (Heidegger, *Pm* 178; see also *Mi* 55, 79)

An *idea* separate from changing entities lends itself to being captured correctly by a proposition, whereas an emerging being does not. Thus the two changes reinforce each other.

Aristotle then solidifies Plato's revolution.

> In the inception, logos as gathering *is* the happening of unconcealment; logos is grounded in unconcealment and is in service to it. But now, logos as assertion becomes the locus of truth in the sense of correctness. We arrive at Aristotle's proposition according to which logos as assertion is what can be true or false. Truth, which was originally, as unconcealment, a happening of the beings themselves . . . now becomes a property of logos. In becoming a property of assertion, truth does not just shift its place; it changes its essence. . . . Truth becomes the correctness of logos. (Heidegger, *IM* 199; see also Heidegger, *CP* 234, §210; Heidegger, *ET* 202; Heidegger, *Mi* 91–92)

At this point, much of Heidegger's earlier analysis of the proposition as an inert object corresponding with a static state of affairs applies, though now without the distinction between readiness-to-hand and presence-at-hand. "In the form of the assertion, logos itself has become just another thing that one comes across. This present-at-hand thing is something handy, something that is handled in order to attain truth as correctness and establish it securely" (Heidegger, *IM* 201–2). Although much of his earlier analysis is preserved, it is now considered a *historical* changeover which happens through Plato and Aristotle's ideas, instead of the earlier attribution to individual Daseins' alterations in attitude.

> A consequence of the transformation is that, from the point of view both of the idea and of assertion, the original essence of truth, *alētheia* (unconcealment), has changed into correctness. . . . The transformation of *phusis* and *logos* into idea and assertion has its inner ground in a transformation of the essence of truth as unconcealment into truth as correctness. . . . Once neither beings nor gathering could be preserved and understood on the basis of unconcealment, only *one* possibility remained: that which had fallen apart and lay there as something present at hand could be brought back together only in a relation that itself had the character of something present at hand. A present-at-hand logos must resemble something else present at hand—beings as the objects of the logos—and be directed by these. (Heidegger, *IM* 203)

The importance of this change cannot be overestimated: history simply "is the transformation of the essence of truth" (Heidegger, *P* 55;

see also 147). He does an impressive job of showing how all of the other elements of realism originate in R2 Correspondence Truth. It is the separation (*chorismos*) of *ideas* from beings that allowed propositions to become the locus of truth, and that also makes us think of the truth-makers as R1 Independent and timeless, features which poorly fit beings emerging out of unconcealedness. *Aletheia* naturally suggests an epistemic conception of truth, where truth bears a necessary relation to human awareness—"the essence of man is essential for the truth of Being" (Heidegger, *BW* 248; see also Heidegger, *CP* 272, §243)—whereas correspondence between two present-at-hand objects implies their independence from each other as well as from an observer. Since the Forms are always the same, there can only be one correct definition of them (R3).

Heidegger spends a surprising amount of time tying R2 Correspondence Truth to R4 Bivalence. It is the change in the nature of truth that leads to bivalence.

> In the transformation of the essence of truth from *aletheia,* by way of the Roman *veritas,* to the medieval *adaequatio, rectitudo,* and *iustitia,* and from there to the modern *certitudo,* to truth as certainty, validity, and assurance, the essence and the character of the opposition between truth and untruth are also altered. The self-evident view that falsity is the only opposite to truth is thereby formed and reinforced. (Heidegger, *P* 57)

This represents a profound historical transformation, not the discovery of a timeless property of truth itself.

> Truth as "correctness" is not of the same essence as truth in the sense of "unconcealedness." The opposition of correctness and incorrectness, validity and invalidity, may very well exhaust the oppositional essence of truth for later thinking and above all for modern thinking. But that decides nothing at all concerning the possible oppositions to "unconcealedness" as thought by the Greeks. . . . We stand too uncritically under the prejudice of the opposition between truth and falsity taken for granted a long time ago. (Heidegger, *P* 26–27; see also 18, 127)

Even if we concede bivalence to correspondence truth, we should not immediately apply it to Unconcealment Truth. In fact, Heidegger explicitly claims that UT is A4, not bivalent, since a being's unconcealment is naturally a matter of degrees.

> The unhidden can therefore be *more* or *less* unhidden. . . . Unhiddenness, therefore, has gradations and levels. "Truth" and "true" is not

> something in itself, such that for everyone it is in every aspect unchangeable and common. It is not the case that everyone, without further ado, has the same right and same strength to every truth. And every truth has its *time*.[40]

Here he rejects R4 Bivalence and follows Hegel and Nietzsche in rejecting R3 Uniqueness as well. Given HPO, there are different truths and truth, like everything, is temporal.

Heidegger rejects bivalence because truth and untruth, conceived as unconcealment and concealment, are inextricably linked rather than mutually exclusive or simply opposed to one another. One of the reasons that Plato is a transitional figure and not wholly within correspondence truth is that the partial memory of the Forms (similar to Heidegger's own pre-ontological awareness of Being) falls in between the bivalent poles of truth and falsity: "That there is something *between* the two is precisely the great *discovery* of Plato" (Heidegger, *ET* 190). Heidegger believes that "untruth *belongs* to the essence of truth. Deconcealment, the overcoming of concealment, happens only through a primordial struggle against hiddenness."[41] They are intertwined with each other, which he sometimes puts in hyperbolic language like "truth, in its essence, is un-truth" (Heidegger, *BW* 179). What he means is that "concealment is not the antithesis of consciousness, but rather concealment belongs to the clearing."[42]

This claim that every revealing is also a concealing is Heidegger's version of Husserl's doctrine of adumbrations, that is, the idea that seeing one side of an object hides the other sides of it. When I look at a box, the front and side that I see block my view of the back and other sides; if I turn it around to see those sides, then the ones that were originally in my view can no longer be seen. In his early work, Heidegger extrapolated this idea to the way that Dasein's revelation of an entity as a present-at-hand object hid it as a ready-to-hand tool, correlatively covering up the primordial essence of Dasein as an engaged agent in favor of the more common conception as theoretical knower. His later phase portrays these changeovers as epochal, which means that the medieval experience of beings as divine creations blocks them from being experienced as Greek self-emerging *physis*, while modern objects hide both of these modes. This is simply how unconcealment works. It becomes distortion, however, if any of these epochal revelations claims permanent, unique truth (R3). This distortion is encouraged by the divorcing of unconcealment from concealment that naturally happens when truth is static correspondence with inert, present objects. Once the beings are just there, their ability to change historically becomes much less evident, and whatever mode we find them in seems natural and permanent.

This static R3 conception of our present understanding of Being as the only one leads to the greatest "vice" or "sin," according to the later Heidegger: taking the revelation of beings for granted or believing them to be the sole true reality. Realism ignores the miraculous and wondrous fact that we are able to experience the world at all by treating truth as a simple matter of beings: you just open your eyes and there they are. Kantian-style anti-realism acknowledges that a lot more goes into apparently simple immediate apprehension, but it too closes down wonder by only allowing one kind of revealing (R3) and giving the credit to the knowing subject (A5). This is aided by R2 Correspondence Truth.

Unconcealment truth was primarily a matter of beings and Being for the pre-Platonics; humans were privileged spectators and favored participants, but nothing more.

> What then do the Greeks understand, pre-philosophically and philosophically, by truth? *Aletheia,* unhiddenness; not hidden, but brought out from hiddenness. So already and from the outset truth as unhiddenness does not pertain to the knowledge and conception of beings, but to beings themselves. . . . From the very beginning, the problem of truth is not a problem concerning knowledge and conception. It only becomes this in a secondary sense, insofar as the knowledge which grasps beings in their unveiledness, unhiddenness, is also for its part "true," i.e., in Greek terms, it is such as to appropriate, communicate, and preserve the unhiddenness of beings. The proposition is not what is primarily true in the sense of unhiddenness, but is the means by which we humans preserve and secure truth, i.e., the deconcealment of beings: *aletheuein.* (Heidegger, *EF* 64)

Initially, human comportment did not bring unconcealment about, but only witnessed its occurrence in beings. "In a way that is self-evident for a Greek, [Plato] quite unambiguously understands *aletheia* not as a property and determination of seeing, of knowledge, nor as a characteristic of knowledge in the sense of a human faculty, but as a determination of what is known, of the things themselves, of the beings" (Heidegger, *ET* 74; see also Heidegger, *EF* 62).

Then Plato focused on and separated the *idea,* so humans' participation through logos took on more importance; it became the knower's responsibility to bring her propositions in line with the *ideas* so as to attain correctness. Heidegger sees this as the beginning of humanism, the anthropocentrism of metaphysics and epistemology that reaches its zenith in his modern "axis of evil": Descartes, Kant, and Nietzsche.

> Concern with human being and with the position of humans amidst beings entirely dominates metaphysics. The beginning of metaphysics in the thought of Plato is at the same time the beginning of "humanism.". . . Human beings, in differing respects but always deliberately, move into a central place among beings. . . . Plato's thinking follows the change in the essence of truth, a change that becomes the history of metaphysics, which in Nietzsche's thinking has entered upon its unconditioned fulfillment. . . . This change in the essence of truth is present as the all-dominating fundamental reality—long established and thus still in place—of the ever-advancing world history of the planet in this most modern of modern times. (Heidegger, *Pm* 181–82; see also Heidegger, *CP* 126, §91)

Whereas unconcealment is a matter of the being's self-emerging, the *idea* brings in the subject's correct grasping, so that the subject's knowing faculties and the proposition now displace the entity as the site of knowledge.

> Only in this Platonic revolution do *noein* and *nous* (apprehending) first get referred essentially to the "idea." The adoption of this orientation to the ideas henceforth determines the essence of apprehension and subsequently the essence of "reason." "Unhiddenness" now means: the unhidden always as what is accessible thanks to the idea's ability to shine. But insofar as the access is necessarily carried out through "seeing," unhiddenness is yoked into a "relation" with seeing, it becomes "relative" to seeing. (Heidegger, *Pm* 173)

This is where the history of Western thought went wrong for Heidegger. This is the beginning of what will culminate in the Kantian Paradigm, where man creates the clearing (A5) and controls beings.

> The priority of *idea* and *idein* over *aletheia* results in a transformation in the essence of truth. Truth becomes *orthotes,* the correctness of apprehending and asserting. With this transformation of the essence of truth there takes place at the same time a change of the locus of truth. As unhiddenness, truth is still a fundamental trait of beings themselves. But as the correctness of the "gaze," it becomes a characteristic of human comportment towards beings. (Heidegger, *Pm* 177; see also Heidegger, *ET* 202; Heidegger, *Mi* 284)

It is now the *idea,* especially the *idea* of the Good in the *Republic,* that makes unconcealment possible, not the other way around (see Heidegger, *Pm*

175). And the linkage of the *ideas* to the human comportment of knowing plants the seeds for the eventual belief in human control over revealing: "The *idea* is the ground that makes *aletheia* possible. . . . Truth has become correctness, and henceforth it will be a characteristic of the knowing of beings" (179). Truth is now anchored in the subject: "Logos has long since been externalized into a faculty of understanding and of reason."[43, 44]

In the modern period, beings have become ob-jects—that which is thrown-against the subject; they are defined by their relation to the subject and, in the Kantian Paradigm, they derive specific features from the constituting powers of the subject (A5). "The weakened meaning of *aletheia* now rebounds on the concept of *being*. Truth is understood as being-correct in the sense of correct assertion . . . ; thus being is also understood as the being of assertion . . . : what is correctly asserted, and *only* this, *is*. Being is thus oriented to the assertion" (Heidegger, *ET* 103; see also Heidegger, *QT* 89; Heidegger, *CP* 130, §91). Only what conforms to the demands of our knowledge, here being describable in assertions, can be admitted as real; to quote one of the most famous aphorisms of analytic philosophy, "To be is to be the value of a variable" (Quine 1980, 15). This is the idealism of the Kantian Paradigm which Heidegger connects to technology, the bête noir of his later thought. As long as we remain trapped within the A5 subject-object relation that is the ultimate legacy of Plato's reconfiguration of truth, we cannot escape our technological age.

> As Plato conceives it, unhiddenness remains harnessed in a relation to looking, apprehending, thinking, and asserting. To follow this relation means to relinquish the essence of unhiddenness. No attempt to ground the essence of unhiddenness in "reason," "spirit," "thinking," "*logos*," or in any kind of "subjectivity," can ever rescue the essence of unhiddenness. (Heidegger, *Pm* 182)

Here Heidegger is claiming that the struggles to work against the Kantian Paradigm while working within it that we examined in part 1 of this book are futile attempts to ground unhiddenness in subjectivity. But this solution merely adds fuel to the fire. He describes A5 here as the act of thinking determining Being:

> Thinking sets itself against Being in such a way that Being is re-presented to thinking, and consequently stands against thinking like an ob-ject. . . . Consequently, thinking is no longer just the opposing member in some new distinction but becomes the basis on which one decides about what stands against it, so much so that Being in general gets interpreted on the

> basis of thinking. . . . In the seemingly irrelevant division *Being and thinking* we have to recognize *that fundamental orientation of the spirit of the West that is the real target of our attack.* (Heidegger, *IM* 123–24, last italics added)

## A5 Active Knower in Modern Metaphysics: "The Real Target of Our Attack"

In "The End of Philosophy and the Task of Thinking," Heidegger claims that both ends of philosophy, its beginning and finish, are particularly instructive periods to examine in order to understand philosophy as a whole; they represent points "in which the whole of philosophy's history is gathered in its uttermost possibility" (Heidegger, *BW* 433). We saw in the preceding section how Heidegger identifies Plato's transformation of A2 Unconcealment Truth into R2 Correspondence Truth with its concomitant R4 Bivalence as the beginning of humanism. Its completion occurs in modern philosophy's doctrines of A5 Active Knower and A1 Dependence, which mark the fulfillment and thus the conclusion of philosophy as metaphysics for him.

In a move that is at odds with what I am calling the Unmooring thesis, Heidegger wants to show that modern philosophy is the "logical" consequence of Plato's humanistic legacy. For Kant,

> as for the Greeks, [A5] thinking (as *Logos*—forms of judgment—categories—reason) gets the upper hand in establishing the perspective for interpreting beings as such. Additionally, following Descartes's procedure, thinking as "thinking" comes to dominate; and beings themselves become [A1] *perceptum* (represented) or *object,* in accordance with the same [legacy] historical reason. Therefore thinking cannot get to a [ICS] ground of Da-sein; i.e., the question of the [A2] truth of be-ing is unaskable here.[45]

The Greeks allowed thinking to get "the upper hand" in the correct ascertainment of the Forms until it came to dominate interpretation completely, eliminating A2 Unconcealment Truth (rendering it "unaskable") and radically altering man and Being.

> The very essence of man itself changes, in that man becomes subject. . . . Man becomes that being upon which all that is, is grounded as regards the manner of its Being and its truth. Man becomes the relational center

> of that which is as such. But this is possible only when the comprehension of what is as a whole changes. (Heidegger, *QT* 128; see also 151; Heidegger, *PR* 76–77)

"What is as a whole" loses R1 Independence to become A1 Dependent when man becomes A5 subject, that is, the one who determines reality. This began with Plato's *ideas,* which can be correctly known separately from beings. The medieval transformation of *ideas* into ideas in the mind of God retains this separation, while its understanding of Being as divine creation took a step toward agent-controlled technology.

> The interpretation of *einai* as *entelecheia* indicates that in the presencing of what is present, presence is completed, that is, presence itself is present pure and simple. . . . Thereafter it is instantly reconstructed in Christian terms—*ens* as *ens creatum*. . . . [When a being is interpreted as *ens creatum* then] a being is what is effected. . . . [When such a being] is interpreted once again [in modernity] . . . now everything refers to the subject, to the consciousness. (Heidegger, *Mi* 257–58, all bracketed comments in original)

Conceiving the universe as a divine product makes it dependent but not on us, restraining the amount of control we should exert out of humility.

Descartes' doctrines of the separation of mind and body, making humans deeply heterogeneous from the rest of the universe, and clear and distinct ideas, making truth depend on what the subject finds impossible to doubt, advanced humanism further (see Heidegger, *WT* 104–5, 116). The conception of truth at play here is clearly different from *aletheia:*

> The *veritas rerum,* the truth of things, is *veritas objectorum,* the truth in the sense of objectivity of objects, not truth as the very being of things presenting themselves. Therefore, here truth does not mean the self-manifestation of what is immediately present. Truth is characterized as what can be ascertained clearly and evidently, [that is,] indubitably certain for a representing ego. (Heidegger, *Zo* 106; see also Heidegger, *Mi* 55, 92)

Truth is determined by what the representing ego finds most difficult to doubt and most helpful in mastering nature, both of which turn out to be the mathematically quantifiable and universally verifiable and repeatable. Kant then made phenomenal reality mind-dependent, which merely brings out what was already implicit in Descartes' epistemology, in Heidegger's view. In an astonishing telescoping of two millennia of the history of philosophy, he writes, "For the Greeks, things appear. For Kant, things appear to me. In the time between them, it has come about that the being has become an ob-ject" (Heidegger, *FoS* 36–37; see also Heidegger, *Zo* 226). This is how Heidegger interprets Kant's claim that Being is not a real predicate: a being's Being is a matter of its being posited (A1) by a subject (A5), which indicates "the pure relationship of the objectivity of objects to the subjectivity of human cognition."[46]

We watched the Kantian Paradigm's vestige of realism in R1 Independent noumena crumble over the 150 years following Kant until reality completely depended on the subject. Nietzsche took this tendency to its logical conclusion by making the (strong) subject's control over reality conscious and voluntary, so that he could explicitly design it for maximal power and control. Since this millennia-long process of subjectivism took such an important step forward with Descartes, Heidegger finds it surprisingly easy to depict Nietzsche as the fulfillment of Descartes.

> Western history has now begun to enter into the completion of that period we call the *modern,* and which is defined by the fact that man becomes the measure and the center of beings. Man is what lies at the bottom of all beings; that is, in modern terms, at the bottom of all objectification and representability. No matter how sharply Nietzsche puts himself time and again against Descartes, whose philosophy grounds modern metaphysics, he turns against Descartes only because the latter *still* does *not* posit man as *subiectum* in a way that is complete and decisive enough. . . . In [the doctrine of the *Übermensch*], Descartes celebrates his supreme triumph.[47]

Descartes was not Cartesian enough; the *Übermensch* actually fulfills Descartes' dream of subjects mastering nature.

Although it is the logical conclusion of a long legacy, modern thought's hubris still shocks Heidegger. "Representation comes to be the tribunal that decides about the beingness of beings and declares that in the future only what is placed before it and through representation and thus is secured for it may be considered a being."[48] Modern A5 Active Knower reinforces R3 Uniqueness, since only that which can be known with certainty is deemed real, while all else is discarded as merely subjective.

> In this method—that is, in this manner of the anticipatory projection of nature as a domain of calculable objects—a decision has already been made, immeasurable in its consequences. For this decision means that everything not exhibiting the characteristics of mathematically determinable objectivity is eliminated as being uncertain, that is, untrue and

> therefore unreal. In other words: The criterion for what truly exists is not being as it manifests itself by itself, but rather exclusively the *ego cogito sum,* and therefore that authoritative kind of truth in the sense of certainty, based upon the subjectivity of the "I think."[49]

This commitment to A5 is the ultimate consequence of Plato's alteration of truth from *aletheia* to R2 Correct Correspondence.

> Of course, the bastion of the prevailing essence of truth, *veritas* and truth as [R2] correctness and certitude, is occluding the [A2] primordial understanding of *aletheia.* This . . . means something momentous, and for our history the only decisive thing: the entirety of beings has in the meantime been transformed in such a way that beings as a whole, and therefore also man, are no longer determined on the basis of the essence of *aletheia.* Consequently, as soon as we hear of concealment and of modes of concealing, we think immediately, and only, of [A5] modes of human activity man himself controls. We do not experience concealment and disclosure as [ICS] events which "come over" beings and man. (Heidegger, *P* 61–62, bracketed comments added)

The A5 view that thinking determines Being is the defining feature of modern thought, yet it is sacrilegious for the later Heidegger. The best way to describe his reaction to it is that he is offended by it; it repels him. He does not base his rejection of it on this personal repugnance, however, but on arguments, two of which I will now discuss.

### R5 Passive Knower: Ontic *Gelassenheit*

Heidegger connects the linchpin of the Kantian Paradigm—A5 Active Knower, that is, the idea that the subject organizes experience—to what he considers to be the defining feature of modern life: technology. He distinguishes between technology as the various mechanical items we use in our daily lives and the *essence* of technology, which is the (ICS) contemporary understanding of Being or the way that entities and we ourselves exist in this epoch (see Heidegger, *BW* 311, 318–19). The essence of technology is the necessary condition for technological machinery; it is only if we can think in certain ways—of problems as needing to be solved through gadgets, of experiments as deciding facts about nature, of materials as capable of being put together to form complex tools, and so on—that we can create technological items at all (see Heidegger, *CP* 92, §67; 88, §61; Heidegger, *Mi* 152). If we saw the various discomforts and inconveniences of daily life as trials placed upon us by God to test our patience and fidelity, or saw reading entrails as the best access to knowledge, or materials as needing to be lovingly preserved in their original state, we would react altogether differently.

The essence of technology—also called "enframing"—reveals the world as *Bestand,* or "standing-reserve," which represents the ultimate stage of objectivity. Objects are bare inert things represented by subjects; *Bestand* consists in completely malleable resources that are readily adapted to whatever needs I happen to have at the moment. *Bestand* stands ready to serve my every whim: water waits at the faucet for me to drink or wash my hands, electricity stands behind the outlet ready for me to plug in various appliances that crouch in the closet for needs to arise, the twenty-four-hour supermarket keeps food fresh in packages until I'm moved to eat. Everything is organized around one's convenience, like an insidious version of *Being and Time*'s worldhood. Although objects are already impoverished, "unworlded" in the early terminology, *Bestand* is further stripped of intrinsic features so that it can fulfill any desire that happens to arise. Plastic takes any shape; electricity powers any device. A transcendental subject constituting objects might seem deeply heterogeneous to bulldozers and bags of Doritos, but Heidegger sees a profound connection. In both cases the subject is the determining center, though one is epistemological and ontological while the other is practical and ontic.

Even this distinction between theory and practice collapses upon examination. The subject determines what can count as an object in order to establish a field of knowable entities, but the explicit purpose behind Descartes' epistemological project was to "make ourselves, as it were, the lords and masters of nature" (Descartes, *PWD* 1:142–43). Heidegger claims that for Descartes, "the point is *control* and *domination* of the process of nature" (Heidegger, *Zo* 105; see also Heidegger, *Mi* 92). Kant, too, places his philosophy in the service of securing science (see Heidegger, *P* 52; Heidegger, *DT* 58–59), albeit with a walled-off preserve for ethical values. Once again, Nietzsche represents the culmination of this process in giving the experience-organizing powers directly to the self for the naked purpose of power for power's sake. Heidegger believes that this confluence of goals indicates something very important about modern metaphysics. Despite the diversity of temperaments and specific details among Descartes, Kant, and Nietzsche,

> all of these differences cannot hide the simple cohesion [legacy] of the whole history of this inquiry into being. . . . History of *this* question concerning being is the history of metaphysics, history of the thinking that thinks being as the being of a being [A5] *from out of and unto a being.* That this inquiry into being is overpowered by beings and not only in its

> beginning (which is the ground for the disempowering of *physis* and *aletheia*), that this priority of beings is [legacy] carried all the way through the history of metaphysics, as essential to metaphysics—this becomes manifest most impressively at the juncture where the question of being is enacted in its purest form since the Greeks: in Kant. Positing [A1] experience as the only decisive domain of beings goes together with the discovery of the transcendental. (Heidegger, *CP* 300, §259, bracketed comments added)

The unity of this drive toward control that was already implicit in A5 is why Heidegger (following Schelling) defines modern Being as will: "Every single being and all beings as a whole have their essential powers in and through the will" (Heidegger, *WCT* 91–92; see also Heidegger, *PLT* 102; Heidegger, *Pm* 231). Nietzsche's greatness was to see this common feature and take it to its logical conclusion of placing the A5 experience-constituting powers of the subject directly under the power of the will (see Heidegger, *WCT* 74, 92), as well as defining both subject and reality as will to power. This then becomes technology: the world is merely material to be fashioned to suit our purposes.

> It is by the positioning that belongs to representation that Nature is brought before man. Man places before himself the world as the whole of everything objective, and he places himself before the world. Man sets up the world toward himself, and delivers Nature over to himself. We must think of this placing-here, this producing, in its broad and multifarious nature. Where Nature is not satisfactory to man's representation, he reframes or redisposes it. . . . The Open becomes an object, and is thus twisted around toward the human being. Over against the world as the object, man stations himself and sets himself up as the one who deliberately pushes through all this producing. (Heidegger, *PLT* 110)

We organize the world to suit ourselves, first with Descartes for our epistemological satisfaction, then with Kant for our scientific and ethical needs (even when the latter frustrate our inclinations), and finally with Nietzsche to achieve power for power's sake. The final emptiness of the drive is the secret force behind all metaphysics, though it is only in Nietzsche that "the command character of the will announces itself. And through it, in the course of modern metaphysics, the long-concealed nature of the long-since existing will as the Being of beings comes to make its appearance" (Heidegger, *PLT* 111).

Showing how the abstract, theoretical claims of anti-realist A5 Active Knower connect to the concrete effects of runaway machinery via the intermediary of the essence of technology as a way of seeing the world (see Heidegger, *CP* 142, §104) is one of the more startling features of Heidegger's later work. If we are the ones who create the access to the world and are responsible for the way the world is (A5), then we can do with it what we like (technology). This attitude underlies his frequent equating of the forgetfulness of Being with nihilism (see, for example, Heidegger, *Pm* 319). Forgetting Being or the clearing means taking credit for our access to beings ourselves, which then eliminates any external constraint on what we do. "Beings *are,* yet they remain abandoned by Being and left to themselves, so as to be mere objects of our contrivance. All goals beyond men and peoples are gone" (Heidegger, *BQ* 159–60; see also 163; Heidegger, *BW* 132; see also Heidegger, *Mi* 14–15). This is where transcendental constitution merges with technology:

> Metaphysically thought, the essence of the Ego consists rather in its [A5] making every other being [A1] something standing over against it, its object, its over-and-against, its projected ob-ject. . . . *Thereby* the Ego proceeds to the totality of beings and presents this to itself as something to be mastered. Only in the reign of subjectivity does there become historically possible an epoch of cosmic discoveries and planetary conquests, for only subjectivity marks off the essential bounds of an unconditioned objectivity and does so ultimately as a claim of its will.[50]

The transition occurs at the "thereby": it is by means of the theory of the subject constituting objects (A5, A1) that Being is forgotten and beings present themselves as to-be-mastered, thus enabling "planetary conquests" (technology).

All that matters in technology is the satisfaction of our desires; eventually even getting what we want submerges into greater efficiency and power for their own sake. Nothing that resists efficiency is recognized or allowed to exist, which is why, in a move that has influenced many postmodernists, Heidegger often uses violent imagery to describe reason. "The determination of truth as correctness is not the indifferent and innocuous theory of a scholastic 'logic' which has been obsolete for ages. Correctness is the calculable adjustment and adaptation of all human behavior to the end of contrivances. Whatever resists these contrivances *will be crushed*" (Heidegger, *BQ* 129, italics added; see also 122; Heidegger, *Pm* 235). It is this violence that leads to his first argument against the technological attitude.

Heidegger is in a tricky situation here. He cannot say that technology or A5 is incorrect or doesn't portray reality accurately because that would violate Historical Phenomenological Ontology, which must acknowledge technology as the reality of our modern times. However, he can say that "the essence of technology, as a destining of revealing, is the danger" (Heidegger, *BW* 333). His first criticism of technology is that although every revealing is a concealing and although each epoch's understanding of Being hides other ways of Being by focusing only on one, enframing does this in a particularly egregious manner (see Heidegger, *IM* 207; Heidegger, *BW* 328, 332, 339). Whereas Greek *physis* left it up to nature how to emerge and medieval *creatio* let God decide how to create the world—both thereby requiring us to be open to how the world presents itself to us—technology puts all the power in our hands. We decide how things will be, and we are on an inevitable slide into making them more and more *bestandlich*—that is, into empty energy reserves ready to take on whatever form our present desires require. Reality loses its inherent richness to melt into a featureless pool of energy or, as he colorfully puts it, "nature becomes a gigantic gasoline station, an energy source for modern technology and industry" (Heidegger, *DT* 50).

If phenomenology contains an ethics, it is a call to a heightened sensitivity to the richness and beauty of the world, a vital gratitude for being open to experience rather than taking our openness for granted, and a commitment to "attentive dwelling" (Heidegger, *BW* 150). This is a descendant of Socrates' description of philosophy as waking people up or Heraclitus's pronouncement that gods reside even in the kitchen, that is, in the most mundane circumstances (see Heidegger, *BW* 256–58). Technology dims this wonder and attention to differences down by letting things show up only insofar as they satisfy our desires and by effacing any details that impede efficiency.

> When destining reigns in the mode of enframing, it is the supreme danger. . . . As soon as what is unconcealed no longer concerns man even as object, but exclusively as standing-reserve, and man in the midst of objectlessness is nothing but the orderer of the standing-reserve, then he comes to the very brink of a precipitous fall. . . . In this way the illusion comes to prevail that everything man encounters exists only insofar as it is his construct. This illusion gives rise in turn to one final delusion: it seems as though man everywhere and always encounters only himself. . . . Where this ordering holds sway, it drives out every other possibility of revealing.[51]

Here Heidegger connects A5 Active Knower with R3 Uniqueness: since we are the orderer, we filter out all ways for beings to be that we find inconvenient. Notice that the lines "everything man encounters exists only insofar as it is his construct . . . man everywhere and always encounters only himself" can be read in terms of either transcendental constitution or technology. The transcendental subject only encounters the phenomena it constitutes, while the city dweller can go for weeks without seeing anything other than buildings and asphalt.

This insulation from anything outside the familiar and useful horrifies Heidegger. In *Being and Time* equipment faded into inconspicuousness when it worked smoothly, leading us to drift into "auto-pilot" and to be awakened from "the oblivious passing of our lives" (Heidegger, *BP* 264) only by breakdowns like anxiety or awareness of death. Now this equipmental inconspicuousness has become tantamount to a technology-induced forgetfulness of Being, that is, the absence of wondrous appreciation of beings' presence to us. The simple fact that a being is "does not become prominent in the equipment; it disappears in usefulness. The more handy a piece of equipment is, the more inconspicuous it remains that, for example, this particular hammer is" (Heidegger, *BW* 190), which is why "the making of equipment never directly effects the happening of truth" (189).

Instrumental inconspicuousness is now portrayed as a sinister danger contributing to the forgetfulness of Being or helping conceal the revelation of Being (see Heidegger, *BW* 132); this is how technology can be considered "false" even within a paradigm defined by HPO and UT. Truth is unconcealment, and technology conceals unconcealment itself. When we are wholly absorbed in manipulating beings, "Being denies its own coming to presence" (Heidegger, *QT* 43) and "conceals revealing itself" (Heidegger, *BW* 333; see also 235). Although this can occur in any historical manifestation—"*in whatever way* the destining of revealing may hold sway, the unconcealment in which everything that is shows itself *at any given time* harbors the danger that man may misconstrue the unconcealed and misinterpret it"[52]—Heidegger sees enframing as particularly prone to hide Being: "Yet when destining reigns in the mode of enframing, it is the *supreme* danger. . . . When enframing holds sway, regulating and securing of the standing-reserve mark *all* revealing. They no longer even let their own fundamental characteristic appear, namely, this revealing as such."[53] Enframing is a particularly jealous clearing which demands that we have no other clearings before it. This is clearly visible in the common belief that science gives us all there is to know about the world and possesses ultimate, definitive answers. Enframing enforces both R3 and forgetfulness of Being.

Enframing gives technological man a false kind of omniscience by filtering out whatever doesn't fit its categories. Heidegger still believes that horizons or pre-ontological understandings (ICS) that project expectations and general parameters for phenomena are necessary for experience, but now he worries about how much they conceal.

> Today a world dominates in which the decisive question runs: How do I have to represent nature in the sequence of its appearances to myself, so that I am in a position to make secure predictions about all and everything? The answer to this question is that it is compulsory to represent nature as a totality of energy particles of existing mass, the reciprocal movements of which are to be mathematically calculable. Descartes already says to the piece of wax that he holds before his eyes: "You are nothing other than an extended, flexible, and mutable thing," and thus I proclaim myself to know everything about you that there is to know of you. (Heidegger, *FoS* 8; see also Heidegger, *BW* 129, 153)

Humans become encased in a shell of self-confirming ways of thinking. When everything we encounter is subsumed within our concepts, we dissolve all alterity into what we expect to see and can understand. Thus, "modern man, Cartesian man, *se solum alloquendo,* only talks to himself" (Heidegger, *FoS* 37; see also Heidegger, *Pm* 307) because "the object is constituted by representation. The representation, namely, that is prior in regards to the object, posits the object across from it, in such a way that the object is never able to first presence from itself."[54]

The active knower is the ontological condition of the modern technological individual who controls and determines reality. Since the active knower shapes what he or she experiences,

> science always encounters only what its kind of representation has admitted beforehand as an object possible for science. . . . The thingness of the thing remains concealed, forgotten. The nature of the thing never comes to light, that is, it never gets a hearing. This is the meaning of our talk about the annihilation of the thing. . . . They have never yet at all been able to appear to thinking as things. (Heidegger, *PLT* 170–71)

In the technological attitude which reveals things only to efface them in the service of greater efficiency, we cut ourselves off from experiencing the way they present themselves, especially those aspects which do not yield efficient comprehensibility or utility.

> Human willing too can be in the mode of self-assertion only by forcing everything under its dominion from the start, even before it can survey it. To such a willing, everything, beforehand and thus subsequently,

> turns irresistibly into material for self-assertive production. The earth and its atmosphere become raw material for self-assertive production.[55]

It isn't the ontic effects of technology like pollution that Heidegger bemoans but the fact that we no longer pay attention to the world around us, that we ignore the richness of detail for the quantifiable, the useful, the *bestandlich.*

As in the mutual interdependence of man and Being, the notion of R5 Passive Knower goes through a kind of rehabilitation here. Heidegger is certainly not returning to a pre-Kantian soft-wax mind which immediately receives pure facts. He still believes that "there are no mere facts, but that a fact is only what it is in the light of the fundamental conception" (Heidegger, *WT* 67), that is, the Impersonal Conceptual Scheme that is the epochal sending of Being. Heidegger's phenomenological alternative to technology's predetermination of what experience must be like is to practice an attentive, patient openness to the particularity of phenomena instead of the distracted, rushed attitude engendered by technology which turns everything into objects, which then sink into *Bestand.* He often describes this attitude in traditional phenomenological terms as eliminating prejudices, "granting the thing, as it were, a free field to display its . . . character directly. Everything that might interpose itself between the thing and us in apprehending and talking about it must first be set aside. Only then do we yield ourselves to the undistorted presencing of the thing."[56] Instead of approaching phenomena with preexisting categories and only acknowledging what fits them, we should draw categories from the various fields of beings, constructing whatever concepts will be most faithful "to the things themselves." His own unorthodox but often illuminating descriptions of things like paintings, bridges, and jugs model this practice.

Heidegger calls this attitude *Gelassenheit,* translated as "releasement" or "letting-be," which he sometimes equates with freedom.[57] Although unmediated perception is impossible, un*prejudiced* perception can be attained with effort. Heidegger encourages what he called in *Being and Time* "a remarkable 'relatedness backward or forward'" (Heidegger, *BT* 28/8) where we (necessarily) use a pre-given horizon of interpretation to approach an entity, but also staunchly remain open to the ways in which it escapes or violates the interpretive horizon we begin with. These *aporiai,* if attended to rather than suppressed or ignored, allow us to refine and expand our initial understanding, even to the point of adding "new existentialia" or new modes of Being.[58] This represents a completion of ED and the empiricism he praised phenomenology for in *Being and Time* but did not completely follow there. This ambition is why "the task for thinking is that of freeing itself and keeping itself free for what is to be thought in order to receive its determination from that" (Heidegger, *TB* 35; see also Heidegger, *FoS* 6; Heidegger, *PR* 86; Heidegger, *ET* 203). It is, rather perversely, a freedom for heteronomy—a flexibility in one's initial interpretive assumptions in order to be open to the voice of beings and Being.[59]

## Heteronomous Thinking

The stated goal of Heidegger's lecture series *What Is Called Thinking?* is "to learn thinking" (Heidegger, *WCT* 14). Philosophy has misunderstood the process of thinking since Plato switched it onto the wrong track so long ago, and now "we moderns . . . can learn thinking only if we radically unlearn what thinking has been traditionally" (8). This unlearning, an heir to the early "destruction" of the tradition, is one reason behind the constant attention he pays to the history of philosophy, particularly its beginning in Plato's doctrine of truth and its end in modern philosophy's A5 doctrine which I discussed in the preceding sections. He reconstructs them in order to deconstruct them, in order to clear the space for his alternate conception of thinking which will be more faithful to the way thought actually occurs and which, as we will see, will supply us with an ethics.

As we have just seen, Heidegger's later conception of thinking emphasizes passivity and receptivity in opposition to the Kantian Paradigm's activity. Even one's activity should now be in the service of creating the conditions for a greater receptivity: "Apprehension in this double sense denotes a process of letting things come to oneself in which one does not simply take things in, but rather takes up a position to receive what shows itself. . . . Apprehension is the receptive bringing-to-stand of the constant that shows itself in itself."[60] Heidegger wants a conception of thinking that will escape technology's willful ignoring of distinctions, its shearing off of details in order to cram phenomena into Procrustean categories for the sake of smooth-running efficiency. He needs a model of thinking that will both be phenomenologically adequate—that is, it will match our experience—and satisfy this sensitive receptivity of *Gelassenheit.*

In the process of learning this new thinking, Heidegger explains learning as the way "to make everything we do answer to whatever essentials address themselves to us" (Heidegger, *WCT* 14). We can already spy some of the main elements of his account of thinking in this definition: essentials address us and we must answer to them. The example of a cabinetmaker's apprentice is brought in to illuminate this idea: "If he is to become a true cabinetmaker, he makes himself answer and respond above all to the different kinds of wood and to the shapes slumbering within wood" (14). In order to become a good woodworker, he cannot simply impose his will upon the wood; it will break, splinter, warp.[61] Like Plato's butcher, he must integrate the features the wood presents as well as the ways "it enters into man's dwelling with all the hidden riches of its nature" (14) into his engagement with it. Working with wood means just that—co-operating *with* the material, responding to it—as well as paying attention to how people interact with wooden products. The will of the worker plays a role, but so must the wood for the product to be good: "In fact, this relatedness to wood is what maintains the whole craft" (14–15). This helps explain Heidegger's preference for Aristotle's doctrine of the four causes, an extended discussion of which opens his essay "The Question Concerning Technology." Aristotle's conception portrays the maker as simply the one who "considers carefully and gathers together" (Heidegger, *BW* 315) the other three causes rather than the sole cause, which is what the efficient cause becomes after medieval philosophy's model of creation ex nihilo and modern science's dismissal of the other causes.

Activities like writing poetry and speaking also get conceived on this model of cooperative or responsive thinking. Heidegger explicitly rejects the romantic genius view which conceives artistic creation on the model of A5 Active Knower by placing all power and control in the subject's hands: "All creation, because it is such a drawing-up, is a drawing, as of water from a spring. Modern subjectivism, to be sure, immediately misinterprets creation, taking it as the sovereign subject's performance of genius" (Heidegger, *BW* 200). The poet, for instance, does not and cannot force words to mean what she wants them to, as Lewis Carroll's Humpty Dumpty thought.[62] Precisely when they are most creative and in control of their craft, poets must be highly sensitive and receptive to the various colorings and connotations of their words in order to choose just the right ones (see 330; Sallis 1970, 26). Mundane speech too is a matter of working within vast systems of vocabulary and grammar that one must first acknowledge before one can construct sentences. This is why Heidegger repeatedly says that speaking is listening: "Every word of mortal speech speaks out of such a listening, and as such a listening. Mortals speak insofar as they listen. . . . This speaking that listens and accepts is responding" (Heidegger, *PLT* 209). This explains his somewhat hyperbolic but important claims that even though "speaking and hearing are customarily set in opposition to one another," he believes that "speech, taken on its own, is hearing. It is listening to the language we speak. . . . It is language that speaks."[63]

Thinking too is conceived as a responding in a disarmed form of the term "co-respondence" (see Heidegger, *WIP* 75–77; Heidegger, *BW* 328). This inescapability of response gives a new sense to *Being and Time*'s thrownness. There it meant that Dasein is always thrown into a specific place and time which set the parameters for the roles it can take up, as well as various personal characteristics such as one's emotional makeup. In the later work, the idea operates at a much deeper, more pervasive level: we are thrown into an epochal way of thinking which determines virtually everything about us and our world. "Always the destining of revealing holds complete sway over men" (Heidegger, *BW* 330), including the fundamental ways we think and experience (see Heidegger, *WCT* 115). As self-evident and inevitable as the laws that govern reason seem to us, they are only one among many possible ways to organize thoughts (A3). Nor could we in principle have chosen them, as Hegel tried to achieve in his historical "hyper-originality."[64] "Reason and its representational activity are only *one* kind of thinking and are by no means self-determined."[65] We could not have determined our own ways of thinking since, in order to do this, we would have already needed a way of thinking which itself could not have been chosen on pain of infinite regress. Every action, thought, and perception requires an interpretive horizon or way of organizing thoughts; thus a horizon must also precede and guide the very attempt to tinker with one's present horizon. Employing the early term of "projecting" as something like making a choice and "enowning" as being thrown into an epochal ICS, Heidegger writes, "In that the thrower projects-open and speaks thinkingly 'from enowning,' it becomes manifest that, the more the thrower projects-open, the more the thrower as thrower is the thrown one" (Heidegger, *CP* 169, §122; see also Heidegger, *Mi* 43, 285). In other words, even the act of choosing brings home to us just how little we have chosen.[66]

Our thinking simply must accept some beginning principles—such as the principle of reason or non-contradiction—in order to think; these are given to us and can be neither justified nor challenged without employing them.

> We find ourselves in a peculiar situation with respect to the laws of thought. For whenever we attempt to call the principles of thinking to mind, they inevitably become a theme of our thinking—and its laws. Behind us, in back of us as it were, the laws of thought lie ever ready and guide every step of our thinking about them. This directive is immediately evident and appears to check every attempt to properly think the laws of thought in a single move. (Heidegger, *PT* 47; see also Heidegger, *WCT* 65; Heidegger, *BW* 324)

Even if we do affect the way we think, it can only be in terms of motives and considerations that we did not choose.[67] In terms of language, for instance, we can invent Esperanto, but only by organizing our efforts in a language that came about naturally: "Humans may be able to invent artificial speech constructions and signs, but only in reference to and in terms of an already spoken language" (Heidegger, *PT* 25; see also Heidegger, *DT* 82–83. Davidson makes the same point at *TLH* 258). Similarly, we can adjust our present way of thinking but only on the basis of another, the way Neurath's boat can only be repaired at sea.

This argument also explains what has been criticized as Heidegger's quietism, summed up in his (in)famous phrase, "Only a god can save us now." In this new conception of thinking, we cannot enact a change in Being on our own: the decision to change must occur to us, the method must strike us as plausible, the goal must appear worthwhile, and so on. We simply cannot make ourselves into the kind of people who would react or perceive in these ways without first finding these reactions and perceptions desirable, and thus already being that kind of people to some extent. Any kind of change we were able to instigate on our own would have to presuppose significant continuity and thus could not be radical: "By itself and on its own, no human calculation and *design* can bring forth a turning in the world's present condition. Especially not, because human design is already formed by this very condition of the world. . . . How then could it [human design] still gain control over it [the world's condition]?" (Heidegger, *Zo* 266, bracketed comments in original; see also Heidegger, *Mi* 192–93). This follows from the completion of A6, so that man is wholly determined by ICS and in no way transcendent or transcendental to the world.

As Julian Young correctly points out,

> Human beings never make their own ultimate horizons of disclosure. . . . This, I think, is a matter not of observation but of logic. Since conspiring or planning is an instance of what Heidegger calls "calculative thinking" [roughly the same as technological thinking], and since thinking of this type always presupposes and happens within a horizon of disclosure, conspiring to create one's ultimate horizon of disclosure would require one to "calculate" before one could "calculate." Human beings and human cultures are, therefore, receptive rather than creative with respect to the modes of presence they inhabit. (Young 2002, 23, bracketed comment added; see also 83)

There is what we might call an irreducible moment of receptivity which precedes and makes possible all activity. This is a logical argument[68] which is most effective when applied to the essence of technology as the view that problems should be fixed by our efforts to maximize efficiency and control. The central problem Descartes wanted to solve was the ineffectiveness of previous modes of thinking for controlling the world, and the solution that struck him was to clear them away in order to construct a new way of thinking. Technology in the sense of machinery was his goal, but

Heidegger points out that the *essence* of technology had to already have shaped his thinking for him to be able to form such a goal and method. In order to be able even to start this project—to desire to control nature and to see previous ways of thinking as an obstruction and as raw material to be re-formed to control reality—he must *already* have been seeing the world in a technological way, that is, as problems to be solved by refashioning means in order to attain ends efficiently, primarily greater control and efficiency. As successful as it was, Descartes' procedure came too late for him to take credit for it. "'On one's own initiative' is already indicative of a way in which being itself lets human beings be in their essence" (Heidegger, *HH* 90).

Nietzsche's rather phenomenological criticism of Descartes' cogito resonates with Heidegger's new model of thinking: "A thought comes when 'it' wishes, and not when 'I' wish, so that it is a falsification of the facts of the case to say that the subject 'I' is the condition of the predicate 'think.' *It* thinks" (Nietzsche, *BGE* §17; see also §192). Here is Heidegger's somewhat more pompous version: "Such thoughts do not first come to be by way of mortal thinking. Rather our mortal thinking is always summoned by that thought to correspond to it or renounce it. We human beings do not come upon thoughts; thoughts rather come to us mortals."[69, 70] This is why in addition to speaking being a listening, thinking is also a response.[71] Although it is we who speak or think, it can only be in reaction to stimulation that we didn't decide to find in need of response and in terms that strike us as appropriate. When we talk about something, we say "the sorts of things that are suggested by what is addressed . . . what the addressed allows to radiate of itself" (Heidegger, *BW* 409). Heidegger believes that this new conception "is beyond activity and passivity as commonly understood" (Heidegger, *BQ* 151; see also Heidegger, *DT* 61). Having been stuck in simplistic notions of freedom and determinism for so long, we lack an adequate vocabulary to discuss it: "We are still far from pondering the essence of action decisively enough" (Heidegger, *BW* 217; see also 330).

The history of philosophy is depicted in line with this view—great thinkers are described like lightning rods who gather up the charge in the air and express it in a concentrated way, rather than as romantic geniuses who are mini-gods that create ex nihilo. "What is great and constant in the thinking of a thinker simply consists in its expressly giving word to what always already resounds" (Heidegger, *PR* 24; see also Heidegger, *N* 4:7; Heidegger, *QT* 54; see also Heidegger, *Mi* 251, 335). Heidegger discusses this idea repeatedly in the work of Nietzsche, for example: "Nietzsche's thought has to plunge into metaphysics because Being radiates its own essence as will to power" (Heidegger, *N* 4:181). Nietzsche came up with the theory that he did because the world showed itself to him in a certain light, suggesting specific ideas, metaphors, and connections which he expressed. He saw things in a certain way which he did not choose and then he put in the words that suggested themselves to him. For Heidegger, great thinkers and artists are more like conduits than creators, a description which succeeds phenomenologically, since it is how artists often describe the experience of in-spiration. "Nietzsche neither made nor chose his way himself, no more than any other thinker ever did. He is sent on his way" (Heidegger, *WCT* 46; see also 65, 164).

This model of thinking incorporates the notion of Impersonal Conceptual Schemes: "That Being itself and how Being itself concerns our thinking does not depend upon our thinking alone. That Being itself, and the manner in which Being itself, strikes a particular thinking, lets such thinking spring forth in springing from Being itself in such a way as to respond to Being as such."[72] We think in particular ways because we are thrown into an epochal understanding of Being that reveals beings in a certain way which makes certain ideas sensible and obvious and others ridiculous and bizarre. As Kierkegaard had already shown, choices require criteria which cannot themselves have been chosen on pain of infinite regress: "Every decision, however, bases itself on something not mastered . . . else it would never be a decision" (Heidegger, *BW* 180). Our acting is and can only be a re-acting or response to how things appear to us: choice means that we choose the option that appears best to us which we didn't choose. Our actions act upon beings in the ways they present themselves as appropriate to be acted upon: "Beings themselves . . . make a claim on us with respect to their aptness to be planned and calculated" (Heidegger, *ID* 35; see also Heidegger, *BW* 320, 384; Heidegger, *N* 4:214).

Thus Heidegger concludes that "the unconcealment itself, within which ordering unfolds, is never a human handiwork. . . . The unconcealment of the unconcealed has already propriated whenever it calls man forth into the modes of revealing allotted to him. When man, in his way, from within unconcealment reveals that which presences, he merely responds to the call of unconcealment" (Heidegger, *BW* 324; see also Heidegger, *PLT* 171). The essence of technology—that is, technology as a way of revealing which enables the human construction of machines—cannot itself be a human construct, but is rather the "mode of revealing allotted to" us, the ICS sent to us in this epoch (see Heidegger, *BW* 326; see also Heidegger, *Mi* 152). The world calls out to modern man to be controlled, materials announce themselves as to-be-put-together-and-used, which is what enables us to engage in technological activity and then conclude that we ourselves are the instigators of the process.[73] "Only to the extent that man for his part is already challenged to exploit the energies of nature can this revealing that orders happen" (Heidegger, *BW* 323; see also Heidegger, *Mi* 12–13). We are in control but, paradoxically, we are not in control of being in control, since this mastery of technology is made possible by the essence of technology's specific way of revealing, which we could not have created.

Describing this paradoxical state of affairs requires strange combinations of active and passive terms: "Man, too, is challenged, that is, *forced to secure* all beings that are his concern as the substance for his planning and calculating" (Heidegger, *ID* 35, italics added). Similarly, "Man *finds himself* placed, on the basis of the being of beings, before the task of *undertaking mastery of the earth*" (Heidegger, *OBT* 188, italics added). In other words, we are required to bend everything to our will; we are ordered to become orderers, forced to force nature into our plan. At the heart and necessary foundation of modern willful autonomy lies heteronomous determination, a fact that unravels technology's self-conception. "Modern technology, as a revealing that orders, is thus no mere human doing. . . . This gathering concentrates man upon ordering the actual as standing-reserve" (Heidegger, *BW* 324). Once again, Heidegger achieves a way to criticize the modern mode of Being without violating HPO by calling it false or unreal. His word for this "challenging claim" of the essence of technology that requires us to reveal beings as *Bestand* is *Ge-stell,* or "enframing."

> Enframing means the gathering together of the setting-upon that sets upon man, i.e., challenges him forth, to reveal the actual, in the mode of ordering, as standing-reserve. Enframing means the way of revealing that holds sway in the essence of modern technology and that is itself nothing technological. . . . Technological activity . . . always merely responds to the challenge of enframing, but it never comprises enframing itself or brings it about. (Heidegger, *BW* 325–26)

We are challenged to challenge nature; we are enframed into the attitude of enframing.

Enframing gives us this technological understanding of Being according to which we are in control of everything as means to ends, which becomes a particularly strong concealment of unconcealment or forgetfulness of Being. It fosters the belief that, like everything else, our mode of revealing is of our making and under our control, thereby blocking the notion of Being as the source of the sendings, that is, the impersonality of ICS. In enframing, the

> totality of the world of technology is interpreted in advance in terms of man, as being of man's making. By this conception of the totality of the

> technological world, we reduce everything down to man. . . . We fail to hear the claim of Being which speaks in the essence of technology. (Heidegger, *ID* 34)

In other words, the problem is precisely the Kantian Paradigm's A5 Active Knower, the idea that it is the subject who opens the clearing and organizes experience rather than "the claim of Being." Under the simultaneous reign of the Kantian Paradigm and technology,

> man . . . exalts himself and postures as lord of the earth. In this way the illusion comes to prevail that everything man encounters exists only insofar as it is his construct. . . . Man stands so decisively in subservience to . . . the challenging-forth of enframing that he does not grasp enframing as a claim, that he fails to see himself as the one spoken to. (Heidegger, *BW* 332)

Viewing ourselves as in control of our thinking and the source of our clearing—which is fallout from the technological way of thinking ("Man stands so decisively in subservience to . . . the challenging-forth of enframing")—blocks the realization that they have been conferred upon us, i.e., that "*es gibt Sein.*" The literal meaning of this phrase—that Being "is given" to us—expresses the idea far better than the more natural translation that "there is Being." While both the Greek sense of *physis* and the medieval view of divine creation forget Being (see Heidegger, *BW* 331), neither does so as completely as modern enframing, since these other understandings of Being attribute the rising to presence of things to some other source than man. This allows for some sort of wonder and gratitude, even if misplaced and misinterpreted. If we are responsible for the clearing, on the other hand, then we owe thanks to no one, we can open it anytime so it's nothing special, and beings are wholly of our making and so at our disposal. Moreover, we can maintain this mode of revealing as long as we like.

However, "if Enframing is a destining of the coming to presence of Being itself [ICS], then we may venture to suppose that Enframing, as [A3] one among Being's modes of coming to presence, changes" (Heidegger, *QT* 37, bracketed comments added). If we are not in control, if we await ICSs to be revealed or sent to us, then the possibility of further epochal revealings can never be ruled out, thus undermining the security of R3. Heidegger hopes to dis-cover Being as the source of the multiple epochal understandings because this replaces A5 with ICS, thus allowing A3 and the attitudes of wonder and gratitude. Thus what we need to do is to think the clearing, that is, to see beings as sent from Being, so that their presence is astonishing and wondrous rather than due to our activity: "It is necessary for thinking to become explicitly aware of the matter here called clearing" (Heidegger, *BW* 442). It is at that point that "the essence, the coming to presence, of Being enters into its own emitting of light" (Heidegger, *QT* 45; see also Heidegger, *BW* 181; Heidegger, *TB* 30)—i.e., that we can become aware of the clearing itself. This would let us see that our way of thinking or revealing beings is only one historical one among many (A3), that it is only a partial truth which conceals as much as it reveals (A4), and that we find ourselves in it and did not make it (ICS). Once again we can see how the Heideggerian Paradigm's ideas fit together to make a coherent whole.

Heidegger follows a line of Hölderlin's poetry to claim that "precisely the essence of technology must harbor in itself the growth of the saving power. But in that case, might not an adequate look into what enframing is, as a destining of revealing, bring the upsurgence of the saving power into appearance?" (Heidegger, *BW* 334; see also Heidegger, *QT* 41; Heidegger, *Mi* 56). Bending technology to our will in order to reduce its harmful effects cannot be the right solution, because this way of overcoming it is itself thoroughly consonant with the technological attitude and so merely proliferates it (see Heidegger, *BW* 313, 339; Heidegger, *OBT* 217). Since enframing means viewing problems as solvable by human action, any attempt on our part to fix it just perpetuates it. Furthermore, the fact that we ourselves are fully constituted by this Impersonal Conceptual Scheme (ED + A6) makes overcoming it by our own efforts difficult, since we are of a piece with it. Our ways of thinking bear the stamp of the modern ICS so completely that any scheme we were to create under its influence would share its character, and thus not constitute a genuinely different set of concepts. Somewhat like Kuhn's normal science, an understanding of Being is self-perpetuating; by the very fact that it gives us our ways of seeing and thinking, it discourages revolutions in them. A transcendental subject who escaped its influence might be able to significantly refashion its concepts "from the outside," but subjects constituted by the ICS can only extend it.

The only way to escape technology is "an adequate look into what enframing is, as a destining of revealing." When he pursues this look, Heidegger finds that the most unusual and innovative feature of technology compared with other epochs is the way the subject conceives of herself in it. Each epoch defines the subject and beings differently, so "the newness in this event by no means consists in the fact that now the position of man in the midst of what is, is an entirely different one in contrast to that of medieval and ancient man. What is decisive is that man himself expressly takes up this position as one constituted by himself" (Heidegger, *QT* 132). There have been several epochal shifts in which humanity found itself occupying a new place, but this is the first time that humans think of themselves as creating their new position the way Descartes does. This is technology's forgetfulness of Being (that is, ICS) in favor of A5's subjectivism.

> We today, and many generations before us, have long forgotten the realm of the unconcealment of beings, although we continually take it for granted. We actually think that a being becomes accessible when an [A5] "I" as subject represents an object. As if the [ICS] open region within whose openness something is made accessible *as* object *for* a subject, and accessibility itself, which can be penetrated and experienced, did not already have to reign here as well![74]

The technological attitude combines with the Kantian Paradigm's conception of the subject as opening the clearing to prevent any awareness of Being (see Heidegger, *PR* 88; Heidegger, *CP* 88, §61). The A5 Active Knower treats the essence of technology—the mode of revealing beings—as itself a kind of technology, that is, a means under our control to be utilized for maximum efficiency and power, which is precisely how both Nietzsche and Descartes present it.

However, this notion of self-founding and self-determination turns out to be technology's Achilles' heel. Heidegger interprets Hölderlin's line to mean that a genuine understanding of technology shows the essence of technology to be a way of revealing that *could not* be something we created or control. The power of technology allows man to "[exalt] himself and [posture] as lord of the earth. In this way the illusion comes to prevail that everything man encounters exists only insofar as it is his construct" (Heidegger, *BW* 332). But thinking about the *essence* of technology makes us realize that this way of revealing itself, which is what empowers us to create machinery, is itself not within our control. We could not have chosen to see the world in this way, nor can we stop seeing things this way by an act of will. The very idea of changing our technological way of thinking demonstrates that we are still determined by this way of thinking. Modern man "does not grasp enframing as a claim, . . . he fails to see himself as the one spoken to . . . so that he *can never* encounter only himself" (Heidegger, *BW* 332; see also Heidegger, *FoS* 63; Heidegger, *Pm* 307). Missing this point is due to confusing technology and the essence of technology—that is, viewing the essence or our epochal clearing as itself something in our power, or believing A5 instead of ICS. We remain trapped in technology because "we forget to ask: What is the ground that enabled modern technology to discover and set free new energies in nature" (Heidegger, *DT* 50; see also Heidegger, *QT* 42–43; Heidegger, *N* 3:181).

Separating the essence of technology from technology is the key insight here because it shows us that our particular horizon—enframing or the essence of technology—is something we are thrown into, something given, granted, or sent to us. We can then acknowledge our dependence or lack of control even over our own incredible amount of control. Heidegger expands the role of thrownness in his later work to become central to his thought, profoundly rejecting the Kantian Paradigm's emphasis on autonomy. In cases of the deepest import, "the decision does not belong to humans. If this is to become clear, what is most important is the insight that man is not a being that makes himself."[75] We must come to terms with the fact that we are thrown into our epochal ways of thinking and experiencing, that even if we change them it can only be on the basis of what we haven't chosen or affected, on an ineliminable moment of passivity.

Heidegger helpfully summarizes the narrative I have been recounting when he describes the turning in his own career, as well as the turning to "the other beginning" that he hopes will occur in the history of thinking and Being as a whole:

> But this is what the other beginning wants to and must achieve: leaping into the truth of be-ing so that be-ing itself grounds humanness. . . . The first beginning [that is, the Greeks] is not mastered; and the truth of be-ing, in spite of its essential shining, is not expressly grounded. And this means that [A5] a *human fore-grasping* (of asserting, of *Techne,* of certainty) sets the standard for the interpretation of the beingness of be-ing. But now the *great turning around* is necessary, which is beyond all "revaluation of all values," that turning around in which beings are not grounded in terms of human being, but rather human being is grounded in terms of [ICS] be-ing. (Heidegger, *CP* 129, §91, bracketed comments added)

Although the first beginning had a *physis-aletheia* structure similar to PO and UT, it wasn't "mastered" and so descended into humanism when Plato's doctrine of Forms transformed UT into correspondence truth. Thus began the legacy that culminated in the extreme A5 subjectivism of the Kantian Paradigm, where "human fore-grasping . . . sets the standard for the interpretation of the beingness of be-ing." The thinking that Heidegger hopes to help usher in—"the great turning around" or "other beginning"—will, on the other hand, "ground humans in Being" or the truth (unconcealment) of be-ing, meaning my ICS and mutual interdependence. In this brief paragraph, Heidegger sketches out the way that what I am calling the Heideggerian Paradigm succeeds the Kantian Paradigm, and sets the stage for the new ways of thinking that follow it.

The essence of technology itself can serve as a catalyst for this new way of thinking if we understand it in terms of Heidegger's new conception of thinking as responsiveness to what is sent. The fact that technology is the worst epoch yet in the sense that it depicts man as most in control and so most conceals Being can actually work to our advantage. If we can show that even this way of thinking defined by total control is not itself under our control, then it can become a particularly powerful demonstration of our dependence and ICS.

> Assuming we could look forward to the possibility that the frame—the mutual challenge of man and Being to enter the calculation of what is calculable—were to address itself to us as the event of appropriation which first surrenders man and Being to their own being; then a path would be open for man to experience beings in a more originary way. (Heidegger, *ID* 40; see also Heidegger, *PLT* 112)

The reason technology in particular has such potential for this switch is that its very emphasis on control can vividly reveal our lack of control. This dependence, although true of all epochs, is especially startling for modernity, since it so precisely inverts its central tenets. This transformation of attitude can then become the basis for a new kind of ethics.

> The essence of technology is in a lofty sense ambiguous. . . . On the one hand, enframing challenges forth into the frenziedness of ordering that blocks every view into the propriative event of revealing and so radically endangers the relation to the essence of truth. . . . On the other hand, enframing propriates for its part in the granting that lets man endure—as yet inexperienced, but perhaps more experienced in the future—that he may be the one who is needed and used for the safekeeping of the essence of truth. (Heidegger, *BW* 338)

Our dependence itself can ground a new kind of ethics based on an inversion of autonomy.

## The Ethics of Thinking

I am a strong *Kehre* reader. I believe that Heidegger's transition—which took place around 1930—not only marks a significant alteration in his own thought, but also forms the hinge on which much of the history of continental philosophy itself turns. Certainly, continuities span the two phases of his thought, and the early work prepares the ground for the later work, especially in the doctrines of Phenomenological Ontology and Unconcealment Truth. But these ideas were compromised in the early work; it isn't until the later work that Heidegger follows through on his own radical insights. Together, the rejection of A5 Active Knower, the abandonment of R6 Realism of the Self in favor of the A6 full immersion of humanity into history, and the making of man constituted along with everything else in an epoch Unmoor the epochs of Being from any anchor, *arche,* or necessary logic whatsoever. Now Heidegger can say that "what the propriating yields [that is, the epochal ICS] . . . is never the effect of a cause, nor the consequence of a reason" (Heidegger, *BW* 415, bracketed comment added). This is a watershed moment in twentieth-century continental philosophy, which sets the stage for later movements such as postmodernism (for example, Lyotard's rejection of meta-narratives and, as we will see in chapter 8, Derrida's deconstruction of metaphysics both embrace the Unmooring) and post-structuralism (as we will see in chapter 7, Foucault's *epistemes* develop the idea of ICS). I do not think it is overstating the significance of this move to portray it the way Heidegger himself does, as one of the great shifts in the history of thought—the first thorough attempt in 2,500 years to embrace a thinking not grounded on the stable, certain foundation of what is really real: "*Any kind* of metaphysics has and must come to an end, if philosophy is to attain its other beginning" (Heidegger, *CP* 121, §85).

Despite its obscurity, the doctrines of the Heideggerian Paradigm fit together into a systematic, coherent view. We transcend particular beings to grasp our epoch's understanding of Being—*physis,* divine creation, and technological *Bestand,* so far—which constitutes the character of the particular entities of an age (ICS). This is the detachment of the constitutive powers of the transcendental subject (A5), who now receives the understandings of Being and changes as they do (A6). Studying the history of philosophy shows A3 Ontological Pluralism—the fact that there have been multiple epochal modes of Being, none of which can be reduced to or derived from each other. These modes cannot be explained or placed in an order or logic, contra Hegel; they simply are and they simply change (though Heidegger does subscribe to the notion of a legacy). As the source of our rationality, they are beyond rational justification. Furthermore, HPO and UT demand that we accept each of these epochal understandings as true and real, rather than insisting on our own as the correct standpoint from which we can see the past as mistakes.

But we have one more important step to take in order to understand Heidegger's later work—the step from the epochal understandings of Being (or beingness) to Being itself, also called the event of appropriation (*Ereignis*), the truth of Being, Beyng, or the clearing at various times.[76] Being itself is the source (though not the cause, which would make it a being) of all the epochs, the "sender" of the sendings. As usual, language gets in the way, requiring many caveats and qualifications: "One can name it an origin, assuming that all ontic-causal overtones are excluded: it is the event [*Ereignis*] of being as condition for the arrival of beings: being lets beings presence" (Heidegger, *FoS* 59; see also Heidegger, *BW* 414–15). This tripartite structure made up of (1) beings, (2) beingness or the understanding of Being, and (3) Being itself is, I believe, the central organizing point of all of Heidegger's later thought, yet it has given rise to a great deal of confusion, much of which could have been averted had he employed a clarified terminology.[77] He himself admits to having created some confusion due to the ambiguity of the word "Being," which can easily apply to both (2) beingness and (3) Being itself[78] (see Heidegger, *OWL* 20, 26–27; Heidegger, *MHC* 44).

Heidegger casts about for a new way of writing to express these difficult ideas—crossing out the word "Being," employing terms like *Ereignis*, "the fourfold," *Spielraum*, "the It gives" (*es gibt*), even coming to reject the ontological difference itself, since it focuses on the difference between beings and beingness: "From the perspective of Appropriation it becomes necessary to free thinking from the ontological difference" (Heidegger, *TB* 37; see also Heidegger, *Mi* 300). There are times, though, when he speaks of the tripartite structure fairly clearly.

> We can say, in summary, that three meanings can be emphasized in "letting-be." The first refers to [1] that which is (to the being). Over against this first sense, there stands another sense for which the attention is drawn less towards *what* is given (towards what is), than towards [2] *the presencing* itself. It then concerns an interpretation of being of the sort given by metaphysics. Within this second emphasis, however, a third has its place, where the stress is now decisively placed upon [3] the *letting* itself, that which *allows* the presencing. . . . In this third meaning, one stands before [3] being *as* being, and no longer before [A3] one of the [2] forms of its destiny. If the emphasis is: *to let* presencing, there is no longer room for the very name of being. *Letting* is then the pure *giving*, which itself refers to the it [*das Es*] that gives, which is understood as *Ereignis*. (Heidegger, *FoS* 59–60, bracketed comments added; see also Heidegger, *PR* 62; Heidegger, *TB* 19)

There are (1) ontic beings, which are just the entities we encounter and deal with day to day. According to ICS, these entities are determined by (2) ontological beingness, that is, an overall defining character which varies from epoch to epoch and which is captured best in the writings of metaphysicians. Finally, there is (3) the very emergence or giving or unconcealment (or truth) of these epochal modes. "In the beingness of beings, metaphysics thinks [2] being, yet without being able to ponder the [3] truth of being" (Heidegger, *Pm* 232, bracketed comments added; see also Heidegger, *Mi* 322, 375). Although most of Heidegger's analyses of the history of philosophy remain at the second level of understandings of Being, his ultimate goal is to point us toward this third level. Ordinary people focus on beings, their experience being guided by an unthematic (pre-ontological) understanding of these entities' epochal beingness. Metaphysicians have always transcended beings to focus explicitly on beingness, but philosophers since the pre-Socratics have forgotten or ignored the third level—Being itself or *Ereignis* (see Heidegger, *BW* 444). "In the beginning of Western thinking, [2] Being is thought, but not [3] the 'It gives' as such. The latter withdraws in favor of [2] the gift which It gives. That [2] gift is thought and conceptualized from then on exclusively with regard to [1] beings."[79]

Studying the history of metaphysics serves the genealogical purpose of teaching us A3—that our way of experiencing the world is contingent, enabling us to resist its insistence that it is the one and only truth. This multiplicity of epochal releasings, however, also points us toward their point of origin or releasement.

> Proper inquiry must be a dialogue in which the [2] ways of hearing and points of view of ancient thinking are contemplated according to [3] their essential origin, so that the [3] call under which [2] past, present, and future thinking—[A3] each in its own way—all stand, might begin to announce itself.[80]

Whereas the switchover between the modes of Being of tools and objects in *Being and Time* pointed to their source in Dasein and society, now the various epochal understandings of Being point to what is beyond them, to their source in appropriation (*Ereignis*) or destiny (*Geschick*), to Being itself. "What is peculiar to [2] Being, that to which Being belongs and in which it remains retained, shows itself in [3] the It gives and its giving as sending. . . . When we explicitly think about [2] Being, the matter itself leads us in a certain sense away from [2] Being, and we think [3] the destiny that gives Being as a gift" (Heidegger, *TB* 10, bracketed comments added). When we think of epochal understandings of Being and realize just how deep they go and how dependent we are on them, we realize that we couldn't have created them (ICS, R5), and we wonder how they could have changed. We cannot accept any intra-epochal explanations—what Heidegger calls onto-theological answers such as that God or man altered them—since these answers themselves only make sense *within* a particular epochal understanding, while we are asking about the origin of epochs as a whole.

The point about this question is that no answer could possibly satisfy it, since any answer would have to take place *within* an epochal understanding: Being itself is "prior to everything. The prior, of which we really can not think . . . because the nature of thinking begins there" (Heidegger, *DT* 83). However, answers are not what he is after. Being itself as the source of the sendings sounds like an answer but actually functions as a placeholder or even a counter-answer, which is one reason why he takes to crossing it out in some of his later works. "There is nothing else to which propriation reverts, nothing in terms of which it might even be explained" (Heidegger, *BW* 415); instead, "it can only be experienced . . . as that which grants" (415). In order to experience this, we need a change in attitude or perspective that instills a new way of relating to the world: "If the answer could be given it would consist in a transformation of thinking, not in a propositional statement about a matter at stake" (Heidegger, *BW* 431; see also Heidegger, *TB* 25–26).

> What prior to everything else first grants unconcealment is the path on which thinking pursues one thing and perceives it: . . . that presencing presences. The clearing grants first of all the possibility of the path to [2] presence, and grants the [3] possible presencing of that presence itself. We must think *alētheia,* unconcealment, as the clearing that first grants Being and thinking and [mutual interdependence] their presencing to and for each other. (Heidegger, *BW* 445, bracketed comments added)

Whereas explanatory reason can apply to beings within an epochal understanding of Being, we need a profound shift in order to think about Being itself, which is another reason Heidegger needs a new conception of thinking. "What alone is singularly decisive is the *experience* of that which is *not* a being and cannot be a being and yet above all raises beings *as* beings unto the openness of its sway" (Heidegger, *Mi* 333). The proper attitude to take toward these sendings is not to analyze them for an inner logic, but to respect their "inexhaustible mystery" (Heidegger, *EGT* 64; see also Heidegger, *BW* 238) by resisting our natural tendency to explain and control: "We never know a mystery by unveiling or analyzing it to death, but only in such a way that we preserve the mystery *as* mystery."[81]

Although technological thinking tries to capture everything there is through comprehension and explanation, the source of rationality cannot be grasped this way. Heidegger rejects Hegel's attempt to order and comprehend history and reason, claiming instead that the changing of an epoch or "the surmounting of a destining of Being . . . each time comes to pass out of the arrival of another destining, a destining that does not allow itself either to be logically and historiographically predicted or to be metaphysically construed as a sequence belonging to a process of history."[82] All that we have is the Unmoored proliferation of epochs of Being, not a rational explanation of any one of them, the combination of them, or the fact that they exist at all. Seeing these radically heterogeneous modes of Being together imparts Heraclitus's insight that eternity is a child playing where "the 'because' withers away in the play. The play is without 'why.' . . . As the abyss it plays the play that, as *Geschick,* passes being and ground/reason to us."[83] The important thing is to stay open to the mysterious fact of presence and keep explanations from extinguishing wonder. When explained, "Being is not acknowledged as Being. Such 'acknowledging' means allowing Being to reign in all its questionableness. . . . But that means to reflect on [3] the origin of presencing" (Heidegger, *N* 4:201, bracketed comment added). Since the series of epochs cannot be organized and placed into the service of a transcendent goal, they can only be viewed as "the ever playful jointure of never resting transformation" (Heidegger, *Pm* 320). We can see premonitions of Derrida here.

The Kantian Paradigm's A5 prevents any sense of gratitude, since this view gives us the credit for Being: "The things for which we owe thanks are not things we have from ourselves. . . . But the thing given to us . . . is thinking. . . . How can we give thanks for this endowment, the gift of being able to think?" (Heidegger, *WCT* 142–43). Taking credit for the clearing amounts to forgetfulness of Being, which eliminates wonder.[84] When we become aware of the gift of thinking and awareness itself that has been bestowed upon us, the proper response is to give the "thanks that alone pays homage to the grace that being has bestowed upon the human essence in thinking" (Heidegger, *Pm* 236). Although we are always already within the clearing, that is, in contact with beings, we take it for granted, ignore it, take credit for it, bypass it for beings, and so on. "We do not reside sufficiently as yet where in reality we already are" (Heidegger, *ID* 33). Heidegger wants us to pay attention to this simplest of all facts in order to celebrate it.[85] Employing terms from *Being and Time*, he says that this "happens only when the openness that makes its advent in thrownness is projected" (Heidegger, *BW* 196). Although we are thrown into many conditions, the most fundamental and general feature we are thrown into is the very ability to have beings present to us at all, which is required for anything else. This is the ultimate transcendental condition for the possibility of any kind of experience whatsoever.

I discussed above how being thrown into an epochal understanding of Being constitutes a deeper, more determining sense of thrownness than the earlier conception of finding oneself in a particular historical period and culture. The later conception also takes on more positive connotations: for one thing, instead of simply being abandoned, we are now thrown by Being. This gives a greater sense of guidance or inheritance now: "History is the transporting of a people into its appointed task as entry into that people's endowment" (Heidegger, *BW* 202; see also Heidegger, *N* 4:196). Furthermore, we are thrown into a way of being that is appropriate to us, that is our own. Since being in the clearing is the ubiquitous condition that underlies all actions and choices, it is not simply an optional role we can choose to take up or not. This is our essence that we are thrown into, a particular "for-the-sake-of-which" set out for us—to be "custodian of the unconcealedness of beings" (Heidegger, *BQ* 163; see also Heidegger, *CP* 169, §122). Now man is thrown into precisely what thrownness had ruled out in *Being and Time:* a "'for the sake of itself,' that is, purely as preserving and guardianship of being" (Heidegger, *CP* 213, §178), which constitutes our essence.[86] There is a specific role or activity that is singled out for us by our nature: since we are the revealer or the being that stands out in the open, we are charged with the "duty" of revealing in the most careful and attentive way possible. Consciously taking up our ability to let beings appear, celebrating it gratefully, and giving beings the kind of careful attention that lets them appear most fully is how I understand "projecting the openness that we are thrown into." These ideas are all summed up in one of Heidegger's most famous phrases: "Man is rather 'thrown' from Being itself into the truth of Being, so that ek-sisting in this fashion he might guard the truth of Being, in order that beings might appear in the light of Being as the beings they are. . . . Man is the shepherd of Being."[87] Ethics *as* phenomenology.

Drawing on the etymology of the word, Heidegger claims that "the name 'ethics,' in keeping with the basic meaning of the word *ēthos,* should now say that 'ethics' ponders the abode of man" (Heidegger, *BW* 258). Since the clearing is "our essential abode in being" (Heidegger, *BCo* 78), thinking about Being "is in itself the original ethics" (Heidegger, *BW* 258). Dwelling in the clearing, then, is our abode, or our true nature, around which a new ethics must be built.

> The granting that sends one way or another into revealing is as such the saving power. For the saving power lets man see and enter into the highest dignity of his essence. This dignity lies in keeping watch over the unconcealment—and with it, from the first, the concealment—of all essential unfolding on this earth. . . . Everything, then, depends upon this: that we ponder this rising and that, recollecting, we watch over it. (Heidegger, *BW* 337; see also 239, 330)

Thus, as I will discuss in the next section, thinking or letting beings appear in attentive dwelling is the way we become who we are or, in his phrase, "thinking and poetizing must return to where, in a certain way, they have always already been but have never yet built. Only through building, however, can we prepare a dwelling in that locality" (Heidegger, *Pm* 319; see also Heidegger, *Mi* 123). This grateful dwelling where we always already are, in the clearing, but by carefully attending it is Heidegger's ethics of thinking.

This ethical attitude is also described in terms of a reciprocal exchange or co-responding between humans and Being: "Originary thinking is the echo of being's favor, of a favor in which a singular event is cleared and lets come to pass: that beings are" (Heidegger, *Pm* 236). Thinking and Being interact by a mutual letting-appear. On the one hand, Being lets beings occur by presenting them to us: "The deepest meaning of being is *letting*. Letting the being be, this is the non-causal meaning of 'letting'" (Heidegger, *FoS* 59). At his best, man resonates to this with *Gelassenheit*, or letting the letting occur, so to speak, which Heidegger often expresses in metaphors of cultivation or nurturing (see Heidegger, *BW* 337, 353; Heidegger, *PLT* 217). Dasein cannot accomplish Being, but the one thing it can do is "to get hold of the counter-resonance of en-ownment . . . and thus first of all to become itself: the preserver of the thrown projecting-open" (Heidegger, *CP* 169, §122). Whereas Being presences beings, we have the ability to bring Being itself to presence by thinking it. Thus our thinking is an echo of Being's revelation in that we reveal its revealing. That is why our "letting beings be, is the *fulfillment and consummation* of the essence of truth in the sense of the disclosure of beings" (Heidegger, *BW* 127, italics added). In this way the mutual interdependence circulates, but now with an ethical charge in which man responds to and repeats Being's own primal event of appearing in his own way. "Thinking accomplishes the relation of Being to the essence of man," where "to accomplish means to unfold something into the fullness of its essence."[88] It is our "duty" to nurture the clearing and allow Being to unfold in all its richness, and in so doing we also accomplish our own essence as revealer.

One of the things that we reveal when we think in this way is that Being, the sender of these ways of thinking, is the groundless ground. It gives the ground on which we think and justify our beliefs and ways of behaving, but it itself cannot be given ultimate justification. Like Nietzsche's Eternal Recurrence, this fact can provoke very different reactions.

> Insofar as being essentially comes to be as ground/reason, it has no ground/reason. However this is not because it founds itself, but because every foundation—even and especially self-founded ones—remain[s] inappropriate to being as ground/reason. . . . Being *qua* being remains ground-less. . . . If we think about this, and if we persist in such thinking, then we notice that we have leaped off from the realm of previous thinking and are in the leap. But do we not fall into the fathomless with this leap? Yes and no. Yes—insofar as being can no longer be given a basis in the sense of beings and explained in terms of beings. No—insofar as being is now finally to be thought *qua* being. As what is to be thought, it becomes, from out of its truth, what gives a measure. The manner in which thinking thinks must conform to this measure. But it is not possible for us to seize upon this measure and what it offers through a com-

> puting and gauging. For us it remains that which is immeasurable. However, so little does the leap allow thinking to fall into the fathomless in the sense of the complete void that in fact it first allows thinking to respond to being *qua* being, that is, to the truth of being. (Heidegger, *PR* 111; see also Heidegger, *P* 49; Heidegger, *Mi* 43)

Being thrown into a way of thinking within a community and epoch is not a curse that prevents us from having genuine thought or truth, but is in fact the only way finite beings are capable of thought. Each epochal understanding sent by Being really does "give a measure" to which "thinking . . . must conform." These measures or laws of thinking are what enable us to put ideas together, evaluate, make decisions, and reach conclusions, and in principle they cannot be gauged by any measure themselves. This groundlessness only seems unsatisfying compared to the "super-justifications" or "hyper-original" self-determination promised by philosophers and prophets for so long.[89] Although the measures are not capable of ultimate justification, they do give us the guidelines for justifying ontic beings and actions. Seen from the impossible vantage point disengaged from all traditions, clearings, and standards, each looks arbitrary, but of course this "view from nowhere" is not our position. Part of our finitude is that our "situatedness" goes all the way down to the core of our thinking and choosing, so that the epochal understanding we are thrown into orients us in all matters. Gadamer describes this well:

> Being so conditioned [by tradition] is not an impairment of historical knowledge, but rather a moment of truth itself. . . . To destroy the phantom of a knowledge that has been freed from the standpoint of the knower must count here without qualification as "scientific." This is precisely the sign of our finitude, remaining mindful of which alone preserves us from delusion. The naïve faith in the objectivity of the historical method was just such a delusion. But what takes its place is not an insipid relativism. What we ourselves are and what we are capable of heeding from the past is not arbitrary and not optional. (Wachterhauser 1994, 29, bracketed comment added; see also Gadamer 1989, 280)

This move overcomes relativism by going through it all the way to the other end. I will return to this topic in my conclusion.

Heidegger calls these various epochal understandings of Being "destinings," though the word could also be translated as "sending" (see Heidegger, *PR* xiv–xv). In German, this word *Geschick* has strong etymological connections to "what is fitting, suitable, appropriate" (*schicklich*) as well as to both "sendings" (*Schicken*) and "history" (*Geschichte*) (Heidegger,

*BW* 329). "When we use the word *Geschick* in connection with being, then we mean that being hails us and clears and lights itself, and in clearing, it furnishes the temporal play-space wherein beings can appear" (Heidegger, *PR* 62). It is what lays out our "space of reasons" (ICS), that is, the measure (*schicklich*) or the way we think and experience which is also the epochal (*Geschichte*) clearing. Although Being itself, of course, is not a benevolent agent who watches over us and has plans for our lives, Heidegger is playing on the comforting and trustworthy connotations of destiny. The sendings are gifts which we should gratefully embrace and cherish, even if there isn't anyone or -thing to be grateful to. Although our thinking must follow the measure laid out by our epochal understanding, we ought to do this with gratitude rather than taking it for granted or demanding grounds for it. He hopes that there "may awaken and found anew our vision of, and trust in, that which grants" (Heidegger, *BW* 340).

It is important to remember that the phrase "groundless ground" has two parts. We tend to focus on the "groundlessness" part, since we are used to philosophers offering absolute grounds, in comparison with which this seems rather paltry. But it *is* a ground—it supplies us with measures which fully enable thinking—and we've never had anything more, no matter what we have been told. As later Wittgenstein and Nietzsche claim, we only find this unsatisfying in comparison with unrealistic metaphysical expectations of what grounds should be like. Although the groundlessness and multiplicity of understandings can be unsettling, they can also help instill the ethical attitude Heidegger is after: "The lucid courage for essential anxiety assures us the enigmatic possibility of experiencing being. For close by essential anxiety as the horror of the abyss dwells awe. Awe cherishes that locality of the human essence within which humans remain at home in that which endures" (Heidegger, *Pm* 234). Just a slight nudge transforms horror at the ultimate meaninglessness of everything—that Being is without why or necessity—into astonished awe that there is Being and meaning at all.

This ethical attitude also promises a solution to nihilism or the loss of value. Heidegger believes that the idea that all values come from human acts of valuing—an ethical A5 Active Knower which comes out in technology—is the ultimate form of nihilism. Technology's focus on fulfilling our desires awards value to things only to the degree that they satiate our cravings.

> Man . . . is continually approaching the brink of the possibility of pursuing and promulgating nothing but what is revealed in ordering, and of deriving all his standards on this basis. Through this the other possibility is blocked—that man might rather be admitted sooner and ever more

> primally to the essence of what is unconcealed and to its unconcealment, in order that he might experience as his essence the requisite belonging to revealing. (Heidegger, *BW* 331)

The strategy for giving our lives worth that naturally presents itself to the Kantian/technological mind is Nietzsche's active nihilism: invent new goals, inject value into the world, inflate our little lives with significance ourselves now that God is dead (see Heidegger, *QT* 67, 95). Nietzsche calls this active nihilism, which he sees as the solution to the valuelessness that most thinkers call nihilism. For Heidegger, "this supposed overcoming is above all the consummation of nihilism."[90]

> It is important to finally realize that precisely through the characterization of something as "a value" what is so valued is robbed of its worth. That is to say, by the assessment of something as a value what is valued is admitted only as an object for man's estimation. But what a thing is in its Being is not exhausted by its being an object, particularly when objectivity takes the form of value. Every valuing, even where it values positively, is a subjectivizing. It does not let beings: be. Rather, valuing lets beings: be valid—solely as the objects of its doing. . . . Thinking in values is the greatest blasphemy imaginable against Being.[91]

Besides the logical incoherence of this model—beings need to appear desirable in order for us to choose to value them, they must present themselves as manipulable and worth manipulating for us to decide to use them—Heidegger believes that this model of personal fulfillment and desire satisfaction actually culminates in the emptiness of modern life, rather than its meaningfulness. "If we merely attempt, on our own authority, to set or seize upon the measure, then it becomes measureless and disintegrates into nothingness" (Heidegger, *HH* 167).

This notion that we determine what is valuable cuts individuals off from anything beyond themselves and their personal wants, thus narrowing and trivializing life. Nietzsche's brilliance was to see this tautological emptiness of autonomy, but his mistake was to embrace it instead of recoiling from it. Descartes started the ball rolling by doubting tradition and rejecting whatever could not pass the "tribunal of reason." Once this epistemological self-reliance is set up, the rest is inevitable: "The ground could not have been anything other than man himself, because the sense of the new freedom forbade him any bond or commitment that did not arise from his own positings" (Heidegger, *N* 4:102; see also Heidegger, *BW* 295–96). The course of modern philosophy follows out this epistemological autonomy to its logical conclusion, which spreads to every corner of modern life: "*All that is left is the solitary superficies of a 'life' that empowers itself to itself for its own sake.* If metaphysics begins as an explicit interpretation of beingness as *idea,* it achieves its uttermost end in the 'revaluation of all values'" (3:176; see also Heidegger, *CP* 348–49, §274).

Taking our cues from anything external is ruled out as heteronomy, but this sheer self-referential or tautological circle where "the will wills itself" (Heidegger, *QT* 77) drains itself of all meaning. To put it simplistically, Nietzsche ontologizes Machiavelli's power for the sake of power outlook: "Under the pressure of the effectiveness of the pure process of empowering of power, goals become superfluous" (Heidegger, *Mi* 17). As finite mortals we simply cannot sustain value in the world by ourselves in such a way that will make a good, meaningful life. We need tradition, rituals, community, and the kinds of natural patterns the ancients called the *cosmos logos.* A5 Active Knower in epistemology means that we only encounter our own concepts in entities and only talk to ourselves in coming to know the world. In ethics, it bleaches the meaning out of our lives.

> The meaninglessness in which the metaphysical articulation of modernity is consummated becomes something we can know as the essential fulfillment of this age only when it is apprehended together with the transformation of man to [R6] *subiectum* and the determination of beings as [A1] the represented and produced character [technology] of the objective. Then it becomes clear that meaninglessness [nihilism] is the prefigured consequence [legacy] of the finality of modern metaphysics in its very beginnings. Truth as certitude becomes the monotony that is injected into beings as a whole when they are served up for man's securing of permanence, man now having been left to his own devices. . . . Truth as [R3] securing univocity grants machination [technology] exclusive pre-eminence. When certitude becomes the one and only, beings alone remain essential; never again beingness itself, to say nothing of its clearing [tripartite structure of Being and forgetfulness of Being]. *When Being lacks the clearing, beings as a whole lack meaning.* (Heidegger, *N* 3:179–80, bracketed comments added)

Heidegger ties together many seemingly disparate theses here to conclude that our own attempts to give our lives meaning are doomed to failure, leaving us with satisfied desires but empty lives. Indeed, the very *attempt* to give life meaning by ourselves shows that, as he often puts it, "the god has fled," that is, community and tradition do not sustain us the way they did in previous ages, since we are flailing about for an alternate source.

As throughout, Heidegger's accounts of technology and epistemology parallel each other, so that fashioning machinery to fulfill our whims, on the one hand, and explaining everything to satisfy our curiosity and master nature, on the other, are of a piece. And both disrupt the traditions he considers so important.

> The unique unleashing of the demand to render reasons threatens everything of humans' being-at-home and robs them of the roots of their subsistence, the roots from out of which every great human age, every world-opening spirit, every molding of the human form has thus far grown. . . . The claim of the mighty Principle [of Reason, i.e., that everything has a reason and thus must be rationally judged] of rendering reasons withdraws the subsistence from contemporary humanity. We could also say that the more decisively humans try to harness the "mega-energies" that would, once and for all, satisfy all human energy needs, the more impoverished becomes the human faculty for building and dwelling in the realm of what is essential. There is an enigmatic interconnection between the demand to render reasons and the withdrawal of roots. (Heidegger, *PR* 30–31, bracketed comment added; see also Heidegger, *DT* 48–49; Heidegger, *OWL* 13)

Heidegger believes that humanity is essentially rooted—we are thrown, we are determined, we receive everything from our tradition, community, Being—and anything of worth or sustaining ability must actively and consciously engage in tradition. "According to our human experience and history, at least as far as I see it, I know that everything essential and everything great originated from the fact that man had a home and was rooted in a tradition" (Heidegger, "OG" 106; see also Heidegger, *Mi* 145).

Traditions give us meaning, but aren't always meaningful in the sense of being explicable or justifiable. Looked at from an external perspective, they are often rather arbitrary—why eat turkey on Thanksgiving? Why use that particular kind of tree for Christmas or drink champagne on New Year's? But imagine how unsettling sitting down to a Thanksgiving meal of hamburgers or toasting the new year with bourbon would be, even if preferable from a purely utilitarian perspective. A tradition gets its resonance merely from being a tradition, from having been interwoven into our lives; it is what is done because it is what has been done every year. As much as this may grate on the nerves of a trained philosopher, it is how humans are. Traditional observance does not supply a practice with *rational* grounding—why should it matter whether it has been done every year? All that should matter is whether it is right—yet this lack does not reduce its impact. It only loses that when one demands reasons for everything, setting oneself up as judge and source of all value, accepting only what makes sense or satisfies conscious desires. When one does this, then even those actions that pass the test lose their meaning.

The solution to nihilism is *Gelassenheit,* both the ontic care-ful attention to things and the ontological respect for the incomprehensibility of Being's sendings. "Releasement toward things and openness to the mystery . . . grant us the possibility of dwelling in the world in a totally different way."[92] We need to remove both metaphysical prejudices—the realist (present-at-hand) notion on the one hand that reality has no intrinsic value or that Platonic, unchanging values exist, and the A5 axiological anti-realism on the other hand which claims that value comes from our projections. Instead, phenomenological attention shows us that in fact the world is full of meaning, even though this meaning can change and we are involved in it. In a way, nihilism is a purely theoretical problem which only arises when we try to justify all of our decisions rationally, the way that for Wittgenstein skepticism only arises when language is on holiday (see Heidegger, *BW* 359). If we dwell where we always already are, that is, pay attention to the way we actually live and the way the world actually presents itself to us, we realize that things are constantly emanating meaningfulness; our lives are bursting with significance. Just as phenomenological descriptions can refute metaphysical or epistemological theories, so pointing out the meaningful world we actually live in can refute nihilism.

We have to remember that meaning doesn't come from us and that we cannot control it, since even those decisions to control are themselves determined by how things present themselves, and that the sustaining traditions represent a groundless ground, that is, they cannot be given ultimate rational justifications. Once we understand these features, we realize that we are immersed in rhythms that guide and support us, supplying us with "those paths and relations in which birth and death, disaster and blessing, victory and disgrace, endurance and decline acquire the shape of destiny for human being. The all-governing expanse of this open relational context is the world of this historical people."[93] The fact that we cannot alter our clearing by ourselves, together with this attitude of trusting gratitude for how things appear, combine to make up what is often called the "quietism" of later Heidegger. His nostalgia or peasant romanticism comes from the fact that traditional methods of, say, farming are deeply integrated with and explicitly need to cooperate with the natural rhythms of the year and weather that help remind us that we are not fully in control, whereas technology tends to efface them, giving us the power to decide matters and thus fostering the illusion of total control.[94]

This is the ethical side of epochal destiny: just as it gives us our way of thinking, so it gives us a way of dwelling, of being at home on this earth we were thrown into, of living with each other in families and communities, of celebrating festivals, worshiping gods, and facing death. This is the solution to nihilism that "gives back to things, to beings, their weight (Being)" (Heidegger, *IM* 12). We make a home of the earth by celebrating the traditions we have been granted, not by trying to create ourselves ex nihilo or choosing only what satisfies our drives. "Only so far as man, ek-sisting into the truth of Being, belongs to Being can there come from Being itself the assignment of those directives that must become law and rule for man. . . . Otherwise all law remains merely something fabricated by human reason" (Heidegger, *BW* 262). Whereas Hegel gets *Sittlichkeit* right—that is, the idea that we derive values and guidance for conduct from our community—he still clings to the Kantian Paradigm's insistence on autonomy by setting up the community's structure itself as the rational, justifiable product of Spirit (see, for example, Hegel, *RH* 53, 79, 95). For Heidegger, this move eliminates precisely those features that allow it to groundlessly ground our lives: "Everything depends on our inhering in this clearing that is propriated by Being itself—never made or conjured by ourselves. We must overcome the compulsion to lay our hands on everything" (Heidegger, *N* 3:181; see also Heidegger, *Mi* 211, 308).

## R6 Realism of the Subject

Although one of the key features of Heidegger's break with his own early work and the Kantian Paradigm is his A6 immersion of the self into multiple historical epochs without any permanent essence, he does end up with a minimal definition of man that remains the same across the epochs: openness to Being. However much this openness may differ from period to period, man must always be open to Being—that is, be able to experience beings—simply in order to be human. This reinstates the R6 Realism of the Subject and its concomitant ethics that he had apparently left behind. Wonder then becomes a new form of authenticity as recapturing or living in accordance with our essence, an attitude that is open to anyone at any point. When we wonder, we become explicitly aware of and consciously embrace the openness that we really are. Becoming aware of the gift of Being means explicitly dwelling where we already are without realizing it, and this takes the form of the traditional ethical argument of living in a way that is appropriate to our essence. Haar argues for this reading in his aptly named *Heidegger and the Essence of Man:* "Does not this formula [of man as open to Being] . . . provide us with the *true* essence of Western man . . . ? Does not Heidegger thereby suggest that there is a true, *transhistorical* essence of man" (Haar 1993, 164, bracketed comment added; see also 174; Kolb 1986, 225–26).

In his later work, Heidegger speaks over and over about the essence of man prodding us to become ourselves, albeit not through our own effort.[95] However, this essence has shrunk to the barest possible point of just the ability to experience or be aware of anything. This awareness changes profoundly across the epochs, as does the self that is aware and the beings one is aware of, but Heidegger has to maintain this one feature of human essence. From it he derives the conception of Being itself as the inexplicable sending of epochal understandings, as well as an ethics of grateful *Gelassenheit*—an impressive amount to get out of this one feature—but he seems to require it as the correct account of the essence of any self. I will discuss this further in the conclusion to this book.

## Conclusion

I have described Heidegger's later work as making a profound break with the Kantian Paradigm and, in important ways, with virtually all of philosophy up to this point. The Heideggerian Paradigm—which still influences continental philosophy today—shows the Kantian Paradigm to be incoherent and the source of contemporary nihilism. His new system maintains an important element of anti-realism in that beings are organized by something like a conceptual scheme, that is, a common character which cannot be derived from the entities themselves. As with Hegel, Nietzsche, and his own early work, the Heideggerian Paradigm subscribes to A3 Ontological Pluralism in that these schemes are multiple, coming closest to Hegel in tying them to historical periods or epochs.

This paradigm transforms A1 Mind-Dependence and the Empirical Directive into mutual interdependence: man and Being intertwine and can only be understood and exist in relation to each other. Not merely an accidental conjunction, the essence of each is simply to be present to the other. Combined with the historical version of A3 and the doctrine of Unconcealment Truth initially presented in *Being and Time,* this leads to Historical Phenomenological Ontology—the claim that only what exists within a historical epoch as formed by that period's understanding of Being is, and that whatever exists within a historical epoch really does exist in that way regardless of its transience. Man too occurs only within the epochs, losing all remnants of Kant's transcendental subjectivity to be different kinds of beings at different periods, thus completing A6 and ED.

Since the subject is wholly constitut*ed* and is so in various ways by the different historical conceptual schemes, it cannot be their constitut*or;* they devolve upon man and world alike. This is Heidegger's new, reformed version of R5 Passive Knower—we receive Impersonal Conceptual Schemes rather than creating or controlling them. They are ultimately incomprehensible, since they give rise to the very structures of comprehension themselves. Unmoored from any permanent ground in a subject, beings, metaphysical entities, God, and so on, all that we have are a series of ways of thinking and living with no possibility of trans-epochal logic, closure, capture, or comprehension. They simply are; all we can do is accept them and, at best, cherish them. Paradoxically, though, this very acceptance itself helps overcome the present structure. Heidegger's attempt to think and live without ultimate grounds or *arche* can be seen as one of the turning points, for better or worse, in the history of philosophy as a whole. The way he arrives at this conclusion, however, is fully intelligible as a reaction to the Kantian Paradigm.

7

# Foucault's History of Truth

> The history of the West cannot be disassociated from the way in which "truth" is produced and inscribes its effects. . . . The history of "truth"—of the power proper to discourses accepted as true—has yet to be written. (Foucault, *FL* 215)

> I try to historicize to the utmost in order to leave as little space as possible to the transcendental. (Foucault, *FL* 99)

I can directly state the basic thesis of this chapter: Foucault works within the Heideggerian Paradigm the way that Hegel, Nietzsche, and to a lesser degree early Heidegger operate within the Kantian Paradigm. Just as Kant presented the first coherent and persuasive complete alternative to realism, so Heidegger's later work marks the first genuine alternative to the Kantian Paradigm, even though it had already been significantly reformed during its reign, as we have seen. This epoch-making shift is the reason for Heidegger's enormous influence: continental philosophers after him must come to grips with his later work as the next major turning point in continental thought after Kant. I will show this influence in detail in the work of Michel Foucault, the post-Heideggerian thinker who wields the greatest cross-disciplinary influence and who is second only to Derrida in sheer philosophical brilliance. The promissory note which I can only issue here due to the limits of the book is that the same influence could be shown in many other prominent post-Heideggerian thinkers.

In this chapter I will show how in point after point Foucault's thought takes place within the Heideggerian Paradigm. He takes his fundamental orientation from it, assuming its outlook and concepts, its problems and issues, and subscribing to most of its major doctrines as outlined in chapter 6. Briefly, Foucault shares with Heidegger a conflicted relationship to Kant as the thinker who opened up the space for essential questions by rejecting realism and positing conceptual schemes, but who immediately closed down this important space by only allowing a single scheme (R3 Uniqueness) located within the subject's faculties (A5 Active Knower). Following later Heidegger, Foucault rescues Kant's promising insights from his compromising anthropocentrism by (1) multiplying the schemes into A3 Ontological Pluralism and tying them to historical epochs, (2) showing how they determine what can count as true or false, leading to A2 and A4 Rejections of Correspondence Truth and Bivalence, and (3) fully rejecting R1 noumena (4) to embrace the full reality of whatever gets formed at the various points in history, that is, Historical Phenomenological Ontology, (5) Unmooring the schemes from the subject to make them (6) Impersonal Conceptual Schemes, as well as (7) rendering the subject A6 fully constituted and changing within history. This brief sketch of Foucault's position shows just how indebted he is to the Heideggerian Paradigm.

Given this enormous affinity between Foucault and Heidegger, it is surprising how little attention has been paid to their relationship in the literature. At the time of this book's composition, only one book and one collection of essays focused on the topic have been published in English.[1] Comments like John Rajchman's that "Foucault's history may be seen to continue, and perhaps to radicalize, Heidegger's challenge to the post-Cartesian philosophy of the subject" (Rajchman 1985, 52),[2] or Derrida's claim that Foucault's almost complete silence on Heidegger "is anything but the empty and inoperative sign of an absence. It *gives* rise or *gives the* place, on the contrary, it marks out the place and the age. . . . No attention to the age or to the problem of the age should lose sight of this" (A. I. Davidson 1997, 85n19), are rarer than they ought to be. Foucault himself claims in one of his last interviews that "Heidegger has always been for me the essential philosopher. . . . My whole philosophical development was determined by my reading of Heidegger" (Foucault, *FL* 470), though he immediately qualifies this somewhat in favor of Nietzsche, as do most commentators (see, for example, McWhorter 1999, 75). In a 1982 lecture, when asked about Lacan's influence on his thought, he turns the subject to Heidegger, in particular on the issue of truth: "There have not been that many people . . . in the twentieth century [who] have posed the question of truth. . . . I see only Heidegger and Lacan. Personally, myself, you must have heard this, I have tried to reflect on all this from the side of Heidegger and starting from Heidegger" (Foucault, *Herm* 189).

Of course, just as Nietzsche and Hegel reformed important features of the Kantian Paradigm, so Foucault introduces significant changes into the Heideggerian Paradigm. Primarily, he vastly increases the amount of historical detail and documentation in his examination of the epochs, paying much more attention to non-philosophical sources than Heidegger does, and gives the entire discussion an ethical/political orientation that is alien to Heidegger's work. But the framework is the same, as I will demonstrate.

## Kant

Foucault's relationship with Kant is complex, just as Heidegger's was. On the one hand, Kant's rejection of realism in favor of conceptual schemes[3] was an extremely important step forward in philosophy, opening up the space for all the important work that followed. Unfortunately, he immediately compromised the potential of this groundbreaking idea by placing the R3 single ahistorical conceptual scheme within the subject.

> What possibilities generated this thought from which everything, up until our time, has seemingly diverted us, but as if to lead us to the point of its returning? . . . Undoubtedly, it can be said that it comes to us through that opening made by Kant in Western philosophy when he articulated, in a manner which is still enigmatic, metaphysical discourse and his reflection on the limits of reason. However, Kant ended by closing this opening when he ultimately relegated all critical investigations to an anthropological question. (Foucault, *LCP* 38; see also Foucault, *OT* 340–41; Hoy 1986, 118)

Foucault's "complementary thesis" to his Ph.D. dissertation translated and commented on Kant's *Anthropology from a Pragmatic Point of View,* in which he sees "the birth of a '*homo criticus,*' whose structure would be essentially different to the man who preceded him" (Macey 1994, 89). In other words, Kant's thought marks an epochal shift in how humanity must be understood. Foucault also specifically identifies Kant as his own intellectual predecessor. Writing under a pseudonym, he says of his own contentious relation to philosophy that

> if Foucault is indeed perfectly at home in the philosophical tradition, it is within the *critical* tradition of Kant, and his undertaking could be called *A Critical History of Thought.* . . . If by thought is meant the act that posits a subject and an object in their various possible relations, a critical history of thought would be an analysis of the conditions under which certain relations between subject and object are formed or modified, to the extent that these relations are constitutive of a possible knowledge. . . . It is not a matter, either, of determining the empirical conditions that at

> a given moment might have permitted the subject in general to become conscious of an object already given in reality. (Foucault, "MF" 314–15)

Foucault follows Kant in rejecting the view of knowledge as simply discovering "an object already given in reality," that is, R1 Independent reality. For the critical tradition that Kant founded and within which Foucault includes himself, the fundamental project of philosophy is to discern the conditions for the possibility of encountering a specific set of objects which cannot be settled by recourse to the objects themselves.

His very early works *Madness and Civilization* and *Mental Illness and Psychology* work within the Kantian Paradigm. The point of these books is to analyze "the constitution of the contemporary experience of madness" (Foucault, *MIP* 68). In line with Kantian anti-realism modified with historical A3 Pluralism, these books claim that the "progress" of scientific knowledge "is not the gradual discovery of the [R1] true nature of madness, but simply the sedimentation of [A1] what the history of the West has made of it for [A3] the last three hundred years. Madness is much more *historical* than is usually believed, and much *younger* too" (69, bracketed comments added). Here we have Foucault's early rejection of the traditional realist conjunction of the R5 Passive Knower perceiving R1 Independent reality in favor of A5 Active Knower, specifically in the realm of psychiatry:

> If mania, if melancholia henceforth assumed the aspects our science knows them by, it is not because in the course of centuries we have learned to [R5] "open our eyes" to [R1] real symptoms; it is not because we have [R5] purified our perception to the point of transparency; it is because in the experience of madness these concepts were [A5] organized around certain [A1] qualitative themes that lent them their unity, gave them their significant coherence, made them finally perceptible. . . . It was the rigor of these themes in their cosmic form—not the approximations of an [R5] observing caution—which [A5] organized the [A1] experience (already almost our own experience) of mania and melancholia.[4]

Like Hegel and Nietzsche, Foucault considers the organizing forms of the experience of madness to be historical, but it is still the subject's contribution which makes madness into the modern concept of mental illness. As the concepts change from medieval tolerant superstition to modern judgmental psychiatry, so the (A1) object perceived alters from village idiot to clinically insane individual. By transferring this entity into a new category, science effects the "confiscation [of madness] in our period in the concept of 'illness'" (Foucault, *MIP* 65). The person used to be subsumed under the category of madness, but is now constituted by the newly formed concept of mental illness and so has been transformed from fool to patient.

Foucault ridicules realist accounts of psychiatry that tell a narrative of the progressive comprehension of an R1 object persisting underneath the various conceptions: "All histories of psychiatry up to the present day have set out to show that the madman of the Middle Ages and the Renaissance was simply an unrecognized mentally ill patient" (Foucault, *MIP* 64). Psychiatry cannot be explained by its object, since it A5 *constitutes* this A1 object.

> If one is to avoid resorting to . . . mythical explanations . . . one must not regard these various aspects of mental illness as [R1] ontological forms. If fact, it is only in history that one can discover the sole concrete a priori from which [A1] mental illness draws, with the empty opening up of its possibility, its necessary figures. (Foucault, *MIP* 84–85, bracketed comments added)

Renaissance madness was not *really* mental illness unrecognized by a barbarous and superstitious people; rather, the contemporary constitution of mental illness "creates" insanity. It is a profound mistake to smugly view modernity as "that happy age when madness was finally recognized and treated according to a truth to which we had too long remained blind" (Foucault, *MC* 241). Mental illness wasn't already there awaiting discovery, but rather was constituted by our culture, and we shouldn't retrospectively project our reality back into the past: "Mental illness has its reality and its value qua illness only within a culture that recognizes it as such" (Foucault, *MIP* 60; see also 84). Hence mental illness is A1 Dependent on certain A5 societal conditions. As Rudi Visker puts it in his excellent discussion of these early books, "The object which psychiatry believes it 'discovered' not only arose historically, but is also dependent on that discovery in a way which excludes a realist interpretation" (Visker 1995, 19).

Within the context of Foucault's oeuvre and the history of continental anti-realism as a whole that we have been tracing, what stands out in this early critique of psychology is the notion of "true" madness which gets distorted and falsified ("confiscated") in modern times as illness. The inappropriateness of scientific concepts

> rendered vain any attempt to treat the whole of madness, the *essence and nature of madness,* in terms of psychology. The very notion of "mental illness" is the expression of an attempt doomed from the outset. What is called "mental illness" is simply *alienated madness,* alienated in the psy-

> chology that it has itself made possible. One day an attempt must be made to study madness as an overall structure—madness freed and disalienated, restored in some sense to its original language. (Foucault, *MIP* 76, first italics added)

Foucault attributes the attempt to restore madness to its "original language" variously to Freud (Foucault, *MC* 198), certain mad artists and poets (Foucault, *MIP* 74–75), and himself (Foucault, *MC* ix). But the point is that he accepts this notion of an "essence and nature of madness" at all and considers the possibility of making contact with it in its "freed and disalienated" state to be coherent. While he warns us not to treat modern mental illness as an R1 "ontological form," this is precisely what the "essence and nature" of madness is. Like Nietzsche's views of the self on my reading, Foucault is not giving up the notion of true madness, but rather trying to correct our understanding of it. He ridicules the notion that the Renaissance madman was really the unrecognized modern mentally ill patient, but ends up simply reversing this idea, asserting that the modern schizophrenic is really the Renaissance madman forced into the ill-fitting straitjacket of mental illness.

Just as Heidegger worked through an early Kantianism in the tension between Dasein's ahistorical essence and complete historicity in *Being and Time,* so Foucault's earliest work enacts his own Oedipal struggle. Many commentators have noticed the Kantian flavor of these early works; Ian Hacking, for example, calls *Madness and Civilization* "an almost Kantian story in which our experience of the mad is a mere phenomenon conditioned by our thought and our history, but there is also a thing-in-itself which can be called madness and which is incorruptible" (Hoy 1986, 29; see also Visker 1995, 25; May 1993, 22). The constitution of "the contemporary experience of madness" (mental illness) is understood here as fitting a preexistent, independent entity (madness) into a specific set of forms, that is, as a content stuffed into a scheme. Foucault differs from Kant in positing a historical diversity of concepts (A3), as well as allowing for the possibility of reaching "noumenal" madness similar to that in Nietzsche's *The Birth of Tragedy,* but he maintains a commitment to R1 Independence. Mental illness may be a human construct but madness isn't, and we might get to know this true madness if we shut down (R5) our present scientific concepts to grasp it in some alternate, more direct fashion.

This vestige of realism forms the target of Derrida's critique: "In writing a history of madness, Foucault has attempted—and this is the greatest merit, but also the very infeasibility of his book—to write a history of madness *itself. Itself.* Of madness itself" (Derrida, *WD* 33). Foucault is buying into what Derrida calls "the metaphysics of presence" by assuming that there is a "unity of an original presence" (40) to madness, that is, a realist essence which subsequently gets covered over or distorted by psychiatry's inappropriate forms. The weakness of this analysis lies in its faith in madness-in-itself and the possibility of access to it: "Everything transpires as if Foucault *knew* what 'madness' means" (41) and considered it "necessary to exhume the virgin and unitary ground" (39).

## No Remainder: The Birth of A1 Dependence in Archaeology

Although stung by Derrida's criticism (Foucault sat silently in the audience while Derrida read the paper quoted above), Foucault came to agree that his earliest books did indeed contain an unacceptable realism. The rest of his work accepts the Heideggerian Paradigm's completion of A1 Dependence in Historical Phenomenological Ontology. Foucault violently rejects a great deal of phenomenology—primarily Husserl's emphasis on an R6 foundational, A5 transcendental subject—but he accepts Heidegger's interpretation of its ontology in which nothing outside of historically fluctuating constitutions can be considered real.[5] Once this position which I am calling HPO has been adopted, concepts like confiscation or distortion cannot even get off the ground because there is nothing independent of these forces for them to distort. His next book, *The Birth of the Clinic,* shows the completion of A1, though it still seems to subscribe to some form of A5 Active Knower by placing the organization of experience within the subject.

Foucault describes *The Birth of the Clinic*—the first work of what he calls his archaeological phase—as a history of "medical perception," and its fundamental target is traditional epistemology's pairing of R5 Passive Knower with R1 Independent objects. We have seen other philosophers tackle this issue, but Foucault's twist is that instead of examining these epistemological assumptions in Plato or Descartes or some other foil from the history of philosophy,[6] he shows these ostensibly esoteric views at work in the way people actually carry out an empirical science—in this case, medicine. Foucault's work represents the most rigorous application of the Empirical Directive in the canon.

Medicine describes its own past the way sciences generally do—as a process of progressive rationality and increasingly faithful attention paid to what is simply in front of the doctor or scientist's eyes, a process which is enabled by enlightened practitioners stripping away the interference of superstitious nonsense.

> Medicine had tended, since the eighteenth century, to recount its own history as if the patient's bedside had always been a place of [R3] constant, stable experience, in contrast to theories and systems, which had been in [A3] perpetual change and [A5] masked beneath their speculation the [R1] purity of clinical evidence. The theoretical, it was thought, was the element of [A3] perpetual change, the starting point of all the historical variations in medical knowledge. . . . At the dawn of mankind, prior to every vain belief, every system, medicine in its entirety consisted of an [R5] immediate relationship between sickness and that which alleviated it. (Foucault, *BC* 54–55, bracketed comments added)

Beneath the accidental historical fluctuations of theories lay illness-in-itself waiting to be discovered by the unprejudiced eye of the clinical gaze. This is just how Hegel describes realist Consciousness' R5 conception of knowing an R1 object: "It has only to *take* it, to confine itself to a pure apprehension of it, and what is thus yielded is the True. If consciousness itself did anything in taking what is given, it would by such adding or subtraction alter the truth" (Hegel, *PS* 70, §116). Truth requires that Consciousness efface itself; it must put aside all beliefs and assumptions, all "theories and systems," in order just to see what is there: "Our approach to the object must also be *immediate* or *receptive;* we must alter nothing in the object as it presents itself" (58, §90). Foucault demonstrates through meticulous historical documentation that practicing physicians were informed by this framework, conceiving of their enlightened gaze as this ideal passive knower: "a pure gaze, prior to all intervention and faithful to the immediate, which it took up without modifying it. . . . The observing gaze refrains from intervening: it is silent and gestureless. Observation leaves things as they are" (Foucault, *BC* 107; see also 121).

Although medicine wants us to believe that its progress has come from the R5 elimination of all concepts—"it is often thought that the clinic originated in that free garden where, by common consent, doctor and patient met, where observation took place, innocent of theories, by the unaided brightness of the gaze" (Foucault, *BC* 52)—what has happened is actually a rearrangement of concepts. Instead of finally seeing what has been there all along (R1) by putting aside all concepts (R5), the doctor is seeing new things (A3) constituted by a new set of concepts (A5). Fundamentally, *The Birth of the Clinic* is a historical Copernican Revolution applied to medicine in keeping with ED.

> The clinic—constantly praised for its [R5] empiricism, the modesty of its attention, and the care with which it silently lets things surface to the observing gaze without disturbing them with discourse—owes its real

> importance to the fact that it is a [A3] reorganization in depth, not only of medical discourse, but of the very possibility of a discourse about disease. The [R5] *restraint* of clinical discourse (its rejection of theory, its abandonment of systems, its lack of a philosophy; all so proudly proclaimed by doctors) reflects the non-verbal conditions on the basis of which it can speak: the common structure that [A5] carves up and articulates what is seen and what is said. (Foucault, *BC* xix, bracketed comments added; see also xiv)

Theories seem dispensable and the apprehension of things appears immediate because the conceptual scheme organizing perception and conception—"the silent configuration in which language finds support" (Foucault, *BC* xi)—is buried so deeply within us and operates so quietly. Just as the wearer of Kant's pink sunglasses believes that everything is pink, so Foucault's physician assumes that things really are as he finds them.

> Behind all this, one supposes that the subject and object of knowledge [R3] remained what they were: their greater proximity and better adjustment simply made it possible for the [R1] object to reveal its own secrets with greater clarity or detail and for the subject to [R5] dispense with illusions that were an obstacle to truth. . . . But this is surely a project on history, an old theory of knowledge [realist epistemology] whose effects and misdeeds have long been known. A more precise historical analysis reveals a quite different principle of adjustment beyond these adjustments: it bears jointly on the type of objects to be known, on the [A5] grid that makes it appear, isolates it, and carves up the elements relevant to a possible epistemic knowledge. . . . What is [A3] modified in giving place to anatomo-clinical medicine is not, therefore, the mere surface of contact between the knowing subject and the known object; it is the more general arrangement of knowledge that determines the reciprocal positions and the connexion between the one who must know and that which is to be known. (Foucault, *BC* 137, bracketed comments added; see also 57; Foucault, *EW* 2:312)

The optical illusion of the conceptual scheme—its transparency—reinforces the commonsense notion that the world comes prepackaged in the groupings we find (R1), which must have always been that way (R3). Realism is hard to shake.

Foucault uses the diversity of epochal perceptions to loosen our realist intuitions.

> At the beginning of the nineteenth century, doctors described what for centuries had remained below the threshold of the visible and the

> expressible, but this did not mean that, after over-indulging in speculation, they had begun to [R5] perceive once again, or that they listened to reason rather than to imagination; it meant that the relation between the visible and invisible—which is necessary to all concrete knowledge—[A3] changed its structure, [A5] revealing through gaze and language what had previously been below and beyond their domain. A new alliance was forged between words and things, enabling one *to see* and *to say*. (Foucault, *BC* xii, bracketed comments added; see also 51, 195–96)

The exposure of historical A3 Ontological Pluralism—the variety of different ways of experiencing disease—indicates that disease isn't an R1 Independent object simply awaiting discovery. Instead, as Hegel said, "as the knowledge changes, so too does the object" (Hegel, *PS* 54, §85), or in Heidegger's words, "what is 'natural' is *not* 'natural' at all, here meaning self-evident for any given ever-existing man. The 'natural' is always historical" (Heidegger, *WT* 39). Here is Foucault's version of this claim:

> It would be untrue, no doubt, to see in late eighteenth-century clinical medicine a mere return to the [R5] purity of a gaze long burdened with false knowledge. . . . [A3] New objects were to present themselves to the medical gaze in the sense that, and at the same time as, the [A6] knowing subject reorganizes himself, changes himself, and begins to function in a new way. It was not, therefore, the conception of disease that changed first and later the way it was recognized [not A3 + R5] . . . but together, and at a deeper level, the relation between the disease and this gaze to which it offers itself and which at the same time it constitutes [(A1 + A3 + A5)].[7]

The subject changes, thus constituting the object disease differently (A6, A5, A3) rather than finally discovering the truth that was always there (R1, R5). Instead of the narrative that portrays knowledge as smoothly approaching reality, Foucault describes "periods that mark an ineradicable chronological threshold [where] . . . it is the forms of visibility that have changed" (Foucault, *BC* 195). These thresholds are the points at which the constituting concepts change and with them the reality that is to be known. The A3 fact that "there have been, and will be, other distributions of illness" (3) is explained by the fact that "a new type of experience was created" (28; see also 137), that is, by a historically changing (A6) Active Knower (A5). These breaks undermine the notion of a smooth progression of knowledge.

Although it retains the Kantian Paradigm's A5, *The Birth of the Clinic* rejects its vestige of R1 Independence. Foucault's earliest works had posited something like a madness in itself, which gets distorted by modern concepts of mental illness but could be reached in its purity by psychoanalysis or art; but he now fully dispenses with anything outside of historical experience. He discusses realist analyses that presuppose R1 in the book's preface, calling them "commentary."

> To comment is to admit by definition an excess of the signified over the signifier; a necessary, unformulated remainder of thought that language has left in the shade—a remainder that is the very essence of that thought, driven outside its secret—but to comment also presupposes that this unspoken element slumbers within speech, and that, by a superabundance proper to the signifier, one may, in questioning it, give voice to a content that was not explicitly signified. . . . Signifier and signified thus assume a substantial autonomy that accords the treasure of a virtual signification to each of them separately; one may even exist without the other. (Foucault, *BC* xvi)

In other words, the signified is that which is spoken about but which maintains an autonomous existence, independent of thought or speech. It would be madness in itself which could be recovered and given a voice on Freud's couch or Artaud's stage, or Davidson's much-maligned content and scheme that can "even exist without the other."

Now, however, Foucault wants "to make a structural analysis of discourses that would evade the fate of commentary by supposing no remainder, nothing in excess of what has been said, but only the fact of its historical appearance" (Foucault, *BC* xvii). Like all of the post-Kantian philosophers we have examined but only completed by Heidegger, he is rejecting the noumenal. From this point on in Foucault's work, only that which occurs within the historical purview of experience will be admitted as real. The transition from the Kantian Paradigm to the Heideggerian has begun.

## Archaeological Historical Ontology

The apex of his archaeological phase in *The Order of Things* and *The Archaeology of Knowledge* marks Foucault's full conversion to the Heideggerian Paradigm. It is here that he passionately pursues A1 Dependence to its limits and Unmoors the epochal conceptual schemes from the subject so as to cast them adrift, that is, exchanging *The Birth of the Clinic*'s vestigial A5 Active Knower for Impersonal Conceptual Scheme. I will discuss A1 in this section and the latter change in the next section.

Although *The Birth of the Clinic* rejected R1 realism under the name of commentary, the focus of that book is on exploding the medical gaze's myth of R5 Passive Knower. In *The Order of Things* and *The Archaeology of Knowledge*, on the other hand, the full implications of the completion of A1 in Historical Phenomenological Ontology—the idea that "one does not subject the multiplicity of statements to the coherence of concepts, and this coherence to the silent recollection of a meta-historical identity" (Foucault, *AK* 62)—take center stage.

In *The Archaeology of Knowledge*—Foucault's analysis of the method of this first phase—he basically concedes Derrida's criticism (without mentioning Derrida by name, though) of the realism in *Madness and Civilization* in using madness as the example to unpack his new commitment to what I'm calling HPO. He selects as targets of his critique phrases strongly reminiscent of his own earlier analysis; for instance: "It would certainly be a mistake to try to discover what could have been said of madness at a particular time by interrogating the being of madness itself, its secret content, its silent, self-enclosed truth" (Foucault, *AK* 32). In a discussion "written against an explicit theme of my book *Madness and Civilization*," he claims that

> there can be no question of interpreting discourse with a view to writing a history of the referent. . . . We are not trying to reconstitute what [R1] madness itself might be, in the form in which it first presented itself to some [R5] primitive, fundamental, deaf, scarcely articulated experience, and in the form in which it was later [A5] organized (translated, deformed, travestied, perhaps even repressed) by discourses. . . . What, in short, we wish to do is to dispense with [R1] "things.". . . To substitute for the enigmatic treasure of 'things' anterior to discourse, the regular formation of objects that emerge only in discourse. (Foucault, *AK* 47, bracketed comments added; see also Foucault, *EW* 2:312, 2:330)

This is very nicely put. Foucault is dispensing with things "anterior to" or independent of discourse by telling a history of the referent as the product (A1) of discourse rather than of its discovery. Madness is not a self-identical thing which can get alienated, confiscated, repressed, or restored to its original language. All of this is conceptually ruled out by archaeology's commitment to HPO.

In an interview, he admits that the notion of repression that he had earlier used requires an independent object whose inherent nature gets repressed or distorted. Just as Heidegger pointed out that the grammar of Nietzsche's accusations of error presupposes the idea of truth, so Foucault now realizes that repression or confiscation is an

> insidious [notion], or at all events I myself have had much more trouble in freeing myself of it. . . . When I wrote *Madness and Civilisation,* I made at least an implicit use of this notion of repression. I think indeed that I was positing the existence of a sort of living, voluble and anxious madness which the mechanisms of power and psychiatry were supposed to have come to repress and reduce to silence. But it seems to me now that the notion of repression is quite inadequate for capturing what is precisely the productive aspect of power.[8]

This earlier commitment to R1 Independence consisted in "the idea that underneath power with its acts of violence and its artifice we should be able to recuperate things themselves in their primitive vivacity" (Foucault, *FL* 221), that is, let disalienated madness speak for itself. Since he rejects the realist ontology which makes the notion of repression coherent, many caricatures of Foucault can be dispelled, as we will see.

Foucault's archaeology deals with the historical constitution of objects; this cannot be considered an alienating or falsifying form thrown over a preexistent entity, but is what we might call the "deep constitution" of the thing as something that can be encountered and studied at all.

> It is not enough for us to [R5] open our eyes, to pay attention, or to be aware, for new objects suddenly to light up and emerge out of the ground. . . . The [R1] object does not await in limbo the order that will free it and enable it to become embodied in a visible and prolix objectivity; it does not pre-exist itself, held back by some obstacle at the first edges of light. [A1] It exists under the positive conditions of a complex group of relations. (Foucault, *AK* 45, bracketed comments added; see also 72)

Like Hegel's Objective Idealism, Foucault has gotten rid of Davidson's form-content dyad, that is, the Kantian notion of a noumenal entity caught in the net of a conceptual scheme. The constitution of objects is not the projection of a form onto an independent but inaccessible object = x. Rather, in line with the Heideggerian Paradigm's HPO, the constitution of entities is so complete that it makes no sense to talk about the objects outside their epoch. Thus Foucault considers it his "essential task . . . to free the history of thought from its subjection to transcendence" (Foucault, *AK* 203; see also 229; Foucault, *FR* 93).

Once we combine A1 Dependence—the rejection of any form of a noumenal remainder—with the view that there are a multiplicity of conceptual schemes (A3) tied to historical periods and that they organize reality (A5 or ICS), we get Heidegger's Historical Phenomenological Ontology, which Foucault sometimes calls Historical Ontology (see Foucault,

*FR* 46, 351). This view is incompatible with seeing the history of science as the progressive uncovering of a permanent object, but must take each actual occurrence and knowledge on its own terms: "In a word, knowledge is not science in the successive displacement of its internal structures; it is the field of its actual history" (Foucault, *EW* 2:326). This view permeates his extremely detailed examination of the changing sciences of (loosely) economics, linguistics, and biology in western Europe throughout the last few centuries in *The Order of Things.* In keeping with his take on the Empirical Directive begun in *The Birth of the Clinic,* Foucault looks for the organizing concepts in the sciences of the day rather than in a transcendental subjectivity or in philosophy.

Carrying the Empirical Directive this far shows Foucault's disagreement with Heidegger (and Nietzsche) about the proper place to look for evidence of historical conceptual schemes. Whereas they consider the famous texts of great philosophers to be the best expressions of epochal schemes,[9] Foucault studies obscure, mundane documents, "the closed and dusty volume that opens with a flight of forgotten words . . . the amassing of minute facts, monuments reduced to infinitesimal fragments" (Foucault, *LCP* 90–91), "texts that have never been read, books which, no sooner printed, were closed and then slept on the shelves and were only taken down centuries later" (Foucault, *SMD* 4). In a method that has influenced the way the discipline of history is practiced, he claims that "it is in directing the resolving power of historical analysis onto official price-lists, title deeds, parish registers, to harbour archives analysed year by year and week by week, that we gradually perceive—beyond battles, decisions, dynasties and assemblies—the emergence of those massive phenomena of secular or multi-secular importance" (Foucault, *AK* 230; see also Foucault, *FR* 76–77; Foucault, *FL* 149). Foucault pieces together something like Heidegger's epochal understandings of Being from examining marginal forgotten texts like prison timetables, handwriting manuals, and contemporary scientific works instead of the great philosophical books of the canon. After giving a detailed account of a period's knowledge, he declares, "Only those who cannot read will be surprised that I have learned such a thing more clearly from Cuvier, Bopp, and Ricardo than from Kant or Hegel" (Foucault, *OT* 307).

Regardless of where he finds his information, HPO is one of the two fundamental doctrines organizing *The Order of Things.* This book traces the changes that took place over the course of several centuries in the study of the subject matters roughly circumscribed as money, language, and life, as well as the relationship of the study of man to these endeavors. The analysis rejects realism from the start, never entertaining the possibility that these bodies of knowledge could simply be matters of just recording an independent reality already divided up into these groups. "It is simply forgotten that man and life and nature are none of them domains that present themselves to the curiosity of knowledge spontaneously and passively" (Foucault, *OT* 72). It is forgotten because their inconspicuous constitution hides itself, so that the entities we encounter appear as if they were always this way by their own nature, requiring of us mere acknowledgment or passive reception (see 132, 220, 252). Foucault consistently rejects the realist strategy of writing a history in terms of what he calls transcendentals or objects transcendent to human discourse and awareness, which would follow the method of "starting with things and saying: the animals being what they are, the plants being such as we see them, how is it that the people of the seventeenth and eighteenth centuries saw them and described them" (Foucault, *FL* 61).

Following the anti-realism initiated by Kant, Foucault believes that what appear to be simple passive processes of perception and knowledge actually involve complicated acts of organization and constitution by something like a conceptual scheme; in his archaeological phase he calls this scheme an *episteme.* To the question, why do people find the world the way they do at various times, why do they group things in those specific relations of similarity and difference, the answer is their *episteme.* This scheme, "as is immediately apparent, is neither determined by an *a priori* and necessary concatenation, nor imposed on us by immediately perceptible contents" (Foucault, *OT* xix). Here he rules out two possible interpretations of the *episteme:* the latter option is the direct imposition of knowledge on us by R5 immediate perception, that is, simple realism. The former "*a priori* and necessary concatenation" would be Kant's R3 Unique scheme residing in the R6 Realist Self. Foucault chooses the Heideggerian Paradigm's third option of the *episteme* which he unpacks as the "historical *a priori*" (xxii). It sets up a particular epistemological space within which certain kinds of things can appear which can then be known in certain ways, thereby forming the condition for the possibility of science. In this way it is "prior" to empirical experience and knowledge of specific entities but, contra Kant, it changes in history. This notion is rather similar to the "*contextually a priori*" that Putnam derives from Quine's "Two Dogmas" paper (Putnam 1983, 95; see also Norris 1997, 162), as well as what Wittgenstein calls "the river-bed of thoughts" which guides our more superficial, empirical beliefs but which can shift over time (Wittgenstein, *OC* §96–97; see also §336).

The narrative of *The Order of Things* describes the "great discontinuities in the *episteme* of Western culture" (Foucault, *OT* xxii; see also 22, 119) which occur when these foundational concepts undergo a transformation. It portrays "these mutations that suddenly decide that things are no longer perceived, describe[d], expressed, characterized, classified, and known in the same way, and that it is no longer wealth, living beings, and discourse that are presented to knowledge in the interstices of words or through their transparency, but beings radically different from them" (217). Since it is the *episteme*'s concepts that constitute the beings that are known and the legitimate modes of knowledge (A5), epistemic changes (A3) are like the shifting of tectonic plates that alter all of the empirical sciences based on them (though Foucault eschews the connotations of depth of the term "archaeology," tracing it to "archive" rather than to the practice of digging up old civilizations; see Foucault, *FL* 57–58, 65; but also Foucault, *OT* xxiv). Archaeology is fundamentally different from traditional ways of doing history: "The problem is no longer one of tradition, of tracing a line, but one of division, of limits; it is no longer one of lasting foundations, but one of transformations that serve as new foundations" (Foucault, *AK* 5). Neither realism nor Kantian anti-realism could explain the radical, incommensurable shifts of what appeared to the passive or the never-changing active perception of people at different times. Rather than self-identifying objects, Foucault claims that only on the table or "grid of identities, similitudes, analogies have we become accustomed to sort out so many different and similar things" (Foucault, *OT* xix; see also xxiv), and it is changes on this level that account for the history of the sciences.[10] Goodman posits a similar idea called version, scheme, or system which lets us "decide whether things are alike . . . a network of labels that organizes, sorts, or classifies items in terms of the types of diversity to be recognized" (Goodman and Elgin 1988, 8; see also Goodman 1978, 8, 13).

Foucault had already hit on the notion of the organization (A5) of madness (A1) by historically changing forms (A3) in his earliest works, leading him to such conclusions as that "the contemporary world makes schizophrenia possible" (Foucault, *MIP* 84). At that point, this represented a "confiscation," since real madness (R1) got distorted by the inappropriate modern concept of mental illness. Now he has fully converted to the Heideggerian Paradigm's Historical Phenomenological Ontology, with "no remainder" outside the epochal or *epistemic* constitution of entities. The *episteme* is Foucault's version of Heidegger's epochal understanding of Being as "the application of a determination of the thing, which is not experientially derived from the thing and yet lies at the base of every determination of the things, making them possible" (Heidegger, *BW* 289; see also Heidegger, *P* 150). In Foucault's words,

> This *a priori* is what, in a given period, delimits in the totality of experience a field of knowledge, defines the mode of being of the objects that appear in that field, provides man's everyday perception with theoretical

> powers, and defines the conditions in which he can sustain a discourse about things that is recognized to be true. (Foucault, *OT* 158)

Since these conceptual schemes change (A3) and so constitute beings differently, and since he has rejected R1, leaving nothing to reality except these variously constituted beings, Foucault is committed to the claim that reality itself changes. He must extend Kant's "highest principle of all synthetic judgments . . . that the conditions of the *possibility of experience* in general are likewise conditions of the *possibility of the objects of experience*" (Kant, *C1* A158/B197) to exclude noumena and therefore any contrast to the qualification "of experience," as Hegel does (see chapter 3). And indeed, we find throughout *The Order of Things* claims that the way things are changes along with the way they are known at these times of *epistemic* transition.

> The entire *episteme* of Western culture found its fundamental arrangements modified. . . . What we must grasp and attempt to reconstitute are the modifications that affected knowledge itself, at that archaic level which makes possible both knowledge itself and the mode of being of what is to be known. (Foucault, *OT* 54)

An *episteme* "defines, then, the general law of beings, and at the same time the conditions under which it is possible to know them,"[11] that is, the simultaneous constitution of knowledge and reality, since these cannot be pried apart without positing a reality independent of our knowledge. This position is entailed by the logic of the Heideggerian Paradigm. If a conceptual scheme constitutes entities roughly the way Kant's concepts and forms of intuition constituted phenomena, but without anything existing besides these constituted entities, then (PO) beings really are whatever the schemes make them. Knowledge and being are one, as Parmenides said so long ago; or logic is metaphysics, as Hegel says; or the equipment is ready-to-hand *in-itself,* as Heidegger writes. Once you add in the fact that these schemes change in history (A3), then the claim that reality itself changes necessarily follows.

And this is exactly what Foucault says: man, life, and nature "constituted an area of empiricity in the Classical age that had not existed until the end of the Renaissance and that was destined to disappear early in the nineteenth century" (Foucault, *OT* 72). The doctrine of HPO is what allows *The Order of Things* to make the shocking claims it is famous for, such as:

> Before the end of the eighteenth century, *man* did not exist—any more than the potency of life, the fecundity of labour, or the historical density

> of language. He is a quite recent creature, which the demiurge of knowledge fabricated with its own hands less than two hundred years ago: but he has grown old so quickly that it has been only too easy to imagine that he had been waiting for thousands of years in the darkness for that moment of illumination in which he would finally be known. (Foucault, *OT* 308; see also 128; Foucault, *FL* 15–16)

Each of these—man, life, labor, and language—is being used here as a technical term for a specific "epochal" incarnation of what we usually think of as a constant stable item. Foucault is claiming that they fundamentally change with each new *episteme,* so much so that we cannot even speak of the same thing persisting across *epistemic* shifts (see Sosa's discussion of Putnam's internal realism in Van Inwagen and Zimmerman 1998, 409). The objects revealed by our present *episteme* seem R3 Unique and R1 Independent but, like early Heidegger's present-at-hand object, this very appearance of independence depends on an *episteme:* "*It is only in the blank space of this grid* that order manifests itself in depth *as though already there,* waiting in silence for the moment of its expression" (Foucault, *OT* xx, italics added; see also 322; Veyne in A. I. Davidson 1997, 160).

Archaeology attempts to dispel this realist illusion.

> Knowledge in its positivity [A3] changes its nature and its form. It would be false—and above all inadequate—to attribute this mutation to the discovery of [R1] hitherto unknown objects. . . . What changed at the turn of the century, and underwent an irremediable modification, was knowledge itself as an anterior and indivisible mode of being [ICS] between the knowing subject and the object of knowledge. . . . Production, life, language—we must not seek to construe these as [R1] objects that [R5] imposed themselves from the outside, as though by their own weight and as a result of some autonomous pressure, upon a body of learning that had ignored them for too long. . . . They are the fundamental modes of knowledge which sustain in their flawless unity the secondary and derived correlation of new sciences and techniques with [A3] unprecedented objects.[12]

Newly discovered entities do not lie dormant outside experience awaiting scientific perception, but actually are "unprecedented objects" constituted by a new *episteme.* They do not exist independently of our investigations, and the history of these sciences should not describe an ever-increasing approach to these silently waiting entities. Instead, archaeology asks "in what new space, and in accordance with what forms, have words, beings, and objects of need taken their places and arranged themselves in relation to one another? What new mode of being must they have received in order to make all these changes possible?" (Foucault, *OT* 220). The fact that he frequently speaks of a new mode of being (see 264, 281) rather than just a new way of thinking about beings shows Foucault's commitment to the Heideggerian Paradigm's HPO.

## Archaeological A6 and ICS: The Death of Man and the Birth of Language

Along with the plurality of the conceptual schemes (A3) common to all of the post-Kantians we have examined, Foucault's archaeological works specifically side with the Heideggerian against the Kantian Paradigm by Unmooring the *epistemes* from the subject. He subscribes to the doctrine of Impersonal Conceptual Schemes by making the *epistemes* independent from the subject. Rather than the transcendental unconstituted source of the constitutive concepts, the archaeological subject is completely dissolved into history and constituted by the various *epistemes* like everything else (A6). Like the later Heidegger, Foucault views A5 Active Knower as a serious mistake, the curse Kant left to the history of philosophy along with his gift of the conceptual scheme.

Foucault defines archaeology's central task as trying to solve

> the crisis in which we have been involved for so long, and which is constantly growing more serious: a crisis that concerns that transcendental reflexion with which philosophy since Kant has identified itself . . . which concerns an anthropological thought that orders all these questions around the question of man's being, and allows us to avoid an analysis of practice; . . . which, above all, concerns the status of the subject. (Foucault, *AK* 204)

Kant's " anthropological" emphasis on the R6 Realist A5 Active Knower as the unchanging source of the single conceptual scheme prevents philosophy from focusing on what we should be studying, the empirical "analysis of practice." Foucault's term for the Kantian Paradigm's Active Knower is "man" and its unfortunate focus is "anthropology," presumably because of Kant's *Anthropology from a Pragmatic Point of View.*

> Anthropology constitutes perhaps the fundamental arrangement that has governed and controlled the path of philosophical thought from Kant until our own day. This arrangement is essential, since it forms part

> of our history; but it is disintegrating before our eyes, since we are beginning to recognize and denounce in it, in a critical mode, both a forgetfulness of the opening that made it possible and a stubborn obstacle standing obstinately in the way of an imminent new form of thought. (Foucault, *OT* 342)

I read "the opening that made it possible" as the rejection of realism in favor of the conceptual schemes embraced by both Foucault and Heidegger, and the "stubborn obstacle" as the insistence on the R3 Uniqueness of the scheme and its placement in the A5 Active Knower. Foucault reaches the strong conclusion that

> we know, in any case, that all efforts to think afresh are in fact directed at that obstacle. . . . It is no longer possible to think in our day other than in the void left by man's disappearance. For this void . . . is nothing more, and nothing less, than the unfolding of a space in which it is once more possible to think. (Foucault, *OT* 342)

The space left when the Kantian Paradigm, organized around an A5 R6 subject, recedes, this space where "it is once more possible to think," is the Heideggerian Paradigm.

Foucault is vehement in his dismissal of the transcendental subject. After endorsing a variety of methods for the analysis of discourse, he goes on to claim indignantly that

> if there is one approach that I do reject, however, it is that (one might call it, broadly speaking, the phenomenological approach) which gives absolute priority to the observing subject, which attributes a constituent role to an act, which places its own point of view at the origin of all historicity—which, in short, leads to a transcendental consciousness. (Foucault, *OT* xiv)

Playing on Kant's famous line about Hume, Foucault calls this A5 approach the "anthropological sleep" (Foucault, *OT* 342; see also Dreyfus and Rabinow 1983, 91), whereas his own "aim is to define a method of historical analysis freed from the anthropological theme" (Foucault, AK 16; see also 7, 15). He does not mince words about how central this issue is to his thought: "The essential task was to free the history of thought from its subjection to transcendence. . . . My aim was to analyse this history, in the discontinuity that no teleology would reduce in advance; to map it in a dispersion that no pre-established horizon would embrace; to allow it to be deployed in an anonymity on which no transcendental constitution would impose the form of the subject" (203). This "subjection to transcendence" he seeks to escape has two possible forms: realist transcendent objects stabilizing knowledge (Plato's inherent joints in nature), and anti-realist transcendental subjectivity anchoring conceptual schemes (Kant's Copernican Revolution). We saw Foucault "dispense with things" or complete A1 in the preceding section of this chapter; here we will examine his fulfillment of A6 and ICS to discard the A5 transcendental subject.

Foucault is perhaps most famous for announcing the death of man. Once we recognize "man" as a technical term, this proclamation amounts to the claim that the active knower of the Kantian paradigm who remains the same (R6) in order to organize experience with universality and necessity "is an invention of recent date. And one perhaps nearing its end" (Foucault, *OT* 387). In an early interview, he explains his statement as

> the death of the subject, of the Subject in capital letters, of the subject as origin and foundation of Knowledge, of Freedom, of Language and History. One can say that all of Western civilization has been subjugated, and philosophers have only certified the fact by referring all thought and all truth to consciousness, to the Self, to the Subject. In the rumbling that shakes us today, perhaps we have to recognize the birth of a world where the subject is not one but split, not sovereign but dependent, not an absolute origin but a function ceaselessly modified. (Foucault, *FL* 67)

Foucault passionately pursues A6—the full immersion of subjectivity into history and its multiplication there. Applying HPO to the subject, he dissolves it into the various forms it has had in different eras with "no remainder." This is the consistent application of Hegel's claim that "in this movement the passive Subject itself perishes; it enters into the differences and the content" (Hegel, *PS* 37, §60), but with no final gathering.

Foucault follows the later Heidegger's inclusion of humanity along with everything else in the pervasive historical flux. *The Order of Things* can be read as, among other things, a detailed demonstration of Heidegger's claim that the "subject-object relation, which [the scientist] took to be most general, is apparently only an historical variation of the relation of man to the thing" (Heidegger, *DT* 78). As Foucault writes,

> Strangely enough, man—the study of whom is supposed by the naïve to be the oldest investigation since Socrates—is probably no more than a kind of rift in the order of things, or, in any case, a configuration whose outlines are determined by the new position he has so recently taken up in the field of knowledge. . . . Man is only a recent invention, a figure not yet two centuries old, a new wrinkle in our knowledge, and . . . he will

> disappear again as soon as that knowledge has discovered a new form. (Foucault, *OT* xxiii)

Rather than sifting through the epochs for a single identity or fitting them together into a Hegelian journey toward the discovery of true subjectivity, Foucault sees history as disrupting any formation of identity. Since he subscribes to HPO, and since he shows that the self changes along with everything else at those points of epochal changeover when "everything that had been presented to view, now takes on a new mode of being" (Foucault, *OT* 264), he concludes that subjectivity itself changes. This is why "before the end of the eighteenth century, *man* did not exist" (308).

Examining archaeology's patient reconstructions of the various *epistemic* humanities has a specific effect on one who accepts HPO. Archaeology does not

> enable us to draw up a table of our distinctive features. . . . It deprives us of our continuities; it dissipates that temporal identity in which we are pleased to look at ourselves when we wish to exorcise the discontinuities of history . . . and where anthropological thought once questioned man's being or subjectivity, it now bursts open the other, and the outside. In this sense, the diagnosis does not establish the fact of our identity by the play of distinctions. It establishes that we are differences. (Foucault, *AK* 131; see also 156)

In my terms, discovering the diversity of understandings of human nature (A3) combined with the commitment to taking what shows itself as what is real (HPO) leads to treating human nature as itself plural and fully historical (A6).

Since the subject has changed fundamentally over the course of history—so deeply that Foucault limits the name "man" to a specific manifestation—we cannot ascribe a foundational or active role to this subject. It has itself been constituted by the various *episteme*'s, so it cannot have constituted them. Jitendra Mohanty describes this reversal of A5 Active Knower into A6 dependent, multiple selves well when he says that "subjectivity itself is constituted, so that it cannot be the source of constitution" (Caputo and Yount 1993, 36). At times, Foucault states this quite directly: "The subject is necessarily situated and dependent, and can never figure as titular (either as transcendental activity, or as empirical consciousness)" (Foucault, *AK* 183; see also Foucault, *FR* 118). Since he also rejects the realist option of things containing inherent natures in favor of the view that entities are organized by a ruling character at a particular time, Foucault makes the Heideggerian move: he shifts the locus of conceptual schemes from the subject to the *episteme,* his version of the epochal clearing or understanding of Being. The *episteme* of an age is the system of thought that brands certain ideas rational, scientific, or true while dismissing others as non-sense or irrelevant. It determines what things show up as and it "is, from beginning to end, historical."[13]

Foucault turns from R1 objects as the determinants of discourse or what can be truly or even sensibly said of them to *epistemes,* preferring "to define these *objects* without reference to the *ground,* the *foundation of things,* but by relating them to the body of rules that enable them to form as objects of a discourse and thus constitute the conditions of their historical appearance."[14] Here discourse constitutes the scientific objects that are studied and known, rather than independent things determining what can be known of them. He also eliminates the A5 transcendental subject as the source of the discursive scheme, since the subject too is constituted by a period's scheme.

> Discourse is not the majestically unfolding manifestation of a [A5] thinking, knowing, speaking subject, but, on the contrary, a totality, in which [A6] the dispersion of the subject and his discontinuity with himself may be determined. . . . I showed earlier that it was neither by "words" nor by [R1] "things" that the regulation of the objects proper to a discursive formation should be defined; similarly, it must now be recognized that it is neither by recourse to a [A5] transcendental subject nor by recourse to a psychological subjectivity that the regulation of its enunciations should be defined. (Foucault, *AK* 55, bracketed comments added; see also Foucault, *FL* 38; Foucault, *LCP* 39)

Both poles, object and subject, must be eliminated as sources that could transcend and found experience or discourse; they are effects rather than causes of the discourse. "The rules of formation operate not only in the mind or consciousness of individuals, but in discourse itself; they operate therefore, according to a sort of uniform anonymity, on all individuals."[15] This commitment to ICS is a constant theme in these books, though where I call the conceptual schemes "impersonal," Foucault's favorite word for them is "anonymous."[16] Archaeology rejects A5 for ICS, so that its project is "to explore scientific discourse not from the point of view of the individuals who are speaking . . . but from the point of view of the rules that come into play in the very existence of such discourse" (Foucault, *OT* xiv).

This is his version of Heidegger's "fundamental ontological inquiry which is reminiscent of Kant, and yet radically different at the same time" (Heidegger, *Zo* 194), since it retains conceptual schemes, but rendered impersonal and historically changing.[17] The death of man means the end of A5 Active Knower, a change Foucault attributes variously to Nietzsche, Sade, and the structuralists (see, for example, Foucault, *EW* 3:247–48, 3:251), but which I attribute to later Heidegger. Now discourse, roughly what is allowed as sensible in an age by its *episteme,* determines the status of all things, including the subject. Along with the *episteme,* this is the Impersonal Conceptual Scheme of the archaeological phase.

> This enunciative domain [that is, roughly discourse] refers neither to an individual subject, nor to some kind of collective consciousness, nor to a [A5] transcendental subjectivity; but . . . is described as an [ICS] anonymous field whose configuration [A6] defines the possible position of speaking subjects. Statements should no longer be situated in relation to a [A5] sovereign subjectivity, but recognize in the [A6] different forms of the speaking subjectivity effects proper to the enunciative field. . . . The analysis of statements operates therefore [ICS] without reference to a cogito. It does not pose the question of the [A5] speaking subject. . . . It is situated at the level of the "it is said." (Foucault, *AK* 122, bracketed comments added; see also 191–92; Foucault, *FL* 48)

Foucault sees a general epochal change from A5 to ICS occurring in his lifetime.[18]

The purpose of tracing the history of A5 man in *The Order of Things* is to speed his demise. Man rose to fill the space left by the end of classical representation—roughly the realist idea that the world sorts itself into neat piles (R3), spontaneously offering up a table of categories (R1) to merely observational knowledge (R5), where "from the very outset, this thought exists within an ontology rendered transparent by the fact that being is offered to representation without interruption" (Foucault, *OT* 206). This conceptual structure functioned perfectly well until an epochal shift introduced an enigmatic historical density into entities which clouded their spontaneous transparency and thus "toppled the whole of Western thought: representation has lost the power to provide a foundation—with its own being, its own deployment . . . for the links that can join its various elements together" (239). Things no longer simply presented themselves in a knowable form, but required something to organize them into this state. In my terms, the realist idea that knowledge is just passively reflecting the Way Things Are was no longer tenable. "The threshold between Classicism and modernity . . . had been definitively crossed when words ceased to intersect with representations and to provide a spontaneous grid for the knowledge of things. At the beginning of the nineteenth century, they rediscovered their ancient, enigmatic density."[19]

This is the great problem of knowledge bequeathed to the modern era by the breakdown of the classical explanation of knowledge: how can knowledge be founded now? Two solutions were simultaneously pursued even though they were incompatible, thus ensuring failure: "The coexistence of Ideology and critical philosophy at the end of the eighteenth century—of Destutt de Tracy and Kant—divides, into two forms of thought, exterior to one another, yet simultaneous, what scientific forms of reflection, on the other hand, hold together in a unity doomed to imminent dissociation" (Foucault, *OT* 240). The tale of modern epistemology as Foucault tells it is a tragic one.

The two strategies to reestablish knowledge that were pursued—the empirical human sciences and transcendental, critical philosophy—are strange mirror images of each other; they could neither absorb each other nor coexist peacefully:

> The new positivity of the sciences of life, language, and economics is in correspondence with the founding of a transcendental philosophy. . . . In their being, they are outside knowledge, but by that very fact they are conditions of knowledge; they correspond to Kant's discovery of a transcendental field and yet they differ from it in two essential points: they are situated with the object and, in a way, beyond it . . . moreover, they concern the domain of *a posteriori* truths and the principles of their synthesis—and not the *a priori* synthesis of all possible experience. (Foucault, *OT* 244)

Kant's critical philosophy attempted to replace realist classical representation with A5 transcendental subjectivity as the condition of the possibility of knowledge: the world doesn't spontaneously present itself in a knowable form, but gets organized into an adequate form by the subject. However, the Empirical Directive had taken effect by this point; the human sciences that study man as object rather than subject had achieved results that could not be ignored.

> In one sense, man is governed by labour, life, and language: his concrete existence finds its determinations in them; it is possible to have access to him only through his words, his organism, the objects he makes—as though it is they who possess the truth in the first place (and they alone perhaps); and he, as soon as he thinks, merely unveils himself to his own eyes in the form of a being who is already, in a necessarily subjacent density, in an irreducible anteriority, a living being, an instrument of production, a vehicle for words which exist before him. All these contents that his knowledge reveals to him as exterior to himself, and older than his own birth, anticipate him, overhang him with all their solidity,

> and traverse him as though he were merely an object of nature. (Foucault, *OT* 313)

The scientific knowledge of such empirical factors profoundly determining us compromises the autonomy and absolute integrity of thought that earlier philosophers had claimed: "The 'I think' has shown itself to be embedded in a density throughout which it is quasi-present, and which it animates, though in an equivocal semi-dormant, semi-wakeful fashion" (Foucault, *OT* 324; see also 331). Our thinking is so deeply influenced by our economic, biological, and linguistic conditions that it becomes difficult to see in what way it is truly ours. Kant's solution of splitting the ego into transcendentally determining and empirically determined aspects, the former of which is free of the influences that determine the latter, is not a workable compromise because it betrays science by having recourse to a "ghost in the machine."

Foucault traces the various futile attempts to reconcile the incompatible aspects of constitutor and constituted, determiner and determined, in man's "ambiguous position as an object of knowledge and as a subject that knows" (Foucault, *OT* 312). He calls this unstable mixture the "strange empirico-transcendental doublet, since he is a being such that knowledge will be attained in him of what renders all knowledge possible" (318).

> The thought that is contemporaneous with us, and with which, willy-nilly, we think, is still largely dominated by the impossibility, brought to light towards the end of the eighteenth century, of basing syntheses in the space of representation, and by the correlative obligation—simultaneous but immediately divided against itself—to open up the transcendental field of subjectivity, and to constitute inversely, beyond the object, what are for us the "quasi-transcendentals" of Life, Labour, and Language. (Foucault, *OT* 250)

Although his solution lies on one side of the dichotomy, Kant's thought embodies this insoluble problem as a whole by trying to encompass both sides of the irreconcilable division at once. The phenomenon-noumenon split simultaneously insists that transcendental subjectivity is free in how it spontaneously organizes experience and that there are causally deterministic influences on empirical humanity which are open to scientific investigation. Modern philosophy consists in the various futile attempts to resolve these aspects, that is, to maintain our autonomy without demoting scientific discoveries about how external forces influence us to mere appearance.

One strategy that particularly intrigues Foucault is the attempt to use various empirical phenomena such as his own chosen subjects of "Life, Labor, and Language" (or the body or history)—the topics of the human sciences—as "quasi-transcendentals"; they are the empirical forces that determine our nature and organize our faculties, but we could comprehend them through the positive sciences and so in a sense get beneath our own foundation, or behind our a priori. Mastering what masters us by knowing it might allow us to acquire a legitimate kind of autonomy, one achieved through the hard work of scholarship rather than just given to ourselves by philosophical hand-waving. Although, for instance, language guides how we think, the science of linguistics can plot this influence exactly and correct for it by fixing the harmful elements of our grammar or even inventing an entirely new language. Similarly, for Marxism humans are determined by our economic structure, so we can control human nature by controlling our economy. Foucault calls this strategy the "analytic of finitude," which is "doing no more, then, than fulfilling with greater care the hasty demands laid down when the attempt was made to make the empirical, in man, stand for the transcendental" (Foucault, *OT* 321). We are enjoined, like Hegel's Spirit at the end of history, to consciously gather up the shapes that have determined us unconsciously, without our participation or awareness, in order to finally be who we are: "The modern *cogito* (and this is why it is not so much the discovery of an evident truth as a ceaseless task constantly to be undertaken afresh) must traverse, duplicate, and reactivate in an explicit form the articulation of thought on everything within it, around it, and beneath it which is not thought" (324; see also 332). But this "interminable to and fro of a double system of reference" (316) cannot work, and its various failures are laid out in the most difficult chapter of *The Order of Things,* "Man and His Doubles," whose details we need not examine here.

Foucault sees man—the A5 organizer of knowledge and experience—waning while a new foundation of knowledge, language, is on the rise. Language will be the autonomous, anonymous region which enables knowledge to take place by sorting out the various types of beings. Subject and language have always been incompatible modes of organization, continuously exchanging places throughout the history of the last few centuries. It was only when classical representation (a form of anonymous language, since it was the spontaneous structuring of reality itself) faded that man could come on the scene (see Foucault, *OT* 311, 339; Foucault, *FL* 17), and it is man's implosion under the weight of the contradictions just discussed that is now creating the space for language.

> The entire modern *episteme* . . . was bound up with the disappearance of Discourse and its featureless reign. . . . If this same language is now

> emerging with greater and greater insistence in a unity that we ought to think but cannot as yet do so, is this not the sign that the whole of this configuration is now about to topple, and that man is in the process of perishing as the being of language continues to shine ever brighter upon our horizon? Since man was constituted at a time when language was doomed to dispersion, will he not be dispersed when language regains its unity? . . . Man had been a figure occurring between two modes of language. (Foucault, *OT* 386)

There can only be one organizer at a time—either A5 man or the ICS anonymous, autonomous *episteme* he calls language here. Around the middle of the twentieth century, Foucault sees the first signs of the former giving way to the latter, that is, A5 Active Knower is being replaced by Impersonal Conceptual Schemes. What I want to point out is that this is *precisely the transition I traced in Heidegger's later work.* Foucault attributes this revolution variously to Nietzsche, Marx, and Freud (Foucault, *FL* 60), the structuralists (63), and to Sade (101), among others, but he also says in a very late interview that Heidegger and Nietzsche "are the two authors whom I've read the most. I think it's important to have a small number of authors with whom one thinks, with whom one works, but on whom one doesn't write."[20]

Indeed, the specific choice of language to stand for ICS as a whole in *The Order of Things* is particularly interesting, as it is perhaps the most important impersonal phenomenon in Heidegger's later work: "Man acts as though *he* were the shaper and master of language, while in fact *language* remains the master of man. Perhaps it is before all else man's subversion of *this* relation of dominance that drives his essential being into alienation" (Heidegger, *BW* 348; see also 410, 423). As we have seen, for Heidegger "it is language that speaks" (411) rather than man. Foucault's discussions of language follow this Heideggerian line: "We are already, before the very least of our words, governed and paralysed by language" (Foucault, *OT* 298). When Foucault claims that language is replacing man in the rise of structuralist sciences, he means that the subject must take up a position that is set out in structures which it has not and could not have created, structures which necessarily precede and even enable its very subjectivity. To be a speaker means to use an inherited grammar and vocabulary; to be a scientist means to set up experiments and write papers in a certain accepted way, even if one introduces innovations. This draws upon both Heidegger's later discussions of language and his early analysis of *das Man,* that is, the idea that one can only be a Dasein by taking up roles that society presents. This is precisely how Foucault describes structuralist linguistics and ethnology, sciences that are doing away with man in favor of language: "At any given instant, the structure proper to individual experience finds a certain number of possible choices (and of excluded possibilities) in the systems of the society" (380).

It is important to Foucault's version of A6 that the subject is not an independent entity who preexists and enters these structures from the outside; rather, what it means to be a subject is to be a nexus of these networks. This is his completion of Heidegger's definition of Dasein as being-in-the-world without any permanent structure of existentialia.

> What is important to me is to show that there are not on the one hand inert discourses, already more than half dead, and then, on the other hand, an all-powerful subject which manipulates them, upsets them, renews them; but that the discoursing subjects belong to the discursive field—they have their place there (and possibilities of their displacements), their function (and possibilities of their functional mutation). The discourse is not the place where pure subjectivity irrupts; it is a space of positions and of differentiated functionings for the subjects. (Foucault, *FL* 38)

The subject isn't in the discursive field like a fish in water, but like salt in water. Although the subject can be conceptually differentiated from the field in that she could have taken and perhaps can still take other options—other words, other roles—she cannot be removed wholesale from the field and still be a subject.

It is the *episteme* that enables us to be subjects at all, as well as to be the specific kinds of subjects that we are, which is why Foucault makes remarks like it is only once a "network of signs" is in place that "Hume has become possible" (Foucault, *OT* 60). Or, even more broadly, "it was this network that made possible the individuals we term Hobbes, Berkeley, Hume, or Condillac" (63). This is his version of Heidegger's habit of using a thinker's name for a matter to be thought rather than as an autonomous thinker, or his point in statements like, "Nietzsche neither made nor chose his way himself, no more than any other thinker ever did. He is sent on his way" (Heidegger, *WCT* 46; see also Heidegger, *BW* 323, 337). It is the *episteme* or epochal understanding of Being that determines what can be said or thought; the individual thinker is its effect, response, or conduit rather than its origin.

Foucault explains how his research strategy is informed by his view of the relationship between individuals and *epistemes* very clearly in the foreword to the English edition of *The Order of Things*.

> I should like to know whether the subjects responsible for scientific discourse are not determined in their situation, their function, their per-

> ceptive capacity, and their practical possibilities by conditions that dominate and even overwhelm them. In short, I tried to explore scientific discourse not from the point of view of the individuals who are speaking, nor from the point of view of the formal structures of what they are saying, but from the point of view of the rules that come into play in the very existence of such discourse.[21]

Foucault resolves the battle between the empirical self determined by the period's ICS and the A5 transcendental determining man in favor of the former. The systems which enable us to think, speak, and inquire are the necessary precondition for us to do things like choosing or creating, including the presumed action of choosing or creating them. The more we investigate them—even with the purpose of mastering them—the more we find that they have already mastered us. "The phenomenological project continually resolves itself, before our eyes, into a description—empirical despite itself—of actual experience, and into an ontology of the unthought that automatically short-circuits the primacy of the 'I think'" (Foucault, *OT* 326).

Foucault summarizes this narrative superbly in an interview from 1969. Because of its clarity, I will quote it at length.

> The nineteenth century was the century . . . when the human sciences were invented. To invent the human sciences apparently meant to make of man the object of a possible knowledge. . . . Yet, in this same nineteenth century one hoped, one dreamed the great eschatological myth of the nineteenth century, which was somehow to make this knowledge of man exist so that man could be liberated by it from his alienations, liberated from all the determinations of which he was not the master, so that he could, thanks to this knowledge of himself, become again or for the first time master of himself, self-possessed. In other words, one made of man an object of knowledge so that man could become subject of his own liberty and of his own existence.
>
> Yet what happened . . . what was discovered was an unconscious that functioned according to mechanisms and according to a topological space that had absolutely nothing to do with what one could expect of the human essence. . . . And similarly for language. . . . By penetrating into language, what did one find? One found structures, correlations, a system that is in some way quasi-logical, and man, in his liberty, in his existence, there again had disappeared. . . . Man disappears in philosophy, not as object of knowledge but as subject of freedom and existence.[22]

This is a very helpful discussion of ideas that appear in a much more difficult form in "Man and His Doubles."

The study of the structures of such entities as the mind, language, and society makes the traditional conception of an autonomous agent freely making choices untenable. As Heidegger said in his reconception of agency, "The decision does not belong to humans. If this is to become clear, what is most important is the insight that man is not a being that makes himself" (Heidegger, *FoS* 56; see also Heidegger, *BW* 180). It is these empirical discoveries, partially due to ED, that fully eliminate the R6 subject as separable from the world and the source of meaning-giving structures (A5). This is why Foucault emphasizes "the discovery of the existence of formal relationships, which can indeed be called structures, exactly in areas that appear in all respects under the control of consciousness, for example in language and formal thought" (Foucault, *FL* 99). He concludes that

> I am not Kantian or Cartesian, precisely because I refuse an equation on the transcendental level between subject and thinking "I." I am convinced that there exist, if not exactly structures, then at least rules for the functioning of knowledge which have arisen in the course of history and within which can be located the various subjects. . . . In all of my work I strive . . . to avoid any reference to this transcendental as a condition of possibility for any knowledge. . . . I try to historicize to the utmost in order to leave as little space as possible to the transcendental. (Foucault, *FL* 98–99)

Despite his structuralist leanings here, the fact that these structures rise and fall historically aligns him with Heidegger against structuralism.

## Archaeological Rejections of Correspondence Truth and Bivalence: Being Within the True

Since an epoch's *episteme* is what determines the mode of Being of the entities to be known at a particular time, it also determines what can and should be studied and the proper method of studying them the way that Kuhn's paradigm does; this culminates in the determination of what assertions will be true. There can be no Truth itself swinging free of what is accepted as true at the time, which means that truth is fully epistemic for Foucault (see Allen 1993, 164). Each period's system determines what can be known and how it can be known, what kinds of questions can be legitimately asked, and what kinds of answers are acceptable. Each creates its own "space of reasons" which limits what can be taken seriously, what may be said without inviting ridicule or scorn, and what can function as a candidate for a true assertion. In an essay from 1970, Foucault calls statements that are properly constructed for their time "within the true" and, as usual, points to just how much this status involves: "A proposition must fulfill some onerous and complex conditions before it can be admitted within a discipline; before it can be pronounced true or false it must be, as Monsieur Canguilhem might say, 'within the true'" (Foucault, *AK* 224; see also Foucault, *PK* 197). This is a deeper epistemological level than bivalent truth and falsity, for it determines the candidates for these values. This alteration in what can count as true rather than simply what is true is how a number of philosophers define conceptual relativism, often in response to Davidson's portrayal of it as merely a redistribution of truth values across the same set of assertions (see Hacking in Hollis and Lukes 1982, 60; Rescher in French, Uehling, and Wettstein 1980, 331–33). If a physician were to diagnose my daughter's sniffles as demonic possession, for instance, this would not be false but nonsense, and possibly grounds for a competency hearing. Such a diagnosis would not come up to the level of falsity within our *episteme,* so to speak; it doesn't play the language-game of contemporary medical discourse well enough even to be wrong. There is a minimal threshold of conformity to an *episteme*'s rules which must be met before bivalence can take hold: "One would only be in the true, however, if one obeyed the rules of some discursive 'policy'" (Foucault, *AK* 224). The *episteme,* not reality out there waiting to be corresponded with, is the necessary condition for knowledge: "There is no knowledge without a particular discursive practice" (183).

Since it is one of his basic tenets that these *epistemes* are profoundly different at different points, Foucault concludes that "the division between true and false . . . is, undoubtedly, a historically constituted division" (Foucault, *AK* 218). Although historical, he denies what many see as the undesirable but inescapable consequence that truth is therefore arbitrary. While Unmoored from a unique, independent reality, Foucault views each period's knowledge as highly structured and rigorously determined; in fact, one of the results of his practice of piecing together a period's *episteme* is precisely to demonstrate that what initially appears incomprehensible to us or simply the result of our predecessors' stupidity actually obeys a logic of its own and studies its own reality. *Epistemes* have "the power of constituting domains of objects, in relation to which one can affirm or deny true or false propositions" (234; see also 182). Since an *episteme* constitutes objects, subjects operating within different ones truthfully describe different domains. Once one grasps the domain of objects available to another age through this kind of careful research, those decisions and observations which initially seemed so alien and bizarre become comprehensible. This is a way that Davidson's improved principle of charity, which seeks intelligibility and understanding rather than simple agreement and which allows for a wide range of influences on the speakers' perceptions and thoughts (see Davidson, *ITI* xix; 282; Davidson, *SIO* 152) can be seen (in principle at least) as rather close to Foucault's work, though this needs much more discussion.

We can also see that Putnam misunderstands Foucault when he says that "Foucault is not arguing that past practices were *more* rational than they look to be, but that all practices are *less* rational, are, in fact, mainly determined by unreason and selfish power" (Putnam 1981, 162). In fact, one of the main points of Foucault's entire oeuvre is to show that earlier practices that seem wholly unintelligible at first glance "possess up to a point their own specific regularities, logic, strategy, self-evidence and 'rationale'" (Foucault, *FL* 276; see also 280; Foucault, *PPC* 105). The difference with Putnam is that Foucault believes that "rationality" has significantly changed throughout history, and he refuses to assume a God's-eye view which would allow him to sort out the genuine forms from the irrational ones: "For me, no given form of rationality is actually reason" (Foucault, *PPC* 35). This does not make these forms *ir*rational, though, since such an accusation presupposes the existence of an ideal that has not been met.

> I do not believe in a kind of founding act whereby reason, in its essence, was discovered or established and from which it was subsequently diverted by such and such an event. I think, in fact, that reason is self-created, which is why I have tried to analyse forms of rationality: different foundations, different creations, different modifications in which rationalities engender one another, oppose and pursue one another. Even so, you cannot assign a point at which reason would have lost sight of its fundamental project, or even a point at which the rational becomes the irrational.[23]

Specific knowledges can be comprehended once one grasps the rules of the language-game played by the knowers of the time, but "the distinction between the rational and its opposite is not pertinent in describing" the rules of the various historical games of truth (Foucault, *EW* 2:324) since, like Heidegger's understandings of Being, these are the source of rationalities themselves, including our own. Putnam retains just the kind of bivalent opposition of rational-irrational and legitimate reason-illegitimate power that Foucault is trying to undermine.

Thinkers in various *epistemes* resemble Kuhn's scientists from different paradigms who work in different worlds, or Heidegger's men who think in terms of different understandings of Being. In a later interview, Foucault says that in *The Order of Things* he was trying to show that "a treatise of medicine written in 1780 and a treatise of pathological anatomy written in 1820 belong to two different worlds. My problem was to ascertain the sets of transformations in the régime of discourses necessary and sufficient for people to use these words rather than those, a particular type of discourse rather than some other type" (Foucault, *PK* 211). Where Heidegger described Galileo and his compatriots seeing different facts when they observed balls dropped from the tower, Foucault makes the same point with Mendel's biological discoveries. Realism's explanation for why people resisted Mendel's obviously true findings is that they stubbornly ignored plain facts or, as in the case of Galileo, were blinded by religious prejudice.

> People have often wondered how on earth nineteenth-century botanists and biologists managed not to see the truth of Mendel's statements. But it was precisely because Mendel spoke of objects, employed methods and placed himself within a theoretical perspective totally alien to the biology of his time. . . . Here was a new object, calling for new conceptual tools, and for fresh theoretical foundations. Mendel spoke the truth, but he was not *dans le vrai* (within the true) of contemporary biological discourse: it simply was not along such lines that objects and biological concepts were formed. A whole change in scale, the deployment of a totally new range of objects in biology was required before Mendel could enter into the true. (Foucault, *AK* 224)

To say that "Mendel spoke the truth" means that from our perspective—thinking within the *episteme* that Foucault shares with Mendel and the reader—his work is both within the true (that is, it makes sense, plays our game, uses the dominant concepts we recognize and thus might be true) and is in fact true. But it did not fit into the contemporary space of biological thought, so at that point it could neither be true nor false. Heidegger's version of this claim is that contemporary "students of physics . . . consider [Newton's principle of inertia] self-evident. . . . During the preceding fifteen hundred years it was not only unknown, but nature and beings in general were experienced in such a way that it would have been senseless" (Heidegger, *BW* 280, bracketed comment added).

To summarize, Foucault rejects realism defined in Dummett's terms as the notion that R1 reality makes propositions R4 Bivalent regardless of human awareness or verification procedures. Furthermore, even if R2 Correspondence Truth has a place here, it would be secondary to the constitution of the domain of entities which can be corresponded to, as Heidegger said. Foucault even phrases the point in Heideggerian terms by calling the *episteme* as the necessary condition of true statements more true than those statements: "The modes of being of order, can be posited as the most fundamental of all . . . always more 'true' than the theories that attempt to give those expressions explicit form, exhaustive application, or philosophical foundation" (Foucault, *OT* xxi; see also Heidegger, *BW* 122).

## Genealogy: A Brief Overview

Once he fully grasps the method he had been working out in his archaeological books and explains it in detail in *The Archaeology of Knowledge,* Foucault discards it, which makes sense according to how he sees the purpose of his work. "My problem is my own transformation. That's the reason also why, when people say, 'well, you thought this a few years ago and now you say something else,' my answer is, (Laughs,) 'Well, do you think I have worked like that all those years to say the same thing and not to be changed?' "[24] As I will discuss below, Foucault sees his work as a means of self-transformation, so that as soon as his method settles down into a stable plan that he can follow out in a foreseeable way, it becomes incapable of fulfilling this function and so needs to be changed. After a few years of relative silence following *The Archaeology of Knowledge,* two books came out in quick succession: *Discipline and Punish* in 1975 and the first volume of *The History of Sexuality* in 1976, both employing a new method he called "genealogy" (this word entered his vocabulary as a description of his new phase around 1971, at least in "Nietzsche, Genealogy, History").

Foucault usually distinguishes this new technique from archaeology by saying that the latter focused on discourse—knowledge claims taking the form of what is said and written—whereas genealogy brings in the non-discursive as well—practices, institutions, buildings, and so on. "Apparatus" sometimes functions as a key term now, differing from the key term of archaeology, *episteme,* in this way:

> The apparatus is thus always inscribed in a play of power, but it is also always linked to certain coordinates of knowledge which issue from it but, to an equal degree, condition it. This is what the apparatus consists in: strategies of relations of forces supporting, and supported by, types of knowledge. . . . What I call an apparatus is a much more general case of the *episteme;* or rather, that the *episteme* is a specifically *discursive* apparatus, whereas the apparatus in its general form is both discursive and non-

> discursive, its elements being much more heterogeneous. (Foucault, *PK* 196–97; see also Foucault, *SMD* 208)

He does not dispense with his earlier work, but incorporates it into a bigger system. Foucault now broadens the scope of his studies to include non-discursive elements, and uses them to construct a more sophisticated analysis of discourse itself.

> Discursive practices are not purely and simply ways of producing discourse. They are embodied in technical processes, in institutions, in patterns for general behavior. . . . The transformation of a discursive practice is linked to a whole range of usually complex modifications that can occur outside of its domain (in the forms of production, in social relationships, in political institutions), inside it (in its techniques for determining its object, in the adjustment and refinement of its concepts, in its accumulation of facts), or to the side of it (in other discursive practices).[25]

He now understands that discourse does not exist in isolation, but is dependent upon and productive of non-discursive power effects, which means that it must be studied within this circuit rather than as a separate layer of history.

This new approach allows him to analyze extremely complex and multifaceted phenomena like "the carceral system [which] combines in a single figure discourses and architectures, coercive regulations and scientific propositions, real social effects and invincible utopias" (Foucault, *DP* 271; see also Foucault, *PK* 194). Although he had already taken a step away from Heidegger's "great books" approach to history by examining marginal, forgotten texts, his archaeological period still focused exclusively on texts. Now he studies a wide spectrum of data: "The extension of the disciplinary methods is inscribed in a broad historical process: the development at about the same time of many other technologies—agronomical, industrial, economic" (Foucault, *DP* 224). He will even show—in some detail—how a "transcendental" issue like the development of the soul arises from such mundane matters as the invention of the rifle and its concomitant types of training (see 162–64)! This can be seen as an extension of his already very strong employment of the Empirical Directive, now expanded to include architecture and practices as well as ignored writings and empirical sciences.

Throughout most of the 1970s, Foucault analyzes these non-discursive practices as well as the effects on and of knowledge, which he collectively calls "power": "The course of study that I have been following until now—roughly since 1970/71—has been concerned with the *how* of power."[26] Although this might sound like a general, theoretical analysis of a metaphysical entity, he decisively rejects this interpretation of what he is doing: "Given that the question 'What is power?' is obviously a theoretical question that would provide an answer to everything, which is just what I don't want to do—the issue is to determine what are, in their mechanisms, effects, their relations, the various power-apparatuses that operate at various levels of society."[27] Foucault uses a kind of ED nominalism to escape the trap of metaphysics, giving extraordinarily detailed, nuanced accounts of very specific mechanisms of power. Although there are significant changes from archaeology, the genealogical analyses are also guided by the basic theses of the Heideggerian Paradigm that he arrived at by the end of his archaeological period. I will briefly run through these primary theses to show genealogy's working commitment to each.

## Genealogical A1 Dependence and A3 Ontological Pluralism

We are prone to believe that the way we find the world is the natural, inevitable way it has always been and must be. Here is how Heidegger describes this prejudice: "It simply no longer occurs to us that everything that we have all known for so long, and all too well, could be otherwise" (Heidegger, *IM* 56; see also Heidegger, *PR* 81). Genealogy provokes the suspicion that this kind of realism is a ruse that has often been used to cover up shameful origins and legitimate oppression; even a brief familiarity with history should prevent belief in the various classes of "natural slaves" that have been proposed through the ages. In "Nietzsche, Genealogy, History"—Foucault's clearest discussion of genealogy and one of the best introductions to his work as a whole—he writes that genealogy "must record the singularity of events outside of any monotonous finality; it must seek them in the most unpromising places, in what we tend to feel is without history" (Foucault, *FR* 76). The "most unpromising places" are precisely those objects that seem most R1 Independent of us and R3 permanent and unchanging, i.e., that appear to fit the realist account best. Genealogy fundamentally opposes the

> attempt to capture the exact essence of things, their purest possibilities, and their carefully protected identities; because this search assumes the existence of [R3] immobile forms that precede the external world of accident and succession. This search is directed to [R1] "that which was already there.". . . If the genealogist refuses to extend his faith in meta-

> physics, if he [ED] listens to history, he finds that there is "something altogether different" behind things: not a timeless and essential secret, but the secret that they [A1] have no essence or that [HPO] their essence was fabricated in a piecemeal fashion from alien forms. (Foucault, *FR* 78, bracketed comments added)

When we follow the Empirical Directive to focus on what actually occurs in history, what we find is not an orderly progression toward the discovery of persistent objects, but "an unstable assemblage of faults, fissures, and heterogeneous layers that threaten the fragile inheritor from within" (Foucault, *FR* 82). Wherever an object or institution tries to pass itself off as permanent, unique, and independent, genealogy shows the wildly different incarnations it has taken and the frequently unpalatable functions it has served.

In this way we discover A3 Pluralism behind every apparently univocal truth or permanent entity. Genealogy "disturbs what was previously considered immobile; it fragments what was thought unified; it shows the heterogeneity of what was imagined consistent with itself" (Foucault, *FR* 82; see also Foucault, *EW* 3:225). His genealogical phase adds the important layer of practices and institutions to his analyses, but these are used to show once again how objects are not independent of us but constituted, now by both knowledge and power: "The history of the 'objectification' of those elements which historians consider as objectively given (if I dare put it thus: of the objectification of objectivities), this is the sort of circle I want to try and investigate" (Foucault, *FL* 286).

A central thesis of the first volume of *The History of Sexuality* is that power, especially political power, has been wrongly conceived as exclusively repressive. This view is called the repressive hypothesis and, as we saw above, Foucault himself subscribed to it in his earliest work. The problem with it is that it presupposes a realist object preexisting the power structure with a specific nature which then gets repressed. In this case, the idea is that human nature's free, natural sexuality (R1) has been trapped and repressed by prudish Victorian morals, mangling and deforming us. Foucault finds this conception wrong for many reasons, and his book unravels this conception of power by pulling on this realist thread. If he can eliminate the notion of an independent sex, then power cannot be defined as repressing it, nor can liberation consist in lifting the weight of repression to allow natural sexuality to resume its original form and express itself spontaneously. Thus the way for the book's central aim of constructing a new conception of power is cleared by its assault on realism.

Near the end of the book Foucault insists that "it is precisely this idea of sex *in itself* that we cannot accept without examination. . . . This idea of sex took form in the different strategies of power and the definite role it played therein" (Foucault, *HS* 152; see also 98). First, like Heidegger's early analysis of presence-at-hand and later of objectivity, Foucault describes the process that defined sex and/or sexuality[28] as an R1 Independently real entity; given his form of the ED, this process occurs within empirical science, in particular psychology, rather than in philosophy. It was here that

> sexuality was defined as being [R1] "by nature": a domain susceptible to pathological processes, and hence one calling for therapeutic or normalizing interventions. . . . The [ICS] "economy" of discourses—their intrinsic technology, the necessities of their operation . . .—this, and not a system of representations, is what determines the essential features of what they have to say. (Foucault, *HS* 68–69, bracketed comments added; see also Foucault, *EW* 1:45; Foucault, *PP* 57–8)

In other words, sexuality got defined by whatever features aided the proliferation of this new science, not by independent reality or "sex in itself." Not, as we will see, that this was done intentionally by a devious conspirator; it's just that those "discoveries" that helped the infant science succeed and spread were taken up and disseminated by those empowered by the science, while those that didn't tended to wither away. Obviously, the foremost characteristic that a subject matter must have in order to deserve its own science and require treatment is being real, natural, not merely psychosomatic. The nature of sexuality was determined "not, however, by reason of some natural property inherent in sex itself, but by virtue of the tactics of power immanent in this discourse."[29] Like Heidegger's account, sexuality's R1 Independence is itself A1 Dependent on ICS scientific discourse and practice.

It is essential to Foucault's project that we dismantle the realist justification of psychology in order to be able to resist its bullying ruse and achieve a properly critical perspective on it. He states his commitment to HPO very clearly: "Sexuality must not be thought of as a kind of natural given which power tries to hold in check, or as an obscure domain which knowledge tries gradually to uncover. It is the name that can be given to a historical construct" (Foucault, *HS* 105; see also Foucault, *FL* 166, 198). This idea then pulls the rug out from under the repressive hypothesis: since sexuality is itself constituted by power, it cannot get repressed by power. Power in many ways takes the place of discourse or the *episteme* as the ICS of genealogy, which means that Foucault actually reverses the repressive hypothesis: "We must cease once and for all to describe the effects of power in negative terms. . . . In fact, power produces; it produces reality; it produces domains of objects" (Foucault, *DP* 194). Power is not essentially a negative force, though it does employ specific local prohibitions within its overall strategies;[30] instead, given its constitutive role in his Heideggerian Paradigm thought, power is fundamentally productive. Foucault insists repeatedly that "the processes of objectification originate in the very tactics of power and of the arrangement of its exercise."[31] This claim that sexuality is dependent on or constituted by the power-knowledge apparatus of psychology, that in the early practices of psychology, "what was involved . . . was the very production of sexuality,"[32] is repeated over and over again in the 159 pages of *The History of Sexuality*.

This commitment to A1 combines with the Empirical Directive's emphasis on history (see Foucault, *HS* 72, 91) to produce A3 Ontological Pluralism. History does not reveal a logical progress toward persistent identities, nor does it allow belief in a transcendent *meta-physis* world. Against interpretations of history as determined by Platonic metaphysics, Christian destiny, or Hegelian Spirit, Foucault organizes his reading of history around the inassimilable event.

> The forces operating in history are not controlled by destiny or regulative mechanisms, but respond to haphazard conflicts. . . . They always appear through the singular randomness of events. . . . The world of effective history knows only one kingdom, without providence or final cause. . . . The world we know is not this ultimately simple configuration where events are reduced to accentuate their essential traits, their final meaning, or their initial and final value. On the contrary, it is a profusion of entangled events. (Foucault, *FR* 88–89; see also Foucault, *PoT* 55)

What we discover from studying the history of any ostensible ahistorical entity is that it has possessed radically divergent meanings at different times which cannot fit together into a consistent package, but must each be acknowledged as real.

Foucault extends the lessons of A3 far, seeing total transformations occurring at these epoch shifts. For instance, the jarring juxtaposition of the brutal torture-execution of Damiens with a bland prison timetable that opens *Discipline and Punish* shows just how radically punitive mentality altered in the eighty years separating the two. Whereas we recoil from the first and find the second humane and unexceptional, Damiens's contemporaries would have found his public torture entertaining and edifying but the timetable mystifying and impossible to obey. What has transpired in those eighty years is that "'crime,' the object with which penal practice is concerned, has profoundly altered: the quality, the nature, in a sense the substance of which the punishable element is made" (Foucault,

*DP* 17; see also 7; Foucault, *EW* 3:70). Similarly, in his Collège de France lectures on psychology, Foucault views the changeover from the church's control of sexuality to psychology's, not as different interpretations of the same object, but as a change in the object itself: "Concupiscence was the sinful soul of the flesh. Since the eighteenth century, the nervous type is the rational and scientific body of this same flesh. The nervous system takes the place of concupiscence by right. It is the material and anatomical version of the old concupiscence."[33] In other words, "as the knowledge changes, so too does the object" (Hegel, *PS* 54, §85). This is A3 Ontological Pluralism as a consequence of A1 Dependence + Empirical Directive, which leads naturally to HPO.

## Genealogical A6 and HPO: "The Historical Ontology of Ourselves"

The main target of genealogy's historical dismantling of realism is the subject. Foucault focuses on the topics of punishment and sexuality, not so much for their intrinsic worth, but because they offer particularly rich insights into modern subjectivity (see Foucault, "MF" 316; Foucault, *SMD* 251–52); he specifically calls *Discipline and Punish* a "history of the modern soul" (Foucault, *DP* 23) and "a genealogy of the modern 'soul' . . . as the present correlative of a certain technology of power over the body" (29; see also Foucault, *HS* 143; Foucault, *PP* 57). These quotes appearing early in his first genealogical book already show that the subject is being treated according to A1 and A3, as discussed in the preceding section: since the book discusses the "modern" soul, telling its history, this implies that it varies (A3), and as a "correlative" of structures of power rather than a self-subsistent entity (A1). In fact, the second quote continues a sentence later with an even more explicit proclamation of A1: the soul "is produced permanently around, on, within the body by the functioning of a power that is exercised on those punished—and, in a more general way, on those one supervises, trains and corrects."

Foucault repeats the genealogical procedure on subjects that he has already applied to transcendent objects, first rejecting realism's R1 and R3 claims of a permanent, ahistorical nature to the self which could get discovered or distorted by knowledge, freed or repressed by power.

> The individual is not to be conceived as a sort of elementary nucleus, a primitive atom, a multiple and inert material on which power comes to fasten or against which it happens to strike, and in so doing subdues or

> crushes individuals. In fact, it is already one of the prime effects of power that certain bodies, certain gestures, certain discourses, certain desires, come to be identified and constituted as individuals. . . . The individual is an effect of power.[34]

Individuals do not exist as subjects previous to power's taking them into its grasp; rather, they are constituted as subjects by the power structure of their time—society, forms of knowledge, forces coming from all directions. Subjects can only exist within this field of power, which makes them A1 Dependent on power; as seen in the quote above, this continues unraveling the repressive conception of power. "It's my hypothesis that the individual is not a pre-given entity which is seized on by the exercise of power. The individual, with his identity and characteristics, is the product of a relation of power exercised over bodies, multiplicities, movements, desires, forces."[35] Just as genealogy fragments objects of study by showing the various heterogeneous incarnations they have had throughout history (A3), its analyses of the subject are

> capable of shattering the unity of man's being. . . . It places within a process of development everything considered immortal in man. . . . A knowledge of history easily disintegrates this unity, depicts its wavering course. . . . Nothing in man—not even his body—is sufficiently stable to serve as the basis for self-recognition. . . . It introduces discontinuity into our very being. (Foucault, *FR* 88)

Foucault explains the purpose of this method in a talk from 1980: "I have tried to get out from the philosophy of the subject through a genealogy of this subject, by studying the constitution of the subject across history which has led us up to the modern concept of the self" (Foucault, *PoT* 176; see also 199). He is using history to disrupt the supposedly ahistorical R6 subject; after all, knowledge "is made for cutting" (Foucault, *FR* 88). Foucault himself, under the guise of the commentator "Maurice Florence," says that

> the first methodological rule for this sort of work is thus the following: to circumvent [R6] anthropological universals to the greatest extent possible, so as to interrogate them in their [A6] historical constitution (and of course also the universals of a humanism that would put forward the rights, privileges, and nature of a human being as an [R6] immediate and nontemporal truth of the subject). It is also necessary to overturn the philosophic procedure of moving back toward the [A5] constitutive subject in which one is seeking an [R3] account of what any object of

> knowledge in general may be; what is required, on the contrary, is to return toward the study of the [ICS] concrete practices by which the [A6] subject is constituted in the immanence of a domain of knowledge. (Foucault, "MF" 317, bracketed comments added)

In addition to showing us the diachronic heterogeneity or trans-epochal differences that subjectivity has had, genealogy also provides an account of how the modern subject became what it is and why this is harmful. History not only explains why R6 Realism of the Subject is wrong, but also how we have come to believe in it and the strategic role it plays, that is, the power effects it wields and the power structures it keeps in place and that keep it in place. I will briefly examine the somewhat different accounts that Foucault's two published genealogical works give of this phenomenon.

*Discipline and Punish* describes how the particular kind of interiority and self-consciousness, as well as conscience, that define modern subjectivity were born from a new method of continuous surveillance which was devised to enforce laws more efficiently. In place of the difficult, politically dangerous, and ineffective method of the public execution—the favored form of punishment for monarchic power—"there is a form of surveillance which requires very little in the way of expenditures. No need for arms, physical violence, or material restraints. Just an observing gaze that each individual feels weighing on him, and ends up internalizing to the point that he is his own overseer: everyone in this way exercises surveillance over and against himself" (Foucault, *FL* 233). Like Freud's theory of the child internalizing her parents into her superego, the criminal/prisoner watches himself because he suspects that he is being watched, stopping his criminal activity himself for fear of being caught (see Foucault, *DP* 201, 217; Foucault, *PP* 47). This preemptive prevention of one's own actions gets upgraded into the constant observation of one's emotions and thoughts, detecting potential behavior in embryo before it flares up.

This continuous and deepening introspective investigation introduces a reflexivity or self-awareness that is distinctive to the modern psyche; it is the digging that hollows out an inside, so to speak. This phenomenon then spreads beyond prison walls by means of the general use of similar observational and training techniques in the army, schools, hospitals, and so on. "Knowable man (soul, individuality, consciousness, conduct, whatever it is called) is the object-effect of this analytical investment, of this domination-observation" (Foucault, *DP* 305; see also 170). Through this internal observation, as well as a new form of training made possible by it, "submissive subjects are produced and a dependable body of knowledge built up about them. This disciplinary technique exercised upon the body had a double effect: a 'soul' to be known and a subjection to be maintained."[36]

Thus a fundamentally new form of A6 subjectivity is produced by a new ICS power structure. Foucault does not just set out to prove that this form of subjectivity has been recently created, rather than being our eternal essence; he also wants to show how it binds us to the present disciplinary-surveillance power structure by "implanting" enforcing agents within us. The more psychology and morality persuade us to identify this "voice of conscience" with our deepest selves (as, for example, Kant informs us that the voice of conscience that tells us to do our duty is our most rational and true self), the less effort the police must expend to keep people from breaking the law. What starts as increased prudent concern over getting caught by a more watchful power morphs into a conscience about doing wrong that we identify as the "better angels of our nature." The more surveillance cameras a store has the fewer guards it needs, true, but the guiltier you feel about stealing, the fewer cameras the store needs. Believing in R6 Realism of the Subject leads us to identify ourselves with this modern self-policing consciousness/conscience which helps society operate smoothly. Modern subjectivity

> is [A1] born rather out of methods of punishment, supervision and constraint. . . . On this reality-reference, various concepts have been constructed and domains of analysis carved out: psyche, subjectivity, personality, consciousness, etc.; on it have been built scientific techniques and discourses, and the moral claims of humanism. But let there be no misunderstanding: it is not that a [R1] real man, the object of knowledge . . . has been substituted for the soul, the illusion of the theologians. The man described for us, whom we are invited to free, is already in himself the [A1] effect of a [ICS] subjection much more profound than himself. A "soul" inhabits him and brings him to existence, which is itself a factor in the mastery that power exercises over the body. [A6] The soul is the effect and instrument of a political anatomy; the soul is the prison of the body. (Foucault, *DP* 29–30, bracketed comments added)

Genealogy thus exposes realism of the subject as not just false—ahistorical, unchanging, transcendent entities are perhaps the only absolute falsehoods for a relativistic system—but a ruse, a way to maintain our willing participation in this power scheme (see Foucault, *DP* 178–79).

*The History of Sexuality* offers an even more intricate account of how the modern subject has been constituted by employing a stronger union of power and knowledge in the arena of sexuality, a much less obvious context to examine power than prisons. Sexuality turns out to be a perfect domain for studying modern subjectivity for two reasons: (1) it has only recently become a scientific topic, so the power effects of claiming scientific knowledge of a subject matter are quite visible here; and (2) with the rise of psychology, sexuality has become the key for the modern examination of the self, coming to represent for many people their true identity. Foucault is especially puzzled by this last feature which, to his astonishment, seems now (at least in the mid-1970s, when the book was written) to be taken as an unquestioned fact. Indeed, the original title of the book was to be "Sex and Truth" (Foucault, *PK* 209).

> The problem in fact is the following: how is it that in a society such as ours, sexuality is not simply that which permits us to reproduce the species, the family, and the individual? Not simply something which procures pleasure and enjoyment? How is it that sexuality has been considered the privileged place where our deepest "truth" is read and expressed? For this is the essential fact: that since Christianity, Western civilization has not stopped saying, "To know who you are, know what your sexuality is about." Sex has always been the center where our "truth" of the human subject has been tied up.[37]

Western society has increasingly come to define subjects in terms of their sexuality and then determined that this identity needs to be approached and captured in terms of knowledge. This movement started (Foucault believes at this point in his career) with the Christian notion of sin of the flesh, which psychology then transformed into conceptions of abnormality and health, while the healing of confession was transferred from the booth to the couch. Of course, this changeover created subtle differences that rippled throughout the entire system, while also maintaining certain continuities. "*Through the medicalization of the effects of confession* . . . the sexual domain was no longer accounted for simply by the notions of error or sin, excess or transgression, but was placed under the rule of the normal and the pathological" (Foucault, *HS* 67; see also 116; Foucault, *EW* 3:166; Foucault, *PP* 114–16, 202). Where Christianity posited the ideal of the saint or God-fearing soul, psychology tries to create the normal human being. Christianity promised heaven, but psychology offers healthy sex, and modern society chose a normal sex life over the afterlife.

As sexuality became our identity and took on greater and greater importance for both the individual and society, it also became more and more worrying; any minor abnormality could destroy a child's future and, ultimately, all of society (via concerns about perverts and repopulation). The need for expert treatment exploded, and these experts needed information in order to make proper diagnoses. Information-gathering becomes the new incarnation of confession, in which the psychologist absolves us of our abnormalities by giving us exercises to do. Our sexuality is our true self, but it has a truer self—*normal* sexuality, how all humans ought to take their pleasure with a specified set of body parts and gendered partners. How we de facto get pleasure doesn't matter; we need to find out how we're *supposed* to get pleasure, which only the experts can tell us once we have told them how we actually do get it.[38] Thus, instead of a repressive regime of censorship and silence broken only by occasional courageous shoutings or furtive whisperings about sexuality, Foucault believes that we've been drowning in talk about sexuality, that "we have since become a singularly confessing society. . . . One goes about telling, with the greatest precision, whatever is most difficult to tell. . . . Western man has become a confessing animal" (Foucault, *HS* 59). He scoffs, "a censorship of sex? There was installed rather an apparatus for producing an ever greater quantity of discourse about sex" (23), creating a demand to be heard that fostered an entire profession of psychologists who "have even offered their ears for hire" (7). The current explosion of blogs where tens of thousands of people write their musings into the ether for anyone to read them is just the logical next step in this process.

What makes this analysis superior to *Discipline and Punish* is the fact that the latter's scheme of an internalization of self-policing still utilizes the repressive conception of power that Foucault is trying to eliminate (see Foucault, *HS* 83–84). The process of subjectification in that book was motivated by a fear of getting caught and punished, just the sort of negative power he criticizes political philosophers for focusing on; in *The History of Sexuality,* on the other hand, the power structure primarily works through pleasure and desire.[39] We obey not out of fear of being caught, but because we want to be normal and healthy, even deriving shudders of excitement from the confession itself (see 45, 71, 77). Psychologists hold out something that we conforming animals (again, echoes of Heidegger's *das Man*) desperately want—normalcy, health—rather than threatening us with what we don't want—punishment, imprisonment. In this fundamentally new structure that Foucault calls bio-power, psychologists and administrators of all kinds promise "the indefinite extension of strength, vigor, health, and life" (125; see also 72) instead of threatening harm. There's nothing remotely like clumsy, brute force going on here.

The ultimate point of his discussion is that we have been formed into this kind of subjectivity because it is a particularly useful mode of subjection for the present power scheme. It isn't our permanent, ahistorical nature that psychologists are finally dis-covering and liberating, but rather a historically contingent and particularly servile form of living that we are being formed into. However, one of the subjection tactics is precisely to convince us that this is our true nature that is finally being liberated so that we may become ourselves. This is why limited, local forms of repression are so useful: they help convince us that expressing this form of subjectivity is a matter of freely flouting authority.

> The obligation to confess is . . . so deeply ingrained in us, that we no longer perceive it as the effect of a power that constrains us; on the contrary, it seems to us that truth, lodged in our most secret nature, "demands" only to surface; that if it fails to do so, this is because a constraint holds it in place, the violence of a power weighs it down, and it can finally be articulated only at the price of a kind of liberation. . . . One has to be completely taken in by this internal ruse of confession in order to attribute a fundamental role to censorship, to taboos regarding speaking and thinking. . . . An immense labor to which the West has submitted generations in order to produce . . . men's subjection: their constitution as subjects in both senses of the word. (Foucault, *HS* 60; see also 85; Foucault, *EW* 3:331)

The double meaning of the word "subjection" is his conclusion (though not his argument). We have been formed into subjects who identify with our sexuality and then get warned by experts of all kinds of dangers if we misuse it. New epidemics arise all the time,[40] provoking the eruption of new crops of experts who then need to gather further information. "These sites radiated discourses aimed at sex, intensifying people's awareness of it as a constant danger, and this in turn created a further incentive to talk about it" (Foucault, *HS* 31). Psychologists traced all effects to a sexual etiology which of course made their own expertise all the more necessary and their methods legitimate: "The principle of sex as a 'cause of any and everything' was the theoretical underside of a confession that had to be thorough, meticulous, and constant, and at the same time operate within a scientific type of practice. The limitless dangers that sex carried with it justified the exhaustive character of the inquisition to which it was subjected" (65–66).

The limitless and extraordinary dangers that sexuality poses required continuous guidance from psychologists and scientific experts in the most intimate of matters, so that the domain of what is medical, and hence subject to medical control and intervention, expanded dramatically. Rather than going to the doctor only for such matters as broken limbs or bleeding, one becomes accustomed to consulting a psychologist for dissatisfaction with sex, or one's life or self or marriage or children, the expert being the one with a knowledge of human nature to guide one onto the path to normalcy and health. It is the experts' claim to knowledge of the R6 Realist Subject that is the key to their power; we follow their advice because we believe it to be informed by a knowledge of our essence (see Foucault, *PP* 134, 185, 340). In other words, belief in an R6 realist essential self is the necessary presupposition that gives the experts with knowledge of it power over us. Plato puts it directly and naively when he argues that philosophers—that is, those who know the Form of humanity and the city—ought to rule, and anyone with enlightened self-interest *wants* to be ruled by those who possess such knowledge of true reality. In turn, psychology defines the normal person as obeying the law, paying taxes, and so on. This is one of the ways that Foucault sees power structures other than the most visible ones of police and governments maintaining political order. The fact that political philosophy still focuses on these more apparent forms of power rather than the subtle ones that construct the kind of citizens who must be in place for governments to be able to function in the first place is why he frequently says that "we need to cut off the King's head: in political theory that has still to be done" (Foucault, *PK* 121).

One might expect Foucault now to attack the experts' power by claiming that we are not *really* this modern self-policing or sexual subject, that this form has been imposed upon us and we need to discover who we really are beneath these distorting or enslaving encumbrances. But of course, that is just what he cannot say. Foucault subscribes to the Historical Phenomenological Ontology of the Heideggerian Paradigm, sometimes describing what he does as "a historical ontology of ourselves" (Foucault, *FR* 46; see also 351). As stated above, *Discipline and Punish* is described as a history of the modern soul, that is, it describes how the subject was produced at specific times by techniques of power—specifically, forms of observation and training. Foucault immediately clarifies this assertion in a very interesting way: "Rather than seeing this soul as the reactivated remnants of an ideology, one would see it as the present correlative of a certain technology of power over the body. It would be wrong to say that the soul is an illusion, or an ideological effect. On the contrary, it exists, it has a reality, it is produced. . . . This is the historical reality of this soul" (Foucault, *DP* 29; see also Foucault, *EW* 3:15; Foucault, *PP* 58). In other words, even though it has been produced and only exists within a power structure (A1), even though there have been other ways of being a subject (A6), this really *is* how we are now. There is no other transcendent or transcendental aspect of subjectivity with which we can compare the present form to find it unreal or inauthentic; the entities of this world are transient and constituted, but they are as real as real gets. From the perspective of realism,

> the individual is no doubt the fictitious atom of an "ideological" representation of society; but he is also a reality fabricated by this specific technology of power that I have called "discipline.". . . Power produces; it produces reality; it produces domains of objects and rituals of truth. The

> individual and the knowledge that may be gained of him belong to this production. (Foucault, *DP* 194)

A correlate of this new conception of power as productive is that it has products, and without anything transcendent to compare them with, they are reality.

Toward the end of *The History of Sexuality,* Foucault engages in an imaginary dialogue with himself, as he did at the end of *The Archaeology of Knowledge,* both being the last books published in one of his phases. One of the objections he raises against his genealogy is the charge of idealism, i.e., that he has "only groundless effects, ramifications without roots, a sexuality without a sex" (Foucault, *HS* 151). In other words, by emphasizing construction and what people believe about sexuality at a certain time so much, he is not acknowledging brute facticity—here the facticity of sex as the body and its genitalia. When he claims that everything about humans changes in history, including our body, he seems to be overlooking the obvious facts of raw physicality which are wholly unaffected by our thoughts or beliefs about them, just as Goodman and Derrida allegedly did not take into account the fact that stars were around before humans. We may have changed our minds at various points in recorded history, but surely we haven't changed our brains, much less other parts of our anatomy.

But this objection misses the force of HPO. Without even the possibility for a genuinely external check on how we experience reality, since any check automatically gets filtered through our experience, beliefs, and so on, we ought to accept that what we experience exists in the way we experience it. Then the claim that nevertheless there *must* be physical or biological constants underlying all the cultural or mental changes is gratuitous speculation, a throwback to something quasi-noumenal. There simply is no reason to posit an additional persistent, imperceptible *physis* beneath the changing, perceived *nomos:* if we do not experience it, it is the wheel that spins without affecting anything else, and if we do experience it, then the idea of a non-cultural *physis* simply becomes one more element of our *nomos,* as sex is for psychology or the present-at-hand is for Dasein. Thus, Foucault replies to this objection that, rather than ignoring the body, in fact he deals with it extensively, but his analysis takes its historicality to be unproblematic.

> Far from the body having to be effaced, what is needed is to make it visible through an analysis in which the biological and the historical are not consecutive to one another . . . but are bound together in an increasingly complex fashion in accordance with the development of the modern technologies of power that take life as their objectives. (Foucault, *HS* 152)

He wants to undermine the traditional binary oppositions of *physis-nomos* or reality-appearance that defined metaphysics for Heidegger, taking in this case the pairing of sex as physical body and sexuality as cultural behaviors and norms. "We must not place sex on the side of reality, and sexuality on that of confused ideas and illusions; *sexuality is a very real historical formation*" (Foucault, *HS* 157, italics added). People have experienced bodies in radically different ways throughout history, as Foucault and his followers show, and we cannot separate independent bodies from these. They are historical as well as real. As we saw, Heidegger claims that treating these features as mutually exclusive rests on a presupposition that ought to be rejected:

> But why should what comes into existence and passes away count as non-being? Only when beingness is already established as constancy and presence. Therefore, beingness is not read off a being or a non-being, but rather a being is projected-open onto this beingness, in order to show itself first of all in the open of this projecting-open *as* a being or a non-being. (Heidegger, *CP* 137, §100)

Despite our ancient tendency to separate out the constant physical from the variable cultural and treat the former as ontologically higher than, prior to, and foundational for the latter, the Heideggerian Paradigm's doctrine of HPO will not allow such a division.

> We believe, in any event, that the body obeys the exclusive laws of physiology and that it escapes the influence of history, but this too is false. The body is molded by a great many distinct regimes; it is broken down by the rhythms of work, rest, and holidays. . . . Nothing in man—not even his body—is sufficiently stable to serve as the basis for self-recognition. (Foucault, *FR* 87; see also 83)

He sums up his position here:

> Might not the historical root of a science lie in [mutual interdependence] that reciprocal genesis of the subject and the object of knowledge? . . . This would imply that [A3] there isn't *one* truth—which [UT] doesn't mean either that this historical is irrational or that this science is illusory. Rather, it confirms the presence of [HPO] a real and intelligible history, of a series of collective rational experiences conforming to [ICS] a set of precise, identifiable rules and resulting in the construction of both [A6] the knowing subject and [A1] the known object. (Foucault, *EW* 3:254, bracketed comments added)

## Genealogical Impersonal Conceptual Scheme: Power-Knowledge

We have seen that like archaeology, genealogy dispenses with A5 transcendental subjectivity along with R1 ahistorical objects; neither pole founds or organizes knowledge. Genealogy considers the subject constituted (A6) rather than constituting (A5).

> One has to dispense with the [A5] constituent subject itself, that's to say, to arrive at an analysis which can account for the [A6] constitution of the subject within a historical framework. And this is what I would call genealogy, that is, a form of history which can account for the constitution of [A1] knowledges, discourses, domains of objects, etc., without having to make reference to a subject which is either [A5] transcendental in relation to the field of events or [R6] runs in its empty sameness throughout the course of history. (Foucault, *PK* 117, bracketed comments added)

We cannot organize experience around the constituent acts of the subject, since it itself is constituted by something else and changes profoundly along with the rest of reality at these historical shifts.

> These "power-knowledge relations" are to be analyzed, therefore, not on the basis of a [A5] subject of knowledge . . . but, on the contrary, the [A6] subject who knows, the [A1] objects to be known and the modalities of knowledge must be regarded as so many effects of these [ICS] fundamental implications of power-knowledge and their [A3] historical transformations. In short, it is not the activity of the [A5] subject of knowledge that produces a corpus of knowledge . . . but [ICS] power-knowledge . . . that determines the forms and possible domains of knowledge.[41]

Instead of the Kantian Paradigm's A5 Active Knower, Foucault follows the Heideggerian Paradigm to make beings, knowledge, and the subject all dependent on an Impersonal Conceptual Scheme. He still understands history as organized by epochal constituting patterns, though in genealogy these are organized and enforced by power relations, institutions, and practices, in addition to the discourses of knowledge that archaeology focused on: apparatuses "crystallize into institutions, they inform individual behaviour, they act as grids for the perception and evaluation of things" (Foucault, *FL* 282). These power structures determine what kind of subjects we are, so we cannot be the source of the conceptual schemes or power structures themselves. Although Foucault is following Heidegger here, he faces a problem that Heidegger did not. Heidegger's description of Being in anthropomorphic terms, such as saying that it "wants" to come to appearance or that it "loves" to hide, could generally be cashed out in "non-metaphorical" language (although parsing out metaphorical from literal in Heidegger's discourse gets rather problematic when pushed on, as he himself would insist on). Foucault's quasi-structuralist anonymity of power, on the other hand—his commitment to ICS—presents a difficulty because teleological notions like tactics and strategy are central to his genealogical analyses. He constantly talks about such features of power schemes as motivations, rewards, strategies, and ruses, and these terms seem much harder to eliminate or cash out in non-anthropomorphic or non-intentional terms.

Foucault clearly sets out the paradox of genealogical ICS in the following quote from *The History of Sexuality:*

> Power relations are both intentional and nonsubjective. . . . They are imbued, through and through, with calculation. . . . But this does not mean that [they result] from the choice or decision of an individual subject; let us not look for the headquarters that presides over its rationality. . . . The logic is perfectly clear, the aims decipherable, and yet it is often the case that no one is there to have invented them, and few who can be said to have formulated them: an implicit characteristic of the great anonymous, almost unspoken strategies.[42]

He explicitly states here that power relations have the characteristics of purpose, calculation, and rationality which seem inescapably bound up with the conscious planning of intelligent agents, while also claiming that they are nonsubjective, anonymous, and were never invented by anyone. Whereas Nietzsche (at least rhetorically) entertained the idea of a sinister cabal of resentful priests intentionally imposing a self-serving conceptual scheme onto their epoch in *On the Genealogy of Morals*—which is highly implausible, but consistent with his placement of concepts under conscious control—Foucault sides with Heidegger's impersonal analysis. The conspiracy theory does not work as an explanation, since the conspirators themselves would have to be constituted in such a way that they desire those specific ends and perceive that tactic as practical and promising, both of which require an already present mentality which couldn't be under their control on pain of infinite regress. Given his ICS, Foucault must reject all conspiracy theory–type analyses that view power as something possessed by those on top and imposed on those below; he believes instead that power "is a machine in which everyone is caught, those who exercise the power as well as those who are subjected to it" (Foucault, *FL*

234; see also Foucault, *PP* 55). This then works in tandem with his rejection of the repressive conception of power: since the psychological treatment of sexuality was promoted as highly beneficial in promising health and normalcy, it was initially available just to the wealthy and powerful, only later trickling down to the less advantaged members of society; exactly the reverse order of what a conspiracy model of power would posit (see Foucault, *HS* 122–27; Foucault, *EW* 3:386).

Foucault follows the Heideggerian Paradigm's shift of what determines knowledge from either R1 things or A5 man to an anonymous, historical organization. It is still a transcendental inquiry, just displaced. Again, Mohanty is right on target in his discussion of Foucault's relation to transcendental philosophy in his first two phases.

> With the pregiven object and the pregiven subject both out, constitution occurs by rules of discourse. But this structuralist theory is soon replaced by the so-called genealogy: all constitution, be it of the subject, of forms of discourse, or of their object domains, is said to be by "power." In view of Foucault's continuing critique of transcendental philosophy . . . what he wants to set aside is only one half of that tradition—namely the priority accorded to subjectivity. The other half he retains, and this is the general theory of constitution. (Caputo and Yount 1993, 35; see also Habermas 1987, 252)

There is a general constitution of knowledge, subject, and things within a period, but it is done by the anonymous or impersonal power-knowledge apparatus.

Foucault offers an ingenious account of how an apparatus can develop subjective or anthropomorphic features such as purposes or ruses without recourse to anything anthropomorphic, like Hegel's Spirit or Nietzsche's diabolical priests. Although I'm not aware of him ever using it, evolution in fact presents a familiar model of just such a process. Evolution posits a continuing clash of random, violent encounters—"a profusion of entangled events"—from which intelligent patterns emerge, patterns which can legitimately be seen as solutions to problems, even though there is no sentient awareness of the problem or conscious decision. Random mutations encounter a variety of environmental pressures, which results in the selection and reinforcement of a few candidates. These propagate, some of their offspring mutate and thus present new possible responses to environmental challenges or constitute environmental challenges to others, and if the original species or one of the mutated varieties meets the new challenges and thus persists, it "solves the problem."

This evolutionary description is quite close to Foucault's account of how power schemes develop. The main difference is that "memes" can change and absorb features from each other much more quickly and fully than genes can. Thus, instead of the descent of a species, Foucault sees a vast, teeming multiplicity of individual, local interactions converging and incorporating each other into broader power structures as they rise.

> The "invention" of this new political anatomy must not be seen as a sudden discovery. It is rather a multiplicity of often minor processes, of different origin and scattered location, which overlap, repeat, or imitate one another, support one another, distinguish themselves from one another according to their domain of application, converge and gradually produce the blueprint of a general method. . . . On almost every occasion, they were adopted in response to particular needs. . . . This did not prevent them being totally inscribed in general and essential transformations. (Foucault, *DP* 138; see also Foucault, *EW* 3:345)

Innumerable interactions between individuals trying to influence each other are constantly occurring; behaviors that succeed are likely to be repeated and refined. Techniques slowly develop which, when particularly successful, spread and become more formalized. When very powerful, these techniques even start re-forming the subjectivities that are subjected to them, thus reinforcing their effectiveness. Once they reach a certain level of generality (of course, none of this allows exact measurement, though Foucault traces the developments in considerable detail), they are likely to encounter other techniques which have proven efficacious on other subpopulations. Like wave formations, sometimes they interfere with each other to cancel out, and sometimes they gear together, reinforcing each other to become an even more wide-ranging technique. The most successful eventually rise to the level of widely acknowledged systems like medicine or monarchy or pedagogy, but they always begin from local interactions rather than from an individual or group that consciously thinks up a plan and goes on to impose it on the masses (though once in place they can always be purposefully wielded). "These tactics were invented and organized according to local conditions and particular urgencies. They were designed piece by piece before a class strategy solidified them into vast and coherent ensembles" (Foucault, *FL* 236; see also 260; Foucault, *PP* 71).

Since "power comes from below" (Foucault, *HS* 94), Foucault's method is to

> make an ascending analysis of power, or in other words begin with its infinitesimal mechanisms, which have their own history, their own trajec-

> tory, their own techniques and tactics, and then look at how these mechanisms of power, which have their own solidity and, in a sense, their own technology, have been and are invested, colonized, used, inflected, transformed, displaced, extended, and so on by increasingly general mechanisms and forms of overall domination. Domination is not something that is pluralized and then has repercussions down below. I think we have to analyze the way in which the phenomena, techniques, and procedures of power come into play at the lowest levels . . . and how more general powers or economic benefits can slip into the play of these technologies of power, which are at once relatively autonomous and infinitesimal. (Foucault, *SMD* 30–31; see also Foucault, *HS* 92–93; Foucault, *EW* 1:59; Foucault, *PK* 99)

Once a technique reaches a high level of generality, individuals who have been at least partially formed by it are invested in it: the experts as well as those who consider themselves benefited will protect it, consciously adapting it to meet new challenges if necessary and possible. If a power technique cannot handle new problems, it will pass away, the way the monarchy's reliance on spectacular executions failed because it allowed both excessive theft of increasingly important property during the birth of capitalism (see Foucault, *DP* 86–89) and political danger in the carnival atmosphere of the execution itself (see 59–65), eventually giving way to the superior methods of imprisonment and surveillance (see Foucault, *SMD* 249–50). Foucault consistently rejects humanitarian explanations of this change in punishment, preferring the evolutionary account that, for example, spectacular public execution simply could not handle new pressures and so "died out," giving way to a new form of punishment which was a more efficient, not more humane, solution to a specific set of problems: the goal was "not to punish less, but to punish better" (Foucault, *DP* 82; see also Foucault, *PP* 29).

It is with this kind of account that Foucault is able to claim that "the objective existed and the strategy was developed, with ever-growing coherence, but without it being necessary to attribute to it a subject which makes the law" (Foucault, *PK* 204; see also 203). Power regimes reform and refine themselves, discover solutions, and adapt to problems without any master planner. If they don't, they fail, the way that species die out. Just as, say, moths evolved wings that look like bird eyes, so power regimes have developed "ruses which are not ultimately played *by* any particular person, but which are none the less lived, and assure the permanence and function of the institution" (38). Thus Foucault can employ the teleological language that makes the best sense of a history purified of all transcendent entities—"it is intelligible and should be susceptible to analysis down to the smallest detail—but this in accordance with the intelligibility of struggles, of strategies and tactics" (Foucault, *FR* 56)—while still maintaining that the power-knowledge structures are impersonal.

## Genealogical A2 and A4 Rejections of Correspondence Truth and Bivalence

Foucault's fascination with truth is a constant theme of his oeuvre, as he himself repeatedly notes: "My general theme isn't society but the discourse of true and false, by which I mean the correlative formation of domains and objects and the verifiable, falsifiable discourses that bear on them."[43] Even though genealogy has removed archaeology's exclusive focus on discourse and knowledge claims, they have hardly disappeared, since they play an essential role in power relations.

> My problem has always been on the side of another category: truth. How did the power unfolding in insanity produce psychiatry's "true" discourse? The same thing applies to sexuality: how to recapture the will to know how power exerted itself on sex? I don't want to write the sociological history of a prohibition but rather the political history of a production of "truth."... The history of the West cannot be dissociated from the way in which "truth" is produced and inscribes its effect.... The history of "truth"—of the power proper to discourses accepted as true—has yet to be written. (Foucault, *FL* 215; see also 220)

The scare quotes here indicate that Foucault is not studying traditional R2 Correspondence Truth between propositions or ideas and R1 Independent reality. Genealogy continues the archaeological notion that a theory or observation must be "within the true" before qualifying as either true or false. "Nothing can exist as an element of knowledge if . . . it . . . does not conform to a set of rules and constraints characteristic, for example, of a given type of scientific discourse in a given period."[44] Obviously, this is neither correspondence with—nor R4 Bivalence determined by—independent, determinate reality. Truth and falsity can only occur once knowable objects are in place; knowledge is of A1 objects constituted by power and so is inseparable from the workings of power itself, the way that Kantian math and science are inseparable from the workings of transcendental subjectivity: "Knowledge follows the advances of power, discovering new objects of knowledge over all the surfaces on which power is exercised" (Foucault, *DP* 204; see also 23; Foucault, *PP* 56, 78). This is the meaning of Foucault's most famous phrase: "power/knowledge." As he insists repeatedly, this conjunction does not mean that the two are identical or that knowledge is "nothing but" power, but rather that they necessarily go together (see Foucault, *FL* 462). Power must constitute objects before knowledge can take hold of them, since they do not just exist on their own.

Although Foucault does not address bivalence directly, the Empirical Directive means that he would not examine bivalence in the abstract, but only within the context of truth structures instantiated within specific institutions. And during his genealogical phase, he shows a propensity for exceptions to bivalence in punishment and sexuality. The central truth-mechanism in the judicial realm is the court's decision as to whether or not the defendant is guilty and thus deserves punishment. Although this seems like a bivalent distinction—either guilty or not—Foucault finds that in the past, evidence, guilt, and punishment were established in degrees, so that a certain amount of evidence determined a degree of guilt rather than a degree of the probability of absolute guilt. This partial guilt then permits a parallel quantity of legitimate punishment, even torture, which can be used to acquire further evidence which increases the guilt and thus the punishment, forming a particularly vicious circle. "Each piece of evidence aroused a particular degree of abomination. . . . Thus a semi-proof did not leave the suspect innocent until such time as it was completed; it made him semi-guilty; slight evidence of a serious crime marked someone as slightly criminal. In short, penal demonstration did not obey a dualistic system: true or false; but a principle of continuous gradation" (Foucault, *DP* 42; see also Foucault, *Ab* 6–7). Sexuality's central bivalence is gender determination, and Foucault is fascinated by the story of a hermaphrodite who initially escapes this coercive identification until societal pressure forces Barbin to settle on either male or female:

> Biological theories of sexuality, juridical conceptions of the individual, forms of administrative control in modern nations, led little by little to rejecting the idea of a mixture of the two sexes in a single body, and consequently to limiting the free choice of indeterminate individuals. Henceforth, everybody was to have one and only one sex. Everybody was to have his or her primary, profound, determined and determining sexual identity.[45]

As we have seen, individual propositions only possess truth and falsity within an era or regime of truth, as in the Heideggerian Paradigm. We cannot simply ask diachronic questions like, "Was the Renaissance madman *actually* a schizophrenic?" since this question illicitly analyzes an object constituted by one set of concepts in terms of a qualitatively different set. This deep heterogeneity prevents any comparison of the various epochal constitutions in terms of "getting it right," since there is no ahistorical remainder outside the historical flux to be accurately portrayed and thus to allow for neutral adjudication between incommensurable periods. Apparatuses or *epistemes* allow us to dispense with both things and subjects while still assigning truth and falsity to propositions. "Power, with the discursive practices that bear it and pronounce its effects, is the producer of knowledge. Power not only creates true discourses, but what is much more important, it creates the constraints that allow us to separate true discourse from false discourse" (Foucault, *FL* 159; see also 280; Foucault, *PK* 197). This is why Foucault can release knowledge from being determined by R1 Independent reality as well as Kant's safeguard in a universal ahistorical (R6) constituting subject (A5) without making it arbitrary or up to individual whim; it is relativism, but not anarchy or the always dreaded "anything goes."

The systems themselves are radically incommensurable and so cannot be ranked by a criterion of truth, as Hegel does, or one of goodness like Nietzsche's health (Foucault, *EW* 2:471). Whereas Hegel claims that the moments of consciousness progressively achieve more and more truth as they approach absolute knowledge, and Nietzsche calls Christianity false and the *Übermensch*'s perspective honest based on the different degrees to which they recognize and express their true nature as will to power, Foucault's work lies in "seeing historically how effects of truth are produced within discourses which in themselves are neither true nor false."[46] Applying the criterion of truth to a discourse or apparatus commits the category mistake of applying a quality that only operates *within* a regime to the regime itself. Since the world has no realist essence or "legible face" (Foucault, *AK* 229), we cannot evaluate the accuracy of these schemes by anything else; the very idea of the R2 accuracy of a conceptual scheme is incoherent.[47]

Foucault's history of truth is the story of how power relations contingently come together at certain times to confer the status of "true" on certain statements, how those statements then play this role in various discourses, and what power effects follow from that status, with special attention paid to those dealing with the subject. Without an extra-contextual reality, constitutive subject, or God's-eye view, what distributes truth and falsity is history's "profusion of entangled events." This is what he means by the epigrammatic line that gives my book its title: "Truth is a thing of this world" (Foucault, *FR* 72). According to UT, truth isn't even ideally or conceivably about *meta-physis* Forms or substances or noumena, but about what we encounter in this world which, as Nietzsche showed in Step Six Physics, is simply the world. Foucault goes farther to claim that truth is not just *about* the world but is itself something *within* the world, that is, "produced only by virtue of multiple forms of constraint. And it induces regular effects of power" (72–73). We have no access to any kind of eternal or trans-human truth; all we have are the shifting claims embedded in multiple institutions with power effects which make up Foucault's subject matter.

> Truth itself forms part of the history of discourse and is like an effect internal to a discourse or a practice. . . . There isn't *one* truth—which doesn't mean either that this history is irrational or that this science is illusory. Rather, it confirms the presence of a real and intelligible history, of a series of collective rational experiences conforming to a set of precise, identifiable rules and resulting in the construction of both the knowing subject and the known object. (Foucault, *EW* 3:253–54)

Without the legitimation of correspondence truth or the world's adjudication among the various ways of describing it, power cannot be separated from truth. If Plato were right, then the philosopher who knows the truth is in contact with reality itself and therefore should rule; power, while de facto external to knowledge, should de jure accompany it. However, if discursive formations are incommensurable (A3) and reality is the product (HPO) of the dominant power structure of the time (ICS), then every "truth" is the result of a Nietzschean struggle of interpretations rather than the disinterested discovery of being (see Foucault, *FR* 85–86). This is why Foucault prefers discussing knowledge in terms of warfare (strategy and tactics) rather than language (meaning). "There are different strategies which are mutually opposed, composed and superposed so as to produce permanent and solid effects" (Foucault, *FL* 281; see also Foucault, *FR* 56–57; Foucault, *SMD* 172–73). There is no innocent knowledge, no bare, unprejudiced intuition of reality itself, though neither is there illicit, falsifying knowledge that distorts true reality, as his early romantic understanding of psychology had depicted it (see Foucault, *HS* 98; Foucault, *EW* 3:343). Without the legitimation of correspondence truth, knowledge is inherently political, including and especially the claim of legitimation by correspondence truth and independent reality. This ethical interpretation of the Heideggerian Paradigm is one of the common links connecting many postmodernists such as Lyotard, Derrida, and Levinas who see violence inherent in the attempt to commensurate different regimes, language-games, and so on in the name of Truth or Reality. I will return to this.

This, of course, means that Foucault cannot claim that he has "gotten it right," that his books capture "what really happened" in opposition to other accounts which are now shown to be false. I think this is what he means by the strange claim that "I am quite aware that I have never written anything but fictions. . . . It seems to me the possibility exists to make fiction work in truth, to induce effects of truth with a discourse of fiction" (Foucault, *FL* 213). He repeats this idea in a later interview:

> What I want to do, and here is the difficulty of trying to do it, is to solve this problem: to work out an interpretation, a reading of a certain reality, which might be such that, on the one hand, this interpretation could produce some of the effects of truth; and on the other hand, these effects of truth could become implements within possible struggles. (Foucault, *FL* 261)

When Foucault says that his writings are fictions, I think he is playing with these terms the way Nietzsche does, meaning that they fail by the standard of R2 Correspondence Truth; he's not trying to tell us what "really happened." But, of course, he does not consider this standard to be coherent.

However, his histories can perfectly well satisfy the sense of truth he accepts as "held to be true within a certain regime of truth or discourse" or "playing the role of true claim with all of the relevant consequences," and thus be believed and have the "effects of truth." Ultimately he is trying to influence some of the ways that we pursue and use historical truth, thus altering our present regime of power-knowledge. Since, as an attempt to reform it, this does not presently fit into our contemporary mode, it is "fictional" or not within the true, but if it succeeds, then it *will* be true once the regime adapts to it. Foucault can say that his early work on madness has already become true since it has had an enormous impact on the way that madness is studied, changing the structure of historiography to accommodate his method, which now is within the true:

> What I do is a kind of historical fiction. In a sense I know very well that what I say is not true. . . . But the book had an effect on the perception of madness. So the book and my thesis have a truth in the nowadays reality. What I am trying to do is to provoke an interference between our reality and the knowledge of our past history. If I succeed, this will have real effects in our present history. My hope is my books become true after they have been written. (Foucault, *FL* 301)

We have to be careful not to exaggerate this claim of fictionality; in order to have the effect he wants, Foucault's work has to obey most contemporary rules of historical research. Much of his audience is composed of professional historians who must respect his scholarship in order to find his work persuasive. More generally, it is a fact in our society that books that can claim a certain kind of scholarly authority written by people with letters after their names have more authority and thus produce more of the power effects he wants. However, he is also using these works to shift historiography and philosophy in new directions, which his astonishing popularity would indicate that he has succeeded in doing. Although they are fictions by the standard of correspondence truth, nothing meets this standard, and if they come to be accepted and play an authoritative role, then there is nothing else to ask for. The belief that there is something more to truth beyond this rests on realism.

This discussion of *Madness and Civilization* is perhaps Foucault's best description of the tightrope he must walk.

> For those who read it and used it—the book constituted a transformation in the historical, theoretical, and moral or ethical relationship we have with madness, the mentally ill, the psychiatric institution, and the very truth of psychiatric discourse. So it's a book that functions as an experience, for its writer and reader alike, much more than as the establishment of a historical truth. For one to be able to have that experience through the book, what it says does need to be true in terms of academic, historically verifiable truth. It can't exactly be a novel. Yet the essential thing is not in the series of those true or historically verifiable findings but, rather, in the experience that the book makes possible. Now, the fact is, this experience is neither true nor false. An experience is always a fiction: it's something that one fabricates oneself, that doesn't exist before and will exist afterward. (Foucault, *EW* 3:243)

This also shows how complex his position is. Those who throw up their hands, concluding that he doesn't or even can't take truth seriously, deeply misunderstand him. Even a more sympathetic commentator like Christopher Norris reads the lesson of *The Order of Things* as stating that scientific disciplines' "specific claims to truth, 'scientific' or otherwise, were seen as nothing more than a species of enabling fiction," and criticizes Foucault because "he relativizes knowledge and truth only in so far as those notions attach to thought-systems other than his own" (1985, 200–201). To accuse something of being "nothing more than . . ." presupposes that it is coherent to think of it being more than that, whereas Foucault allows no other conception of truth. I hope I have disproved the latter assertion adequately.

## The Undefined Work of Freedom

The first volume of *The History of Sexuality* is subtitled "An Introduction" because it was intended to be the beginning of a six-book series of genealogical analyses of modern sexuality. However, just as Foucault found that fully unpacking his method in *The Archaeology of Knowledge* killed the interest it held for him, so this long-range project with locked-in topics for each volume lost its appeal once it was laid out as a predetermined path. So instead of pursuing his announced project on sexuality, he once again underwent a period of (published) silence (he continued his lectures, which now give us tremendously valuable insight into his thought in this period) to emerge some eight years later with two books in quick succession, written in a new style. In both of his career shifts, the method he had been using came to appear inadequately narrow, forcing him to expand his focus. The third and final phase of Foucault's career adds to archaeology's concentration on discursive knowledge and genealogy's non-discursive power and institutions the third axis of the analysis of subjectivity, or "the forms within which individuals are able, are obliged, to recognize themselves as subjects" (Foucault, *UP* 4). Besides determining that he had to go much farther back in time than ever before, he discovered that he

> had to undertake a third shift, in order to analyze what is termed "the subject." It seemed appropriate to look for the forms and modalities of the relation to self by which the individual constitutes and recognizes himself *qua* subject. . . . I felt obliged to study the games of truth in the relationship of self with self and the forming of oneself as a subject, taking as my domain of reference and field of investigation what might be called "the history of desiring man."[48]

This third period, often called ethics or subjectivity, examines the ways that subjects constitute themselves as a specific type of subject.

The relationship of this final phase to the earlier two has been a source of much discussion among scholars, although Foucault himself sees it as a natural development. He writes of "the efforts one makes to alter one's way of looking at things," concluding that "sure of having traveled far, one finds that one is looking down on oneself from above. . . . I seem to have gained a better perspective on the way I worked—gropingly, and by means of different or successive fragments—on this project, whose goal is a history of truth" (Foucault, *UP* 11). Just as he viewed genealogy as a logical extension of archaeology ("when I think back now, I ask myself what else it was that I was talking about, in *Madness and Civilization* or *The Birth of the Clinic,* but power?" [Foucault, *FR* 57; see also Foucault, *EW* 3:283]), so now he believes that ethics brings out what was implicit in the earlier two periods: "The goal of my work during the last twenty years [has] not been to analyze the phenomena of power. . . . My objective, instead, has been to create a history of the different modes by which, in our culture, human beings are made subjects."[49] The subject constitutes itself through "games of truth" (Foucault, *UP* 6) as well as practices and institutions, which means that ethics incorporates the results and methods of both archaeology and genealogy (see 11–12).

Speaking of subjects constituting themselves here is a departure from the way Foucault had earlier written about the constitution of subjectivity, and it represents the most original contribution of the late phase. There are commentators, such as Béatrice Han in her recent study *Foucault's Critical Project,* who view this late discussion of the subject's activity upon itself as a revival of a Kantian kind of transcendental autonomy that his earlier work had successfully put to rest, claiming that this new "idea of a sovereign 'self-consciousness' seems to contradict that of the genesis of forms of subjectivity within power-knowledge" (Han 2002, 169). She sees a serious incompatibility between this last phase, on the one hand, and his genealogical work, which

> radically contradicts the notion of a reflective self-constitution in which the subject would stand as master of itself and an author of the problematizations in which it recognizes itself. . . . The Foucauldian analysis of subjectivity therefore appears to oscillate in a contradictory manner, between a definition of subjectivity as "self-creation," on the one hand, and on the other hand, the need, in order to understand the games of truth through which recognition itself operates, to go back to the practices of power of which subjects are not masters. . . . It is very difficult to say if, for him, the subject is constituting or constituted. (Han 2002, 172)

This analysis misunderstands Foucault's late phase, which actually offers the beginnings (though he did not get a chance to develop it fully) of a conception of subjectivity in line with the later Heidegger's, a subjectivity that is both constituted and constituting.[50]

Han sets up a caricature of Foucault's late conception of subjectivity as sovereign self-creator, master and author of itself. Such a conception is as alien to Foucault's last works as it was to his early ones. Just months before his death in 1984, he said in an interview:

> I don't think there is actually a [A5] sovereign, founding subject, a [R6] universal form of subject that one could find everywhere. I am very skeptical and very hostile toward this conception of the subject. I think on the contrary that the [A6] subject is constituted through practices of subjection . . . starting of course from [ED] a number of rules, styles and conventions that are found in the culture. (Foucault, *FL* 452, bracketed comments added)

In that same year, he explicitly distinguishes the "self-author" model of the subject from his own: "If I am now interested in how the subject constitutes itself in an active fashion through practices of the self, these practices are nevertheless not something invented by the individual himself. They are models that he finds in his culture and that are proposed, suggested, imposed upon him by his culture, his society and his social group" (Foucault, *FL* 440–41). There is nothing like self-mastery or self-creation, since the subject can only draw these constituting forces from outside itself. Once again Foucault's analysis resembles Heidegger's discussion of Dasein's thrownness into a range of projects offered by *das Man* in order to define itself or, in the later work, man's listening to language in order to speak.

Foucault never wavers in his rejection of a preexisting subject. In a late interview he explains that

> what I rejected was the idea of starting out with a theory of the subject—as is done, for example, in phenomenology or existentialism—and, on the basis of this theory, asking how a given form of knowledge was possible. What I wanted to try to show was how the subject constituted itself in one specific form or another, as a mad or a healthy subject, as a delinquent or non-delinquent subject, through certain practices that were also games of truth, practices of power, etc. (Foucault, *FL* 440)

Throughout his work he considers the subject an effect; there is no transcendent or transcendental subject anywhere in Foucault's thought, at least not after the very first texts. The innovation introduced in this third phase that has thrown off Han is that whereas his earlier work was locked into a third-person perspective on the subject—seeing it only from the outside, perhaps to compensate for phenomenology's first-person perspective—he now incorporates internal experience as well. This first-person perspective cannot be authoritative for him the way it was for Husserl's Cartesian-style phenomenology, but neither need it be entirely excluded. The genealogical descriptions of the subject from the outside present her in passive terms as being formed or constituted by forces imposed upon her; without dispensing with the phenomena established in the first two phases, the ethical works add an account of the internal experience of this formation in active terms. We still receive these practices from our society, often under great pressure, but now Foucault is also interested in the ways that we *participate* in applying them to ourselves. This participation is nothing like having absolute control over them or creating them to achieve a Hegelian self-creation, but neither is it negligible or just a ruse of power, as it had been up to now.

In an important explanation from a 1980 lecture, Foucault discusses his transition from a genealogical focus on the third-person perspective, which is called "domination" here, to his ethical emphasis on the first-person perspective, called "techniques of the self."

> Since my project was concerned with the knowledge of the subject, I thought that the techniques of domination were the most important. . . . But, analyzing the experience of sexuality, I became more and more aware that there is in all societies . . . another type of techniques: techniques which permit individuals to perform, by their own means, a certain number of operations on their own bodies, on their own souls, on their own thoughts, on their own conduct, and this in such a way that they transform themselves. . . . Let's call this kind of techniques a techniques or technology of the self. *I think that if one wants to analyze the genealogy of the subject in Western civilization, he has to take into account not only techniques of domination but also techniques of the self.* Let's say: he has to take into account *the interaction between those two types of techniques*—techniques of domination and techniques of the self. (Foucault, *PoT* 180–81, italics added; see also Foucault, *EW* 1:177)

Here he clearly distinguishes the two types of techniques, but describes them as complementary modes of analysis. In fact, he concludes that genealogy requires the study of ethics just to be good genealogy, since the way we are formed and the way we form ourselves "interact," similar to the way he earlier concluded that knowledge and power are inseparable.

This move to the self's applying techniques to itself can be seen as the extension of his new, non-repressive conception of power. "When I was studying asylums, prisons, and so on, I insisted, I think, too much on the techniques of domination. . . . Power consists in complex relations: these relations involve a set of rational techniques, and the efficiency of those techniques is due to a subtle integration of coercion-technologies and self-technologies" (Foucault, *PoT* 182). Focusing on the third-person perspective leads to a coercive understanding of power, just what his work on sexuality's cultivation of introspection and seeking out of expert advice in order to achieve health undermines. Since they are perceived as beneficial practices, these are not only sought out by the subjects but actively applied to themselves. Now he is capitalizing on these genealogical insights by examining how domination intertwines with the self-constituting, first-person perspective, which allows a more positive sense of selfhood than seemed possible in his earlier work. This does not discard the domination his genealogical studies revealed, but rather complements it with a new layer in order to give a more nuanced analysis, just as power refined his archaeological studies which had concentrated too much on discourse.

We do not start as pre-given, ahistorical subjects but rather get formed into the subjectivity that is standard at the time largely through positive and negative feedback, very little of which is conscious or intentional on anyone's side. The subject "is not a substance. It is a form, and this form is not primarily or always identical to itself. . . . It is precisely the historical constitution of these various forms of the subject in relation to the games of truth that interests me" (Foucault, *FL* 440; see also Foucault, *TS* 18; Foucault, *Herm* 486). The epoch's games of truth (the study of which takes the place of archaeology) determine the features that characterize its various identities, while its practices (taking the place of genealogy) provide the rituals used to mold itself into these types of beings. There is no Kantian autonomy here in the sense of acting without causes external to oneself, if only because there is no original inside which could either preserve its purity or be invaded from an outside. Indeed, we can only get an "inside" from the "outside," making the strict dichotomy necessary for autonomy meaningless. What has changed in the move from genealogy to ethics is that Foucault now sees the potential for participation in the process to be more than merely a sham, so that we might be able to take a genuine ownership of the self that is constituted. But this is by no means a hyper-original or metaphysically spontaneous self-creation.

Unfortunately, the two published works of this period that explore these important changes in his views, volumes 2 and 3 of *The History of Sexuality*, while better than most believe, are still inferior books by Foucault's standards, quite possibly rushed to get into publication before his death. In order to get a full sense of his last phase, we have to piece together ideas from many sources, certainly using these two books but also various interviews and presentations. What interests Foucault here is the relationship that developed between the contemporary mode of subjectivity in the West and (1) the changing *games of truth* concerning sexuality associated first with the church and then with the human sciences, especially psychology, and (2) the changing *practices* these institutions offer people to make themselves into the right kind of sexual being, especially confession and its heir in psychoanalysis. Seeing how these topics are the successors to archaeology and genealogy shows how this phase can be seen as something of a culmination of his career (see Foucault, *UP* 11–12). I will follow this narrative in some detail, both to reconstruct his last phase which, partially due to the incomplete state of the published analyses, has not received the attention it deserves, and to get insight into one of the central problems of Foucault's work: how can he justify the changes he is trying to motivate?

In a moment of intellectual autobiography, Foucault describes how as a student he resented the dominance of "the philosophy of the subject," especially Husserl's phenomenology, that "set as its task *par excellence* the foundation of all knowledge and the principle of all signification as stemming from the meaningful subject" (Foucault, *PoT* 174), that is, what I call A5 Active Knower. Liking neither of the alternatives popular at the time, logical positivism and structuralism, he explains his path this way: "I have tried to get out from the philosophy of the subject through a genealogy of this subject, by studying the constitution of the subject across history which has led us up to the modern concept of the self" (Foucault, *PoT* 176; see also 199; Foucault, *EW* 1:176–77). By showing how this A6 subject has itself been constituted, he demonstrates that it cannot be the Kantian or Husserlian source of all meaning (A5), but itself depends upon something else for its meaning, what I am calling ICS. The historical variations of these schemes and their vulnerability to the influence of "events" distinguish his views from structuralism.

This method comes to focus on the history of science because "all the practices by which the subject is defined and transformed are accompanied by the formation of certain types of knowledge, and in the West, for a variety of reasons, knowledge tends to be organized around forms and norms that are more or less scientific" (Foucault, *PoT* 177). Employing what he learned from archaeology, he realizes that self-constitution cannot be separated from what is considered truth, and one of the key features of our particular games of truth is that they have increasingly valorized the scientific. This is due in no small degree to its claim that its achievement of R5 Passive objectivity grants it access to R1 Independent reality as it R2 really is. Non-scientific knowledge is not taken seriously in our society, as philosophers are painfully aware; people will only organize their self-constitutions on the basis of information certified by experts with scientific accreditations. However, Foucault is "not trying to do history of sciences in general, but only of those which sought to construct a scientific knowledge of the subject" (177). Unlike Heidegger, who deals with the hard sciences, Foucault only studies the human sciences, since it is these that primarily influence subjects. He explicitly contrasts Heidegger's study of the way "it was through an increasing obsession with *technē* as the only way to arrive at an understanding of *objects,* that the West lost touch with Being" with his own work as an attempt to "turn the question around and ask which techniques and practices constitute the Western concept of the *subject,* giving it its characteristic split of truth and error, freedom and constraint" (178–79, italics added). This depiction is rather unfair, since Heidegger insists that every question of Being is also a question of man, but notice that turning a question around is a matter of changing emphasis within a framework that is held constant.

Foucault's histories are to function as "a diagnosis of what we are," which amounts to "another kind of critical philosophy . . . that seeks the conditions and the indefinite possibilities of transforming the subject, of transforming ourselves" (Foucault, *PoT* 179; see also Foucault, *TS* 146). This is a frequent theme in his work: we look to history to reveal the frailty and variability of the features in ourselves that we usually assume are permanent and unassailable.

> The work of the intellectual is to show that what is, does not have to be what it is. . . . The return to history makes sense in the respect that history shows that that which is [A3] not always was so. It unites casual movements into threads of a fragile and uncertain history. Thus things [A1] were formed which give the impression of the greatest [R3] self-evidence. . . . Because they are made they can be unmade—of course, assuming we know how they were made. (Foucault, *FL* 359, bracketed comments added; see also Foucault, *FR* 335)

This certainly is "another kind of critical philosophy," since it actually inverts Kantian autonomy and the standard take on ethics that I have discussed above. This standard view commands us to seek out those aspects of ourselves which are permanent, ahistorical, universal *physis* so that we can become who we are, that is, take them up consciously and live them deliberately.

For Foucault, the goal is not to achieve authenticity by discovering our essence or recovering our true selves, but to free ourselves of the very idea of essence, to transgress anything that presents itself as our true, necessary, permanent self.

> If the Kantian question was that of knowing what limits knowledge has to renounce transgressing, it seems to me that the critical question today has to be turned back into a positive one: in what is given to us as universal, necessary, obligatory, what place is occupied by whatever is singular, contingent, and the product of arbitrary constraints? The point, in brief, is to transform the critique conducted in the form of necessary limitation into a practical critique that takes the form of a possible transgression. (Foucault, *FR* 45)

This is a reversal of traditional ethics, so that the purpose of his late work is to teach us how to become what we are not.

> Criticism is no longer going to be practiced in the search for [R6] formal structures with universal value, but rather as a [ED] historical investigation into the [ICS] events that have led us to constitute ourselves and to recognize ourselves as subjects of what we are doing, thinking, and saying. In that sense, this criticism is not transcendental. . . . It will sepa-

> rate out, from the contingency that has made us what we are, the possibility of no longer being, doing, or thinking what we are, do, or think. . . . It is seeking to give new impetus, as far and wide as possible, to the undefined work of freedom. (Foucault, *FR* 45–46, bracketed comments added; see also 50, 335; Foucault, *Herm* 253n)

As we saw, Heidegger turned from his early "search for formal structures with universal value" to immerse the A6 self in history, so that "not every way of being a self is necessarily subjectivity."[51] After a brief flirtation with romantic realism at the beginning of his career, Foucault maintains A6 throughout the rest of it. "I would call subjectivization the process through which results the constitution of a subject, or more exactly, of a subjectivity which is obviously only one of the given possibilities of organizing a consciousness of self" (Foucault, *FL* 472; see also Foucault, *EW* 3:327).

This kind of "counter-criticism" or becoming what one is not requires "the historical ontology of ourselves" (Foucault, *FR* 46), since it is history that shows us A6, that is, that A3 Pluralism applies to the subject, that there have been many different forms of subjectivity, so that our present mode is contingent, meaning that we can assume other forms. Furthermore, history shows us specifically how our modern subjectivity has been formed, thus teaching us how to re-form or unmake it. He sums up both of these points:

> There is, I think, a fundamental heterogeneity here that should warn us against any retrospective projection. And I would say that whoever wishes to study the history of subjectivity—or rather, the history of the relations between the subject and truth—will have to try to uncover the very long and slow transformation of an apparatus of subjectivity. (Foucault, *Herm* 319; see also 462, 486)

An important point here, mentioned above, is that genealogy or historical ontology is not entirely negative, pointing only to contingency and the possibility of other alternatives. Given HPO, we *are* this form of subjectivity today; the fact that we can and perhaps should (more on that below) become otherwise in no way undermines our present identity (see Foucault, *FS* 171–72). Studying history is simultaneously learning who we are and learning that we do not have to be this kind of being, and HPO allows Foucault to make both of these claims simultaneously.

As the first volume of *The History of Sexuality* already showed, psychology identifies modern humanity's deep self with its sexuality and requires a form of confession in order to reveal and cure abnormalities. The study of this specific practice of confession is what draws Foucault into the distant past, through Christianity into ancient Greece. It is this feature of modern subjectivity that organizes his entire late study, namely, psychology's game of truth that identifies the self and its health with its sexuality as known by science as the heir to confession. "I would wish . . . to take [a particular form of psychological confession] as a point of departure for a more general reflection on this practice of confession, and on the postulate, which is generally accepted in Western societies, that one needs for his own salvation to know as exactly as possible who he is" (Foucault, *PoT* 173, bracketed comment added).

Despite its vast importance and self-evidence in our eyes, Foucault wants to portray this connection between our essence, well-being, and sexuality as a contingent linkage rather than an inevitable fact[52] about reality by telling a detailed narrative of the process by which it came about.

> The question posed is then this: How is it that within Western Christian culture the government of men requires, on the part of those who are led, in addition to acts of obedience and submission, "acts of truth," which have this particular character that not only is the subject required to speak truthfully, but to speak truthfully about himself and his faults, his desires, the state of his soul etc.? How was a type of government of men formed where one is required not simply to obey, but to demonstrate in stating it, that which one is. (Foucault, *RC* 154; see also Foucault, *EW* 1:179; Foucault, *Herm* 253)

The first volume of *The History of Sexuality* described modern psychology's location of a person's deep identity in their sexuality as a great innovation, with only brief allusions to precedents in the Christian confessional. Now he realizes that Christianity has been preparing this connection for centuries: "Christianity is a confession. This means that Christianity belongs to a very special type of religion—those which impose obligations of truth on those who practice them. . . . Everyone in Christianity has the duty to explore who he is, what is happening within himself" (Foucault, *RC* 182; see also Foucault, *TS* 40; Foucault, *PoT* 201). This is how the edict "know yourself" came to take over and infect "take care of yourself," which did not have to be connected to or based on knowledge.[53] The revelation explored at length in the late work is that this linkage was forged long ago, though it has gone through significant transformations: "It is a fact, a mysterious fact, that [in] this indefinite spiral of truth and reality in the self sexuality has been of major importance since the first centuries of our era. It has become more and more important. Why is there such a fundamental connection between sexuality, subjectivity and truth obligation?" (Foucault, *RC* 183). Furthermore, this issue is of the utmost importance: "Why are we concerned with truth, and more so than with the care of the self? And why must the care of the self occur only through the concern for truth? I think we are touching on a fundamental question here, what I would call *the* question for the West: How did it come about that all of Western culture began to revolve around this obligation of truth?"[54]

Foucault's study of subjectivization practices tries to demonstrate how differently the ancient Greeks organized sexuality and subjects than we do today.[55] Although the practices of self-examination and confession to a master are formally similar to modern introspection and psychoanalysis, the Greek versions of these practices lacked the particular relationship to truth and scientific knowledge that defines ours. Commenting on the shift from ancient to Christian (which also preserves certain elements), he writes that "several themes, principles, or notions may be found in the one and the other alike, true; but for all that, they do not have the same place or the same value within them" (Foucault, *UP* 21). Transferring an element to a new system alters its significance, texture, and, of particular importance in this case, its relation to truth. "In ancient philosophy self-examination and confession may be considered [a] truth-game, and an important truth-game, but the objective of this truth-game is not to discover a secret reality inside the individual. The objective of this truth-game is to turn the individual into a place where truth can appear and act as a real force" (Foucault, *PoT* 195; see also Foucault, *EW* 1:104). The most important change traced by Foucault is that the Christian version subscribes to R6 Realism of the Self, thus introducing a preexisting self which we must discover and interpret rather than create, whereas "in the Hellenistic or Roman philosophy, you see that the self is not something that has to be discovered or deciphered as a very obscure text. . . . The self doesn't have to be discovered but to be constituted, to be constituted through the force of truth."[56]

Foucault distinguishes several elements of epochal ethical systems (often citing four—see Foucault, *FR* 352–56; Foucault, *UP* 91–93) in order to give a finely grained analysis of what changes when they pass; this could be seen as a criticism or refinement of Heidegger's monolithic conception of a single wholly dominant understanding of Being for each epoch, a conception Foucault himself followed in his archaeological phase. Now he insists that some elements can be carried over to another period, but that they take on new significance in this new holistic context, altered by the fact that other elements change drastically. The only way to grasp these transitions in their richness of detail is by distinguishing all of the threads and following each one in the ways that they change and the ways they remain stable (see Foucault, *UP* 29). In particular, he wants to separate the codes of what is allowed and disallowed—which have gotten a disproportionate amount of attention—from the other elements, such as the relation to oneself, the ideal or goal one seeks, and so on. "I am not supposing that the codes are unimportant. But one notices that they ultimately revolve around a rather small number of rather simple principles. . . . On the other hand . . . there is a whole rich and complex field of historicity in the way the individual is summoned to recognize himself as an ethical subject of sexual conduct."[57] Foucault's analyses aim to show how these other elements differed enormously between ancient Greek, Christian, and modern ethics, the same three epochs Heidegger employs.

Rather than organizing their ethics around a preexisting self which must be discovered in bivalently true or false information, the Greeks conceived of ethics aesthetically. The goal of their practices was the creation of a beautiful self rather than the discovery of the real R6 self, and this ideal was achieved through self-mastery rather than through Christian purity or modern psychological normalcy. Foucault is quite clear that he finds a great deal about Greek ethics "quite disgusting" (Foucault, *FR* 346) and, like Heidegger, is in no way recommending a return to this former way of life (see 250, 343, 347). But he is utterly enthralled by the fact that in their ethics "the reason for making this choice was the will to live a beautiful life, and to leave to others memories of a beautiful existence."[58] As a radical alternative to discovering a preexisting structure for normalcy or following divine rules to gain entrance into heaven, "the idea of the *bios* as a material for an aesthetic piece of art is something which fascinates me. The idea also that ethics can be a very strong structure of existence, without any relation with the juridical per se, with an authoritarian system, with a disciplinary structure. All that is very interesting" (348).

The key features of Greek ethics for Foucault are its central value of self-mastery and its goal of a beautiful life. One wants to constitute oneself as master of oneself, which entails keeping one's desires from becoming excessive to the point of overpowering one's will; the specific details of the object of desire, such as the gender of one's sexual partners, matters less than whether the desire itself is under control (see Foucault, *UP* 44–45, 85–86). This goal is worthy because it is beautiful and noble, not because God commands it or because it is what normal people do. This marks a profoundly different relationship between the self's sexuality and truth from ours. The modern subject *is* her sexuality; its nature is her truth. This is why verdicts of perversion are so deeply damaging.

> The nineteenth-century homosexual became a personage. . . . Nothing that went into his total composition was unaffected by his sexuality. It was everywhere present in him: at the root of all his actions because it was their insidious and indefinitely active principle. . . . It was consub-

> stantial with him, less as a habitual sin than as a singular nature. . . . The sodomite had been a temporary aberration; the homosexual was now a species. (Foucault, *HS* 43)

Sexuality is not an action one does, but the identity modern subjects are,[59] so that knowing oneself requires knowing one's sexuality, "the soul's most secret and determinant part" (Foucault, *HS* 124). For the Greeks, on the other hand,

> the preference for boys or girls was easily recognized as a character trait: men could be distinguished by the pleasure they were most fond of; a matter of taste that could lend itself to humorous treatment, *not a matter of topology involving the individual's very nature, the truth of his desire, or the natural legitimacy of his predilection*. . . . The enjoyment of boys and of women *did not constitute two classificatory categories* between which individuals could be distributed. (Foucault, *UP* 190, italics added; see also Foucault, *FR* 349)

It is just this change in the definition of the subject and its relation to the truth of their sexuality that Foucault is tracing.

The turning point in the story comes when the practices of confession are altered by Christianity, "the cradle of Western hermeneutics of the self."[60] Foucault focuses on the changes that occurred in monasteries where, unlike in Greek ethics, "the supreme good is not the mastership of oneself; the supreme good in monastic life is the contemplation of God. The obligation of the monk is continuously to turn his thoughts to that single point which is God, and his obligation is also to make sure that his heart, his soul, and the eye of his soul are pure enough to see God" (Foucault, *PoT* 214). The Greek emphasis on political duties foregrounded a worldly self-mastery that qualified one to assume mastery over others—family, slaves, and polis (see Foucault, *FS* 144; Foucault, *UP* 60, 75–77). In the monastery, on the other hand, what matters is purity of thought which God—the original Panopticon—is continuously monitoring. This results in the fact that "in monastic life . . . self-examination . . . is much more concerned with thoughts than with actions" (Foucault, *PoT* 214–15). This begins the practice of deep extensive introspection and, in response, a rich private internal life sprang up to be watched.

The first volume of *The History of Sexuality* had already noted that confession shifted its focus from actions to thoughts and desires after the Council of Trent. This increased the attention individuals paid to their interior lives but, ironically, the more they examined them the more elaborate these became; introspective confession ended up developing precisely the desirous interior life it was supposed to be stamping out (Foucault, *HS* 18–21; see also Foucault, *PP* 41, 63–68). Now Foucault tells this story in much more detail, primarily examining the important fifth-century monk John Cassian's exacting models of self-examination and confession, which led those in the monasteries to "a never-ending struggle over the movements of our thoughts . . . over its simplest manifestations, over the factors that can activate it" (Foucault, *RC* 193). Instead of the Greek goal of beautiful self-mastery that was reasonably definable and attainable, now "man must do no less than keep ceaseless watch over his thoughts and bodily movements day and night" (195; see also Foucault, *TS* 45). The interminable self-analysis engaged in by these solitary contemplatives with vast stretches of time on their hands then receives further fuel with the entrance of Satan. Thoughts must now be examined not only for their intrinsic quality of either purity or pollution but also for their source; even apparently good thoughts could be evil if originating from the wrong agent. "It is a question of seizing the movement of thoughts . . . of examining quite deeply in order to seize and decipher the origin from which it comes (from God, oneself or the Devil) and to carry out a sorting process."[61]

These factors all add up to A6: "the apparition of a new kind of self, or at least a new kind of relationship to our selves" (Foucault, *PoT* 227). Of course, these two are not different: a new technology or practice is precisely what constitutes a new kind of self for the late Foucault (the subject is the "correlative of a certain technology of power," as *Discipline and Punish* has it), and Christianity has given the Greek practices a very new significance. "What man needs, if he does not want to be the victim of his own thoughts, is a perpetual work of hermeneutics. The function of this hermeneutics is to discover the reality hidden inside the thought" (220; see also Foucault, *TS* 46). The new features of this practice are that it is never-ending, that it seeks a preexisting reality (R6), and that it plugs into a specific truth game.

> The spiritual struggle against libido . . . consists . . . in turning our eyes continuously downwards or inwards to decipher, among the movements of the soul, which ones come from the libido. . . . The task is not only an issue of mastership but also a question of the diagnosis of truth and illusion. It requires a permanent hermeneutics of oneself. . . . The criterion of purity does not consist in keeping control of oneself even in the presence of the most desirable people: it consists in discovering the truth in myself.[62]

This is a profound change in the conception of ethics, from actions to be mastered to thoughts to be deciphered, from a self to be created to an identity to be known. Furthermore, the purpose of all of this knowledge is to give up the self that is discovered: "This new Christian self had to be constantly examined because in this self were lodged concupiscence and desires of the flesh. From that moment on, the self was no longer something to be made but something to be renounced and deciphered."[63]

Modernity, especially psychology, then appropriates much of this Christian model, but with two important changes. First, it renounces the renunciation of the self, completely reversing Christianity's scornful self-abnegation into a cultivation of and obsession with the self. Instead of discovering it in order to efface it, now subjectivity is sought for the sake of identification, normalization, and maximizing health.

> One of the great problems of Western culture has been to find the possibility of founding the hermeneutics of the self not, as it was the case in early Christianity, on the sacrifice of the self but, on the contrary, on a positive, on the theoretical and practical, emergence of the self. That was the aim of judicial institutions, that was the aim also of medical and psychiatric practices, that was the aim of political and philosophical theory—to constitute the ground of subjectivity as the root of a positive self, what we could call the permanent anthropologism of Western thought.[64]

Modernity's second major change is that rather than linking knowledge of the self to religious salvation, it connected it to science and especially to psychology's ideal of sexual normalcy (see Foucault, *FL* 377). The only legitimate knowledge of the self now is scientific knowledge, which sets out the norm we seek to attain. One of the reasons ancient Greece is a particularly useful topic of study is that it undermines the apparent necessity of the modern connection of the investigation into the self to psychology because it was a time "when the effect of scientific knowledge and the complexity of normative systems were less" (Foucault, *FR* 339). As a proponent of HPO, Foucault's claim cannot be that we have made a terrible mistake and we must recover a truth that the Greeks got right, but rather that both kinds of truth games are possible. Neither is necessary or essential to the very nature of being human, since it's all a matter of what occurs contingently in history.

The power of this genealogical A3 Ontological Pluralism lies in demonstrating the contingency of what we tend to assume is necessary or permanent:

> My idea is that it's not at all necessary to relate ethical problems to scientific knowledge. Among the cultural inventions of mankind there is a treasury of devices, techniques, ideas, procedures, and so on, that can-

> not exactly be reactivated, but at least constitute, or help to constitute, a certain point of view which can be very useful as a tool for analyzing what's going on now—and to change it. (Foucault, *FR* 349–50)

These past techniques cannot be "reactivated" as if we could simply become Greek, but the fact that alternatives have existed contradicts the R6 Realism of the Subject we have been indoctrinated into believing. There have been profoundly different forms of subjectivity, and since actuality implies possibility, there can be other fundamentally different forms. "If we compare that to our experience now . . . we can wonder whether this [connection] wasn't a historical event, one which was not at all necessary, not linked to human nature, or to any anthropological necessity" (Foucault, *FR* 347; see also Foucault, *FL* 318). When asked in a late interview if his *History of Sexuality* contains an ethics, Foucault replies:

> if you mean by ethics a code which would tell us how to act, then of course *The History of Sexuality* is not an ethics. But if by ethics you mean the relationship you have to yourself when you act, then I would say that it intends to be an ethics, or at least to show what could be an ethics of sexual behavior. It would be one which would not be dominated by the problem of the deep truth of the reality of our sex life. (Foucault, *FL* 380)

What his books show us is that the way we relate to ourselves does not have to be mediated by psychology or any notion of a deep unique truth or independent reality. This relationship has been constructed historically and so can be taken apart. It is not necessary to think of the self as the kind of being that has a deep reality; we can embrace A6 instead:

> What we need to do is not to recover our lost identity, or liberate our imprisoned nature, or discover our fundamental truth; rather, it is to move toward something altogether different. . . . In my judgment, what ought to be produced is not man as nature supposedly designed him, or as his essence ordains him to be—we need to produce something that doesn't exist yet, without being able to know what it will be. (Foucault, *EW* 3:275; see also Foucault, *PPC* 166)

This genealogical use of A3 also points to an important distinction between the continental and analytic forms of anti-realism. Many analytic philosophers who discuss alternative conceptual schemes tend to do so by means of thought experiments. When he discusses conceptual schemes, for instance, Davidson writes about what might be believed by Saturnians and Plutonians (see Davidson, *ITI* 186), "little green men and women from Mars" (Davidson, *TLH* 56), or the highly artificial Orwellian imposition of physicalist language (Davidson, *ITI* 188–89). Even when discussing Quine's field translator in the jungle, Davidson makes no use of actual anthropological methodology or data, as Michael N. Forster points out.[65] Eli Hirsch, an analytic philosopher who works on how "language divides up reality in a certain way," sums up this methodological practice when he explains near the beginning of *Dividing Reality* that "actual languages differ somewhat in how they divide reality. The relevant normative intuitions, however, arise most vividly, not when we compare actual languages, but when we compare a given actual language, such as English, to certain imagined languages that are radically different from it" (Hirsch 1993, 3–4). Even if actual languages embody alternative conceptual schemes, in other words, imaginary languages offer superior conditions for study. This approach then leads to such problems as when Robert Kraut discusses Rorty's story of the "Antipodeans" (Rorty 1979, chapter 2) and "Sellars' myth about a community of Rylean behaviorists" as possible holders of alternate schemes, but has to pause to wonder "perhaps, on closer scrutiny, it isn't clear that we really can envisage such non-standard and attenuated conceptual repertoires; but neither is it clear that we can't" (Lepore 1986, 410). In other words, it is hard to decide whether humans are capable of entertaining such deviant schemes, though Davidson for one considers himself capable of settling the issue.

Perhaps the analysis of the conceptual possibility of alternate conceptual schemes is influenced by the fact that it is being considered entirely in hypothetical terms. As I argued in my discussion of the early Heidegger's analysis of being-with, when studied phenomenologically, that is, carefully attending to the concrete situation of people communicating with each other in the world, the possibility that Davidson's radical interpretation must always take seriously that the speaker is not rational and not speaking intelligibly becomes vastly less likely. This then allows much more leeway in allowing divergent meaning to speakers' statements. For Foucault's genealogical purposes which persist into his third phase, he needs to use actual historical ways of thinking and living; former actuality implies possibility much more persuasively than mere conceptual possibility does. And these historical documents also carry a strong presumption of meaningfulness with them. This kind of reconstruction requires a great deal of work, whether one concentrates on philosophical texts the way Heidegger does or on marginal texts and institutions and buildings like Foucault. Nothing is more alien to this way of thinking than Davidson's claim that human conceptual systems and beliefs[66] must be deeply homogeneous so that, for example, all one needs in order to make Kuhn's different paradigms commensurable is "Webster's dictionary" (Davidson,

*ITI* 189). Davidson integrates this homogeneity so deeply into humanity as a whole that no matter what the differences, "the radical interpreter . . . can assume he and [his informants] share most basic concepts. Thus a first guess is apt to be right, though there can be no assurance of this" (Davidson, *Prob* 144; see also Davidson, *PDD* 308–9). We can see here a profound difference with postmodern continental thinkers who insist on the radically other.[67]

## R6 Free Realism of the Subject

We now have a better idea of what Foucault is doing and how he is doing it. He is trying to show that the truths, institutions, and identities we generally take as natural and permanent—that is, in a realist way—are actually historically constituted and thus contingent and therefore susceptible to change.

> Recourse to history . . . is meaningful to the extent that history serves to show how that-which-is has not always been; i.e., that the things which seem most evident to us are always formed in the confluence of encounters and chances, during the course of a precarious and fragile history. . . . They reside on a base of human practice and human history; and . . . since these things have been made, they can be unmade, as long as we know how it was that they were made. (Foucault, *PPC* 37; see also Foucault, *EW* 3:323)

Before we can act, we must rid ourselves of the realism that sustains our belief in the permanence of these features or that keeps our revolutions superficial, altering only surface features while leaving intact our core identities, which are the real effects and footholds of power.[68]

This activist motivation marks an important difference between Foucault's thought and analytic anti-realism. For instance, Michael Dummett interprets Wittgenstein in a way that places him fairly close to Foucault as claiming that "it is vain and presumptuous to attempt to see reality through God's eyes: all we can do is to describe our own practices as we can view them through our own eyes. . . . We cannot intelligibly talk about what is true independently of what we recognize as true" (Clark and Hale 1994, 55–57). Dummett goes on to show how this position amounts to a kind of idealism that merges with realism, similar to the way I explained Hegel's Objective Idealism or HPO. He concludes that "if realism and idealism, or, as I am here preferring to say, externalism and internalism, coincide, there can be no harm in being an externalist. The externalist has an advantage over the internalist, in that, of certain things that we say, it is our practice to claim that they represent how things are in themselves, independently of how we apprehend them" (57). In other words, if their content converges there is no real difference in the positions, and realism enjoys the tie-breaker of having common sense on its side.

This is just where Foucault disagrees. Even though he subscribes to HPO and thus views the entities he studies as fully real, it is extremely important to him to deny the realist doctrines R1 and R3—that is, the claims that reality has a natural, proper, permanent way of being in itself, wholly independent of us. The reason for this comes out in his comment in a late interview that "my point is not that everything is bad, but that everything is dangerous. . . . If everything is dangerous, then we always have something to do. So my position leads not to apathy but to a hyper- and pessimistic activism" (Foucault, *FR* 343). Although UT and HPO prevent him from claiming that the present form of subjectivity, maintained and legitimated by realism, is false, he does find it dangerous.

> The large, ill-defined, and confused family of "abnormal individuals," the fear of which haunts the end of the nineteenth century, does not merely mark a phase of uncertainty or a somewhat unfortunate episode in the history of psychopathology. *It was formed in correlation with a set of institutions of control and a series of mechanisms of surveillance and distribution, and . . . it gives rise to laughable theoretical constructions that nonetheless have harshly real effects.* (Foucault, *Ab* 323, italics added; see also Foucault, *PP* 39, 340)

The category of abnormality is parasitic on the category of normality, which is a definition of the R6 true, real nature of humanity that we all should strive to achieve. The experts' power derives from their knowledge of this essence, their ability to measure individuals' divergence from the ideal, and their capacity to bring these misfits into the warm fold of healthy normalcy. What is significant here is that on the basis of claiming to know the R1 reality of mental illnesses and R6 human nature, the human sciences underwrite locking people up. At the very least, many grow up convinced that they are horribly abnormal.[69] Although we must be careful not to reduce Foucault's thought to personal motivations, we can certainly see why anti-realism would be particularly persuasive to a gay man studying psychology at a time when homosexuality was officially categorized as a mental illness.

This is the harm that realism holds, the "harshly real effects" unseen by Dummett but which Foucault's historical studies try to highlight and disarm: "Historical analysis is a way of avoiding the sacralization of theory: it allows one to erase the threshold of scientific untouchability" (Foucault, *FL* 198). Even if the content of realism and idealism meet in HPO, the "perlocutionary force" (see Austin 1975, 99–102) of realist statements can be devastating. If we reject realism to embrace A6, however, "my optimism would consist . . . in saying that so many things can be changed, fragile as they are, bound up more with circumstances than necessities, more arbitrary than self-evident, more a matter of complex, but temporary, historical circumstances than with inevitable anthropological constants" (Foucault, *PPC* 156; see also Foucault, *FL* 312). Without the absolute legitimation of independent, unique reality, incommensurable views lack a neutral means of adjudication. If one wins out over the other, this cannot be the result of free rational convincing because even the conception of rationality is under dispute. This is why many postmodernists believe that reconciling incommensurable ways of thinking necessarily entails violence.[70] Interestingly, Wittgenstein agrees that heterogeneous language-games cannot be resolved rationally, since rationality only takes place within a language-game. If we try to convince someone operating with a different language-game, "we should be trying to give him our picture of the world. This would happen through a kind of *persuasion*" (Wittgenstein, *OC* §262, italics in original). He even employs violent imagery to describe it: "Is it wrong for them to consult an oracle and be guided by it?—If we call this 'wrong' aren't we using our language-game as a base from which to *combat* theirs?"[71]

However, Foucault runs into a serious problem here, one that has been pointed out by many commentators.[72] The point of all of his work is to provoke and enable deep changes.

> A critique is not a matter of saying that things are not right as they are. It is a matter of pointing out on what kinds of assumptions, what kinds of familiar, unchallenged, unconsidered modes of thought the practices that we accept rest. . . . Criticism is a matter of flushing out that thought and trying to change it: to show that things are not as self-evident as one believed. . . . As soon as one can no longer think things as one formerly thought them transformation becomes both very urgent, very difficult, and quite possible. (Foucault, *PPC* 154–55)

In line with his ethics of counter-criticism where one becomes what one is not, he wants to motivate his readers to change their form of subjectivity, but given his allegiance to the Heideggerian Paradigm's Historical Phenomenological Ontology, he is also committed to the claim that the present form of subjectivity is fully real. This is actually who we are even if it has been historically formed and could change. If this is the case, though, why should we change it?

Obviously, arguments based on autonomy, authenticity, or the liberation of our inner nature are ruled out; since our identity has been constructed by power, freeing and appropriating this self cannot be the key to freedom. "The man described for us, whom we are invited to free, is already in himself the effect of a subjection much more profound than himself" (Foucault, *DP* 30). Similarly, when we "liberate" our sexuality, we "think we are affirming the rights of our sex against all power, when in fact we are fastened to the deployment of sexuality" (Foucault, *HS* 157), since this sexuality is a foothold for psychology to mold us into obedient subjects. "The object 'sexuality' is in reality an instrument formed a long while ago, and one which has constituted a centuries-long apparatus of subjection" (Foucault, *PK* 219). Using concepts like authenticity, liberation, and identity politics to rebel against the powers that be ends up reinscribing these power forms even more deeply. "I have always been somewhat suspicious of the notion of liberation, because if it is not treated with precautions and within certain limits, one runs the risk of falling back on the idea that there exists a human nature or base that, as a consequence of certain historical, economic and social process, has been concealed, alienated or imprisoned in and by mechanisms of repression."[73] Since the idea of liberation requires R6 Realism of the Subject, it has to go along with its parasite notion of repression.

Personal identity functions as a tool of repression when experts tell us that we have an essence which only they can reveal to us. Authenticity, freedom, and normalcy can all be ours as long as we conform to the prescribed norms. But the question is, how can Foucault condemn this? If he subscribes to HPO, then we really *are* these identities regardless of their contingency and constitution by power. Indeed, since he has ruled out the very idea of a natural identity, how can he employ notions like prison or constraint at all, as in comments like this: "We have to be liberated from this kind of subjectivity. We are prisoners of certain conceptions about ourselves and our behavior. We have to liberate our own subjectivity, our own relation to ourselves" (Foucault, *FL* 298; see also Hoy 1986, 61; Butler 1999, 123, 129)? What is this "we" that is imprisoned within contemporary modes of subjectivity? How can there be anything to us beyond how we are shaped by modern power/knowledge structures to be trapped? Foucault repudiated his early R6 realism—the idea that there was a madness in itself that could be repressed or distorted—in favor of HPO—that whatever exists at a period is reality. However, these doctrines seem to rob his critique of its ability to generate precisely the kinds of values or criteria he needs to condemn the modern form of subjectivity. He is usually consistent in abdicating these vestiges of realism: "It is not that the beautiful totality of the individual is amputated, repressed, altered by our social order, it is rather that the individual is carefully fabricated in it."[74] And yet he still speaks of being trapped or imprisoned.[75]

I think that behind Foucault's many criticisms of modern subjectivity we can spy a belief in some kind of human nature which does get mistreated or deformed. Of course, this cannot be any specific historical form, since subjects have and can take on many forms. The specific target of Foucault's criticism is the reification of *any* specific identity as the realist R1 and R3 truth of subjectivity itself, that is, R6 in general. Each era claims to be the one true absolute essence in a tendency that seems endemic to regimes of truth, partly as an illusion natural to the process and partly as a legitimating tool of power. These realist justifications enforce present power formations and prevent change by labeling experimenters abnormal, deviants, or perverts and by promising health and normalcy to those who conform. Foucault's fundamental criticism of these epochs is the fact that they claim to be the only possible order (R3), rather than just one among an indefinite number of possibilities (A3). He is not claiming that any particular regime is false, but that others are always possible yet are blocked by the rigid adherence to one scheme as the sole truth. "We must make the intelligible appear against a background of emptiness, and deny its necessity. We must think that what exists is far from filling all possible spaces" (Foucault, *FL* 312). Here Foucault repeats Heidegger's move when he claimed that every clearing is also a concealing and criticized technology because it "drives out every other possibility of revealing" (Heidegger, *BW* 332), or Nietzsche's promise that "there are a thousand paths that have never yet been trodden—a thousand healths and hidden isles of life. Even now, man and man's earth are unexhausted and undiscovered" (Nietzsche, *Z* 189).

Foucault motivates this call to continuous change by relying on a particular conception of human freedom. Just as Nietzsche's accusation that Christianity lies relied on the grammar of truth, so Foucault's description of constituted identities as prisons carries with it the notion of something free that is being imprisoned. Caputo describes this structure well:

> The claim that every historical constitution is a contingency that threatens to become a historical "trap" means that something is being trapped. The idea that no particular historical constitution is exhaustive or totalizing means that there is always a residue, an irreducibility, a fragment that cannot be incorporated . . . a purely negative, always historical capacity for being-otherwise, which is what Foucault means by freedom.[76]

The reason that the congealing of power relations is bad is that it conflicts with the essential human ability always to be something other, to create new ways of thinking and being. Just as Heidegger rests with a minimal essence of man as the clearing which enables the epochal understandings of Being, so Foucault ends up with the basic condition for the possibility of never-ending historical transformations of subjectivity. For both philosophers, their minimal residue of R6 Realism of the Subject occurs precisely where they engage in a Kantian transcendental inquiry into conditions, though for them it is the conditions for the possibility of ever-changing historical truths (A3) rather than of the one necessary and universal truth (R3).

With this definition of the self, we have gone as far from traditional R6 as possible while still retaining a form of it. Foucault makes the essence of human nature an anti- or counter-essence, the ability to transgress anything prescribed as our necessary or true identity. Our identity is precisely the ability to refuse and contradict any specific identity. As he says in an interview, his conception of the self comes close to Nietzsche (Foucault, *FR* 351), though I would say it is actually more Nietzschean than Nietzsche himself, since I argue above that will to power has too much content (see chapter 4). Foucault has completely inverted Kantian autonomy, since we must reject any identity that has gotten stuck to us in the process of history, and yet, in a strange way, he still retains a paradoxical version of it. The reason we "must" dissolve these identities is that actually, beneath them, we *are* this amorphous, thrashing freedom, this drive to become otherwise which any description will confine. It is this counter-identity, which is really the deepest of all identities, that insists that we break through all the other identities; we must become what we are not because *that* becoming is what we are.

This freedom then forms the ground for Foucault's evaluations. The constant note sounded in his various criticisms of our identities is not the fact that they have been constituted, since HPO and A6 render this innocuous, but rather their fixedness, their rigidity, their constraint on our ability to change or choose new ones. The theme of "fixing" recurs throughout his discussions, as if he is haunted by claustrophobia. "The examination that places individuals in a field of surveillance also situates them in a network of writing; it engages them in a whole mass of documents that *capture and fix them*" (Foucault, *DP* 189, italics added). "Discipline fixes; it arrests or regulates movements" (219; see also Foucault, *Ab* 46; Foucault, *FL* 228; Foucault, *PP* 21, 75). He expresses horror at the Freudian analysis of focusing children's sexuality on their genitals, thus closing down their ability to let pleasure flow freely throughout their body (Foucault, *FL* 219). These view are surprisingly similar to Sartre's famous discussion of the way the look freezes one's identity and curtails freedom: "Thus I, who in so far as I am my possibles, am what I am not and am not what I am—behold now I *am* somebody!" (Sartre 1992, 353). One can imagine this cry coming from the mouth of Herculine Barbin, the hermaphrodite who gets fixed in a web of sexual classifications, cutting her off from "the happy limbo of a non-identity" (Foucault, *HB* xiii) where s/he could (ideally) pass through differently gendered areas unimpeded.

In another late interview, Foucault discusses a topic which his interviewer suggests could be "the fundamental criteria of what you have called a new ethics" (Foucault, *FL* 447). Although power relations are ubiquitous and inescapable—meaning that Foucault's hope is not for the impossible utopia of a society without power relations—he defines one particular type as

> states of domination in which the power relations, instead of being mobile, allowing the various participants to adopt strategies modifying them, remain blocked, frozen. When an individual or a social group succeeds in blocking a field of power relations, immobilizing them and preventing any reversibility of movement by economic, political or military means, one is faced with what may be called a state of domination. (Foucault, *FL* 434)

In opposition to these particularly restrictive forms of power, Foucault's goal is "the *ethos,* the practice of the self, that will allow us to play these games of power with as little domination as possible" (Foucault, *FL* 446).

In another interview, he again dismisses the impossible ideal of a "culture without restraints," instead employing the criterion of

> whether the system of constraints in which a society functions leaves individuals the liberty to transform the system. . . . A system of constraint becomes truly intolerable when the individuals who are affected by it don't have the means of modifying it. This can happen when such a system becomes intangible as a result of its being considered a moral or religious imperative, or a necessary consequence of medical science. (Foucault, *FL* 327; see also 386–87, 441–42)

He seems to be exploring a formal criterion that could evaluate and compare epochs, namely, the degree of domination versus fluidity in relations of power. Minimal domination would require a regime to renounce realist claims to the one, absolute truth which naturally freezes relations and restricts options, in order to allow people to modify their selves as works of art. This allows people to be otherwise, to invent new forms of subjectivity without being branded criminals or mad, and to create new types of pleasure without being sinners or perverts (unless that's what they want to be). This is another reason why he is so interested in Greek ethics. Since their central value—beauty instead of truth—doesn't obey R2 Correspondence to a set ideal or R4 Bivalent determination if one has achieved success, it is much more variable, and "the search for a form of morality that would be acceptable to everyone—in the sense that everyone would have to submit to it—strikes me as catastrophic" (Foucault, *FL* 473; see also Foucault, *UP* 21, 62). Thus, Foucault opts for almost a kind of compatibilism: there is no Kantian autonomy since the subject is always already influenced, but her participation in mobile power relations can be understood as freedom.

Paradoxically, his counter-critical ethics takes the traditional form of authenticity—uncover your true self that you may live in accord with it. He has determined human nature to be the inability ever to be determined once and for all as any specific nature. Although this is as distant as one can get from a traditional realist essence, it is still what we really are, which in turn determines what kind of behavior is appropriate to this anti-identical identity. Foucault himself sums up the paradox nicely: "My way of being no longer the same is, by definition, the most singular part of what I am" (Foucault, *EW* 3:444). He frequently describes his ideal life that would be in accord with this kind of self: "What can the ethics of an intellectual be . . . if not that: to render oneself permanently capable of self-detachment" (Foucault, *FL* 461; see also 455; Foucault, *PoT* 230–31).

Philosophy itself gets defined in these terms: "In what does [philosophy] consist, if not in the endeavor to know how and to what extent it might be possible to think differently, instead of legitimating what is already known? . . . . It is entitled to explore what might be changed, in its own thought, through the practice of a knowledge that is foreign to it" (Foucault, *UP* 9). Just as Heidegger seeks a new way of thinking that will fundamentally alter the essence of man, so Foucault considers self-transformation to be the essential function of philosophy, a process that he understands as freedom. "I shall thus characterize the philosophical ethos appropriate to the critical ontology of ourselves as a historico-practical test of the limits that we may go beyond, and thus as work carried out by ourselves upon ourselves as free beings" (Foucault, *FR* 47). Foucault does make the process more active, though, never telling us to wait for a god to save us.

> From this philosophy comes the movement through which, not without effort and fumblings, dreams and illusions, one detaches oneself from what are the received truths and seeks other rules of the game. From philosophy comes the displacement and transformation of the limits of

> thought, the modification of received values and all the work done to think otherwise, to do something else, to become other than what one is. (Foucault, *FL* 306–7; see also 385; Foucault, *FR* 50)

It is perhaps the great irony of Foucault's work that it is only through this philosophical endeavor to become what we are not that we truly become who we are.

## Conclusion

I have tried to show in this chapter that Foucault is best read as a disciple of Heidegger, and that the later Heidegger's influence on him is more general and more illuminating than, for example, Nietzsche's. Although Foucault admires Kant for rejecting realism and introducing the idea of conceptual schemes, he criticizes Kant for putting philosophy into an "anthropological sleep" by limiting the schemes to one (R3) situated within a universal (R6), transcendentally constituting subject (A5). The process of language coming to dominate in the wake (in both senses) of man traced in *The Order of Things,* although described in terms of structuralism and specific disciplines (ED) there, parallels the ascendancy of the Heideggerian Paradigm over the Kantian Paradigm in philosophy. Foucault embraces this revolution, positing a new candidate for an Impersonal Conceptual Scheme in each of his three phases rather than relying on an active knower, even in the last phase when the subject is allowed to participate to some degree in his own subjectification. Moreover, this subject changes profoundly over time (A6), especially in relation to particular human sciences (ED). This is probably Foucault's greatest contribution to the discussion, and his extreme commitment to ED is one reason for his enormous influence outside philosophy, though the more I have studied his late work the more convinced I have become that he was on the verge of a very important new conception of agency before he died.

# Post

8

# Derrida

> The step "outside philosophy" is much more difficult to conceive than is generally imagined by those who think they made it long ago with cavalier ease, and who in general are swallowed up in metaphysics in the entire body of discourse which they claim to have disengaged from it. (Derrida, *WD* 284)
>
> In the beginning, in principle, was the post, and I will never get over it. (Derrida, *PC* 29)

Jacques Derrida is certainly the most misunderstood and casually misconstrued philosopher of recent times, and the thinker who has provoked the strongest reactions across the analytic-continental divide. He presently holds the dubious position, occupied before him at various times by Hegel, Nietzsche, and Heidegger, of being the poster child for everything that's wrong with continental thought, if not Western civilization as a whole. Such certainly is the verdict rendered by nineteen philosophers, including Quine, in a highly unorthodox protest of Cambridge's plan to award Derrida an honorary degree. Characterizing their view as how Derrida appears "in the eyes of philosophers," or at least "certainly among those working in leading departments of philosophy throughout the world," they assert that his writings consist of "tricks and gimmicks. . . . His works employ a written style that defies comprehension. . . . Where coherent assertions are being made at all, these are either false or trivial." The conclusion is that his work as a whole amounts to "little more than semi-intelligible attacks upon the values of reason, truth, and scholarship" (Derrida, *PoI* 420–21).

Derrida often comments on the irony that these criticisms (which he has suffered throughout his career) frequently commit the very sins they attribute to him (see Davis and Schleifer 1994, 334; Derrida, *Ltd* 153). In particular, he is accused of contempt for responsible scholarship and careful reading by people who have barely read a page of his books, who justify their accusations by attributing to him views that are explicitly denied in his books, supported by quotes that do not appear in them, as in fact occurs in the Cambridge letter (see Derrida, *PoI* 404). This reaches its zenith in Searle's astonishing criticism that "Derrida's eccentric reading of the history of Western philosophy, a reading according to which philosophers are supposed to be roundly condemning writing, while privileging spoken language, is not grounded on an actual reading of the texts of the leading figures in the philosophical tradition."[1] Eccentric no doubt, but if any major figure has ever *read* the texts of the tradition, it is Derrida (see Cavell 1995, 70). His writings are certainly difficult, and they demand considerable knowledge of the history of philosophy if one is to appreciate their finer points, but why should he not be forgiven the difficulty that inevitably accompanies any kind of specialization? Why isn't he entitled to expect the appropriate effort and background from his readers, two factors conspicuously lacking in those most passionate in their denunciation? A similar complaint that high-level symbolic logic, much less theoretical physics, made no sense to an unschooled student would not be taken seriously, yet the most advanced continental philosophy of the second half of the twentieth century must be immediately intelligible to those untrained in the tradition (see Derrida, *PoI* 115–16, 176–77). Searle's "Reply to Derrida" (1977) demonstrates how little effort Searle had put into his reading since, as Derrida easily shows in *Limited Inc,* Searle repeatedly uses Derrida's own arguments to attack him (see Derrida, *Ltd* 46–47, 98).

One reason for the difficulty of Derrida's writing, especially for analytic readers, is that, like all of the continental figures I have discussed, Derrida is taking part in a larger conversation that loses a great deal for those unfamiliar with what he is responding to. Deconstruction takes this tendency even farther in its version of the Empirical Directive, in that philosophical texts form its essential subjects of study.[2] Deconstruction is "intentional" in that there is no such thing as deconstruction as such, only deconstruction of particular texts: "Nothing is less lonely and thinkable on its own. . . . 'Deconstruction' would always go *with,* together with *something* else" (Royle 2000, 282; see also Derrida, *Ltd* 141; Staten 1986, 31). Thus, the less familiar one is with these works, the more obscure Derrida's readings will be (although his deconstructions are meant to render these works and figures unfamiliar).

Despite the common impression that he appeared out of nowhere or merely "translat[es] into the academic sphere tricks and gimmicks similar to those of the Dadaists" (Derrida, *PoI* 420), that he is a misplaced literary theorist, psychoanalyst, or, well, something, Derrida cannot be understood without the philosophical context and concerns that he works within and on. He himself states that "my work would have no sense outside its explicit, recurrent, and systematic references to Plato, Aristotle, Descartes, Kant, Hegel, Nietzsche, Husserl, Heidegger, and several other authors" (411; see also Norris 1987, 156). Although he refuses any simple identification, including being a philosopher, he says that "I always place myself in relation to philosophy" (Derrida, *PoI* 412; see also Derrida, *TFS* 48; Rapaport 1989, 22). Saussure, Nietzsche, and Levinas are certainly important to him, but it is the later Heidegger who wields the greatest influence on his work; he even derives the term "deconstruction" from Heidegger's terms *Destruktion* and *Ab-bau*.[3] In the terms of my scheme, I will show that Derrida is working on the Heideggerian Paradigm, though he is not exactly working *within* it. One of the reasons Derrida is both so difficult and so interesting and important is that he problematizes some of this paradigm's central tenets similar to the way the later Heidegger worked to escape the Kantian Paradigm, thus pointing the way to a new form of philosophy.

This makes his work both very exciting and extremely challenging, since he is trying to depart from some of the most basic stabilizing assumptions that have governed the entire history of philosophy the way Heidegger did, releasing his writing from constraints and notions we take so much for granted that we are not even aware of them. The question of how to do philosophy in a profoundly new way never strays far from his thought. Speaking of Bataille in terms applicable to his own work, he asks, "How, after having exhausted the discourse of philosophy, can one inscribe in the lexicon and syntax of a language, our language, which was also the language of philosophy, that which nevertheless exceeds the oppositions of concepts governed by this communal logic? Necessary and impossible, this excess had to fold discourse into strange shapes."[4] He also makes the point that, in general, challenging earlier ways of arguing and doing philosophy has always been part of doing philosophy, so that doing philosophy in radically new ways is one of the most traditional practices we have. Our discipline has the peculiarity of never settling down into what Kuhn calls a "normal" science, and its history is littered with cries of foul play when someone changes the rules, though, in retrospect, many of these figures are considered our greatest thinkers.[5] As strange as they are, almost anyone who has worked through Derrida's texts leaves with no doubt that they are marked by the highest level of rigor; it is just a rigor that works along very different lines than we are used to.

This chapter will try to fill in a little of the background conversation to help make the ideas Derrida is reacting to and the general trajectory of his thought more visible. Derrida's revolutionary innovations do make this chapter more hesitant and sketchy than the others. Partly because Derrida has written so much and I feel less certain of his corpus than of the other thinkers I have discussed, partly because Derrida's very topic of opening onto a new way of thinking is inherently tentative and suggestive, and partly because we have so little distance from which to evaluate his accomplishment, this chapter will be in the nature of hypotheses, educated guesses, and extrapolations. This is fitting for the final chapter of a book which now turns from the reconstruction of a history to the always foolish art of prognostication; besides, no other tone fits writing about Derrida.

Derrida's work consists largely in the deconstruction of the history of philosophy as a necessary precursor to stepping beyond it, though that step, as we will see, can never exactly go beyond. He defines this history as the era of the metaphysics of presence because its "matrix . . . is the determination of Being as *presence* in all senses of this word" (Derrida, *WD* 279). Those who have read my book to this point will not be surprised that I interpret this metaphysics of presence as a form of realism.

## Realism: The Metaphysics of Presence

Derrida's treatment of realism is peculiar, among other reasons, because he transposes the issue into terms of speech and writing, especially in his early work (that is, through the early 1970s). This is one of the features of his work that particularly irritates Searle. After quoting Culler quoting Derrida stating that the privileging of the *phonè* or spoken word over writing "has necessarily dominated the history of the world during an entire epoch" (from Derrida, *G* 8), Searle comments:

> On the face of it, this claim is bizarre. This distinction between speech and writing is simply not very important to Plato, Aristotle, Aquinas, Descartes, Kant, Spinoza, Leibniz, Hume, etc. . . . Notice that all these philosophers address themselves to issues such as universal and particular, transcendental and empirical, etc. For these philosophers these issues neither arise from the distinction between the oral and the written nor depend on the "privileged" status of the oral. (Madison 1993, 174–75)

Well, yes, "on the face of it" this topic is "simply" not very important "for these philosophers," but Derrida's method is to look beyond what is on the face of texts. He tries to peel back the obvious meaning of a text to find marginal elements that initially appear trivial but which, when carefully attended to, become tremendously illuminating. He often finds minor figures, lesser texts of major figures, or footnotes and offhand comments to be the most telling.[6]

Derrida's general view is that writings are governed by systems of thought that inevitably end up asserting views opposite to their general thesis, usually at a point when the author lets his guard down. He occasionally compares this process to unconscious forces that bubble up during sleep or distraction in easily dismissed phenomena such as jokes or slips of the tongue. For instance, when Heidegger makes a certain claim which is then undermined by the specific examples he uses to illustrate it, Derrida comments that "the choice of examples can be read beyond that meaning [that is, what one consciously means to say]. This supposes a completely other protocol of reading, an other logic, an other rhetoric, a hermeneutic not only broadened but restructured by taking into account what would be called, to go quickly and in a word doubtless problematic, the 'unconscious.'"[7] Thus what texts "simply" say "on the face of it" is precisely not what deconstruction takes as authoritative; it often unravels the initial sense, though always through careful attention to what can be found within the text (ED). "This comprehension of the sign in and of itself, in its immediate materiality as a sign, if I may so call it, is only the first moment but also the indispensable condition of all hermeneutics and of any claim to transition from the sign to the signified. When one attempts, in a general way, to pass from an obvious to a latent language, one must first be rigorously sure of the obvious meaning" (Derrida, *WD* 32).

Just as Freud found previously ignored dream imagery to be the "royal road to the unconscious," Derrida believes that what philosophers say about writing is a particularly helpful clue to their thought as a whole. The fact that this topic seems metaphysically innocuous makes it all the easier for unexamined presuppositions to "pool up" here, so to speak. The exact status of "writing" within his works is a little difficult to pin down. Derrida does explicitly distinguish between writing in the "narrow," "vulgar," or "common" sense, what we would usually call the literal sense (but see Derrida, *G* 89), and what he sometimes calls "arche-writing" (almost synonymous with trace, spacing, *différance*), a "concept" that shares some of common writing's characteristics but that functions somewhat like a transcendental condition for many things (I will discuss this in detail below). Keeping strictly to this distinction, we could say that although writing in the narrow sense might play a very minor role in these philosophers' works, arche-writing is deeply involved.[8] Derrida does not stop here, but goes on to show how frequently the topics of speech and writing actually appear in these works, and often loaded up with startlingly high significance (see, for example, 130, 201). These two strategies of showing how the structure of arguments involves the transcendental condition arche-writing and of pointing out the presence of literal speech and writing work together, because writing in the narrow sense shares important characteristics with arche-writing: "Writing is one of the representatives of the trace in general."[9] It is because of this relationship that philosophical presuppositions about arche-writing concerning the metaphysics of presence tend to emerge when philosophers discuss the topic of writing. A thinker's treatment of writing is a symptom of their commitment to the more pervasive background metaphysics of presence. This is how Derrida justifies claims about the centrality of writing that can certainly look bizarre, such as that Plato's attack on writing is "the philosophical movement par excellence" (Derrida, *MP* 316; see also 311), or that "the meditation upon writing and the deconstruction of the history of philosophy become inseparable" (Derrida, *G* 86; see also Derrida, *Dis* 111).

The basic relationship between speech and writing in the metaphysics of presence is phonocentric, meaning that throughout the history of philosophy the latter is constantly denigrated in favor of the former. "*The history of* (the only) *metaphysics* . . . has always been . . . the debasement of writing, and its repression outside 'full' speech."[10] This debasement is in no way accidental or contingent, but is entailed by a deeply held system of ideas. "The privilege of the *phonè* does not depend upon a choice that could have been avoided. It responds to a moment of *economy*."[11] The very structure of the metaphysics of presence leads to these views.

The metaphysics of presence gives a realist explanation of the transcendental conditions for the possibility of meaning. In order for there to be meaning, in this view, there must be things out there that words can hook on to in a determinate fashion. The referents must be R1 Independent of thought and language; in Derrida's preferred semiological terms, "the signified has no need of the signifier to be what it is" (Derrida, *G* 73). Because the object referred to transcends and is wholly separate from the system of signifiers that refer to it, Derrida calls it the transcendental signified.

> Realism or sensualism—"empiricism"—are modifications of logocentrism. . . . [The transcendental signified] then becomes an ultimate referent, according to the classical logic implied by the value of referent, or it becomes an "objective reality" absolutely "anterior" to any work of the mark, the semantic content of a form of presence which guarantees the movement of the text in general from the outside. (Derrida, *Pos* 64–65, bracketed comment added; see also Derrida, "SOR" 113)

It is absolutely anterior in that it is the world that prods us into naming it; language does not bring about being (R5), nor can it affect it in any way without compromising its own truth. This view is absolutely central to the history of philosophy.

> First there is what is, "reality," the thing itself . . . then there is, imitating these, . . . the inscription or transcription of the thing itself. . . . And obviously, according to "logic" itself . . . what is imitated is more real, more essential, more true, etc., than what imitates. It is anterior and superior to it. . . . Doubtless this order will appear to be contested, even inverted, in the course of history, and on several occasions. But never have the absolute distinguishability between imitated and imitator, and the anteriority of the first over the second, been displaced by any metaphysical system. . . . This order of appearance is . . . the order of truth. (Derrida, *Dis* 191–92)

Words get their significance from the prior existence of things which are wholly different from and do not depend upon language. Metaphysics thus posits "a *concept signified in and of itself,* a concept simply present for thought, independent of a relationship to language, that is, of a relationship to a system of signifiers . . . what I have proposed to call a 'transcendental signified,' which in and of itself, in its essence, would refer to no signifier, would exceed the chain of signs, and would no longer itself function as a signifier" (Derrida, *Pos* 19–20). Language becomes merely the signifier, a dispensable tool used to indicate but which in no way affects the indicated (a rose by any other name . . .).

Reality is fully present; it is what it is (R3) and with no need to be referred to (R1). Since the very distinction between signifier and signified already brings in the possibility of confusion, in that signifiers can lack referents or get linked to the wrong ones, the ideal situation would be to dispense with signs altogether and simply bask in the direct presence of the things themselves. The perfect language would be the one Jonathan Swift imagined, where people carry around bags of objects which they silently show each other, occasionally squeezing for emphasis. Ironically, such a situation would create enormous miscommunication (à la Wittgenstein's thoughts on ostensive definitions), so the best alternative is talking to oneself in the pure saturated meaningfulness of one's own mind. Here there is no chance for misunderstanding because there is no intermediary of signs. This is the zenith of phonocentrism: speech is better than writing, and internal speech is best of all because it grants maximal control over meaning and minimal distance between (indeed, identity of) communicators.

> *Phonè,* in effect, is the signifying substance *given to consciousness* as that which is most intimately tied to the thought of the signified concept. From this point of view, the voice is consciousness itself. When I speak, not only am I conscious of being present for what I think, but I am con-

> scious also of keeping as close as possible to my thought, or to the "concept," a signifier that does not fall into the world, a signifier that I hear as soon as I emit it, that seems to depend upon my pure and free spontaneity, requiring the use of no instrument, no accessory, no force taken from the world. Not only do the signifier and the signified seem to unite, but also, in this confusion, the signifier seems to erase itself or to become transparent, in order to allow the concept to present itself as what it is, referring to nothing other than its presence. The exteriority of the signifier seems reduced. Naturally this experience is a lure, but a lure whose necessity has organized an entire structure, or an entire epoch.[12]

Within my mind words are not needed as I simply point to my referents in a pellucid plenum of pure significance.

In normal speech, the R3 determinateness of the external world guarantees the determinateness of language, since the signifiers are directly connected to their signifieds. Again using terms of writing to talk about metaphysics, Derrida writes, "The idea of the book is the idea of a totality, finite or infinite, of the signifier; this totality of the signifier cannot be a totality, unless a [R3] totality constituted by the signified preexists it, [R5] supervises its inscriptions and its signs, and is [R1] independent of it in its ideality" (Derrida, *G* 18, bracketed comments added; see also Derrida, *Dis* 44). Language should only R5 passively record R3 determinate R1 preexisting reality (see Derrida, *G* 167, 312; Derrida, *MP* 71). The category "dogs" derives its legitimacy from the fact that it merely reflects a really existing set of objects—the set of all dogs—and this category won't change, since it is aligned with the inherent joints of reality. The existence of a referent wholly outside the circulation of signs enables a unique account of the world and a language with determinate meanings. "The transcendental signified . . . would place a reassuring end to the reference from sign to sign. I have identified logocentrism and the metaphysics of presence as the exigent, powerful, systematic, and irrepressible desire for such a signified."[13] If things simply are what they are, then attaching signs to them imbues the words with univocal meanings.

Furthermore, if the meaning of words derives solely from being joined to the joints of reality rather than from interconnections among the words themselves, then it can be transported without loss into any language, like Quine's myth of the museum where translation amounts to just switching labels on self-identical exhibits (Derrida, "SOR" 113). This is why translation serves as another "royal" indication for Derrida: "The theme of a transcendental signified took shape within the horizon of an absolutely pure, transparent, and unequivocal translatability" (Derrida, *Pos* 20; compare Heidegger's philosophical dictum: "Tell me what you think of translation, and I will tell you who you are" [Heidegger, *HH* 63]). If extra-linguistic reality (R1) secures a determinate meaning (R3) which can then be perfectly translated, then language is R5 Passive; it does not affect the meanings it contains, but allows them to be passed between sterile containers which do not affect their contents in any way. Derrida considers this concept endemic to philosophy.

> What does the philosopher say when he is being a philosopher? He says: What matters is truth or meaning, and since meaning is [R1] before or beyond language, it follows that it is translatable. [R5] Meaning has the commanding role, and consequently one must be able to fix its [R3] univocality or, in any case, to master its plurivocality. If this plurivocality can be mastered, then translation, understood as the transport of a semantic content into another signifying form, is possible. There is no philosophy unless translation in this latter sense is possible. Therefore the thesis of philosophy is translatability in this common sense, that is, as the transfer of a meaning or a truth from one language to another without [R5] any essential harm being done.[14]

Although it seems a minor issue, belief in pure translation indicates a realist belief in determinate meaning (R3) unaffected by words (R5), a meaning that consciousness can comprehend and master entirely, which explains philosophy's susceptibility to this ideal.

Writing represents the ultimate danger in this scheme because it is defined by the absence of subject and object; the writer isn't there or else she would speak, and the referent isn't there or it would simply be pointed out. At least the potential absence of both is "*required* by the general structure of signification" (Derrida, *SP* 93; see also Derrida, *MP* 313; Derrida, *Ltd* 48–50), and without their presence keeping everything in place, A3 slippage and confusion are likely to ensue. In this way, at least for philosophy, "the root of evil is writing . . . absence of the object, absence of the interlocutor" (Derrida, *AF* 126–27; see also Derrida, *G* 130, 201). This economy or system of thought leads one either to condemn writing because it is A5 Active and thus interferes with determinate meaning (see Derrida, *G* 36, 170), or to demand that it be R5 Passive, that it "never have the least effect on the structure and content of the meaning (of ideas) that it will have to vehiculate. The same content, previously communicated by gestures and sounds, henceforth will be transmitted by writing."[15] Again, philosophy is particularly prone to this way of thinking: "The philosophical text, although it is in fact always written, includes, precisely as its philosophical specificity, the project of effacing itself in the face of the signified content which it transports."[16] This is the textual form of R5 Passivity: in order to dis-cover preexisting reality without distorting it, which would falsify it, language must have no effect on meaning, ideally to the point of virtual disappearance.

For a very brief examination of these ideas in practice, let us look for the metaphysics of presence in the work of the grandfather of analytic philosophy, Gottlob Frege. Derrida argues that "the maintenance of the rigorous distinction—an essential and juridical distinction—between the *signans* and the *signatum*" (Derrida, *Pos* 19) brings everything else in its wake; since this is the seed from which the entire plant grows, we should look for it in Frege's writings. And in fact one of the central mistakes that Frege's work on mathematics seeks to correct is the problem that "the signs used for the numbers are explained to be the numbers themselves." Rather than a minor misstep, Frege considers this a deep confusion which prevents all clear thought on the subject: "How on earth there can be a definition where there is no question about connexions between sign and thing signified by it is a puzzle. We merge the sign and what it signifies as far as possible, without making any distinction between them. . . . Where people are satisfied with such superficialities, there is, of course, no basis for a deeper understanding" (Geach and Black 1960, 144; see also 113). This is not just any mistake, but one that "of course" robs those who make it of any "basis for a deeper understanding." Frege concludes the introduction to his *Grundgesetze* by stating that its task is in no small part to clear up this confusion. "People have managed to mistake numerals for numbers, names for the things named, the mere devices of arithmetic for its proper subject-matter. Such experiences teach us how necessary it is to demand the highest exactness in manner of speech and writing. And I have taken pains to do justice to such demands" (151).

Such exactness is not merely a matter of style for Frege, but determines whether language itself is meaningful or not. "The laws of logic presuppose concepts with sharp boundaries, and therefore also complete definitions for names of functions. . . . Every symbol must be completely defined at a stroke, so that, as we say, it acquires a reference" (Geach and Black 1960, 170; see also 159, 105). As briefly discussed in chapter 1, this notion of complete, absolutely delineated concepts is the necessary condition for signs to have reference. It is natural language's great flaw that it allows expressions which lack this feature, prompting the hope for a superior language.

> Languages have the fault of containing expressions which fail to designate an object. . . . A logically perfect language (*Begriffsschrift*) should satisfy the conditions, that every expression grammatically well constructed as a proper name out of signs already introduced shall in fact

> designate an object, and that no new sign shall be introduced as a proper name without being secured a reference.[17]

A sign's link to an external referent is essential. Referenceless expressions could satisfy aesthetic purposes by remaining at the level of sense, since other sentences can determine the facts about Odysseus, but this exemption does not extend to serious business: "The question of truth would cause us to abandon aesthetic delight for an attitude of scientific investigation. Hence it is a matter of no concern to us whether the name 'Odysseus,' for instance, has reference, so long as we accept the poem as a work of art. It is the striving for truth that drives us always to advance from the sense to the reference" (Geach and Black 1960, 63). In other words, for the purposes of play or "delight" the mere circulation of signifiers suffices, but when it is a "question of truth" we must put away childish things and exit the circle of signifiers to ground our thought in the actual signified. "It is necessary that formulas express a sense and that the rules be grounded in the reference of the signs. The end must be knowledge and it must determine everything that happens" (188; see also 22). Such, as Derrida says, is "the order of truth." Thus, the distinction between signifier and signified is absolutely essential so that signifiers can be grounded (R2) in the signified (R1): "The properties of the numbers are mirrored in corresponding properties of the signs" (196). Frege does not underestimate the importance of this move: "For, after all, the central tenet of formal arithmetic is that the numerical figures are mere figures, and not signs. For figures, arbitrary rules could be stipulated, but in the case of signs the rules follow from what they stand for" (231). Math is true because we cannot just do whatever we want, as we can with these marks; its possibilities are determined (R5) by numbers themselves (R1).

Once this stability of meaning has been secured by tying all signs to referents, the way is cleared for perfect translation. As long as lossless transference of meaning between expressions is not possible, we know that the expressions themselves are interfering (A5) with the contents of thoughts, thus compromising their objectivity and representing a failure of truth. Frege insists on the importance of this point: "We must never forget that different sentences may express the same thought" (Geach and Black 1960, 49). In fact, just as Derrida says, Frege makes the very possibility of logic rest upon transparent translation.

> We must not fail to recognize that the same sense, the same thought, may be variously expressed; thus the difference does not here concern the sense, but only the apprehension, shading, or colouring of the thought, and is irrelevant for logic. It is possible for one sentence to give

> no more and no less information than another; and, for all the multiplicity of languages, mankind has a common stock of thoughts. If all transformation of the expression were forbidden on the plea that this would alter the content as well, *logic would simply be crippled; for the task of logic can hardly be performed without trying to recognize the thought in its manifold guises.* (Geach and Black 1960, 46n, italics added; see also 59)

Frege's well-known distinction between sense and reference allows us to compensate for any slippage among diverse senses by calibrating them to the univocal reference. Although different people may associate different senses with the name "Aristotle" depending on what they happen to know about him, "so long as the reference remains the same, such variations of sense may be tolerated, although they are to be avoided in the theoretical structure of a demonstrative science and ought not to occur in a perfect language" (Geach and Black 1960, 58n; see also 22). The possible drift of signifiers can always be stopped and fixed by grounding them in the signified that transcends mere signs. Since they can always be cross-referenced to reality, expressions from any language or period can be made commensurable. Hence perfect translation is a criterion of good thought and precise logic.

None of this is merely fortuitous, in Derrida's opinion. He claims that "this scheme has a general value and governs all discourses, from the moment that they make the smallest appeal to any of these notions."[18] Like Hegel, Derrida believes that there is an intrinsic logic to these ideas, so that as soon as someone starts thinking this way he gets pulled into its gravitational field. Indeed, this is one aspect of Derrida's version of the Impersonal Conceptual Scheme. This also justifies the rather surprising emphasis he places on the topic of writing. Since this topic triggers so many of the ideas and values that animate this system, watching how philosophers deal with it is particularly illuminating. The fact that the authors might not consider it central to their work (though Derrida repeatedly finds authors making extraordinary claims about the topic) is irrelevant, since he is not trying to reproduce the author's conception of what he was doing but rather, in a quasi-structuralist fashion, to reconstruct the system of ideas that informs and organizes the writing (see Derrida, *G* 158, 163).

## A1 and A6: The Play of Signifiers

It is important to determine the status of deconstruction carefully. As Derrida protests over and over, it is not negative or destructive; he generally deconstructs texts that he considers important and that he admires or even loves (see, for example, Derrida, *EO* 85–87; Derrida, *TFS* 63). Moreover, to deconstruct a text is certainly not to attack it, nor exactly to challenge the truth of its claims. "I hope my intention is clear. I think Saussure's reasons are good. I do not question, *on the level on which he says it,* the truth of *what Saussure says* in such a tone. . . . I would rather announce the limits and the presuppositions of what seems here to be self-evident."[19] The main criticism Derrida brings to bear on the authors is that their commitment to the metaphysics of presence "is situated . . . by an entire naïve philosophy of the idea-sign" (Derrida, *G* 277; see also 296). The deconstructed claims are not so much false as naive or insufficiently analyzed; when rigorously examined, the oppositions that structure the discourse cannot be maintained in any kind of pure mutual exclusivity (see, for example, Derrida, *Ltd* 117).

Like Heidegger and Foucault, Derrida situates a text's claims within a system that structures its ideas, "bracketing" its truth claims by limiting their validity to the confines of that system. The concepts he analyzes "have meaning only within a closure of the game" (Derrida, *G* 245), while deconstruction consists in the analysis of the rules of the game, that is, the context that opens and organizes the text's claims.

> One of the definitions of what is called deconstruction would be the effort to take this limitless context into account, to pay the sharpest and broadest attention possible to context, and thus to an incessant movement of recontextualization. The phrase which for some has become a sort of slogan, in general so badly understood, of deconstruction ("there is nothing outside the text"), means nothing else: there is nothing outside context.[20]

This (in)famous slogan that "there is nothing outside the text" (from Derrida, *G* 158) is a restatement of A1 Dependence: we cannot get outside of thoughts, systems, ideas to reach reality itself; any discussion of reality itself takes place within some determining context or other (see Dasenbrock 1993, 106; Staten 1986, 21, 157).

> What is called "objectivity," scientific for instance (in which I firmly believe, in a given situation), imposes itself only within a context which is extremely vast, old, powerfully established, stabilized or rooted in a network of conventions (for instance, those of language) and yet which still remains a context. And the emergence of the value of objectivity (and hence of so many others) also belongs to a context. . . . That does not in the slightest discredit them. In the name of what, of which other "truth," moreover, would it? (Derrida, *Ltd* 136)

This quote moves directly to Phenomenological Ontology (in my sense of the term; I am not imputing any commitment to traditional phenomenology to Derrida). Objectivity arises within a context instead of being the outside of all contexts, although this does not discredit it or entail any kind of knee-jerk rejection. In order to reject it, we would need a higher, "truer truth" in the name of which we could condemn this paltry excuse for truth. Condemned to immanence as we are, what has traditionally been considered objective (that is, science, disengaged theory, and so on) becomes one context among others. It does not get automatically attacked, but neither does it have a trump card as that which bypasses subjectivity to plug directly into reality itself; it must take its place among all the other contexts, to be evaluated in a comparison that it will sometimes win and sometimes lose. In a nice statement of the movement common to Objective Idealism, Step Six Physics, and PO, Derrida comments on Heideggger that "a thought which seeks to go to its very end in its language, to the end of what [it] envisages under the name of original finitude or finitude of Being, therefore should abandon not only the words and themes of the finite and the infinite, but also, which is doubtless *impossible,* everything that they govern in language" (Derrida, *WD* 318n70).

The rejection of our access to R1 Independent reality, that is, the transcendent signified, and in fact the very coherence of such a thing is a constant theme in Derrida's work, often expressed in the terminology of writing.

> We are no longer credulous enough to believe that we are setting out from things themselves by avoiding "texts" simply by avoiding quotation or the appearance of "commentary." The most apparently direct writing, the most directly concrete, personal writing which is supposedly in direct contact with the "thing itself," this writing is "on credit": subjected to the authority of a commentary or a re-editing that it is not even capable of reading.[21]

The thought of the absolutely exterior (to the text, language, or thought) or the origin often gets described in what he calls the "the new logic of the 'supplement'" (Derrida, *G* 7), or the trace. This is the same paradoxical logic of early Heidegger's dependent present-at-hand objects that present themselves as always having been there independently of us, or Foucault's discussion of the scientific ICS where "it is only in the blank space of this grid that order manifests itself in depth as though already there, waiting in silence for the moment of its expression" (Foucault, *OT* xx). Here is Derrida's description:

> If reading must not be content with [R5] doubling the text, it cannot legitimately transgress the text toward something other than it, toward a [R1] referent (a reality that is metaphysical, historical, psychobiographical, etc.) or toward a signified outside the text whose content could take place, could have taken place outside of language, that is to say, in the sense that we give here to that word, outside of writing in general. . . . In what one calls the real life of these existences "of flesh and bone," beyond and behind what one believes can be circumscribed as Rousseau's text, [PO] there has never been anything but writing; there have never been anything but supplements, substitutive significations which could only come forth in a chain of differential references, the "real" supervening, and being added only while taking on meaning from a trace. . . . We have read, *in the text,* that the absolute present, Nature, that which words like "real mother" name, have always already escaped.[22]

It is only "in the text" that we read about the real world outside of the text. "This is the heart of the matter—everything that is exterior in relation to the book, everything that is negative as concerns the book, is produced *within the book.* The exit from the book, the other and the threshold, are all articulated *within the book.* The other and the threshold can only be written, can only affirm themselves in writing. One emerges from the book only within the book" (Derrida, *WD* 76).

Although the common understanding of causality demands that the origin precede and cause its linguistic trace (see Derrida, *WD* 129), Derrida adamantly rejects such a clean distinction and priority. "The first impulse of what is called 'deconstruction' carries it toward this 'critique' of the phantasm or the axiom of purity, or toward the analytical decomposition of a purification that would lead back to the indecomposable simplicity of the origin" (Derrida, *MO* 46; see also Derrida, *Pos* 26; Derrida, *Dis* 330). Metaphysical systems demand an R1 origin, an *arche* to ground themselves (see Derrida, *MP* 63; Derrida, *PC* 270). But no purely exterior origin can be grasped since, like the raw sensory material in Kant's epistemology, we only get it already cooked. The very notion of pure reality-in-itself is a posit of the system, "the 'real,' the 'originary,' the 'true,' the 'present,' being constituted only on the rebound" (Derrida, *Dis* 323). A transcendental signified or the notion of something "outside the text"—that is, wholly untouched by human thought or description—is itself part of the text—that is, an idea, a description, a posit, or a characterization. "Is the concept of origin, or of the fundamental signified, anything but a function, indispensable but situated, inscribed, within the system of signification? . . . The fundamental signified, the meaning of the being represented, even less the thing itself, will never be given us in person, outside the sign or outside play" (Derrida, *G* 266; see also Derrida, *Dis* 35–36, 298–99). We have the function of signs referring to an external world, but our access to this world is always mediated by more signs. This amounts to "a reference without a referent" (Derrida, *Dis* 206), rather like Davidson's "correspondence without confrontation" (Davidson, *SIO* 137), or his comment that theories of language "will, of course, contain a recursion on a concept like satisfaction of reference. But these notions we must treat as theoretical constructs whose function is exhausted in stating the truth conditions for sentences. . . . None of this is open to direct confrontation with the evidence" (Davidson, *ITI* 223). This view is in keeping with many of the rejections of noumena that we have seen: Hegel claimed that "both of them, subjectivity as well as objectivity, are certainly thoughts" (Hegel, *HL* 255, §192R); Nietzsche said that "'it is considered' is the real 'it is,' the sole 'this is'" (Nietzsche, *WTP* 556); and Heidegger showed that "the 'in-itself' is not an original character; it still has a phenomenal genesis" (Heidegger, *HCT* 218). Here is Derrida's version: "This reference to the meaning of a signified thinkable and possible outside of all signifiers remains dependent upon the onto-theo-teleology that I have just evoked" (Derrida, *G* 73; see also 7).

It is easy to misconstrue Derrida's infamous slogan into an extreme "textual idealism" similar to a common view of Hegel's thought. However, the doctrine I am calling Phenomenological Ontology shows how misguided such interpretations are, misinterpretations which exasperate Derrida in their frequency.

> The concept of text or of context which guides me embraces and does not exclude the world, reality, history. Once again (and this probably makes a thousand times I have had to repeat this, but when will it finally be heard, and why this resistance?): as I understand it (and I have explained why), the text is not the book, it is not confined in a volume itself confined to the library. It does not suspend reference—to history, to the world, to reality, to being, and especially not to the other, since to say of history, of the world, of reality, that they always appear in an experience, hence in a movement of interpretation which contextualizes them according to a network of differences and hence of referral to the other, is surely to recall that alterity (difference) is irreducible. (Derrida, *Ltd* 137; see also Derrida, *TFS* 76)

Derrida is not denying reality, but pointing out that our relation to any kind of reality is inevitably mediated by all kinds of interconnected influences such that we can never comprehend them in their entirety or correct for them. Similar claims have been made by all of the continental philosophers I have discussed, including Kant, as well as such thinkers as Kuhn, Goodman, and (middle-period) Putnam; even Davidson's notion of triangulation and coherence truth suggests such ideas, as Samuel C. Wheeler III tirelessly points out. Nelson Goodman says, "We are confined to ways of describing whatever is described. Our universe, so to speak, consists of these ways rather than of a world or of worlds."[23] Derrida puts the point like this: "From the moment that the sign appears, that is to say from the very beginning, there is no chance of encountering anywhere the purity of 'reality'" because "the signified . . . is *always already in the position of the signifier*."[24] This doesn't mean that we do not encounter reality, just that we need to wean ourselves off of the traditional metaphysical understanding of reality as R1 Independent of and cleanly external to everything human or linguistic.

> The concept of text I propose is limited neither to the graphic, nor to the book, nor even to discourse, and even less to the semantic, representational, symbolic, ideal, or ideological sphere. What I call "text" implies all the structures called "real," "economic," "historical," socio-institutional, in short: all possible referents. Another way of recalling once again that "there is nothing outside the text." That does not mean that all referents are suspended, denied, or enclosed in a book, as people have claimed, or have been naïve enough to believe and to have accused me of believing. But it does mean that every referent, all reality has the structure of a differential trace, and that one cannot refer to this "real" except in an interpretive experience. The latter neither yields meaning nor assumes it except in a movement of differential referring. That's all.[25]

This is no simple or direct realism, of course; there are too many quotation marks. But neither is it a simple or extreme idealism. We encounter the world, but as referents, under descriptions.

Just as there is no*thing* outside the text, neither is there any*one* out there either. Like later Heidegger and Foucault, Derrida views subjectivity as a variable effect of systems (A6), rather than a timeless natural structure preceding and determining them (R6). Metaphysics insists on some form of transcendental subjectivity fully present and transparent to itself which can grasp its meanings instantly, without any chance of messages going awry in the tangled medium of words. In this phonocentric ideal there is no gap where the message could get lost, and hence no need of signs to facilitate comprehension.

> The voice *is heard* (understood) . . . closest to the self as the absolute effacement of the signifier: pure auto-affection . . . which does not borrow

> from outside of itself, in the world or in "reality," any accessory signifier, any substance of expression foreign to its own spontaneity. It is the unique experience of the signified producing itself spontaneously, from within the self, and nevertheless, as signified concept, in the element of ideality or universality. The unworldly character of this substance of expression is constitutive of this ideality. . . . This illusion is the history of truth.[26]

This is the dream of full self-presence, in which consciousness imbues signifiers with a significance it controls utterly. The subject's meaning-giving faculties would be spontaneous and wholly envelop the movement of signs, controlling them and giving them determinate meaning (R3).

However, Derrida embraces the Heideggerian Paradigm's new version of R5 Passive Knower. According to this view, we are not the autonomous source of the organizing structures of experience but recipients of them, rendering us deeply dependent on what we have been "thrown" into. Derrida even uses later Heideggerian terms of gratitude at one point to describe the ethos of his work as a whole: "Everything I do, especially when I am writing, resembles a game of blindman's bluff: the one who is writing . . . holds out his hand like a blind man seeking to touch the one whom he could thank for the gift of a language, for the very words in which he declares himself ready to give thanks" (Derrida, *MO* 64), tying Heidegger's *es gibt die Sprache* to his own meditations on the gift just a few pages later (67; see also Derrida, *GT* 80–81). He agrees with the Heideggerian Paradigm that our ability to think and experience is always shaped by ideas and structures we have inherited without choosing them, focusing on language as Heidegger and Foucault did as well. The experience of one's native language, for instance, "would be ostensibly *autonomous,* because I have to speak this law and appropriate it in order to understand it *as if* I was giving it to myself, but it remains necessarily *heteronomous*."[27] It is this quasi-structuralist view that leads Derrida to the Heideggerian Paradigm's A6 rejection of the R6 Realist A5 Active Subject: "The concept of *subjectivity* belongs *a priori and in general* to the order of the *constituted*. . . . There is no constituting subjectivity" (Derrida, *SP* 84–85n9, italics in original; see also Derrida, *PoI* 219).

Derrida emphasizes how R5 dependent we are on the systems of thought we inherit. "The writer writes *in* a language and *in* a logic whose proper system, laws, and life his discourse by definition cannot dominate absolutely. He uses them only by letting himself, after a fashion and up to a point, be governed by the system."[28] Here he follows Heidegger's idea that "it is language that speaks" (Heidegger, *BW* 411; see also 348, 423) rather than man. Derrida is explicit about his alignment with what I am calling the Heideggerian Paradigm, including identifying Foucault and the doctrine of A6 they all share:

> It is immediately evident that what I have said on the subject, what Heidegger, above all, was the first to say, on the connection between metaphysics and humanism, theology and humanism, everything in my work that follows paths opened up by Heidegger also implies this "disappearance" of man. But here there would also be a problem of language. . . . However, I am indeed fundamentally in agreement with Michel Foucault, from the Heideggerian standpoint that I have indicated. (Wood and Bernasconi 1988, 86)

Instead of being the transcendental origin and controller of language (A5), "the subject (in its identity with itself, or eventually in its consciousness of its identity with itself, its self-consciousness) is inscribed in language, is a 'function' of language, becomes a *speaking* subject only by making its speech conform—even in so-called 'creation,' or in so-called 'transgression'—to the system of the rules of language" (Derrida, *MP* 15; see also Derrida, *Pos* 29; Derrida, *G* 68; see also 141; Derrida, *SP* 93). This feature so deeply determines the subject that we cannot even say that a subject preexists language, but should rather see it as an effect of language. "The self does not exist, it is not present to itself before that which engages it in this way and which is not it. There is not a constituted subject that engages itself at a given moment in writing for some reason or other. It is *given* by writing" (Derrida, *PoI* 347; see also Derrida, *SP* 82). Derrida rejects the traditional notion of an autonomous ego with determinable boundaries in general.[29]

Like later Heidegger and Foucault, Derrida does not use philosophers' names to refer to individuals, since they are not so much the creators of their thoughts as a conduit or a nexus of influences. Instead these terms represent "the name of a problem" (Derrida, *G* 99), since "at the 'origin' of every speech act, there can only be Societies which are (more or less) anonymous . . . a multitude of instances, if not of 'subjects,' of meanings highly vulnerable to parasitism—all phenomena that the 'conscious ego' of the speaker and the hearer (the ultimate instances of speech act theory) is incapable of incorporating."[30] Neither is there a unique, timeless structure of subjectivity. Since it is an effect of writing, different contexts will construct it differently: "The I of *I recall* is produced and uttered in different ways depending on the language in question. It never precedes them; therefore it is not independent of language in general" (Derrida, *MO* 29).

Thus Derrida is committed to both A1 and A6: neither thing nor subject exceeds or precedes writing (or language or experience) in order to serve as anchor or ruler of discourse. "Nothing—no present and in-*different* being—thus precedes *différance* and spacing. There is no subject who is agent, author, and master of *différance*. . . . Subjectivity—like objectivity—is an effect of *différance*, an effect inscribed in a system of *différance*" (Derrida, *Pos* 28; see also Derrida, *MP* 13; Derrida, *GT* 24). The next step, though radical, follows from this. Previously the goal of R3 Uniqueness, that is, a determinate set of meanings ensuring lucid comprehensibility and communication, had been secured either by the realist strategy of linking signifiers to transcendental signifieds, that is, the world independent of our language and thoughts that could therefore support the entire structure; or by the Kantian strategy of an active subject controlling all organizing structures. If these are both removed, however, "one would have to give up a concept of language regulated by deep semantic anchoring points" (Derrida, *GT* 48). With both world and subject constituted by the signs, "no transcendent truth present outside the field of writing can govern theologically the totality of the field" (Derrida, *MP* 7; see also Derrida, *Pos* 44).

With no appeal to external reality, transcendental subjectivity, or any *arche* whatsoever, Derrida radically extends the Heideggerian Paradigm's Unmooring, that is, the idea that nothing can impose closure on the limitless potential for new possibilities or slippage of meaning, which he sometimes calls "play": "The absence of the transcendental signified extends the domain and the play of signification infinitely."[31] What he means by this is that without a determinate independent reality to anchor words or an active subject to maintain them, their meaning is subject to semantic drift where words that once meant one thing gradually shift to mean something completely different. "Every sign . . . can break with every given context, and engender infinitely new contexts in an absolutely nonsaturable fashion" (Derrida, *MP* 320). While unnoticeable on a day-to-day basis, this drift vividly confronts us when we try to read, say, Shakespeare. If the referents are themselves A1 products of these drifting words, then the movement of meaning perpetuates itself and there can be no control that is wholly external to the process.

> The ties between words, concepts, and things, truth and reference, are not *absolutely* and purely guaranteed by some metacontextuality or metadiscursivity. However stabilized, complex, and overdetermined it may be, there is a context and one that is only relatively *firm*, neither absolutely solid nor entirely closed, without being purely and simply identical to itself. In it there is a margin of play, of difference, an opening. (Derrida, *Ltd* 151; see also Derrida, *Dis* 262)

Derrida compares this view to a modified Hegelianism, that is, Hegel's notion of history as knowledge, being, and subjectivity changing together, but now without the final gathering into a totality (see Derrida, *WD* 274–

75; Derrida, *G* 298, Derrida, *Gl* 17). Without the R1 "transcendental signified, which, at one time or another, would place a reassuring end to the reference from sign to sign" and thus serve as a ground, "no ground of nonsignification—understood as insignificance or an intuition of a present truth—stretches out to give it foundation under the play and the coming into being of signs" (Derrida, *G* 49, 48).

This view has implications for his method. Authorial intent is greatly reduced as a determining cause of—and so key to—the meaning of a text. Instead texts often, perhaps always, resist what the author wants them to say, which means that reading must go beyond what texts say "on the face of it."

> The presumed subject of the sentence might always say, through using the "supplement," more, less, or something other than what he *would mean*. The question is therefore not only of Rousseau's writing but also of our reading. . . . The reading must always aim at a certain relationship, unperceived by the writer, between what he commands and what he does not command of the patterns of the language that he uses. (Derrida, *G* 157–58; see also Derrida, *Pos* 94; Derrida, *Ltd* 62)

A great deal of *Of Grammatology* in fact is taken up with showing the difference between what Rousseau (among others) wants to say and what his writing, betraying his intentions, ends up stating or committing him to.[32]

## ICS: *Différance* and Iterability

With neither independent transcendent signifieds nor active transcendental subjects to give signifiers their meaning, Derrida turns to Saussure's device of signs' internal differences to generate it. In light of the fact that "there is no constituting subjectivity," as quoted above, "the very concept of constitution itself must be deconstructed" (Derrida, *SP* 85n9), which is what his Saussurean impersonal constitution of meaning amounts to. Individual units of language get their significance by differing from all other units within a language. Each one is what it is by *not* being what the others are; as Spinoza said, every definition is a negation, an idea Derrida expresses as "difference is articulation" (Derrida, *G* 66) and "articulation . . . is the origin of languages" (315). A system of meaning or a language bootstraps itself to significance through the mutual repulsion of its elements, the various contents creating an articulation by distinguishing themselves from other members, rather than attaching themselves to R1 objects out there in the world. So "what is discovered here is that there is no nucleus of meaning, no conceptual atom, but that the concept is produced within the tissue of differences" (Derrida, *WD* 267; see also Derrida, *G* 69, 89).

In this way a massive referential network of differences can produce meaning without touching the "ground" of an independent reality, creating Derrida's version of a groundless ground. "Every sign—verbal or otherwise—may be used at different levels, in configurations and functions which are never prescribed by its 'essence,' but emerge from a play of differences" (Derrida, *WD* 220; see also 25). However, whereas Hegel's system was a closed circle which assured self-coincidence, totality, finality, stability, and so on, Derrida's anti-systems *cannot* coincide; the end points miss each other by a small but essential gap. This gap is what initiates the meaning-generating circulation, but it also ensures that no meaning is ever final or self-identical. He often calls this source of meaning-producing differences *différance.* This term derives from a combination of "differing" and "deferring,"[33] because it is the circulating *differings* between words that generate meaning but, without the unambiguous correspondence with independent reality, absolute meaning that would be invulnerable to semantic drift is permanently *deferred.*

This network of differences is the Impersonal constitutive source of any particular Conceptual Scheme.

> *Différance* is also the production, if it can still be put this way, of these differences, of the diacriticity that the linguistics generated by Saussure, and all the structural sciences modeled upon it, have recalled is the condition for any signification and any structure. These differences—and, for example, the taxonomical science which they may occasion—are the effects of *différance;* they are neither [R1] inscribed in the heavens, nor [R5] in the brain, which does not mean that they are [A5] produced by the activity of some speaking subject. (Derrida, *Pos* 9, bracketed comments added; see also Wood and Bernasconi 1988, 85)

*Différance* is the spacing of those initial differences that separate and articulate words and things, thus enabling us to think and speak. Derrida allows neither the realist explanation that these distinctions are in the things themselves, nor the Kantian claim that they are imposed upon the world by us. Instead, differences occur in the middle voice, "undecided *between* the active and the passive . . . saying an operation that is not an operation, an operation that cannot be conceived either as passion or as the action of a subject or an object, or on the basis of the categories of agent or patient. . . . For the middle voice, a certain nontransitivity may be what philosophy, at its outset, distributed into an active and a passive voice."[34] Although philosophy has "distributed [it] into an active and a passive voice," that is, attributed the designation of identity to either objects (R1) or subjects (A5), Derrida follows the Heideggerian Paradigm in conceiving of it as impersonal.

> What is written as *différance,* then, will be the playing movement that "produces"—by means of something that is not simply an activity—these differences. . . . Since language, which Saussure says is a classification, has not [R1] fallen from the sky, its differences [A1] have been produced, are produced effects, but they are effects which do not find their cause in [A5] a subject or [R1] a substance. (Derrida, *MP* 11, bracketed comments added; see also Derrida, *FWT* 170; Derrida, *EO* 116)

Derrida is explicit that *différance* or spacing fulfills the role that used to be played by the constitutive agent (A5): "Spacing . . . carries the meaning of a productive, positive, generative force. Like dissemination, like *différance* it carries along with it a *genetic* motif" (Derrida, *Pos* 106n42; see also 27).

Although fully successful in creating meaning for a time, these systems are fated to shake apart and mutate due to Derrida's account of meaning. If words could correspond to independent reality, then determinate meaning would be secured by a simple "Fido"—Fido relationship; as long as the real dog faithfully stays, the word maintains its stable meaning. However, Derrida has denied that anything is outside the text; he has brought Fido into the linguistic house of Being, so to speak (see, for example, Derrida, *Dis* 43). This releases an indefinite play or semantic drift, since there are no extra-semantic anchors to keep meanings in place, leaving language "open to the most radical grafting, open to deformation, transformations, expropriation" (Derrida, *MO* 65; see also Derrida, *PC* 261). Metaphysics has always sought to limit this play in the futile dream of "a fundamental immobility and a reassuring certitude, which itself is beyond the reach of play. And on the basis of this certitude anxiety can be mastered" (Derrida, *WD* 279; see also Derrida, *MP* 247). Instead of this impossible determinateness, Derrida proposes the attitude that "*affirms* (I do not say produces or controls) endless substitution, it neither arrests nor controls play . . . but without the metaphysical or romantic pathos of negativity" (Derrida, *Pos* 86; see also Derrida, *WD* 292; Derrida, *Dis* 268; Derrida, *PC* 121). This is not an unfortunate state that we must resign ourselves to because perfect stability is incoherent and, if possible, would be incapable of generating meaning anyway.

*Différance* creates the possibility of meaning by instigating the articulating differences while simultaneously rendering the direct confrontation with the referent impossible; that is, it forever defers full presence or self-identical meaning. It enables the meaning we have while preventing the meaning we dream of. "The desire of presence . . . carries in itself the destiny of its non-satisfaction. *Différance* produces what it forbids, makes possible the very thing that it makes impossible" (Derrida, *G* 143). Although genuine meanings and identities do emerge from this roiling network, they are riven by differences and are inherently unstable, allowing nothing permanent or atemporal but "only *stabilization in process*" (Derrida, *GT* 95; see also Derrida, *Pos* 107n42). This is how Derrida's Phenomenological Ontology becomes Historical:

> I take into account and believe that it is necessary to account for this stability. . . . On the other hand, to account for a certain stability (by essence always provisional and finite) is precisely not to speak of eternity or of absolute solidity; it is to take into account a historicity, a nonnaturalness, of ethics, of politics, of institutionality, etc. If recalling this is to put radically into question the stability of contexts, then, yes, I do that. I say that there is no stability that is absolute, eternal, intangible, natural, etc. . . . A stability is not an immutability; it is by definition always destabilizable. (Derrida, *Ltd* 151; see also Derrida, *DN* 13–14)

Although it is less prominent in his work, Derrida does subscribe to the view held by both later Heidegger and Foucault that the structures in our experience that appear permanent are merely historical forces that have become temporarily congealed. "If I speak of great stability, it is in order to emphasize that this semantic level is neither originary, nor ahistorical, nor simple, nor self-identical in any of its elements, nor even entirely semantic or significant. Such stabilization is relative, even if it is sometimes so great as to seem immutable and permanent. It is the momentary result of a whole history of relations of force" (Derrida, *Ltd* 145; see also Derrida, *FWT* 37; Derrida, *MO* 9).

Derrida believes that systems of ideas inherently contain contradictions, which deconstruction merely brings to the surface.[35] Attributing the effects to an impersonal process, he claims that "it is not I who deconstruct; rather, something I call 'deconstruction' happens to the experience of a world, a culture, a philosophic tradition: 'it' deconstructs."[36] Thus, just as Hegel stood by and watched moments of consciousness discover their own weaknesses and surpass themselves according to the logic of history, so Derrida merely has "to watch the configuration of our problem, along with its theoretical and historical conditions, take shape by means of the logic implicit in this text" (Derrida, *MP* 210).

Derrida's version of the Empirical Directive helps illuminate this self-deconstruction of texts. With nothing outside of actual linguistic practice to guide and guarantee the meaning of words, we must look to actual usage in order to understand language. This is why Derrida claims that in our escape from metaphysical conceptions of language and meaning, "the *departure* is radically empiricist."[37] This commitment keeps us from looking beyond the text to ground our practices in something transcendent—independent referents, metaphysically conceived linguistic rules, types, Forms, God—demanding instead that we pay extremely close attention to what actually occurs in language. This is why he wants to read, for example, Rousseau's work "as a *text* and not as a document. . . . One cannot abstract from the written text to rush to the signified it *would mean*" (Derrida, *G* 149–50; see also Derrida, *WD* 32). We must not "sublime" our language into something ideal but should "consider only usage, play, and the contextual functionings of idioms."[38]

Derrida admires Austin partly because of his commitment to this "radically empirical" method; if any movement should simply take language as it finds it without sifting out proper from improper instances, ordinary language philosophy should. However, Derrida is disappointed that Austin retreats from his stated commitment to it.

> Austin's procedure is rather remarkable, and typical of the philosophical tradition that he prefers to have little to do with. It consists in recognizing that the possibility of the negative (here, the *infelicities*) is certainly a structural possibility, that failure is an essential risk in the operations under consideration; and then, with an almost *immediately simultaneous* gesture made in the name of a kind of ideal regulation, an exclusion of this risk as an accidental, exterior one that teaches us nothing about the language phenomenon under consideration.[39]

If these are inherent structural possibilities that are built into language, then an empirical account of language should accept them as full-fledged linguistic entities rather than second-class citizens (HPO). "Why determine as 'marginal' what can always go on in 'real life,' which is, to my knowledge, the only place from where a theory of language can draw its 'facts,' its 'examples,' its 'objects?'"[40] Derrida is trying to be *extra* ordinary, that is, true to the ethos of ordinary language philosophy, which he believes Austin compromises by discriminating among instances of language usage. To be fully empirical, we must accept how people talk as successful instances of language rather than discriminating between authentic and inauthentic uses (Derrida, *TP* 63; see also 327; Derrida, *MP* xxiii). This attitude helps keep us from unconsciously relying on assumptions about what we should be seeing, so that we can see what is there. Coming to the text with a worked-out theory blinds one to what is on the page; it "predestine[s] one's reading" (Derrida, *PC* 4; see also Derrida, *TP* 334).

Derrida's radical linguistic empiricism attends to all aspects of linguistic behavior and everything on the page, allowing him to notice phenomena that appear insignificant. This is one reason he spends so much time on features that most of us pass by without even noticing, items which initially strike many as intentionally bizarre to even discuss (see Derrida, *Ltd* 44, 70), such as Searle's signature and copyright (see 30–31, 34, 45). Without a clean and certain distinction between signifier and signified (see, for example, Derrida, *G* 159; Wood and Bernasconi 1988, 88) that filters out the insignificant from the significant, Derrida pays attention to all that appears on the page. And if one follows his works to the end, he usually makes some very interesting and illuminating points out of these discussions that seem so strange at the beginning.

Derrida insists on understanding linguistic phenomena only in terms of what actually transpires (ED) without appealing to what ought to occur by the "sublimed" rules or by assumptions about textual form and transcendental signified. To put this in other terms, all we have are tokens; types emerge from actual linguistic use and, as wholly dependent on the tokens, they cannot completely regulate their functioning nor escape their drift. Linguistic rules do not govern usage from a transcendent and transcendental position immune from changes in actual use, but rather form part of a feedback loop between rules and use. We see this every year when new dictionaries come out: they are authoritative in that they tell us the correct spelling, meaning, and so on, but they must accommodate new words and changes in meaning that bubble up from the babble of the hoi polloi (Derrida, "SOR" 133–34; see also Staten 1986, 22)

Derrida captures this movement in "the strange alogical logic of what I call 'iterability'" (Derrida, *Ltd* 119; see also 48). This logic means first that signs must be "iterable," or able to function in multiple contexts. A genuinely single-use word, the ultimate proper name which only names a single thing at a single time, would be impossible, since understanding the thing requires locating it within a grid of universal qualities, thus undermining its utter uniqueness: "The name is the appellation of a singularity but also, in the possibility of repeating this appellation, it is the effacement of that singularity."[41] It is the ability to recognize a sign in different contexts as the "same" that gives it the identity and expressive power necessary to function as language (see Derrida, *MP* 318; Derrida, *SP* 50); this process is what leads us to think of such ideal entities as types transcending and governing all practice. As discussed above, Derrida strongly rejects anything beyond the text, viewing meaning as an effect of the network of mutually differing elements (A1). However, since each text embodies at least a slightly different network, every (con)text will imbue the "same" sign with at least a slightly different meaning. Derrida sums up this claim when he says that "iterability alters, contaminating parasitically what it identifies and enables to repeat 'itself'" (Derrida, *Ltd* 62). If an individual sign derives its meaning holistically from its context of internally distinguishing elements, its meaning will shift as it is placed in networks of different compositions.

Thus the very repetition of the same places an in-principle limit on this sameness, leading to play or an inherent drift of meaning.

> Iterability supposes a minimal remainder (as well as a minimum of idealization) in order that the identity of the *selfsame* be repeatable and identifiable *in, through,* and even *in view of* its alteration. For the structure of iteration—and this is another of its decisive traits—implies *both* identity *and* difference. . . . The iterability of an element divides its own identity a priori, even without taking into account the fact that this identity can only *determine* or delimit itself through differential relations to other elements and that it hence bears the mark of this difference. . . . The remainder, although indispensable, is never that of a full or fulfilling presence.[42]

The possibility of placing a mark into a new context of elements is inherent to language; a sign can only function if it can be the same in different sentences. Since identity arises out of the Saussurean "differential relations to other elements," though, each new context changes its identity. The sign does have a "minimal" identity, but not the way it has been traditionally conceived, since "the very iterability which constitutes their identity never permits them to be a unity of self-identity" (Derrida, *MP* 318). Without an unchangeable (R3) external object (R1) to cling to (R2), the sign's meaning relies on an inherently unstable and mobile circulation of meaning. Therefore, the idea that "there is nothing outside the text" fundamentally changes the way we understand what is "inside" the text. "If there is thus no [R3] thematic unity or overall meaning to reappropriate [ED] beyond the textual instances, no [R3] total message located in some [R1] imaginary order, [A5] intentionality, or lived experience, then the text is no longer the [R2] expression or representation (felicitous or otherwise) of any *truth*" (Derrida, *Dis* 262, bracketed comments added; see also Royle 2000, 293).

Since types arise from and wholly depend upon the behavior of tokens which have now been shown to be indefinitely mutable, the meanings that a token may take on can never be contained or controlled in advance or in principle. There simply is no way to limit, predict, or exhaustively encompass the contexts a sign might enter, and since these are what determine its meaning, the same goes for the possibilities of play or semantic drift its meaning is subject to. This adds up to the conclusion that iterability "marks the essential and ideal limit of all pure idealization."[43] These endless possibilities for new meanings (albeit usually occurring in a gradual, overlapping, ship-of-Theseus way) are integral to the very structure and possibility of linguistic meaning, and yet they do not behave according to traditional logic and ontology.

> Every sign . . . can break with every given context, and engender infinitely new contexts in an absolutely nonsaturable fashion. . . . There are only contexts without any center of absolute anchoring. This citationality, duplication, or duplicity, this iterability of the mark is not an accident or an anomaly, but is that (normal/abnormal) without which a mark could no longer even have a so-called "normal" functioning.[44]

Since the possibility of an endless change in their meaning is built into the very conditions for words to have meaning at all (an un-iterable word cannot function), the idea of an original meaning is inapplicable.

Derrida's "only contexts without any center" is his version of the PO paradoxical notion of masks or interpretation all the way down without an original, what he sometimes calls an "originary supplement" (Derrida, *G* 313; see also Derrida, *SP* 87). Inspired by Levinas's notion of the trace, this structure appears in many forms in Derrida's works. For instance, he says that there was no original speech to which writing happened, but that language has always been writing (see Derrida, *G* 37); or that since every reading is an interpreting (see 163; Derrida, *FWT* 171; Derrida, *Ltd* 146), there is no such thing as the intrinsic meaning of a text (see Derrida, *MO* 25; Derrida, *Dis* 355) nor an original language before translation.[45] He summarizes the traditional realist view and his own here:

> Sometimes repetition, classically, [R5] repeats [R1] something that precedes it . . . repetition succeeds a first thing, an original, a primary, a prior, the repeated itself which in and of itself is supposed to be foreign to what is repetitive or repeating in repetition. As it is also imagined that a narrative relates something that would be previous and foreign to itself, or in any event independent of it. . . . In the classical hypothesis, repetition in general would be secondary and derivative. But sometimes, according to a logic that is other, and non-classical, repetition is "original," and induces, through an unlimited propagation of itself, a general deconstruction: not only of the entire classical ontology of repetition, along with all the distinctions recalled a moment ago, but also of the entire psychic construction . . . insuring the integrity of the organization. . . . Two

> logics then, with an incalculable effect. (Derrida, *PC* 351–52, bracketed comments added; see also 383)

Due to his reputation, it is important to emphasize that whatever Derrida does with a text must be completely anchored in what is on the page (ED), preventing the "anything goes" interpretation he is frequently accused of. "These texts are not to be read according to a hermeneutical or exegetical method which would seek out [R1] a finished signified beneath a textual surface. Reading is [A5] transformational. . . . But this transformation cannot be executed however one wishes. It requires protocols of reading."[46]

Let us now return to the deconstructive reading of Frege in light of these new points. Frege's aim is to construct an ideal logical notation modeled on mathematics that will make logical connections maximally perspicuous by eliminating the confusions of ordinary language. The various connotations and subjective feelings that words conjure up, all of their perlocutionary and illocutionary effects, must be sifted out to leave behind the precipitate of hard, thick meaning. "In my formalized language . . . only that part of judgments which affects the *possible inferences* is taken into consideration. Whatever is needed for a valid inference is fully expressed; what is not needed is for the most part not indicated" (Geach and Black 1960, 3). He calls the logically relevant information the "conceptual content," which is cleanly separable from all other elements of language (see 11, 22, 61) and which forms the content of translation, as discussed above. This ideal language must be able to contain meaning in a perfectly lucid manner such that it will be "fully expressed" or completely present to the listener with minimal misunderstanding (R5). Ordinary language hides or distorts its conceptual content, hindering its direct presentation, which shows that such "languages are unreliable on logical questions. It is indeed not the least of the logician's tasks to indicate the pitfalls laid by language in the way of the thinker" (126; see also 58; Burge 2005, 219). The methodological project then falls out of these ideas: "It is therefore highly important to devise a mathematical language that combines the most rigorous accuracy with the greatest possible brevity."[47]

This project is organized by a strong hierarchical dichotomy between ideal and ordinary language, where the latter is infected with misleading and confusing subjective phenomena (which he calls representations) while the former is capable of attaining objectivity (senses). As he pursues his goal, however, Frege discovers that he cannot maintain this division with the strictness he requires. This comes out, for instance, when he discusses the work of another scholar who tries to maintain this kind of strict distinction.

> Kerry holds that no logical rules can be based on linguistic distinctions; but my own way of doing this is something that nobody can avoid who lays down such rules at all; for we cannot come to an understanding with one another apart from language, and so in the end we must always rely on other people's understanding words, inflexions, and sentence-construction in essentially the same way as ourselves. As I said before, I was not trying to give a definition, but only hints; and to this end I appealed to the general feeling for the German language. It is here very much to my advantage that there is such good accord between the linguistic distinction and the real one. (Geach and Black 1960, 45; see also Burge 2005, 250)

Whereas Frege had been determined to keep logical laws pure and uncontaminated by ordinary language, here he admits that mutual understanding requires a necessary detour not just through ordinary language, but even the particular, local, temporal-spatial phenomenon of a national tongue. Although he had wanted to sift out subjective phenomena such as "feelings" from the conceptual content, Frege here appeals to his readers' "general feeling" for German to guide their comprehension of his necessarily dark utterances. In order to construct a language in which meaning is "fully expressed," Frege confesses, "I must confine myself to hinting at what I have in mind by means of a metaphorical expression, and here I rely on my reader's agreeing to meet me half-way" (Geach and Black 1960, 115; see also 55). Frege has to resort to metaphors, and his readers must consult their feeling for his particular idiom in order to grasp them, in order to create an absolutely literal language, all of which is based on the view that communication should need neither idiom nor feeling. Frege is forced to this "necessary detour" (another of Derrida's favorite concepts) of hints and metaphors that do not say what he wants them to because language betrays him (especially on the topic of logical simples); he finds that his writing, well, deconstructs itself: "By a kind of necessity of language, my expressions, taken literally, sometimes miss my thought; I mention an object, when what I intend is a concept. I fully realize that in such cases I was relying upon a reader who would be ready to meet me half-way—who does not begrudge a pinch of salt" (54; see also Burge 2005, 245).

Frege is forced into this situation because of a problem that arises from his distinction between objects and concepts. Objects or arguments are entities that are complete in themselves; they are the things that are, with existence being construed rather broadly. Concepts or functions, on the other hand, are predicates or descriptions of objects which are intrinsically incomplete; in Frege's famous phrase, they are "unsaturated." Concepts have a hole in them which, when filled by an object, form a complete thought. If every part of language were complete, combinations of words could only form lists instead of sentences (see A. W. Moore 2000, 359). It is the fact that the parts are complementary that allows them to snap together to form units that refer and are true or false, and this requires that one of them be incomplete.

> Not all the parts of a thought can be complete; at least one must be "unsaturated," or predicative; otherwise they would not hold together. . . . Only because their sense is thus "unsaturated" are they capable of serving as a link. Only when they have been supplemented in this twofold respect do we get a complete sense, a thought. . . . It is thus easy to see that the difficulty arising from the "unsaturatedness" of one part of the thought can indeed be shifted, but not avoided. "Complete" and "unsaturated" are of course only figures of speech; but all that I wish or am able to do here is to give hints. . . . On thorough investigation it will be found that the obstacle is essential, and founded on the nature of our language; that we cannot avoid a certain inappropriateness of linguistic expression; and that there is nothing for it but to realize this and always take it into account. (Geach and Black 1960, 54–55; see also 24)

Frege believes that this complementarity must be intrinsic to thoughts or words, since he fundamentally rejects any kind of Kantian transcendental subjectivity which could synthesize the subject and predicate into a judgment (see Geach and Black 1960, 127, 131–32). That view would weave the subject into the very foundations of logic, thus tainting the topic with subjectivity. In other words, if our mental activity were required (A5), the catastrophe of psychologism would ensue. (I discuss this further in my conclusion.) Instead, concepts and objects naturally snap together, like nuts and bolts or, as Derrida might comment in one of his jauntier moods, like male and female genitalia where one part must be open to the other if conception is to take place.[48]

The problem comes when we talk about concepts because this puts them in the subject place of an assertion, thus treating them as objects. In an Aristotelian vein, only objects qua saturated entities can properly serve as subjects of assertions, whereas the unsaturated concepts are strictly forbidden this role; otherwise the division between the two would spring leaks and concepts could get saturated, eliminating their ability to combine with objects to form thoughts. As Frege puts it in rather an understatement, "language is here in a predicament" (Geach and Black 1960, 46), since we seem to talk about concepts all the time with smashing success.[49] Worse still, we must do so in the very place where, above all others, such transgressions should never occur, namely, in laying the foundations of logic: "In logical discussions one quite often needs to assert something about a concept . . . but the concept as such cannot play this part, in view of its predicative nature" (46). To top it all off, just setting up the distinction between concepts and objects that then gets undermined entails defining concepts as incapable of serving as subjects of assertions, which of course is already an assertion about concepts. The proscription transgresses itself in its very proscribing! This well-known "concept of the horse" problem, which seems to pose a greater and more immediate threat to Frege's work than does Russell's paradox, arises from the attempt to draw an inviolable distinction, just the kind of thing that deconstruction claims will inevitably implode. And it is "the nature of our language" that forces Frege to use "figures of speech; but all that I wish or am able to do here is to give hints."

What does this mean for Frege? As I stated above, deconstruction is not an attack or any kind of destruction. Derrida might occasionally underplay the critical element in it, but many overplay it. If the deconstruction is effective, it does not refute Frege or suggest anything like the idea that his work is wrong. Derrida points to the elements in someone's work that come back on them against their will when repressed; in Frege's words, "by a kind of necessity of language, my expressions, taken literally, sometimes miss my thought." Now deconstruction does represent a criticism of ambitions or claims to absolute purity, so I think Derrida would conclude that Frege's dreams of a formalized language containing only the conceptual content "fully expressed" are naive and impossible, a fairly noncontroversial position these days. What is so interesting is that Frege himself shows this by admitting that he must rely on German, even his readers' feeling for German, in order to appreciate his metaphors and hints, in the service of constructing a pellucid, completely neutral language. Derrida, on the other hand, explicitly embraces the "compromised" nature of real communication: "Philosophy finds its element in so-called natural language. It has never been able to formalize itself integrally in an artificial language," which is one reason why "I only ever write in French and . . . I attach great importance to this fact, as to all problems concerning idiom, natural and national language" (Derrida, *PoI* 225, 416; Derrida, *TFS* 11).

In fact, Derrida perfectly captures Frege's problem (without, as far as I know, ever giving a detailed analysis of his work):

> That philosophy is written and written in an idiom, was for a long time disavowed by the philosopher, whether because he claimed to transcend his idiom in view of a sort of universal and transparent language, or whether because—and this amounts to the same thing—he considers the natural language in which he speaks to be an empirical accident and

> not an experience tied to the exercise of thought. But this disavowal is never assured, constant; it is, like every disavowal, caught up in contradiction. The philosopher has indeed to recognize that philosophy does not take place outside of a natural language. . . . There comes a moment in which one can no longer dissociate the concept from the word in some way. Sometimes this link between the concept and the word imports metaphors.[50]

Frege's naïveté consists in the fact that he does not follow his own advice "that we cannot avoid a certain inappropriateness of linguistic expression; and that there is nothing for it but to realize this and always take it into account." He realizes that they are inevitable, but still treats the "flaws" of spatial-temporal particular language like early Wittgenstein's ladder that must be discarded once climbed, that is, as a completely external, accidental means that can, at least in theory, be fully separated from logic. After all, "we are taking 'judgment' to mean, not an act performed by a definite man at a definite time, but something timelessly true, even if its being true is not acknowledged by any human being" (Geach and Black 1960, 126n). The kind of analysis Frege is concerned with "has nothing to do with time; its applicability to occurrences in time is irrelevant" (107; see also 134; Burge 2005, 213, 247), an idealization that allows him to ignore the fact he otherwise admits as important, that "we *cannot* come to an understanding with one another apart from language, and so *in the end we must always* rely on other people's understanding words, inflexions, and sentence-construction in essentially the same way as ourselves" (Geach and Black 1960, 45, italics added). This is also facilitated by the signifier/signified distinction, since "while the actual numbers are timeless, numerical figures arise and pass away in time" (227). Burge writes that "a trademark of a sense of Fregean thought component is that it can in principle be expressed on indefinitely many occasions. For nothing in its expression or in its being thought affects its referential relations. . . . Its relations to its referent(s) is atemporal and depends purely on its own nature and the inventory of the world" (Burge 2005, 237–38), precisely the opposite of Derrida's notion of iterability (ED). If time-bound signs are merely an aid to grasping the timeless numbers, problems with signs can be admitted while simultaneously bracketed as unessential. Deconstruction, on the other hand, tries to follow Frege's line about realizing the inherent perplexities of language and "always tak[ing them] into account." Here is how Derrida describes the general attitude:

> Deconstruction therefore finds itself at the heart of what you call "tensions." It is a question of assuming these tensions, of "living" them as

> much as of "understanding" them. Those who fear and wish to deny the inescapable necessity of these transformations try to see in deconstruction the agent responsible for such changes, when in my eyes it is above all else a question of trying to understand them, of interpreting them, so as to respond to them in the most responsible fashion possible. (Derrida, *PoI* 413)

## Quasi-Transcendental Arguments

In the wake of so much criticism of Derrida's work, particularly the common claim that it is neither philosophical nor even relevant to philosophy, discussions of his status abound. One debate on this issue that is particularly interesting for my purposes occurs between Christopher Norris and Richard Rorty. Both agree that at least Derrida's early work (roughly through the early 1970s) should be considered "real philosophy," meaning that it contains recognizable arguments that can be rationally analyzed and evaluated and that take up traditional philosophical topics. In particular, both depict Derrida as engaging in a Kantian-style transcendental inquiry into the conditions of the possibility of language or meaning. Norris writes that his

> arguments amount to a form of Kantian transcendental deduction. That is to say, they pose the question: what must be the necessary *presuppositions* of our thinking about language if language is to make any kind of coherent or intelligible sense? . . . Where these objections [made by Derrida's opponents] miss the mark is in not discerning how rigorously Derrida argues his way in following out the various contradictory entailments of the texts he reads. . . . The route of detailed argument by which those conclusions are arrived at is one that philosophers should recognize, since it takes the form (as with Derrida on Husserl) of a transcendental deduction, albeit to what must seem decidedly counterintuitive ends.[51]

Norris's main point against those who would eject Derrida from the discipline is that his work in fact counts as a philosophical enterprise which simply ends up with "counterintuitive" conclusions, hardly a distinctive characteristic. If one actually studies these early texts, one will find a real philosopher.

Rorty's responds that, alas, it is so; the early work does supply transcendental arguments, but he argues that that is its *flaw,* not its virtue.[52] Derrida's "counterintuitive" conclusions should prevent him from employing the type of transcendental argument Norris saddles him with in a misguided attempt to give him legitimacy. Norris has unintentionally buried Derrida, not praised him, or rather buried him by praising.

> Insofar as Derrida remains faithful to the nominalism he shares with Strawson, transcendental arguments will not permit him to infer the existence of such quasi entities as "différance," "trace" and "archi-writing." Insofar as he does not remain faithful to it, he is just one more metaphysician. A philosopher cannot, as Derrida does, set his face against totalization, insist that the possibilities of recontextualization are boundless, and nonetheless offer transcendental arguments. For how could he hope to grasp *the conditions of possibility of all possible contexts?* . . . I think it . . . important to insist that Derrida is *not* giving rigorous arguments against logocentrism. (Dasenbrock 1989, 208; see also Rorty 1982, 100; 1991b, 119)

Rorty considers Derrida's mid-1970s texts such as *The Post Card* superior to the early works because these media fit the message; these middle texts no longer try to *argue* against logocentrism, but just attempt to write in a non-logocentric way. Metaphysics is a Chinese finger trap; the harder you pull away, the stronger its grip. Since reason is essential to this system, using reason to escape it ends up reaffirming it, so their arguments actually compromise the early "philosophical" works. Rorty makes similar distinctions between the early and later phases of both Wittgenstein and Heidegger.[53]

This debate is particularly interesting for my discussion because of Kant's status in my narrative: the Heideggerian Paradigm is attempting to escape his shadow, and it is just at the point of transcendental arguments that the two representatives of the Heideggerian Paradigm I discuss above get bogged down. Though they qualify their claims, both the later Heidegger and Foucault seem to appeal to some condition of everything else (Being, power) which is in some way outside of changing history, and both rely on a minimal essential definition of the self (R6) as openness to new possibilities for the rest of their thought to be thoroughly historical, as well as for Foucault to justify his more prescriptive moments. The fact that these thinkers encounter problems precisely when they engage in Kantian transcendental arguments suggests that this might be an Achilles' heel of the Heideggerian Paradigm, the element of the Kantian Paradigm it could not shake off, the way that the Kantian Paradigm retained vestiges of realism. In light of this, the fact that Derrida is accused of being at his most conservative, and even of compromising what is revolutionary in his thought, on just this same topic is intriguing. If he gets sucked into the same trap as later Heidegger and Foucault, then we could classify Derrida as another member of the Heideggerian Paradigm. On the other hand, if he can solve it, then perhaps his thought can open the way for a new approach or even a new paradigm that escapes this flaw.

Derrida's susceptibility comes from using the kinds of terms that Rorty nominates as the necessary condition for other important phenomena, that is, arche-writing, trace, and above all, *différance.* And indeed, as the original self-differentiation that is the source of all further differences, *différance* is frequently described as the necessary condition for articulation, enabling entities to be distinct from one another and thus to be themselves which allows us to know and name them. In other words, like Being itself, *différance* is "what makes possible the presentation of the being-present."[54] Derrida defines *différance* variously as the condition of "temporalization as well as relationship with the other and language" (Derrida, *G* 60; see also Derrida, *Ltd* 129), of the "sensible plenitude" and "all that one calls sign" (Derrida, *G* 62; see also Derrida, *WD* 71), "the positive *sciences*" (Derrida, *G* 63), "the opposition of presence and absence" (143), "languages" (268; see also 315), and "nominal effects" (Derrida, *MP* 26). *Différance* is "the very opening of the space in which ontotheology—philosophy—produces its system and its history" (6), and, of course, "this movement of *différance* is not something that happens to a transcendental subject; it produces a subject" (Derrida, *SP* 82). In order to do Heidegger one better, it even "is the condition for there being an *envoi,* possibly an *envoi* of being, a dispensation or a gift of being and time, of the present and of representation" (Derrida, "SOR" 136). His commitment to the indefinitely open future should prevent any totalities, but Derrida speaks of "the structure of textuality in general . . . This is how a text always comes about" (Derrida, *EO* 51; see also Derrida, *Ltd* 48; Derrida, *Dis* 290). He writes that *différance* operates everywhere (see, for example, Derrida 2000a, 404), concluding that "for me, *life is différance*" (407). He calls iterability a structure that is "universal and necessary"[55] and asks rhetorically, "Wouldn't the apocalyptic be a transcendental condition of all discourse, of all experience even, of every mark or every trace?" (Fenves 1993, 156–57; see also Derrida, *PoI* 83, 208–9).

What makes such contentions particularly problematic for Derrida, as Rorty points out, is that his frequent assertions about such phenomena as iterability opening language up to absolutely unforeseeable possibilities should keep him from making any claims about the totality of discourse (see Derrida, *Ltd* 100, 116, 137). The philosopher's "fundamental project [is] to render an account of all possible discourses and all possible arts. He wants to situate himself in a place where everything done and said can be thought, theorized, and finally mastered by him" (Derrida, *PoI* 140; see also Derrida, *G* 18; Derrida, *DN* 13). This project, which Derrida wants to reject as incoherent, sounds uncomfortably like what he proposes to do, as discussed in the previous paragraph. Derrida is arguing that all possible discourse is marked in advance by features that render it *un*controllable in principle, but this still attributes features to *all* possible discourse, experience, and so on, even if it is to deny that they can be characterized in any straightforward way once and for all. Echoing Heidegger's criticism of Nietzsche, Derrida frequently says, "Frontal critiques always let themselves be turned back and reappropriated into philosophy" (Derrida, *PoI* 82).

Derrida is fully aware of the metaphysical pedigree and potential entanglements of transcendental arguments and, accordingly, he is careful to put the notion of origin he is using in question. Indeed, this challenge is one of the ways he defines deconstruction: "What is put into question is precisely the quest for a rightful beginning, an absolute point of departure. . . . The problematic of writing is opened by putting into question the value *arkhē*."[56] Certainly these strange terms do not function as straightforward traditional foundations or starting points (see Derrida, *G* 74; Derrida, *WD* 203; Derrida, *MP* 6), which is at least one reason why he often uses the qualified term "quasi-transcendental."[57] He tells the reader that his analysis "does not amount to saying that this law has the simplicity of a logical or transcendental principle" (Derrida, *Ltd* 92; see also 100; Derrida, *PC* 191–92), frequently denying traditional features to his terms: "Have I not indefatigably repeated—and I would dare say demonstrated—that the trace is neither a ground, nor a foundation, nor an origin, and that in no case can it provide for a manifest or disguised onto-theology" (Derrida, *Pos* 52; see also 40, 106n37; Derrida, *TP* 12; Derrida, "SOR" 136).

Derrida is here following Heidegger's attempts to render Being itself (see chapter 6) impervious to metaphysical or onto-theological interpretations. The ontological difference insists that Being can *in no way* be a being, not even the highest being, so it cannot be a necessary condition in the sense of cause or foundation, in the way God is the origin of the universe for much of traditional metaphysics. That would amount to ontotheology, which explains Being by recourse to a being such as God. Derrida uses a version of the ontological difference to prevent his terms from being placed into "a manifest or disguised onto-theology": "*The trace itself does not exist.* (To exist is to be, to be an entity, a being-present)."[58] Since these phenomena like *différance* are never fully present or self-identical, the argument goes, they are not entities and thus cannot function as transcendental conditions. Metaphysics is inherently metaphysics of presence, which only applies to entities that purport to be fully present and self-identical. Since Derrida's terms break down such notions, they slip through the fingers of metaphysical thought: "*No concept of metaphysics can describe*" trace and *différance* (Derrida, *G* 65). A fortiori they cannot be fitted into a traditional metaphysical structure like a transcendental inquiry. In retrospect, Heidegger can be seen as foreshadowing this Derridean language: "The origin of the difference can no longer be thought of within the scope of metaphysics" (Heidegger, *ID* 71; see also Derrida, *SNS* 121). The problem with Derrida's argument is that these qualifications by themselves do not disqualify such terms from serving as transcendental conditions; they just require a modified form of it. Indeed, Heidegger takes these qualifications into account, while still applying the concept of origin: "One can name [being] an origin, assuming that all ontic-causal overtones are excluded: it is the event of being as condition for the arrival of beings" (Heidegger, *FoS* 59). M. C. Dillon makes the excellent point that Kant's transcendental unity of apperception performs many of the same functions as Derrida's *différance,* and it too cannot be considered a being on Kant's system, but this does not stop it from functioning as a, or indeed, the paradigmatic transcendental condition (Madison 1993, 199–200).

Derrida rejects metaphysical interpretations of his claims, and certainly he avoids any traditional onto-theological meaning, but let us examine whether he avoids using them as *any* kind of origin or transcendental condition. *Différance* is not a thing, nor is it separate from its "effects," which prevents it from being an onto-theological or transcendent source; it is

> the playing movement that "produces"—by means of something that is not simply an activity—differences, these effects of difference. This does not mean that the *différance* that produces differences is somehow before them, in a simple and unmodified—in-different—present. *Différance* is the non-full, non-simple, structured and differentiating origin of differences. Thus, the name "origin" no longer suits it. (Derrida, *MP* 11; see also Derrida, *G* 60)

Rather than saying that origin as such no longer suits *différance,* however, it seems more appropriate to say that it cannot be understood as an onto-theological or realist origin the way the "Paralogism" prevents us from viewing the subject as a thing. These various phenomena do seem to function as origins and transcendental conditions, however. Derrida repeatedly states that these perform the genetic or constitutive condition role in traditional metaphysical systems: "In a conceptuality adhering to classical strictures '*différance*' would be said to designate a constitutive, productive, and originary causality, the process of scission and division which would produce or constitute different things or differences" (Derrida, *MP* 8–9; see also 12; Derrida, *Ltd* 153). He makes it a kind of constituting agent

(ICS): "It is not the question of a constituted difference here, but rather, before all determination of the content, of the *pure* movement which produces difference. *The (pure) trace is differance*" (Derrida, *G* 62). This does not automatically saddle him with all the baggage of traditional metaphysics, but he certainly appears to be pursuing a transcendental inquiry in the manner of the Heideggerian Paradigm, as qualified with the ontological difference.

> Differences appear among the elements or rather produce them, make them emerge as such and constitute the *texts,* the chains, and the systems of traces. . . . The unheard difference between the appearing and the appearance (between the "world" and "lived experience") is the condition of all other differences, of all other traces, and *it is already a trace. . . . The trace is in fact the absolute origin of sense in general. Which amounts to saying once again that there is no absolute origin of sense in general.* (Derrida, *G* 65)

We see here the denial that the trace represents an origin in the traditional sense, along with the claim that it still functions as an origin. As with Heidegger and Foucault, this notion of an unsurpassable source is what drives Derrida to make his most metaphysical and essentialist pronouncements: "Essentially and lawfully, every concept is inscribed in a chain or in a system within which it refers to the other, to other concepts, by means of the systematic play of differences. Such a play, *différance,* is thus no longer simply a concept, but rather the possibility of conceptuality, of a conceptual process and system in general" (Derrida, *MP* 11).

## A Certain Heidegger

But of course, nothing is ever simple when it comes to Derrida's thought: "All of this remains to be carefully modulated. Never all or nothing, that is one simple thing that must be said about access to the text" (Derrida, *PoI* 175). His texts seem riddled with these transcendental arguments in which the transcendental origin is not a present being but still functions as a necessary condition for all Xs. As mentioned above, these kinds of arguments present a particular problem for thinkers of the Heideggerian Paradigm, so if Derrida were to get tripped up here it would be par for the course. On the other hand, if he can engage this issue in such a way that leaves his work uncompromised by it (not a very Derridean notion, I realize), his work might loosen this conceptual knot and point the way to a new form of thought.

To explore Derrida's take on transcendental arguments, I want to shift the ground. Whereas Norris and Rorty locate Derrida relative to Kant, I will examine his thought in relation to Heidegger, my candidate for the next seminal thinker in continental philosophy after Kant. In my narrative, Heidegger and Kant are the figures who constructed the frameworks from which the others took their bearings and within which they worked, even when they criticize or extend their respective paradigms. Here my guiding hypothesis is that Derrida's relationship to Heidegger resembles the later Heidegger's to Kant: Heidegger's thought represents a deeply divided legacy for Derrida, as Kant's was for Heidegger. For each, the predecessor's work is inescapable in that it opened up the paths of thought that will be pursued, but at the same time the earlier thinker remained mired in some of the very problems that he identified and tried to escape. In both cases, the task is to think through the issues more thoroughly in order to escape these problems more successfully than the pathbreaker did. Thus, in Derrida's encounter with[59] Heidegger we can perhaps begin to make out the outlines of a new paradigm for continental thought. Derrida sums up this task here:

> To read ["the texts of the history of metaphysics"], certainly, within the opening of the Heideggerian breakthrough, which is *the only thought excess of metaphysics as such,* but also to read them, occasionally, and faithfully, *beyond certain propositions or conclusions within which the Heideggerian breakthrough has had to constrain itself,* propositions or conclusions which it has had to call upon or take its support from. (Derrida, *MP* 62, italics and bracketed comment added)

This double reading, both with and against the earlier figure, applies equally to Heidegger's relation to Kant in his founding of a new paradigm which he described as "reminiscent of Kant, and yet radically different at the same time" (Heidegger, *Zo* 194). At one point, Derrida describes his move as "simultaneously very far from and very near to Heidegger's" (Derrida, *PC* 66).

Just as Kant was the unavoidable groundbreaking figure for the Heideggerian Paradigm, so Derrida frequently writes of Heidegger's unique position, calling his work "uncircumventable" (Derrida, *MP* 22; see also Derrida, *TP* 262; Derrida, "SOR" 124; Derrida, *G* 24), since "what I have attempted to do would not have been possible without the opening of Heidegger's questions" (Derrida, *Pos* 9). The key advance that Heidegger made is that he came closer to getting beyond metaphysics and subjected this enterprise to a closer examination than anyone else. Therefore the texts of metaphysics must be read "within the opening of the Heideggerian breakthrough" because this is "the only thought excess of metaphysics as such."[60]

However, just as Kant's epoch-making rejection of realism was compromised by his remnants of realism, so Derrida considers Heidegger's texts riddled with the metaphysics he tried to twist free of.[61] This is not surprising, given his view of the tenacity of metaphysics: "Metaphysics always returns. . . . Is this not what Heidegger will never finally be able to avoid, the unavoidable itself?" (Derrida, *OS* 40–41; see also Derrida, *SP* 74n4). Thus "the Heideggerian breakthrough," like the Kantian breakthrough, is marked by internal tension. Derrida's task is to exploit Heidegger's postmetaphysical resources while exposing his metaphysical vestiges, just as thinkers from Hegel through Heidegger were inspired by Kantian ideas to work through the Kantian Paradigm's traces of realism: "Despite this debt to Heidegger's thought, or rather because of it, I attempt to locate in Heidegger's text—which, no more than any other, is not homogeneous, continuous, everywhere equal to the greatest force and to all the consequences of its questions—the signs of a belonging to metaphysics" (Derrida, *Pos* 10; see also Derrida, *G* 12, 22).

As is appropriate to such a divided subject matter, Derrida's relationship to Heidegger is deeply ambiguous. He cannot simply surpass "the Heideggerian breakthrough" because this body of work more than any other thematizes the history of metaphysics and the escape from it: "From the moment one is having it out with [*s'explique avec*] Heidegger in a critical or deconstructive fashion, must one not continue to recognize a certain necessity of his thinking, its character, which is inaugural in so many respects, and especially what remains to come for us in its deciphering? This is a task of thinking" (Derrida, *PoI* 183–84; see also 223). But that work's failures mean that it must be handled with care, for it may contain structural flaws that prevent success and so must be carefully avoided. In a demonstration of the way texts can deconstruct themselves, it is in the name of and by means of certain aspects of Heidegger's thought that Derrida attacks others: "I never 'criticize' Heidegger without recalling that that can be done from other places in his own text. His text could not be homogeneous."[62] This double view can be summed up in a phrase Derrida uses when listing figures suggestive of "places of transcendence, of an absolute elsewhere, therefore, in the eye of Graeco-Latino-Christian Western philosophy, but yet *inside it.*" Among the figures who help him think about escaping philosophy, he does not mention Heidegger *simpliciter*, but rather "a certain Heidegger" (Derrida, *MO* 71).

Interestingly, Derrida's own most metaphysical moments, that is, his transcendental arguments, often come when he engages in transcendental competition with Heidegger, an attempt to play, in David Kolb's phrase, "the game of standing furthest back" (Kolb 1986, 251). Whereas Heidegger believes that in Being he has found the absolutely first condition of everything—since we have to be aware of whatever we are talking about or have it in the clearing just in order to discuss it—Derrida wants to find what precedes and enables even that. "Are not the thought of the *meaning* or *truth* of Being, the determination of *différance* as the ontico-ontological difference, difference thought within the horizon of the question *of Being,* still intrametaphysical effects of *différance?* . . . *Différance,* in a certain and very strange way, (is) 'older' than the ontological difference or than the truth of Being."[63] Derrida is trying to outdo Heidegger's transcendental argument by making his own key terms—*différance,* trace, and so on—the necessary condition for Heidegger's necessary condition of everything else. The ontological difference between Being and beings is itself a form of spacing or differentiating, making it posterior to Derrida's own transcendental of the origin of all differences. As important as the clearing is, Heidegger always insists that we need to be able to distinguish the clearing from what is within it, presencing from what is present, in order to achieve the awareness that he is trying to account for; this makes his argument rest upon differentiation. Furthermore, if Being and thinking are linguistic, as Heidegger often argues, then Derrida can make a good case that they presuppose language and hence arche-writing: "The fact of language is probably *the only fact* ultimately to resist all parenthetization" (Derrida, *WD* 37, italics added). Thus, in an Oedipal gesture, Derrida insists that even "Being must be conceived as presence or absence on the basis of the possibility of play and not the other way around" (292).

## "A Writing or Reading Which Must Carry Us Beyond"

The overall pattern traced by the history of continental anti-realism that I have been describing is that of the progressive erosion of realism. Simplifying greatly, Kant inaugurates the process by shifting what determines knowledge from independent reality (R1) to active subjectivity (A5), but he maintains both noumena (R1) to escape the paradoxes of full-blown idealism and realism of the transcendental subject (R6) in order to preserve necessary and universal knowledge (R3). The philosophers of the Kantian Paradigm then weaken these realist elements with, in my account, Hegel doing a better job of undermining noumena (R1) and Nietzsche being more successful on realist subjectivity (R6). The later Heidegger makes the next major turn in this narrative by completely immersing the subject into history (A6) and transferring the constitutive and knowledge-determining powers to historically changing Impersonal Conceptual Schemes (A3), which determine humanity's essence along with the rest of reality (R5). According to the inertia of this narrative up to this point, Derrida should move ahead by attacking the most realist element of the Heideggerian Paradigm.

The component of the Heideggerian Paradigm that Derrida zeroes in on is ICS. The later Heidegger's epochal meanings of Being (and Foucault's *epistemes,* and so on) are what take the constitutive pressure off of the subject, so to speak, constituting her rather than making her the constitutor (A5), while still maintaining reality's dependence (A1). And since these schemes change throughout history, so does the form of subjectivity (A6) and the nature of reality (A3). ICS is in many ways the linchpin of the Heideggerian Paradigm, similar to the position held by active transcendental subjectivity in the Kantian Paradigm. As discussed above, Heidegger's ontological difference keeps these schemes from being portrayed metaphysically, that is, as beings like Forms or ideas in the mind of God.

Derrida's objection (put into my terms) is that these Impersonal Conceptual Schemes still partake too much of R3 Uniqueness. Although they are multiple and change over the course of history (A3), each one monolithically determines the characteristics of virtually everything that is during its reign. While Heidegger's later work detaches the experience-structuring concepts from the quasi-transcendental subject of Dasein, Derrida believes that the ICS retains too much of the metaphysics of *Being and Time.* For one thing, the later work maintains an R6 Realist determination of the essence of man. Even though this essence has been attenuated to mere receptivity to Being, any essence brings the problematic structure of the early existential analysis and ideal of authenticity in its wake:

> The ontological distance from *Dasein* to what *Dasein* is as ek-sistence and to the *Da* of *Sein,* the distance that first was given as ontic proximity, must be reduced by the thinking of the truth of Being. Whence, in Heidegger's discourse, the dominance of an entire metaphorics of proximity, of simple and immediate presence, a metaphorics associating the proximity of Being with the values of neighboring, shelter, house, service, guard, voice, and listening. (Derrida, *MP* 130; see also Derrida, *PoI* 258; Derrida, *TP* 358)

Heidegger's later work is still organized around the authentic reappropriation of our true nature, now understood as openness to and guardianship of Being. Derrida's criticism often centers on "the thinking of gathering upon which Heidegger insists so much," which preserves much of the early work's Dasein-centered metaphysics.[64]

The more important criticism, though, is of the conceptual schemes themselves. "Henceforth, along with the theme of time, all the themes that are dependent upon it (and, par excellence, those of *Dasein,* of finitude, of historicity) will no longer constitute the transcendental horizon of the question of Being, but in transition will be *reconstituted* on the basis of the theme of the epochality of Being."[65] It is the very idea of conceptual schemes that bothers Derrida, so Heidegger's moves of transferring them from the A5 subject to impersonal Being, changing them from apparently one permanent set (R3) to an indefinitely open succession (A3), rendering them abyssal by giving up any attempt to account for them, are all secondary issues; these alterations all rest on and maintain ("reconstitute") a deeper metaphysical/realist notion that must be challenged.

The Heideggerian Paradigm employs these temporarily stable systems to establish truth and meaning in the place of an R1 Independent reality, differing from Kant by making them impersonal rather than based in the active subject and changing across history (A3) rather than singular and permanent. But for Derrida, this notion is still too close to the Kantian R3 conceptual scheme.

> The notion of a linguistic *system,* even if opposed to the notions of logical system, of system of categories . . . would never have been possible outside the history (and) of the concepts of metaphysics as theory, *epistēmē,* etc. Whatever the displacements, breaks, and secondary discontinuities of every kind (and they surely have to be taken very strictly into account), this filiation has never been absolutely interrupted. (Derrida, *MP* 180; see also Wheeler 2000, 23–24)

He grants that the Heideggerian Paradigm places qualifications—"displacements, breaks, and . . . discontinuities"—on the notion of a "system of categories" (and notice the references to the ICS terms of both the later Heidegger ["history of metaphysics"] and Foucault ["*epistēmē*"]), but nevertheless these modifications remain "secondary." The structures are still too determinate, their boundaries too clearly drawn, and their power too assured to have escaped Kant's lingering metaphysics. The systems are, well, too systematic; they are too stable and run too smoothly to have broken with metaphysics: "What is in question here is the systematic totality of our conceptuality" (Wood and Bernasconi 1988, 84).[66] Derrida uses several strategies to eradicate the Heideggerian Paradigm's remnant of R3. I will distinguish three of them, though they do tend to merge into each other.

First, he demands that we "prepare, beyond our logos, for a *différance* so violent that it can be interpellated neither as the epochality of Being nor as the ontological difference. . . . As rigorously as possible we must permit to appear/disappear the trace of what exceeds the truth of Being" (Derrida, *MP* 22–23; see also Derrida, *G* 14). Although a truth of Being is supposed to encompass all that can be experienced or thought during a particular epoch, Derrida believes that the various "phenomena" he discusses—trace, *différance,* supplement, and so on—cannot be thought in terms of concepts, indicating an essential limit to any supposedly comprehensive system (see Derrida, *G* 65). This first criticism of Heidegger resembles Levinas's insistence that we cannot (and ethically ought not) fit our experience of other people into categories: "It is above all a matter of finding a place where the human no longer concerns us from the perspective of the horizon of being."[67] Levinas sets up the paradox that the extra-horizonal perspective that would be able to do justice (in both senses of the word) to the other would be a matter of "thinking more than what is thought while nevertheless conserving it in its excessive relation to thought. The idea of the infinite consists in grasping the ungraspable while nevertheless guaranteeing its status as ungraspable."[68]

In a manner similar to Heidegger's criticism of A5, Derrida is concerned that concepts screen out genuine alterity. Commenting on Levinas, he writes that "concepts suppose an anticipation, a horizon within which alterity is amortized as soon as it is announced precisely because it has let itself be foreseen. The infinitely-other cannot be bound by a concept."[69] Derrida is trying to create a category of the uncategorizable, that is, "phenomena" that initially and sometimes continue to resist our attempts to classify them in any simple or definitive way. Two examples of this category are what he calls the "monstrous" (Derrida, *PoI* 386; Derrida, *WD* 293) and the future which, if comprehensible to us today, would merely be an extension of the present and so not a genuine future at all.[70] It is Derrida's repugnance at this drive toward cognitive domestication that makes whatever can resist it attractive, such as the undecidable words I will discuss below, or ideas like the gift that "interrupts economy. . . . It announces itself, gives itself to be thought as the impossible" (Derrida, *GT* 7). These incomprehensible phenomena cannot be prepared for within an a priori set of concepts but must (R5) break through our system of thoughts to create room for new ideas. We need

> a perception that is absolutely surprised by the encounter with what it perceives, beyond its horizon of anticipation—which already appears phenomenologically impossible. . . . The gift as event must be irruptive. . . . They must therefore tear the fabric, interrupt the continuum of a nar-

rative that nevertheless they call for, they must perturb the order of causalities. (Derrida, *GT* 122–23; see also Derrida, *Ap* 34; Derrida, *Gl* 59–60, 243)

Although Heidegger paved the way for these ideas by rendering Being itself radically mysterious and incommensurable with all metaphysical concepts, his mistake lies in giving the epochal meanings of Being too much power and stability, allowing them to organize all beings within a period unproblematically. His treatment of art marks a notable exception. The first section of "The Origin of the Work of Art" is a running narrative of art's refusal to be pigeonholed into either of the non-Dasein categories from *Being and Time,* equipment and thing. When he does come up with a definition of art, it is marked by internal strife and includes "earth," i.e., that which resists and eludes all attempts to comprehend it: "It shows itself only when it remains undisclosed and unexplained. Earth thus shatters every attempt to penetrate it" (Heidegger, *BW* 172). Here Heidegger comes much closer to Derrida's thoughts than in his discussions of epochal ICS.

Derrida's second assault on the Heideggerian Paradigm's ICS emerges from his style of reading. As discussed above, Derrida is deeply committed to highly rigorous standards of reading, repeatedly repudiating the "anything goes" style of interpretation that sometimes goes on in his name. He demands the greatest possible background knowledge and the closest possible attention given to the text, "otherwise, one could indeed say just anything at all and I have never accepted saying, or encouraging others to say, just anything at all, nor have I argued for indeterminacy as such."[71] Indeed, he insists that readers honor "the values of coherence, truth, demonstration, and so forth" even to ensure that whatever unorthodox conclusions arrived at are legitimately reached and not the results of shortcuts (Derrida, *PoI* 198–99; Derrida, *TFS* 43).

However, there is a reason that these silly views are so frequently associated with him; there is some resemblance to some of his basic tenets about reading and interpretation, albeit misconstrued and "greatly overestimated in my texts in the United States" (Derrida, *Ltd* 115). Derrida considers it essential to be as responsible as possible to "the rigor of the discipline" (Derrida, *PoI* 414; see also Derrida, *G* 158) and to what is actually on the page. However, this responsibility, using the same wordplay as Heidegger, means responding to the text, not R5 Passively reflecting it. In fact, Derrida holds that the simple faithful reflection of the content of a text is impossible; metaphysics "delud[es] itself, too, in wanting to look at the text without touching it, without laying a hand on the 'object,' without risking—which is the only chance of entering into the game, by getting a few fingers caught—the addition of some new thread. Adding, here, is nothing other than giving to read. . . . Reading *is* writing."[72] Reading is A5 Active or always already interpretive. Unfortunately for the dream of traditional philosophy, any kind of "translation is transformative" (Derrida, *PoI* 274), echoing Heidegger's famous saying that "every translation is already an interpretation."[73]

Derrida's theory of iterability renders the simple reproduction of meaning (R5) without affecting it impossible. Since signifiers do not get their significance from connections (R2) to independent (R1) and determinant (R3) objects, but rather from the self-differentiating network of differences (ICS), or *différance,* placing an apparently self-identical linguistic unit (R3) such as a phrase, sentence, or paragraph into a new context necessarily affects its meaning. "Iteration . . . is at work, constantly *altering* . . . whatever it seems to reproduce. . . . Iteration alters, something new takes place" (Derrida, *Ltd* 40; see also Derrida, *TP* 243). Citation is an illuminating instance of iteration because it seems to reproduce the original mark for mark, yet merely placing the text in a new context shines a new light on it, bringing out different elements or making new connections. "One can always lift a written syntagma from the interlocking chain in which it is caught or given without making it lose every possibility of functioning. . . . Eventually, one may recognize other such possibilities in it by inscribing or *grafting* it into other chains. No context can enclose it. Nor can any code" (Derrida, *MP* 317; see also Royle 2000, 293). This is not a particularly esoteric or rare occurrence. We read secondary literature about works we have read many times and perhaps taught or even written on in order to see them anew, to be reintroduced to them, to gather new insights into what we know so well. Arranging passages into a new pattern stitched together by discussions that try to show new connections among them can teach profoundly new ideas about very familiar texts (this is obviously what this book tries to do). Derrida uses the term "doubling commentary" to suggest "not a moment of [R5] simple reflective recording that would transcribe the [R1] originary and true layer of a text's intentional meaning, a meaning that is [R3] univocal and self-identical, a layer upon which or after which active interpretation would finally begin. No, this commentary is *already* an [A5] interpretation" (Derrida, *Ltd* 143, bracketed comments added; see also 146; Derrida, *Dis* 64).

We can see a fascinating illustration of this idea in Borges's "Pierre Menard, Author of the *Quixote,*" a short story I have found Derrida mentioning only once, and then just to comment on how French it is (Derrida, *EO* 99). It tells the story of a twentieth-century author who, eschewing updates of classics that place famous protagonists in contemporary settings, decides not "to compose another *Don Quixote*—which would be easy—but *the Don Quixote.* It is unnecessary to add that his aim was never to produce a mechanical transcription of the original; he did not propose to copy it. His admirable ambition was to produce pages which would coincide—word for word and line for line—with those of Miguel de Cervantes" (Borges 1962, 48–49). Menard succeeds in writing on his own "the ninth and thirty-eighth chapters of Part One of *Don Quixote* and a fragment of the twenty-second chapter" (48), and the effect is surprising. "The text of Cervantes and that of Menard are verbally identical, but the second is almost infinitely richer. . . . It is a revelation to compare the *Don Quixote* of Menard with that of Cervantes" (52). Borges then juxtaposes the two, quoting the "same passage" word for word, but first as written by Cervantes and then by Menard, finding that the passages' divergent authorship thoroughly alters the impression they make. Speaking of the phrase, "truth, whose mother is history," Borges sniffs, "written in the seventeenth century, written by the 'ingenious layman' Cervantes, this enumeration is a mere rhetorical eulogy of history" (53). But "on the other hand," written by Menard, "a contemporary of . . . Bertrand Russell" and William James, "the idea is astounding" (52–53). "Equally vivid is the contrast in styles," since Menard's use of this "archaic style" can only be an "affectation," whereas the seventeenth-century Cervantes "handles easily the ordinary Spanish of his time" (53). Borges concludes that this experiment "has enriched, by means of a new technique, the hesitant and rudimentary art of reading: the technique is one of deliberate anachronism and erroneous attributions" (54). Readers can now imagine well-worn books to be written at different times, in different orders, or by different authors than they actually were and explore how such alterations would change their perceptions of the works.

This is quite different from Derrida's technique, but it helps illuminate it a bit. By bringing the same text into relation with a different author in a different time period, Borges makes "identical" passages from *Don Quixote* look and feel quite different, demonstrating the importance of context. Although the thought experiment only works if the passages are "the same," by the end the process begins to wear down our trust in such notions. Derrida's claim is that without transcendent types to safeguard meaning and usage from a position beyond their actual employment, every iteration of linguistic tokens alters their meaning by placing them in a new context, even if only slightly. Each instance must allow us to recognize them as the same sign for them to function, but we should understand this sameness in a new way, specifically, not as empirical instances participating in a Type, the closet Platonism he sees still hanging over much philosophy of language. If types are generated out of the circulation of tokens, then they are open to indefinite change, though this will almost always be a slow drift, the kind of overlapping ship-of-Theseus shift that we in fact see occurring in language all the time.

This brings us back to the topic of play. This contextual generation of word meaning without external control in which each context can bring out new elements also applies to texts, giving rise to an interpretive drift. To repeat, it isn't that one can say anything one wants; interpretation must be rigorously based on what is on the page. But Derrida's claim is that when one reads closely without the presuppositions that screen out certain elements as unimportant or meaningless, one finds that texts are open to much broader ranges of interpretation than we usually think. We tend to settle on a very narrow set of meanings for a text, or often just one: the literal meaning (see Derrida, *G* 18; Derrida, *Dis* 44). But Derrida denies that such a thing exists, insisting and frequently demonstrating that there is no way to close off in advance what meanings can be derived from any text, even in perfect compliance with traditional codes of reading. Again, this can be seen fairly innocuously in the way great scholars often disagree about very basic interpretive issues.

Derrida is saying that there are and can be no inherent limits to what readers can make of texts, even in accordance with the most rigorous application of the most traditional rules. Although this is true of all texts, he tries to show this by focusing on words or phrases that explicitly defy R3 determination, that are "rigorously undecidable" (Derrida, *Gl* 2), such as *pharmakon,* which means either "poison" or "cure," or the note, "I have forgotten my umbrella," which was "found, isolated in quotation marks, among Nietzsche's unpublished manuscripts. . . . There is no infallible way of knowing the occasion of this sample or what it could have been later grafted onto. We never will know *for sure* what Nietzsche wanted to say or do when he noted these words, nor even that he actually *wanted* anything" (Derrida, *SNS* 123). Given philosophy's general insistence on clear literal meaning, its demand for "the reassuring and absolute rule, the norm of this polysemia" (Derrida, *MP* xxvii; see also Derrida, "SOR" 113), such instances of "undecidable" significance are a source of great "hermeneutic anxiety" (Derrida, *EO* 170). Indeed, the possible impossibility of definitive meaning is the textual counterpart to Dasein's angst-inducing death in *Being and Time.* "It is always possible that it means nothing at all or that it has no decidable meaning. There is no end to its parodying play with meaning, grafted here and there, beyond any contextual body or finite code. . . . The hermeneut cannot but be provoked and disconcerted by its play" (Derrida, *SNS* 131–33).

Philosophy recoils from such indeterminability, since its dream of perfect translation and complete comprehension requires that expressions have a determinate (R3) and separable (R1) conceptual content, as we saw with Frege.

> One must be able to fix its univocality. . . . If this plurivocality can be mastered, then translation, understood as the transport of a semantic content into another signifying form, is possible. There is no philosophy unless translation in this latter sense is possible. . . . *Wherever translation in this sense has failed, it is nothing less than philosophy that finds itself defeated.* This is precisely what I tried to deal with in "Plato's Pharmacy" by means of a certain number of words such as *pharmakon,* whose body is in itself *a constant challenge to philosophy.* Philosophical discourse cannot master a word meaning two things at the same time and which therefore cannot be translated without an essential loss. Whether one translates *pharmakon* as "poison" or "remedy" . . . the undecidability is going to be lost. So, *pharmakon* is one of the limits . . . marking the limit of philosophy as translation.[74]

Undecidables defy translation, exposing the ineliminable limit of determinate meaning, and so challenge many of philosophy's basic assumptions. Although most visible in such undecidables, Derrida holds that this principle applies everywhere, making interpretive drift ubiquitous and uncontrollable. And what is true of words or sentences extends to entire texts: "The hypothesis that the totality of Nietzsche's text, in some monstrous way, might well be of the type 'I have forgotten my umbrella' cannot be denied. Which is tantamount to saying that there is no 'totality to Nietzsche's text'" (Derrida, *SNS* 133–35; see also Derrida, *MP* 248). There can be no closure to what readers can legitimately make of a text, no final decisive interpretation, and since there is nothing more to the text than what is made of it (PO), it has nothing like a stable identity (R3). This does not mean that we cannot derive meaning from texts or that we cannot evaluate interpretations as better and worse, but it does mean that the idea of *the* meaning of a text that is fixed once and for all must be discarded.

Whatever the implications this interpretive drift might have for a discipline like literary criticism, it has devastating consequences for the Heideggerian Paradigm. Derrida lays down the gauntlet with sweeping claims like this one about the theme of woman, which has irreducibly multiple meanings (A3) in Nietzsche's writings: "Everywhere operative, and most especially in Nietzsche's text, this graphic, which describes a margin where the control over meaning or code is without recourse, poses the *limit to the relevance of the hermeneutic or systematic question*" (Derrida, *SNS* 99, italics added). Recall that Heidegger's later work, largely followed by Foucault, posits Conceptual Schemes as Impersonal, that is, beyond the control or creation of any groups or individuals who are rather its effects, and that these schemes are both stable and all-encompassing for the epoch they reign over. For Heidegger, "metaphysics is the truth of beings as such and as a whole."[75] Metaphysical systems represent the best expression of each epoch's truth of Being, its ICS. We reconstruct a period's conceptual scheme by consulting its metaphysical works, and we grasp our own era's clearing through the writings of the figures most attuned to it, particularly the last metaphysician, Nietzsche.

> Metaphysics is not a human artifact. . . . Thinkers are in each case preeminently situated in the unconcealment that the Being of beings prepares for them. As a result of its historical essence, "Nietzsche's metaphysics," that is to say, the truth of beings as such and as a whole, which has now been preserved in words derived from his fundamental position, is the fundamental trait of the history of our age. (Heidegger, *N* 3:249–50)

Nietzsche's system, which Heidegger patiently pieces together across some 1,200 pages, gives us the best insight into the meaning of Being of our time.

But iterability demonstrates that "there is no such thing either as the truth of Nietzsche, or of Nietzsche's text" (Derrida, *SNS* 103). Nietzsche's works can be interpreted and reinterpreted in innumerable ways, as he perhaps intended, which undermines Heidegger's massive history of Being. This narrative is built out of the reconstructions of each epoch's system as derived from its texts, but Derrida rules out any determinate meaning to these texts: "The *written* text of philosophy . . . overflows and cracks its meaning" (Derrida, *MP* xxiii). As powerful and insightful as Heidegger's readings are, someone else could subject the same texts to very different readings and come up with a completely different history. In fact, this is just what Derrida himself does in "*Ousia* and *Grammē:* Note on a Note from *Being and Time.*" He focuses here on Heidegger's reading of Aristotle's interpretation of time; the fact that this is a poor theory of time based on the present or the now point and that "every subsequent account of time . . . has been essentially determined by it" (Heidegger, *BT* 49/26) lends tremendous importance to Heidegger's innovative and superior theory. Reading Aristotle as poisoning the tradition with the wrong kind of temporality allows Heidegger to claim the role of curing philosophy with his analysis.

Derrida's critique points out that Aristotle's text contains "both an instability and several possibilities of overturning; and we may wonder whether *Sein und Zeit* has not, in a way, arrested them" (Derrida, *MP* 49). There is play in Aristotle's writings which allows other interpretations on this issue. Derrida grants the legitimacy and interest of Heidegger's reading, but insists that the same texts can be read completely differently, in particular, as anticipating a great deal of Heidegger's own "corrective" views. Adding insult to injury, he claims, conversely, that Heidegger's texts can be shown to contain traces of the bad temporality.

> *Physics IV* doubtless confirms the Heideggerian de-limitation. Without a doubt, Aristotle thinks time on the basis of *ousia* as *parousia,* on the basis of the now, the point, etc. And yet an entire reading could be organized that would repeat in Aristotle's text *both* this limitation *and* its opposite. And which [would] make it appear that the de-limitation is still governed by the same concepts as the limitation. (Derrida, *MP* 61; see also Derrida, *Gl* 198)

Rather than just stating that this is possible, Derrida actually gives both readings in some detail, which I will not go into here. He makes the same point—that texts can be read in indefinitely many ways—about Rousseau (Derrida, *G* 307), Plato (Derrida, *Dis* 84), Hegel (Derrida, *Gl* 199), and Descartes as a criticism of Foucault's reading of him in *Madness and Civilization* (Derrida, *FWT* 12). The general claim is that "it is always possible for a text to become new, since the blanks open up its structure to an indefinitely disseminated transformation."[76] The specific point that Derrida is at pains to demonstrate, though, is that undecidability infects just those texts on just those issues that Heidegger has to claim definitive interpretations of in order for his history of Being to work. If he is to anoint himself the one who comes after metaphysics, Heidegger must be able to define the age of metaphysics and draw a clear line around it, that he may place most thinkers inside and himself outside. But Derrida blurs such clean divisions between the inside and the outside or the metaphysical and the non- or post-metaphysical (Derrida, *PC* 21, 38). Where Heidegger tried to define and delimit the history of metaphysics by tying all of it to a "vulgar" understanding of time, Derrida believes that the inherent polysemy of texts implies that "every text of metaphysics carries within itself, for example, *both* the so-called 'vulgar' concept of time *and* the resources that will be borrowed from the system of metaphysics in order to criticize that concept" (Derrida, *MP* 60; see also Derrida, *G* 72). This applies just as much to Heidegger as it does to Aristotle, completely disrupting all attempts to place one inside and the other outside the history of metaphysics. Speaking of a double reading of the *Enneads,* he writes that

> henceforth, the closure of metaphysics . . . would not occur *round* [R3] a homogeneous and continuous field of metaphysics. Rather, it would fis-

> sure the structure and history of metaphysics, *organically* inscribing and systematically *articulating* the traces of the *before* and the *after* both from within and without metaphysics. Thereby proposing an infinite, and infinitely surprising, reading. An irreducible rupture and excess can always be produced within an era, at a certain point of its text. (Derrida, *MP* 172n16, bracketed comment added; see also Derrida, *Gl* 229)

This undecidable plurivocality applies to all of Heidegger's themes: "One could multiply such questions around the concept of finitude, around the point of departure in the existential analytic of *Dasein* . . . , etc. If we have chosen to examine the opposition that structures the concept of temporality, it is because the entire existential analytic leads back to it" (Derrida, *MP* 63–64). Although only early topics are listed here, Derrida's attack undermines Heidegger's later work as well; this is shown by the fact that at the start of the essay, the terms listed in the footnote that forms the ostensible subject of Derrida's essay follow Heidegger "throughout an itinerary that covers more than forty years" (33n6). Heidegger's technique of reconstructing the epochal ICS requires that the data used, metaphysical texts, be determinable; it is through this construction of the history of metaphysics that he locates his own position as *post*-metaphysical. Derrida denies that this is true, which, he believes, undermines Heidegger's entire endeavor: "Wherever this being-together or with itself of the *envoi* [sending] of being divides itself, defies the *legein* [gathering], frustrates the destination of the *envoi*, is not the whole schema of Heidegger's reading challengeable in principle, deconstructed from a historical point of view?" (Derrida, "SOR" 131).

Taking the objection a step further, Derrida argues that this attempt to escape metaphysics not only fails but is itself the main metaphysical remnant in Heidegger's work: "The thought of the *meaning* or *truth* of Being . . . [is] still intrametaphysical."[77] This is why he repeatedly distances himself from this element of the Heideggerian Paradigm: "The tradition was not homogeneous. . . . I have often said how problematic I find the idea of Metaphysics, capital M, and the Heideggerian schema of the epochality of Being or of the reassembled unity of a history of Being."[78] This also goes for the epochal shifts between the multiple conceptual schemes which both Foucault and Heidegger are able to locate: "I am very mistrustful whenever people identify historical breaks or when they say, 'This begins there.' I have never done that" (Derrida, *EO* 84; see also Derrida, *FWT* 12; Derrida, *Pos* 24). This is why Derrida is particularly interested in Heidegger's reading of Nietzsche; it represents Heidegger's attempt to, so to speak, close the book on metaphysics by showing that all possible variations on the being-becoming dyad have now been exhausted. Heidegger's endeavor to find *the* truth of Nietzsche's text as the end of metaphysics is possibly the supreme gesture of metaphysics itself.

When I introduced Derrida's focus on the topic of writing, I explained his emphasis by showing how this subject could almost function as a kind of symbol or symptom of a philosopher's commitment to the metaphysics of presence. The fact that the Heideggerian Paradigm explicitly bases its reconstructions of ICSs on texts makes Derrida's theories directly relevant to Heidegger's later thought. His claim is that "in the text there are fissures or resources that cannot be dominated by the systematic discourse."[79] This makes any kind of narrative too unstable to allow the teller to emerge triumphantly outside of the systems it encompasses. "Western metaphysics . . . is articulated, in its diverse epochs, according to schemas of implication that are not as easily mastered as is sometimes believed: Whence the illusions of the break, the mirages of the new . . . the archeological lure" (Derrida, *MP* 140). Although Foucault bases his thought less on great works and less exclusively on discourse in general after his archaeological period, he too needs definitive interpretations of whatever phenomena he takes as his evidence. He is not writing the history of metaphysics in order to be outside of it, but he does want to establish the *epistemes* of various periods. For Derrida, insisting on the stability of a scheme, even one that is temporary and groundless, betrays a metaphysical impulse; deconstruction shows that every system is multifaceted and open. He says of his own reading of Descartes that differs from Foucault's, "The consequences of this are unlimited, not only for the interpretation of Descartes, which is certainly important, but also for the protocols of reading and the methodological or epistemological apparatus in *L'Histoire de la folie*" (Derrida, *FWT* 12), which also characterizes the Heideggerian Paradigm.

## Quasi-Transcendental Arguments Revisited

Derrida's third strategy in his assault on the Heideggerian Paradigm's Impersonal Conceptual Scheme employs his quasi-transcendental arguments. The schemes are the conditions for the possibility of all beings, and it initially looked like Derrida adopted some version of this argument which formed his own residue of traditional philosophy, realism, metaphysics, and so on. As discussed above, *différance* fits the traditional role of a transcendental condition in many ways: as the vibrating event of self-differentiation, it generates all other meaning- and presence-conferring identities while being previous or anterior to them (though not separate from them). When we look at the way it actually performs this role, however, we find that its very "nature" changes the structure of the traditional transcendental argument, twisting it into a new and paradoxical shape. His favorite formula for this new structure is that it is simultaneously the condition for both the possibility *and the impossibility* of various phenomena, which alters the standard transcendental argument in important ways:

> I am trying to interrogate the tradition of the concepts of possibility and impossibility that we are inheriting, trying to free it, or rather, to go a little further than what, in transcendental philosophy and elsewhere, we usually understand by those words. In particular, I am trying to think how the only possible x should occur under the form of the impossible. . . . I am trying to elaborate a logic, and I would call this a "logic," in which the only possible x (and I mean here any *rigorous concept* of x) is "the impossible x."[80]

Although this idea originally comes from what has been known as "transcendental philosophy," it does not simply repeat this move but is "trying to free it, or rather, to go a little further." Accordingly, "that's why it is not simply Kantian—although it has something to do with Kant" (Derrida, 2000b, 352). Derrida explains a number of phenomena in terms of this idea, such as hospitality, forgiveness, determining a date, the "Postal Principle," and the gift, discussions of which would take me too far afield here.

As far as I can tell, *différance* was the first quasi-transcendental condition. It makes systems of meaning possible while also preventing any kind of full, determinate meaning. "*Différance* produces what it forbids, makes possible the very thing that it makes impossible" (Derrida, *G* 143). It is this impossibility of fully coherent systems, that is, their inability to be genuinely systematic in such a way that all the ends meet up to let meaning circulate without loss or change (see Derrida, *WD* 271), that accounts for their "auto-deconstruction." This inherent and inescapable instability undermines all systems, including Heidegger's epochal understandings of Being, making them unsustainable even as temporary abyssal systems of meaning.

> Deconstruction, without being anti-systematic, is on the contrary, and nevertheless, not only a search for, but itself a consequence of, the fact that the system is impossible; it often consists, regularly or recurrently, in making appear—in each alleged system, in each self-interpretation of and by a system—a force of dislocation, a limit in the totalization. . . . It

> has been a question of showing that the system does not work, and that this dysfunction not only interrupts the system but itself accounts for the desire for system. (Derrida, *TFS* 4; see also Derrida, *PoI* 212)

There is no such thing as a self-consistent system of meaning for Derrida, and insisting on one is a sign of metaphysics or realism. Systems exist and function, but with fatal "flaws" (the scare quotes question the application of the concept of flaw when there can be no flawless instance) built in so that they necessarily break down and mutate into new systems (Caputo gives a similar reading at Madison 1993, 157, 161).

*Différance* creates meaning and at the same time renders it radically unstable, far more unstable than the Heideggerian Paradigm's epochs that can rule for centuries. "Textuality being constituted by differences and by differences from differences, it is by nature absolutely heterogeneous and is constantly *composing with the forces that tend to annihilate it*" (Derrida, *Dis* 98, italics added). The fact that each signifier's significance emerges from and stands on a trembling mass of differences rather than on a stable R2 connection to an independent signified means that each identity can dissolve back again or reform in a very different way. This raises A3 Ontological Pluralism to a higher power than just having a succession of different forms under various schemes:

> Differance, the disappearance of any originary presence, is *at once* the condition of possibility *and* the condition of impossibility of truth. . . . What is is not what it is, identical and identical to itself, unique, unless it *adds to itself* the possibility of being *repeated* as such. And its identity is hollowed out by that addition, withdraws itself in the supplement that presents it. (Derrida, *Dis* 168; see also Derrida, *DN* 13–14).

This quote brings in what we might call the necessary anticipation of iterability. Signs must be repeatable in multiple contexts in order to have meaning at all. But varying a sign's textual environment changes its meaning, since this derives entirely from the context. Derrida concludes that the sign or text's inherent and necessary mutability robs it of any definite meaning in advance, retroactively, so to speak. Thus, iterability is the condition of the possibility of meaning but simultaneously renders any stable or full meaning impossible. "On the one hand, repetition is that without which there would be no truth. . . . But on the other hand, repetition is the very movement of non-truth: the presence of what is gets lost, disperses itself" (Derrida, *Dis* 168; see also Derrida, *Ltd* 59, 129) through play, semantic drift, or dissemination. On the one hand, "*différance* is the systematic play of differences, of the traces of differences, of the *spacing* by means of which elements are related to each other . . . without which the 'full' terms would not signify," but on the other hand, "the play of differences supposes, in effect, syntheses and referrals which forbid at any moment, or in any sense, that a simple element be *present* in and of itself, referring only to itself" (Derrida, *Pos* 27, 26).

The "phenomena" Derrida fastens upon, that is, trace, *différance,* iterability, and so on, function as quasi-transcendental rather than transcendental conditions by enabling features such as meaning or different objects or subjects, but simultaneously interfering with them.

> The structure of iteration—and this is another of its decisive traits—implies *both* identity *and* difference. . . . The iterability of an element divides its own identity a priori, even without taking into account the fact that this identity can only *determine* or delimit itself through differential relations to other elements and that it hence bears the mark of this difference. It is because this iterability is differential, within each individual "element" as well as between the "elements," because it splits each element while constituting it, because it marks it with an articulatory break, that the remainder, although indispensable, is never that of a full or fulfilling presence: it is a differential structure escaping the logic of presence or the (simple or dialectical) opposition of presence and absence, upon which opposition the idea of permanence depends. (Derrida, *Ltd* 53; see also Derrida, *MP* 13)

Such enabling phenomena cannot function simply as "principle, condition of possibility, or 'radical' foundation; for the structure of iterability divides and guts such radicality" (Derrida, *Ltd* 93; see also Derrida, *GT* 7; Wood and Bernasconi 1988, 85). This goes farther than merely saying that these terms are not beings, as the ontological difference defense did; it claims that they prevent the phenomena from forming the way the metaphysics of presence conceives of them. Thus the "competition between randomness and code disrupts the very systematicity of the system while it also, however, regulates the restless, unstable interplay of the system" (Smith and Kerrigan 1984, 2).

According to this third strategy, regardless of conceptual schemes' basis in undecidable texts, their grounding in quasi-transcendentals makes them much less stable than later Heidegger or Foucault take them to be. Using key terms from both Foucault and Heidegger, Derrida argues that "the movement of any archaeology, like that of any eschatology, is an accomplice of this reduction of the structurality of structure and always attempts to conceive of structure on the basis of a full presence which is beyond play."[81] But such a move to insulate a scheme from shifting cannot work because "the concept of centered structure—although it represents coherence itself, the condition of the *epistēmē* as philosophy or science—is contradictorily coherent" (Derrida, *WD* 279), that is, it only circulates on the basis of intrinsic instabilities. Therefore, the conceptual schemes can never be sources of homogeneous constitution and truth, but are intrinsically riven with diverse forces working against each other. Once again using both Foucaultian and Heideggerian terms: "Each and every time, *epoch,* context, culture, each and every national, historical or *disciplinary* moment, has a certain coherence, but also a certain heterogeneity" (Derrida, *TFS* 15, italics added).

In general, Derrida considers the historical breaks between ICS too clean: "Foucault's typical gesture consists in hardening into an opposition a more complicated play of differences that stretches along a more extended time. . . . Foucault sets up as ruptures and binary oppositions a range of more complex differences" (Derrida, *FWT* 12; see also 7). Despite his commitment to the messy details, Foucault ends up simplifying them into systematic structures with fairly decisive beginning and end points. Derrida makes the same objection to *Madness and Civilization,* where the goal of liberating madness requires a determinate history of its internment, similar to Heidegger's history of metaphysics. Derrida challenges this eschatological liberation by disrupting the history it is meant to liberate us from. On one end of the story, the crisis that reason enters by excluding madness canot be located at a specific historical date, but "has always begun and is interminable. . . . If it is classic, it is not so in the sense of the *classical age* but in the sense of eternal and essential classicism" (Derrida, *WD* 62). At the other end, since Foucault is able to write so empathetically of madness, "we must assume that a certain liberation of madness has gotten underway, that psychiatry has opened itself up, however minimally, and that the concept of madness as unreason, if it ever had a unity, has been dislocated. And that a project such as Foucault's can find its historical origin and passageway in the opening produced by this dislocation" (38). Foucault's very attempt to give the mad a voice shows that psychiatry has not fully silenced it. The relevant point for us is that disturbing the narrative destroys the unity of madness and makes any simple position relative to it impossible.

Foucault also overestimates the organizational power of an ICS and its homogeneity; they always contain counterforces that disrupt the relationships and orders that Foucault spies.[82] This power of dissemination or play "uproots such a text—but also every other . . . both from its author . . . and from the all-powerful constraint of a mythic *episteme*" (Derrida, *AF* 48). As usual, Derrida considers this endemic to writing (see 118, 124) and claims, in a pointed reference to Foucault's method, that "frivolity defies all archeology" (119; see also 62–63). Even something as apparently settled as Descartes' cogito contains an element "which I maintain cannot be enclosed in a factual and determined historical structure, for it is the project of exceeding every finite and determined totality" (Derrida, *WD* 60; see also 57; Derrida, *TP* 243–47). Foucault's project is compromised in advance by the indefinite redescribability of conceptual systems and their history, so that Derrida rejects both the *episteme* and "the epochality of Being, in Heidegger's sense," since they take place "within what would be recognizably called 'history,' an orientable history with periods, ages, or revolutions, mutations" (Derrida, *PoI* 358; see also Derrida, *WD* 291; Derrida, *SP* 102). The intrinsic instability of systems leads Derrida to reject the kind of epochal history that is central to the Heideggerian Paradigm: "Deconstruction . . . mistrusts any sort of periodization" (Derrida, *TFS* 9; see also 6; Derrida 1989b, 15). Indeed, "despite all appearances to the contrary, the concept of history has always been a rational one. It is the meaning of 'history' or *archia* that should have been questioned first, perhaps. A writing that exceeds, by questioning them, the values 'origin,' 'reason,' and 'history' could not be contained within the *metaphysical closure of an archaeology*" (Derrida, *WD* 36, italics added).

Derrida's enigmatic work *The Post Card* applies the logic of the supplement to letters, stating that "in the beginning, in principle, was the post, and I will never get over it" (Derrida, *PC* 29). This means that rather than an original subject matter antecedent to the letter, there are messages or "posts" all the way down; experience is always already mediated. But this idea then plays on the other meaning of the word "post" to undermine the before and after—the after is in the beginning, just as Heidegger's "post"-metaphysical analysis of time is already contained in the heart of metaphysics, in Aristotle's discussion, or as Foucault's liberation of madness can be found within its internment. And this makes all ordering and escape indeterminate.

> If the post (technology, position, "metaphysics") is announced at the "first" *envoi,* then there is no longer A metaphysics, etc. . . . nor even AN *envoi,* but *envois* without destination. For to coordinate the different epochs, halts, determinations, in a word the entire history of Being with a destination of Being is perhaps the most outlandish postal lure. There is not even the post or the *envoi,* there are *posts* and *envois.* And this movement . . . seems to me simultaneously very far from and very near to Heidegger's. (Derrida, *PC* 66; see also 191)

This reads Heidegger's Unmooring against his own regressive notions of gathering and destiny. Since any post-metaphysics can be read as within metaphysics, we can never come up with the definitive history of metaphysics, nor can we step outside of it, thus Heidegger's very attempt to escape is his most metaphysical moment

Referring to what I have called Heidegger's later turn from the Kantian Paradigm by dissolving man into history (A6) through the reliance on a thinner essence or "truth" of man (R6), Derrida writes, "*The thinking of the end of man, therefore, is always already prescribed in metaphysics, in the thinking of the truth of man.* What is difficult to think today is an end of man which would not be organized by a dialectics of truth and negativity" (Derrida, *MP* 121; see also Derrida, *OS* 55). As we saw, Heidegger's later work is compromised by his commitment to a deep true essence of man as openness to Being, even though he uses this to reject all particular historical contents as definitions of subjectivity. Derrida acknowledges the difficulty of finding an escape that does not carry "along with it the whole of metaphysics" (Derrida, *WD* 281). Simple or direct attempts to reject or step outside of metaphysics "in a discontinuous and irruptive fashion, by brutally placing oneself outside, and by affirming an absolute break and difference," employ and thus extend its very concepts, "thereby inhabiting more naively and more strictly than ever the inside one declares one has deserted."[83] Heidegger's destruction of the history of metaphysics relies on the notions of a determinate meaning to this history and its decisive end, with clear boundaries that mark texts as simply inside or outside of it, all of which is highly metaphysical.[84] This means that "the step 'outside philosophy' is much more difficult to conceive than is generally imagined by those who think they made it long ago with cavalier ease, and who in general are swallowed up in metaphysics in the entire body of discourse which they claim to have disengaged from it" (Derrida, *WD* 284).

Derrida's reversal of Heidegger's readings is important here. After laying out his own reading of Aristotle on time, and generalizing this to the claim that "every text of metaphysics carries within itself" both the traditional, metaphysical notion of time and at least the sources for the radical Heideggerian challenge, Derrida writes that "it is on the basis of this formal necessity that one must reflect upon the conditions for a discourse exceeding metaphysics" (Derrida, *MP* 60–61). What he means by this is, as he puts it somewhat blandly, "the 'logic' of every relation to the outside is very complex and surprising" (135). Once the integrity and closed definitions of conceptual systems have been fatally compromised, the boundaries or breaks between them are undermined as well. This theme of the deconstruction of the outside/inside binary runs throughout Derrida's writings.[85] Because texts, authors, and concepts cannot be simply classified as metaphysical or not, nor as occupying a specific place in an overall history of Being, the "end" of metaphysics cannot be located. This means that the entire project of placing oneself outside of it is impossible. "There is no simple 'after' philosophy, just as there is no contemporaneity, nor any simple transition to a non-philosophical discourse that would leave philosophy behind" (Derrida, *TFS* 10). In addition to textual undecidability, the internal instability or the *différance* inherent in any system of meaning prevents the kind of definitive classification used by the Heideggerian Paradigm to escape metaphysics, "regularly [changing] transgressions into 'false exits'" (Derrida, *MP* 135; see also Derrida, *WD* 252; Derrida, *PC* 20–21).

> What we must be wary of, I repeat, is the *metaphysical* concept of history. This is the concept of history as the history of meaning. . . . The closure of metaphysics, above all, is not a circle surrounding a homogeneous field, a field homogeneous with itself on its inside, whose outside then would be homogeneous also. . . . I have never believed that there were *metaphysical* concepts *in and of themselves*. No concept is by itself, and consequently in and of itself, metaphysical, outside all the textual work in which it is inscribed. . . . The concept of history . . . can always be reappropriated by metaphysics. (Derrida, *Pos* 56–57; see also Derrida, *Dis* 6)

Instead, given his view of the indefinite openness of texts (strategy two) and the inherent instability of systems (strategy three), "there is not one single history, a general history, but rather histories *different* in their type, rhythm, mode of inscription" (Derrida, *Pos* 58). Thus, attempts to settle the history of metaphysics once and for all so as to place oneself outside it cannot succeed in principle.

Derrida argues that Heidegger's later history of philosophy inherits a considerable amount of the problematic structure of his early analysis of authentic Dasein. Just as Dasein's "true" authentic way of living and experiencing or understanding time was distinguished from and prioritized over inauthentic time, so the conception of metaphysics as a limited historical era requires a pristine pre-metaphysical time to which this catastrophe happened and promises the eschatological possibility of a post-metaphysical time to come. This contradicts Heidegger's more general commitment to Historical Phenomenological Ontology, i.e., that whatever appears is real. What many commentators (including myself) would like to view as an unfortunate but isolatable feature of Heidegger's later thought, sometimes called his nostalgia, is for Derrida deeply woven into his understanding of metaphysics in the historical meanings of Being. Derrida sees a structural continuity between the early goal of Dasein's reappropriation of its deep nature and the later search through the history of philosophy for "something like an archi-originary intactness that has been basically forgotten."[86] As discussed in chapter 5, Derrida rejects the early Heidegger's structural distinction between authentic and inauthentic Dasein (see Derrida, *MP* 63; Derrida, *Ap* 14, 77), and now we see his rejection of its counterpart in the later work's history of philosophy as a Fall (see Derrida, *OS* 110; Derrida, *PC* 192).

With Heidegger's attempt to escape labeled a "false exit," Derrida's alternative solution is that the only way to get outside metaphysics is to problematize the very notion of going outside.

> There *is not* a transgression, if one understands by that a pure and simple landing into a beyond of metaphysics. . . . Even in aggressions or transgressions, we are consorting with a code to which metaphysics is tied irreducibly, such that every transgressive gesture reencloses us—precisely by giving us a hold on the closure of metaphysics—within this closure. But, by means of the work done on one side and the other of the limit the field inside is modified. . . . Transgression implies that the limit is always at work. . . . The thought that exceeds meaning and meaning-as-hearing-oneself-speak by interrogating them—this thought, announced in grammatology, is given precisely as the thought for which there is not sure opposition between the outside and inside. At the conclusion of a certain work, even the concepts of excess or of transgression become suspect.[87]

Since each text can be read in indefinitely many different ways, works that seem to be purely metaphysical can be read against metaphysics, meaning that "the limit is always at work." "As always, the dissension is internal. The exterior (is) the interior" (Derrida, *WD* 39). This means, on the one hand, that resistance to metaphysics can be found "within" its history, at its heart; the tools of its construction are always the tools for its "destruction" as well. On the other hand, there is no "other beginning," no distinct language or thinking that is post- or anti-metaphysical by its nature, place in history, or distinctness from early eras, since these can always be used to alternate purposes and read in different ways. Derrida is erasing the notion of a boundary.

Instead of going beyond or outside philosophy, deconstruction undermines the opposition between inside and outside by demonstrating the radical heterogeneity contained within every text and conceptual system: "In the beginning, in principle, is the post." Because of this, there is neither need nor ability to take a step beyond metaphysics; by releasing their usually overlooked disruptive features, deconstruction attacks the metaphysical assumption of conceptual schemes having a stable meaning which underlies the very notion of a beyond. "The passage beyond philosophy does not consist in turning the page of philosophy (which usually amounts to philosophizing badly), but in continuing to read philosophers *in a certain way*" (Derrida, *WD* 288, italics in original). Because all texts and systems have these instabilities, they are already deconstructing themselves. Derrida is just showing us what we usually ignore or, in an almost Freudian way, repress: "For the present and for some time to come, the movement of that schema will only be capable of working over the language of metaphysics from within, from a certain sphere of problems inside that language. No doubt this work has always already begun" (Derrida, *SP* 51–52; see also 57n6).

This is another reason for his version of the Empirical Directive, that is, the idea that deconstruction has no positive content of its own, but is only a way of reading texts. Like Hegel's phenomenology, the work is going on and we just free it.

> The movements of deconstruction do not destroy structures from the outside. They are not possible and effective, nor can they take accurate aim, except by inhabiting those structures. Inhabiting them *in a certain way*, because one always inhabits, and all the more when one does not suspect it. Operating necessarily from the inside, borrowing all the strategic and economic resources of subversion from the old structure, borrowing them structurally, that is to say without being able to isolate their elements and atoms, the enterprise of deconstruction always in a certain way falls prey to its own work. (Derrida, *G* 24; see also Derrida, *WD* 36)

Thus, deconstruction "must borrow its resources from the logic it deconstructs" (Derrida, *G* 314; see also Derrida, *MO* 59; Derrida, *WD* 280), both because it has none of its own and because every apparently metaphysical text contains counterforces ready to be used. Derrida's peculiar ways of reading are attempts to free these internal tensions from an almost willful blindness on our part to suppress contradictions and find univocal meanings (see Derrida, *G* 245): "Since no text is homogeneous (this has become for me a sort of categorical axiom, the charter of all my interpretations), it can be legitimate, and is even necessary, to do a reading of it that is divided, differentiated, even contradictory in appearance" (Derrida, *FWT* 171; see also Derrida, *Dis* 6).

Deconstruction means to reside "within" metaphysics, reading the tradition from an oblique angle rather than rejecting it; straightforward rejections extend the same ideas, whereas a slight disruption or displacement that ensures the ends of the circles miss each other devastates the system. "Since the revolution against reason, from the moment it is articulated, can operate only *within* reason, it always has the limited scope of what is called, precisely in the language of a department of *internal* affairs, a disturbance."[88] Derrida wants "to attempt an exit and a deconstruction without changing terrain, by repeating what is implicit in the founding concepts and the original problematic, by using against the edifice the instruments or stones available in the house" (Derrida, *MP* 135). Of course, using these traditional ideas and texts runs the constant risk of falling into their way of thinking, of getting pulled into the gravitational field of their implications.

> Since these concepts are indispensable for unsettling the heritage to which they belong, we should be even less prone to renounce them. Within the closure, by an oblique and always perilous movement, constantly risking falling back within what is being deconstructed, it is necessary to surround the critical concepts with a careful and thorough discourse—to mark the conditions, the medium, and the limits of their effectiveness. (Derrida, *G* 14; see also Derrida, *WD* 263; Derrida, *Dis* 5)

Derrida is trying to avoid both using metaphysical concepts in their metaphysical sense and inventing a new set of concepts which has a tendency to become merely a mask for the old concepts. He is trying to use the old concepts and texts against themselves, or rather to show that they are always already working against themselves and are written in undecidably multiple ways. In keeping with what I wrote above, I would say that he does occasionally fall into fairly straightforward transcendental arguments, for instance.

But when he succeeds in using these concepts against themselves, he is able to "disturb" the system more successfully than Heidegger did, thus solving one of the main problems of the Heideggerian Paradigm and leading the way to a new paradigm. Of course, it is part of this very theory not to convict Heidegger (or anyone else) of metaphysics in a wholesale manner. Rather, Heidegger represents the exemplary case of someone on the edge, both inside and outside. After all, it was Heidegger who wrote that "metaphysics cannot be abolished like an opinion. One can by no means leave it behind as a doctrine no longer believed and represented. . . . We may not presume to stand outside of metaphysics because we surmise the ending of metaphysics. For metaphysics overcome in this way does not disappear. It returns transformed, and remains in dominance."[89] At the end of philosophy, thinking does not move on to an entirely new subject matter for Heidegger, but "finds itself moved to review the whole history of philosophy" (Heidegger, *BW* 436; see also Heidegger, *Pm* 321). There are also times when Heidegger denies that metaphysics as the forgetting of

Being is a contingent event that occurs to a fully present awareness of Being, and so could be reversed or cured:

> Oblivion does not simply *befall* the essence of being, as something apparently separate from the latter. It belongs to the issue of being itself, prevails as a destiny of its essence. Correctly thought, oblivion, the concealing of the as yet unrevealed essence (in the verbal sense of essential unfolding) of being [crossed out], shelters untapped treasures and is the promise of a find that awaits only the appropriate seeking. (Heidegger, *Pm* 314, bracketed comment added; Derrida praises this idea at *TFS* 83)

In other words, the oblivion or forgetting of Being which defines metaphysics is intrinsic to Being, and even marks a positive legacy or inheritance to us if we can learn to read these texts the right way, which is exactly what so much of Heidegger's work consists of. His problem, besides his commitment to ICS, would be that he thinks we can find what has been lost: although "philosophy knows nothing of the clearing," "it is necessary for thinking to become explicitly aware of the matter here called clearing" (Heidegger, *BW* 443, 442).

## Conclusion

The rejection of realist accounts of both independent objects (R1) and transcendental subjects (R6) is basic to Derrida's thought. There is nothing outside the text because our experience is always linguistically mediated; this makes both subject and object effects of language, rather than entities that precede it from the outside to master or anchor it. Language impersonally structures our selves and our world, and our actions depend on passively taking on these structures (R5). In lieu of correspondence (R2) with an external world (R1), meaning gets generated by elements differing from each other, a process that creates meaning while permanently deferring the full presence of referents that would constitute ultimate meaning. This is Derrida's quasi-transcendental argument. *Différance* is the condition of both the possibility and the impossibility of meaning; it enables these systems while simultaneously and by the very same function interfering with or disturbing their operation. This ensures that all systems are "flawed," leading to their tendency to operate in multiple ways—such as texts being capable of very different interpretations—and their inevitable mutation into other forms. In fact, this changes the very idea of mutation, since the system has no stable identity in the first place to change; each system is simultaneously many things at once.

In this way, Derrida overcomes the Heideggerian Paradigm's difficulties with transcendental arguments. While he takes certain insights from the idea of ICS and does believe that systems do successfully operate in this off-balance improvisational manner, the profound instabilities he sees at their heart (or lack thereof) finally frees this notion from the trappings of Kant's version of conceptual schemes. Derrida's reformation of the notion is far deeper than the Heideggerian Paradigm's changes, giving it a strange new shape that more successfully escapes the lingering vestiges of realism.

# Conclusion: Anthropology from Two Kantian Points of View; or, A Tale of Two Kants

> That division is entirely correct, provided there is also a difference in kind between the concepts that assign to the principles of this rational cognition their respective objects. (Kant, "On the Division of Philosophy," introduction to *Critique of Judgment* 9/171)

The hypothesis that has organized this book from the outset is that Kant, as the figure who precedes the analytic-continental split, could serve as a common ground on which the two traditions can recognize each other's work as sufficiently similar or overlapping in nature to make a dialogue between them both practical and profitable. I have used Kant as a kind of Rosetta stone to cast continental thought in a vocabulary that would be more readily intelligible and demonstrably relevant to analytic philosophers. However, in endeavors such as these, we must always be careful not to lose distinctions by overemphasizing similarities. Indeed, my attempts to establish that the two branches have been talking about a common topic has more than historical interest only if they have different things to say about it, so that they might learn from each other.

Accordingly, I will conclude this study of what is common to both analytic and continental thought with a brief discussion of their differences, in particular the different ways they have approached this shared topic. And just as I used Kant's work to organize my analysis of the former, I will also use it for the latter purpose. To pursue my analogy a step further, the fact that the Rosetta stone contains a single message enables translation, but its precise juxtaposition of diverse languages also makes it a particularly useful site for examining the languages' specific differences.

Although Kant insists on the deep systematic harmony of his thought as a whole, the first two *Critiques* present accounts that differ in important ways. There is, of course, the conflict between scientific determinism and ethical freedom which is only disarmed by the two perspectives of phenomena and noumena. But even if the two *Critiques*' accounts are logically compatible, they are informed by and impart profoundly different *outlooks,* a rather vague notion that picks up some of the less definable senses of Kuhn's notion of the paradigm, such as the ethos of a discipline, the sense of how to do it, and what its goal should be, derived in this case from particular conceptions of human thought. It is here that I see the seeds for the analytic-continental split.

The first *Critique,*[1] which I have focused on as the origin of the type of anti-realism I have treated in this book, portrays humanity as torn between absolute epistemological limits and unquenchable yearnings for the metaphysical knowledge that reason dangles before us. Scientific knowledge is universal yet essentially limited to our epistemological perspective, and we simply have to make our peace with the fact that we cannot escape this perspective, albeit a peace endlessly renegotiated. Autonomy too is characterized by this tension. On the one hand, the first *Critique*'s anti-realism gives the knower autonomy in that we organize the realm of knowable phenomena, rather than objects dictating their natures to our passive wax tablet of a mind. On the other hand, it places a profound and essential limit on this autonomy by instructing us to accommodate ourselves to our inborn forms and concepts. Objects must correspond to our conditions of knowledge, but we in turn must make our investigations correspond to the conditions uncovered by critical philosophy. In Heidegger's phrase, we are "thrown" into our forms, concepts, and ideas, and our "epistemological duty," so to speak, is to submit to them.

Nor does Kant allow for the kind of ersatz choice that Hegel does, through retrospective justification or explanation of these structures of our faculties as the best or only possible or inevitable ones. "This peculiarity of our understanding, that it can produce *a priori* unity of apperception solely by means of the categories, and only by such and so many, is as little capable of further explanation as why we have just these and no other functions of judgment, or why space and time are the only forms of our possible intuition" (Kant, *C1* B145–46; see also Kant, *PFM* 65/318). We explain nature's regularity by recourse to the faculty of understanding (A5), but Kant rules out explanations of understanding and intuition, since they are the sources of all intelligibility themselves. This is, necessarily, where explanations bottom out: "Human insight is at an end as soon as we arrive at fundamental powers or faculties, for their possibility can in no way be understood" (Kant, *C2* 48/46–47). Karl Ameriks calls this part of Kant's "modesty": "Kant is perfectly willing to allow that various basic aspects of experience remain inexplicable primitives. . . . Transcendental idealism . . . is not an account that even purports to give any positive 'explanation' of how we come to have the basic powers of mind that we exhibit" (Ameriks 2000a, 62–63).

Their brute facticity renders our faculties ultimately contingent; Kant repeatedly states that our type of intuition[2] and understanding[3] are not the only ones possible, allowing both divine and alien alternatives as fully coherent, if unimaginable, possibilities. This makes our knowledge "universal for us," that is, holding for all beings constituted like us or intersubjectively ubiquitous, but not holding for beings without these faculties. "We cannot judge in regard to the intuitions of other thinking beings, whether they are bound by the same conditions as those which limit our intuition and which *for us are universally valid*" (Kant, *C1* A27/B43, italics added). The epistemological agent is completely dependent on these structures and, if he is to acquire genuine knowledge, he must acknowledge this dependency and refuse to step beyond it. The great danger to be resisted here is that "speculative reason, presumptuously overreaches itself" (Kant, *C2* 3/4) by ignoring the essential limitations on our knowledge to believe that it can reach reality itself. However, although our transcendental structures and the knowledge they produce are ultimately unjustifiable and contingent, this is genuine knowledge and must be respected as such. Critical philosophy uncovers the conditions of our experience and tells us to accept them. This is Kant at his most Humean; despite important changes, the first *Critique* follows the spirit of Hume's guiding anti-rationalist epigram: "Be a philosopher; but, amidst all your philosophy, be still a man" (Hume 1978, 9).

Kant's ethical thought, on the other hand, portrays humans as torn between following empirical inclinations and rational conscience, even when these coincide on the same action. His objection to basing ethics on inclinations is due not merely to their selfishness, but also to the fact that they come from the empirical and phenomenal side of the self. This makes them external to our true self, as well as leaving them subject to physical, cultural, psychological, and historical causal processes which compromise our freedom and, importantly for my purposes, infect ethics with contingency and variability. "In morals, the proper and inestimable worth of an absolutely good will consists precisely in the freedom of the principle of action from all influences from contingent grounds which only experience can furnish."[4] Our empirical inclinations are consistently described as "foreign causes" or "alien influences" (Kant, *FMM* 63/445, 65/448) which compromise both our autonomy and the universality of their commands. For autonomy and universality, we can only obey laws issued from "our proper self."[5] Whereas Kant bases his theoretical work on structures that are particular to humans, thus limiting the scope of phenomenal knowledge, ethics demands an absolute universality which requires that its laws be unaffected by anything specific to us. "A completely isolated metaphysics of morals, mixed with no anthropology . . . is not only an indispensable substrate of all theoretically sound and definite knowledge of duties; it is also a desideratum of the highest importance to the actual fulfillment of its precepts."[6]

To achieve such unconditioned universality, Kant derives the moral law from the mere form of rationality, that is, "universal conformity to law as such."[7] Ethics is generated out of pure logic by making virtue equivalent to self-consistency and vice the self-contradiction of illicitly excepting oneself from universal laws.[8] This derivation from pure logic makes the moral law necessary and binding on *all* rational beings.

> Everyone must admit that a law, if it is to hold morally (i.e., as a ground of obligation), must imply absolute necessity; he must admit that the command: Thou shalt not lie, does not apply to men only as if other rational beings had no need to observe it. . . . The ground of obligation here must not be sought in the nature of man or in the circumstances in which he is placed but a priori solely in the concepts of pure reason.[9]

Kant explicitly rules out for ethics the "universal for us" status based on the particularities of our constitution that he happily awards to scientific laws: "For reason to give law it is required that reason need presuppose only itself, because the rule is objectively and universally valid only when it holds without any contingent subjective conditions which differentiate one rational being from another."[10] Since the moral law derives from logic, it is open to the kind of ultimate explanation that the cognitive structures are not, and it is absolutely universal, since all rational beings have access to it.[11] Whereas our theoretical "duty" is to accept what is specific to our constitution, in ethics we must use logic to slice through all that is on the side of the empirical, and which therefore qualifies as contingent, particular, and external causes (the physical, the cultural, the psychological, the historical), in order to act on pure unconditioned reason (Kant, *FMM* 43/426, 26–27/410–11; Kant, *C2* 74/70–71).

Unlike the cognitive version, our practical autonomy is complete and uncompromised: "Reason must regard itself as the author of its principles, independently of alien influences" (Kant, *FMM* 65/448). The practical agent is burdened with an alien empirical side, that is, the inclinations which can be extended to include any empirical causal influences, such as history, society, gender, and so on. But her duty is to become as noumenal as possible in order to base her decisions on factors that escape these contingent, causal, temporal influences. Indeed, Kant even holds out the holy will as the model we should strive for and can almost become at our best (Kant, *C2* 125/118; see also 33/32). This is Kant at his least Humean: amidst all your actions, be solely a rational agent, ignoring what is merely human about yourself.[12]

This practical schema considers the aspects of ourselves that we merely find rather than make to be alien, external, and heteronomous, while what we choose and can justify is our true self. If we were to apply this scheme to the theoretical structure, we would find (as the idealists did) that the experience-organizing forms and concepts would actually have the same status as the inclinations. Although they are transcendental instead of empirical, we are thrown into our forms, concepts, and ideas without justification or reason, rendering them merely local or binding only on us. Yet the first *Critique* accepts their authority. It tells us to resist reason's temptation to be something other than human, that we should submit to the particular mental organization that we happen to find in ourselves in order to secure knowledge even if it is only "for us . . . universally valid." The practical obligation, on the other hand, is to follow reason's demand not to base our decisions on what is human and particular about us, but to use logic to cut through the merely local and contingent, in order to act on the purely rational that escapes time and conditions. This even applies to what is intersubjectively common, like the desire for happiness. This parallel between the structures of our faculties in the theoretical work and our inclinations in the ethical is far from perfect; for one thing, the former are transcendental, while the latter are empirical. What is interesting is that while they share the features of particularity and radical contingency, Kant's reactions to them are directly opposed: we are required to accept our faculties and their resultant knowledge in theoretical inquiries, while we must ignore all that is specific to us and our species in ethical action. I am not asserting that Kant is contradicting himself, since the schemes apply to different topics, but rather that, taken as models, these two schemes impart very different conceptions of human thought and philosophy.

The Janus-faced mask I have placed on Kant has probably fallen off by now. My claim is that continental thought follows the spirit of his epistemology, while analytic thought follows the practical (which is rather ironic, given analytic philosophy's emphasis on epistemology and continental's insistence on the ubiquity of the ethical). Continental thought embodies the spirit of Kant's theoretical work: we are essentially finite beings conditioned by forces beyond our control, and the job of philosophy is to help us understand these, not overcome them; there is nothing beyond them. Analytic philosophy takes up the ethical ethos: although we may be conditioned by accidental features, philosophy uses reason to pierce these conditions so that we can find truth which escapes their influence. I will unpack this interpretation for each branch and then relate it to my main subject of anti-realism.

As discussed in chapter 5, Heidegger views his early work as an extension and expansion of the first *Critique* which he reads, at its deepest level, as a powerful analysis of human finitude. This is not a matter of our "deficiencies" or liability to error, "rather, this finitude lies in the essential structure of knowledge itself" (Heidegger, *KPM* 15). Heidegger interprets Kant's theory of the active organization of experience, the linchpin of his anti-realism, as a measure of our finitude in that we need structuring horizons to orient our experience. Heidegger calls our organization of experience an understanding of Being and claims that this structure, "which thoroughly dominates human existence . . . manifests itself as the innermost ground of human finitude. . . . Only because the understanding of Being is the most finitude [*sic*] in what is finite, can it also make possible the so-called 'creative' capacities of the finite human creature" (160–61). We always find ourselves already under way, necessarily beginning from a previous orientation that enables us to gather information or have experience at all. Just as Neurath's boat cannot now be brought into dry dock for a complete overhaul, so it was never launched virginally into the water. We were always already structured to think in certain ways by the unchosen fore-structures of understanding; they can be changed, but only on the basis of input and consideration that they themselves determine. "We constantly and always already reside in such prior viewpoints" (Heidegger, *PIK* 158). Heidegger stresses the fact that the particular structures that enable all of our activity are not of our making, thus siding with Kant against Hegel's demand for a "hyper-originality," in Pippin's term. "In attempting to lay the ground for Metaphysics, Kant was pressed in a way that makes the proper foundation into an abyss" (Heidegger, *KPM* 202; see also 207, 151). The transcendental faculties are the foundation of all knowledge, but an abyssal foundation or groundless ground (*abgründlich Grund*), since they themselves lack ultimate justification. Kant's first *Critique* exposes the inevitable spade-turning end to all explanations.[13]

Heidegger's account of Dasein captures the tension inherent in the first *Critique*'s account of knowledge in that "in the 'double meaning' of 'care,' what we have in view is a *single* basic state in its essentially twofold structure of thrown projection" (Heidegger, *BT* 243/199; see also 188/148, 265/223). We are thrown into our ways of projecting, that is, the ways we can understand the world around us and the actions we can take, which makes even our activity dependent upon an ineliminable moment of passive reception. In other words, "all projection—and consequently, even all of man's 'creative' activity—is *thrown,* i.e., it is determined by the dependency of Dasein on the being already in the totality, a dependency over which Dasein itself does not have control" (Heidegger, *KPM* 165).

The lesson Heidegger draws from the first *Critique* is that we should acknowledge this finitude rather than fighting it, that in fact philosophy itself is a matter of coming to grips with this finitude, whether it be our mortality or our epistemological limits. "It is not a matter of . . . extinguish[ing] finitude, but rather the reverse. It is precisely a question of becoming certain of this finitude in order to hold oneself in it" (Heidegger, *KPM* 152; see also 203). The fundamental purpose of philosophy is to "hold oneself" in finitude, not a bad description of the first *Critique*'s moral that we must shun rationalist ambitions to know reality in itself. Where the first *Critique* legitimates knowledge of phenomena as genuine knowledge, Heidegger takes it a step further with PO and UT to conclude that in principle there is nothing more to be known (see Heidegger, *PIK* 68–69; see also Heidegger, *KPM* 88). The first *Critique* is a radical new founding of philosophy, since it rejects the God's-eye perspective in favor of an exclusively human one. "*The general horizon of the problematic of the Critique* is, according to our interpretation, *human Dasein with respect to its understanding of being*" (Heidegger, *PIK* 48; see also 13). It is only the vestiges of realism in Kant's framework that leave room for "noumenon-envy," which is why Heidegger and the idealists feel that they are completing the spirit of his work by eliminating this idea.

On the side of the "subject,"[14] the first *Critique* permanently compromises autonomy and leaves us inextricably "in-the-world" (ED). However, as Heidegger interprets it, the features and structures we are thrown into are not some accidental external casing, but our real selves.

> Dasein is something that has been thrown; it has been brought into its "there," but *not* of its own accord. . . . To this entity it has been delivered over, and as such it can exist solely as the entity which it is. . . . Although it has *not* laid that basis *itself*, it reposes in the weight of it. . . . And how *is* Dasein this thrown basis? Only in that it projects itself upon possibilities into which it has been thrown. The Self, which as such has to lay the basis for itself, can *never* get that basis into its power; and yet, as existing, it must take over Being-a-basis. . . . It has been *released* from its basis, *not through* itself but *to* itself, so as to be *as this basis*. (Heidegger, *BT* 329–30/284–85)

Thrownness rules out traditional notions of autonomy. However, there is no other kind of Dasein than a thrown in-the-world one, no other content but what we can pick up from the empirical, contingent, historically situated society we happen to live in. To be authentic is "to understand this thrownness as the null basis which it has to take up into existence" (Heidegger, *BT* 333/287). On the one hand, the basis of our lives is "null," meaning that we have been thrown into our circumstances without our consent and without ultimate reasons for them. But on the other hand, these circumstances make us who we are, and there is nothing else to us. This is why "*authentic Being-one's-Self* does not rest upon an exceptional condition of the subject, a condition that has been detached from the 'they'; *it is rather an existentiell modification of the 'they.'*"[15] With the completion of A6 and ED (which does not take place in his early work), we are what we make of ourselves in the situation we find ourselves in, a situation that includes our particular abilities, tastes, preferences, gender, society, and so on. These features inevitably guide our choices, though in principle we could not have chosen them: "Every decision, however, bases itself on something not mastered . . . else it would never be a decision" (Heidegger, *BW* 180; see also 330, 361). Heidegger applies Kant's theoretical move to the notion of the self as a whole. Just as the first *Critique* tells us to accept knowledge produced by our contingent faculties as genuine knowledge, so Heidegger claims that the features and structures we are thrown into are our real selves.

Turning to the other side, the underlying structure of Kant's ethical thought is isomorphic with and very much in the same spirit as one of the founding gestures of analytic philosophy, namely Frege's rejection of psychologism. Frege was deeply concerned about psychologism and, by an interesting coincidence, attacks it in his review of Husserl's *Philosophy of Arithmetic,* one of the earliest points of contact between analytic and continental thought. He wants to stop "the devastation caused by the influx of psychology into logic . . . a widespread philosophical disease" (Frege 1972, 337; see also 323). Any influence exerted by the ways we happen to think would compromise the necessary realism of the realm of logic: "Our act of judgment [R5] can in no way alter the make-up of a thought. We can only recognize [R1] what is there. A true thought [R5] cannot be affected by our act of judgment."[16] The view that mental acts affect—or effect—true thoughts results from confusing private representations with the objective world, that is, (variously) concept, thought, or object: "If people consider, instead of things themselves, only subjective representations of them, only their own mental images—then all the more delicate distinctions in the things themselves are naturally lost, and others appear instead which are logically quite worthless. . . . The finer distinctions in the subject-matter become obliterated in psychological logic" (Geach and Black 1960, 146; see also Frege 1972, 324–25, 335).

Frege objects to psychologism because any involvement of the mind's contingent features in determining logical truth limits its scope, condemning us to relativism in encounters with differently structured minds.

This is precisely the kind of restriction entailed and accepted by the first *Critique*'s account of scientific laws. As Michael Dummett writes,

> Psychologism cannot, on his view, account for the objective validity of arguments; if my thinking processes differ from yours, or human ones from Martian ones, then validity for me may fail to coincide with validity for you, validity for human beings with validity for Martians; there would be no standard by which one could be deemed right as opposed to the other. In the same way, psychologism destroys objective truth: the truth of a thought can no longer be distinguished from its being recognized as true. (Dummett 1981, 64)

Indeed, it is central to Dummett's influential reading of Frege that the psychologism he was targeting had its source in Kantian idealism (see Dummett 1981, 500, 503; Burge 2005, 69). Dummett quotes a passage from the preface to the *Grundgesetze* about possible ways to justify logic in which Frege clearly rejects the first *Critique*'s strategy for justifying math and science.

> Stepping away from logic, one may say: we are compelled to make judgments *by our nature* and by external circumstances, and, when we judge, we cannot reject this law—e.g., that of identity—but must acknowledge it, unless we wish to bring our thought into confusion and finally renounce all judgment. I do not wish either to dispute or to endorse this view; I wish only to observe that we do not here have a logical deduction. What is given is not a ground for the law's being true, but for our taking it to be true. Moreover, *this impossibility of rejecting the law, which holds for us, does not in the least prevent us from supposing beings who do reject it;* but it prevents us from supposing that such beings are right to do so; and it also prevents us from doubting whether it is we or they who are right. (Dummett 1981, 510, italics added)

As we saw, in the first *Critique* Kant conceded the possibility of other forms of intuition and understanding, but nonetheless endorsed ours as producing genuine knowledge. The second *Critique,* on the other hand, is in line with Frege in insisting on a stronger form of authority. Ethics of course cannot be based on happiness because it is variable, but this is not the only reason: "Suppose that finite rational beings were unanimous in the kind of objects their feelings of pleasure and pain had, and even in the means of obtaining the former and preventing the latter. Even then they could not set up the principle of self-love as a practical law, for the unanimity itself would be merely contingent" (Kant, *C2* 25/26). Even if all agents did possess the same inclinations, this commonality would still be ethically invalid because the mere fact of agreement is ultimately contingent. Our cognitive faculties too possess merely contingent unanimity, but they are allowed to set up laws.

For Frege, psychologically deriving logic from actual thought processes would ruin its purity and its ability to command. Intersubjective ubiquity is not enough here. This is the same reasoning Kant applied to the moral law:

> Everyone must admit that a law, if it is to hold morally (i.e., as a ground of obligation), must imply absolute necessity. . . . The ground of obligation here must not be sought in the nature of man or in the circumstances in which he is placed but a priori solely in the concepts of pure reason. . . . Applied to man, it borrows nothing from knowledge of him (anthropology) but gives man, as a rational being, a priori laws. (Kant, *FMM* 5/389; see also 59/442; Kant, *C2* 97/93)

Once its transcendence is secured, logic can then slice through the varying and contingent features that happen to make people think the way they do in order to determine the laws that track truth. We must go outside the factors that have come to situate us by chance in order to plug into that which escapes the fluctuating and fallible causal chains of history and psychology. Logic concerns the transcendent realm of truth, rather than the empirical field of belief, just as ethics concerns what we ought to do rather than what we actually do. Frege says that "we are taking 'judgment' to mean, not an act performed by a definite man at a definite time, but something timelessly true, even if its being true is not acknowledged by any human being,"[17] in the same way as "it is, in fact, absolutely impossible by experience to discern with complete certainty a single case in which the maxim of an action, however much it might conform to duty, rested solely on moral grounds" (Kant, *FMM* 23/406; see also 36/419; Kant, *C2* 31/31).

This captures a common ethos of analytic thought.[18] Rather than incorporating the contingent features that condition our beliefs, we judge them by the higher standard of Truth itself, which transcends us. Reason, and especially for early analytic philosophy, logic, enables us to achieve genuine knowledge, something fundamentally different from what our culture or species tends to or even must believe. This is the realist conception of truth. Burge writes that "truth-values . . . formed Frege's answer to Kant's dictum that there could be no knowledge of objects without intuitions. Frege held that commitment to mind-independent objects is inseparable from the very act of judging something to be true. The idea is surely the quintessential distillation of the ambitions of rationalist epistemology" (Burge 2005, 131–32). Dummett, in *Origins of Analytical Philosophy,* claims that Frege's view that "thoughts and their constituent senses form a 'third realm' of timeless and immutable entities which do not depend for their existence on being grasped or expressed" creates a "non-psychological direction given to the analysis of concepts and of propositions . . . [which] was to lead to analytical philosophy" (Dummett 1994, 23, 25; see also C. O. Hill 1991, 13, 29). This way of thinking may also have contributed to analytic philosophy's general lack of emphasis on time and history, as briefly discussed in chapter 1.

The question from the continental or first *Critique* perspective is, what business do finite creatures like us have laying claim to timeless truth that transcends all human conditions? Continental philosophers have given up the "real world" as a fable and, completing A1 and PO, this means that what we come to know under imperfect, changing conditions is not an ersatz substitute but simply truth. Truth is a thing of this world. As Derrida puts it, "The emergence of the value of objectivity (and hence of so many others) also belongs to a context. . . . That does not in the slightest discredit them. In the name of what, of which other 'truth,' moreover, would it?" (Derrida, *Ltd* 136). For Foucault's notion of power/knowledge, the fact that a person's authority influences whether or not their utterances become accepted "does not mean that what the person says is not true, which is what most people believe. When you tell people that there may be a relationship between truth and power, they say: 'So it isn't truth after all!'" (Foucault, *FL* 446). Rather, his work tries "to take account of the fact that discourse has not only a meaning or a truth, but a history, and a specific history that does not refer it back to the laws of an alien development" (Foucault, *AK* 127; see also 117; Foucault, *EW* 3:253–54). For the development to be alien, we would need a pristine Truth.

The rejection of the transcendent and the atemporal is central to all of Heidegger's thought. His early work bears a certain resemblance to psychologism by studying the way the existentials or the structures of Dasein affect thought. Dasein is closer to Kant's transcendental subjectivity than empirical humanity or noumenal intelligence, which issues the categorical imperative from outside of time that holds for all rational beings.

> Doubt, error, and conviction are not primarily objects of empirical determination; rather, as comportments of human Dasein, they are subject to a unique ontological investigation, which is not psychological and empirical. In view of Husserl's investigations we see here a lot more clearly that, whereas logic is not to be replaced by psychology, it does presup-

> pose an investigation of what is called thinking as such. The clarification of these modes of comportments is the task of phenomenology. (Heidegger, *PIK* 122)

The thinker's constitution inescapably affects how she thinks, even her attempts to correct her thinking; this is why the existential analysis of Dasein is fundamental ontology, or the necessary foundation to the study of everything else.

> Philosophy is the conceptual knowledge of a fundamental realm of phenomena—indeed a conceptual knowledge which must necessarily be grounded in and guided by a self-knowledge of human Dasein. But therein lies the fact that all conceptual disclosure and conceptual enlightenment must necessarily and primarily establish itself in a realm wherein the conceptual as such lives, i.e., in the rational in the widest sense, in transcendental apperception, in the sphere of freedom of reason—or in what we call the existence of Dasein. Therefore, all philosophical conceptual knowledge of Dasein, even when this knowledge is not directly related to the phenomena of existence, are necessarily *existentials*. (Heidegger, *PIK* 269)

Heidegger considers this approach the legacy of the first *Critique* (see Heidegger, *PIK* 277). When Kant moved to the second edition of the first *Critique* as well as the second *Critique,* however, "ethicality was . . . grasped as pure, i.e., as neither conditioned by nor even made for the factical, empirical human being. This personal-ontological problem of a finite pure reason in general admittedly was not able to tolerate in proximity to itself that which recalls the specific constitution of a determinate kind of realization of a finite rational creature in general" (Heidegger, *KPM* 118). This move away from our "specific constitution" is a mistake for Heidegger, since knowledge is an activity of specific, conditioned, temporal knowers.

Once Heidegger's later work removes the remnants of transcendental subjectivity haunting Dasein, the factors that determine the thinker encompass a great deal: social and cultural influences, gender, race, history can all affect knowledge without compromising it because there is no independent reality or truth that gets dirtied when we touch it. There is nothing else we can point to or think coherently about that can provide an invidious comparison. With no access to an absolute reality or truth that transcends our perspectives, some form of relativism is common in continental thought. At the same time, though, this "situatedness" also saves us from extreme or nihilistic relativism, since the paralyzing view that all perspectives or views are equal is itself only available to a God's-eye view. Along with never reaching reality in itself, being situated also means necessarily starting from preferences, opinions, unconsciously absorbed ways of doing things. None of these can be a candidate for absolute truth, but neither do they thereby fade into a grey neutrality among which we can choose by a whim. This is a false dichotomy that has been forced on us by a long history of demands for hyper-justification in comparison with which anything else seems worthless.

Gadamer, a figure I have not discussed but who fits my schema well, explains this move nicely. He firmly believes that "we are always situated within traditions. . . . It is always part of us" (Gadamer 1989, 282), which leads him to conclude that "*understanding is, essentially, a historically effected event*" (300). We are therefore cut off from an ahistorical, final transcendent truth: "It is part of these particular conditions of truth that we have no absolute, certain standards, even when it comes to research, to distinguish genuine accomplishment from empty pretension" (Wachterhauser 1994, 28). However,

> being so conditioned is not an impairment of historical knowledge, but rather a moment of truth itself. . . . This is precisely the sign of our finitude, remaining mindful of which alone preserves us from delusion. The naïve faith in the objectivity of the historical method was just such a delusion. But what takes its place is not an insipid relativism. What we ourselves are and what we are capable of heeding from the past is not arbitrary and not optional. (Wachterhauser 1994, 29; see also Gadamer 1989, 280)

Our situatedness prevents contact with the really real which could tell us the truth once and for all, but it also prevents us from the free fall of nihilistic relativism where all is the same. What we find interesting, relevant, good, reasonable, and so on is part of the total situation we are thrown into. We can reform these initial views—indeed, Gadamerian hermeneutics is precisely the pursuit of such corrections—but this endeavor and the evaluation of correctness itself can only take place on the basis of a previous orientation. This is the middle ground onto which we are thrown.

This tension that Heidegger locates in the first *Critique* and that is an effect of anti-realism is, I believe, one of the paradigmatic gestures of continental thought. It is the tension between, on the one hand, the passive reception of features which, according to traditional views and Kant's practical thought, precludes them from being part of our true self or legitimate thought; and, on the other hand, the ED and A6 acknowledgment that there can be nothing more to us than what these influences have made us, that even what we make of ourselves occurs in their wake. This tension is explored by all of the continental figures featured in this book. We have already seen early Heidegger's analysis of thrownness and nullity. Although this work prioritizes the future over the past, history becomes important as the essence of the finitude that defines us and as the source of all content for our selfhood. Following Nietzsche, he calls this phenomenon fate: "This is how we designate Dasein's primordial historicizing, which lies in authentic resoluteness and in which Dasein *hands* itself *down* to itself, free for death, in a possibility which it has inherited and yet chosen" (Heidegger, *BT* 435/384). This last phrase combining inheritance and choice perfectly captures the paradox that Nietzsche's notion of *amor fati* shares.

Nietzsche's idea of eternal return ratchets up the tension, since in this context, what I as this individual instantiation have inherited is in some sense what the primal "first" me chose. Conversely, I should view my present choices as the legacy I am leaving to my future selves. What is ultimately at issue here is reconciling the will's thrashing demand for total autonomy with its insurmountable roots in facticity or thrownness: "'It was'—that is the name of the will's gnashing of teeth and most secret melancholy. Powerless against what has been done, he is an angry spectator of all that is past. The will cannot will backwards" (Nietzsche, *Z* 2.20). One solution to this frustrating inability to take control of one's thrownness is to seek an escape from time altogether, to invent a timeless realm and abuse the temporal changing world by comparison: "This, indeed this alone, is what *revenge* is: the will's ill will against time and its 'it was.' . . . Until eventually madness preached, 'Everything passes away; therefore everything deserves to pass away. . . . Alas, where is redemption from the flux of things and from the punishment called existence?'" (2.20). Instead of this mad search for a fabulous transcendence, Nietzsche hopes for a "reconciliation with time" brought about by *amor fati:* "To recreate all 'it was' into a 'thus I willed it'—that alone should I call redemption" (2.20). Redemption consists not in being redeemed *from* time, but in being reconciled *with* time so that one loves one's fate, chooses one's inheritance, and becomes what one is.

The fundamental task of Hegel's entire *Phenomenology of Spirit* is for natural consciousness, that is, the thinking self of the present, to re-collect and internalize the shapes of consciousness that have already occurred and made consciousness capable of this recollection, somewhat like Proust's writing about what enabled him to become a writer.

> This past existence is the already acquired property of universal Spirit which constitutes the Substance of the individual, and hence appears externally to him as his inorganic nature. In this respect formative education, regarded from the side of the individual, consists in his acquiring

> what thus lies at hand, devouring his inorganic nature, and taking possession of it for himself. (Hegel, *PS* 16, §28)

Education means explicitly appropriating the moments of consciousness which Spirit has already been through unaware, making what we are "in-itself" become "for us" in "the process in which Spirit *becomes* what it is *in itself*" (Hegel, *PS* 487, §802; see also 14, §25). Although it originally occurred without my personal input, this process allows me to comprehend it and, most importantly, to assent to it and thus "choose" it.

One of the main goals of the Heideggerian Paradigm is to develop a conception of agency that can incorporate a pervasive thrownness in order to supersede the opposition between freedom and determinism. The fact that philosophy circles around these alternatives is why Heidegger believes that "we are still far from pondering the essence of action decisively enough" (Heidegger, *BW* 217). The later Heidegger says that "history is the transporting of a people into its appointed task as entry into that people's endowment" (202). This does not mean that a being, the Great Being, puts us on earth to fulfill a purpose, but rather that whatever situation we find ourselves within functions as our fate/character. I spent some time in chapter 7 discussing how Foucault's late work explored a conception of subjectivity that could allow for a form of freedom that starts from entirely empirical, caused influences. This self would be a nexus of historical, society, cultural forces that at a certain point of complexity becomes involved in the process of its own formation, forming a feedback loop.

Although Derrida's thought is often seen as simply iconoclastic, he says that "whether it's a question of life or work or thought . . . I have always recognized myself in the figure of the heir—and more and more so, in a way that is more and more deliberate, and often happy" (Derrida, *FWT* 3; see also Derrida 2000a, 405). The role of the heir is complex, however, at least when the inheritance is an Oedipal discipline like philosophy which virtually consists in criticizing one's influences. Derrida defines the role as being under a "double injunction, a contradictory assignation: It is necessary first of all to know and to know how to *reaffirm* what comes 'before us,' which we therefore receive even before choosing, and to behave in this respect as a free subject" (Derrida, *FWT* 3; see also 52). On the other hand, the process of appropriating this past "means not simply accepting this heritage but relaunching it otherwise and keeping it alive. Not choosing it (since what characterizes a heritage is first of all that one does not choose it; it is what violently elects us), but choosing to keep it alive" (3). And it is here that the paradox reappears, since "this reaffirmation, which both continues and interrupts, resembles (at least) an election, a selection, a decision. One's own *as* that of the other" (4; see also Derrida, *PoI* 204; Derrida, *TFS* 85). We are necessarily determined by forces "outside" of us, but this does not stop them from being our own, since there is no inside to be invaded.

This move repeats Heidegger's analysis of Kant quite closely:

> If our heritage assigns contradictory tasks to us (to receive and yet to choose, to welcome what comes before us and yet to reinterpret it, etc.), this is because it is a testimony to our finitude. Only a finite being inherits, and his finitude *obliges* him. . . . But the same finitude obliges one to choose, to prefer, to sacrifice, to exclude, to let go and leave behind. Precisely in order to respond to the call that preceded him. (Derrida, *FWT* 5; see also Derrida, *PoI* 130; Derrida, *DN* 6)

It is fidelity to the spirit of philosophy that compels us to betray the tradition of philosophy in the sense of attacking those who have taught us the most; there is no higher tribute. In this way, "what is the most decided, the most firmly decided is the decision to maintain the greatest possible tension between the two poles of the contradiction . . . faithfulness and filial lack of piety" (Derrida, *PoI* 151; see also Derrida, *TFS* 43).

Furthermore, the only way to create something new is to cannibalize what we find in the tradition. This is why Derrida believes that "every discourse is *bricoleur.* . . . The engineer is a myth [that is, a] subject who supposedly would be the absolute origin of his own discourse" (Derrida, *WD* 285; Derrida, *TFS* 69).

> The only weakness of *bricolage*—but, seen as a weakness is it not irremediable?—is a total inability to justify itself in its own discourse. The already-there-ness of instruments and of concepts cannot be undone or reinvented. . . . In the best of cases, the discourse of *bricolage* can confess itself, confess in itself its desire and its defeat, provoke the thought of the essence and the necessity of the already-there, recognize that the most radical discourse, the most inventive and systematic engineer are surprised and circumvented by a history, a language, etc., a *world* . . . from which they must borrow their tools, if only to destroy the former machine. (Derrida, *G* 138–39)

Once again, the concepts are always already there and unjustifiable, but these are not reasons to reject them, since, after all, "is it not irremediable?" Nor does he claim any exemption from these conditions for his own work. Derrida insists that deconstruction

> analyzes [finite contexts] without claiming any absolute overview. . . . To the extent to which it—by virtue of its discourse, its socio-institutional situation, its language, the historical inscription of its gestures, etc.—is itself rooted in a given context (but, as always, in one that is differentiated and mobile), it does not renounce (it neither can nor ought to do so) the "values" that are dominant in this context. (Derrida, *Ltd* 137, bracketed comment added; see also Derrida, *G* 160)

The context is "differentiated and mobile," thus containing within itself the tools and the impetus for its own criticism, but this cannot be done from outside of the context, from an "absolute overview" which would allow us to renounce wholesale the contexts that determine our outlook.

As many have noted, the present division between analytic and continental philosophy is overdetermined, being drawn by such diverse factors as geography, style of writing, style of argumentation, figures referred to, and topics discussed. The analysis offered in this conclusion classifies philosophical works by their ethos, an admittedly vague but I think useful notion that combines certain philosophical tenets with how the thinker understands what he is doing and how to do it. To discover a particular philosopher's place, we would ask how he conceives of his work and the goal of philosophy. Is he after timeless truth that escapes the contingent empirical factors that happen to have made him what he is, even if only as an inaccessible ideal, or does he view truth as itself the product of such factors? The founding fathers of analytic philosophy—Frege, Russell, and Moore—favor the former approach, which is in line with the perspective of the second *Critique,* whereas the first great continental figure—Hegel—insists that truth is temporal and historical, following out the implications of the first *Critique.*

This way of defining the branches would not leave the respective rosters exactly the way they are at present, but would require some reshuffling. Husserl, at least up until his final works when he started engaging with Heidegger's thought, and Habermas would both count as more analytic than continental by this definition. This conclusion is not startling; Husserl has always been one of the more easily assimilated continental thinkers (for example, in Dummett's historical work), and of all contemporary "continental" philosophers Habermas is probably taken the most seriously and engaged with the most by analytic thinkers. From the other side, committed anti-realists who carry the doctrine through to its logical conclusion like Michael Dummett or Nelson Goodman would be more continental. Quine's willingness to allow logic to be reformulated under sufficient empirical pressure (see Quine 1980, 43) at least brings him within striking range of the other side. But by far the most continental of the important analytic philosophers would be the later Wittgenstein. Wittgenstein's insistence on paring away everything that smells of the sublime or the transcendent, his commitment to basing his thought only on the vicissitudes of human life, and his acceptance of the deeply counterintuitive conclusions that follow from this approach strike me as deeply continental.[19] Although many analytic philosophers claim to be committed to such a purely empirical study, the presence of the notion of a timeless truth betrays traces of metaphysics.

The history of continental philosophy I have traced represents a far-reaching development of Kant's founding rejection of realism. These thinkers inherit his anti-realism and extend it, working out its problems and clearing it of remnants of realism, which turns out to be an extremely complicated task. The views of truth and reality that emerge from this process can appear paradoxical and even irrational, but we must understand that they are the result of two hundred years of analysis and debate. While not inevitable, these ideas are the logical conclusion of a great many arguments that build on each other and thus can only be fully grasped with the proper understanding of the context. Overall, I think the continental thinkers carry out the implications of anti-realism further and more consistently than do their analytic counterparts.

# Notes

## Introduction

1. In a show of (perhaps misplaced) courtesy, Leibniz withheld publication of the book when Locke's death prevented him from responding to its criticisms.

2. The only notable encounter between significant thinkers from the two traditions (ignoring Carnap's take on Heidegger) is that between Derrida and Searle, and perhaps the only thing they could agree on is that their encounter does not represent "a confrontation between two prominent philosophical traditions" (Searle 1977, 198; see also Derrida, *Ltd* 71). Gilbert Ryle's intelligent and informed review of *Being and Time* (reprinted in Murray 1978, 53–64), though short, also comes to mind as a counterexample.

3. Kevin Mulligan suggests that "the almost complete absence of debate between Continental and Analytical philosophers . . . is a historical curiosity; it is difficult to think of a similar example of widespread, almost complete mutual isolation and indifference between philosophical communities" (Mulligan 1991, 118). In 1971, Richard J. Bernstein defined the epoch in terms of this split: "The dominant characteristic of our philosophic age is one of ignorance and suspicion of different philosophic styles and movements, usually mixed with disdain, and a stubborn conviction that one's own way of philosophizing is the only worthwhile way" (Bernstein 1971, 3).

4. Rorty 1982, 228. Despite his frequent claims of finding similar conclusions in continental and post-positivist analytic philosophy, Rorty justifies his disinterest in bringing the camps together by claiming that no such common topics exist: "We should not fuss about 'building bridges' between analytic and Continental philosophy. Such a project would make sense if, as is sometimes said, the two sides were attacking common problems with different 'methods.' But . . . there are no such common problems" (Rorty 1982, 225–26). J. J. Ross similarly criticizes Dummett's strategy of going back to Frege and Husserl after attending a lecture on Levinas that he found "mystifying": "Could communication have been established between Dummett and Levinas by going back to the point of divergence. . . . I doubt it. The whole *problématique* that concerned Levinas, in the article referred to by the lecturer, had no connection with anything in which Dummett might have been interested. Only if there had been a common question which concerned them both would Levinas and Dummett have been able to compare their respective answers, collate their reference to common authorities, of the past or the present, and to agree or disagree" (Biletzki and Matar 1998, 67).

5. To give just one prominent analytic philosopher's recent evaluation of its importance, Crispin Wright has written, "There is no more fundamental philosophical task confronting us at the present time than to see our way clear to disposing of, or sustaining, the anti-realist challenge in different areas of discourse" (Wright 1993, 106).

6. James Conant attributes a similar strategy of finding in Kant the resources to "heal this rift" to Hilary Putnam (Putnam 1990, xxxiii), but I cannot find any evidence of this attempt in Putnam's work. Although he does occasionally talk about continental figures, it is usually to hold them up as examples of thought gone wrong. Tom Rockmore recently wrote a book arguing that "consciously or more often unconsciously, the main thinkers in the twentieth century are in dialogue with each other on the basis of a shared Kantian tradition, which they understand in different ways" (Rockmore 2006, 19; see also 161). Christopher Norris identifies anti-realism as a topic that has united figures across the divide, including several I discuss here (Norris 1997, 1–2).

7. Kant's influence on analytic philosophy is receiving more attention as more philosophers analyze the history of this tradition; see, for example, Hanna 2001, 11 (see 121): "It is scarcely an exaggeration to say that the inner drama of analytic philosophy from Frege to Quine and beyond is its century-long love-hate relationship with Kant's theoretical philosophy." For just one example of the "beyond," Davidson discusses his influences in his "Intellectual Autobiography," saying that "Kant's influence has been the most pervasive, but it runs so deep that I have seldom acknowledged it in print" (Davidson, *PDD* 64).

8. Heidegger's description of his strategy for interpreting the unity of Kant's mental faculties by way of their common root in the imagination in the opening quote of this introduction describes my approach to Kant as the common, sustaining root of both traditions nicely: "If . . . it has the character of a root, then it must be ground in such a way that it lets the stems grow out from itself, lending them support and stability. . . . It unveils how this root is the root for both stems" (Heidegger, *KPM* 97; see also Rorty 1979, 161).

9. I have listed all of the theses that are used throughout, along with representative quotes, in the Guide to Matrices at the beginning of the book.

## Chapter 1

1. Austin 1962, 70. Alston makes the same comment at 2002, 97.

2. Gerald Vision opens his book with the sweeping claim, "From its inception to the present, philosophy may be viewed as a series of struggles between various realisms and anti-realisms" (Vision 1988, 3).

3. Putnam 1981, 49 (bracketed numbers added); see also Putnam 1983, 205; Putnam 1990, 30–31. See Moran 2000, 75, for a discussion of these as separate theses, as well as a comparison with Hartry Field's formulation in Field 1982.

4. Devitt 1997, 15–16. See also Devitt in French, Uehling, and Wettstein 1988, 159–60; Fine 1996, 137, 155; Alston 2002, 1; Miller in Alston 2002, 13; Lynch in Alston 2002, 59.

5. Quoted in Kirkham 1995, 170.

6. See, for example, Putnam's remark: "Before Kant almost every philosopher subscribed to the view that truth is some kind of correspondence between ideas and 'what is the case'" (Putnam 1978, 1).

7. See Nicholas Rescher: "Philosophical realism as a general doctrine maintains that there is a domain of mind-independent existence and that we can obtain *some* reliable knowledge of it" (Rescher 2000, 93). He goes so far as to call them the "two indispensable and inseparable constituents" of physical realism (105). See also, for example, French, Uehling, and Wettstein 1988, 114; Walker 1989, 3, 21; Papineau 1987, 10; Fine 1996, 129, 137, 152; Russell 1959b, 121, 128.

8. Although Dummett finds the "characterization of realism . . . in terms of truth" more "illuminating" than it would be if done "in terms of reference," he also believes that "unless we take reference into account, we shall not succeed in including under our general characterization of realism every philosophical doctrine that has traditionally been so labeled" (Dummett 1981, 441). Hence he includes both issues in his definition: "The fundamental thesis of realism, as we have been considering it so far, is that we really do succeed in referring to external objects, existing independently of our knowledge of them, and that the statements we make about them carry a meaning of such a kind that they are rendered true or false by an objective reality the constitution of which is, again, independent of our knowledge. This is a thesis concerning the theory of meaning" (446). He simply decides that the latter criterion of bivalence is the best way to determine the former metaphysical issue.

9. In Lynch 2001a, 57; see also Alston 2002, 4; Searle 1995, 154–55, 199.

10. Hartry Field does not believe that this claim follows from realism. See Field 1982.

11. Curtis Brown responds that the world can be mind-independent (R1) yet still contain objects that can be accurately classified or depicted in many ways, thus rejecting R3. He calls this position "moderate realism," which claims that there can be multiple true descriptions of the single, determinate, independent world (in French, Uehling, and Wettstein 1988, 147–48). However, this still presupposes a single set of entities which then get organized differently, as Davidson points out: "The notion of organization applies only to pluralities. But whatever plurality we take experience to consist in . . . we will have to individuate according to familiar principles" (Davidson, *ITI* 192). This is also Putnam's point in his Cookie Dough metaphor that I will discuss below (see Putnam 1987, 34–36).

12. There is a reading of Heraclitus that places his conception of logos quite close to Plato's Forms, but this is not the place to discuss this.

13. My colleague Colin Anderson frequently reminds me that there is a significant body of Plato interpretation which interprets the Forms as a kind of heuristic tool which lacks the determinate finality I am attributing to it here.

14. Kolakowski 1969, 46. I owe this quote to Brown 1988.

15. Peter Hylton has shown in detail how Russell and Moore's strong acceptance of bivalence constitutes part of their rejection of idealism. See, for example, Hylton 1990, 10.

16. In Geach and Black 1960, 159. In his later work, Wittgenstein describes the

feeling he was under: "The sense of a sentence—one would like to say—may, of course, leave this or that open, but the sentence must nevertheless have *a* definite sense. An indefinite sense—that would really not be a sense *at all*" (Wittgenstein, *PI* §99; see also §71, §88).

17. Dummett 1991, 15; see also Dummett 1981, 433, 441; 1993, 230, 465.

18. Dummett 1991, 9; see also Dummett 1978, 155; Dummett 1981, 434, 505; Lynch 2001a, 244. Dummett moves from the excluded middle to bivalence in his career. For a brief discussion, see Dummett 1981, 435–36, 471–72; Van Cleve 1999, 219; Putnam 1983, 84.

19. Wittgenstein *Tractatus*, 4.023; see also 3.01, 3.23, 3.25, 3.251, 3.42, 4.1, 4.2, 4.25, 4.26, 4.3. See also ter Hark in Moyal-Sharrock 2004, 127.

20. Ralph C. S. Walker claims that one can be a realist and reject bivalence if "the world was intrinsically vague in such a way as to make some quite specific claims . . . neither determinately true, nor determinately false" (Walker 1989, 32), though it seems that whether or not the world is intrinsically vague would be bivalently true or false (see Dummett 1993, 468).

21. As stated above, this is not the only possible kind of realist, but it is by far the most natural and populous species.

22. Aristotle, *De anima* 429b30; see also Marx 1971, 74. Aristotle's agent or active intellect might count as an exception to this interpretation, but his doctrine on this point is too obscure to undermine the many points at which he clearly subscribes to a passive intellect receiving sensory data.

23. This view of science as worship resurfaces forcefully in the modern age in Leibniz's thought.

24. Russell 1996, 456; see also Russell 1959b, 74. Besides the difference between Russell's logical versus Kant's intuitive grounding of math (Frege had already worked on a logical rather than intuitive grounding for arithmetic; see Geach and Black 1960, 138, 148), another issue for Russell is the idea that space necessarily involves contradictions, which, if true, brings in Kantian antinomies and Hegelian dialectic, as well as rendering both space and geometry subjective. See Hylton 1990, chapters 3–5, for a helpful discussion of these matters.

25. Russell 1996, 450–51; see also Frege in Geach and Black 1960, 122, 127, 131, 145.

26. Russell introduces Kant in his *History of Western Philosophy* this way: "Immanuel Kant (1724–1804) is generally considered the greatest of modern philosophers. I cannot myself agree with this estimate, but it would be foolish not to recognize his great importance" (Russell 1945, 704). This importance, however, turns out to resemble the historical importance of diseases and wars; in the next paragraph, "Hume . . . awakened him from his dogmatic slumbers—so at least he says, but the awakening was only temporary, and he soon invented a soporific which enabled him to sleep again" (704). The effect of Kant's thought on himself was only sleep, but on his disciple Fichte it was "insanity, and, from this extreme, philosophy has been attempting, ever since, to escape into the world of every-day common sense" (xxi; see also 718).

27. Russell 1959a, 42; see also 121; Biletzki and Matar 1998, 15, 42.

28. Russell 1929, 259–60 (bracketed comment added); see also Russell 1945,

834. This attitude is still voiced half a century later. Quine, the leading analytic philosopher of his day, in an essay written for a general audience, presents the same discovery of rigorous logical analysis as what will solve (or dissolve) problems that previous generations could not: "A striking trait of scientific philosophy . . . has been the use, increasingly, of the powerful new logic. This has made for a deepening of insights and a sharpening of problems and solutions. . . . It has been appreciated increasingly in the past sixty years that our traditional introspective notions—our notions of meaning, idea, concept, essence, all undisciplined and undefined—afford a hopelessly flabby and unmanageable foundation for a theory of the world. Control is gained by focusing on words" (Quine 1981, 191–92).

29. Russell 1945, 834; see also Russell 1959b, 14–15; in Ayer 1959, 33. When discussing, and quoting at length, his early idealist works in *My Philosophical Development,* Russell has a moment of insight into his own philosophical character: "I had when I was younger—perhaps I still have—an almost unbelievable optimism as to the finality of my own theories" (Russell 1959b, 41). Even in the context of reviewing his many errors, however, this self-awareness does not stop him from continuing to assert his present views without qualification, resembling nothing more than Hegel's depiction of natural consciousness that continually corrects itself, thus realizing that experience itself is constantly changing, but constantly forgetting this by seizing on the latest conclusion as the right and final answer (see Hegel, *PS* 64, §109).

30. This kind of dismissal of the past is not limited to early, logically oriented analytic philosophy. Peter Strawson, for instance, describes one of the two sources of the tremendous excitement that ordinary language philosophy held for him when he first started philosophy: "In the face of this refined examination of actual linguistic practice, a lot of traditional philosophical theorizing began to look extraordinarily crude, like an assemblage of huge, crude mistakes. And it was, of course, extremely exhilarating to see these huge and imposing edifices of thought just crumbling away, or tumbling down, to the tune of this fairly modest sort of piping" (Magee 1986, 147–48).

31. Putnam's former student James Conant actually raises his eyebrows about "the following peculiar feature of his pedagogic practice: he would usually motivate the approach he wished to take to a contemporary philosophical issue through a discussion of the work of some philosopher whom he admired. One's first fleeting impression would therefore perhaps be of someone unable to arrive at ideas of his own" (Putnam 1990, xvi).

## Chapter 2

1. John R. Searle claims that metaphysical realism and correspondence truth form a conception that "is so fundamental that to some extent it defines [the Western intellectual tradition]" (Searle 1993, 57; see also 60). This leaves Kant in a rather awkward position.

2. Of course, this will also serve as Hegel's objection to Kant's critical solution to skepticism.

3. On this dilemma, see Carr 1999, 104; and Stroud's "The Allure of Idealism," in Stroud 2000.

4. Linda Martín Alcoff points out that the words "real" and "royalty" share a common root (Alcoff 1996, 201).

5. The common attribution to Bacon of this violent imagery of "putting nature on the rack" is questionable.

6. This is one of the key passages for Putnam's interpretation of Kant. See Putnam 1981, 61–64.

7. Wordsworth echoes this sentiment a few years later: "This I feel, / That from thyself it is that thou must give / Else never canst receive." I owe this quote to Abrams 1953, 63.

8. Kant, *C1* A158/B197; see also Kant, *PFM* 44/296, 53/306, 65–66/319.

9. Heidegger, *PIK* 115, 127, 201. Of course, Heidegger sometimes goes farther than this, denying that the work concerns epistemology at all (see Heidegger, *BP* 128).

10. Kolb 1986, 41; see also Beck 1969, 462; Hyppolite 1974, 145; Weatherston 2002, 33.

11. Actually, Putnam is willing to somewhat question this claim. In 1981 he solidly claims that Kant "does not doubt that there is *some* mind-independent reality" (Putnam 1981, 61), but he later wavers: "I think that almost all of the *Critique of Pure Reason* is compatible with a reading in which one is not at all committed to a Noumenal World, or even, as I said, to the intelligibility of thoughts about noumena" (Putnam 1987, 41). In a rather Heideggerian move, he later claims that "in the first Critique Kant himself repeatedly comes to the very point of seeing that the notion of a 'thing in itself' is empty, and always backs away from his own recognition of that fact; but still, there *is* some recognition of that fact, I would claim, even at moments in the first Critique" (Putnam 1995, 29).

12. See Allais 2003, 375, 379; Schaper and Vossenkuhl 1989, 235; M. Clark 1990, 55.

13. See Blattner 1999, 251–52, and Priest 2002, 81–82, for discussions of this well-known criticism, but see also Van Cleve 1999, 137–38, for a possible defense.

14. Hume's dry comment on Descartes' committing of this "fallacy" is delicious: "To have recourse to the veracity of the supreme Being, in order to prove the veracity of our senses, is surely making a very unexpected circuit" (Hume 1975, 153).

15. Practical postulates of God are a different matter, of course.

16. H. Allison 1983, 7; see also 8, 242; Putnam 1981, 61; Rudd 2003, 53.

17. As we will see in chapter 4, this is close to Nietzsche's anti-realism. See Stevenson and Walker 1983, 161.

18. See Mulligan 1991, 117: "Taking German idealism seriously is, I suggest, one of the marks of Continental Philosophy. One symptom of this is the out of hand dismissal of realism by Continental Philosophers." Of course, I would disagree with this if "out of hand" means without reasons or argumentation.

19. Kant, *C1* A58/B82; see also A191/B236, A237/B296, A642/B670.

20. Some commentators believe that Kant holds noumenal correspondence to be intelligible, just impossible for humans, and thus "in some of his moods at least, Kant was by Dummett's standards a realist, i.e., a believer in knowledge-

transcendent truths" (Stevenson and Walker 1983, 140). Walker goes farther than this: "In admitting things in themselves, which can be speculated about but never known, [Kant] admits a class of truths about the noumenal world which are verification-transcendent in the most radical fashion possible" (157). See also Ameriks 2000b, 258.

21. I owe this quote to Van Cleve 1999, 215; and McCumber 2003, 79n21.

22. Quoted in Schaper and Vossenkuhl 1989, 144, and cited there as R5642, 18:281 (all bracketed comments in original).

23. These are the kinds of questions that Nelson Goodman is brilliant at posing. See, for example, Goodman 1978, 130–40.

24. See in Lynch 2001a, 273; Blackburn 1984, 233–35; Hylton in Beiser 1993, 453–54.

25. Moran 2000, 89; see also McDowell 1996, 9, 34. Sellars makes the same point, for example, in Beck 1969, 188.

26. Interestingly, Kant himself suggests a proto-Hegelian interpretation of "external" sensation as a merely posited limit concept: "Understanding accordingly limits sensibility, but does not thereby extend its own sphere. In the process of warning the latter that it must not presume to claim applicability to things-in-themselves but only to appearances, it does indeed think for itself an object in itself, but only as transcendental object. . . . The representation remains for us empty, and is of no service except to mark the limits of our sensible knowledge" (Kant, *C1* A288/B344–45; see also Hanna 2001, 115).

27. Kant, *C1* A150/B190 (my italics); see also A125; Kant, *PFM* 39/291; Kant 1992, 557–58.

28. Stevenson and Walker 1983, 141; see also 157; Walker 1989, 63, 102–3; Kemp Smith 1984, 36.

29. There are some suggestions that alien races could possess different faculties (see Kant, *C1* A27/B43, B72, B139, B148–49, A230–31/B283). Certainly, all humans have the same faculties for Kant.

30. Allen 1993, 28; see also Putnam 1987, 43; Moran 2000, 82–84; Van Cleve 1999, 214.

31. Putnam views the different perspectives in each *Critique* as a "*hint* of conceptual relativity" (Putnam 1987, 43) and finds "especially in the third Critique and in Kant's postcritical writings, a *tendency* towards genuine pluralism, which Kant perhaps resisted, but which nevertheless surfaces in his work" (Putnam 1991, 30). Van Cleve (1999, 220–25) and Carl Posy (1983, 81–94, and 1984, 115–34) discuss the antinomies as possible exceptions to bivalence, which I will not be discussing in detail for Kant. Dummett concludes that since there is no meaningful answer to questions about "spatial, temporal or causal" relations among noumena, Kant is not committed to the ubiquitous application of bivalence (Dummett 1981, 472).

32. Interestingly, in his important paper which attempts to show "the impossibility of demonstrating a schema's uniqueness" by exhaustively refuting all possible methods for establishing it (Beck 1969, 233–34), Körner leaves out Kant's actual strategy of proving that this particular one is our necessary projection. Körner seems only interested in refuting a schema (that is, a conceptual scheme) con-

ceived in a transcendentally realist manner, whose impossibility, of course, Kant would concede. See Körner 1970, 72.

33. Houlgate 1991, 8; see also Habermas 1971, 15; Hanna 2001, 58, 65; McCumber in Comay and McCumber 1999, 3.

34. See Kant, *C1* Bxxiv, A71/B96, A73/B98, A79/B105, A338/B396, A462/B490, A591/B619, A804/B832; Kant, *PFM* 49/306, 51/308, 64/322, 71/329–30.

35. Carr 1999, 43; see also 34, 56, 65, 107, 122, 126; Ameriks 2000b, 55, 169; H. Allison 1983, 290; Kolb 1986, 17; Schürmann 1979, 161.

36. See Kant, *C1* A22/B37, B157, B157n.a, B421.

37. Hyppolite 1974, 143; see also 26, 94; Stewart 2000, 20; Guyer in Beiser 1993, 185, 208n12; Sherover 1971, 66, 89; Rosen 1982, 114; Lear 1998, 252.

38. See Kant, *C1* A463–64, A404; see also Schaper and Vossenkuhl 1989, 278; Carr 1999, 43, 63; Van Cleve 1999, 176.

39. Heidegger, *PIK* 258; see also Heidegger, *N* 1:123; Heidegger, *HCT* 233–34; Heidegger, *PIK* 268; Heidegger, *BP* 55, 125; Heidegger, *KPM* 117.

40. Kant, *C1* A112; see also A107, A116, A123, A129, B133. See Pippin 1989, 19; Guyer 1987, 82; Schaper and Vossenkuhl 1989, 255.

41. Bertrand Russell puts this nicely: in investigating Kantian space, "we only push one stage farther back the region of 'mere fact,' for the constitution of our minds remains still a mere fact" (Russell 1996, 454).

42. See Kant, *C1* B422; Kant, *FMM* 68–69/451. The idealists try to achieve just this kind of self-creation through history. See the next chapter.

43. See Ameriks 2000a, 264; Schaper and Vossenkuhl 1989, 7; Walker 1978, 131; Dahlstrom 1984, 189; Stevenson and Walker 1983, 172.

44. In Beck 1969, 457. C. G. Prado writes that "there is no getting around how Kant permanently changed debate about truth by altering our understanding of perception from one of direct apprehension to one of perception as a complexly interactive process" (Prado 2006, 11).

## Chapter 3

1. M. Westphal 1998, 1; see also Pinkard 2002, 218; Beiser 1993, 114; Gadamer 1976a, 76; McDowell 1996, 111.

2. Hegel, *RH* 51; see also 69, 90; Hegel, *HL* 199, §140R; Hegel, *PS* 10, §18.

3. Here I need to state the obligatory qualification that I am skipping over many interesting figures in this rich period, and indeed throughout my book. Limitations of space, time, and my own intelligence require selectivity. Of course I do not mean to indicate that the story I am telling is the only one that can be told, only that it is a good, true, and illuminating one.

4. M. Westphal 1998, 115; see also 137; Habermas 1971, 25. We can see from this that Putnam importantly misunderstands Hegel when he accuses Hegel of "[losing] sight of the immanence of reason, of the fact that reason is always relative to context and institution" (Putnam 1983, 234). This is a serious misreading of Hegel, though admittedly some of his language does suggest such a reading. Ironically, a book by a prominent Hegel scholar published just a few years after

Putnam's comment contains a chapter titled "Context and the Immanence of Rationality in Hegel's Phenomenology"! (Houlgate 1986, chapter 7). See Rockmore in Denker and Vater 2003, 342: "Hegel elaborates a 'thick,' thoroughly contextualized view of the human. . . . As human beings, we are not transcendent to, but immanent in, our world."

5. This project only gets fully worked out in *Science of Logic,* but the necessary historical introduction takes place in the *Phenomenology.*

6. Hegel, *HL* 66, §41R1; see also 40, §24R2. This strategy is sometimes considered Hegel's solution to the ancient skeptical Problem of the Criterion. See K. R. Westphal 2003b, 153–55; K. R. Westphal 1989, 11–16; Forster 1998, 152–61.

7. In his introduction to a collection of Putnam's papers, his former student James Conant describes his surprise at Putnam's teaching method: "I came to know Putnam first as a teacher of philosophy. I attended his classes at Harvard and was *repeatedly struck* by the following *peculiar* feature of his pedagogic practice: he would usually motivate the approach he wished to take to a contemporary philosophical issue through a discussion of the work of some philosopher whom he admired. One's first fleeting impression would therefore perhaps be of someone unable to arrive at ideas of his own—an impression, however, that would vanish as one came to realize that Putnam's readings of philosophers tended to be no less *idiosyncratic* than his own approach to philosophical problems" (Putnam 1990, xvi, all italics mine). Why this would be so peculiar and suspicious is rather puzzling, unless these are merely the thoughts of the youthful student. Even if one does not go so far as Hegel or Heidegger to believe that philosophy itself or even all thought is necessarily embedded in a historical context motivated by predecessors, it still seems a fairly natural way to conceive of what one is doing.

8. See Houlgate 1991, 28–32, for a brief, clear discussion of this topic; see also Kolb 1986, 209–10; Beiser 1993, 277–79.

9. This is a little more complicated when it comes to the first section of the book, "Consciousness." There is dispute over whether these are actually historical periods (as argued in chapters 9 and 10 of Forster 1998) or not (as argued by Hartmann in MacIntyre 1972). See Pinkard 2002, 229n13, for a more in-depth discussion and more references.

10. Note that the word "consciousness" is used both to refer to the first phase of Spirit's development and as a fairly neutral term for the mind in general. I will adopt the artificial convention of capitalizing it when using it in the first sense, for the sake of clarity.

11. Kenneth R. Westphal has made an extended defense of the view that Hegel is a realist, particularly in *Hegel's Epistemological Realism.* In order to defend this position, however, he has recourse to some extensive reinterpretations and rather baroque charts which I find unpersuasive. He notes that "Hegel's adoption of realism has gone all but unnoticed in the literature" (K. R. Westphal 1989, 266n.33).

12. We have to keep in mind that throughout this section Hegel is describing how Consciousness takes itself, not what it really is, that is, what Hegel or the phenomenological observer understands it to be.

13. Hegel, *PS* 150, §247. This quote actually describes Observing Reason, a

later shape of consciousness, but it repeats some of the mistakes of "Consciousness," especially since it is the first subsection of "Reason," just as "Consciousness" is the first section of the book as a whole. Placement within sections often indicates parallels with similarly placed sections and subsections in the *Phenomenology*.

14. Flay says that for consciousness "the subject or knower plays no active role in knowledge and experience, but is only passive and receptive, and thus depends wholly upon the object for truth" (Flay 1984, 38). For Hyppolite, "the object . . . is posited as being completely external to consciousness which has but to receive it passively" (Hyppolite 1974, 66). See Inwood 1985, 55; M. Westphal 1998, 66, 79; Heidegger, *HPS* 22, 49, 61, 84, 101, 129, 142.

15. I feel a little guilty at using Kierkegaard's wonderful wit to praise Hegel rather than to bury him, but Kierkegaard did misunderstand Hegel to a large degree.

16. Of course, this is not simple abandonment but an *aufhebung;* we will see how realism is preserved in the final stage of the process.

17. Houlgate 1991, 6–7; see also Houlgate 1986, 130; Lamb 1980, 91; M. Westphal 1998, xix; Pippin 1997, 18; Heidegger, *Pm* 333.

18. In fact, one of Hegel's innovations was to explore subjectivity in all of its arenas, but these are all interconnected to the shape of consciousness, so this approach still holds. See Hyppolite 1974, 10, 579; Forster 1998, 122, 365.

19. Forster 1998, 361; see also Houlgate 1986, 151; M. Westphal 1998, 88n8; Rockmore in Denker and Vater 2003, 339. Besides, Kant's view gives rise to oddities: if phenomena have always behaved in a Newtonian fashion, why did it take so long to note these regularities? Why did Euclid figure out math so much earlier than Newton determined science if they are both tracing the effects of permanent structures of the mind?

20. Pippin 1999, 73; see also Kolb 1986, 28, 31; Houlgate 1991, 9; Stewart 2000, 18; Cutrofello 1994, 5.

21. This formulation still depends on the subject-object dichotomy, which gets overcome, as I will discuss below.

22. See Stewart 2000, 27, 47; Forster 1998, chapter 10; Pippin 1989, 94; Houlgate 1991, 6; K. R. Westphal 1989, 92.

23. Notice that he says that Spirit has its existence "as" history, rather than "in" history. I think Heidegger misunderstands this in his discussion in *Being and Time* §82, though his focus is not on the *Phenomenology* there.

24. Sellars 1963, 148. See, for example, Solomon in Inwood 1985, 32; Stevenson and Walker 1983, 166; Rockmore 2001, 359–66.

25. See Pippin 1989, 127; Pippin 1999, 66; Pinkard 2002, 259; Ameriks 2000a, 227; Inwood 1985, 47. This rejection of the very coherence of the given makes Davidson's criticisms of the very idea of conceptual schemes less relevant to Hegel, as I will return to below. Forster makes something like this specific point at Forster 1998, 379–80, and offers important criticisms of Davidson's article in all of chapter 10. See also in Shook 2003, 38.

26. See, for example, Kant, *C1* A190/B235, A288/B344. Putnam claims that Kant already rejects the given (1987, 43), but Van Kirk (1984) shows persuasively that, if nothing else, Kant's "Refutation of Idealism" refutes this claim.

27. Though see Ameriks 2000b, 258, for a resurrection of the "neglected alternative," that is, the idea that noumena could coincide with the structures of our mind. This is also how Kenneth R. Westphal imputes the view to Hegel that the nature of truth is correspondence, though not the criterion. See K. R. Westphal 2003a 51, 70–71; K. R. Westphal 2003b 168, 172.

28. Actually, it began before Hegel with people like Fichte and Reinhold, but I am picking it up with Hegel, because I find his formulation particularly powerful and because of limitations of space.

29. See Pippin 1989, 6; Stewart 2000, 10; Schaper and Vossenkuhl 1989, 168; Hyppolite 1974, 144; Putnam 1990, 261; Norris 2002, 15.

30. As in his work on induction, Goodman is following an argument Hume put forward, specifically, against Lockean substance which lacks all qualities but counts as true reality: "Bereave matter of all its intelligible qualities, both primary and secondary, you in a manner annhihilate it, and leave only a certain unknown, inexplicable *something*, as the cause of our perceptions; a notion so imperfect, that no sceptic will think it worth while to contend against it" (Hume 1975, 155). Obviously this criticism applies to Kant's noumena as well.

31. See Hegel, *PS* 98, §159; 246, §409. Although the qualification "for consciousness" remains here, the progress to Absolute Knowing eliminates it, as I will show. Here is Jon Stewart on this issue: "When we abstract from our cognitive faculties to imagine the thing-in-itself, then we simultaneously do away with objectivity itself, since it is these faculties which determine objectivity in the first place. Thus, we are left with an 'utter abstraction' that has no content" (Stewart 2000, 26–27; see also M. Westphal 1998, 212; Forster 156n72).

32. Wittgenstein, *PI* §194; see also §96, §132, §195; Wittgenstein, *RFM* 40, §1.8; Rudd 2003, 89.

33. See Nagel 1986, 106; see also Dummett, in Clark and Hale 1994, 59.

34. Of course, there are significant differences between Wittgenstein and Hegel. For instance, Hegel believes that ideas possess an inner logic which, if violated, must eventually be discovered by self-contradictions that eventually force corrections upon users. Wittgenstein, on the other hand, believes that communities determine meaning and the logic of ideas, and that anything external to our language-games underdetermines the "decisions" communities reach in the use of words. See Houlgate 1986, 172–74, for a brief discussion of this topic.

35. This is strikingly similar to Putnam's internalist view as well: "In an internalist view also, signs do not intrinsically correspond to objects, independently of how those signs are employed and by whom. But a sign that is actually employed in a particular way by a particular community of users can correspond to particular objects *within the conceptual scheme of those users*. 'Objects' do not exist independently of conceptual schemes. *We* cut up the world into objects when we introduce one or another scheme of description. Since the objects *and* the signs are alike *internal* to the scheme of description, it is possible to say what matches what" (Putnam 1981, 52).

36. Hegel, *HL* 67–68, §41R2; see also Hegel, *DFS* 96, 187; Kolb 1986, 41; Wartenberg, in Beiser 1993, 116.

37. Of course, Wittgenstein uses this same argument in the preface to the *Trac-*

*tatus* to justify transforming the critical project of drawing a limit to thought into drawing the limit of "the expression of thoughts: for in order to be able to draw a limit to thought, we should have to find both sides of the limit thinkable (i.e., we should have to be able to think what cannot be thought" (Wittgenstein 2001, 3).

38. Davidson, *ITI* 198; see also Rorty 1998, 87. Where he would disagree is with Davidson's claim that there cannot be fundamentally divergent ways of experiencing the world and with the claim that our touch is "unmediated."

39. Other critics have noticed this similarity. Alasdair MacIntyre writes that Davidson repeats "the substance of Hegel's demonstration of the illegitimacy of any dualism which tears apart conceptual schemes on the one hand and the world on the other," but instead of having to eradicate all talk of conceptual schemes, Hegel "gave its canonical form both to the idea of a conceptual scheme and to that of alternative and incompatible conceptual schemes, and he did so without ever violating his own ban on the illegitimate dualist scheme/content and scheme/world distinctions" (in Krausz 1989, 183, 184; see also Forster 1998, 380; Lear 1998, 300).

40. Russell bequeathed analytic philosophy this misunderstanding of Hegel: "We shall understand by [idealism] the doctrine that whatever exists, or at any rate whatever can be known to exist, must be in some sense mental" (Russell 1959b, 37). Moore, too, for here is how his "Refutation of Idealism" begins: "Modern idealism, if it asserts any general conclusion about the universe at all, asserts that it is *spiritual*. . . . The idealist means to assert that [chairs and tables and mountains] are *in some sense* neither lifeless nor unconscious, as they certainly seem to be; . . . When the whole universe is declared to be spiritual, it is meant not only that it is in some sense *conscious*, but that it has what we recognize in ourselves as the *higher* forms of consciousness" (Moore 1965, 1). Hegel explicitly rejects this silly interpretation of his thought: "To speak of thought or objective thought as the heart and soul of the world, may seem to be ascribing consciousness to the things of nature. We feel a certain repugnance against making thought the inward function of things" (Hegel, *HL* 37, §24R). He goes on to explain that he means that the world is intelligible, that is, that it follows laws we can understand.

41. Hegel, *HL* 37, §24R1; see also 70, §42R3; 114, §80R; 201, §142R; 228, §163R2.

42. This is the anti-realist reading of Wittgenstein's claim that "*essence* is expressed in grammar" (*PI* §371). Whereas in the *Tractatus* there was an independent structure to the world which grammar pictured, the later Wittgenstein finds R1 Independence incoherent, so that what we express about the world is its essence by default.

43. This can also be understood as Hegel's commitment to the internalist view of justification, that is, that one must be aware of and understand the reasons that justify a belief in order for it to be justified, using "truth" for "knowledge" here: "Truth, to deserve the name, must authenticate its own truth: which authentication, here within the sphere of logic, is given, when the notion demonstrates itself to be what is mediated by and with itself" (Hegel, *HL* 122, §83R; see also 222, §159R).

44. Here Putnam accurately detects a Hegelian resonance in his work.

45. Or in Quine's famous formulation, "To be is to be the value of a variable" (Quine 1980, 15). See Dummett 1993, 465: "What reality consists in is not deter-

mined just by what objects there are, but by what propositions hold good: the world is the totality of facts, not of things. This was the reason for the concentration on acceptance or rejection of the principle of bivalence."

46. The same point applies to Paul Guyer's claim that Hegel was inspired to derive all categories from "some single concept" in order to "justify a claim to necessity" from "his immediate predecessors" Reinhold and Fichte (Beiser 1993, 187). This historical influence may be accurate, but the philosophical point of compromising autonomy would hold true regardless.

47. See Dudley 2002, 72; Houlgate 1986 123.

48. See Forster 1998, 173; Körner in Beck 1969, 233–34; McCumber 1993, 5.

49. Heidegger, *FoS* 18; see also Heidegger, *HPS* 105. Kant then shrank from this abyss in his second edition of the *Critique,* as well as in the second *Critique,* according to Heidegger. As we will see in chapter 6 and my conclusion, Heidegger sides with Kant here, holding that we must accept this abyss of explanation.

50. Pippin 1999, 65–66; see also Schaper and Vossenkuhl 1989, 258–61; Gadamer 1976a, 37; Forster 1998, 170–71.

51. Hegel, *PS* 37, §60 (bracketed comments added). Note that Hegel is talking here of any subject, that is, anything that supports predicates, not just the thinking self, though it certainly applies to that subject as well.

52. Sellars 1963, 127, 16. Strangely, Putnam seems completely unaware of any precedent to his social externalism: "Another important feature of both Kripke's theory and mine is that reference is determined *socially*. . . . The idea that the extensions of our terms are fixed by collective practices and not by concepts in our individual heads is a sharp departure from the way meaning has been viewed ever since the seventeenth century" (Putnam 1983, 75).

53. Hegel, *HL* 25, §19; see also 184, §306; 261, §436; Hegel, *RH* 53.

54. Hegel, *PS* 20, §34 (italics added); see also 17, §29; 50, §79; 51, §80; Hegel, *RH* 95; Hegel, *HL* 20, §15.

55. See Derrida, *WD* 268, 275, 271; Marx 1971, 62–63, 106; Heidegger, *OBT* 149–50; Caputo 1987, 18; Haar 1993, 69.

56. Hegel, *PS* 491, §806; see also Hegel, *HL* 43–45, §24R3; 221, §159; 276, §213R.

57. See Kolb 1986, 43, 79, 81, 91, 206–7, 243; Stewart 2000, 459; Kojève 1969, 109.

58. Hegel, *PS* 12, §22; see also 10, §18; 19, §32; 21, §37.

59. This is reminiscent of Husserl's distinction in "The Origin of Geometry."

60. Hegel, *PS* 23, §39; see also Hegel, *HL* 41, §24R2; 237, §172R; 276, §213R.

61. Davidson describes conceptual scheme change as "when the speakers of a language come to accept as true an important range of sentences they previously took to be false" (Davidson, *ITI* 188), which then changes the words' meanings. The same range of sentences would have to be available to each speaker, the only differences being where the Ts and Fs are placed. Nicholas Rescher points out that this misconstrues alternate conceptual schemes; their divergence does not consist in different assignments of truth and falsity to the same set of sentences, but rather in having different candidates for truth and falsity (in French, Uehling, and Wettstein 1980, 331–34). Hacking makes the same point in Hollis and Lukes 1982, 60.

62. Hegel credits Kant for having discovered antinomies, but criticizes him for misinterpreting them as based on a confusion which must be cleared up. See Hegel, *HL* 77, §47; 78, §48R; 99, §160.

## Chapter 4

1. Nietzsche, *BGE* 6; see also 23, 187; Nietzsche, *EH* 1.2.

2. Nietzsche, *WTP* 560; see also 559; Dreyfus and Hall 1992, 237; Heidegger, *N* 4:79.

3. Nietzsche, *BGE* 10. Michael Steven Green claims that this is a reference to the little-known neo-Kantian philosopher Afrikan Spir, who, according to the central argument of his book, had a significant impact on Nietzsche. See Green 2002.

4. See, for example, Hales and Welshon 2000, 59.

5. See Nietzsche, *WTP* 477, 484, 487, 547; Nietzsche, *BGE* 17, 54. Compare Ryle's analysis of how grammar misleads us to hypostatize the mind as a separate entity in *The Concept of Mind* and Russell's discussion of how "the subject-predicate logic" of our language leads to a "substance-attribute metaphysic," even though it is an accidental feature of our syntax: "Language misleads us both by its vocabulary and by its syntax. We must be on our guard in both respects if our logic is not to lead to a false metaphysic" (Ayer 1959, 38).

6. There are also many passages where he attacks Kant, calling him "that most deformed concept-cripple of all time" (Nietzsche, *TI* 8.7) and stating that "my concept of the philosopher is worlds removed from any concept that would include even a Kant" (Nietzsche, *EH* 3.2.3; see also Nietzsche, *WTP* 553; Nietzsche, *D*, preface 3; Nietzsche, *BGE* 54; Nietzsche, *TI* 4; Nietzsche, *A* 10). Hales and Welshon claim that "there are few targets in Nietzsche's work more virulently attacked than Kant" (Hales and Welshon 2000, 77). However, they use this to argue against Kantian interpretations of Nietzsche (especially the argument I will make below that, despite his twistings, he still retains something of a noumenal realm), although they themselves see strong parallels with Kant in other ways (see 119). This relies on Nietzsche's pronouncements too literally, something they do throughout their book, as if he might not be Oedipally distancing himself from a thinker who wielded too much influence over himself, or might not have the same perspective on his own work that we do.

7. Nietzsche, *BGE* 16, 20, 268; Nietzsche, *WTP* 562; Nietzsche, *TI* 482.

8. Nietzsche, *WTP* 523, 565; Houlgate 1986, 44.

9. Nietzsche, *TI* 495; see also Nietzsche, *WTP* 495, 606, 634.

10. See Danto 1965, 95, 40; Vaihinger in Conway 1998, 416–17n10, 403; Megill 1985, 53; Heidegger, *N* 3:95–96; Wilcox 1974, 98, 141; Lingis 1989, 98–99; Hales and Welshon 2000, 119; Ansell Pearson 1991, 32; Houlgate 1986, 258n75; Conway 1990, 99; Pippin 1999, 95–96, 153; Cutrofello 1994, 140n29; Desmond in Gallagher 1997, 78–79.

11. See also George J. Stack's "Kant, Lange, and Nietzsche: Critique of Knowledge," in Ansell Pearson 1991, for more on the connection with Lange.

12. R. K. Hill 2003, 131. Two slight disagreements with this remark: I think

Nietzsche talks more about concepts than about the Aesthetic's space and time, and he emphasizes the increase of power over Darwin's focus on mere survival and propagation of the species.

13. Nietzsche, *WTP* 480; see also 498, 503; Nietzsche, *HATH* 1.16.

14. Nietzsche, *WTP* 517–18; see also 494, 507, 574.

15. In Breazeale 1979, 65; see also Richardson 1996, 224n8, 243; Houlgate 1991, 7; Stevenson and Walker 1983, 161; Ansell Pearson 1991, 36; R. K. Hill 2003. 183–84.

16. Nietzsche, *BGE* 4. We are also condemned to untruth because the fluctuating chaos of reality simply cannot be captured in thoughts or language. See Nietzsche, *WTP* 715; Houlgate 1986, 45. This idea that thoughts and words cannot represent becoming contains echoes of Kant's claim that we cannot have a thought of the spontaneous transcendental subject, at Kant, *C1* B157n.a.

17. Wilcox 1974, 42; see also Danto 1965, 81; Richardson and Leiter 2001, 109n39; Hales and Welshon 2000, 15; Schacht 1983, 52, 74; D. B. Allison 1977, 6.

18. Nietzsche, *GS* 121; see also 110–11; Nietzsche, *WTP* 172, 455, 487; Leiter in Schacht 1994, 341.

19. Putnam makes a similar point in defending his own conceptual relativity: "The interest relativity of ascriptions of reference (and causality) shows that there are alternative right descriptions of the world with respect to reference (and causality), but not that reference (and causality) are 'not in the world.' What is absurd is absolutizing any of the alternative right descriptions" (in Clark and Hale 1994, 291n20).

20. Nietzsche, *WTP* 600; see also 565; Nietzsche, *Z* 3.11.2; Nietzsche, *GS* 373.

21. See Kolakowski 1969, 63; Havas in Dreyfus and Hall 1992, 237; Pippin 1999, 153.

22. Nietzsche, *WTP* 515–16; see also 535, 584, 585A; Nietzsche, *GS* 111.

23. Quine's commitment to indefinite revisionism in "Two Dogmas" seems sympathetic with this view (see Quine 1980, 43), though he says in another book that "whoever denies the law of excluded middle changes the subject. In repudiating '*p* or ~*p*' he is indeed giving up classical negation, or perhaps alternation, or both; and he may have his reasons" (Quine 1970, 83). At Quine 1992, 36, he leaves the issue open: "In particular, quantum mechanics invites logical deviations. . . . When the dust has settled, we may find that the very notion of existence, the old one, has had its day. . . . Whether to say at that point that we have gained new insight into existence, or that we have outgrown the notion and reapplied the term, is a question of terminology." Davidson makes similar arguments about changing the subject at Davidson, *EAE* 221–23, 237, 273.

24. Nietzsche, *BGE* 34; see also Green 2002, 113; Richardson 1996, 278, 290; Heidegger, *N* 3:107; Hales and Welshon 2000, 51–52.

25. Nietzsche would have found the Copenhagen interpretation of quantum mechanics the zenith of this movement. See Kosso 1998, 14: "Quantum mechanics has made metaphysical anti-realists of many physicists." See Putnam 1990, 5, 11.

26. See Houlgate 1986, 183–84; Richardson 1996, 121, 263.

27. Heidegger, *N* 2:230; see also Schacht 1983, 192–93; Houlgate 1986, 63, 91; Haar 1996, 49, 63.

28. Heidegger, *Pm* 179; see also Heidegger, *N* 3:35, 3:37, 3:64, 3:124, 3:126, 3:235–36, 3:246, 4:132.

29. See Houlgate 1986, 48–49; Schacht 1983, 64, 96; Richardson 1996, 32, 77, 90; Green 2002, 7, 20; Danto 1965, 96, 80; Solomon 1988, 117.

30. R. K. Hill 2003, 195; see also Schacht 1983, 107, 108, 114; Richardson 1996, 108.

31. I use the *Nachlass* extensively here because first, the fact that it contains so many worthwhile passages of philosophy justifies its study on its own, even if it reduces claims about "what Nietzsche really thought," and second, because when used in conjunction with the published work it can be very illuminating, especially for my issues.

32. See Schacht 1983, 349; Richardson 1996, 27, 109, 142, 282; Wilcox 1974, 76.

33. In D. B. Allison 1977, 27; see also Schrift 1990, 42; Heidegger, *N* 3:82; Haar 1996, 51, 63.

34. Although Nietzsche often praises internal organization, unified rule, that is, "style" (Nietzsche, *GS* 290), this never goes so far as to eliminate all internal diversity or to close off future changes. "In contrast to the animals, man has cultivated an abundance of *contrary* drives and impulses within himself: thanks to this synthesis, he is master of the earth.—Moralities are the expression of locally limited orders of rank in his multifarious world of drives, so man should not perish through their contradictions. . . . The highest man would have the greatest multiplicity of drives, in the relatively greatest strength that can be endured. Indeed, where the plant 'man' shows himself strongest one finds instincts that conflict powerfully (for example, in Shakespeare), but are controlled" (Nietzsche, *WTP* 966; see also Nietzsche, *BGE* 212). Here it is quite clear that being in control does not preclude significant conflict.

35. Nietzsche, *WTP* 558. Alternatively, this quote can also be interpreted as a metaphysical view of a thing as the sum of its effects, which would then not solve the problem at hand; see, for example, *WTP* 557.

36. Nietzsche, *WTP* 473, from 1886–87; see also 567. This could alternately be read as a genealogical criticism of the in-itself.

37. See Richardson and Leiter 2001, 312; M. Clark 1990, 113–14, 117; Conway 1990, 97; Lacoue-Labarthe 1993, 5–9.

38. Peter Poellner claims that Nietzsche only has a pragmatic refutation of noumena, never attacking the idea's conceptual coherence. But he is rather selective in his supporting quotations. He writes: "Even in the well-known passage from *Twilight of the Idols* sometimes used as evidence for Nietzsche's rejection of the notion of a thing in itself as self-contradictory, what he in fact explicitly says is *not* that it is incoherent, but that knowledge of what it purports to apply to would be *futile*" (Richardson and Leiter 2001, 114). Poellner then quotes only Step Five! Step Five is indeed a pragmatic refutation, but if Nietzsche had been satisfied with that objection, he would not have added a further step, just as Poellner does not.

39. Quoted in Ansell Pearson 1991, 69 as K.G.W., VII, 3, 40 (53).

40. In D. B. Allison 1977, 15; see also Haar 1993, 86; M. Clark 1990, 109, 134; Ansell Pearson 1991, 293; Conway 1990, 101; Lacoue-Labarthe 1993, 16.

41. I am indebted to discussions with John Koritansky for this insight.

42. Derrida, *G* 19; see also Derrida, *MP* 136; Derrida, *EO* 8–9, 14, 46; Derrida, *SNS* 77.

43. Although Derrida consistently states that one of his goals in his many readings of Nietzsche is to save him from Heidegger's metaphysical reading, Derrida also recognizes that "the arguments of Heidegger's mighty tome [that is, *Nietzsche*] are much less simple than is generally admitted" (Derrida, *SNS* 73, bracketed comment added; see also 79).

44. Compare Nagel's "View from Nowhere."

## Chapter 5

1. Gilbert Ryle concluded a review published in *Mind* right after *Being and Time* was published that was balanced but expressed strong admiration: "Though I deplore the damage wrought upon his Metaphysics by the presuppositions which Heidegger has unconsciously inherited [Ryle reads him as too much under the influence of Husserl], I have nothing but admiration for his special undertaking and for such of his achievements in it as I can follow. . . . He shows himself to be a thinker of real importance by the immense subtlety and searchingness of his examination of consciousness, by the boldness and originality of his methods and conclusions, and by the unflagging energy with which he tries to think beyond the stock categories of orthodox philosophy and psychology" (in Murray 1978, 64, bracketed comment added). He then ends the review with a concern that Heidegger's later work would end in "a windy mysticism," a view that came to be commonly held in analytic circles, accompanied by a qualification that would be virtually unthinkable today for a major analytic figure to publish in the pages of *Mind:* "I hazard this opinion with humility and with reservations since I am well aware how far I have fallen short of understanding this difficult work" (64).

2. One of the more interesting features of Ryle's review of *Being and Time,* besides how familiar he is with the general field of phenomenology, is that he actually criticizes Heidegger for ignoring the fact that "the attempt to derive our knowledge of 'things' from our practical attitude towards tools breaks down; for to use a tool involves knowledge of what it is, what can be done [with] it, and what wants doing" (Murray 1978, 63).

3. Note that "existence" is used as a technical term for Dasein's way of Being, rather than just being real. Thus, to say that only Dasein *exists* is not solipsism, but merely means that nothing else has this mode of Being, even though many other things are real.

4. Notice how similar his discussion is to Nietzsche's on this topic.

5. This is a little simplistic; this stage still allows for an intermediate stage of repair. Full presence-at-hand would be a step farther removed from *praxis,* as discussed in Heidegger, *BT* §69b.

6. On this topic, see Rorty 1991b, 36, 38; Dreyfus and Hall 1992, 73, 87; Carman 2003, 158, 166; Richardson 1986, 67, 167; Dreyfus 1991, 262–63, 280.

7. Heidegger, *BT* 34/13; see also 244/200, 274/231, 361/313, 424/372.

8. Heidegger, *BP* 280; see also 228, 274; Heidegger, *PIS* 439–40, 38–39/17.

9. Heidegger, *PIK* 289; see also 48, 252; Heidegger, *KPM* 141–42. This similarity with Kant's project has not gone unnoticed by critics. See Versényi 1965, 23; Caputo 1987, 98; Macomber 1967, 29; Rorty 1989, 109–10; Richardson 1986, 12–13; Guignon 1993, 6; Blattner 1999, 261; Weatherston 2002, 25; Sherover 1971; Carman 2003, 11–13, 155; Lafont 2000, xiii, 154; Wolin 1990, 70; Glazebrook 2000, 39, 42; Wrathall and Malpas 2000, 44; Carr 1999, 130; Okrent 1988, 28, 271; Schürmann 1987, 143; Rudd 2003, 69.

10. Heidegger distinguishes three slightly different modes of inconspicuousness and of conspicuousness, but the distinctions do not matter for my presentations, so I will group them all under these titles.

11. Of course, this presencing is broadly understood as temporally diverse, rather than occurring only or even primarily in the present tense and as present to more aspects of us than just cognition.

12. See Sheehan 2001, 191.

13. Heidegger, *HCT* 112. Compare with Hegel: "Everything actual, in so far as it is true, is the Idea. . . . Every individual being is some one aspect of the Idea. . . . It is only in them altogether and in their relation that the notion is realized" (Hegel, *HL* 275, §213), and "the world is itself the idea" (Hegel, *HL* 291, §234R).

14. Compare Husserl: "It must always be borne in mind here that *whatever physical things are*—the only physical things about which we can make statements, the only ones about the being or non-being, the being-thus or being-otherwise of which we can disagree and make rational decisions—*they are as experienceable physical things.* . . . One must not let oneself be deceived by speaking of the physical thing as transcending consciousness or as 'existing in itself.' . . . This is true of any conceivable kind of transcendence which could be treated as either an actuality or a possibility. *An object existing in itself is never one with which consciousness or the Ego pertaining to consciousness has nothing to do*" (Husserl 1982, §47).

15. Heidegger, *BP* 175; see also 66, 69, 124, 157, 167, 255, 297; Heidegger, *BT* 170/132; Heidegger, *KPM* 165; Heidegger, *HCT* 166–67, 222–23.

16. Heidegger, *BT* 116/84; see also 141/106, 190–91/150; Heidegger, *BP* 164; Heidegger, *HCT* 191.

17. Heidegger, *BT* 101/71; see also Heidegger, *BP* 293; Heidegger, *OHF* 69, 73.

18. Hegel, *PS* 56–57, §89; see also Guignon 1983, 130, 175, 193, 203.

19. Heidegger, *HCT* 254–55; see also 207, 213, 231; Heidegger, *TDP* 41.

20. See Carman 2003, 136, 157, 168, 201–2; Vallicella 1983, 42; Cerbone 1995, 414; De Boer 2000, 170; Okrent 1988, 78; Olafson 1998, 48.

21. See Heidegger, *BT* 269/227; Heidegger, *PIS* 11, 17; Heidegger, *HCT* 217; Heidegger, *BP* 169, 175, 219, 221, 222–23; Heidegger, *MFL* 129, 194–95; Heidegger, *PIK* 19.

22. Something like this strategy is taken by Frede in Donagan, Perovich, and Wedin 1986, 137; Blattner 1994, 194; Dreyfus and Spinosa 1999, 72n16.

23. There is one commentator I found who would not consider this a problem in any way. Graham Harman makes the astonishing claim that "Heidegger turns out to be *the* philosopher of the noumenal" (Harman 2002, 160). He paren-

thetically continues that he uses this term "mostly for shock value, since there will turn out to be a crucial difference between Heidegger and Kant on this point," but the view is deeply integrated into his reading: "'Realism' will probably always be a loaded term that awakens dozens of misconceptions; for this reason, it should be avoided whenever possible. But if there were ever a philosopher who respected the force of a reality absolutely distinct from its conditions of being perceived, Martin Heidegger is that philosopher" (120). Harman does not state that he is only saying *this* for shock value.

24. One way to read the above passage is as a foreshadowing of the temporality of readiness-to-hand, specifically, that Dasein always fits entities into a past-present-future scheme (or schematism) upon encountering them. This still fits in nicely with my reading, since it requires Dasein for the entities to be temporal and thus to be what they are (see Heidegger, *HCT* 197, 214).

25. Heidegger, *HCT* 218; see also 197; Heidegger, *BP* 157; Heidegger, *MFL* 166; Van Buren 2002, 116; Dreyfus and Hall 1992, 93.

26. Heidegger, *PlS* 174–75; see also Heidegger, *BP* 206–7. This also shows that Graham Priest's criticism is wrong: "Heidegger simply identifies Logic with the received logical theory of his day, forgetting that it, too, is a product of a fallible history. It is an irony that a thinker of the acuity of Heidegger, who was so critical of his historical heritage, should have been blind to the possibility that people had got Logic wrong, which logical investigations in the second half of the twentieth century have shown to be a very real possibility" (Priest 2002, 248).

27. Heidegger, *MFL* 216–17; see also Heidegger, *BP* 210; Heidegger, *PlS* 125; Heidegger, *IPR* 14.

28. See Heidegger, *IPR* 26. Gadamer follows him in this. He rejects the similarity that Davidson finds in their views, responding (among other things): "Even the model proposition that Davidson employs—'snow is white'—seems strange to me from this viewpoint. Who uttered this, even if it is true?" (Hahn 1997, 127–28).

29. In several of his discussions from these early works, Heidegger complicates matters by using actual pictures as his examples, when his point is that we have no experience of a *mental* picture. Although one of his points is to contrast the experience of a real picture with our experiences to show the difference, it can confuse matters.

30. Davidson writes an anti-Cartesian (see Davidson, *Prob* 17; Davidson, *SIO* 47) passage that could be seamlessly dropped into any of a dozen of Heidegger's works: "There is a picture of the mind which has become so ingrained in our philosophical tradition that it is almost impossible to escape its influence. . . . The mind is a theater in which the conscious self watches a passing show (the shadows on the wall). The show consists of 'appearances,' sense data, qualia, what is 'given' in experience. What appear on the stage are not the ordinary objects in the world that the outer eye registers and the heart loves, but their purported representatives. Whatever we know about the world outside depends on what we can glean from the inner clues" (Davidson, *SIO* 34). Davidson is attacking the vulnerability of Quine's "proximal" stimulus to skepticism, but the similarity with Heidegger is striking.

31. Heidegger, *MFL* 125–26; see also Heidegger, *HCT* 35, 210, 266; Heidegger, *BT* 207/164; Heidegger, *BP* 208–9; Wrathall 1999, 75; Wolin 1993, 250; Versényi 1965, 34–35.

32. Heidegger, *BW* 122; see also 127; Heidegger, *KPM* 87; Heidegger, *BT* 261/218; Heidegger, *MFL* 217; Heidegger, *PlS* 350.

33. We can see an echo of this idea in Husserl's line, "so much illusion, so much being" (Husserl 1950, §46). Heidegger explicitly endorses this idea in 1938: "Illusion is still the clearing, is still be-ing" (Heidegger, *Mi* 94, §39).

34. Blattner suggests that Heidegger hints at "life" as a fourth distinct mode. See Blattner 1999.

35. It is not fully developed in *Being and Time,* but one way to place a closure on the modes of Being would be to link them directly to the temporal dimensions, thus permanently limiting them to three. This reading would emphasize Heidegger's Kantianism over his phenomenology.

36. I see no need to restrict possible disclosures to complementary ones, unless he means this term in the quantum mechanical sense of incompatible qualities shared by the same entity, such as light being both wave and particle.

37. Heidegger, *BT* 265/223; see also 60/36; Heidegger, *IPR* 29; Heidegger, *BP* 322; Heidegger, *BW* 105, 128; Sallis 1995b, 100.

38. See Sherover 1971, 241; Carman 2003, 180; Lafont 2000, 39, 77; Wolin 1990, 70.

39. Heidegger, *TDP* 56; see also 174; Sartre 1993. There is also a parallel here with the *Tractatus*'s solipsism: "I am my world. . . . Where *in* the world is a metaphysical subject to be found? You will say that this is exactly like the case of the eye and the visual field. But really you do *not* see the eye" (Wittgenstein 2001, 5.63, 5.633). Saul A. Kripke attributes Wittgenstein's view to the influence of Lichtenberg (see Kripke 1982, postscript, esp. 123n7).

40. Heidegger, *BP* 297; see also 278; Heidegger, *HCT* 238, 246; Heidegger, *BT* 156/120, 162/125.

41. One could even draw out a comparison here between the inability of external features to tell me what to do and Hegel's criticism of Kant's attempt to anchor experience on raw data. This argument, which Kierkegaard's *Fear and Trembling* and much of Sartre's work explores, shows the inescapability of freedom by demonstrating that factors weigh upon our decisions only after being assigned a weight by us, similar to the way sensory data gets synthesized before it can tell us about the external world.

42. See Heidegger, *BT* 119/86, 145/110–11, 160/123, 410/359; Heidegger, *BP* 277, 295.

43. Derrida, *SNS* 117; see also Derrida, *Pos* 54; Derrida, *MP* 64n39, 129n25; Derrida, *GT* 162; Derrida, *OS* 55; Derrida, *Ap* 77.

44. "Consciousness" is Sartre's term for Dasein, along with the "for-itself."

45. Heidegger, *BP* 227; see also Heidegger, *BT* 171/133, 274/231, 275/232, 276/233, 279/236, 293/249, 309/264, 351/304, 370/323.

46. It also seems that love could serve as a less angst-ridden candidate for playing this role, since I like to think that my wife and friends love me for me, not just because I show up regularly, earn money, tell amusing anecdotes, and so on. How-

ever, one could argue that if I hadn't come along, someone else would have married my wife, impregnated her, befriended my friends, and so on.

47. Heidegger, *FCM* 103; see also 82, 117, 121.

48. Heidegger, *HCT* 197; see also 319; Heidegger, *BT* 39/17; Heidegger, *BP* 16, 228.

49. Richardson 1986, 127; Pöggeler 1970, 287; Caputo 1987, 89; Caputo 1993, 172; Löwith 1995, 72; Rorty 1989, 110; Rorty 1991b, 42; Murray 1978, 331, 344–45.

50. See Guignon 1983, 215. The very end of what we have of *Being and Time* hints at this openness, which puts into question the answer posited at the beginning of the book: "Does *time* itself manifest itself as the horizon of *Being*?" (Heidegger, *BT* 488/437).

51. Interested readers are directed to forthcoming papers of mine which go into these topics in much greater detail; readers uninterested in Davidson's criticism can skip this section without losing the thread of the book's overall narrative.

52. See Dreyfus 1991; Haugeland in Dreyfus and Hall 1992; Mark Okrent's comments on Haugeland's piece in Okrent 1988, 293–94n19; Okrent 1989; Nulty 2003; Malpas 1992, 4, 264. There was even an NEH Summer Institute on "Heidegger and Davidson: Critics of Cartesianism" at the University of California, Santa Cruz, in 1990 that was attended by, among others, Davidson.

53. Davidson, *PDD* 729; see also Quine 1969, 26–27, 81; Quine 1987, 8; Quine 1992, 38.

54. By "theory of truth" Davidson does not mean an account of the nature of truth, but rather an attempt to grasp the meaning of a specific sentence by determining its truth conditions in a Tarskian T-sentence (see Davidson, "SCT" 289).

55. Davidson, "SCT" 301; see also Davidson, *SIO* 77, 174, 182, 215; Davidson, *Prob* 65, 183; Davidson, *TLH* 245. The public theory of meaning is "the nothing is hidden thesis" that Jerry Fodor and Ernest Lepore attribute to Davidson (see Stoecker 1993, 71).

56. Davidson, *SIO* 147–48 (bracketed comments added); see also Davidson, *TLH* 62, 107; Davidson, *RD* 82n5, 84; Davidson, *PDD* 80; Davidson, *ITI* 279.

57. In this way, Davidson's employment differs from that of Richard Grandy, who justifies his version, called the principle of humanity, as a "pragmatic constraint": "If a translation tells us that the other person's beliefs and desires are connected in a way that is too bizarre for us to make sense of, then the translation is *useless for our purposes*" (Grandy 1973, 443, italics added). The ontological or constitutive consequences also distinguish him from Martin Hollis, who claims that agreement on basic propositions must form a "bridgehead" for translation. For Hollis, this has no effect on what the speaker *really* means, just on what the interpreter must take her to mean: "What is *per impossible* here is not—or not without long argument—that S might see as red what the enquirer sees as green. It is, rather, the idea that translation can occur without there being the same facts of the world described in the two languages. Equally the moral is not so much that there is a single, objective and neutral world as that translation needs to presuppose one. Whether or not the world is a fact, it is an indispensable presupposition" (in Hollis and Lukes 1982, 74). Following Quine, Davidson gives no credence to the notion of what a speaker really means independently of what interpreters can take them to mean. Nor will

he end up allowing a distinction between "indispensable presuppositions" of translation and metaphysics.

58. Davidson, *Prob* 184; see also Davidson, *ITI* 27, 62, 197; Davidson, *Prob* 36, 50, 169–70, 190; Davidson, "SCT" 320; Davidson, *PDD* 600; though see also Davidson, *Prob* 184.

59. If a speaker cannot be interpreted, then her words have no meaning and there are no grounds for imputing rationality to her; reciprocally, to be capable of speech is to be interpretable by a rational being, which requires the interpreter to find the speaker rational. Davidson (who began his career as a classicist) thus rejoins the ancient meanings of logos: to be capable of speech and to be rational are one.

60. Davidson frequently distinguishes his work from Quine's, among other ways, by saying that he applies the principle of charity more broadly than Quine. See Davidson, *ITI* xix, 153, 228; Davidson, *SIO* 148.

61. Davidson, *ITI* 137; see also Davidson, *Prob* 98, 148, 157; Davidson, *TLH* 45.

62. Hahn 1999, 240; see also 246. In response to these (and other) criticisms, Davidson sometimes claims that his analyses of communication are not and never were intended to describe how this phenomenon actually works (see Davidson, *TLH* 111–12; Davidson, "SCT" 324–25; Davidson, *Prob* 127–28; Davidson, *RD* 81). However, I believe and have tried to show above that he did make such claims for radical interpretation. Furthermore, if his arguments are so disconnected from the actual workings of communication, even to the degree that by his own admission other explanations of successful communication might be possible (see Davidson, *RD* 79, 264; Davidson, *PDD* 331; Davidson, "SCT" 325n67), then the explanations or arguments derived from them do not seem capable of supporting the strong claims he wants them to. A full discussion of this, though, would take much too long; see Livingston in Dasenbrock 1993, 269–70, 275, for a good analysis of this topic.

63. Others have voiced these criticisms. Carlos Pereda makes no. 1 in Pereda 1998, 82; Andreas Kemmerling supports no. 2 in Stoecker 1993, 100–102; Stephen Mulhall makes all three criticisms in Mulhall 1987, 319–22, and 1990, 100–104; McDowell makes no. 2 in Malpas, Arnswald, and Kertscher 2002, 185; Hans-Johann Glock makes no. 2 in Glock 2003, 352; Rorty points out no. 3 in Rorty 1997, 62–64; and Dreyfus makes no. 3 central to his overall unfavorable comparison of Davidson with Heidegger in Dreyfus 1980.

64. This is one of the more curious features of Ryle's review of *Being and Time*. One would expect him to be highly receptive to this idea, but although he is generally sensitive to and appreciative of the book (see Murray 1978, 64), his main criticism here is that Heidegger overlooks the fact that knowing-how presupposes a more theoretical form of knowledge (see 63)!

65. Heidegger, *PIK* 16; see also Heidegger, *HCT* 185, 168–69, 187, 191; Heidegger, *BT* 95/67, 98/69, 104/74, 405/354; Heidegger, *BP* 165, 309; Dreyfus 1991, 51, 93.

66. Heidegger, *BT* 207/164; see also Heidegger, *PlS* 288; Heidegger, *HCT* 266; Heidegger, *BP* 208–9; Heidegger, *BW* 151–52, 408; Heidegger, *EGT* 64–66.

67. Although I have found a few commentators note how different Heideg-

ger's account of understanding is from Davidson's (see Dreyfus 1991, 218–19, 268; Nulty 2003, 34; Gustafsson 1998, 451), as far as I know only Stephen Mulhall points out this residue of empiricism: "Davidson's commitment to the notion of bare sounds and bare movements as the experiential basis from which any understanding of human speech and action must arise is strikingly analogous to empiricist sense-datum theories of knowledge. In both, it is presupposed that everyday experience of the world can be illuminatingly viewed as a logical or theoretical construction out of brute data—'the given'. . . . Even those who lead the hunt for empiricist dogmas can find that the task of extirpation must begin at home" (Mulhall 1990, 105–6; see also Mulhall 1987, 321–22).

68. Davidson, *SIO* 42; see also Davidson, *TLH* 56–58; Davidson, "Ext" 1–2; Davidson, *PDD* 105. Besides the problem of skepticism, Davidson also occasionally mentions the Sellarsian problem of the given, i.e., that the empirical input is incoherently pressed into serving both causal and justificatory purposes. See Davidson, "KPV" 286–87.

69. John Haugeland hits the nail on the head in his comparison of Heidegger and Davidson when he argues that Davidsonian interpretation is not ubiquitous, but arises only in instances of Heideggerian breakdown. However, he discusses this only in a few sentences in a footnote (in Dreyfus and Hall 1992, 42n24) to his influential essay, whose conclusion about the two philosophers is that "despite these significant differences [not the one treated in the footnote], the convergences are at least as important" (31, bracketed comment added). Mark Okrent comments on Haugeland's paper: "What makes it so good is that it articulates quite clearly why it is that some of us think that Heidegger and Donald Davidson share a great deal in common" (Okrent 1989, 75). I am claiming that this difference, among others, renders the two far less compatible than many critics have made them out.

70. See Davidson, *RD* 117, 145; Davidson, *TMK* 72; see also Davidson, *ITI* 196; Davidson, *RD* 158.

71. Heidegger, *HCT* 187; see also Heidegger, *MFL* 134; Heidegger, *BT* 58–56/59, 246/202; Heidegger, *IPR* 40, 60–61.

72. Davidson, *PDD* 225; see also Davidson, *TMK* 88; Quine 1966, 220; Russell 1959b, 200, 206.

73. Ian Hacking dryly comments on this passage: "Oddly, this is a question that seems never to surface for me" (Lepore 1986, 450).

74. Wittgenstein, *OC* §110; see also §148, §196, §204, §232, §344, §431; Wittgenstein, *Zet* §277, §416; Wittgenstein, RPP §151; Wittgenstein, *LWP* 2:21.

75. Wittgenstein, *RFM* 333, §4.31; see also 323, §6.21; Wittgenstein, *RPP* §314, §453; Wittgenstein, *Zet* §314–15; Wittgenstein, *OC* §148, §166, §212, §471.

76. Wittgenstein, *RFM* 341, §6.38; see also Wittgenstein, *OC* §46, §510–11; Wittgenstein, *RPP* §257, §723.

77. Davidson has on occasion allowed that de facto we do use other evidence such as earlier utterances, clothes, companions, and so on, a fact he points out to Fodor and Lepore with some indignation (Davidson, *RD* 81), but this doesn't change the fundamental point that "still, we can agree that pinning matters down must in the end depend on the details of speech behavior" (Davidson, *SIO* 115), and that evidence must be available to the radically ignorant interpreter.

78. Davidson, "Ext" 1–2; see also Davidson, *SIO* 42, 144–45; Davidson, *TLH* 56–58; Davidson, *PDD* 105.

79. Jeff Malpas's *Donald Davidson and the Mirror of Meaning*, which treats the connections between Heidegger and Davidson at some length, makes holism the key to understanding Davidson.

80. See Davidson, "KVP" 288. I assume Davidson would agree with Heidegger's pithy query: "The question of whether there is a world at all and whether its Being can be proved, makes no sense if it is raised by *Dasein* as Being-in-the-world; and who else would raise it?" (Heidegger, *BT* 246–47/202; see also Heidegger, *IPR* 241).

81. Interestingly, there are times when Davidson allows for this kind of immediate seeing rather than theoretical explicit interpretation (see Davidson, *PDD* 254; Davidson, *TLH* 137; Davidson, "KVP" 290).

82. Davidson's "improved" principle of charity, which aims at intelligibility in rather than agreement with the speaker (see Davidson, *ITI* xix, 282–83; Davidson, *PDD* 307), allows for a reconstruction of Davidson's thought that places him in much greater sympathy with conceptual schemes. Fully explaining this, as I do in my forthcoming articles, would take up too much space here and, besides, he does not consistently stick to it (see Davidson, *SIO* 211).

## Chapter 6

1. I will qualify this at the end of this chapter.

2. Heidegger, *BW* 294–95; Heidegger, *PR* 94; Heidegger, *N* 4:10, 4:48, 4:53; Heidegger, *Mi* 302.

3. Heidegger, *N* 2:80; see also 2:131; Heidegger, *PR* 55, 87; Heidegger, *ET* 150; Heidegger, *FoS* 61; Heidegger, *HH* 123.

4. This is reminiscent of Nietzsche's claim that "there are a thousand paths that have never yet been trodden—a thousand healths and hidden isles of life. Even now, man and man's earth are unexhausted and undiscovered" (Nietzsche, *Z* 189).

5. One interesting point is that while Heidegger can make no pronouncements about how the history of Being must occur, he does comment on its predilection for continuing to change. In a quasi-Hegelian move, he says that "that which has the character of destining moves, in itself, at any given time, toward a special moment that sends it into another destining, in which, however, it is not simply submerged and lost" (Heidegger, *QT* 37; see also Heidegger, *PT* 69). These epochs seem to possess an intrinsic impetus to self-overcoming, to changing-over into another period. In discussing Anaximander again, he says that "being is overcoming the unfit, that means not insisting upon endurance, because transition belongs to the essence of being" (Heidegger, *BCo* 105; see also 98). I'm not sure he has the right to make such claims, however.

6. Heidegger, *N* 3:19; see also 3:4–5, 2:186; Heidegger, *EGT* 78.

7. Heidegger, *N* 3:56; see also Heidegger, *Mi* 199. Heidegger even claims that "compared to [our encounter with Heraclitus's *polemos*], world wars remain superficial" (Heidegger, *Pm* 321; see also Heidegger, *WCT* 66; Derrida, *PoI* 310)!

8. Heidegger, *QT* 117; see also Heidegger, *IM* 110; Heidegger, *BQ* 48; Heidegger, *AM* 67.

9. In Horwich 1993, 330 (bracketed comment added); see also Kuhn 1970, 170, 206. Many have noted the similarities between Kuhn and continental thought, including Kuhn himself: "The philosophy I knew and had been exposed to, and the people in my environment to talk to, were all of them out of the English logical empiricist tradition, in one way or another. This was a tradition which by and large had no use for the continental and particularly the German philosophical tradition. I think, in some sense or other, I can be described as in some part having reinvented that tradition for myself" (Kuhn 2000, 321).

10. Strauss 1989, 38–39; see also von Herrmann in Macann 1996, 182; Pöggeler 1998, 43; Thomson 2005, 9, 114n76; Elden in Milchman and Rosenberg 2003, 194.

11. Heidegger, *ID* 66–67; see also Heidegger, *N* 3:164; Heidegger, *BW* 186, 436; Heidegger, *PR* 105.

12. Heidegger, *BW* 238; see also Heidegger, *CP* 123, §87; 168, §120; Heidegger, *EGT* 27.

13. This is also a way to understand Heidegger's constant insistence in the later work that Being is linguistic (see, for example, Heidegger, *BW* 413–14). Since humans need language to grasp reality, reality itself is permeated with language.

14. Heidegger, *BW* 332; see also *BW* 131, 335, 339.

15. Heidegger, *QT* 127; see also Heidegger, *PR* 27; Heidegger, *Zo* 25, 80; Heidegger, WCT 62.

16. Heidegger, *Zo* 110; see also 94; Heidegger, *PT* 28–29. Heidegger could count Davidson as an ally in this fight with his theory of anomalous monism: "The fact that the mental vocabulary is not fit for inclusion in sciences like physics or physiology cannot in itself be taken as impugning the reality of the states, events, and objects it is used to describe. . . . Physics does not speak to the interests that demand other ways of characterizing things" (Davidson, *SIO* 72). Davidson's views that mental events are identical with physical events and that each mental event can individually be causally explained would not be acceptable to Heidegger, however.

17. Gadamer 1981, 104; see also Gadamer 1976b, 50, 207; Gadamer 1981, 41; Gadamer 1994, 21; Gadamer 1989, 255; in Michelfelder and Palmer 1989, 23, 104; in Sallis 1995a, 94.

18. I will retain "man" as a technical term despite its sexist connotations, since it is so deeply embedded in Heidegger's work.

19. Heidegger, *BW* 186; see also 217, 234, 240, 260; Heidegger, *P* 147; Heidegger, *N* 4:152; Heidegger, *BCo* 62; Heidegger, *PR* 69; Heidegger, *OBT* 99; Heidegger, *WCT* 126; Heidegger, *Pm* 279, 294; Heidegger, *HH* 91; Heidegger, *Mi* 185.

20. Putnam briefly echoes this argument decades later to undermine the notion of reference that is required by realism: "If the mind does not have the ability to grasp external things or forms directly, then no *mental* act can give it the ability to single out a correspondence (or anything else external, for that matter)" (Putnam 1983, 207).

21. Heidegger, *BW* 329; see also 211, 248; Heidegger, *WCT* 121; Heidegger,

*DT* 83; Heidegger, *Zo* 176–77; Heidegger, *BW* 412; Heidegger, *CP* 169, §122, 177, §133, 179, §135, 201, §164; Heidegger, *BQ* 179; Heidegger, *QT* 38–39, 145–47.

22. Heidegger, *WCT* 79; see also 106, 144; Heidegger, *N* 4:216; Heidegger, *PR* 70, 94; Heidegger, *Pm* 283; Heidegger, *TB* 12.

23. Heidegger, *ID* 31–32; see also Heidegger, *BW* 228–29, 235; Heidegger, *DT* 84; Heidegger, *Zo* 176–80; Heidegger, *CP* 169, §123.

24. Heidegger, *BW* 217; see also 240, 256, 416; Heidegger, *P* 76–77; Heidegger, *N* 4:218; Heidegger, *HH* 91.

25. Note that at other times Heidegger denies subjectivistic readings of *Being and Time.* See, for example, Heidegger, *PR* 86; Heidegger, *CP* 182–83, §138; Heidegger, *TB* 27; Heidegger, *Zo* 116, 191; Heidegger, *BW* 138; Heidegger, *Mi* 123, 188. At times he says that he needed to use metaphysical language in order to be understood in a metaphysical time, but he was using it precisely in order to overcome it. "*Sein und Zeit,* which can only be *one* exigent pathway among other possible pathways, *must* unavoidably look like 'metaphysics' and 'anthropology,' nay it has to make itself initially 'understandable' with the help of 'metaphysics' and 'anthropology' by going through them, which means that *Sein und Zeit* has to reckon with all possible and proximate misunderstandings" (Heidegger, *Mi* 125; see also 187). According to this self-reading, *Being and Time* did escape metaphysics but only by going through it, which inevitably leads less adept readers to misinterpret it as stuck there. As can be seen, I am one of those unfortunate readers.

26. Heidegger, *CP* 168, §120; see also 227, §202; Heidegger, *BQ* 80, 181; Heidegger, *FoS* 8; Heidegger, *P* 7; Heidegger, *BW* 238; Haar 1993, 176.

27. Heidegger, *N* 4:145; see also Heidegger, *BCo* 66; Heidegger, *WT* 106; Heidegger, *WIP* 87.

28. See Kant, *PFM* 65/318; Kant, *C1* B145–46; Kant, *C2* 48/46–47; Kant, *C1* A122; Heidegger, *BT* 271/228, 330/284; Heidegger, *N* 3:119; Heidegger, *FoS* 18; Heidegger, *PR* 65; De Boer 2000, 211.

29. As we will see, Derrida uses this term to describe some of his basic terms as well.

30. Heidegger, *TB* 52; see also Heidegger, *BW* 433; Heidegger, *IM* 30. This view is a possible inspiration for Jean-François Lyotard's suspicion of meta-narratives.

31. Wittgenstein, *Zet* §358. See Forster 2004 for an informative discussion of this issue.

32. Wittgenstein, *OC* §148; see also §204, §475; Wittgenstein, *PI* §217, §87, §211–13; see also 200, §485.

33. For those interested, my next book will be an extended analysis of the relationship between Wittgenstein and Heidegger's thought.

34. Heidegger, *BW* 176–77; see also 122, 446–47; Heidegger, *ET* 86; Heidegger, *BQ* 19, 82, 103; Heidegger, *WIT* 189; Heidegger, *CP* 252, §233.

35. Though there are still occasional mentions of the parallel accounts, such as this: "By recalling the beginning (*aletheia*) as well as by being mindful of the ground of the possibility of correctness (*adaequatio*), we come across the same thing: *the openness of the open*" (Heidegger, *CP* 237, §214).

36. See Heidegger, *BQ* 15–16, where he ridicules claims that the naturalness

of thinking in terms of correspondence explains its historical longevity, rather than the other way around.

37. Heidegger, *P* 55; see also 50, 62; Heidegger, *CP* 236, §213; Heidegger, *IM* 46, 62, 96–97, 130, 132–33, 201; Heidegger, *Pm* 168, 180, 280; Heidegger, *BQ* 14, 103; Heidegger, *N* 1:149, 3:34; Heidegger, *Mi* 331.

38. Though at least at one point Heidegger is explicitly "nostalgic" in John D. Caputo's sense, that is, he seems to think that the Greeks got it right in a trans-epochal way: "The reciprocal counter-essence between *aletheia* and *lethe* holds sway as the basic feature of beings as a whole, in the midst of which Greek humanity endures its history. It is almost as if what was always already nearby and experienced is explicitly put into words only in the age of the completion of Greek humanity" (Heidegger, *P* 88). Though contrast with this: "There is no destinal epoch of enowning. . . . For the Greeks, being *as* being was neither thought nor raised as a question" (Heidegger, *FoS* 61).

39. Heidegger, *BQ* 106; see also 102; Heidegger, *ET* 9, 74, 86; Heidegger, *Pm* 182; Heidegger, *EF* 62, 64, 76.

40. Heidegger, *ET* 25; see also 91, 93, 226.

41. Heidegger, *ET* 67; see also 104; Heidegger, *BW* 128, 448; Heidegger, *CP* 174, §129; Heidegger, *Mi* 193, 229.

42. Heidegger, *Zo* 182. Although he usually rejects the term "consciousness," he uses it here in order to bring his work into relation with Freud in a discussion with the psychologist Medard Boss.

43. Heidegger, *IM* 187. Note that towards the end of his career, perhaps under pressure from objections raised by the eminent Plato scholar Friedländer, Heidegger abandoned his historical account: "We must acknowledge the fact that *alētheia,* unconcealment in the sense of the clearing of presence, was originally experienced only as *orthotēs,* as the correctness of representations and statements. But then the assertion about the essential transformation of truth, that is, from unconcealment to correctness, is also untenable" (Heidegger, *BW* 447). However, this is the account he held for most of his career and that has become influential as his official doctrine.

44. Poetry is the best model we still have of an alternate form of discourse: "An example of an outstanding non-objectifying thinking and speaking is poetry" (Heidegger, *PT* 30). Poetry does not deal with entities as objects or impose expectations, but opens itself to the things that they are, allowing itself to be surprised, and bending language to accommodate the things' particularities. The poet renounces control by being sensitively attuned to the nuances of language and receptive to the unnoticed aspects of the world. As Wallace Stevens put it in "Study of Two Pears": "The pears are not viols, / Nudes or bottles. / They resemble nothing else. . . . The pears are not seen / As the observer wills." (I owe this quote to Ken Alpern.) Furthermore, poetry escapes questions of correctness and correspondence (see Rorty 1991b, 36, 38). Although poems can be judged better and worse, there is no "correct" poetic representation of an entity or event; there can be many good poems about a single thing which differ dramatically, thus escaping R2–R4. "The responding in which man authentically listens to the appeal of language is that which speaks in the element of poetry. The more poetic a poet is—

the freer (that is, the more open and ready for the unforeseen) his saying—the greater is the purity with which he submits what he says to an ever more painstaking listening, and the further what he says is from the mere propositional statement that is dealt with solely in regard to its correctness or incorrectness" (Heidegger, *PLT* 216).

45. Heidegger, *CP* 179, §134 (bracketed comments added); see also 221, §193; Heidegger, *P* 103; Heidegger, *DT* 58–59.

46. Heidegger, *Pm* 354; see also 343, 361; Heidegger, *QT* 107, 150, 167; Heidegger, *FoS* 76; Heidegger, *PR* 23; Heidegger, *BW* 440.

47. Heidegger, *N* 4:28 (bracketed comment added); see also 4:86, 4:103; Heidegger, *Pm* 300.

48. Heidegger, *N* 3:219; see also 3:239, 4:84; Heidegger, *PR* 27, 55, 77, 119; Heidegger, *Zo* 128; Heidegger, *CP* 76, §52; Heidegger, *BW* 303.

49. Heidegger, *Zo* 107; see also Heidegger, *BW* 302; Heidegger, *IM* 190, 210, 216.

50. Heidegger, *P* 137 (italics and bracketed comments added): see also 156; Heidegger, *N* 3:178, 3:190–91, 4:241; Heidegger, *QT* 79–80.

51. Heidegger, *BW* 332; see also 131–32; Heidegger, *DT* 56; Heidegger, *PR* 80; Heidegger, *Mi* 137. Once again we can note an important overlap here with Levinas. Levinas too warns of the dangers inherent in "the myth of a legislative consciousness" (Levinas 1996, 14) for whom "knowledge is a relation of the *Same* with the *Other* in which the Other is reduced to the Same and divested of its strangeness, in which thinking relates itself to the other but the other is no longer other as such. . . . It is perhaps this adequation of knowledge to the entity which permits it to be said that one only learns what one already knows, that nothing absolutely new, nothing other, nothing strange, nothing transcendent, could either affect or truly enlarge a mind committed to contemplating everything" (151).

52. Heidegger, *BW* 331 (all italics added); see also "the destining of revealing is as such, *in every one of its modes,* and therefore necessarily, *danger*" (331, first italics added).

53. Heidegger, *BW* 332–33 (italics added); see also 339; Heidegger, *QT* 37, 41, 43.

54. Heidegger, *FoS* 72; see also 75; Heidegger, *N* 3:89. Here we can again see how Levinas's relation with the Other parallels Heidegger's relation with Being and beings.

55. Heidegger, *PLT* 111; see also Heidegger, *QT* 84, 100; Heidegger, *BW* 172, 228–29; Heidegger, *P* 75.

56. Heidegger, *BW* 151; see also 156–57, 170, 194; Heidegger, *FoS* 80; Heidegger, *Zo* 62, 71; Heidegger, *CP* 316, §262; Heidegger, *PT* 25.

57. See Heidegger, *BW* 125; Heidegger, *BQ* 120–21, 133; Heidegger, *IM* 137.

58. See Haugeland's "Truth and Finitude: Heidegger's Transcendental Existentialism" in Wrathall and Malpas 2000, for a helpful comparison of this attitude in early Heidegger and Kuhn.

59. The best example of this method is the first section of "The Origin of the Work of Art," where Heidegger's attempts to fit an artwork into the categories of object and tool fail to account for its distinctiveness, leading him to create an entirely new category for works of art with its own terms. The fact that the inadequate

categories happen to be the two non-Dasein modes of Being from *Being and Time* could be a tacit self-criticism.

60. Heidegger, *IM* 147; see also Heidegger, *DT* 82; Heidegger, *PT* 27; Heidegger, *H* 125; Heidegger, *WCT* 203, 209.

61. Note that he *could* simply impose his will on a substance like plastic, which shows that plastic is much better *Bestand* than wood and explains why "the making of [technology] never directly effects the happening of truth" (Heidegger, *BW* 189), substituting "technology" for "equipment" here. Plastic offers little resistance to our will and so does not require us to respond to much outside of our desires.

62. Heidegger would thus disagree with Davidson's optimism about the speaker's ability to do away with linguistic conventions and create new ones, "the power of innovation and creativity in the use of language" (Davidson, *TLH* 143). The reason such linguistic innovations succeed, Heidegger would say, is that they strike deeper chords that individual speakers do not create, else such new phrases could not communicate at all. At one point, Davidson comes close to agreeing with this point. In discussing the way words change meaning in conversations such as Socratic *elenchus,* he states that "a stubbornly deviant learner, on the other hand, may have an insight into a deep similarity of cases that others have missed, and she may carry the community with her. This is exactly what Socrates does, or attempts to do, when he tries to persuade his companions to stop using the word 'just' to apply to acts in which someone returns harm for harm, and to apply it instead to acts that return benefit for harm" (259). Rather than "sheer invention" (143) like a malaprop or an arbitrary imposition like Humpty Dumpty's (and Keith Donnellan's) redefinition of "glory" (see 97), these are motivated (even if unpredictable) shifts in meaning that bring to the surface connections that had not been noticed or emphasized before.

63. Heidegger, *BW* 410–11; see also 418, 423; Heidegger, *PR* 96; Heidegger, *N* 4:200; Heidegger, *PT* 25; Heidegger, *PLT* 181; Gadamer 1976b, 50.

64. Hegel notices the problem that Heidegger deals with (especially in *PR*), namely, the ungroundedness of thought and logic, and how this is in tension with logic's self-conception: "The manner in which Formal Logic establishes this law of thought [that is, the law of sufficient ground] sets a bad example to other sciences. Formal Logic asks these sciences not to accept their subject-matter as it is immediately given; and yet herself lays down a law of thought without deducing it." However, he goes on to claim that showing how these laws "are really grades in the self-determination of thought" is both "the true business of logic" and the means by which "they are understood and demonstrated" (Hegel, *HL* 176, §121R, bracketed comment added).

65. Heidegger, *Pm* 293; see also 235; Heidegger, *WCT* 154; Heidegger, *N* 4:22; Heidegger, *CP* 325, §265.

66. Hegel, the thinker who anticipated Heidegger's conception of ICS, also discovered this antinomy of freedom. See Hegel, *HL* 206, §145R; 220, §158R. As I will discuss in the next chapter, I think that at the time of his death, Foucault was working on a conception of subjectivity that would have accommodated these issues.

67. This idea was touched on with the concepts of guilt and nullity in *Being and Time* (Heidegger, *BT* 330/284).

68. The analytic philosopher of free will Galen Strawson makes the same argument (in wonderfully clear terms) which he calls the Basic Argument, though his focus is on the issue of moral responsibility (Strawson 1994). He bemoans the fact that this argument is so little known and given so little attention. He should have looked at more continental philosophy than Sartre as a (correct) target of this argument to see that Heidegger offered it decades ago, placing it into continental work ever since.

69. Heidegger, *PR* 53; see also Heidegger, *PLT* 6; Heidegger, *PT* 53; Heidegger, *BW* 372.

70. Once again, we can make a connection with Wittgenstein, who often uses the act of searching for the right word as an example of a moment when we assume we are being very active and conscious, but if we pay close (phenomenological) attention, in fact often little in the way of thought or decision occurs. "But I do not always have to make judgments, give explanations; often I might only say: 'It simply isn't right yet.' I am dissatisfied, I go on looking. At last a word comes: '*That's* it!' *Sometimes* I can say why" (Wittgenstein, *PI* II.xi, p. 186). These are cases where "in philosophy one is in constant danger of producing . . . a myth of mental processes. Instead of simply saying what anyone knows and must admit" (Wittgenstein, *Zet* §211).

71. See Heidegger, *BW* 220, 411, 418, 423; Heidegger, *Pm* 236; Heidegger, *CP* 325, §265; Heidegger, *P* 49; Heidegger, *OWL* 76; Heidegger, *N* 3:187, 3:214; Heidegger, *PR* 47, 96; Heidegger, *PLT* 181, 209.

72. Heidegger, *Pm* 279; see also Heidegger, *BW* 217, 384; Heidegger, *IM* 166–67.

73. To put it in terms of the *Euthyphro*'s piety dilemma, in *Being and Time* tools were usable because Dasein (projected goals which required equipment and so) used them; now man is called to use tools because they present themselves as to-be-used.

74. Heidegger, *N* 4:93 (bracketed comments added); see also 3:240, 4:89, 4:108, 4:139; Heidegger, *PLT* 111, 127; Heidegger, *PR* 80; Heidegger, *WT* 97.

75. Heidegger, *FoS* 56; see also Heidegger, *WCT* 115, 126, 142; Heidegger, *OWL* 76; Heidegger, *BW* 136; Heidegger, *CP* 167, §120.

76. Heidegger is not consistent with these terms, and his grasp of this issue evolved over his career, reaching maturity in the 1940s, I believe.

77. See Sheehan 2001 for a good discussion of this topic. See also Thomson 2000.

78. The German word for "a being," *das Seiende,* is not the same as the word for "Being," *Sein.*

79. Heidegger, *TB* 8 (bracketed comments added); see also Heidegger, *EGT* 51; Heidegger, *BW* 443; Heidegger, *N* 3:189–90.

80. Heidegger, *EGT* 86 (bracketed comments added); see also Heidegger, *P* 113; Heidegger, *PR* 61; Heidegger, *Pm* 302; Heidegger, *BW* 436.

81. Heidegger, *EHP* 43; see also Heidegger, *QT* 45; Heidegger, *EGT* 51, 93; Heidegger, *PT* 56; Heidegger, *BW* 136, 448; Heidegger, *Pm* 310; Heidegger, *OWL* 13.

82. Heidegger, *QT* 39; see also 44; Heidegger, *PR* 108; Heidegger, *BW* 335; Caputo 1987, 115, 180–81; Caputo 1993, 30; Schürmann 1987, 130.

83. Heidegger, *PR* 113. Hegel again anticipates both Heidegger (and Derrida) here. Since there is nothing outside of Spirit's self-creation, there can be no goal external to the process to make it "serious." Furthermore, the act of creation leads to the reabsorption of what is created. Thus Hegel describes all of reality as a kind of play: "The movement of the notion is as it were to be looked upon merely as play: the other which it sets up is in reality not an other" (Hegel, *HL* 225, §161R).

84. See Heidegger, *EGT* 26, 87, 99, 122; Heidegger, *BW* 263, 448; Heidegger, *CP* 180, §136; Heidegger, *BQ* 178.

85. See Heidegger, *BQ* 132; Heidegger, *BW* 329; Heidegger, *Pm* 257.

86. See Heidegger, *BW* 241, 338; Heidegger, *EGT* 36; Heidegger, *IM* 186; Heidegger, *Mi* 211.

87. Heidegger, *BW* 234; see also 231, 245, 252, 259.

88. Heidegger, *BW* 217; see also 245; Heidegger, *EGT* 36; Krell 1986, 92.

89. Of course, one could simply ask of these metaphysical or onto-theological justifications what the imprimatur of a god or a Form adds to the way we do things. What is actually gained with the magic words "omniscience" or "Reality Itself"? See Thomas Nagel's "The Absurd" in Nagel 1979, for an interesting analytic expression of this idea.

90. Heidegger, *QT* 104; see also Heidegger, *N* 4:44. This is a little confusing; what Nietzsche calls passive nihilism is what most thinkers, including Heidegger, simply call nihilism, and what Nietzsche calls active nihilism is in his opinion the overcoming of the loss of values which most simply call nihilism. Heidegger is claiming that this overcoming (Nietzsche's active nihilism) does not cure but actually exacerbates the problem (Nietzsche's passive nihilism).

91. Heidegger, *BW* 251; see also Heidegger, *QT* 102–3, 134; Heidegger, *N* 4:203.

92. Heidegger, *DT* 55; see also Heidegger, *CP* 163, §118; Heidegger, *Pm* 308; Heidegger, *WCT* 121; Heidegger, *PR* 86; Heidegger, *TB* 23.

93. Heidegger, *BW* 167; see also 169–70, 187–88, 337; Heidegger, *ET* 155; Heidegger, *CP* 98, §72; Heidegger, *IM* 11; Heidegger, *EHP* 56.

94. "The countryman knows that his possessions stand under the constant menace of the weather, yet he finds that everything around him is at peace and delightful. He waits confidently for the future gift of the field and the grapevine. Fruit and man are protected in the favor that permeates earth and heaven and that grants something which will remain" (Heidegger, *EHP* 74; see also Heidegger, *BW* 159, 320). The point isn't the romanticized picture of the happy farmer, but his awareness of the degree to which he is participating in a larger "system," such as the fourfold or Aristotle's four causes, rather than controlling the entire process from the outside. Heidegger does believe that we can have the proper attitude toward technological items; it is just a little harder than with traditional tools (see Heidegger, *DT* 54).

95. See Heidegger, *BW* 256, 416; Heidegger, *N* 1:194, 4:94; Heidegger, *FoS* 73; Heidegger, *CP* 163, §118; 169, §122; 211, §175; Heidegger, *Mi* 176, 192–93; Heidegger, *HH* 76; Heidegger, *ET* 153; Sheehan in Polt and Fried 2001, 13; Thomson 2001, 260; Thomson 2005, 170; Haar 1993, 61; Kolb 1986, 181.

## Chapter 7

1. Elden 2001; Milchman and Rosenberg 2003.

2. On the connections between the two and the dearth of critical attention, see Rajchman 1985, 109; Elden 2001, 1; Milchman and Rosenberg 2003, 1; Clifford in Dallery and Scott 1990, 107; Okrent 1988, 278.

3. As well as his focus on his contemporary situation in "What Is Enlightenment?" (see Foucault, *FR* 38), though I won't be discussing this.

4. Foucault, *MC* 130–31 (bracketed comments added); see also 135, 224, 243.

5. See, for example, Dreyfus and Rabinow 1983, 109: Foucault "studies the emergence of a battle which defines and clears a space. Subjects do not first preexist and later enter into combat or harmony. In genealogy subjects emerge on a field of battle and play their roles, there and there alone. The world is not a play which simply masks a truer reality that exists behind the scenes. It is as it appears."

6. See Foucault, *SMD* 173: "We should always be wary of blaming poor old Plato for everything we want to banish."

7. Foucault, *BC* 89–90 (bracketed comments added); see also xv. Compare also with an even more direct echo of Heidegger's claim from a 1982 lecture: "We pose the question of the subject in the realm of practice . . . quite spontaneously—I do not mean 'quite naturally,' but I should say rather 'quite historically,' and through a necessity that weighs heavily on us" (Foucault, *Herm* 318).

8. Foucault, *PK* 118–19; see also 108, 183; Foucault, *FL* 198, 201; Foucault, *AK* 68.

9. See, for example, Nietzsche, *Z* 1.12, 2.18; Heidegger, *N* 3:4, 3:19.

10. Kuhn himself notes the similarity of his history of science with Foucault's archaeology at 2000 14n2.

11. Foucault, *OT* 74; see also 158, 208, 217.

12. Foucault, *OT* 252–53 (bracketed comments added); see also 344–45, 387; Foucault, *AK* 41; Foucault, *FL* 95.

13. Foucault, *AK* 117. Some commentators have noted the similarity to Heidegger's clearing. See Dreyfus 1996, 4; Dreyfus and Rabinow 1983, 122; Rajchman 1985, 116; Schürmann 1987, 318n14; Kolb 1986, 149. Given its centrality to science, the *episteme* also bears a resemblance to Kuhn's paradigm.

14. Foucault, *AK* 47–48; see also 41, 54, 72, 191.

15. Foucault, *AK* 63; see also 129; Foucault, *FL* 40, 58.

16. See Foucault, *AK* 60, 117, 121, 210; Foucault, *FL* 49.

17. Some commentators have noted the simultaneous Kantian influence and change. See Hoy 1986, 33; Hacking 2002, 5; D'Amico 1989, 90; Flynn 1989, 137; Rajchman 1985, 103; Bearn in Krausz 1989, 223.

18. See Foucault, *LCP* 42; Foucault, *FL* 60, 63, 99, 101; Foucault, *OT* 342, 385–87.

19. Foucault, *OT* 304; see also 337, 340, 345.

20. Foucault, *FL* 470. See Foucault, *AK* 110–11, for an extraordinarily Heideggerian formulation of language: "Although the statement cannot be hidden, it is not visible either. . . . Perhaps it is like the over-familiar that constantly eludes one. . . . It has this quasi-invisibility of the 'there is,' which is effaced in the very

thing of which one can say: 'there is this or that thing'. . . . In the examination of language, one must suspend, not only the point of view of the 'signified' (we are used to this by now), but also that of the 'signifier,' and so reveal the fact that, here and there, in relation to possible domains of objects and subjects, in relation to other possible formulations and re-uses, there is *language*."

21. Foucault, *OT* xiii–xiv; see also 200, 275, 345.

22. Foucault, *FL* 52–53; see also 59; Foucault, *EW* 2:301, 2:332–33. Gadamer, Heidegger's third great disciple along with Foucault and Derrida, gives a similar narrative: "The almost mythical status of self-consciousness—which was adopted in its apodictic self-certainty and elevated to the status origin and justification of all validity, and the ideal of an ultimate grounding in general, over which apriorism and empiricism fight—loses its credibility in the face of the priority of the domain of language, a domain that we cannot undermine and in which all consciousness and all knowledge articulates itself. From Nietzsche we learned to doubt the grounding of truth in the self-certainty of self-consciousness. Through Freud we became acquainted with the astonishing scientific discoveries that resulted from taking these doubts seriously. And in Heidegger's fundamental critique of the concept of consciousness we have seen the conceptual prejudice that stems from Greek Logos-philosophy and that, in the modern turn, put the concept of the subject in the center. All of this lent a certain primacy to the 'linguisticality' of our experience of the world. Over against the illusion of self-consciousness as well as the naïveté of a positive concept of facts, the midworld of language has proven itself to be the true dimension of that which is given" (Michelfelder and Palmer 1989, 29).

23. Foucault, *PPC* 29; see also Foucault, *FL* 355; Foucault, *EW* 3:299, 3:313. This can also be read as a criticism of Heidegger's more nostalgic moments.

24. Foucault, *FL* 379; see also 450, 455; Foucault, *AK* 17; Foucault, *EW* 3:239–40.

25. Foucault, *LCP* 200; see also Foucault, *EW* 1:12, 2:308, 2:314, 2:324.

26. Foucault, *PK* 92; see also Foucault, *SMD* 24; Foucault, *EW* 3:224, 3:336.

27. Foucault, *SMD* 13; see also Foucault, *FL* 258–60; Foucault, *EW* 3:324, 3:340; Foucault, *PP* 4.

28. Generally (though he does not stick to this distinction throughout), Foucault uses "sex" as a technical term to refer to the parts of the body that have been grouped together as sexual, such as the genitalia, whereas "sexuality" refers to the social and behavioral manifestations that get grouped together under the head of "sexual," similar to the common use of the term "gender" when opposed to "sex." He believes that neither grouping is inherently necessary or historically stable. While this insight seems less plausible when applied to sex, he does not think that the two categories can be completely separated. There are no R1 Independent facts about sex; we get to sex only through sexuality. It is a dichotomy that can shed light but ultimately must be deconstructed.

29. Foucault, *HS* 70; see also 155; Foucault, *FL* 208; Armstrong 1992, 187.

30. See Foucault, *HS* 12, 21, 27, 30, 32, 49, 55, 61, 131.

31. Foucault, *DP* 102; see also Foucault, *HS* 72, 94; Foucault, *Ab* 52.

32. Foucault, *HS* 105; see also 44, 48, 114, 127; Foucault, *Ab* 202; Foucault, *PK* 210, 219; Foucault, *FR* 62; Caputo and Yount 1993, 247–48; Visker 1995, 111.

33. Foucault, *Ab* 223; see also 147; Foucault, *PK* 211; Foucault, *EW* 1:89, 1:99; Foucault, *PP* 7.

34. Foucault, *PK* 98; see also Foucault, *PK* 97; Foucault, *SMD* 29–30, 45. For discussions of Foucault's rejection of an essential human nature, see Hutton in Foucault, *TS* 127; Rorty 1991b, 197; Dreyfus and Rabinow 1983, 258; Bernstein 1992, 146; Rajchman 1985, 101; Flynn 1989, 135; Hacking in Hoy 1986, 36; McWhorter 1999, 30–31.

35. Foucault, *PK* 74; see also Foucault, *SMD* 28; Foucault, *FL* 158, 165; Foucault, *EW* 3:2–4; Foucault, *PP* 15, 56, 238.

36. Foucault, *DP* 295; see also 141, 155; Foucault, *EW* 3:254; Foucault, *PP* 52, 56.

37. Foucault, *FL* 214; see also 201; Foucault, *HS* 69, 78, 124, 155–56; Foucault, *HB* vii–x; Foucault, *EW* 1:81.

38. In this way, sexuality also functions as an incoherent empirical-transcendental doublet, since normalcy is an empirical generalization of what people de facto do, but also a normative prescription of what people de jure ought to do. If the facts about sexual behavior are derived from actual behavior, then that would seem to be what holds the authority, overruling prescriptions, even if they are derived from what most people do.

39. See Foucault, *HS* 83–84. In Foucault *DP*, the main transition is a refinement in the techniques of power itself from the costly and inefficient threat of public punishment to the efficient and ubiquitous sense of being watched; in *HS*, on the other hand, Foucault talks of a change in the understanding of power which, at least in the period under discussion there, has never been repressive.

40. As uncharitable as speculation about such matters is, it is hard not to wonder whether Foucault's reportedly defiant behavior in the face of early warnings about AIDS was at least partially influenced by his deep suspicion of medical expertise and concocted dangers of sexuality, especially since this suspicion was initially not uncommon.

41. Foucault, *DP* 27–28 (bracketed comments added); see also 185, 209; Foucault, *LCP* 200–201; Foucault, *EW* 1:8, 1:12; Foucault, *PP* 13.

42. Foucault, *HS* 94–95; see also Foucault, PK 159; Foucault, *SMD* 28; Foucault, *Ab* 236.

43. Foucault, *FL* 285. On Foucault's analysis of truth, see Allen 1993, 164; Flynn 1989, 135; Foucault, "MF" 315; Dreyfus and Rabinow 1983, 31.

44. Foucault, *PoT* 52; see also Foucault, *Ab* 130; Foucault, *PK* 112; Foucault, *SMD* 164.

45. Foucault, *HB* viii; see also Foucault, *Ab* 71. In his last phase he will become fascinated with "ancient medical regimens" of sexual acts, partially because "instead of being organized according to the binary form of permitted and forbidden, they suggest a constant oscillation between more and less" (Foucault, *UP* 116). However, see Foucault, *PP* 266, 305–6.

46. Foucault, *PK* 118. As with Heidegger, we can see resonances here with the later Wittgenstein: "If the true is what is grounded, then the ground is not *true*, nor yet false" (Wittgenstein, *OC* §205).

47. This is why Carl G. Hempel's contribution to the *Starmaking* discussion of Goodman's work seems so wrong to me. He states: "In the search for scientifically

right versions, the stubbornness of facts shows itself in the realization that we cannot well use just any criteria we please. If, for example, we were to measure the duration of an event by the number of pulse beats of the Dalai Lama during that event, we would obtain a world version in which the rate of change of all processes would depend on the Dalai Lama's state of health; thus, during periods of what is usually called increased pulse rate, the axial rotation of the earth would be slower, the period of every pendulum would be longer, etc., than during periods of a normal pulse. In addition to containing these curious causal connections, the version in question would have the grave flaw of not permitting the formulation of any general and reasonably simple laws of nature. . . . I think he does not do full justice to the stubbornness of facts" (McCormick 1996, 131). This view assumes that there are ahistorical, acultural standards of non-curious connections and simple laws, as if there were not innumerable ways to "do full justice to the stubbornness of facts." Quine showed this in formal terms to analytic philosophy, while Foucault finds actual historical cases of "curious connections."

48. Foucault, *UP* 6; see also Foucault, *FL* 450; Foucault, *PoT* 179–80; Foucault, *FR* 48–49, 338.

49. Foucault, *EW* 3:326; see also 1:88, 1:177; Foucault, *FL* 450–51.

50. Han believes that Heidegger offered Foucault promising solutions to his problems, but that Foucault did not follow his lead (see Han 2002, 57–59). Obviously, I disagree with the latter part of this claim.

51. Heidegger, *P* 138; see also Heidegger, *Pm* 285, 334; Heidegger, *QT* 153; Heidegger, *DT* 77–78.

52. At Foucault, *UP* 3, he describes the de-familiarization and suspension of presuppositions about sexuality that he is attempting at the beginning of his study as a kind of "bracketing." Derrida might see here an invocation of the muses, especially at the beginning of an epic about the Greeks.

53. See Foucault, *TS* 22; Foucault, *EW* 1:93; Foucault, *Herm* 419, 461.

54. Foucault, *FL* 444; see also Foucault, *Herm* 253, 364, 408.

55. See late support for A3 and A6 at Foucault, *FL* 363; Foucault, *UP* 35, 187, 250; Foucault, *Herm* 462.

56. Foucault, *PoT* 197; see also Foucault, *FR* 341, 361; Foucault, *RC* 184; Foucault, *CS* 239–40.

57. Foucault, *UP* 32; see also 250; Foucault, *PoT* 197; Foucault, *EW* 1:180; Foucault, *Herm* 13, 112, 251, 365, 446.

58. Foucault, *FR* 341; see also Foucault, *UP* 89–91; Foucault, *CS* 185; Foucault, *Herm* 424; Foucault, *FS* 166.

59. One can see hints of Sartre here.

60. Foucault, *PoT* 200. He does suggest at one point at least (Foucault, *FS* 96–97) that the Socratic elenchus is an important predecessor in demanding a one-on-one account of a person's bios, to say nothing of Socrates' claim, particularly in the *Apology*, that Socrates had been charged by god to help people with the state of their souls, as well as the insistence on rituals of purification in, for example, the *Phaedo*.

61. Foucault, *RC* 156; see also 187; Foucault, *PoT* 221; Foucault, *FR* 361; Foucault, *EW* 1:84; Foucault, *Herm* 218, 422, 503; Foucault, *UP* 41.

62. Foucault, *RC* 186–87; see also 196; Foucault, *FR* 358; Foucault, *CS* 68; Foucault, *Herm* 256.

63. Foucault, *FR* 366; see also Foucault, *PoT* 226; Foucault, *RC* 183; Foucault, *FR* 362; Foucault, *EW* 1:84, 3:310–11; Foucault, *FS* 143–44.

64. Foucault, *PoT* 228; see also Foucault, *EW* 3:334. In keeping with ED, Foucault even suggests that this use of the self to produce truth is a source of what I have called A5 Active Knower, where understanding the subject's transcendental structures is the key to comprehending all of knowledge (see Foucault, *FR* 371; Foucault, *FS* 107).

65. Forster 1998, 407. This is particularly surprising given the fact that Davidson has done extensive empirical psychological work in his field, though he rarely refers to or, explicitly at least, uses it in his philosophy.

66. Despite Davidson's rhetoric in "On the Very Idea of a Conceptual Scheme" he does not abandon the idea of conceptual schemes, and despite his improved principle of charity he still claims that the vast majority of beliefs are and must be shared.

67. I am presently working on a paper exploring this difference.

68. See Foucault, *LCP* 228; Foucault, *PPC* 154–56; Foucault, *FL* 423; Foucault, *Herm* 252.

69. For a fascinating account of this phenomenon along with a good analysis of Foucault, see Ladelle McWhorter's *Bodies and Pleasures: Foucault and the Politics of Sexual Normalization.*

70. See Lyotard 1988; Levinas 1969, 72–73; Levinas 1996, 23; Derrida, *G* 127, Derrida 2000c, 15.

71. Wittgenstein, *OC* §609 (italics in original); see also §92, §217, §233, §610–12.

72. See, for example, Fraser 1981; Taylor in Hoy 1986; Habermas in Hoy 1986; Habermas 1987, 286; Cutrofello 1994, 27, 83.

73. Foucault, *FL* 433; see also 218, 369; Foucault, *HS* 60; Foucault, *FR* 245, 343, 350, 362.

74. Foucault, *DP* 217; see also Foucault, *FL* 354–55; Foucault, *PPC* 29, 35; Foucault, *PP* 56–57.

75. See Foucault, *FL* 68, 73; Foucault, *DP* 176; Foucault, *EW* 3:200.

76. In Caputo and Yount 1993, 253; see also Bernstein 1992, 164; Rajchman 1985, 62, 122–23.

## Chapter 8

1. In Madison 1993, 178. Searle protests that a critical response to his review by Mackey "is guilty of precisely the sort of misrepresentation that he accuses me of" since it expands his claim, meant only to apply to *Of Grammatology,* to "the absurd view that Derrida has never discussed any other philosophers on any other subjects in any other of his works" (273n2). However, Searle describes what he is doing in the section where this comment on Derrida's reading appears as "a *general assessment* of the deconstruction of the distinction between speech and writ-

ing" (178, italics added). The more important issue, though, isn't about whether Derrida "discusses" anyone else, but whether he "grounds" his thought on "an actual reading" of "leading" figures. In other words, does he (1) pick important figures, (2) read them well rather than willfully, and (3) make a solid case for his assertions based on the evidence he finds in these texts. I assume that Searle stands by his denial of these points throughout Derrida's work.

2. This is one of the two main features that Rorty finds objectionable in Derrida's thought. I will discuss the other below. See in Dasenbrock 1989, 205–6, 213.

3. Derrida, *EO* 86–87; Derrida, *PoI* 212; Derrida, *FWT* 165; in Wood and Bernasconi 1988, 1; in Sallis 1993, 180.

4. Derrida, *WD* 252–53; see also Derrida, *Ltd* 55; Derrida, *PoI* 188, 429; Derrida, *SP* 102; Derrida, "SOR" 137. His style is perhaps at its most disorienting in the works from the mid-1970s, for example, parts of *Dissemination, Glas,* and *The Post Card.*

5. See Derrida, *PoI* 217, 376, 411; Derrida, *TFS* 54–55.

6. This is why one aspect of Searle's criticism, i.e., that Derrida was not grounding his thought on "the leading figures in the philosophical tradition," shows a misunderstanding of Derrida's thought. Derrida says repeatedly that, while he does work on the "major" figures, he is also extremely interested in "rooting out minor or marginalized texts" (Derrida, *PoI* 85; see also 224, 244; Derrida, *G* 162; Derrida, *WD* 32; Derrida, *Ltd* 44; Derrida, *TFS* 4–5; Derrida, *FWT* 7).

7. Sallis 1993, 217; see also Derrida, *Ltd* 73–74; Derrida, *Dis* 150; Derrida, *TP* 63–64, 306, 368.

8. Inconsistently, Searle follows up his objection that speech and writing play almost no role in the great philosophers' works with a criticism that Derrida's claims are cheap, since they are just "based on a redefinition" of speech and writing (Madison 1993, 178). Certainly redefinitions can be criticized, but if Searle recognizes that this is what Derrida is doing, then he should not express dismay and outrage that Derrida finds the issue where Searle does not. Either Derrida is using these terms in their normal meanings and Searle can complain that these philosophers did not address these issues, or Derrida is redefining them and can claim that the philosophers are addressing these terms so defined, and Searle can attack the redefinition, but I don't think he can attack both simultaneously.

9. Derrida, *G* 167; see also 56; Derrida, *WD* 267; Staten 1986, 61.

10. Derrida, *G* 3; see also 11–12, 29–30; Derrida, *SP* 16; Derrida, *MP* 73.

11. Derrida, *G* 7; see also 99, 120, 166, 198, 283; Derrida, *SP* 99; Derrida, *Dis* 4, 76; Derrida, "SOR" 114; Derrida, *PC* 468–89.

12. Derrida, *Pos* 22; see also Derrida, *SP* 16, 22, 40, 76; Derrida, *G* 98, 138, 166; Derrida, *PC* 194, 465; Derrida, *Gl* 250, 253; Derrida, *MP* xix, 73, 297.

13. Derrida, *G* 49; see also 159. Compare with the *Tractatus* 2.0211: "If the world had no substance, then whether a proposition had sense would depend on whether another proposition was true."

14. Derrida, *EO* 120 (bracketed comments added); see also 56, 140; Fenves 1993, 123.

15. Derrida, *MP* 312; see also Derrida, *G* 8, 167, 294–95, 312.

16. Derrida, *G* 160; see also 286; Derrida, *SP* 51; Derrida, *PoI* 135, 374; Wood and Bernasconi 1988, 88–89; Derrida, *PC* 23; Derrida, *MP* 221, 229, 257.

17. Geach and Black 1960, 69–70; see also 58, 104; Burge 2005, 132.

18. Derrida, *G* 198; see also 166, 283; Derrida, *Dis* 4, 149.

19. Derrida, *G* 39 (italics in original); see also Derrida, *MP* 187; Derrida, *PoI* 357; Derrida, *PC* 232; Staten 1986, 155.

20. Derrida, *Ltd* 136; see also Derrida, *PoI* 171, 372–73; Royle 2000, 293; Wheeler 2000, 21, 152, 166.

21. Derrida, *GT* 100; see also Derrida, *G* 49; Derrida, *Pos* 28; Derrida, *Dis* 4–5, 209–10; Derrida, *PC* 27, 192.

22. Derrida, *G* 159 (bracketed comments added, italics in original); see also 61, 167, 243, 288; Derrida, *MO* 64; Derrida, *GT* 121–22, 170; Derrida, *EO* 152–53; Derrida, *Dis* 128, 193, 258.

23. Goodman 1978, 3. Despite portraying himself as a peacemaker between the camps, when Putnam notes a similarity between Derrida and Goodman, this does not strike him as an opportunity for comparison and dialogue, but rather as evidence of how the latter "has reached conclusions in some ways *perilously* close to Derrida's" (Putnam 1992, 109, italics added).

24. Derrida, *G* 91, 73; see also Derrida, *Dis* 328; Derrida, *SP* 49; Derrida, *PC* 191.

25. Derrida, *Ltd* 148; see also Derrida, *Pos* 44, 91; Derrida, *Dis* 335; Derrida, *PoI* 356.

26. Derrida, *G* 20; see also 98, 138, 153–54, 166, 286, 289; Derrida, *SP* 22.

27. Derrida, *MO* 39; see also Derrida, *Pos* 59–60; Derrida, *TFS* 84–85; Derrida 1995b 91; Derrida, *PC* 100, 171, 186; Derrida, *FWT* 5; Derrida, "SOR" 136.

28. Derrida, *G* 158; see also Derrida, *MO* 23; Derrida, *Dis* 96, 129, 340; Derrida, *PoI* 384.

29. See Derrida, *FWT* 48–49, 52, 112, 176; Derrida, *EO* 53, 184; Fenves 1993, 151, 166; Derrida, *MO* 60; Derrida 2000a, 404; Derrida 2000c, 29; Derrida, *Ltd* 76; Derrida, *WD* 226–27; Derrida, *GT* 123, 156; Derrida, *Dis* 299.

30. Derrida, *Ltd* 75–76; see also 36; Derrida, *G* 246; Derrida, *FWT* 65; Derrida, *MP* 21, 266; Derrida, "SOR" 135; Derrida, *AF* 59; Derrida, *EO* 30, 32; Derrida, *Dis* 95, 183. This also fits in with one of the overarching, guiding thoughts of this book and continental thought in general, namely, that individual thinkers can only think by means of the issues of other philosophers, even when they are being innovative and original (how else is one to know what is original, after all?). This is one reason why doing philosophy and the history of philosophy are not separated by most continental philosophers.

31. Derrida, *WD* 280; see also 274, 289; Derrida, *G* 50, 157; Derrida, *PC* 261; Derrida, *Ltd* 149; Derrida, *MP* 317; Derrida, *Dis* 89; Derrida, *EO* 69.

32. See Derrida, *G* 195, 200, 215, 216–17, 229, 243, 246, 275, 313; Derrida, *SP* 52; Derrida, *Dis* 11.

33. See, for example, Derrida, *SP* 88; Derrida, *Ltd* 56; Derrida, *Pos* 8–9; Derrida, *WD* 78; Derrida, *MP* 8.

34. Derrida, *MP* 9; see also 134; Derrida, *TP* 119; Wood and Bernasconi 1988, 84; Llewelyn 1986, 74.

35. Derrida, *WD* 264; see also 20, 284; Derrida, *SP* 57n6; Derrida, *MP* 60; Derrida, *DN* 9; Derrida, *AF* 118, 124.

36. Derrida, *TFS* 80; see also Derrida, *Pos* 68; Derrida 2000c, 139; Derrida, *PoI*

82, 356; Royle 2000, 282–83; Wood and Bernasconi 1988, 4; Caputo in Madison 1993, 163.

37. Derrida, *G* 162, though this does not mean the traditional version of empiricism, which will be subject to deconstruction as well (see Derrida, *MP* 192; Derrida, *SP* 45n4).

38. Derrida, *GT* 48; see also 4; Derrida, *TFS* 48; Derrida, *Ltd* 105; Wheeler 2000, 18, 63, 168.

39. Derrida, *MP* 323; see also 326–27; Derrida, *Ltd* 48, 77, 82, 89–90, 133. Stanley Cavell offers an interesting rebuttal to Derrida's charge that actually brings Austin's views much closer to Derrida's. Cavell argues that Austin's many discussions of such topics as excuses and insincerity show him to be deeply convinced of and concerned with the permanent structural possibilities of all the ways in which our speech "misfires," just the issue Derrida thinks Austin underplays. Interestingly, Cavell employs a Derridean method of reading by starting from Austin's apparently unimportant and universally ignored quotation of the *Hyppolytus* (see Cavell 1995, 52–53, 79).

40. Derrida, *Ltd* 125; see also 127; Derrida, *Gl* 94. Derrida makes a parallel criticism of Husserl, whose phenomenology should equally refrain from such selective attention, at Derrida, *SP* 20–21, 101.

41. Derrida, *PoI* 389–90. Derrida makes the same point about dates (see 378). Although not reached for the same reasons, this idea makes an interesting comparison with Wittgenstein's claim that "it is not possible that there should have been only one occasion on which only one person obeyed a rule" (Wittgenstein, *PI* §199). Glendinning 1998 has an excellent discussion of this similarity.

42. Derrida, *Ltd* 53; see also 40, 79, 119, 129; Derrida 2000a, 402; Derrida, *TFS* 72.

43. Derrida, *Ltd* 119; see also 64, 70, 100, 115–16, 137; Derrida, *G* 244. I assume that it is an "ideal" limit because, as mentioned, language still requires a minimal identity of the "same" sign across contexts.

44. Derrida, *MP* 320–21; see also Derrida, *SNS* 123, 133; Derrida, *PoI* 175.

45. Derrida, *MO* 61; Derrida, *EO* 152–53; Wood and Bernasconi 1988, 5. Other examples of the originary supplement would be a mirror without a preceding object to reflect, citations without a primary text cited, an echo before the original voice (Derrida, *Dis* 316, 323), the Nietzschean "perspectives with no reference outside perspective" (Derrida, *TP* 244), a graft or prosthesis "without a body proper" (Derrida, *Dis* 11; Derrida, *MO*), representation before perception (Derrida, *SP* 45n4), or, in a specific example he analyzes, copies without an original (Derrida, *TP* 195, 220). In all of these examples, "all oppositions based on the distinction between the original and the derived, the simple and the repeated, the first and the second, etc., lose their pertinence from the moment everything 'begins' by following a vestige" (Derrida, *Dis* 330).

46. Derrida, *Pos* 63; see also Derrida, *Ltd* 143–44; Derrida, *PoI* 198–99, 349; Derrida, *G* 149–50, 158; Derrida, *WD* 32, 44; Derrida, *Ltd* 115–16, 144–45, 148; Derrida, *Dis* 54, 64; Derrida, *TFS* 48.

47. Geach and Black 1960, 116. One point that does not fit the strict Derridean schema is the rest of this quote: "To this end a symbolic language would be

best adapted, by means of which we could directly express thoughts in *written or printed symbols without the intervention of spoken language*" (116, italics added). Here Frege finds that the precision of writing makes it superior to speech, apparently escaping phonocentrism. However, Derrida is ready for this, showing how Rousseau makes a similar point: "While distrusting writing, and indeed because of that distrust, Rousseau wants to exhaust all its univocity, clarity, precision. These values are negative when they chill the expression of passion; but they are positive when they avoid trouble, ambiguity" (Derrida, *G* 227; see also 166). In other words, writing in the narrow sense can sometimes possess phonocentric value, but only to the extent that its precision undoes the harmful effects of arche-writing. Writing's exactitude can make the signifiers particularly transparent as possible (R5), thus letting the signified become as present as possible. This actually retains the structure of phonocentrism, even if, paradoxically, by valuing writing in the common sense. "A precise and exact language should be absolutely univocal and literal: non-metaphorical. The language is written, and pro-regresses, to the extent that it masters or effaces the figure in itself" (271). Literal writing maintains the values of phonocentrism; only an embrace of phenomena such as metaphors or undecidable words would truly allow for arche-writing. Although I find this fairly convincing, one does begin to suspect that Derrida's deconstruction is "unfalsifiable." The next question, though, is to what degree this is a criterion relevant to his work. I will address this issue below.

48. See Derrida, *Dis* 152. At the risk of going even farther out on an allusive limb, I am reminded here of chapter 11 of the *Tao Te Ching:* "We shape clay into a pot, / but it is the emptiness inside / that holds whatever we want. / We hammer wood for a house, / but it is the inner space / that makes it livable. / We work with being, / but non-being is what we use" (Mitchell 1988). Heidegger echoes this idea in his discussion of a jug; although in one sense it consists of solid clay, in another sense "the empty space, this nothing of the jug, is what the jug is as the holding vessel" (Heidegger, *PLT* 169).

49. The later Wittgenstein would say that this is precisely why language is *not* in a predicament.

50. Derrida, *PoI* 374; see also Derrida, *MP* 221, 229, 244; Derrida, *FWT* 18.

51. In Dasenbrock 1989, 194; see also 201; Norris 1987, 94, 183; Norris 1997, 4, 83. Many commentators read Derrida as pursuing a transcendental inquiry. See Dews 1995, 129; A. W. Moore 2000, 362; Habermas 1987, 181; Rorty 1991b, 93–94, 101; Wood in Wood and Bernasconi 1988, 64; Gasché 1986, 2, 147, 184, 198; Gasché in Arac, Godzich, and Martin 1983, 161. In response to Rorty's use of Gasché 1986 to bolster his own depiction of early Derrida as a transcendental philosopher, Gasché qualifies these descriptions in Gasché 1994, for example, at 4, 19, and 49. However, the later volume retains a great deal of this same language.

52. Though Rorty was once concerned to defend Heidegger from the same charge. See Rorty 1982, 39–40.

53. Quoted, for example, in Rorty's discussion of Derrida at 1982, 101; see also in Dasenbrock 1989, 214n9; Rorty 1991b, 128.

54. Derrida, *MP* 6. This quote is qualified in a way I will discuss below; see also Derrida, *SP* 65; Derrida, *G* 166.

55. Derrida, *Ltd* 70; see also 57, 62; Derrida, *FWT* 174; Derrida, *PoI* 224.

56. Derrida, *MP* 6; see also 63; Derrida, *MO* 46; Wood and Bernasconi 1988, 85.

57. See Derrida 2001a 406; Derrida 1999, 25, 34; Derrida, *MO* 26. In *Glas,* he asks if there is not always an unassimilable element to every system that plays "an almost transcendental role" (Derrida, *Gl* 151–62). Although he certainly adheres to the inherent incompletability of systems (see 166), this description is triply qualified by calling it "almost" transcendental, putting it into a question, and splitting that question by eleven pages of text.

58. Derrida, *G* 167; see also 62; Derrida 2000b, 383; Derrida, *PoI* 208, 210, 322; Derrida, *Dis* 109; Derrida, *WD* 270; Derrida, *TP* 81, 145; Derrida, *TFS* 34; Wood and Bernasconi 1988, 85. This is how Derrida qualifies the *MP* 6 quote mentioned above; he crosses through the first "is" in the sentence, "If *différance* is (and I also cross out the 'is') what makes possible the presentation of the being-present, it is never presented as such." Although it functions as a transcendental condition, *différance* is not a being capable of becoming present. Conveying this by crossing out the "is" is an obvious allusion to Heidegger's crossing out the word "Being" in his later work: "The crossing out of this word initially has only a preventive role, namely, that of preventing the almost ineradicable habit of representing 'being' as something standing somewhere on its own that then on occasion first comes face-to-face with human beings" (Heidegger, *Pm* 310). Heidegger crosses out "Being" in order to prevent the onto-theological confusion of the ontological difference or, without the jargon, treating Being as if it were an object that has the option of either coming into contact with us or staying away, instead of the mere fact of the presence of things to us. This presence is not an entity and cannot cease without ourselves ending, that is, Mutual Interdependence.

59. Derrida likes the German word *Auseinandersetzung* to describe his relationship to Heidegger and tries to render it into French with *explication avec,* most literally translated as "explanation with." Richard Wolin's translation of this phrase as "simple interpretation," as well as his rendition of the entire sentence containing it, is one of Derrida's more serious concerns about Wolin's translation, though he has many other concerns as well (see Derrida, *PoI* 182–83, 441–42).

60. Derrida, *MP* 62; see also 123; Derrida, *Pos* 54; Derrida, *DN* 14; Derrida, *WD* 280; Derrida, *SP* 26n5; Marrati 2005, 123.

61. See Derrida, *G* 12, 143; Derrida, *MP* 48; Derrida, *EO* 114; Sallis 1987, 181, 193–94; Derrida, *Pos* 55.

62. Sallis 1987, 189; see also Derrida, *PoI* 182, 311–12; Derrida, *TFS* 9; Derrida, *Pos* 10; Derrida, *MP* 65, 108, 135; Derrida, *WD* 281–82; Derrida, *OS* 107–8.

63. Derrida, *MP* 22; see also 67; Derrida, *SP* 67; Derrida, *G* 23, 143; Derrida, *Dis* 352; Derrida, "SOR" 136; Derrida, *PC* 66.

64. In Royle 2000, 291; see also Derrida, *PoI* 131, 305; Derrida, *FWT* 80–81; Derrida, *DN* 14; Derrida, *FWT* 81; Derrida, "SOR" 115, 130, 136; Marrati 2005, 122.

65. Derrida, *MP* 64 (italics added); see also 136; Derrida, *WD* 36, 198; Derrida, *Pos* 54; Derrida, *TFS* 7; Derrida, *Ap* 79.

66. Derrida, *EO* 175; see also Derrida, *Ltd* 53; Derrida, *PoI* 360; Derrida 1999, 80; Derrida, *FWT* 5.

67. Levinas 1996, 8; see also 74; Levinas 1985, 90; Derrida, *TFS* 83–84.

68. Levinas 1996, 19; see also 70, 76; Levinas 1969, 62; Derrida, *WD* 273.

69. Derrida, *WD* 95; see also *WD* 103, 114; Derrida, *PoI* 360; Derrida, *FWT* 51, 59; Derrida 1999, 115; Derrida 2000c, 77; Derrida, *FWT* 5.

70. Derrida, *PoI* 387; see also Derrida, *G* 5; Derrida 1999, 77; Derrida, *TFS* 20–21, 83–84; Derrida, *FWT* 4; Derrida, "SOR" 137. Another name for this category is "the unnameable." See Derrida, *G* 14, 286; Derrida, *WD* 293; Derrida 2000c 25.

71. Derrida, *Ltd* 144–45; see also 148; Derrida, *Dis* 54, 64; Derrida, *TFS* 48.

72. Derrida, *Dis* 63; see also Derrida, *G* 163; Derrida, *Pos* 63; Derrida, *TP* 303; Derrida, *Gl* 5.

73. Heidegger, *WCT* 174; see also, for example, Heidegger, *BW* 149, 226, 233, 256.

74. Derrida, *EO* 120 (italics added); see also 170; Derrida, *SNS* 51; Derrida, *Dis* 70, 97–98, 138, 221; Derrida, *TP* 381.

75. Heidegger, *N* 3:187; see also, for example, 3:19; Heidegger, *BW* 294–95; Foucault, *OT* 168; though see also Foucault, *EW* 1:9.

76. Derrida, *Dis* 345. This is why the apparent unfalsifiability of Derrida's readings alluded to above might not pose a problem for him. Although he does think interpretation is answerable to the text, that "data" profoundly underdetermine what we make of it. Since it can be interpreted in many ways, a crucial test of a reading is rather difficult. There are obvious parallels to Quine's critique of Popper here.

77. Derrida, *MP* 22; see also 51; Derrida, *WD* 24; Derrida, *Dis* 352.

78. Derrida, *PoI* 224; see also 265, 285, 358; Derrida, *Pos* 56; Wood and Bernasconi 1988, 4.

79. Derrida, *PoI* 82; see also Derrida, *G* 102; Derrida, *Dis* 126; Derrida, *WD* 308n3; Derrida, *Gl* 229.

80. Derrida 2000b, 353; see also Derrida, *FWT* 170; Derrida, *SP* 65–66; Derrida, *TP* 73; Derrida, *MP* 219; Derrida, *PC* 29; Royle 2000, 300.

81. Derrida, *WD* 279; see also in Fenves 1993, 146; Derrida, *Dis* 333–34. Many of Derrida's criticisms are explicitly directed at structuralism, but he also says that he was reacting to Foucault as well. See, for example, Derrida, *PoI* 416.

82. Whether this is a fair characterization of Foucault, or for that matter of Heidegger, is an issue I will not take up here.

83. Derrida, *MP* 135; see also Derrida, *PoI* 82; Derrida, *Dis* 207; Derrida, *TFS* 33; Derrida, *Gl* 233.

84. This is a little unfair to the subtleties of Heidegger's reading of Nietzsche.

85. See Derrida, *G* 215, 314; Derrida 1999, 76, 80; Derrida 2000a, 404; Derrida, *Dis* 5, 128, 229, 316.

86. Derrida, *EO* 114; see also Derrida, *OS* 69; Derrida, *MO* 62; Sallis 1987, 193–94.

87. Derrida, *Pos* 12; see also Derrida, *PoI* 257; Fenves 1993, 168; Derrida, *SNS* 117–19; Derrida, *SP* 128n14; Derrida, *MP* 215.

88. Derrida, *WD* 36; see also 267–68, 289; Derrida, *G* 154, 314; Derrida 2000a, 403.

89. Heidegger 1973, 85. See also Heidegger, *Mi* 354: "The overcoming of machination cannot be brought about immediately through some kind of de-

struction or even by 'refuting' metaphysics. All immediate negation leads to nothing." Compare this with Derrida, "SOR" 113. David Wood also quotes this passage as a particularly Derridean moment in Silverman and Aylesworth 1990, 56. Interestingly, Heidegger presents his most Derridean book—his reading of Kant in *KPM*—in terms startlingly similar to Derrida's description of his purpose in reading Aristotle against Heidegger: "The interpretation of Kant's transcendental philosophy with a view to 'schematism' and 'the power of imagination' *exaggerates* deliberately in order to show that already *within* the history of metaphysics itself there is the necessity of a rigorous transformation of the question of metaphysics" (Heidegger, *Mi* 335).

## Conclusion

1. For the sake of convenience, throughout the conclusion I will be using the perspective of the first *Critique* to denote both the actual *Critique of Pure Reason* and the *Prolegomena to Any Future Metaphysics,* in other words, Kant's general views on speculative or theoretical reason. Similarly, the second *Critique* view refers to both the *Critique of Practical Reason* and the *Foundations of the Metaphysics of Morals,* that is, the practical perspective.

2. Kant, *C1* B72, A230/B283, A286/B342.

3. Kant, *C1* B138–39, A230/B283, though see B148.

4. Kant, *FMM* 43/426. Kant concedes at one point that some experience may be required to apply the law (5/389) and perhaps for judgments about imperfect duties, but he contradicts this requirement at another point (Kant, *C2* 38/36) and repeatedly insists on the need for a pure philosophy of morals (Kant, *FMM* 26n/410, 59/442; Kant, *C2* 8–9/8).

5. Kant, *FMM* 79/460–61; see also 75–76/457, 64/447; Kant, *C2* 34/33, C2 90/86–87.

6. Kant, *FMM* 26–27/410–11; see also Kant, *C2* 74/70–71.

7. Kant, *FMM* 18/402; see also 37–38/421; Kant, *C2* 26/27.

8. "When we observe ourselves in any transgression of a duty, we find that we do not actually will that our maxim should become a universal law. That is impossible for us; rather, the contrary of this maxim should remain as a law generally, and we only take the liberty of making an exception to it for ourselves. . . . Consequently, if we weighed everything from one and the same standpoint, namely, reason, we would come upon a contradiction in our will, viz., that a certain principle is objectively necessary as a universal law and yet subjectively does not hold universally but rather admits exceptions" (Kant, *FMM* 41/424; see also 72/455).

9. Kant, *FMM* 5/389; see also 24/408, 28/412, 42/425, 44/427; Kant, *C2* 15/15, 17/19, 32/32, 85/81.

10. Kant, *C2* 19/20–21; see also 24/25. This quote, ruling out *any* distinctions among rational beings, shows that it is not the *empirical* nature of anthropology that he is rejecting.

11. Kant's claim that we come across the moral law as a "fact of reason" which admits of no further explanation or deduction (see Kant, *C2* 36/35, 47–49/46–

47, 57/55) strikes me as incompatible with his actual "deductions" of the categorical imperative from the form of universal lawfulness.

12. Indeed, Kant even holds out the holy will as the model we should strive for and can almost achieve when we shut off inclinations (see Kant, *C2* 125/118, 33/32).

13. Heidegger even quotes *C1* B145–46, Kant's discussion of the inexplicability of our transcendental faculties at *PIK* 99, though he does not make as much of this passage as my reading would expect him to.

14. Heidegger roughly equates Dasein with Kant's subject at Heidegger, *PIK* 226, 283.

15. Heidegger, *BT* 168/130; see also 213/169, 220/176, 224/179, 312/267, 318/273, 344/298, 346/299, 403/352, 435/383.

16. In Geach and Black 1960, 122 (bracketed comments added); see also 128, 145; Burge 2005, 132.

17. In Geach and Black 1960, 126; see also 107, 134; Burge 2005, 213, 237, 247.

18. This view was stronger and more prevalent before about 1950, but it still underlies much thought after this point to various degrees. Even recent thinkers such as Davidson or Putnam who reject correspondence with independent reality dismiss the notion that truth can change out of hand. See Davidson, "SCT" 307–8; Davidson, *TMK* 17–18; Putnam 1981, x, 54–55; Putnam 1983, xvii, 84, 86; Putnam 1988, 115; Putnam 1990, 41, 115; in Clark and Hale 1994, 242. Obviously, this claim needs a great deal of unpacking to justify it.

19. As mentioned above, my next book will be an in-depth analysis of Wittgenstein and Heidegger.

# Bibliography

## Authors Cited by Abbreviations


Davidson, Donald. "Comments on Karlovy Vary Papers." In Kotatko, Pagin, and Segal 2001, 285–307.

———. *Essays on Actions and Events.* 2nd ed. Oxford: Clarendon, 2001.

———. "Externalisms." In Kotatko, Pagin, and Segal 2001, 1–16.

———. *Inquiries into Truth and Interpretation.* 2nd ed. Oxford: Clarendon, 2001.

———. *Problems of Rationality.* Oxford: Clarendon, 2004.

———. "Radical Interpretation Interpreted." In *Philosophical Perspectives 8: Logic and Language,* 121–28. Ed. James E. Tomberlin. Atascadero, Calif.: Ridgeview, 1994.

———. "The Structure and Content of Truth." *Journal of Philosophy* 87, no. 6 (June 1990): 279–328.

———. *Subjective, Intersubjective, Objective.* Oxford: Clarendon, 2001.

———. *Truth, Language, and History.* Oxford: Clarendon, 2005.

Derrida, Jacques. *Adieu to Emmanuel Levinas.* Trans. Pascale-Anne Brault and Michael Naas. Stanford: Stanford University Press, 1999.

———. *Aporias.* Trans. Thomas Dutoit. Stanford: Stanford University Press, 1993.

———. *The Archaeology of the Frivolous: Reading Condillac.* Trans. John P. Leavey Jr. Lincoln: University of Nebraska Press, 1980.

———. *Deconstruction in a Nutshell: A Conversation with Jacques Derrida.* Ed. John D. Caputo. New York: Fordham University Press, 1997.

———. "Derrida's Response to Baldwin." *Ratio* 13, no. 4 (December): 401–6, 2000a.

———. "Discussion." *Ratio* 13, no. 4 (December): 345–54, 373–86, 2000b.

———. *Dissemination.* Trans. Barbara Johnson. Chicago: University of Chicago Press, 1981.

———. *The Ear of the Other: Otobiography, Transference, Translation.* Trans. Peggy Kamuf and Avital Ronnell. Lincoln: University of Nebraska Press, 1985.

———. *For What Tomorrow . . . A Dialogue.* Trans. Jeff Fort. Stanford: Stanford University Press, 2004.

———. *The Gift of Death.* Trans. David Wills. Chicago: University of Chicago Press, 1995b.

———. *Given Time: I. Counterfeit Money.* Trans. Peggy Kamuf. Chicago: University of Chicago Press, 1992.

———. *Glas.* Trans. John P. Leavey Jr. and Richard Rand. Lincoln: University of Nebraska Press, 1986.

———. *Limited Inc.* Ed. Gerald Graff. Evanston, Ill.: Northwestern University Press, 1988.

———. *Margins of Philosophy.* Trans. Alan Bass. Chicago: University of Chicago Press, 1982.

———. *Mémoires for Paul de Man.* Rev. ed. Trans. Cecile Lindsay, Jonathan Culler, Eduardo Cadava, and Peggy Kamuf. New York: Columbia University Press, 1989b.

———. *Monolingualism of the Other; or, The Prosthesis of Origin.* Trans. Patrick Mensah. Stanford: Stanford University Press, 1998.

———. *Of Grammatology.* Corr. ed. Trans. Gayatri Chakravorty Spivak. Baltimore: The Johns Hopkins University Press, 1976, 1997.

———. *Of Hospitality.* Trans. Rachel Bowlby. Stanford: Stanford University Press, 2000c.

———. *Of Spirit: Heidegger and the Question.* Trans. Geoffrey Bennington and Rachel Bowlby. Chicago: University of Chicago Press, 1989a.

———. *Points . . . Interviews, 1974–1994.* Trans. Peggy Kamuf et al. Stanford: Stanford University Press, 1995.

———. *Positions.* Trans. Alan Bass. Chicago: University of Chicago Press, 1981.

———. *The Post Card: From Socrates to Freud and Beyond.* Trans. Alan Bass. Chicago: University of Chicago Press, 1987.

———. "Sending: On Representation." In Ormiston and Schrift, 1990.

———. *Speech and Phenomena and Other Essays on Husserl's Theory of Signs.* Trans. David B. Allison. Evanston, Ill.: Northwestern University Press, 1973.

———. *Spurs/Nietzsche's Styles.* Trans. Barbara Harlow. Chicago: University of Chicago Press, 1979.

———. *A Taste for the Secret.* Coauthored with Maurizio Ferraris. Ed. Giacomo Donis and David Webb. Trans. Giacomo Donis. Malden, Mass.: Polity, 2001.

———. *The Truth in Painting.* Trans. Geoffrey Bennington and Ian McLeod. Chicago: University of Chicago Press, 1987.

———. *Writing and Difference.* Trans. Alan Bass. Chicago: University of Chicago Press, 1978.

Descartes, René. *The Philosophical Writings of Descartes.* 3 vols. Trans. John Cottingham, Robert Stoothoff, and Dugald Murdoch. New York: Cambridge University Press, 1985.

Foucault, Michel. *Abnormal: Lectures at the Collège de France, 1974–1975.* Ed. Valerio Marchetti and Antonella Salomoni. Trans. Graham Burchell. New York: Picador, 2003.
———. *The Archaeology of Knowledge.* Trans. A. M. Sheridan Smith. New York: Harper Colophon Books, 1972.
———. *The Birth of the Clinic: An Archaeology of Medical Perception.* Trans. A. M. Sheridan Smith. New York: Vintage Books, 1994.
———. *The Care of the Self.* Vol. 3 of *The History of Sexuality.* Trans. Robert Hurley. New York: Vintage Books, 1988.
———. "Dream, Imagination and Existence." Foreword to *Dream and Existence,* ed. Keith Hoeller. Atlantic Highlands, N.J.: Humanities, 1993.
———. *Discipline and Punish: The Birth of the Prison.* Trans. Alan Sheridan. New York: Vintage Books, 1995.
———. *Essential Works of Foucault, 1954–1984.* 3 vols. Series ed. Paul Rabinow. New York: New Press, 1998.
———. *Fearless Speech.* Ed. Joseph Pearson. Los Angeles: Semiotext(e), 2001.
———. *Foucault/Blanchot.* Trans. Jeffrey Mehlman and Brian Massumi. New York: Zone Books, 1990.
———. *Foucault Live: Collected Interviews, 1961–1984.* Ed. Sylvere Lotringer. Trans. Lysa Hochroth and John Johnston. New York: Semiotext(e), 1996.
———. "Foucault, Michel, 1926–." This article appears under the title "Maurice Florence." In Gutting 1994, 314–19.
———. *The Foucault Reader.* Ed. Paul Rabinow. New York: Pantheon Books, 1984.
———. *Herculine Barbin: Being the Recently Discovered Memoirs of a Nineteenth-Century French Hermaphrodite.* Trans. Richard McDougall. New York: Pantheon Books, 1980.
———. *The Hermeneutics of the Subject: Lectures at the Collège de France, 1981–1982.* Ed. Frédéric Gros. Trans. Graham Burchell. New York: Palgrave Macmillan, 2005.
———. *The History of Sexuality: An Introduction.* Vol. 1 of *The History of Sexuality.* Trans. Robert Hurley. New York: Vintage Books, 1978.
———. *Language, Counter-Memory, Practice: Selected Essays and Interviews.* Ed. Donald F. Bouchard. Trans. Donald F. Bouchard and Sherry Simon. Ithaca: Cornell University Press, 1977.
———. *Madness and Civilization: A History of Insanity in the Age of Reason.* Trans. Richard Howard. New York: Vintage Books, 1988.
———. *Mental Illness and Psychology.* Trans. Alan Sheridan. Berkeley and Los Angeles: University of California Press, 1987.
———. *The Order of Things: An Archaeology of the Human Sciences.* New York: Vintage Books, 1970.
———. *The Politics of Truth.* Ed. Sylvere Lotringer and Lysa Hochroth. New York: Semiotext(e), 1997.
———. *Politics, Philosophy, Culture: Interviews and Other Writings, 1977–1984.* Ed. Lawrence D. Kritzman. Trans. Alan Sheridan et al. New York: Routledge, 1988.

———. *Power/Knowledge: Selected Interviews and Other Writings, 1972–1977.* Ed. Colin Gordon. Trans. Colin Gordon et al. New York: Pantheon Books, 1980.

———. *Psychiatric Power: Lectures at the Collège de France, 1973–1974.* Ed. Jacques Lagrange. Trans. Graham Burchell. New York: Palgrave Macmillan, 2006.

———. "Questions of Method: An Interview with Michel Foucault." In Baynes, Bohman, and McCarthy 1987, 100–117.

———. *Religion and Culture.* Ed. Jeremy R. Carrette. New York: Routledge, 1999.

———. *"Society Must Be Defended": Lectures at the Collège de France 1975–1976.* Ed. Mauro Bertani and Alessandro Fontana. Trans. David Macey. New York: Picador, 2003.

———. *Technologies of the Self: A Seminar with Michel Foucault.* Ed. Luther H. Martin, Huck Gutman, and Patrick H. Hutton. Amherst: University of Massachusetts Press, 1988.

———. *The Use of Pleasure.* Vol. 2 of *The History of Sexuality.* Trans. Robert Hurley. New York: Vintage Books, 1985.

Hegel, G. W. F. *The Difference Between Fichte's and Schelling's System of Philosophy.* Trans. H. S. Harris and Walter Cerf. Albany: State University of New York Press, 1977.

———. *Hegel's Logic.* Trans. William Wallace. Oxford: Clarendon, 1975.

———. *Lectures on the History of Philosophy.* Vol. 3. Trans. R. F. Brown and J. M. Stewart. Berkeley and Los Angeles: University of California Press, 1990.

———. *Phenomenology of Spirit.* Trans. A. V. Miller. New York: Oxford University Press, 1977.

———. Preface and Introduction to the *Phenomenology of Mind.* Ed. Lawrence S. Stepelevich. Trans. J. B. Baillie. New York: Macmillan, 1990.

———. *Reason in History: A General Introduction to the Philosophy of History.* Trans. Robert S. Hartman. Englewood Cliffs, N.J.: Prentice Hall, 1953.

Heidegger, Martin. *Aristotle's "Metaphysics" Θ 1–3: On the Essence and Actuality of Force.* Trans. Walter Brogan and Peter Warnek. Bloomington: Indiana University Press, 1995.

———. *Basic Concepts.* Trans. Gary E. Aylesworth. Bloomington: Indiana University Press, 1993.

———. *The Basic Problems of Phenomenology.* Trans. Albert Hofstadter. Bloomington: Indiana University Press, 1982.

———. *Basic Questions of Philosophy: Selected "Problems" of "Logic."* Trans. Richard Rojcewicz and André Schuwer. Bloomington: Indiana University Press, 1994.

———. *Basic Writings.* Rev. ed. Ed. David Farrell Krell. San Francisco: HarperSanFrancisco, 1993.

———. *Being and Time.* Trans. John Macquarrie and Edward Robinson. San Francisco: HarperSanFrancisco, 1962.

———. *Contributions to Philosophy (From Enowning).* Trans. Parvis Emad and Kenneth Maly. Bloomington: Indiana University Press, 1999.

———. *Discourse on Thinking.* Trans. John M. Anderson and E. Hans Freund. San Francisco: Harper Torchbooks, 1966.

———. *Early Greek Thinking: The Dawn of Western Philosophy.* Trans. David Farrell Krell and Frank A. Capuzzi. San Francisco: HarperSanFrancisco, 1975.

———. *Elucidations of Hölderlin's Poetry.* Trans. Keith Hoeller. Amherst, Mass.: Humanity Books, 2000.

———. *The End of Philosophy.* Trans. Joan Stambaugh. New York: Harper and Row, 1973.

———. *The Essence of Human Freedom: An Introduction to Philosophy.* Trans. Ted Sadler. New York: Continuum, 2002.

———. *The Essence of Truth: On Plato's Cave Allegory and "Theaetetus."* Trans. Ted Sadler. New York: Continuum, 2002.

———. *Four Seminars.* Trans. Andrew Mitchell and François Raffoul. Bloomington: Indiana University Press, 2003.

———. *The Fundamental Concepts of Metaphysics: World, Finitude, Solitude.* Trans. William McNeill and Nicholas Walker. Bloomington: Indiana University Press, 2001.

———. *Hegel's Concept of Experience.* New York: Harper and Row, 1970.

———. *Hegel's "Phenomenology of Spirit."* Trans. Parvis Emad and Kenneth Maly. Bloomington: Indiana University Press, 1994.

———. *Heraclitus Seminar.* Coauthored wth Eugene Fink. Trans. Charles H. Siebert. Evanston, Ill.: Northwestern University Press, 1993.

———. *History of the Concept of Time.* Trans. Theodore Kisiel. Bloomington: Indiana University Press, 1985.

———. *Hölderlin's Hymn "The Ister."* Trans. William McNeill and Julia Davis. Bloomington: Indiana University Press, 1996.

———. *Identity and Difference.* Trans. Joan Stambaugh. New York: Harper Torchbooks, 1969.

———. *An Introduction to Metaphysics.* Trans. Ralph Manheim. New Haven: Yale University Press, 1959.

———. *Introduction to Phenomenological Research.* Trans. Daniel O. Dahlstrom. Bloomington: Indiana University Press, 2005.

———. *Kant and the Problem of Metaphysics.* 5th enl. ed. Trans. Richard Taft. Bloomington: Indiana University Press, 1990.

———. *Martin Heidegger in Conversation.* Ed. Richard Wisser. Trans. B. Srinivasa Murthy. New Delhi: Arnold-Heinemann, 1977.

———. *The Metaphysical Foundations of Logic.* Trans. Michael Heim. Bloomington: Indiana University Press, 1992.

———. *Mindfulness.* Trans. Parvis Emad and Thomas Kalary. New York: Continuum, 2002.

———. *Nietzsche.* 4 vols. Ed. David Farrell Krell. San Francisco: HarperSanFrancisco, 1979, 1984, 1987, and 1982.

———. *Off the Beaten Track.* Trans. and ed. Julian Young and Kenneth Haynes. New York: Cambridge University Press, 2002.

———. *On the Way to Language.* Trans. Peter D. Hertz and Joan Stambaugh. San Francisco: HarperSanFrancisco, 1971.

———. *On Time and Being.* Trans. Joan Stambaugh. New York: Harper Torchbooks, 1972.

———. "'Only a God Can Save Us': *Der Spiegel*'s Interview with Martin Heidegger." In Wolin 1993, 91–116.

———. *Ontology: The Hermeneutics of Facticity.* Trans. John van Buren. Bloomington: Indiana University Press, 1999.

———. *Parmenides.* Trans. Richard Rojcewicz and André Schuwer. Bloomington: Indiana University Press, 1992.

———. *Pathmarks.* Ed. William McNeill. Cambridge: Cambridge University Press, 1998.

———. *Phenomenological Interpretation of Kant's "Critique of Pure Reason."* Trans. Parvis Emad and Thomas Kalary. Bloomington: Indiana University Press, 1997.

———. *The Piety of Thinking.* Trans. James G. Hart and John C. Maraldo. Bloomington: Indiana University Press, 1976.

———. *Plato's "Sophist."* Trans. Richard Rojcewicz and André Schuwer. Bloomington: Indiana University Press, 1997.

———. *Poetry, Language, Thought.* Trans. Albert Hofstadter. New York: Harper and Row, 1971.

———. *The Principle of Reason.* Trans. Reginald Lilly. Bloomington: Indiana University Press, 1991.

———. *The Question Concerning Technology and Other Essays.* Trans. William Lovitt. New York: Harper Torchbooks, 1977.

———. *Supplements: From the Earliest Essays to "Being and Time" and Beyond.* Ed. John van Buren. Albany: State University of New York Press, 2002.

———. *Towards the Definition of Philosophy.* Trans. Ted Sadler. New York: Athlone, 2000.

———. *What Is a Thing?* Trans. W. B. Barton Jr. and Vera Deutsch. Chicago: Henry Regnery, 1967.

———. *What Is Called Thinking?* Trans. Fred Wieck and J. Glenn Gray. New York: Harper and Row, 1968.

———. *What Is Philosophy?* Trans. Jean T. Wilde and William Kluback. New Haven, Conn.: New College and University Press, 1956.

———. *Zollikon Seminars: Protocols—Conversations—Letters.* Trans. Franz Mayr and Richard Askay. Evanston, Ill.: Northwestern University Press, 2001.

Kant, Immanuel. *Critique of Judgment.* Trans. Werner S. Pluhar. Indianapolis: Hackett, 1987.

———. *Critique of Practical Reason.* 3rd ed. Trans. Lewis White Beck. Upper Saddle River, N.J.: Library of Liberal Arts, 1993.

———. *Critique of Pure Reason.* Trans. Norman Kemp Smith. New York: St. Martin's, 1965.

———. *Foundations of the Metaphysics of Morals.* 2nd ed. Trans. Lewis White Beck. Upper Saddle River, N.J.: Library of Liberal Arts, 1995.

———. *Lectures on Logic.* Trans. and ed. J. Michael Young. New York: Cambridge University Press, 1992.

———. *Prolegomena to Any Future Metaphysics.* Trans. James W. Ellington. Indianapolis: Hackett, 1977.

Nietzsche, Friedrich. *Beyond Good and Evil: Prelude to a Philosophy of the Future.* Trans. Walter Kaufmann. New York: Vintage Books, 1966.

———. *Daybreak: Thoughts on the Prejudices of Morality.* Trans. R. J. Hollingdale. New York: Cambridge University Press, 1982.

———. *The Gay Science.* Trans. Walter Kaufmann. New York: Vintage Books, 1974.

———. *Human, All Too Human: A Book for Free Spirits.* Trans. R. J. Hollingdale. New York: Cambridge University Press, 1986.

———. *On the Genealogy of Morals/Ecce Homo.* Trans. Walter Kaufmann and R. J. Hollingdale. New York: Vintage Books, 1967.

———. *The Portable Nietzsche.* Ed. and trans. Walter Kaufmann. New York: Penguin Books, 1954.

———. *The Will to Power.* Ed. Walter Kaufmann. Trans. Walter Kaufmann and R. J. Hollingdale. New York: Vintage Books, 1968.

Wittgenstein, Ludwig. *Culture and Value.* Trans. Peter Winch. Chicago: University of Chicago Press, 1980a.

———. *Last Writings on the Philosophy of Psychology, Volume One: Preliminary Studies for Part 2 of "Philosophical Investigations."* Ed. G. H. von Wright and Heikki Nyman. Trans. C. G. Luckhardt and Maximilian A. E. Aue. Chicago: University of Chicago Press, 1982.

———. *Last Writings on the Philosophy of Psychology, Volume Two: The Inner and the Outer.* Ed. G. H. von Wright and Heikki Nyman. Trans. C. G. Luckhardt and Maximilian A. E. Aue. Cambridge, Mass.: Blackwell, 1992.

———. *On Certainty.* Ed. G. E. M. Anscombe and G. H. von Wright. Trans. Denis Paul and G. E. M. Anscombe. New York: Harper Torchbooks, 1969.

———. *Philosophical Investigations.* 3rd ed., rev. trans. Trans. G. E. M. Anscombe. Madsen, Mass.: Blackwell, 2001.

———. *Remarks on the Foundations of Mathematics.* Rev. ed. Ed. G. H. von Wright, R. Rhees, and G. E. M. Anscombe. Cambridge, Mass.: MIT Press, 1983.

———. *Remarks on the Philosophy of Psychology.* Vol. 1. Ed. G. E. M. Anscombe and G. H. von Wright. Trans. G. E. M. Anscombe. Chicago: University of Chicago Press, 1980b.

———. *Remarks on the Philosophy of Psychology.* Vol. 2. Ed. G. H. von Wright and Heikki Nyman. Trans. C. G. Luckhardt and Maximilian A. E. Aue. Chicago: University of Chicago Press, 1980c.

———. *Tractatus Logico-Philosophicus.* Trans. D. F. Pears and B. F. McGuinness. New York: Routledge, 2001.

———. *Zettel.* Ed. G. E. M. Anscombe and G. H. von Wright. Trans. G. E. M. Anscombe. Berkeley: University of California Press, 1970.

## Other Authors

Abela, Paul. 1996. "Putnam's Internal Realism and Kant's Empirical Realism: The Case for a Divorce." *Idealistic Studies* 26, no. 1 (Winter/Spring): 45–56.

Abrams, M. H. 1953. *The Mirror and the Lamp: Romantic Theory and the Critical Tradition.* New York: Oxford University Press.

Alcoff, Linda Martín. 1996. *Real Knowing: New Versions of the Coherence Theory.* Ithaca: Cornell University Press.

Allais, Lucy. 2003. "Kant's Transcendental Idealism and Contemporary Anti-Realism." *International Journal of Philosophical Studies* 11, no. 4: 369–92.

Allen, Barry. 1993. *Truth in Philosophy.* Cambridge, Mass.: Harvard University Press.

Allison, David B., ed. 1977. *The New Nietzsche.* New York: Dell.

Allison, Henry. 1983. *Kant's Transcendental Idealism: An Interpretation and Defense.* New Haven: Yale University Press.

Alston, William P., ed. 2002. *Realism and Antirealism.* Ithaca: Cornell University Press.

Ameriks, Karl. 2000a. *Kant and the Fate of Autonomy: Problems in the Appropriation of the Critical Philosophy.* New York: Cambridge University Press.

———. 2000b. *Kant's Theory of Mind: An Analysis of the Paralogisms of Pure Reason.* 2nd ed. Oxford: Clarendon.

Anderson, Walter Truett, ed. 1995. *The Truth about the Truth: De-confusing and Reconstructing the Postmodern World.* New York: G. P. Putnam's Sons.

Ansell Pearson, Keith, ed. 1991. *Nietzsche and Modern German Thought.* New York: Routledge.

Apel, Karl-Otto. 1999. *From a Transcendental-Semiotic Point of View.* New York: Manchester University Press.

Arac, Jonathan, Wlad Godzich, and Wallace Martin, eds. 1983. *The Yale Critics: Deconstruction in America.* Minneapolis: University of Minnesota Press.

Armstrong, Timothy J., trans. 1992. *Michel Foucault, Philosopher.* New York: Routledge.

Augustine. 1961. *Confessions.* Trans. R. S. Pine-Coffin. New York: Penguin Books.

Austin, J. L. 1962. *Sense and Sensibilia.* G. J. Warnock, reconstructed. New York: Oxford University Press.

———. 1975. *How to Do Things with Words.* 2nd ed. Ed. J. O. Urmson and Marina Sbisà. Cambridge, Mass.: Harvard University Press.

Ayer, A. J., ed. 1959. *Logical Positivism.* New York: Free Press.

Bacon, Francis. 1960. *The New Organon and Related Writings.* Ed. Fulton H. Anderson. New York: Macmillan.

Bambauch, Charles R. 1995. *Heidegger, Dilthey, and the Crisis of Historicism.* New York: Cornell University Press.

Baynes, Kenneth, James Bohman, and Thomas McCarthy, eds. 1987. *After Philosophy: End or Transformation?* Cambridge, Mass.: Cambridge University Press.

Beck, Lewis W., ed. 1969. *Kant Studies Today.* La Salle, Ill.: Open Court.

Beiser, Frederick C., ed. 1993. *The Cambridge Companion to Hegel.* New York: Cambridge University Press.

Bernauer, James W. 1990. *Michel Foucault's Force of Flight: Toward an Ethics of Thought.* Atlantic Highlands, N.J.: Humanities.

Bernauer, James, and David Rasmussen, eds. 1994. *The Final Foucault.* Cambridge, Mass.: MIT Press.

Bernstein, Richard J. 1971. *Praxis and Action: Contemporary Philosophies of Human Activity.* Philadelphia: University of Pennsylvania Press.

———. 1988. *Beyond Objectivism and Relativism: Science, Hermeneutics, and Praxis.* Philadelphia: University of Pennsylvania Press.

———. 1992. *The New Constellation: The Ethical-Political Horizons of Modernity/Postmodernity.* Cambridge, Mass.: MIT Press.

Biletzki, Anat, and Anta Matar, eds. 1998. *The Story of Analytic Philosophy: Plot and Heroes.* New York: Routledge.

Blackburn, Simon. 1984. *Spreading the Word: Groundings in the Philosophy of Language.* Oxford: Clarendon.

Blattner, William D. 1994. "Is Heidegger a Kantian Idealist?" *Inquiry* 37:185–201.

———. 1999. *Heidegger's Temporal Idealism.* New York: Cambridge University Press.

Borges, Jorge Luis. 1962. *Ficciones.* Ed. Anthony Kerrigan. New York: Grove Press.

Brandl, Johannes, and Wolfgang L. Gombocz, eds. 1989. *The Mind of Donald Davidson.* Grazer Philosophische Studien, vol. 36. Atlanta: Rodopi.

Breazeale, Daniel, ed. and trans. 1979. *Philosophy and Truth: Selections from Nietzsche's Notebooks of the Early 1970s.* Atlantic Highlands, N.J.: Humanities.

Brown, Curtis. 1988. "Internal Realism: Transcendental Idealism?" *Midwest Studies in Philosophy* 12:145–55.

Burge, Tyler. 2005. *Truth, Thought, Reason: Essays on Frege.* New York: Oxford University Press.

Butler, Judith. 1999. *Gender Trouble: Feminism and the Subversion of Identity.* 10th anniversary edition. New York: Routledge.

Caputo, John D. 1983. "The Thought of Being and the Conversation of Mankind: The Case of Heidegger and Rorty." *Review of Metaphysics* 36 (March): 661–85.

———. 1987. *Radical Hermeneutics: Repetition, Deconstruction, and the Hermeneutic Project.* Indianapolis: Indiana University Press.

———. 1993. *Demythologizing Heidegger.* Indianapolis: Indiana University Press.

Caputo, John, and Mark Yount, eds. 1993. *Foucault and the Critique of Institutions.* University Park: Pennsylvania State University Press.

Carman, Taylor. 2003. *Heidegger's Analytic: Interpretation, Discourse, and Authenticity in "Being and Time."* New York: Cambridge University Press.

Carr, David. 1999. *The Paradox of Subjectivity: The Self in the Transcendental Tradition.* New York: Oxford University Press.

Cavell, Stanley. 1990. *Conditions Handsome and Unhandsome: The Constitution of Emersonian Perfectionism.* Chicago: University of Chicago Press.

———. 1995. *Philosophical Passages: Wittgenstein, Emerson, Austin, Derrida.* Cambridge: Blackwell.

Cerbone, David R. 1995. "World, World-Entry, and Realism in Early Heidegger." *Inquiry* 38:401–21.

Clark, A. J. 1985. "Why Kant Couldn't Be an Anti-Realist." *Analysis* 45 (January): 61–63.

Clark, Maudemarie. 1990. *Nietzsche on Truth and Philosophy.* New York: Cambridge University Press.

Clark, Peter, and Bob Hale, eds. 1994. *Reading Putnam.* Cambridge: Blackwell.

Comay, Rebecca, and John McCumber. 1999. *Endings: Questions of Memory in Hegel and Heidegger.* Evanston, Ill.: Northwestern University Press.

Conway, Daniel W. 1990. "Beyond Realism: Nietzsche's New Infinite." *International Studies in Philosophy* 22, no. 2: 93–109.

———, ed. 1998. *Nietzsche: Critical Assessments.* Vol. 2. New York: Routledge.

Cook, Daniel J. 1973. *Language in the Philosophy of Hegel.* The Hague: Mouton.

Cooper, David E. 1992. "Inverting the Image: Dreyfus's Commentary on Heidegger." *Inquiry* 35 (June): 233–48.

———. 1993. "Postmodernism and 'The End of Philosophy.'" *International Journal of Philosophical Studies* 1, no. 1 (March): 49–59.

Cutrofello, Andrew. 1994. *Discipline and Critique: Kant, Poststructuralism, and the Problem of Resistance.* Albany: State University of New York Press.

Dahlstrom, Daniel O., ed. 1984. *Realism.* Proceedings of the American Catholic Philosophical Association, vol. 59. Washington, D.C.: National Office of the American Catholic Philosophical Association.

Dallery, Arleen B., and Charles E. Scott. 1990. *Crises in Continental Philosophy.* Albany: State University of New York Press.

D'Amico, Robert. 1989. *Historicism and Knowledge.* New York: Routledge.

Danto, Arthur C. 1965. *Nietzsche as Philosopher.* New York: Columbia University Press.

Dasenbrock, Reed Way, ed. 1989. *Redrawing the Lines: Analytic Philosophy, Deconstruction, and Literary Theory.* Minneapolis: University of Minnesota Press.

———. 1993. *Literary Theory after Davidson.* University Park: Pennsylvania State University Press.

Davidson, Arnold I., ed. 1997. *Foucault and His Interlocutors.* Chicago: University of Chicago Press.

Davis, Robert Con, and Ronald Schleifer, eds. 1994. *Contemporary Literary Criticism: Literary and Cultural Studies.* 3rd ed. New York: Longman.

De Boer, Karin. 2000. *Thinking in the Light of Time: Heidegger's Encounter with Hegel.* Albany: State University of New York Press.

Deleuze, Gilles. 1983. *Nietzsche and Philosophy.* Trans. Hugh Tomlinson. New York: Columbia University Press.

———. 1984. *Kant's Critical Philosophy.* Minneapolis: University of Minnesota Press.

Denker, Alfred, and Michael Vater, eds. 2003. *Hegel's "Phenomenology of Spirit": New Critical Essays.* New York: Humanity Books.

Derrida, Jacques, and Maurizio Ferraris. 2001. *A Taste for the Secret.* Trans. Giacomo Donis. Cambridge: Polity.

Devitt, Michael. 1997. *Realism and Truth.* 2nd ed. Princeton: Princeton University Press.

Dews, Peter. 1995. *The Limits of Disenchantment: Essays on Contemporary European Philosophy.* New York: Verso.

Donagan, A., A. N. Perovich Jr., and M. V. Wedin, eds. 1986. *Human Nature and Natural Knowledge.* Boston: D. Reidel.

Dreyfus, Hubert L. 1980. "Holism and Hermeneutics." *Review of Metaphysics* 34 (September): 3–23.

———. 1984. "Beyond Hermeneutics: Interpretation in Late Heidegger and Recent Foucault." In *Hermeneutics: Questions and Prospects,* ed. Gary Shapiro and Alan Sica, 66–83. Amherst: University of Massachusetts Press.

———. 1991. *Being-in-the-World: A Commentary on Heidegger's "Being and Time," Division I.* Cambridge, Mass.: MIT Press.

———. 1996. "Being and Power: Heidegger and Foucault." *International Journal of Philosophical Studies* 4, no. 1 (March): 1–16.

Dreyfus, Hubert L., and Harrison Hall, eds. 1992. *Heidegger: A Critical Reader.* Cambridge: Blackwell.

Dreyfus, Hubert L., and Paul Rabinow. 1983. *Michel Foucault: Beyond Structuralism and Hermeneutics.* 2nd ed. Chicago: University of Chicago Press.

Dreyfus, Hubert L., and Charles Spinosa. 1999. "Coping with Things-in-Themselves: A Practice-Based Phenomenological Argument for Realism." *Inquiry* 42, no. 1: 49–78.

Dudley, Will. 2002. *Hegel, Nietzsche, and Philosophy: Thinking Freedom.* New York: Cambridge University Press.

Dummett, Michael. 1978. *Truth and Other Enigmas.* Cambridge, Mass.: Harvard University Press.

———. 1981. *The Interpretation of Frege's Philosophy.* Cambridge, Mass.: Harvard University Press.

———. 1991. *The Logical Basis of Metaphysics.* Cambridge, Mass.: Harvard University Press.

———. 1993. *The Seas of Language.* Oxford: Clarendon.

———. 1994. *Origins of Analytical Philosophy.* Cambridge, Mass.: Harvard University Press.

Edwards, James C. 1990. *The Authority of Language: Heidegger, Wittgenstein, and the Threat of Philosophical Nihilism.* Tampa: University of South Florida Press.

Elden, Stuart. 2001. *Mapping the Present: Heidegger, Foucault and the Project of a Spatial History.* New York: Continuum.

Elgin, Catherine Z. 1997. *Between the Absolute and the Arbitrary.* Ithaca: Cornell University Press.

Engel, Pascal. 1991. "Interpretation Without Hermeneutics: A Plea against Ecumenism." *Topoi* 10:137–46.

Farrell, Frank B. 1994. *Subjectivity, Realism and Postmodernism: The Recovery of the World in Recent Philosophy.* New York: Cambridge University Press.

Fell, Joseph P. 1979. *Heidegger and Sartre: An Essay on Being and Place.* New York: Columbia University Press.

Fenves, Peter, ed. 1993. *Raising the Tone of Philosophy: Late Essays by Immanuel Kant, Transformative Critique by Jacques Derrida.* Baltimore: The Johns Hopkins University Press.

Field, Hartry. 1982. "Realism and Relativism." *Journal of Philosophy* 79, no. 10 (October): 553–67.

Findlay, J. N. 1958. *Hegel: A Re-examination.* New York: Oxford University Press.

———. 1981. *Kant and the Transcendental Object: A Hermeneutic Study.* Oxford: Oxford University Press.

Fine, Arthur. 1996. *The Shaky Game: Einstein, Realism, and the Quantum Theory.* 2nd ed. Chicago: University of Chicago Press.

Flay, Joseph C. 1984. *Hegel's Quest for Certainty.* Albany: State University of New York Press.

Flynn, Thomas R. 1989. "Foucault and Historical Nominalism." In *Phenomenology and Beyond: The Self and Its Language,* ed. H. A. Durfee and D. F. T. Rodier, 134–47. Boston: Kluwer Academic.

Fodor, Jerry, and Ernest Lepore. 1994. "Is Radical Interpretation Possible?" In *Philosophical Perspectives Eight: Logic and Language,* ed. James E. Tomberlin, 101–19. Atascadero, Calif.: Ridgeview.

Forster, Michael. 1998. *Hegel's Idea of a "Phenomenology of Spirit."* Chicago: University of Chicago Press.

———. 2004. *Wittgenstein on the Arbitrariness of Grammar.* Princeton: Princeton University Press.

Fraser, Nancy. 1981. "Foucault on Modern Power: Empirical Insights and Normative Confusions." *Praxis International* 1, no. 3 (1981): 272–87.

Frege, Gottlob. 1972. "Review of Dr. E. Husserl's *Philosophy of Arithmetic.*" *Mind,* n.s., 81, no. 323 (July): 321–37.

French, Peter A., Theodore E. Uehling Jr., and Howard K. Wettstein, eds. 1980. *Studies in Epistemology.* Vol. 5 of *Midwest Studies in Philosophy.* Minneapolis: University of Minnesota Press.

———. 1988. *Realism and Antirealism.* Vol. 12 of *Midwest Studies in Philosophy.* Minneapolis: University of Minnesota Press.

Fynsk, Christopher. 1993. *Heidegger: Thought and Historicity.* Exp. ed. Ithaca: Cornell University Press.

Gadamer, Hans-Georg. 1976a. *Hegel's Dialectic: Five Hermeneutical Studies.* Trans. P. Christopher Smith. New Haven: Yale University Press.

———. 1976b. *Philosophical Hermeneutics.* Trans. and ed. David E. Linge. Berkeley and Los Angeles: University of California Press.

———. 1981. *Reason in the Age of Science.* Trans. Frederick G. Lawrence. Cambridge, Mass.: MIT Press.

———. 1989. *Truth and Method.* 2nd rev. ed. Trans. Joel Weinsheimer and Donald G. Marshall. New York: Continuum.

———. 1994. *Heidegger's Ways.* Trans. John W. Stanley. Albany: State University of New York Press.

———. 1998. *The Beginning of Philosophy.* Trans. Rod Coltman. New York: Continuum.

Gallagher, Shaun, ed. 1997. *Hegel, History, and Interpretation.* Albany: State University of New York Press.

Gasché, Rodolphe. 1986. *The Tain of the Mirror: Derrida and the Philosophy of Reflection.* Cambridge, Mass.: Harvard University Press.

Geach, Peter, and Max Black, eds. 1960. *Translations from the Philosophical Writings of Gottlob Frege.* Oxford: Basil Blackwell.

Gellner, Ernest. 1959. *Words and Things.* New York: Penguin Books.

Glendinning, Simon. 1998. *On Being with Others: Heidegger—Derrida—Wittgenstein.* New York: Routledge.

Glock, Hans-Johann. 2003. "Critical Notice of *Subjective, Intersubjective, Objective.*" *Philosophical Investigations* 26, no. 4 (October): 348–60.

Gilson, Etienne. 1941. *God and Philosophy.* New Haven: Yale University Press.

———. 1952. *Being and Some Philosophers.* 2nd ed. Toronto: Pontifical Institute of Mediaeval Studies.

Glazebrook, Trish. 2000. *Heidegger's Philosophy of Science.* New York: Fordham University Press.

Goodman, Nelson. 1978. *Ways of Worldmaking.* Indianapolis: Hackett.

Goodman, Nelson, and Catherine Z. Elgin. 1988. *Reconceptions in Philosophy and Other Arts and Sciences.* Indianapolis: Hackett.

Grandy, Richard. 1973. "Reference, Meaning, and Belief." *Journal of Philosophy* 70, no. 14 (August 16): 439–52.

Green, Michael Steven. 2002. *Nietzsche and the Transcendental Tradition.* Chicago: University of Chicago Press.

Grene, Marjorie. 1966. *The Knower and the Known.* New York: Basic Books.

———. 1995. *A Philosophical Testament.* Chicago: Open Court.

Guignon, Charles B. 1983. *Heidegger and the Problem of Knowledge.* Indianapolis: Hackett.

———, ed. 1993. *The Cambridge Companion to Heidegger.* New York: Cambridge University Press.

Gustafsson, Martin. 1998. "Systematic Meaning and Linguistic Diversity: The Place of Meaning-Theories in Davidson's Later Philosophy." *Inquiry* 41: 435–53.

Gutting, Gary. 1989. *Michel Foucault's Archaeology of Scientific Reason.* New York: Cambridge University Press.

———, ed. 1994. *The Cambridge Companion to Foucault.* New York: Cambridge University Press.

Guyer, Paul. 1987. *Kant and the Claims of Knowledge.* New York: Cambridge University Press.

Haar, Michel. 1987. *The Song of the Earth: Heidegger and the Grounds of the History of Being.* Trans. Reginald Lilly. Indianapolis: Indiana University Press.

———. 1993. *Heidegger and the Essence of Man.* Trans. William McNeill. Albany: State University of New York Press.

———. 1996. *Nietzsche and Metaphysics.* Trans. and ed. Michael Gendre. Albany: State University of New York Press.

Habermas, Jürgen. 1971. *Knowledge and Human Interests.* Trans. Jeremy J. Shapiro. Boston: Beacon.

———. 1987. *The Philosophical Discourse of Modernity: Twelve Lectures.* Trans. Frederick Lawrence. Cambridge, Mass.: MIT Press.

———. 1992. *Postmetaphysical Thinking: Philosophical Essays.* Trans. William Mark Hohengarten. Cambridge, Mass.: Cambridge University Press.

Hacker, P. M. S. 1996. *Wittgenstein's Place in Twentieth-Century Analytic Philosophy.* Cambridge, Mass.: Blackwell.

Hacking, Ian. 2002. *Historical Ontology.* Cambridge, Mass.: Harvard University Press.

Hahn, Lewis Edwin, ed. 1997. *The Philosophy of Hans-Georg Gadamer.* Library of Living Philosophers, vol. 24. Chicago: Open Court.

———. 1999. *The Philosophy of Donald Davidson.* Library of Living Philosophers, vol. 27. Chicago: Open Court.

Haldane, John, and Crispin Wright, eds. 1993. *Reality, Representation, and Projection.* New York: Oxford University Press.

Hales, Steven D., and Rex Welshon. 2000. *Nietzsche's Perspectivism.* Chicago: University of Illinois Press.

Hamilton, Edith, and Huntington Cairns, eds. 1961. *The Collected Dialogues of Plato.* Princeton: Princeton University Press.

Han, Béatrice. 2002. *Foucault's Critical Project: Between the Transcendental and the Historical.* Trans. Edward Pile. Stanford: Stanford University Press.

Hanna, Robert. 2001. *Kant and the Foundations of Analytic Philosophy.* Oxford: Clarendon.

Hanson, Norwood Russell. 1958. *Patterns of Discovery.* New York: Cambridge University Press.

Harman, Graham. 2002. *Tool-Being: Heidegger and the Metaphysics of Objects.* Chicago: Open Court.

Henderson, David K. 1993. *Interpretation and Explanation in the Human Sciences.* Albany: State University of New York Press.

Hill, Claire Ortiz. 1991. *Word and Object in Husserl, Frege, and Russell: The Roots of Twentieth-Century Philosophy.* Athens: Ohio University Press.

Hill, R. Kevin. 1990. "Foucault's Critique of Heidegger." *Philosophy Today* 34 (Winter): 324–41.

———. 2003. *Nietzsche's Critiques: The Kantian Foundations of His Thought.* Oxford: Clarendon.

Hirsch, Eli. 1993. *Dividing Reality.* New York: Oxford University Press.

Hoffman, Piotr. 2000. "Heidegger and the Problem of Idealism." *Inquiry* 43, no. 4: 403–12.

Hollinger, Robert, ed. 1985. *Hermeneutics and Praxis.* Notre Dame: University of Notre Dame Press.

Hollis, Martin, and Steven Lukes, eds. 1982. *Rationality and Relativism.* Cambridge, Mass.: MIT Press.

Horwich, Paul, ed. 1993. *World Changes: Thomas Kuhn and the Nature of Science.* Cambridge, Mass.: MIT Press.

Houlgate, Stephen. 1986. *Hegel, Nietzsche and the Criticism of Metaphysics.* New York: Cambridge University Press.

———. 1991. *Freedom, Truth and History: An Introduction to Hegel's Philosophy.* New York: Routledge.

Hoy, David Couzens. 1986. *Foucault: A Critical Reader.* Cambridge: Blackwell.
Hume, David. 1975. *Enquiries.* 3rd ed. Ed. P. H. Nidditch. Oxford: Clarendon.
———. 1978. *A Treatise of Human Nature.* 2nd ed. Ed. L. A. Selby-Bigge and P. H. Nidditch. New York: Clarendon.
Husserl, Edmund. 1950. *Cartesian Meditations: An Introduction to Phenomenology.* Trans. Dorion Cairns. Boston: Kluwer Academic.
———. 1982. *Ideas Pertaining to a Pure Phenomenology and to a Phenomenological Philosophy.* Bk. 1. Trans. F. Kersten. Boston: Kluwer Academic.
———. 1997. *Psychological and Transcendental Phenomenology and the Confrontation with Heidegger, 1927–1931.* Ed. and trans. Thomas Sheehan and Richard E. Palmer. Boston: Kluwer Academic.
Hylton, Peter. 1990. *Russell, Idealism, and the Emergence of Analytic Philosophy.* New York: Clarendon.
Hyppolite, Jean. 1974. *Genesis and Structure of Hegel's "Phenomenology of Spirit."* Trans. Samuel Cherniak and John Heckman. Evanston, Ill.: Northwestern University Press.
Ijsseling, S. 1986. "Foucault with Heidegger." *Man and World* 19, no. 4: 413–24.
Inwood, Michael, ed. 1985. *Hegel.* New York: Oxford University Press.
James, William. 1963. *Pragmatism and Other Essays.* New York: Washington Square.
Jencks, Charles. 1987. *What Is Post-Modernism?* 2nd ed., rev. and enl. New York: St. Martin's.
Kaufmann, Walter. 1974. *Nietzsche: Philosopher, Psychologist, Antichrist.* 4th ed. Princeton: Princeton University Press.
Kemp Smith, Norman. 1941. *The Philosophy of David Hume: A Critical Study of Its Origins and Central Doctrines.* London: Macmillan.
———. 1984. *Commentary to Kant's "Critique of Pure Reason."* 2nd ed., rev. and exp. Atlantic Highlands N.J.: Humanities.
Kierkegaard, Søren. 1992. *Concluding Unscientific Postscript to "Philosophical Fragments."* Ed. and trans. Howard V. Hong and Edna V. Hong. Princeton: Princeton University Press.
Kirkham, Richard L. 1995. *Theories of Truth: A Critical Introduction.* Cambridge, Mass.: MIT Press.
Kitcher, Patricia. 1990. *Kant's Transcendental Psychology.* New York: Oxford University Press.
Kojève, Alexandre. 1969. *Introduction to the Reading of Hegel: Lectures on the "Phenomenology of Spirit."* Ed. Allan Bloom. Trans. James H. Nichols Jr. Ithaca: Cornell University Press.
Kolakowski, Leszek. 1969. *Towards a Marxist Humanism: Essays on the Left Today.* Trans. Jane Zielonko Peel. New York: Grove Press.
Kolb, David. 1986. *The Critique of Pure Modernity: Hegel, Heidegger, and After.* Chicago: University of Chicago Press.
Körner, Stephan. 1970. *Categorial Frameworks.* Oxford: Basil Blackwell.
Kosso, Peter. 1998. *Appearance and Reality: An Introduction to the Philosophy of Physics.* New York: Oxford University Press.
Kotatko, Petr, Peter Pagin, and Gabriel Segal, eds. 2001. *Interpreting Davidson.* Stanford: CSLI.

Krausz, Michael, ed. 1989. *Relativism: Interpretation and Confrontation.* Notre Dame: University of Notre Dame Press.

Krell, David Farrell. 1986. *Intimations of Mortality: Time, Truth, and Finitude in Heidegger's Thinking of Being.* University Park: Pennsylvania State University Press.

Kripke, Saul. 1982. *Wittgenstein on Rules and Private Language: An Elementary Exposition.* Cambridge, Mass.: Harvard University Press.

Kuhn, Thomas S. 1970. *The Structure of Scientific Revolutions.* 2nd enl. ed. Chicago: University of Chicago Press.

———. 2000. *The Road since Structure: Philosophical Essays, 1970–1993, with an Autobiographical Interview.* Ed. James Conant and John Haugeland. Chicago: University of Chicago Press.

Kulp, Christopher B., ed. 1997. *Realism/Antirealism and Epistemology.* New York: Rowman and Littlefield.

Lacoue-Labarthe, Philippe. 1993. *The Subject of Philosophy.* Ed. Thomas Trezise. Minneapolis: University of Minnesota Press.

Lafont, Cristina. 2000. *Heidegger, Language, and World-Disclosure.* New York: Cambridge University Press.

Lamb, David. 1980. *Hegel: From Foundation to System.* Boston: Martinus Nijhoff.

Lawson, Hilary, and Lisa Appignanesi, eds. 1989. *Dismantling Truth: Reality in the Post-Modern World.* London: Weidenfeld and Nicolson.

Lear, Jonathan. 1984. "The Disappearing 'We.'" *Proceedings of the Aristotelian Society,* suppl. vol. 58: 219–42.

———. 1998. *Open Minded: Working Out the Logic of the Soul.* Cambridge, Mass.: Harvard University Press.

Lepore, Ernest, ed. 1986. *Truth and Interpretation: Perspectives on the Philosophy of Donald Davidson.* New York: Basil Blackwell.

Levinas, Emmanuel. 1969. *Totality and Infinity.* Trans. Alphonso Lingis. Pittsburgh: Duquesne University Press.

———. 1985. *Ethics and Infinity.* Trans. Richard A. Cohen. Pittsburgh: Duquesne University Press.

———. 1994. *Outside the Subject.* Trans. Michael B. Smith. Stanford: Stanford University Press.

———. 1996. *Basic Philosophical Writings.* Ed. Adriaan T. Peperzak, Simon Critchley, and Robert Bernasconi. Bloomington: Indiana University Press.

———. 1998. *Entre Nous: Thinking-of-the-Other.* Trans. Michael B. Smith and Barbara Harshav. New York: Columbia University Press.

Lewis, David. 1983. *Philosophical Papers.* Vol. 1. New York: Oxford University Press.

Lingis, Alphonso. 1989. *Deathbound Subjectivity.* Indianapolis: Indiana University Press.

Llewelyn, John. 1986. *Derrida on the Threshold of Sense.* New York: St. Martin's.

Locke, John. 1959. *An Essay Concerning Human Understanding.* 2 vols. Ed. Alexander Campbell Fraser. New York: Dover.

Löwith, Karl. 1994. *My Life in Germany Before and After 1933: A Report.* Trans. Elizabeth King. Chicago: University of Illinois Press.

———. 1995. *Martin Heidegger and European Nihilism.* Trans. Gary Steiner. New York: Columbia University Press.

Ludwig, Kirk, ed. 2003. *Donald Davidson: Contemporary Philosophy in Focus.* New York: Cambridge University Press.
Luntley, Michael. 1995. *Reason, Truth and Self: The Postmodern Reconditioned.* New York: Routledge.
Lynch, Michael P. 2001a. *The Nature of Truth: Classic and Contemporary Perspectives.* Cambridge, Mass.: MIT Press.
———, ed. 2001b. *Truth in Context: An Essay on Pluralism and Objectivity.* Cambridge, Mass.: MIT Press.
Lyotard, Jean-François. 1984. *The Postmodern Condition: A Report on Knowledge.* Trans. Geoff Bennington and Brian Massumi. Minneapolis: University of Minnesota Press.
———. 1988. *The Differend: Phrases in Dispute.* Minneapolis: University of Minnesota Press.
Macann, Christopher, ed. 1996. *Critical Heidegger.* New York: Routledge.
Macey, David. 1994. *The Lives of Michel Foucault.* London: Vintage Books.
MacIntyre, Alasdair, ed. 1972. *Hegel: A Collection of Critical Essays.* Garden City: Doubleday.
———. 1984. *After Virtue.* 2nd ed. Notre Dame: University of Notre Dame Press.
———. 1988. *Whose Justice? Which Rationality?* Notre Dame: University of Notre Dame Press.
Macomber, W. B. 1967. *The Anatomy of Disillusion: Martin Heidegger's Notion of Truth.* Evanston, Ill.: Northwestern University Press.
Madison, Gary B., ed. 1993. *Working through Derrida.* Evanston, Ill.: Northwestern University Press.
Magee, Bryan. 1986. *Modern British Philosophy.* New York: Oxford University Press.
Magnus, Bernd, and Kathleen M. Higgins, eds. 1996. *The Cambridge Companion to Nietzsche.* New York: Cambridge University Press.
Mahon, Michael. 1992. *Foucault's Nietzschean Genealogy: Truth, Power, and the Subject.* New York: State University of New York Press.
Malpas, Jeff. 1992. *Donald Davidson and the Mirror of Meaning: Holism, Truth, Interpretation.* New York: Cambridge University Press.
———, ed. 2003. *From Kant to Davidson: Philosophy and the Idea of the Transcendental.* New York: Routledge.
Malpas, Jeff, Ulrich Arnswald, and Jens Kertscher, eds. 2002. *Gadamer's Century: Essays in Honor of Hans-Georg Gadamer.* Cambridge, Mass.: MIT Press.
Margolis, Joseph. 2003. *The Unraveling of Scientism: American Philosophy at the End of the Twentieth Century.* Ithaca: Cornell University Press.
Marrati, Paola. 2005. *Genesis and Trace: Derrida Reading Husserl and Heidegger.* Stanford: Stanford University Press.
Marx, Werner. 1971. *Heidegger and the Tradition.* Trans. Theodore Kisiel and Murray Greene. Evanston, Ill.: Northwestern University Press.
May, Todd. 1993. *Between Genealogy and Epistemology: Psychology, Politics, and Knowledge in the Thought of Michel Foucault.* University Park: Pennsylvania State University Press.
McCormick, Peter J., ed. 1996. *Starmaking: Realism, Anti-Realism, and Irrealism.* Cambridge, Mass.: MIT Press.

McCumber, John. 1993. *The Company of Words: Hegel, Language, and Systematic Philosophy.* Evanston, Ill.: Northwestern University Press.

———. 1996. "Time in the Ditch: American Philosophy and the McCarthy Era." *Diacritics* 26, no. 1: 33–49.

———. 2002. "The Temporal Turn in German Idealism: Hegel and After." *Research in Phenomenology* 32:44–59.

———. 2003. "Just in Time: Toward a New American Philosophy." *Continental Philosophy Review* 36:61–80.

———. 2005. *Reshaping Reason: Toward a New Philosophy.* Bloomington: Indiana University Press.

McDermid, Douglas. 1998. "Putnam on Kant on Truth: Correspondence or Coherence?" *Idealistic Studies* 28, no. 1–2 (Winter/Spring): 17–34.

McDowell, John. 1996. *Mind and World.* Cambridge, Mass.: Harvard University Press.

McGinn, Colin. 1977. "Charity, Interpretation, and Belief." *Journal of Philosophy* 74, no. 9 (September): 521–35.

McKeon, Richard, ed. 1941. *The Basic Works of Aristotle.* New York: Random House.

McWhorter, Ladelle. 1999. *Bodies and Pleasures: Foucault and the Politics of Sexual Normalization.* Indianapolis: Indiana University Press.

Megill, Allan. 1985. *Prophets of Extremity: Nietzsche, Heidegger, Foucault, Derrida.* Berkeley and Los Angeles: University of California Press.

Mensch, James Richard. 1996. *Knowing and Being: A Postmodern Reversal.* University Park: Pennsylvania State University Press.

Merleau-Ponty, Maurice. 1962. *Phenomenology of Perception.* Trans. Colin Smith. New York: Humanities.

Michelfelder, Diane P., and Richard E. Palmer, eds. 1989. *Dialogue and Deconstruction: The Gadamer-Derrida Encounter.* Albany: State University of New York Press.

Milchman, Alan, and Alan Rosenberg, eds. 2003. *Foucault and Heidegger: Critical Encounters.* Minneapolis: University of Minnesota Press.

Mitchell, Stephen. 1988. *Tao Te Ching.* New York: Harper and Row.

Moore, A. W. 2000. "Arguing with Derrida." *Ratio* 13, no. 4 (December): 355–73.

Moore, G. E. 1965. *Philosophical Studies.* Totowa: Littlefield, Adams.

Moran, Dermot. 2000. "Hilary Putnam and Immanuel Kant: Two 'Internal Realists'?" *Synthese* 123, no. 1 (April): 65–104.

Morick, Harold, ed. 1967. *Wittgenstein and the Problem of Other Minds.* Atlantic Highlands, N.J.: Humanities.

Moyal-Sharrock, Danièle. 2004. *The Third Wittgenstein: The Post-Investigations Works.* Burlington: Ashgate.

Mulhall, Stephen. 1987. "Davidson on Interpretation and Understanding." *Philosophical Quarterly* 37, no. 148 (July): 319–22.

———. 1990. *On Being in the World: Wittgenstein and Heidegger on Seeing Aspects.* New York: Routledge.

Mulligan, Kevin. 1991. "Introduction: On the History of Continental Philosophy." *Topoi* 10:115–20.

Murray, Michael, ed. 1978. *Heidegger and Modern Philosophy.* New Haven: Yale University Press.

Nagel, Thomas. 1979. *Moral Questions.* New York: Cambridge University Press.
———. 1986. *The View from Nowhere.* New York: Oxford University Press.
Nahm, Milton C. 1964. *Selections from Early Greek Philosophy.* Englewood Cliffs, N.J.: Prentice-Hall.
Nehamas, Alexander. 1985. *Nietzsche: Life as Literature.* Cambridge, Mass.: Harvard University Press.
Norris, Christopher. 1985. *The Contest of Faculties: Philosophy and Theory after Deconstruction.* New York: Methuen.
———. 1987. *Derrida.* Cambridge, Mass.: Harvard University Press.
———. 1994. *Truth and the Ethics of Criticism.* New York: Manchester University Press.
———. 1997. *New Idols of the Cave: On the Limits of Anti-Realism.* New York: Manchester University Press.
———. 2002. *Hilary Putnam: Realism, Reason, and the Uses of Uncertainty.* New York: Manchester University Press.
Nulty, Timothy J. 2003. "Davidson and Disclosedness: An Analysis of Heideggerian and Davidsonian Truth." *Idealistic Studies* 33, no. 1: 25–38.
Ogilvy, James A. 1975. "Reflections on the Absolute." *Review of Metaphysics* 28, no. 3: 520–46.
Okrent, Mark. 1988. *Heidegger's Pragmatism: Understanding, Being, and the Critique of Metaphysics.* Ithaca: Cornell University Press.
———. 1989. "Heidegger and Davidson (and Haugeland)." *Southern Journal of Philosophy* 28, suppl., 75–81.
Olafson, Frederick A. 1998. "Being, Truth, and Presence in Heidegger's Thought." *Inquiry* 41, no. 1: 45–64.
O'Neil, Brian. 1974. *Epistemological Direct Realism in Descartes' Philosophy.* Albuquerque: University of New Mexico Press.
Ormiston, Gayle L., and Alan D. Schrift, eds. 1990. *Transforming the Hermeneutic Context: From Nietzsche to Nancy.* Albany: State University of New York Press.
Palmer, Richard E. 1969. *Hermeneutics.* Evanston, Ill.: Northwestern University Press.
Papineau, David. 1987. *Reality and Representation.* New York: Basil Blackwell.
Pereda, Carlos. 1998. *Crítica: Revista Hispanoamericana de Filosofía* 30, no. 88 (April): 73–91.
Pinkard, Terry. 2002. *German Philosophy, 1760–1860: The Legacy of Idealism.* New York: Cambridge University Press.
Pippin, Robert B. 1989. *Hegel's Idealism: The Satisfactions of Self-Consciousness.* New York: Cambridge University Press.
———. 1997. *Idealism as Modernism: Hegelian Variations.* New York: Cambridge University Press.
———. 1999. *Modernism as a Philosophical Problem: On the Dissatisfactions of European High Culture.* 2nd ed. Cambridge, Mass.: Basil Blackwell.
Plantinga, Alvin. 1982. "How to Be an Anti-Realist." *Proceedings of the American Philosophical Association* 56, no. 1 (September): 47–70.
Pöggeler, Otto. 1970. "Heidegger Today." *Southern Journal of Philosophy* 7:273–306.
———. 1998. *The Paths of Heidegger's Life and Thought.* Trans. John Bailiff. Amherst, Mass.: Humanity Books.

Polanyi, Michael. 1966. *The Tacit Dimension.* New York: Anchor Books.

Polt, Richard, and Gregory Fried, eds. 2001. *A Companion to Heidegger's "Introduction to Metaphysics."* New Haven: Yale University Press.

Posy, Carl. 1983. "Dancing to the Antinomy: A Proposal for Transcendental Idealism." *American Philosophical Quarterly* 20, no. 1 (January): 81–94.

———. 1984. "Kant's Mathematical Realism." *The Monist* 67, no. 1 (January): 115–34.

Prado, C. G., ed. 2003. *A House Divided: Comparing Analytic and Continental Philosophy.* New York: Humanity Books.

———. 2006. *Searle and Foucault on Truth.* New York: Cambridge University Press.

Prauss, Gerold. 1999. *Knowing and Doing in Heidegger's "Being and Time."* Trans. Gary Steiner and Jeffrey S. Turner. Amherst, Mass.: Humanity Books.

Preyer, Gerhard, Frank Siebelt, and Alexander Ulfig, eds. 1994. *Language, Mind and Epistemology: On Donald Davidson's Philosophy.* Boston: Kluwer Academic.

Priest, Graham. 2002. *Beyond the Limits of Thought.* 2nd ed. New York: Oxford University Press.

Putnam, Hilary. 1975. *Mind, Language and Reality.* Vol. 2 of *Philosophical Papers.* New York: Cambridge University Press.

———. 1978. *Meaning and the Moral Sciences.* Boston: Routledge and Kegan Paul.

———. 1981. *Reason, Truth, and History.* New York: Cambridge University Press.

———. 1983. *Realism and Reason.* Vol. 3 of *Philosophical Papers.* New York: Cambridge University Press.

———. 1987. *The Many Faces of Realism.* La Salle, Ill.: Open Court.

———. 1988. *Representation and Reality.* Cambridge, Mass.: MIT Press.

———. 1990. *Realism with a Human Face.* Ed. James Conant. Cambridge, Mass.: Harvard University Press.

———. 1992. *Renewing Philosophy.* Cambridge, Mass.: Harvard University Press.

———. 1994a. "Sense, Nonsense, and the Senses: An Inquiry into the Powers of the Human Mind." *Journal of Philosophy* 91, no. 9 (September): 445–517.

———. 1994b. *Words and Life.* Ed. James Conant. Cambridge, Mass.: Harvard University Press.

———. 1995. *Pragmatism: An Open Question.* Cambridge: Blackwell.

Quine, Willard van Orman. 1960. *Word and Object.* Cambridge, Mass.: MIT Press.

———. 1966. *The Ways of Paradox and Other Essays.* New York: Random House.

———. 1969. *Ontological Relativity and Other Essays.* New York: Columbia University Press.

———. 1970. *Philosophy of Logic.* Englewood Cliffs, N.J.: Prentice-Hall.

———. 1980. *From a Logical Point of View: Nine Logico-Philosophical Essays.* 2nd rev. ed. Cambridge, Mass.: Harvard University Press.

———. 1981. *Theories and Things.* Cambridge, Mass.: Harvard University Press.

———. 1987. "Indeterminacy of Translation Again." *Journal of Philosophy* 84, no. 1 (January): 5–10.

———. 1992. *Pursuit of Truth.* Rev ed. Cambridge, Mass.: Harvard University Press.

Rajchman, John. 1985. *Michel Foucault: The Freedom of Philosophy.* New York: Columbia University Press.

Ramberg, Bjørn T. 1989. *Donald Davidson's Philosophy of Language: An Introduction.* New York: Basil Blackwell.

Rapaport, Herman. 1989. *Heidegger and Derrida: Reflections on Time and Language.* Lincoln: University of Nebraska Press.

Rescher, Nicholas. 2000. *Nature and Understanding: The Metaphysics and Method of Science.* Oxford: Clarendon.

Richardson, John. 1986. *Existential Epistemology: A Heideggerian Critique of the Cartesian Project.* Oxford: Clarendon.

———. 1996. *Nietzsche's System.* New York: Oxford University Press.

Richardson, John, and Brian Leiter, eds. 2001. *Nietzsche: Oxford Readings in Philosophy.* New York: Oxford University Press.

Ricoeur, Paul. 1974. *The Conflict of Interpretations.* Ed. Don Ihde. Evanston, Ill.: Northwestern University Press.

Rockmore, Tom. 1986. *Hegel's Circular Epistemology.* Bloomington: Indiana University Press.

———. 2001. "Analytic Philosophy and the Hegelian Turn." *Review of Metaphysics* 55 (December): 339–70.

———. 2006. *In Kant's Wake: Philosophy in the Twentieth Century.* Malden, Mass.: Blackwell.

Rorty, Richard. 1979. *Philosophy and the Mirror of Nature.* Princeton: Princeton University Press.

———. 1982. *Consequences of Pragmatism: Essays, 1972–1980.* Minneapolis: University of Minnesota Press.

———. 1989. *Contingency, Irony, Solidarity.* New York: Cambridge University Press.

———. 1991a. *Objectivity, Relativism, and Truth.* Vol. 1 of *Philosophical Papers.* New York: Cambridge University Press.

———. 1991b. *Essays on Heidegger and Others.* Vol. 2 of *Philosophical Papers.* New York: Cambridge University Press.

———, ed. 1992. *The Linguistic Turn: Essays in Philosophical Method with Two Retrospective Essays.* Chicago: University of Chicago Press.

———. 1998. "Davidson Between Wittgenstein and Tarski." *Crítica: Revista Hispanoamericana de Filosofía* 30, no. 88 (April): 49–71.

———. 1998. *Philosophical Papers, Volume 3: Truth and Progress.* New York: Cambridge University Press.

Rosen, Michael. 1982. *Hegel's Dialectic and Its Criticism.* New York: Cambridge University Press.

Rosenberg, Jay F. 1980. *One World and Our Knowledge of It: The Problematic of Realism in Post-Kantian Perspective.* Boston: D. Reidel.

Royle, Nicholas, ed. 2000. *Deconstructions: A User's Guide.* New York: Palgrave Macmillan.

Rudd, Anthony. 2003. *Expressing the World: Skepticism, Wittgenstein, and Heidegger.* Chicago: Open Court.

Russell, Bertrand. 1929. *Our Knowledge of the External World.* New York: W. W. Norton.

———. 1945. *A History of Western Philosophy.* New York: Simon and Schuster.

———. 1959a. *My Philosophical Development.* New York: Simon and Schuster.

———. 1959b. *The Problems of Philosophy.* New York: Oxford University Press.

———. 1996. *The Principles of Mathematics.* New York: W. W. Norton.

Sallis, John, ed. 1970. *Heidegger and the Path of Thinking.* Pittsburgh: Duquesne University Press.

———, ed. 1978. *Radical Phenomenology: Essays in Honor of Martin Heidegger.* Atlantic Highlands, N.J.: Humanities.

———, ed. 1987. *Deconstruction and Philosophy: The Texts of Jacques Derrida.* Chicago: University of Chicago Press.

———, ed. 1993. *Reading Heidegger.* Indianapolis: Indiana University Press.

———. 1995a. *Delimitations: Phenomenology and the End of Metaphysics.* 2nd ed. Indianapolis: Indiana University Press.

———. 1995b. *Double Truth.* Albany: State University of New York Press.

Sartre, Jean-Paul. 1992. *Being and Nothingness: A Phenomenological Essay on Ontology.* Trans. Hazel E. Barnes. New York: Washington Square.

———. 1993. *The Transcendence of the Ego: An Existentialist Theory of Consciousness.* Trans. Forrest Williams and Robert Kirkpatrick. New York: Hill and Wang.

Schacht, Richard. 1983. *Nietzsche: Arguments of the Philosophers.* New York: Routledge.

———, ed. 1994. *Nietzsche, Genealogy, Morality: Essays on Nietzsche's "On the Genealogy of Morals."* Berkeley and Los Angeles: University of California Press.

Schaper, Eva, and Wilhelm Vossenkuhl, eds. 1989. *Reading Kant: New Perspectives on Transcendental Arguments and Critical Philosophy.* New York: Basil Blackwell.

Schrift, Alan D. 1990. *Nietzsche and the Question of Interpretation: Between Hermeneutics and Deconstruction.* New York: Routledge.

Schürmann, Reiner. 1979. "Anti-Humanism: Reflections on the Turn towards the Post-Modern Epoch." *Man and World* 12, no. 2: 160–77.

———. 1987. *Heidegger on Being and Acting: From Principles to Anarchy.* Bloomington: Indiana University Press.

Scott, Charles E. 1984. "Speech and the Unspeakable in the 'Place' of the Unconscious." *Human Studies* 7:39–54.

———. 1990. *The Question of Ethics: Nietzsche, Foucault, Heidegger.* Indianapolis: Indiana University Press.

Searle, John R. 1977. "Reiterating the Differences: A Reply to Derrida." *Glyph* 1: 198–208.

———. 1993. "Rationality and Realism: What Is at Stake?" *Daedalus* 122, no. 4 (Fall): pp. 55–83.

———. 1995. *The Construction of Social Reality.* New York: Free Press.

Sellars, Wilfrid. 1963. *Science, Perception and Reality.* Atascadero, Calif.: Ridgeview.

———. 1974. *Essays in Philosophy and Its History.* Boston: D. Reidel.

Sheehan, Thomas. 2001. "A Paradigm Shift in Heidegger Research." *Continental Philosophy Review* 34:183–202.

Sherover, Charles M. 1971. *Heidegger, Kant, and Time.* Bloomington: Indiana University Press.

Shook, John R., ed. 2003. *Pragmatic Naturalism and Realism.* Amherst, Mass.: Prometheus Books.

Silverman, Hugh J., and Gary E. Aylesworth, eds. 1990. *The Textual Sublime: Deconstruction and Its Differences.* Albany: State University of New York Press.

Small, Robin. 2001. *Nietzsche in Context.* Burlington: Ashgate.

Smith, Joseph H., and William Kerrigan, eds. 1984. *Taking Chances: Derrida, Psychoanalysis, and Literature.* Baltimore: The Johns Hopkins University Press.

Soames, Scott. 2003. *Philosophical Analysis in the Twentieth Century, Volume I: The Dawn of Analysis.* Princeton: Princeton University Press.

Solomon, Robert, ed. 1973. *Nietzsche: A Collection of Critical Essays.* New York: Anchor Books.

———. 1988. *Continental Philosophy since 1750: The Rise and Fall of the Self.* New York: Oxford University Press.

———. 2005. *Existentialism.* 2nd ed. New York: Oxford University Press.

Solomon, Robert C., and Kathleen M. Higgins, eds. 1988. *Reading Nietzsche.* New York: Oxford University Press.

Staten, Henry. 1986. *Wittgenstein and Derrida.* Lincoln: University of Nebraska Press.

Stern, Robert, ed. 1999. *Transcendental Arguments: Problems and Prospects.* New York: Oxford University Press.

Stevenson, Leslie, and Ralph Walker. 1983. "Empirical Realism and Transcendental Anti-Realism." *Aristotelian Society,* suppl. vol. 57: 131–77.

Stewart, Jon. 2000. *The Unity of Hegel's "Phenomenology of Spirit": A Systematic Interpretation.* Evanston, Ill.: Northwestern University Press.

Stoecker, Ralf, ed. 1993. *Reflecting Davidson: Donald Davidson Responding to an International Forum of Philosophers.* New York: De Gruyter.

Strauss, Leo. 1989. *The Rebirth of Classical Political Rationalism: An Introduction to the Thought of Leo Strauss: Essays and Lectures.* Ed. Thomas L. Pangle. Chicago: University of Chicago Press.

Strawson, Galen. 1994. "The Impossibility of Moral Responsibility." *Philosophical Studies* 75:5–24.

Strawson, P. F. 1966. *The Bounds of Sense: An Essay on Kant's "Critique of Pure Reason."* London: Methuen.

———. 1985. *Skepticism and Naturalism: Some Varieties.* New York: Columbia University Press.

Stroud, Barry. 2000. *Understanding Human Knowledge: Philosophical Essays.* New York: Oxford University Press.

Taylor, Charles. 1975. *Hegel.* New York: Cambridge University Press.

———. 1987. "Overcoming Epistemology." In Baynes, Bohman, and McCarthy, 464–88.

———. 1989. *Sources of the Self: The Making of the Modern Identity.* Cambridge, Mass.: Harvard University Press.

Taylor, Mark C. 1987. *Altarity.* Chicago: University of Chicago Press.

Thomson, Iain. 2000. "Ontotheology? Understanding Heidegger's Destruktion of Metaphysics." *International Journal of Philosophical Studies* 8, no. 3: 297–327.

———. 2001. "Heidegger on Ontological Education; or, How We Become What We Are." *Inquiry* 44, no. 3: 243–68.

———. 2003. "The Philosophical Fugue: Understanding the Structure and Goal of Heidegger's *Beiträge.*" *Journal of the British Society for Phenomenology* 34, no. 1: 57–73.

———. 2005. *Heidegger on Ontotheology: Technology and the Politics of Education.* New York: Cambridge University Press.

Vallicella, William F. 1983. "Kant, Heidegger, and the Problem of the Thing in Itself." *International Philosophical Quarterly* 23:35–43.

Van Buren, John, ed. 2002. *Supplements: From the Earliest Essays to "Being and Time" and Beyond.* Albany: State University of New York Press.

Van Cleve, James. 1999. *Problems from Kant.* New York: Oxford University Press.

Van Inwagen, Peter, and Dean W. Zimmerman. 1998. *Metaphysics: The Big Questions.* Malden, Mass.: Blackwell.

Van Kirk, Carol A. 1984. "Kant's Reply to Putnam." *Idealistic Studies* 14, no. 1 (January): 13–23.

Verene, Donald Phillip. 1985. *Hegel's Recollection: A Study of Images in the "Phenomenology of Spirit."* Albany: State University of New York Press.

Vermazen, Bruce. 1983. "The Intelligibility of Massive Error." *Philosophical Quarterly* 33, no. 130 (January): 69–74.

Versényi, Laszlo. 1965. *Heidegger, Being, and Truth.* New Haven: Yale University Press.

Vesey, Godfrey, ed. 1974. *Understanding Wittgenstein.* Ithaca: Cornell University Press.

Vision, Gerald. 1988. *Modern Anti-Realism and Manufactured Truth.* New York: Routledge.

Visker, Rudi. 1991. "From Foucault to Heidegger: A One-Way Ticket?" *Research in Phenomenology* 21:116–40.

———. 1995. *Michel Foucault: Genealogy as Critique.* Trans. Chris Turner. New York: Verso.

Wachterhauser, Brice R., ed. 1994. *Hermeneutics and Truth.* Evanston, Ill.: Northwestern University Press.

Walker, Ralph C. S. 1978. *Kant: The Arguments of the Philosophers.* Boston: Routledge and Kegan Paul.

———. 1989. *The Coherence Theory of Truth: Realism, Anti-Realism, Idealism.* New York: Routledge.

———. 1995. "Verificationism, Anti-Realism, and Idealism." *European Journal of Philosophy* 3, no. 3: 257–72.

Weatherston, Martin. 2002. *Heidegger's Interpretation of Kant: Categories, Imagination and Temporality.* New York: Palgrave Macmillan.

Weinsheimer, Joel. 2000. "Charity Militant: Gadamer, Davidson, and Post-critical Hermeneutics." *Revue Internationale de Philosophie* 3, no. 213: 405–22.

Welton, Donn, ed. 1999. *The Essential Husserl: Basic Writings in Transcendental Phenomenology.* Bloomington: Indiana University Press.

Westphal, Kenneth R. 1989. *Hegel's Epistemological Realism.* Philosophical Studies Series, vol. 43. Dordrecht: Kluwer.

———. 2003a. *Hegel's Epistemology: A Philosophical Introduction to the "Phenomenology of Spirit."* Indianapolis: Hackett.

———. 2003b. "Hegel's Manifold Response to Scepticism in the *Phenomenology of Spirit.*" *Proceedings of the Aristotelian Society* 104, no. 1: 149–78.

Westphal, Merold. 1998. *History and Truth in Hegel's "Phenomenology."* 3rd ed. Bloomington: Indiana University Press.

Wheeler III, Samuel C. 2000. *Deconstruction as Analytic Philosophy.* Stanford: Stanford University Press.
Wilcox, John T. 1974. *Truth and Value in Nietzsche: A Study of His Metaethics and Epistemology.* Ann Arbor: University of Michigan Press.
Williams, Bernard. 1978. *Descartes: The Project of Pure Enquiry.* New York: Penguin Books.
———. 1985. *Ethics and the Limits of Philosophy.* Cambridge, Mass.: Harvard University Press.
Wilson, Bryan R., ed. 1970. *Rationality.* Oxford: Basil Blackwell.
Wolin, Richard. 1990. *The Politics of Being: The Political Thought of Martin Heidegger.* New York: Columbia University Press.
———, ed. 1993. *The Heidegger Controversy: A Critical Reader.* Cambridge, Mass.: MIT Press.
Wood, Allen W., ed. 1984. *Self and Nature in Kant's Philosophy.* Ithaca: Cornell University Press.
Wood, David, and Robert Bernasconi, eds. 1988. *Derrida and "Différance."* Evanston, Ill.: Northwestern University Press.
Wrathall, Mark A. 1999. "Heidegger and Truth as Correspondence." *International Journal of Philosophical Studies* 7, no. 1: 69–88.
Wrathall, Mark A., and Jeff Malpas, eds. 2000. *Heidegger, Coping, and Cognitive Science: Essays in Honor of Hubert L. Dreyfus, Volume 2.* Cambridge, Mass.: MIT Press.
Wright, Crispin. 1993. *Realism, Meaning and Truth.* 2nd ed. Cambridge: Blackwell.
Yolton, John W. 1996. *Perception and Reality: A History from Descartes to Kant.* Ithaca: Cornell University Press.
Young, Julian. 2002. *Heidegger's Later Philosophy.* New York: Cambridge University Press.
Zeglen, Ursula M., ed. 1999. *Donald Davidson: Truth, Meaning and Knowledge.* New York: Routledge.
Ziff, Paul. 1970. "A Response to 'Stimulus Meaning.'" *Philosophical Review* 79, no. 1 (January): 63–74.

# Index

# About the Author

Lee Braver is chair of the department of philosophy at Hiram College in Ohio.